Mortgage Lending

principles &practices

8th edition

HONDROS LEARNING™

HONDROS LEARNING™

4140 Executive Parkway

Westerville, Ohio 43081

www.hondroslearning.com

20 19 18   1 2 3

ISBN: 978-1-59844-317-2

For more information on or to purchase our products, please visit www.hondroslearning.com.

NMLS Rules of Conduct

Rules of Conduct for NMLS Approved Pre-Licensure (PE) and Continuing Education (CE) Courses

The Secure and Fair Enforcement for Mortgage Licensing Act (SAFE Act), requires that state-licensed MLOs complete pre-licensing (PE) and continuing education (CE) courses as a condition to be licensed. The SAFE Act also requires that all education completed as a condition for state licensure be NMLS approved. Since 2009 NMLS has established course design, approval, and delivery standards which NMLS approved course providers are required to meet. To further ensure students meet the education requirements of the SAFE Act, NMLS has established a Rules of Conduct (ROC). The ROC, which have been approved by the NMLS Mortgage Testing & Education Board, and the NMLS Policy Committee, both of which are comprised of state regulators, are intended to stress that NMLS approved education be delivered and completed with integrity.

Rules of Conduct

As an individual completing either pre-licensure education (PE) or continuing education (CE), I agree to abide by the following rules of conduct:

1. I attest that I am the person who I say I am and that all my course registration information is accurate.

2. I acknowledge that I will be required to show a current government issued form of identification prior to, and during the course, and/or be required to answer questions that are intended to verify/validate my identity prior to, and during the course.

3. I understand that the SAFE Act and state laws require me to spend a specific amount of time in specific subject areas. Accordingly, I will not attempt to circumvent the requirements of any NMLS approved course.

4. I will not divulge my login ID or password or other login credential(s) to another individual for any online course.

5. I will not seek or attempt to seek outside assistance to complete the course.

6. I will not give or attempt to give assistance to any person who is registered to take an NMLS approved pre-licensure or continuing education course.

7. I will not engage in any conduct that creates a disturbance or interferes with the administration of the course or other students' learning.

8. I will not engage in any conduct that would be contrary to good character or reputation, or engage in any behavior that would cause the public to believe that I would not operate in the mortgage loan business lawfully, honestly or fairly.

9. I will not engage in any conduct that is dishonest, fraudulent, or would adversely impact the integrity of the course(s) I am completing and the conditions for which I am seeking licensure or renewal of licensure.

I understand that NMLS approved course providers are not authorized by NMLS to grant exceptions to these rules and that I alone am responsible for my conduct under these rules. I also understand that these rules are in addition to whatever applicable rules my course provider may have.

I understand that the course provider or others may report any alleged violations to NMLS and that NMLS may conduct an investigation into alleged violations and that it may report alleged violations to the state(s) in which I am seeking licensure or maintain licenses, or to other states.

I further understand that the results of any investigation into my alleged violation(s) may subject me to disciplinary actions by the state(s) or the State Regulatory Registry (SRR), including removal of any course from my NMLS record, and/or denial or revocation of my license(s).

Table of Contents

Preface

This textbook offers a comprehensive introduction and review of mortgage lending principles & practices including:

- Federal mortgage-related laws
- General information about mortgage programs and products
- Mortgage loan origination activities
- Ethics expected of mortgage professionals
- Content related to MLO license laws and regulations

The textbook provides you an overview about the mortgage industry, but not everything will be contained within these pages. It is common for a Mortgage Loan Originator (MLO) to continue learning, even after years of experience.

The principles and practices covered in the textbook are a foundation that will help prepare you to become a capable and qualified mortgage professional. It will enable you to stay current with the changes in federal laws, products, guidelines, and procedures in the mortgage industry. We encourage you to accept the challenge presented to you and become a true mortgage professional. Share your knowledge effectively with customers, deliver quality customer service to your clients, and continually demonstrate ethical behavior in your business practices.

Preface

A mortgage loan is one of the biggest financial commitments a person will make in his or her lifetime. Because of this, mortgage professionals must be knowledgeable, ethical, and customer focused when it comes to providing home loans.

As a mortgage professional, you will guide clients through the process of applying for a loan, facilitating this by seeking potential clients, and assisting them in the application process. Steps involved include:

- Gathering and evaluating information about a customer's financial status for informed decision making,
- Explaining the features and benefits of the different loan programs available,
- Ensuring consumers select the program that is right for them,
- Preparing the loan closing package, and
- Closing the loan.

Not only do mortgage loan originators facilitate first mortgages, they can also help consumers refinance loans and obtain second mortgages. The steps involved in both of these processes closely match those listed above.

Mortgage loan originators also develop relationships with commercial and residential real estate agencies as well as with other mortgage professionals as a way of developing business by referral. Referral sources may come from a wide variety of places—satisfied customers, mortgage industry professionals, and your own personal associations.

Using this Text

Mortgage Lending Principles and Practices was designed to give you the information you need to successfully enter the mortgage field. Contained here is a thorough discussion of ***federal lending legislation***, including financial disclosure laws, privacy protection and consumer identification laws, and prohibited predatory lending laws. The textbook also presents a primer on types of loan products and finance instruments—including ***conventional*** and ***nontraditional*** loan programs and financing. The important topic of ***ethical issues*** is also covered, including a look at fair lending, mortgage fraud, and advertising.

Whether used in the classroom or for self-study, you will find the information presented in a clear and concise manner. The author has provided key terms, examples, chapter summaries, and quizzes, as well as mortgage exercises and case studies to reinforce the concepts presented. Once you have completed your prelicensing course or self-study program, keep this book handy as a valuable reference tool for your new mortgage career.

Hondros Learning

Hondros Learning™ is a leading provider of classroom materials for mortgage prelicensing and continuing education. Together with Hondros College, we have provided training and educational products for more than one million students.

Our *National Mortgage Lending CompuCram*® online exam-prep is the perfect companion to this book. CompuCram® is a self-paced question and answer program designed to help you study for the national mortgage lending exam. For more information about CompuCram or any of our other products, please visit www.hondroslearning.com or www.compucram.com.

Acknowledgments

Hondros Learning™ thanks the following experts for their valuable contributions and assistance in developing this text:

Gary N. Smith, CMC., NMLS Approved Mortgage Instructor & Licensed MLO, Mortgage Compliance Consultant

Ben Katz, NMLS Approved Mortgage Instructor & Licensed MLO, NYS Certified Real Estate Instructor

Linda Williams, CEO at Mortgage Compliance Expert, Regulatory Compliance Specialist, Technical Writer

Mortgage Lending Overview

Mortgage lending is a profession that requires knowledge of many disciplines, including real estate, banking, property valuation, and others to be effective. This chapter provides an overview of the mortgage lending industry, beginning with a brief history of mortgage lending in the United States. As we will discuss, federal legislation transformed a period of uncertainty into the thriving mortgage industry we have today. The role of the primary mortgage market and how it developed and has been sustained and affected by the secondary mortgage market will be reviewed. This chapter also introduces the enactment of the Dodd-Frank Act and its effect on the mortgage lending industry. Finally, we will introduce federal disclosure regulations, privacy protections, and the prohibition of predatory lending.

After completing this chapter, you will be able to:

- Identify historical events that shaped today's mortgage industry.
- Contrast the primary mortgage market and secondary mortgage market.
- Identify entities involved in the primary and secondary mortgage markets.
- Identify the regulatory agencies involved in mortgage lending.
- Discuss the seeds of the subprime mortgage crisis.
- Discuss the history of the Dodd-Frank Act and the state of the mortgage market preceding its passage into legislation.
- Identify disclosure provisions of federal laws related to mortgage lending.
- Identify regulations to protect the privacy of consumers.
- Describe regulations that address predatory lending.
- Define regulatory requirements for mortgage loan originators.

Key Terms

Alt-A Loan

Average Prime Offer Rate (APOR)

Consumer Financial Protection Bureau (CFPB)

Correspondent

Demand Deposits

Disintermediation

Dodd-Frank Wall Street Reform and Consumer Protection Act

Federal Deposit Insurance Corporation (FDIC)

Federal Home Loan Mortgage Corporation (Freddie Mac)

Federal Housing Finance Agency (FHFA)

Federal National Mortgage Association (Fannie Mae)

Government National Mortgage Association (Ginnie Mae)

Government-Sponsored Enterprise (GSE)

Loan Processor

Mortgage

Mortgage-Backed Security (MBS)

Mortgage Banker

Mortgage Broker

Mortgage Loan Originator (MLO)

Payment Shock

Primary Mortgage Market

Secondary Mortgage Markets

Securitization

Service Release Premium (SRP)

Subprime Loans

Table Funding

Underwriter

Citations

Citations throughout this textbook refer to different statutes and regulations. Federal statutes (e.g., Dodd-Frank Act, Real Estate Settlement Procedures Act of 1974, etc.) designate legislation passed by Congress. Federal regulations (e.g., Regulation X/RESPA, Regulation Z/TILA) designate rules or other requirements specified by government departments/agencies that are responsible for the administration of the regulations.

The wording may be the same in both a statute and regulation; however, the wording in a regulation may also expand on the wording of a statute, based on the government entity's explanation or interpretation of the statute as part of its administration of the law.

CFR stands for "Code of Federal Regulations" in legislative terminology.

Concepts of Mortgage Lending

In the past decade, mortgage lending laws and regulations have increased dramatically and enforcement of a majority of laws and regulations has been transferred to one government entity, the Consumer Financial Protection Bureau (CFPB).

The guidelines and regulations that guide us today are a result of legislation designed to protect residential borrowers, who are likely making the single, largest investment of their lives. With the mortgage fraud issues that occurred in previous years, legislative action resulted in the promulgation of new rules that sought to increase the level of oversight of mortgage loan originators (MLOs) and to regain the borrowing public's confidence in the mortgage industry and the loan products offered to them.

With the advent of frequent changes to the lawful way MLOs may conduct their daily tasks, it is imperative that MLOs stay informed about all regulation changes and guidelines that are in place to guide them in serving the public.

It is the purpose of this prelicensing education course to give you the foundation upon which to build your knowledge. Once licensed, MLOs must stay current on all aspects of mortgage lending through ongoing research of the different regulations and agency guidelines (especially the CFPB, see http://www.consumerfinance.gov).

Importance of Understanding Mortgage Lending Concepts

As a student preparing to begin this course of study, it is critical to embrace and understand the concepts of mortgage law, regulations, and principles. The retention of knowledge and the comprehension of the information and lessons in these chapters is more than a matter of memorization; it is a necessity to know the underlying foundation of the content's principles. A successful MLO will know and understand the regulations and laws, and the *intent* of the law as well. Understanding the history of the mortgage industry provides a solid basis for comprehending the concepts that have prevailed through time and serve as a guide for the MLO's success.

Adherence to the laws, regulations, and industry guidelines that are in place today are more important than ever. Assisting the public with their mortgage needs by educating them, using industry knowledge to provide them with suitable and appropriate mortgage products, and adhering to the principles and regulations of mortgage lending are essential in the industry.

When studying and learning these principles, look for the concepts and history behind the law, as well as the regulations and guidelines that are in place today. That is the key to success!

Seeds of Today's Mortgage Industry

In the United States from the 1900s through the 1930s, buying a home was a much different process than it is today. The modern mortgage industry began as a method of rehabilitating an economy decimated by the Great Depression. Most of today's underwriting standards have been around for less than 80 years. Prior to the late 1930's, today's mortgage professional would be taken aback at what a mortgage loan looked like.

Following independence from England, property ownership in the United States became available to a larger portion of the public. However, having severed ties with England, the new nation had effectively cut off its major source of financial support. Since the economy in most of the United States at that time was agricultural, very few individuals or businesses had sufficient capital to act as a large-scale lender. Many merchants gradually stepped into this role and would lend locally.

Most early mortgages were short-term (generally 3-5 years) interest-only loans, which did not pay down the principal of the loan. The loan amounts were usually for no more than 50% of the home's value, requiring homeowners to have substantial assets to obtain financing. This kept many people in perpetual debt due to the need to repeatedly refinance their home purchase. If they were unable to pay off or reborrow at the end of the loan term, they lost their home in foreclosure. Due to the risks involved, many insurance companies became mortgage lenders and sought out groups of investors to spread the risk and rewards.

Several events led to the mortgage industry we have today. During the Great Depression, the economic instability allowed very few Americans to buy homes. Not only were they without personal financial resources to do so, but many banks were unable to lend funds due to a lack of capital reserves. Indeed, banks were unable to refinance mortgages that were being paid in a timely manner, resulting in widespread foreclosures.

First, even before the Great Depression, the Federal Reserve Act of 1913 created the **Federal Reserve System**. This Act established *a federal charter for banks that permitted them to make real estate loans*. Although these loans were initially the short-term, high down payment loans just referenced, the Act established the framework for government involvement with mortgage lending. Furthermore, the Federal Reserve Act was instrumental in implementing a system for the government to influence interest rates. Other significant banking legislation followed:

- The **Federal Home Loan Bank Act of 1932**, passed during the height of the Great Depression, established **Federal Home Loan Banks**, which had the authority to lend money to thrifts—savings and loan associations (S & Ls), credit unions, and savings banks—so that they could finance home mortgages in their neighborhoods.

- The **Banking Act of 1933**, also known as the Glass-Steagall Act, created the **Federal Deposit Insurance Corporation** (FDIC) to insure depositors against bank default. This was an important step in enticing people to, once again, save their money in banks. This allowed the banks to have a continued source of funds to make more home mortgage loans.

- The **National Housing Act of 1934** extended this protection to savings and loan depositors with the creation of the **Federal Savings and Loan Insurance Corporation** (FSLIC). After the savings and loan crisis of the 1980s exhausted FSLIC reserves, it was abolished by the federal **Financial Institutions Reform Recovery and Enforcement Act** (FIRREA) in 1989. FIRREA transferred all assets previously held by FSLIC to the Savings Association Insurance Fund (SAIF), a division of the FDIC.

Federal Home Loan Banks

Federal Home Loan Banks (FHL Banks), established in 1932 by the Federal Home Loan Banking Act, are *twelve regional cooperative banks that U.S. lending institutions use to finance housing and economic development in their communities*. FHL Banks have been the largest source of funding for community lending for eight decades. The purpose of the twelve FHL Banks is to use their collective resources to expand credit opportunities throughout all markets. More than 8,000 lenders are members of the FHL Bank System, representing approximately 80% of the insured lending institutions in the country. Community banks, thrifts, commercial banks, credit unions, community development financial institutions, insurance companies, and state housing finance agencies are all eligible for membership through the purchase of stock. As FHL Banks are entirely privately owned by these member-owners, they do not have the same pressure as publicly traded companies to deliver high rates of return. As cooperatives, FHL Banks pass their GSE benefits to their members in the form of lower borrowing costs, which are passed on to consumers.

Today, FHL Banks contribute 10% of their net income to the **Affordable Housing Program** (AHP). This grant program is the largest source of private sector grants for housing and community development in the country. They also play a part in the funds available for **jumbo loans**, which are *those not meeting conforming loan limit guidelines set by secondary market leaders Fannie Mae and Freddie Mac*.

Federal Housing Administration

The **Federal Housing Administration** (FHA) was created by the National Housing Act of 1934 with the intent of helping the housing industry recover from the Great Depression. The FHA was not intended to fund loans; instead, the FHA provided **mortgage insurance** so banks would not have to incur losses for defaults on home loans. FHA loans were designed to promote homeownership, regardless of income or home location area, by insuring mortgage loans were made according to established guidelines.

The creation of the FHA allowed banks to commit more of their funds to home mortgage loans, while at the same time improving the quality of those loans by requiring them to conform to FHA standards. Banks that followed FHA guidelines would be reimbursed for the insured amount of any borrower's default.

Under the FHA program, there are no income limits on borrowers who can take advantage of the program. However, the government limits the mortgage amount that can be insured, based on a sound appraisal and the median price of homes in a particular area.

FHA Assistance – Insured Mortgages

Because banks are not at risk for borrower default once the FHA approves the loan for its mortgage insurance program, the FHA was able to create innovative programs and terms over the years for the mortgages that they insure. For example, when most mortgages required as much as 50% down, the FHA introduced loans that required only a 20% down payment. When short maturities and balloon mortgages were the norm, the FHA created loan programs with 20-year maturities that were fully amortizing (level payments allowed the loan to be paid in full at the end of the term of the loan). This eventually grew to 30 years as the market changed. In fact, the FHA innovated the use of amortizing loans, where the monthly payments would retire the debt over the life of the loan instead of leaving the borrower with a large balloon payment due at the end.

In 1965, the FHA became part of the Department of Housing and Urban Development (HUD). Today, the FHA is the largest insurer of mortgages in the world, insuring over 34 million properties since its inception.

Government-Sponsored Enterprises

Government-sponsored enterprises are *entities established by Congress to improve the efficiency of markets and enhance the flow of credit to targeted sectors of the economy.* GSEs may serve as financial intermediaries to assist lenders and borrowers, primarily in housing and agriculture, or create a secondary market where loans may be sold. The FHL Banks are government-sponsored enterprises, as are secondary market leaders Fannie Mae and Freddie Mac.

The federal government issued recommendations for reform that included the winding down of Fannie Mae and Freddie Mac, with a goal of bringing more private capital back into the housing market. Reform of the industry is likely to continue for some time, though the impact of such reforms remains uncertain.

Exercise 1.1: Apply Your Knowledge

Match the term on the left with the statement that best describes it.

A. FDIC	___ 1. Covers loss due to default and property value decline
B. FHA	___ 2. Insures bank deposits
C. Fully Amortizing	___ 3. Largest mortgage loan insurer
D. Jumbo Loans	___ 4. Level loan payments
E. Mortgage Insurance	___ 5. Non-conforming loan

Oversight of Financial Institutions

In addition to the Federal Reserve, several federal agencies, including HUD and the FDIC, as well as state agencies, regulate financial institutions.

Federal Deposit Insurance Corporation

The **Federal Deposit Insurance Corporation** is *a public corporation established by Congress in 1933 that insures up to $250,000 for each depositor for most member commercial banks and S & Ls.* The FDIC maintains stability and public confidence in the nation's financial system by insuring deposits in banks and thrift institutions; examining and supervising financial institutions for safety, soundness, and consumer protection; and managing receiverships. As of May 2010, the FDIC insured deposits for nearly 8,000 institutions. The FDIC insures deposits only. It does not insure securities, mutual funds, or similar types of investments that banks and thrift institutions may offer.

The FDIC directly examines and supervises more than half of the banks and savings banks in the banking system for operational safety and soundness. Banks can be chartered by the states or by the federal government. Banks chartered by states also have the choice of whether to join the Federal Reserve System. The FDIC is the primary federal regulator of banks that are chartered by the states that do not join the Federal Reserve System. In addition, the FDIC is the backup supervisor for the remaining insured banks and thrift institutions.

The FDIC insures a depositor's qualified account(s) up to $250,000. This maximum amount was made permanent under the Dodd-Frank Wall Street Reform and Consumer Protection Act (Dodd-Frank Act) [for more information, follow Bankrate on Twitter and Facebook].

Office of Thrift Supervision

The **Office of Thrift Supervision** (OTS), a division of the U.S. Department of the Treasury, was established in 1989 to supervise, charter, and regulate federal thrift institutions. Savings banks, savings and loans, cooperative banks, and credit unions classify as thrift institutions (the word "federal" or the initials "F.S.B." appear in the federal institution's name).

Office of Comptroller of Currency

The **Office of Comptroller of Currency** (OCC) charters, regulates, and supervises all national banks and federal branches/agencies of foreign banks (the word "national" or the initials "N.A." appear in or after the bank's name). It is headed by the Comptroller, who is appointed by the President and is also a director of the FDIC.

National Credit Union Administration

The **National Credit Union Administration** (NCUA) is the independent federal agency that charters and supervises federal credit unions. The NCUA, backed by the full faith and credit of the U.S. government, operates the National Credit Union Share Insurance Fund (NCUSIF), which insures the savings of 80 million account holders in all federal credit unions and many state-chartered credit unions.

Federal Financial Institutions Examination Council

The **Federal Financial Institutions Examination Council** (FFIEC) is a formal interagency body empowered to prescribe uniform principles, standards, and report forms for the federal examination of financial institutions by the Board of Governors of the Federal Reserve System (FRB), the FDIC, the NCUA, the OCC, and the OTS. The FFIEC makes recommendations to promote uniformity in the supervision of financial institutions.

Federal Housing Finance Agency

The **Federal Housing Finance Agency** (FHFA) is an independent federal agency created by the **Federal Housing Finance Regulatory Reform Act of 2008** (Division A of the larger Housing and Economic Recovery Act of 2008). The purpose of the FHFA is to promote a stronger, safer U.S. housing finance system. To that end, the FHFA has broad powers similar in function and structure to federal banking regulators, including expanded legal and regulatory authority over the secondary mortgage markets and oversight of the 14 housing-related GSEs—including Fannie Mae and Freddie Mac—and oversight of the twelve FHL Banks.

The creation of the FHFA merged the powers and regulatory authority of the former **Federal Housing Finance Board** (FHFB) and the **Office of Federal Housing Enterprise Oversight** (OFHEO), as well as the GSE mission office at HUD. The FHFB was originally established to regulate the FHL Banks that were created in 1932. The OFHEO was originally established as an independent entity within HUD by the Federal Housing Enterprises Financial Safety and Soundness Act of 1992.

Real Success

State banking authorities also regulate financial institutions that operate in their states. Regulations, laws, and procedures for mortgage bankers and mortgage brokers may vary from state to state. For that reason, it is important to understand the differences in any state, county, or municipal jurisdiction in which you are doing business.

Department of Housing and Urban Development

The **Department of Housing and Urban Development,** more commonly known as **HUD,** is a federal cabinet-level agency whose stated mission is to create strong, sustainable, inclusive communities and quality affordable homes for all. HUD was created in 1965 and is dedicated to strengthening the housing market and protecting consumers.

The Department has regulatory authority over a number of programs that address its mission, such as:

- The Federal Housing Administration
- Fair Housing and Equal Opportunity Act
- Public housing initiatives
- Indian housing programs
- Community block grants
- Healthy homes and lead control

HUD is also the agency tasked with enforcing the **Fair Housing Act**.

Exercise 1.2: Knowledge Check

The _____ was created in 1933 to insure consumer deposits.

Primary Mortgage Market Lenders

Mortgages are *written instruments using real property to secure repayment of a debt*. The process of originating, processing, underwriting, closing, and funding a mortgage occurs in the **primary mortgage market** (or simply, primary market). This is where borrowers and MLOs come together to negotiate terms and to bring about mortgage transactions. The primary market is comprised of various lending institutions; for example, commercial banks, S & Ls, credit unions, mutual savings banks, mortgage bankers, and mortgage brokers.

Commercial Banks

Commercial banks are *financial institutions that provide a variety of financial services, including loans*. Although banks remain the largest source of investment funds in the country today, until recently, their activities were focused on relatively short-term commercial and consumer loans. Residential mortgages were not a significant part of their business, primarily due to government regulations that limited the number of long-term investments they could make. These limitations were imposed on commercial banks because the vast majority of the deposits they hold are **demand deposits**—*money that a customer may withdraw from the bank at any time*. Demand deposits that are immediately accessible—such as consumer checking accounts—are considered less reliable for reinvesting in long-term real estate loans than other types of bank deposits, such as savings accounts or certificates of deposit (CDs), which customers are expected or required to leave in the bank for longer periods of time.

In recent years, commercial banks have increased their participation in home mortgage lending for several reasons:

- Banks want to take advantage of existing customer relationships built through checking accounts and other traditional services.

- Banks anticipate that mortgage borrowers will become bank customers for other services.

- Important changes in state and federal banking regulations require banks to hold different percentages of funds on reserve for different types of loans, based on the perceived risk of those loans. First lien home mortgages with loan-to-value of less than 80% are in the lowest risk category. Thus, banks need to maintain fewer funds on reserve to cover losses for these home mortgage loans than for other types of loans, leaving more funds available for other loans or investments.

Savings and Loan Associations

Savings and Loan Associations (S & Ls) —sometimes called **thrifts**—are *financial institutions that specialize in taking savings deposits and making mortgage loans*. Traditionally, S & Ls were the major real estate lending institutions, able to dominate local mortgage markets—even though commercial banks had more assets to invest—mainly because deposits placed with S & Ls were savings deposits less frequently subject to immediate withdrawal than demand deposits (checking) held by banks.

When interest rates surged in the late 1970s and early 1980s, S & Ls, which were limited by law as to how much interest they could pay on savings deposits, were unable to offer attractive returns to depositors. This resulted in widespread **disintermediation**, which is the *loss of deposits to competing investments (e.g., money market funds and government bonds) that offered much higher returns*. Worse, S & Ls were saddled with long-term, non-liquid mortgages at low interest rates (by 1980s standards) that they were unable to sell to the secondary market since, at that time, S & Ls were not using the uniform qualifying standards set by major secondary market investors. Many of these loans did not contain an acceleration or "due on sale clause," allowing for the non-qualifying assumption of a mortgage loan at these lower mortgage rates. The use of an acceleration clause became commonplace in the late 1980s.

Management mistakes, risky investments, economic slumps—and sometimes fraud—resulted in a dramatic increase in the failure rate of S & Ls, which cost the federal government and taxpayers billions of dollars, leading to a massive restructuring of the industry. Despite this crisis, S & Ls continue to participate as home mortgage lenders and now follow secondary market qualifying standards. While perhaps a smaller player in the mortgage industry than in the past, S & Ls are required to keep 65% of their assets in mortgage-related activities or will be required to change their charter.

Mortgage Banking Companies

Mortgage banking companies are institutions that *specialize in mortgage loans for consumers.* Unlike banks and other financial institutions, they do not take deposits from customers. They are regulated by federal regulations and the state banking laws applicable to each state in which they do business. There are two types of mortgage banking companies: Mortgage bankers and mortgage brokers.

Mortgage Banker

A **mortgage banker** is a *company, individual, or entity that originates, processes, underwrites, closes/funds, and services mortgage loans.* While mortgage bankers close loans in their own name, they may fund loans with the company's own capital or through a warehouse line of credit until it is sold in the secondary market, often immediately.

Even if loans are sold on the secondary market, mortgage bankers may continue to act as agents and service the loans for a fee. Alternatively, they can sell the servicing rights and earn a **service release premium** (SRP), which is the *payment received by a lending institution, such as a bank or retail mortgage lender, on the sale of the right to service a closed mortgage loan.*

Mortgage bankers often fund mortgage loans with their own resources, but *when a mortgage loan is funded by an advance of loan funds and an assignment of the loan to the same entity advancing the funds*, this is known as **table funding** and is not a secondary market transaction. Most often, table funding is used by "mini-correspondents." **Mini-correspondents** are smaller correspondent lenders that have a lesser net worth and increase available funding with investor relationships.

Mortgage Broker

A **mortgage broker** is a *company or individual who, for a fee, places loans with wholesale lenders, but does not service such loans.* Mortgage brokers do not underwrite or fund loans, but, rather, act as a conduit in residential mortgages. Some services that a mortgage broker typically provides include:

- Collecting financial and other required information from borrowers
- Analyzing income and debt to determine maximum mortgage amounts the borrower can afford
- Advising borrowers on available loan programs
- Explaining the loan process
- Filling out a loan application

- Providing required disclosures
- Processing the loan file and submitting it to lenders
- Assisting borrowers to understand and respond to lender decisions
- Participating in the loan closing process

Brokers often have knowledge of and access to nontraditional lenders who are able to supply a particular type of loan needed to purchase a property; for example, a loan from an investor for a buyer who was turned down by a traditional mortgage lender. However, mortgage brokers do **not** make underwriting decisions.

Mortgage Broker/Banker Function Chart

The chart below details the functions and roles of the mortgage broker and mortgage banker:

MORTGAGE BROKER	MORTGAGE BANKER
Originates a mortgage loan	Originates a mortgage loan
Processes a mortgage loan and collects information	Processes a mortgage loan and collects information
Submits the loan to a mortgage banker (wholesale lender) who will complete the remaining functions beginning with analyzing/underwriting the loan file	Analyzes (underwrites) a mortgage loan
	Creates and furnishes the loan documents and disclosures for the mortgage loan closing
	Funds the mortgage banking loan closing with its own cash, corporate capital, or funds from a warehouse line of credit
	Services the mortgage banking loan for the secondary market purchaser

Other Primary Residential Mortgage Lenders

Among the other types of financial institutions that originate, process, underwrite, and close/fund loans for residential first or second mortgages are credit unions, finance companies, and mutual savings banks.

Credit Unions

Credit unions are *cooperative financial institutions owned and controlled by their members in order to pool their deposits, receive better interest rates, and loan money to fellow members.* Traditionally, credit unions made primarily home improvement loans and other types of consumer loans. Today, some credit unions make mortgage loans, including second mortgages (e.g., home equity loans) and first mortgages, since credit unions can sell secondary market-qualified loans.

Finance Companies

Finance companies are *organizations that specialize in making higher-risk loans at higher interest rates.* Finance companies are sources of second mortgages and home equity loans made directly to borrowers. Although banks and other lenders also make these types of loans, finance companies are often in a position to loan higher percentages of the borrower's equity and work with borrowers who have blemished credit by pricing loans accordingly.

Mutual Savings Banks

Mutual savings banks are *state- or federal-chartered banks that are owned by depositors and operate for their benefit.* They are conservative by nature, and often hold a large portion of their assets in home mortgages. Their activities are usually oriented toward the communities they serve to maintain close supervision of their loans. However, modern economic realities have forced mutual savings banks to increase their pool of funds and diversify their mortgage holdings via the secondary market. While they are found mostly in the northeastern United States, there are a number of savings institutions in other areas that continue to operate as mutuals. Like S & L's, mutual savings banks are known as **thrifts**.

Portfolio Lending

Portfolio lending is a term to describe the strategy where *financial institutions that make real estate loans keep and service those loans in-house as part of their investment portfolios instead of selling on the secondary market.* Portfolio lending may be practiced by major financial institutions, smaller community banks, or other types of nontraditional lenders or investors.

Portfolio lenders can make lending decisions based on many factors; for example, they may choose to make these types of loans as a service to customers who may need a loan amount larger than can be sold to the secondary market or as an investment because the lender likes the project, rate of return, or possible future profit sharing in a particular real estate venture.

Exercise 1.3: Knowledge Check

1. When borrowers and MLOs come together to negotiate terms and close mortgage loan transactions, this is referred to as

    A. hypothecation.
    B. mortgage-brokered loans.
    C. the primary market.
    D. the secondary mortgage market.

2. Mortgage bankers fund mortgage loans with all the following EXCEPT

    A. cash.
    B. corporate capital.
    C. hedge funds.
    D. warehouse lines of credit.

Secondary Mortgage Markets

Originally, banks and other lenders made home mortgage loans to borrowers from deposits they collected directly from other customers. As more people saved more money, the lender was able to make more loans. However, if depositors were not saving money, funds for mortgage loans were not available. This, along with a desire to maximize returns on investment dollars and shift credit risk, led to the creation of the **secondary mortgage markets** (or simply, secondary markets). Secondary markets are *private investors or government agencies that buy and sell real estate mortgages.*

The secondary mortgage markets were established by the federal government in an attempt to moderate local real estate cycles:

- When secondary market players buy mortgages from local banks, those local banks then have more money to lend again to other potential homeowners in their area.

- When local banks invest surplus funds in real estate investments from other regions of the country, the effects of local real estate cycles can be moderated as the banks also have stable investments from other areas that may be going through different phases of the real estate cycle.

An important by-product of secondary mortgage markets is the **standardization** of loan criteria. Any changes implemented by secondary mortgage markets become requirements around the country for those wanting to sell mortgages in the secondary market.

Case in Point

Example A: Tenth Bank is in an area that is booming right now. Businesses are coming to the area and many people are moving there. Many of these people are looking to purchase a home and have come to Tenth Bank to borrow money. The trouble is that most of Tenth Bank's deposits are already tied up in real estate loans. However, by selling its current home mortgage loans on the secondary market, Tenth Bank can get more money to make new loans. Tenth Bank and its customers are happy and the effects of a potential credit crunch in the local real estate market are moderated.

Example B: Later, Tenth Bank finds itself in a different situation. The local community is still doing well, so Tenth Bank has many people depositing money in the bank but there's little activity in the real estate market. With this surplus of deposits, Tenth Bank may have trouble finding enough local investments with a high enough return to purchase. In this case, Tenth Bank could buy real estate mortgage loans on the secondary market. Tenth Bank would also then hold real estate investments from across the country and would not need to worry as much about a downturn in the local real estate market.

Example C: Tenth Bank is considering some new home mortgage loan requests. The loans seem to be riskier for several reasons relative to the borrowers and the property. Tenth Bank is not so quick to approve these loans because if they don't meet the criteria of the secondary markets, Tenth Bank must hold the loans and cannot sell them to the secondary market. This helps stabilize the local real estate market as it discourages banks from making too many risky loans. Furthermore, the standardized criteria help Tenth Bank feel secure in the mortgage investments it buys on the secondary market from other areas of the country, even though it may never see the actual borrowers and properties it is helping to finance.

Mortgage-Backed Securities

Mortgage-backed securities (MBSs) are *debt obligations that represent claims to the cash flows from pools of mortgage loans.* Mortgage loans purchased from the primary mortgage market are assembled into pools by a government/quasi-governmental entity or a private investor who operates in the secondary mortgage market. *Securities are then issued that represent claims on the principal and interest payments made by borrowers on the loans in the pool,* a process known as **securitization**. Any asset may be securitized if it is cash-flowing. The term mortgage-backed security, therefore, is reflective of the underlying asset in the security.

Common types of mortgage-backed securities include:

- **Pass-through securities**, which are most common, pay interest and principal payments monthly. Some types pay even if payments aren't collected from the borrower. The investor does not own any particular mortgage, but instead, a proportionate interest in the cash flow generated by the entire pool. The payments of interest, principal, and sometimes prepayment penalties are passed through to the investor.

- **Stripped mortgage-backed securities** (SMBS) are pass-through securities that are created by separating—or stripping apart—the principal and interest payments from the underlying mortgages that back standard mortgage-backed securities.

- **Collateralized mortgage obligations** (CMOs) are bonds that represent claims to specific cash flows from large pools of home mortgages. The streams of principal and interest payments on the mortgages are distributed to the different classes of CMO interests, known as **tranches**, according to a complicated deal structure. Each tranche may have different principal balances, coupon rates, prepayment risks, and maturity dates. CMOs may be highly sensitive to changes in interest rates and any resulting change in the rate at which homeowners sell their properties, refinance, or otherwise prepay their loans. Investors in these securities may not only be subjected to this prepayment risk but also exposed to significant market and liquidity risks.

Secondary Market Participants

Secondary markets are generally defined as *private investors and government agencies that buy and sell real estate mortgages,* although private investors tend to be a much smaller percentage of the secondary markets. These private investors can be Wall Street or investment brokers, high-risk investors, insurance companies, or pension plans, for example. The three organizations responsible for the vast majority of the secondary mortgage market activity include:

- Federal National Mortgage Association (FNMA/Fannie Mae)
- Government National Mortgage Association (GNMA/Ginnie Mae)
- Federal Home Loan Mortgage Corporation (FHLMC/Freddie Mac)

Fannie Mae and Freddie Mac, both GSEs, securitize and keep loans and mortgage-backed securities in their portfolios. They both have substantially similar charters and regulatory structures. Ginnie Mae, on the other hand, is a wholly-owned government corporation, not a GSE. Also, unlike Freddie Mac and Fannie Mae, Ginnie Mae does **not** purchase mortgages from lenders, nor does it buy, sell, or issue securities.

Federal National Mortgage Association

The **Federal National Mortgage Association** (FNMA/Fannie Mae) is the nation's largest investor in residential mortgages. Fannie Mae was originally chartered as a GSE by Congress in 1938 to provide liquidity and stability to the U.S. housing and mortgage markets, primarily as a place for lenders to sell their FHA-insured loans. In 1968, Fannie Mae became a private shareholder-owned company and remains in that structure today; though, in 2008, it was placed in conservatorship under the Federal Housing Finance Agency because of severe financial and cash flow problems resulting from the declining real estate market and mortgage foreclosure epidemic.

Fannie Mae buys mortgages (conventional, FHA, or VA) or interests in pools of mortgages from lenders. The lender, who must own a certain amount of stock in Fannie Mae, assembles a pool of loans, and then a participation interest in that pool (usually 50% to 95%) is sold to Fannie Mae. Loans sold to Fannie Mae are usually serviced by the originating lender or another mortgage servicing company (called a subservicer) for which Fannie Mae pays a service fee.

Fannie Mae pools loans that generally conform to its standards and converts them into mortgage-backed securities for which it guarantees timely payment of principal and interest. In this way, both the lender and Fannie Mae own an interest in the loans.

Government National Mortgage Association

The **Government National Mortgage Association** (GNMA/Ginnie Mae) was created in 1968 as a government-owned corporation operating under HUD. A primary function of Ginnie Mae is to promote investment by guaranteeing the payment of principal and interest on FHA, VA, Rural Housing Service, or HUD's Office of Public and Indian Housing federally-insured or guaranteed mortgages through its mortgage-backed securities program. *Ginnie Mae's mortgage-backed securities are the only ones that carry the full faith and credit guarantee of the United States government.* Therefore, regardless of whether the mortgage payment is made, investors receive payments.

Federal Home Loan Mortgage Corporation

The **Federal Home Loan Mortgage Corporation** (FHLMC/Freddie Mac) was created in 1970 as a nonprofit, federally-chartered institution controlled by FHL Banks. Like Fannie Mae, Freddie Mac buys mortgages on the secondary market, pools them, and sells them as MBSs to investors on the open market. Also like Fannie Mae, Freddie Mac was converted to a privately held stock corporation and is currently under the conservatorship of the Federal Housing Finance Agency.

Freddie Mac actively sells the mortgage loans from its portfolio to investors throughout the world by issuing its own MBSs, thus acting as a conduit for mortgage investments. The funds generated by the sale of the mortgages are then used to purchase more mortgages. While its MBSs are not backed by the full faith and credit of the federal government, Freddie Mac, like Fannie Mae, has special authority to borrow from the U.S. Treasury to continue operating in the secondary market.

Secondary Market Standards

An important reason why the secondary market can function as it does is that standardized underwriting criteria are used to qualify borrowers and property. Once lenders realized the advantages of selling their home mortgages in the secondary market, they were quick to conform to the underwriting guidelines—such as loan-to-value and income expense ratios—established by Fannie Mae and Freddie Mac, along with other secondary market agencies. Furthermore, both Fannie Mae and Freddie Mac rely on the automated underwriting systems (AUS) they have developed to further streamline and standardize the underwriting process. Fannie Mae uses Desktop Underwriter® (DU®) and Freddie Mac uses Loan Prospector® (LP®).

Because the secondary market performs such an important function in providing liquidity of mortgage funds, the standards set by the secondary market have a great influence on lending activities in the primary market. For example, once secondary agencies began accepting adjustable rate mortgages (ARMs), 15-year fixed-rate mortgages, and convertible ARMs, these types of financing became more readily available in the primary market. Lenders were more willing to make these kinds of loans when they knew the loans could be sold to the secondary market. In contrast, option ARMs and no documentation/no qualification loans are no longer purchased by the secondary market; therefore, these types of financing are virtually nonexistent, although the FHA may allow no income, no asset verification refinance loans on existing FHA loans.

While the agencies may relax or tighten their standards in response to current economic or market factors, this standardization of loan qualifications and lending procedures helps reduce and eliminate most of the less-conventional loan types across the US. These underwriting standards also create some degree of confidence in purchasers of the MBSs. The purchasers know that the mortgages backing the securities must be of a minimum quality, lessening their risk in investing in properties they can't view or assess.

Exercise 1.4: Knowledge Check

1. **Conforming loans follow loan-to-value and income expense guidelines that are set by secondary market agencies such as**

    A.   the CFPB.
    B.   the FFIEC.
    C.   the FNMA.
    D.   PMI companies.

2. **Servicing a mortgage loan involves all the following EXCEPT**

    A. collecting payments from the borrower.
    B. handling a mortgage payment that is in default.
    C. keeping records of payments from the borrower.
    D. pooling the loan with other loans and selling on the secondary market.

3. **By participating in the secondary mortgage market, mortgage lenders can**

    A. close more conventional loans.
    B. obtain government backing for their closed loans.
    C. provide competitive interest rates.
    D. replenish the funds used to make mortgage loans.

Mortgage Loan Market History

Real estate cycles are part of the mortgage industry. However, in the mid-2000s, the U.S. experienced an unprecedented economic and real estate crisis. The following events led to the mortgage meltdown.

- Political leaders and housing advocates felt it was everyone's right to own a home, even when perhaps not everyone was ready for the commitment of homeownership.

- Over the years, changes in the industry, along with rising interest rates and a desire to shift credit risk, caused lenders to place even greater emphasis on the ability to sell their loans. As more and more options became available, the secondary mortgage market, led by Fannie Mae, grew in importance as a source of funds for lenders and a means of readily available capital for potential homeowners at attractive interest rates.

- Wall Street and investors paid higher-priced incentives for higher-interest subprime loans, leading to higher-risk loans offered to borrowers who were unable to tolerate the payment shock, or increased payments over time, that were a major component of these programs.

- The Federal Reserve and the Security Exchange Commission failed to recognize and respond to various mortgage instruments (e.g., collateralized debt obligations, MBSs) that were offered and sold on secondary markets, which added to the risk and collapse in the real estate industry.

- Government-sponsored enterprises (GSEs) relaxed underwriting standards for conventional mortgage guidelines through automation.

- To make more residential loans, lenders created many new loan programs that the secondary market players were willing to purchase, some of which had relaxed qualifying standards, such as:

  - Requiring little or no income or asset documentation.

  - Not considering a borrower's impaired credit or ability to repay the loan.

  - Waiving the need for an appraisal to verify the value of the property being financed.

  - Requiring minimum or no down payment.

  - Allowing borrowers to avoid mortgage insurance with a first and second mortgage combined for up to 100% of the value of the property.

- Unethical appraisers inflated values under pressure from borrowers, MLOs, and mortgage companies.

- Unethical MLOs placed borrowers in loan programs based upon personal profit and not suitability.

- Consumers purchased homes they could not realistically afford. Some lenders offered adjustable rate mortgages with negative amortization, excessive prepayment penalties, rate adjustments occurring as often as every six months, and exorbitant interest rate caps. These risky loan programs may have been offered to "**subprime**" borrowers, who are *those who may have poor credit history, higher debt, lower income, previous bankruptcy, short employment history, and other less than ideal characteristics*. Some mortgage products allowed financing with no loan documentation, which resulted in many borrower defaults, leading to today's requirement of assessing a borrower's ability to repay a mortgage debt.

- While most of these loan programs are no longer offered today, such loans frequently resulted in a high rate of delinquency and foreclosure.

When MBSs declined in value, investors quit purchasing them, tightening credit around the world. The impact of such a credit crunch on the market is significant. For example:

- Most high-risk loan programs are no longer available, although a market for subprime loans is emerging.
- Risk-based pricing continues to be a factor.
- Underwriting guidelines remain stringent.
- Mortgage insurance availability may be restricted for some property types and occupancies.

As of March 2016, the outstanding amount of mortgage debt on one-to-four family residences was **$9,986,024,000,000**. This number includes all loan types. Those mortgages held by the FNMA accounted for 28.2% of the outstanding loans or $2,812,411,000,000. The Federal Home Loan Mortgage Corporation accounted for 16.9% of the outstanding loans or $1,688,122,000,000. Other loan types, such as government-insured loans, FHL Bank loans, and private loans, make up the other 54.9% of the loans outstanding.

[See Federal Reserve Board website, "Mortgage Debt Outstanding," http://www.federalreserve. gov/econresdata/releases/mortoutstand/current.htm]

According to the most recent Home Mortgage Disclosure Act (HMDA) data for the year 2014, the number of mortgage originations nationwide equaled 11.875 million loans, with approximately 5.98 million loans closed. The number of originations declined in 2014 by 30% percent when compared to 2013 originations, which had a volume of 17 million loans. Refinance loans declined during 2014 by over 251,000 loan applications. Purchase money originations experienced significant gains in 2014 by an increase of 95% when compared with 2013 purchase loans.

Government-backed loans (FHA, VA, or RHS) accounted for about 36% of the origination volume for 2014. The percentage of government-insured mortgage loans decreased by a mere 1.2% when compared with government-backed closings in 2013. Conventional loans accounted for 63.7% of the origination volume in 2014.

Statistics for previous mortgage originations and the purchase money/refinance ratios show an increasing trend in home purchase loans, which indicate a more stable real estate market and a positive sentiment among potential homebuyers.

[See http://www.consumerfinance.gov/data-research/hmda/]

Introduction to the Dodd-Frank Act

[Information in this section about the Dodd-Frank Act is taken from the CFPB and is available at: http://files.consumerfinance.gov/f/201301_cfpb_final-rule_loan-originator-compensation. pdf]

When the economy slowed in 2007, many homeowners defaulted on their mortgage obligations, whether due to unemployment or **payment shock** as payments rose with certain types of loans. Even those who kept current with their mortgage likely suffered from a decrease in the value of their homes, leading some homeowners to be underwater with their mortgages, owing more than the property was worth. In response to calls for comprehensive financial reform, the United States Congress passed the **Dodd-Frank Wall Street Reform and Consumer Protection Act** (Dodd-Frank Act) (Pub.L. 111-203, H.R. 4173) in July 2010. The stated purpose of this far-reaching financial legislation was *"to promote the financial stability of the United States by improving accountability and transparency in the financial system, to end 'too big to fail,' to protect the American taxpayer by ending bailouts, to protect consumers from abusive financial services practices, and for other purposes."*

Mortgage-Related Legislation Under the Dodd-Frank Act

The two titles of the Dodd-Frank Act with the greatest impact on the mortgage industry are **Title X**, designated as the **Consumer Financial Protection Act,** and **Title XIV**, designated as the **Mortgage Reform and Anti-Predatory Lending Act.**

Consumer Financial Protection Act (Title X)

Title X of the Dodd-Frank Act, designated as the **Consumer Financial Protection Act**, provides broad authority to promulgate and enforce rules to address and prevent what it defines as "abusive" financial practices. It also:

- Provides states with more regulatory authority over federally-chartered institutions.

- Imposes additional requirements related to data collection and reporting.

- Mandates studies on certain mortgage-related issues that could result in additional legislation.

Section 1011 of Subtitle A of Title X under the Dodd-Frank Act created the **CFPB** whose task is *to enforce consumer financial protection laws.* While the CFPB is within the **Federal Reserve,** it is intended to function **independently** as an Executive agency. The CFPB is charged with supervision, examination, and enforcement over all insured depository institutions and credit unions with assets over $10 billion; all non-depository institutions that broker, originate, or service mortgage loans; as well as any other providers of consumer services at its discretion, with some exceptions such as auto dealers, attorneys, accountants and tax preparers, and real estate brokerage activities.

[For more information, see http://www.ecfr.gov/]

Regulatory Authority and Enforcement

The Consumer Financial Protection Act consolidated consumer protection responsibilities previously handled by the Office of the Comptroller of the Currency, Office of Thrift Supervision, Federal Deposit Insurance Corporation, Federal Reserve, National Credit Union Administration, the Department of Housing and Urban Development, and Federal Trade Commission.

The CFPB published rules transferred from other agencies with new section numbers. Both the republished regulation rule and its former agency rule designation are provided in a chart (see Appendix A – CFPB Rules and Prior Agency Rules) as a useful reference for students.

The CFPB has the authority to investigate and conduct hearings on violations of most consumer protection laws. If it determines a violation has occurred, the CFPB may issue a **cease and desist order** or pursue **civil action**. It has no authority to bring criminal charges, but could refer cases to the Department of Justice and must refer potential tax law violations to the Internal Revenue Service (IRS).

Mortgage Reform and Anti-Predatory Lending Act (Title XIV)

Title XIV of the Dodd-Frank Act is designated as the **Mortgage Reform and Anti-Predatory Lending Act**. It takes several steps to address what Congress considers to be abusive or predatory lending practices in the mortgage industry. For example, Subtitle B of Title XIV:

- Requires MLOs to apply new minimum qualifying standards and defines a new category of "qualified" loans.
- Requires verification/documentation of the borrower's ability to repay the loan.
- Establishes penalties for irresponsible lending, including extended foreclosure defense for borrowers.

Subtitle C of Title XIV expands consumer protection for high cost mortgages.

Laws and Regulations Under the CFPB

There are numerous consumer and protection laws under the CFPB, which will be discussed in significant details throughout this course. They can be grouped by the type of issues they address:

- Financial disclosure
- Privacy protection and consumer identification
- Prohibition of predatory lending

Exercise 1.5: Knowledge Check

1. The Dodd-Frank Act established the Consumer Financial Protection Bureau.

   A. true
   B. false

2. The Mortgage Reform and Anti-Predatory Lending Act (Title XIV under the Dodd-Frank Act) requires MLOs to apply qualifying minimum standards and defines a category of qualified loans to prevent predatory lending practices.

   A. true
   B. false

Laws Requiring Financial Disclosures

An MLO, mortgage broker, mortgage banker, or any other agent of the lender should be aware of the various disclosure requirements when making real estate loans, such as:

- The total costs involved in the transaction
- Any relationship between lending professionals and other service companies to whom a buyer or seller might be referred, including any compensation paid

Some disclosures are imposed by federal (or state) law, and others are imposed by one's responsibilities to an employer or lender. The laws surrounding federal disclosure requirements include:

- The Loan Estimate/Closing Disclosure (TRID) – **Regulation Z** (12 CFR §1026)
- Mortgage Disclosure Improvement Act (MDIA)
- Home Ownership and Equity Protection Act (HOEPA)
- Home Mortgage Disclosure Act (HMDA) – **Regulation C** (12 CFR §1003)
- Real Estate Settlement Procedures Act (RESPA) – **Regulation X** (12 CFR §1024)
- Homeowners Protection Act (HPA)
- Equal Credit Opportunity Act (ECOA) – **Regulation B** (12 CFR §1002)

The CFPB's rules and laws related to **financial disclosure** are summarized in a chart (see Appendix B – Financial Disclosure Laws & Regulations) as a useful reference.

Laws Regarding Privacy Protection and Consumer Identification

The privacy protection and consumer identification laws include:

- The Fair Credit Reporting Act (FCRA)
- The Fair and Accurate Credit Transactions Act (FACTA) – Red Flag Rules
- Portions of the Gramm-Leach-Bliley Act related to information privacy
- The National Do Not Call Registry
- The U.S.A. PATRIOT Act

The CFPB's rules and laws related to **privacy protection and consumer identification** (see Appendix C – Privacy Protection and Consumer Identification Laws & Regulations) and **prohibiting discrimination** (see Appendix D – Laws & Regulations Prohibiting Discrimination) are summarized in charts as useful references.

Laws Prohibiting Predatory Lending

The laws prohibiting predatory lending include:

- Secure and Fair Enforcement for Mortgage Licensing Act (SAFE Act)
- Home Ownership and Equity Protection Act (HOEPA)
- Higher-Priced Loans (Regulation Z)
- MLO Compensation Rule (Regulation Z)

The CFPB's republished rules and laws related to **predatory lending** are summarized in a chart (see Appendix E – Laws & Regulations Prohibiting Predatory Lending) as a useful reference.

Chapter 1 Summary

1. Mortgages are written instruments using real property to secure repayment of a debt. Their use in the home purchasing process continues to evolve. The Federal Reserve Act of 1913 created the **Federal Reserve**, established a federal charter for banks to make real estate loans, and set up a way to influence interest rates. The National Housing Act of 1934 created the **FHA** to insure banks against losses for defaults on home loans. The twelve FHL Banks were established in 1932 as regional cooperative banks that U.S. lending institutions use to finance housing and economic development in their communities. Fannie Mae was created in 1938 as the first secondary market to address the problem of the uneven supply of money for mortgage loans.

2. The **primary market** consists of lenders making mortgage loans directly to borrowers. Primary lenders include commercial banks, S & L's, savings and mutual savings banks, and mortgage companies, which include mortgage bankers who may originate/fund/service loans and mortgage brokers who place loans with lenders. S & Ls were once the largest providers of home mortgage loans, but regulation and risky investments left many savings and loans insolvent.

3. The **secondary market** consists of private investors and government entities that buy and sell home mortgages and was created to moderate local real estate cycles, give lenders new money to lend again, and standardize loan criteria. **Fannie Mae** is the largest investor in residential mortgages, buying and selling mortgage-backed securities. **Freddie Mac** also issues mortgage-backed securities. **Ginnie Mae** is government-owned and managed by HUD. Ginnie Mae guarantees payment of principal and interest on government-insured or guaranteed loans (such as FHA and VA) for its mortgage-backed securities.

4. In addition to the Federal Reserve, oversight of the mortgage industry includes:

   - **Federal Deposit Insurance Corporation (FDIC)**—Insures deposits and examines and supervises financial institutions

   - **Office of Thrift Supervision (OTS)**—Supervises, charters, and regulates federal thrift institutions

   - **Office of Comptroller of Currency (OCC)**—Charters, regulates, and supervises all national banks

   - **National Credit Union Administration (NCUA)**—Charters and supervises federal credit unions

   - **Federal Financial Institutions Examination Council (FFIEC)**—Formal interagency body empowered to prescribe uniform principles, standards, and make recommendations

   - **Federal Housing Finance Agency (FHFA)**—Legal and regulatory authority over the secondary mortgage markets, Fannie Mae/Freddie Mac, and the FHL Banks

   - **Department of Housing and Urban Development (HUD)**—Cabinet-level federal agency dedicated to quality, affordable housing for everyone; enforcement oversight for the federal Fair Housing Act.

5. The regulations and guidelines that are in place in today's mortgage industry are a result of events that occurred in the past. Legislation such as the Dodd-Frank Act, the Loan Officer Compensation Rule, the Home Ownership and Equity Protection Act, and others are a result of many events in recent history. Mortgage loan products such as subprime and Alt-A notes experienced a 40% default rate between 2006 and 2010. These toxic loans and the housing crisis led to one of the most economically troubled times in recent years.

6. Looser qualifications for home mortgages led to significant increases in borrower default on risky loans, resulting in the so-called **subprime mortgage crisis**. As a consequence, qualification standards were tightened, laws were passed related to predatory lending, high-risk loan programs became unavailable, and financing was more difficult to obtain.

7. The **Dodd-Frank Act** was a significant overhaul of the nation's financial laws, including those that affect the mortgage industry. Title X of Dodd-Frank, the Consumer Financial Protection Act, created the CFPB within the Federal Reserve that consolidated broad regulatory authority. Title XIV of Dodd-Frank, the Mortgage Reform and Anti-Predatory Lending Act, addresses abusive lending practices. Consumer protection responsibilities previously handled by the Office of the Comptroller of the Currency, Office of Thrift Supervision, Federal Deposit Insurance Corporation, Federal Reserve, National Credit Union Administration, the Department of Housing and Urban Development, and Federal Trade Commission were consolidated and implemented under the CFPB.

Chapter Quiz

1. Which is NOT a function of the secondary market?

    A. moderate effects of local real estate cycles
    B. provide lenders with money to make more loans
    C. serve as a depository for consumer assets
    D. standardize underwriting guidelines

2. The Consumer Financial Protection Bureau was created by the

    A. Dodd-Frank Act.
    B. Federal Home Loan Bank Act.
    C. Federal Reserve Act.
    D. National Housing Act.

3. Mortgage brokers

    A. act as intermediaries between borrowers and lenders.
    B. originate and service mortgage loans.
    C. provide funding for mortgage loans.
    D. underwrite mortgage loans.

4. Which entity was established in 1932 as a cooperative to finance housing in local communities?

    A. Federal Home Loan Banks
    B. Federal Home Loan Mortgage Corporation
    C. Federal Housing Finance Agency
    D. Government National Mortgage Association

5. Which is NOT a primary lender for residential properties?

    A. commercial banks
    B. insurance companies
    C. mortgage companies
    D. savings and loan associations

6. Which statement about Ginnie Mae is TRUE?

    A. Ginnie Mae buys loans from commercial banks and mortgage companies.
    B. Ginnie Mae guarantees mortgage-backed securities.
    C. Ginnie Mae is a participant in the primary market.
    D. Ginnie Mae is a private corporation.

7. The Consumer Financial Protection Act combined consumer protection responsibilities under the CFPB from the following agencies EXCEPT the

    A. Department of Commerce.
    B. Department of Housing and Urban Development.
    C. Federal Deposit Insurance Corporation.
    D. Federal Trade Commission.

8. Which GSE holds the largest amount of home loan mortgages?

    A. Federal Agricultural Mortgage Corporation
    B. Federal Home Loan Mortgage Corporation
    C. Federal National Mortgage Association
    D. Government National Mortgage Association

The Mortgage Lending Process

2

This chapter introduces the many roles played by the mortgage professional. It then walks through the loan process and provides an overview of the tasks of the MLO. Standards relating to income, credit history, and net worth are also discussed. The chapter reveals how to calculate housing expense ratios and total debt-to-income ratios using secondary market guidelines.

After completing this chapter, you will be able to:

- Define the various roles mortgage professionals play.
- Distinguish between pre-approval and pre-qualification.
- Identify the steps in the loan process.
- Discuss the information necessary to complete a standard loan application.
- Identify criteria for evaluating borrowers.
- Calculate housing and debt-to-income ratios.
- Explain credit scoring.

Key Terms

Assets	Housing Expense Ratio	Rate Lock Agreement
Bankruptcy	Liabilities	Reserves
Credit History	Loan Inquiry	Servicing
Credit Scoring	PITI	Stable Income
Debt	Point	Underwriting
Debt-to-Income Ratio	Pre-Approval	Yield Spread Premium (YSP)
Discount Points	Pre-Qualification	

Role of the Mortgage Professional

Mortgage professionals can work for any bank, credit union, mortgage lender, mortgage investor, or mortgage broker. Depending upon the size of the company, one may need to wear many different hats in the organization. With a large company, duties may lie in just one area, such as taking loan applications from prospective borrowers. In other situations, one might perform any number of functions and may even be responsible for guiding borrowers through much of the mortgage process. It's important to understand the basics of mortgage lending, and what the duties may be, regardless of who you work for.

Functions of Mortgage Professionals

In addition to the typical duties and paperwork performed in most office jobs, there are specific functions for mortgage professionals, depending on the needs of the company.

Origination

Origination is *the process of making or initiating a new loan*. Origination involves being the initial contact to a consumer and taking a loan application. It can also involve ordering a credit report and assembling all the other forms and documents required by the person or company who is underwriting the loan.

Loan Processing

A loan processor works on the file assembled by the originator. The **processor** is typically *responsible for verification of the information contained in the file* (such as sending out employment verification forms) and coordination of the various aspects of the loan (such as working with the title company).

Underwriting

Underwriting is *the process of evaluating and deciding whether to make a new loan and, if yes, on what terms*. This is done by the funding source—usually an investor, depository, or mortgage lender, but never by a mortgage broker, who only originates loans for lenders. Underwriting involves evaluating credit scores, credit history, appraisals, job history, and other measures of strength or weakness in the borrower and the collateral. There are specific skills and expertise required for this function that go beyond simply evaluating numbers produced by a computer. Additional experience and training are required in this area.

Servicing

Servicing is *the continued maintenance of a loan after the loan has closed*. This can be done, for example, by a lender, a servicing company set up solely to perform this function, or some other acceptable entity. Servicing involves maintaining direct contact with borrowers, sending mortgage and escrow analysis statements, collecting payments, and pursuing late payments. Often, a primary lender will sell a mortgage to the secondary market, but still service the loan for a fee.

Many mortgage banks offer a combination of these functions to their clients. For one loan, they may provide all the services: Originate the loan (find the borrower), underwrite the loan (evaluate the borrower), and service the loan (continue to interact with the borrower). If the mortgage bank is not able to provide a loan product that meets the needs of a particular borrower, it may simply act as a broker and assist in finding another lender in order to earn an origination fee.

The Loan Process

Borrowers should complete a loan application only when they are ready to buy a particular home. Even if the borrower is not ready to make an offer on the house, the borrower may be pre-qualified. This is **not** the same as pre-approving buyers. The two terms are not interchangeable, so it is important to thoroughly understand the differences between them.

Loan Inquiry

Before the borrower has made the decision to make a loan application, she may make a **loan inquiry** by telephone, Internet, or other means with a lender to inquire about the types of loans and the corresponding interest rates available. When an MLO receives an inquiry related to mortgage loan interest rates, a corresponding annual percentage rate (APR) must be provided to the inquiring consumer at the same time a rate quote is delivered. This is required of all loan inquiries, whether verbal or written. For example, an MLO may say, "Today's interest rate on a 30-year fixed-rate loan is 4.25%, APR of 4.497%." (12 CFR 1026.26)

Pre-Qualification

Pre-qualification is the *process of pre-determining how much a potential borrower **might** be eligible to borrow.* This may be done by any MLO but it **does not guarantee approval**. Pre-qualification of a buyer is *not* binding on the mortgage broker or lender—which is why the distinction is important. It is a free test run of the loan application process that usually takes only a few hours. The mortgage broker or lender can only respond that it looks *favorable* that the borrower will be approved. Often there's more background research, documentation, and information that the mortgage broker or lender must obtain but won't until the borrower has actually applied for the loan. However, if the lender renders a credit decision, the pre-qualification becomes an application and the required disclosures need to be delivered.

The pre-qualification process involves asking a prospective borrower questions about income and debts. A credit report may be ordered by an MLO or the borrower may just be asked questions about her financial situation. An MLO's pre-qualification of a prospective borrower may be as simple as making sure that the borrower has a steady job and no glaring credit report problems; for example, no recent bankruptcy. Often, an MLO will compute the borrower's income and debt ratios to get an idea of the maximum mortgage loan payment she may be able to afford.

Some lenders or mortgage brokers offer a loan pre-qualification form, often created by the local real estate board, which is not binding. Assuming a credit decision is not anticipated as a result of this, it does not trigger required disclosures. MLOs may also provide a closing cost worksheet while the loan is still in the pre-qualification state.

Pre-Approval

Pre-approval is *the process by which a lender determines if a potential borrower can be financed through the lender and for what amount of money.* The lender is rendering a credit decision. A mortgage broker *cannot* give a borrower a pre-approval; only the lender who is going to fund the mortgage loan can provide a pre-approval. For a pre-approval:

- A borrower goes through most of the same steps in the loan process, such as completing an application and providing documentation of income and assets.

- A lender is stating that the prospective borrower's situation has been investigated and, provided all circumstances stay the same, the lender is willing to loan a certain amount of money to purchase a house. This is especially helpful when working with a buyer because it is a powerful negotiation tool in getting an offer accepted by a seller and may be a requirement of contract acceptance.

Of course, a borrower's circumstances can and do change, which is why there are always conditions listed on a pre-approval. Depending upon internal pre-approval procedures, some pre-approvals are more specific and binding. This is where experience is helpful, and an MLO should take advantage of the wisdom and experience the employer and other senior mortgage professionals can offer. Pre-approvals are always in writing and always follow the policies and procedures established by the employer or mortgage lender.

Completing an application in anticipation of a credit decision triggers federally-mandated disclosures. For example, in order to submit a loan application for pre-approval, the borrower must be given a **Loan Estimate**, which binds the MLO to its terms.

Information related to a loan application must also be reported on the Loan Application Register (LAR) to comply with the **Home Mortgage Disclosure Act (HMDA)**.

Traditional Steps

The real estate loan approval process traditionally consists of four steps:

1. Consulting with the mortgage loan originator

2. Completing a loan application

3. Processing a loan application

4. Analyzing the borrower and property

Real Success

Traditionally, borrowers went to an MLO's office for face-to-face meetings. These days, many MLOs visit prospective borrowers at home or at work. The Internet has changed this process as well—many of these steps can now be done quickly and conveniently online or by other electronic means. Answering initial questions, completing a loan application, getting final approval, and closing the loan can all be done electronically. Most of this chapter looks at the process from the traditional approach of meeting with the borrower face-to-face. Keep in mind that regardless of how the application is obtained, the mechanics of the loan process, the steps taken, information needed, and end result are still the same.

Consulting with the MLO

Whether a prospective borrower wishes to consult in person or online, the first step is to choose the right MLO. If a borrower already has a relationship with someone, this may be a good place to start. On the other hand, if a borrower has past credit problems, it may be helpful to use a mortgage company that deals with many different lenders, although in today's tight market and stringent credit score qualifying standards, this is not the fix for credit issues it once was. As a borrower decides how to proceed with applying for her loan, MLOs should remember these points:

- Do not interject your opinion into the situation. Let the applicant's job history and credit dictate the course of action you suggest. This is especially important if you are an MLO representing many different lenders and loan programs.

- Always let the client or customer have the final say as to how she applies for a loan and with whom.

- If you work with more than one investor or company program, always consult with your mortgage company or employer regarding their policies before giving any type of advice or recommendation.

- Provide mortgage loan options for the consumer to choose from, which is required by the MLO Comp Rule (discussed in a later chapter).

After the lender is selected, initial discussions usually involve the various types of mortgages the lender offers (e.g., 30-year, 15-year, fixed-rate, ARM) so the borrower can decide which loan best suits his needs. A borrower needs to give the lender a good deal of personal and financial data on which the lender will base the lending decision. Providing the borrower with a complete list of required documents and reviewing these documents early in the application helps speed up the approval process.

When the goal is an actual loan approval (not pre-approval) for a purchase, the **sales contract** will be examined as well. The MLO wants to ensure that it's possible to comply with the terms of the agreement. Of particular concern are the **financing commitment date** and the **closing date**. A contract may call for a closing date that is too early to be realistic. If it's impossible for the lender to meet the closing date, a more feasible date can be agreed upon by all parties to the contract to avoid frustration. Loan fees and pricing adjustments may also be listed in the sales agreement.

Interest Rates

One topic that inevitably arises very early in a borrower's conversations with an MLO is the **interest rate**, which is the *amount charged by a lender to a borrower for the use of assets, expressed as a percentage of the loan amount (the principal)*. When considering interest rates, you may hear the term **basis point**, which is 1/100th of a percentage point. For example, 325 basis points equal 3.25% or 3 1/4%.

A couple of other terms to keep in mind when discussing interest rates with a borrower:

- **Par rate** is a term that describes *the rate without discounts or points that lenders offer only to mortgage brokers*, also known as the "wholesale" rate, that does not create an additional charge or provide for a credit for the borrower.

- **Rate Lock (Lock-In Agreement).** This is a commitment guaranteed by a lender that an interest rate will not change on a specific loan for a specific period of time. Since a **lock-in agreement** generally requires that the loan close by a specific date, the anticipated close date should be carefully considered. If a loan does not close before the expiration of the rate lock, a borrower may be required to pay a rate lock extension fee to extend the locked interest rate for a period of time. If current interest rates are lower, a borrower may be required to close at the previously locked, higher interest rate. In either situation, a borrower most often will receive the "worst" of the market, that is, the advantage will be to the lender. Remember that when a borrower enters into a rate lock agreement, he agrees to accept the locked interest rate, even if interest rates decline after locking, in most instances.

- **Float.** Between the time of application and closing, a borrower may choose to bet on interest rates decreasing by electing to float. Floating is essentially *choosing not to lock the interest rate.* Since it is the borrower's responsibility to lock his rate before closing, choosing to float is considered risky and may result in a higher interest rate.

Common Fees Associated with Real Estate Loans

In addition to the interest, there are other fees associated with processing a real estate loan; for example, fees for obtaining a borrower's credit bureau report, securing a property appraisal report, and completing inspections. Other items like title insurance and recording fees are paid if and when a loan closes. Fees that occur only when a loan closes are likely to be paid out of closing funds, but other early expenses incurred must be paid even if the loan doesn't close and are referred to as "POC" or *paid outside of closing* costs.

Lender's return (lender's yield) is the *total amount of money the lender can make from a loan in relation to the amount invested.*

- Most of the lender's return is accounted for as a result of interest paid by the borrower over the term of the loan.

- Another opportunity for a lender to recognize return is at closing when the fees are collected from the borrower.

- A lender could also recognize a return during the loan term through servicing fees or by collecting a fee for those loans that allow a prepayment penalty if the borrower pays off the loan before two years after the loan is closed.

A lender is generally only interested in the total amount of money it will make from the loan, not necessarily its source.

Title XIV of the Dodd-Frank Act (Pub.L. 111-203, H.R. 4173), which is designated as the Mortgage Reform and Anti-Predatory Lending Act, prohibits any direct or indirect compensation to an MLO that varies based on the terms of the loan, other than the amount of principal loan amount (Dodd-Frank Act §1403 (c)(1)). Final rules that address this provision are covered in more detail in a later chapter.

Loan Origination Fees

For loans that actually close, lenders may charge a loan **origination fee** to *cover the administrative costs of making and processing the loan,* including setting up the loan on the lender's books. Such fees may be referred to collectively as **points.** A point is simply *one percent of the loan amount.* So, for example, on a $120,000 loan, the borrower would have to pay an additional $1,200 for every point the lender charged as an origination fee. Points can be charged for many reasons, such as closing fees, underwriting fees, documentation fees, etc., but all points serve to help increase the lender's return. MLOs base loan fees on what the current market will bear.

 State processing fees may not always be included in the origination fee. Some brokers and lenders may charge a separate loan processing fee.

Another factor the lender considers when determining the number of points charged on a loan is the sale of the loan on the secondary market. For example, a lender may need to sell a loan at a discount to compensate that secondary market buyer for the time value of money.

The lender can attempt to make up some of any loss by charging the borrower **discount points**. Alternatively, in a competitive environment, some of those fees may even be waived as the lender can sell the loan on the secondary market at a premium. It all depends on the current market and interest rate of the loan.

An MLO must set the fees to offset the **actual costs and expenses** incurred in the origination of the loan. If not, they can be fined for **upcharging** the borrower, which is *profiting from a third party or lender fee.*

Real Success

MLOs can collect a credit report fee at application, but no other fees may be collected until the Loan Estimate disclosure is delivered to the borrower (within three business days of the MLO's receipt of a completed loan application) and the borrower indicates his intention to proceed with the transaction. At that point, other transaction fees—such as for an appraisal—may be charged.

Discount Points

Discount points represent a ***pre-payment of interest*** *at the beginning of a loan for* ***reducing the note interest rate*** *charged for some defined period of the life of the loan.* This essentially shifts the timing of when the lender collects its fees for making the loan. With discount points, the borrower pays *more* out-of-pocket upfront in order to pay *less* out-of-pocket later. Discount points, especially if paid by the seller, could allow the borrower to qualify for a loan that would otherwise be impossible to get.

By charging discount points up front, the lender is able to make up the required return on investment that is lost by making the loan **below par rate**. However, it's important to know that to be legitimate, the discount points must reflect a **bona fide reduction** to the market or par rate that is reasonably consistent with established industry norms and practices for secondary market transactions. In other words, a lender could not quote a higher interest rate than the borrower would qualify for, and then offer discount points to lower it.

Although paying discount points to get a lower interest rate would seem to be of benefit primarily to the buyer, discount points can also benefit the seller. Who pays the points is open to negotiation; a seller or builder may be willing to pay discount points to make the property more marketable.

How the discount is priced, in other words, how many points it takes to buy the rate down is based on many assumptions and calculations by the lender, primary of which is an assumption as to how long the loan might last and where interest rates are headed. Generally, lenders assume that the typical 30-year loan is either paid off when a property is sold or refinanced within eight to 12 years and will price its discount points with that in mind.

The difference between origination "points" and discount points is apparent on the Loan Estimate. All origination points must be lumped together as the origination fee on the Loan Estimate while discount points used to buy down the rate must be indicated as a **charge** the borrower incurs for the interest rate selected. This allows the borrower to make an informed decision about the rate options available and the impact on the loan.

Yield Spread Premium

Yield spread premium (YSP) (lender credits) is *a tool that an MLO can use to **lower the upfront cash out-of-pocket expenses at closing*** for a borrower in exchange for **higher monthly out-of-pocket payments** required by a higher interest rate. Like discount points, YSP also shifts the timing of the out-of-pocket fees that a borrower pays to a lender for the privilege of getting a loan, but with YSP, the borrower pays *less* out-of-pocket upfront and *more* out-of-pocket later.

Lender credits must be disclosed to the borrower on the Loan Estimate as a **credit** the borrower receives for the interest rate selected. This allows the borrower to make an informed decision about the rate options available and the impact on the loan.

Qualifying Standards

When an MLO first meets with a potential borrower (for pre-qualification or pre-approval), he will likely perform an analysis of the current or allowable monthly housing expense based on the borrower's gross income and debt. This provides the MLO—and the borrower—with a realistic understanding of what mortgage payment the borrower may be able to afford.

There are two qualifying standards:

- Housing expense ratio
- Total debt-to-income ratio (sometimes called total expense debt ratio or total debt service ratio)

Both ratios may be considered in the underwriting analysis, although some automated underwriting systems (AUS) rely only on the debt-to-income ratio. Underwriting is addressed in more detail later in this chapter.

Besides gross income, the key element needed to determine these ratios is **PITI**, which is an acronym for a mortgage payment that is the sum of monthly **p**rincipal, **i**nterest, **t**axes (property taxes and perhaps mandatory special assessments, if applicable), and **i**nsurance (homeowners hazard/flood insurance and mortgage insurance, if applicable). When the collateral property requires **association fees** as a condition of ownership; for example, as with a condominium; the association fees must be taken into consideration and PITI adjusted to get the complete housing expense.

Qualifying standards may vary from lender to lender but with increased lender dependence on the national secondary market, **the majority of lenders throughout the country have incorporated into their conventional loan underwriting procedures the standards set by the major secondary market investors, specifically Fannie Mae and Freddie Mac.** Of course, if the loan being contemplated is to be made in conjunction with the FHA or VA, those underwriting standards must be applied (underwriting standards for conventional loans and FHA and VA loans will be discussed in more detail in later chapters).

Housing Expense Ratio

A borrower's housing expense ratio, also called the **front-end ratio**, is the *relationship of the borrower's total monthly housing expense to gross income expressed as a percentage*:

Total Housing Expense ÷ Gross Income = Housing Expense Ratio %

Conventional lenders consider a borrower's income adequate for a loan if the proposed total mortgage payment of PITI does not exceed **28%** of stable monthly gross income. **Stable monthly income**, which is covered in more detail later, is *a borrower's monthly income that can reasonably be expected to continue in the future.* This is usually a borrower's **gross monthly income** from primary employment and any other acceptable income.

Case in Point

Mark has a stable monthly gross income of $2,900 and the house he wants to buy would have a monthly mortgage payment of $700:

| $2,900 | **Stable Monthly Gross Income** |
| $ 700 | **Proposed Mortgage Payment (PITI + association fees, if required)** |

$700 ÷ $2,900 = 0.24 or 24%

His housing expense ratio in this example is 24%, which is acceptable for a conventional loan since it's below 28%.

Total Debt-to-Income Ratio

A borrower's total debt-to-income ratio (DTI), also known as the **back-end ratio**, is the relationship of the borrower's total monthly debt obligations (including PITI housing and long-term debts) to gross income expressed as a percentage.

Total Debt ÷ Gross Income = Total Debt-to-Income Ratio %

Conventional lenders want to be sure the borrower's housing expenses (as explained previously), plus any installment debts with 10 or more payments left or other debt that will not be cancelled, do not exceed **36% of stable monthly gross income**. Here, alimony, child support, or any other court-ordered obligations the borrower has must count as debt against this ratio. Debts with fewer than ten payments remaining may still be counted against the borrower if the monthly payment exceeds 5% of the borrower's gross monthly income.

There are different methods of calculating a borrower's student loan payment for use in the total debt-to-income ratio, according to the type of loan a borrower will use (VA, FHA, conventional). But regardless of the loan type, student loan repayment must always be considered in the back-end ratio calculation.

Case in Point

$2,900	Stable Monthly Gross Income
$700	Proposed Mortgage Payment (PITI + association fees, if required)
$225	Auto Payment (18 payments left)
+ $100	Child Support
$1,025	Total

$1,025 ÷ $2,900 = 0.35 or 35%

The borrower's total DTI ratio in this example is 35%, which is acceptable for a conventional loan since it's below 36%.

When the underwriter considers both ratios, the borrower must generally qualify under **both**.

Using Ratios to Determine Maximum Mortgage Payment

Using the housing expense ratio and debt-to-income ratio, it's easy to determine the maximum mortgage payment for which a borrower should qualify. To determine the maximum mortgage payment allowable under the first ratio, take the borrower's stable monthly income and multiply it by the maximum housing expense ratio (28% or 0.28 for conventional loans).

To determine the figure that represents the largest mortgage payment allowed under the second ratio, take the borrower's stable monthly income and multiply it by the maximum total debt-to-income ratio (36% or 0.36 for conventional loans). This provides the amount of total long-term debts the borrower is permitted to have. Use this dollar amount and subtract the monthly long-term obligations of the borrower (not including mortgage PITI payments).

The total debt-to-income ratio is a more realistic measure of the borrower's ability to support the loan payments because it considers *all* the borrower's recurring financial obligations, which means that the maximum mortgage payment allowed is likely to be smaller than if only the housing ratio were considered. When the underwriter considers both ratios, the **smaller of the two** is the maximum mortgage payment allowable.

Exercise 2.1: Apply Your Knowledge

Directions: Consider the following scenario, and then write your responses.

Scenario: Mary Smith has a stable monthly gross income of $3,200. She has three long-term monthly debt obligations: $220 car payment, $75 personal loan payment, and $50 revolving charge card payment.

1. What's the maximum monthly mortgage payment for which she can qualify?

_____

_____

_____

_____

2. What steps could Mary take to qualify for a larger mortgage payment?

_____

_____

_____

_____

Completing the Uniform Residential Loan Application (URLA)

Lenders expect the loans they make to be repaid in a timely manner without collection or foreclosure; thus, employment stability, income potential, history of debt management, and assets are important considerations. A loan application is designed to elicit responses that detail the borrower's history, trends, and attitude as a means of trying to predict future loan repayment behavior.

The **Uniform Residential Loan Application (URLA)** (Fannie Mae **Form 1003** or Freddie Mac **Form 65**) is a form a lender requires a potential borrower to complete that allows the lender to collect pertinent information about the borrower and the property. An application may either be in writing or electronically submitted, including a written record of an oral application. The borrower typically completes a loan application during the initial consultation with the MLO.

There is a great deal of information asked; therefore, attention to detail when completing the application is advised. If the borrower doesn't provide all necessary data during the initial consultation, the missing information must be provided at a later date, which may delay the loan process.

When is an Application an "Application?"

According to TILA/RESPA [see 12 CFR §1024.2 Definitions.], a **complete application** is defined as the *submission of a borrower's financial information in anticipation of a credit decision* relating to a federally-related mortgage loan that includes:

- Borrower's name
- Income calculated as gross monthly income
- Social Security number to obtain a credit report
- Address of the subject property
- Estimate of the value of the property
- Loan amount applied for

A complete application triggers federal disclosure requirements.

Co-Borrowers

The first portion of Form 1003 discusses requirements for borrowers and co-borrowers. A **co-borrower** is simply *a person who signs a note along with another primary borrower and accepts a joint obligation to repay the loan*. Co-borrowers have joint ownership interest in the security property as indicated on the title. A **co-signor**, on the other hand, is *a credit applicant who does not have ownership interest in the security property as indicated on the title but signs the note*. The most common co-borrower is a spouse. Non-occupant parents may also be co-borrowers or co-signors as they lend an established earnings pattern and financial status to their children who otherwise may be unable to purchase a home.

Co-borrowers must have credit history and assets acceptable to the underwriter. Furthermore, if the co-borrower does not reside in the collateral property, he must be able to support both his own housing expense *plus* a proportionate share, if not all, of the proposed housing expense for the applicant. Marginal co-borrowers, therefore, should not be relied on heavily and may do more harm than good.

If there is a co-borrower, the applicant must indicate whether the co-borrower's income or assets will be used for qualifying, in which case the co-borrower's information must be included on the application. Generally, spouses have merged assets and credit and therefore are able to use the same application.

When you have two unmarried adults on a mortgage application:

- You must determine whether their assets and liabilities are sufficiently joined so the information can be meaningfully and fairly presented on a combined basis. If yes, they can complete a single application.

- If the co-borrowers do not have joint assets and liabilities, separate applications should be used. For privacy purposes, credit reports and information disclosed on the mortgage application should be handled separately.

Section I: Type of Mortgage and Terms of Loan

Section I details the specific **mortgage option** a borrower has chosen from those offered by the lender, including loan amount, rate, and term.

Section II: Property Information and Purpose of Loan

Section II asks for detailed information about the **subject property**.

For a **purchase**, the MLO needs to see the sales contract for the home the borrower wants to buy. It's critical to complete as much information in this section as possible, paying particular attention to the property address (to confirm that it agrees with the sales agreement/tax bill), the number of units, and property type (owner-occupied or investment). It's also necessary to document the source of the down payment, including any secondary financing being used to purchase the property.

For a **refinance**, as much of the existing information as possible about the property must be completed to provide the lender with an idea of improvements that have been made, which may increase value.

- **Title.** The borrower should indicate the manner in which title will be held and what name(s) will hold the title to the property. If unsure, he may need to ask an attorney. **Do not assume or advise.**

- **Occupancy.** Occupancy of the property will determine the interest rate, available programs, and overall risk of the loan. Generally, investment loans are a higher risk than owner-occupied loans.

 Loans insured by the FHA require that the borrower establish bona fide occupancy of the home as the borrower's principal residence within **60 days** of signing the security instrument, with continued occupancy for at least one year.

Uniform Residential Loan Application

This application is designed to be completed by the applicant(s) with the Lender's assistance. Applicants should complete this form as "Borrower" or "Co-Borrower," as applicable. Co-Borrower information must also be provided (and the appropriate box checked) when ☐ the income or assets of a person other than the Borrower (including the Borrower's spouse) will be used as a basis for loan qualification or ☐ the income or assets of the Borrower's spouse or other person who has community property rights pursuant to state law will not be used as a basis for loan qualification, but his or her liabilities must be considered because the spouse or other person has community property rights pursuant to applicable law and Borrower resides in a community property state, the security property is located in a community property state, or the Borrower is relying on other property located in a community property state as a basis for repayment of the loan.

If this is an application for joint credit, Borrower and Co-Borrower each agree that we intend to apply for joint credit (sign below):

Borrower	Co-Borrower

I. TYPE OF MORTGAGE AND TERMS OF LOAN

Mortgage Applied for:	☐ VA ☒ FHA	☐ Conventional ☐ USDA/Rural Housing Service	☐ Other (explain):	Agency Case Number 412-2563210	Lender Case Number 013-213141

Amount $ 148,006.00	Interest Rate 5.750 %	No. of Months 360	Amortization Type:	☒ Fixed Rate ☐ GPM	☐ Other (explain): ☐ ARM (type):

II. PROPERTY INFORMATION AND PURPOSE OF LOAN

Subject Property Address (street, city, state & ZIP) 100 Rutland Ct, Columbus, OH 43230 County: Franklin	No. of Units 1
Legal Description of Subject Property (attach description if necessary) SEE PRELIMINARY TITLE REPORT	Year Built 1989

Purpose of Loan	☒ Purchase ☐ Construction ☐ Refinance ☐ Construction-Permanent	☐ Other (explain):	Property will be: ☒ Primary Residence ☐ Secondary Residence ☐ Investment

Complete this line if construction or construction-permanent loan.

Year Lot Acquired	Original Cost $	Amount Existing Liens $	(a) Present Value of Lot $	(b) Cost of Improvements $	Total (a + b) $ 0.00

Complete this line if this is a refinance loan.

Year Acquired	Original Cost $	Amount Existing Liens $	Purpose of Refinance	Describe Improvements ☐ made ☐ to be made Cost: $

Title will be held in what Name(s) John A Doe Sr, Jane B Doe	Manner in which Title will be held Joint tenants	Estate will be held in: ☒ Fee Simple ☐ Leasehold (show expiration date)

Source of Down Payment, Settlement Charges, and/or Subordinate Financing (explain)

III. BORROWER INFORMATION

Borrower	Co-Borrower
Borrower's Name (include Jr. or Sr. if applicable) John A Doe Sr	Co-Borrower's Name (include Jr. or Sr. if applicable) Jane B Doe

Social Security Number 123-45-6789	Home Phone (incl. area code) 614-555-2121	DOB (mm/dd/yyyy) 01/02/1965	Yrs. School 16	Social Security Number 987-65-4321	Home Phone (incl. area code) 614-555-2121	DOB (mm/dd/yyyy) 02/15/1965	Yrs. School 16

☒ Married ☐ Unmarried (include ☐ Separated single, divorced, widowed)	Dependents (not listed by Co-Borrower) no. 2 ages 10, 8	☒ Married ☐ Unmarried (include ☐ Separated single, divorced, widowed)	Dependents (not listed by Borrower) no. ages

Present Address (street, city, state, ZIP) ☐ Own ☒ Rent 1Y No. Yrs. 54 Elm St, Columbus, OH 43231	Present Address (street, city, state, ZIP) ☐ Own ☒ Rent 1Y No. Yrs. 54 Elm St, Columbus, OH 43231
Mailing Address, if different from Present Address	Mailing Address, if different from Present Address

If residing at present address for less than two years, complete the following:

Former Address (street, city, state, ZIP) ☐ Own ☒ Rent ___ No. Yrs. 100 Cranberry St, Reynoldsburg, OH 43069	Former Address (street, city, state, ZIP) ☐ Own ☒ Rent ___ No. Yrs. 100 Cranberry St, Reynoldsburg, OH 43069

IV. EMPLOYMENT INFORMATION

Borrower	Co-Borrower
Name & Address of Employer ☐ Self Employed Yrs. on this job 1Y3M AAA Corp 800 Corporate Dr Columbus, OH 43231	Yrs. employed in this line of work/profession 8	Name & Address of Employer ☐ Self Employed Yrs. on this job 4Y0M Janes Dog Day Care 5522 N Hamilton Rd Columbus, OH 43231	Yrs. employed in this line of work/profession 4

Position/Title/Type of Business VP Sales/Information Technology	Business Phone (incl. area code) 614-895-8888	Position/Title/Type of Business Owner/Dog Day Care & boarding	Business Phone (incl. area code) 742-515-2222

If employed in current position for less than two years or if currently employed in more than one position, complete the following:

Uniform Residential Loan Application
Freddie Mac Form 65   7/05 (rev.6/09)   Page 1 of 5   Fannie Mae Form 1003   7/05 (rev.6/09)

37

Borrower			IV. EMPLOYMENT INFORMATION (cont'd)		Co-Borrower	
Name & Address of Employer	☐ Self Employed	Dates (from – to) 04/01/2006 - 01/⊞	Name & Address of Employer	☐ Self Employed	Dates (from – to)	
ZZZ Info Tech 878 Wharton Rd Columbus, OH 43206		Monthly Income $ 6,500.00			Monthly Income $	
Position/Title/Type of Business VP Sales/Information Technology	Business Phone (incl. area code) 614-999-5648		Position/Title/Type of Business	Business Phone (incl. area code)		
Name & Address of Employer	☐ Self Employed	Dates (from – to)	Name & Address of Employer	☐ Self Employed	Dates (from – to)	
		Monthly Income $			Monthly Income $	
Position/Title/Type of Business	Business Phone (incl. area code)		Position/Title/Type of Business	Business Phone (incl. area code)		

V. MONTHLY INCOME AND COMBINED HOUSING EXPENSE INFORMATION

Gross Monthly Income	Borrower	Co-Borrower	Total	Combined Monthly Housing Expense	Present	Proposed
Base Empl. Income*	$ 7,000.00	$	$ 7,000.00	Rent	$ 950.00	
Overtime			0.00	First Mortgage (P&I)		$ 863.72
Bonuses			0.00	Other Financing (P&I)		
Commissions			0.00	Hazard Insurance		55.00
Dividends/Interest			0.00	Real Estate Taxes		156.25
Net Rental Income			0.00	Mortgage Insurance		65.96
Other (before completing, see the notice in "describe other income," below)		2,950.00	2,950.00	Homeowner Assn. Dues		45.00
				Other:		155.00
Total	$ 7,000.00	$ 2,950.00	$ 9,950.00	Total	$ 950.00	$ 1,340.93

* Self Employed Borrower(s) may be required to provide additional documentation such as tax returns and financial statements.

Describe Other Income

Notice: **Alimony, child support, or separate maintenance income need not be revealed if the Borrower (B) or Co-Borrower (C) does not choose to have it considered for repaying this loan.**

B/C		Monthly Amount
C	2 year net profit + depreciation average (see taxes)	$ 2,950.00

VI. ASSETS AND LIABILITIES

This Statement and any applicable supporting schedules may be completed jointly by both married and unmarried Co-Borrowers if their assets and liabilities are sufficiently joined so that the Statement can be meaningfully and fairly presented on a combined basis; otherwise, separate Statements and Schedules are required. If the Co-Borrower section was completed about a non-applicant spouse or other person, this Statement and supporting schedules must be completed about that spouse or other person also.

Completed ☐ Jointly ☐ Not Jointly

ASSETS	Cash or Market Value	Liabilities and Pledged Assets. List the creditor's name, address, and account number for all outstanding debts, including automobile loans, revolving charge accounts, real estate loans, alimony, child support, stock pledges, etc. Use continuation sheet, if necessary. Indicate by (*) those liabilities, which will be satisfied upon sale of real estate owned or upon refinancing of the subject property.		
Description				
Cash deposit toward purchase held by: Earnest Money	$ 500.00			
List checking and savings accounts below		LIABILITIES	Monthly Payment & Months Left to Pay	Unpaid Balance
Name and address of Bank, S&L, or Credit Union Columbus Bank Co verifications 1212 Broad Columbus, OH 43206		Name and address of Company Chase	$ Payment/Months 195.00/100	$ 6,500.00
Acct. no. 2352652	$ 8,591.00	Acct. no.		
Name and address of Bank, S&L, or Credit Union Columbus Bank Co verifications 1212 Broad ⊞		Name and address of Company Wells Fargo	$ Payment/Months 295.00/32	$ 9,560.00
Acct. no. 1212552	$ 12,975.00	Acct. no.		
Name and address of Bank, S&L, or Credit Union		Name and address of Company Sallie mae	$ Payment/Months 155.00/120	$ 18,950.00
Acct. no.	$	Acct. no.		

Uniform Residential Loan Application
Freddie Mac Form 65 7/05 (rev. 6/09)   Page 2 of 5   Fannie Mae Form 1003 7/05 (rev.6/09)

38

VI. ASSETS AND LIABILITIES (cont'd)

Name and address of Bank, S&L, or Credit Union		Name and address of Company	$ Payment/Months	$
		Ford Motor	490.00	4,850.00
Acct. no.	$	Acct. no.		
Stocks & Bonds (Company name/ number & description)	$	Name and address of Company	$ Payment/Months	$
		Acct. no.		
Life insurance net cash value	$	Name and address of Company	$ Payment/Months	$
Face amount: $ 100,000.00	5,500.00			
Subtotal Liquid Assets	$ 27,566.00			
Real estate owned (enter market value from schedule of real estate owned)	$			
Vested interest in retirement fund	$ 15,205.00			
Net worth of business(es) owned (attach financial statement)	$	Acct. no.		
Automobiles owned (make and year) 2007 Ford Explorer 2005 Honda 2000	$ 16,000.00	Alimony/Child Support/Separate Maintenance Payments Owed to:	$	
Other Assets (itemize)	$	Job-Related Expense (child care, union dues, etc.)	$	
		Total Monthly Payments	$	
Total Assets a. $ 58,771.00		Net Worth (a minus b) ▶ $ 18,911.00	**Total Liabilities b.** $ 39,860.00	

Schedule of Real Estate Owned (If additional properties are owned, use continuation sheet.)

Property Address (enter S if sold, PS if pending sale or R if rental being held for income) ▼	Type of Property	Present Market Value	Amount of Mortgages & Liens	Gross Rental Income	Mortgage Payments	Insurance, Maintenance, Taxes & Misc.	Net Rental Income
		$	$	$	$	$	$
Totals		$ 0.00	$ 0.00	$ 0.00	$ 0.00	$ 0.00	$

List any additional names under which credit has previously been received and indicate appropriate creditor name(s) and account number(s):

Alternate Name	Creditor Name	Account Number

VII. DETAILS OF TRANSACTION / VIII. DECLARATIONS

	VII. DETAILS OF TRANSACTION		VIII. DECLARATIONS	Borrower Yes No	Co-Borrower Yes No
a.	Purchase price	$ 150,000.00	If you answer "Yes" to any questions a through i, please use continuation sheet for explanation.		
b.	Alterations, improvements, repairs		a. Are there any outstanding judgments against you?	☐ ☑	☐ ☑
c.	Land (if acquired separately)		b. Have you been declared bankrupt within the past 7 years?	☐ ☑	☐ ☑
d.	Refinance (incl. debts to be paid off)		c. Have you had property foreclosed upon or given title or deed in lieu thereof in the last 7 years?	☐ ☑	☐ ☑
e.	Estimated prepaid items	1,165.70	d. Are you a party to a lawsuit?	☐ ☑	☐ ☑
f.	Estimated closing costs	6,693.57	e. Have you directly or indirectly been obligated on any loan which resulted in foreclosure, transfer of title in lieu of foreclosure, or judgment?	☐ ☑	☐ ☑
g.	PMI, MIP, Funding Fee	3,256.88	(This would include such loans as home mortgage loans, SBA loans, home improvement loans, educational loans, manufactured (mobile) home loans, any mortgage, financial obligation, bond, or loan guarantee. If "Yes," provide details, including date, name, and address of Lender, FHA or VA case number, if any, and reasons for the action.)		
h.	Discount (if Borrower will pay)				
i.	Total costs (add items a through h)	161,116.15			

Uniform Residential Loan Application
Freddie Mac Form 65   7/05 (rev.6/09)   Page 3 of 5   Fannie Mae Form 1003   7/05 (rev.6/09)

VII. DETAILS OF TRANSACTION			VIII. DECLARATIONS					

			If you answer "Yes" to any question a through i, please use continuation sheet for explanation.		Borrower		Co-Borrower	
					Yes	No	Yes	No
j.	Subordinate financing		f.	Are you presently delinquent or in default on any Federal debt or any other loan, mortgage, financial obligation, bond, or loan guarantee?	☐	☑	☐	☑
k.	Borrower's closing costs paid by Seller	4,500.00	g.	Are you obligated to pay alimony, child support, or separate maintenance?	☐	☑	☐	☐
			h.	Is any part of the down payment borrowed?	☐	☑	☐	☑
l.	Other Credits (explain) Cash Deposit on Sales Contract	500.00	i.	Are you a co-maker or endorser on a note?	☐	☑	☐	☑
m.	Loan amount (exclude PMI, MIP, Funding Fee financed)	144,750.00	--- j.	Are you a U.S. citizen?	☑	☐	☑	☐
n.	PMI, MIP, Funding Fee financed	3,256.00	k.	Are you a permanent resident alien?	☐	☑	☐	☑
o.	Loan amount (add m & n)	148,006.00	l.	**Do you intend to occupy the property as your primary residence?** If Yes," complete question m below.	☑	☐	☑	☐
p.	Cash from/to Borrower (subtract j, k, l & o from i)	8,110.15	m.	Have you had an ownership interest in a property in the last three years? (1) What type of property did you own—principal residence (PR), second home (SH), or investment property (IP)? _____ (2) How did you hold title to the home— by yourself (S), jointly with your spouse (SP), or jointly with another person (O)? _____	☐	☑	☐	☑

IX. ACKNOWLEDGEMENT AND AGREEMENT

Each of the undersigned specifically represents to Lender and to Lender's actual or potential agents, brokers, processors, attorneys, insurers, servicers, successors and assigns and agrees and acknowledges that: (1) the information provided in this application is true and correct as of the date set forth opposite my signature and that any intentional or negligent misrepresentation of this information contained in this application may result in civil liability, including monetary damages, to any person who may suffer any loss due to reliance upon any misrepresentation that I have made on this application, and/or in criminal penalties including, but not limited to, fine or imprisonment or both under the provisions of Title 18, United States Code, Sec. 1001, et seq.; (2) the loan requested pursuant to this application (the "Loan") will be secured by a mortgage or deed of trust on the property described in this application; (3) the property will not be used for any illegal or prohibited purpose or use; (4) all statements made in this application are made for the purpose of obtaining a residential mortgage loan; (5) the property will be occupied as indicated in this application; (6) the Lender, its servicers, successors or assigns may retain the original and/or an electronic record of this application, whether or not the Loan is approved; (7) the Lender and its agents, brokers, insurers, servicers, successors, and assigns may continuously rely on the information contained in the application, and I am obligated to amend and/or supplement the information provided in this application if any of the material facts that I have represented herein should change prior to closing of the Loan; (8) in the event that my payments on the Loan become delinquent, the Lender, its servicers, successors or assigns may, in addition to any other rights and remedies that it may have relating to such delinquency, report my name and account information to one or more consumer reporting agencies; (9) ownership of the Loan and/or administration of the Loan account may be transferred with such notice as may be required by law; (10) neither Lender nor its agents, brokers, insurers, servicers, successors or assigns has made any representation or warranty, express or implied, to me regarding the property or the condition or value of the property; and (11) my transmission of this application as an "electronic record" containing my "electronic signature," as those terms are defined in applicable federal and/or state laws (excluding audio and video recordings), or my facsimile transmission of this application containing a facsimile of my signature, shall be as effective, enforceable and valid as if a paper version of this application were delivered containing my original written signature.

Acknowledgement. Each of the undersigned hereby acknowledges that any owner of the Loan, its servicers, successors and assigns, may verify or reverify any information contained in this application or obtain any information or data relating to the Loan, for any legitimate business purpose through any source, including a source named in this application or a consumer reporting agency.

Borrower's Signature X	Date	Co-Borrower's Signature X	Date

X. INFORMATION FOR GOVERNMENT MONITORING PURPOSES

The following information is requested by the Federal Government for certain types of loans related to a dwelling in order to monitor the lender's compliance with equal credit opportunity, fair housing and home mortgage disclosure laws. You are not required to furnish this information, but are encouraged to do so. The law provides that a lender may not discriminate either on the basis of this information, or on whether you choose to furnish it. If you furnish the information, please provide both ethnicity and race. For race, you may check more than one designation. If you do not furnish ethnicity, race, or sex, under Federal regulations, this lender is required to note the information on the basis of visual observation and surname if you have made this application in person. If you do not wish to furnish the information, please check the box below. (Lender must review the above material to assure that the disclosures satisfy all requirements to which the lender is subject under applicable state law for the particular type of loan applied for.)

BORROWER	☐ I do not wish to furnish this information		CO-BORROWER	☑ I do not wish to furnish this information	
Ethnicity:	☐ Hispanic or Latino ☑ Not Hispanic or Latino		Ethnicity:	☐ Hispanic or Latino ☑ Not Hispanic or Latino	
Race:	☐ American Indian or Alaska Native ☐ Asian ☐ Black or African American ☐ Native Hawaiian or Other Pacific Islander ☑ White		Race:	☐ American Indian or Alaska Native ☐ Asian ☐ Black or African American ☐ Native Hawaiian or Other Pacific Islander ☑ White	
Sex:	☐ Female ☑ Male		Sex:	☑ Female ☐ Male	

To be Completed by Loan Originator:
This information was provided:
☐ In a face-to-face interview
☐ In a telephone interview
☑ By the applicant and submitted by fax or mail
☐ By the applicant and submitted via e-mail or the Internet

Loan Originator's Signature X		Date
Loan Originator's Name (print or type) Jim Smith	Loan Originator Identifier LO.001111	Loan Originator's Phone Number (including area code) 614-255-7777
Loan Origination Company's Name XYZ Mortgage Co	Loan Origination Company Identifier 11-111111	Loan Origination Company's Address 525 Metro Pl, Columbus, OH 43222

Uniform Residential Loan Application
Freddie Mac Form 65   7/05 (rev.6/09)

Fannie Mae Form 1003   7/05 (rev.6/09)

CONTINUATION SHEET/RESIDENTIAL LOAN APPLICATION

Use this continuation sheet if you need more space to complete the Residential Loan Application. Mark **B** f or Borrower or **C** for Co-Borrower.	Borrower:	Agency Case Number: 412-2563210
	Co-Borrower:	Lender Case Number: 013-213141

I/We fully understand that it is a Federal crime punishable by fine or imprisonment, or both, to knowingly make any false statements concerning any of the above facts as applicable under the provisions of Title 18, United States Code, Section 1001, et seq.

Borrower's Signature	Date	Co-Borrower's Signature	Date
X		X	

Uniform Residential Loan Application
Freddie Mac Form 65   7/05 (rev.6/09)   Page 5 of 5   Fannie Mae Form 1003   7/05 (rev.6/09)

41

Section III: Borrower Information

Section III requests **personal information** about the borrower and, if applicable, co-borrower: Name, address, phone number, Social Security number, age, schooling, marital status, etc. When inquiring about a borrower's marital status, MLOs must comply with the Equal Credit Opportunity Act (12 C.F.R. § 202.2(u)) definitions:

- Married
- Unmarried (which includes persons who are single, divorced, or widowed)
- Separated

The application also asks how many dependents the borrower must support. If there are co-borrowers with joint dependents, it's necessary to indicate the number of dependents only for the primary borrower.

If the borrower has resided at her present address for two years or less, previous address information—and whether the borrower owned or rented—must also be provided. This information is also required from the co-borrower, if applicable. MLOs may ask for contact information for lenders, landlords, or rental agents.

Section IV: Employment Information

Section IV requires the borrower to provide details about all current and previous **employment** over a **two-year period**, including years on the job, position, type of business, and contact information. Frequent job changes within the same field and with consistent or increasing income are *not* detrimental to the mortgage decision. The borrower must be able to explain any gaps in employment over one month.

A borrower must indicate if she is **self-employed**, which is defined as owning **25%** or more of the business. Employment information is also required from the co-borrower, if applicable.

Section V: Monthly Income and Combined Housing Expense Information

Section V provides spaces for base **employment gross income**, overtime, bonuses, commissions, dividends, interest, net rental income, and income from any other sources. Income derived from alimony or child support does *not* need to be disclosed unless the borrower wants this considered as income to help qualify for a larger loan. Also, note that a borrower who is self-employed may need to supply additional supporting documents, such as personal tax returns, corporate tax returns, or financial statements, to show income.

Monthly housing expenses, such as rent, mortgage payments, secondary financing, insurance, real estate taxes, etc., are included as well. The lender wants to see what the borrower is currently paying and what the proposed total payment would be for the new mortgage to gauge the potential extra burden of the new loan. This allows underwriters to evaluate the possibility that payment shock could result from a large increase in housing without accumulated assets to support it.

Section VI: Assets and Liabilities

In Section VI, the borrower must list all assets and liabilities to determine net worth. **Assets** are *items of value*, such as cash on hand, checking or savings accounts, stocks, bonds, cash value of insurance policies, equity in real estate, retirement funds, automobiles, and personal property.

Liabilities are *financial obligations owed by a borrower.* Liabilities include the following:

- **Debts** are *any recurring monetary obligation that will not be cancelled* (e.g., monthly bills). The borrower must list all debts—installment loans, credit cards, mortgages, collections, slow pays, judgments, student loans (even if currently deferred), etc. The lender generally will not consider installment loan debt with **less than ten monthly payments** remaining (except for leases, which always count regardless of how few payments remain) or unless the payments on those installment loans significantly affect the borrower's ability to meet credit obligations.

- While any equity in a pledged asset that may be collateral on another loan, such as real estate, would be considered an asset, the **amount owed** on the asset would be considered a liability against the borrower's net worth.

- The borrower must also reveal **alimony** or **child support** *required to be paid* as a liability and should be prepared to produce a copy of a divorce decree for verification.

Lenders obtain a credit bureau report and compare liabilities listed on the application. If a liability is not listed on the credit report, the payment information needs to be verified.

Net worth is determined by *subtracting liabilities from total assets.* Most lenders feel that a borrower's net worth is a good indicator of creditworthiness. A high net worth shows an ability to manage money and may help offset other marginal items on an application. Furthermore, liquid assets that can be sold in an emergency to make payments can give a lender an added feeling of security in making a loan.

Section VII: Details of the Transaction

In Section VII, the MLO estimates what **funds** are required by the borrower at closing by adding and subtracting items such as purchase price, prepaid items (e.g., escrows for taxes, insurance, etc.), estimated closing costs, mortgage insurance, loan amount, etc. The borrower also needs to reveal secondary financing, closing costs to be paid by the seller, and any other credits, such as equity from selling her current home and deposits being held by a broker or title company.

Section VIII: Declarations

In Section VIII, the borrower (and any co-borrower) must respond to critical questions about:

- Outstanding judgments, bankruptcies, foreclosures, lawsuits, etc.
- Delinquency or defaults on any federal debt or other loan
- Obligations to pay alimony or child support
- Borrowed funds used for any part of the down payment
- Co-signers on any other debts
- Citizenship or permanent residency status
- Intentions to occupy the property as a primary residence
- Ownership interest in other properties in the past three years

Section IX: Acknowledgment and Agreement

For Section IX, the borrower (and co-borrower, if applicable) must date and sign the application to acknowledge that she has answered everything truthfully. By signing the application, the borrower acknowledges 11 disclosures, so she should take the time to read and understand this section. Both the MLO and the applicant(s) are responsible for ensuring the information contained in the application is truthful, accurate, and complete.

Section X: Information for Government Monitoring Purposes

Section X is used by the government to monitor lender compliance with equal credit and equal housing laws. The Equal Credit Opportunity Act prohibits discrimination in granting credit based on age, sex, race, marital status, color, religion, national origin, and receipt of public assistance. When meeting with a borrower face-to-face, the MLO must complete this section if the applicant declines to supply the requested information. The MLO must note the applicant's ethnicity, race, and sex on the basis of visual observation and surname to the best possible extent.

The MLO is required to sign the application. Contact information, as well as the MLO's NMLS unique identifier, must also be included.

Special Notice for Balloon Mortgages

A **balloon mortgage** is *a loan that has level monthly payments that fully amortize over a stated term, but provides for a lump-sum payment due at the end of an earlier specified term.* Fannie Mae requires MLOs using the 1003 URLA to insert a special notice regarding the nature of the balloon features on Form 1003 or in a separate attachment if the loan includes this feature. If an attachment is used, the borrower(s) must sign the attachment. The following language must be inserted using capital letters:

"THIS LOAN MUST EITHER BE PAID IN FULL AT MATURITY OR REFINANCED TO A MARKET LEVEL FIXED-RATE MORTGAGE. YOU MUST REPAY THE ENTIRE PRINCIPAL BALANCE OF THE LOAN AND UNPAID INTEREST THEN DUE IF YOU DO NOT QUALIFY FOR THE CONDITIONAL RIGHT TO REFINANCE AS SPECIFIED IN THE NOTE ADDENDUM AND MORTGAGE RIDER. THE LENDER IS UNDER NO OBLIGATION TO REFINANCE THE LOAN IF QUALIFICATION CONDITIONS ARE NOT MET. YOU WILL, THEREFORE, BE REQUIRED TO MAKE PAYMENT OUT OF OTHER ASSETS THAT YOU MAY OWN, OR YOU WILL HAVE TO FIND A LENDER, WHICH MAY BE THE LENDER YOU HAVE THIS LOAN WITH, WILLING TO LEND YOU THE MONEY. IF YOU REFINANCE THIS LOAN AT MATURITY, YOU MAY HAVE TO PAY SOME OR ALL OF THE CLOSING COSTS NORMALLY ASSOCIATED WITH A NEW LOAN EVEN IF YOU OBTAIN REFINANCING FROM THE SAME LENDER."

See: https://www.efanniemae.com/sf/formsdocs/forms/1003.jsp

Signing the Application: Electronic Signatures

The Electronic Signatures in Global and National Commerce Act regulates the use of electronic signatures and records in interstate and foreign commerce. It ensures the validity and the legality of contracts and documents entered into by electronic methods. **A party to a contract cannot be forced to use electronic signature methods** and *may sign in ink,* also called a "**wet signature**." One party can use the electronic signature method and the other party to the contract can retain the right to sign the documents personally. In the same manner, a person who chooses to sign electronically cannot be denied legal effect, validity, or enforceability solely because his signature is in an electronic format.

The consumer must receive disclosure information:

- Regarding his rights to have a legible copy of the document provided to him.
- Disclosing when consent applies.
- Describing procedures to implement and withdraw permission for electronic signatures on documents.
- Including a statement informing the consumer of the hardware and software requirements to facilitate electronic signatures.

If a statute, rule, or regulation requires that a contract or other record that contains electronic signatures or the authorization to sign electronically requires a retention period, that condition is met by the retention of the electronic record of the information in the contract. It must remain accessible to all parties who are entitled by law to access the documents.

A person can withdraw his consent to electronic signatures *at any time* during the process. Withdrawal of permission does not affect the validity of previously executed documents that were electronically signed while the permission of the consumer was in effect.

Processing the Loan Application

Once the application has been properly completed and the required disclosures have been delivered to and accepted by the borrower, the lender can begin gathering other pertinent information to validate the data. This task is often delegated to the **loan processor**. A loan processor is *the person who will independently verify the information provided by the borrower*. For example, a borrower states that she works for ABC Widget Company and provides an address and phone number for the company. The loan processor will obtain the address and phone number from an independent source, such as a company website, white page listing, or other source, and perform a verbal verification of employment or mail/email a written verification of employment. The loan processor gathers all the information and assembles the loan file into a package that is presented to the underwriter for evaluation and a loan decision.

Some loan processors accept a borrower's check stubs or W-2 forms, copies of bank statements, and other documents; others use verification forms that are sent out to the borrower's employer, banks, other creditors, and any previous mortgage lender. A **credit report** is ordered (if not obtained at the time of prequalification by the MLO) and a **preliminary title report** prepared.

An approved **appraisal management company** is also contacted to appraise the property. Appraisal management companies (AMC's) were initially mandated by the FDIC and in 2011, the authority and enforcement for AMC's were assumed by the CFPB. This standard requires that appraisers have independence of other parties and regulates MLO communication with the appraisal firm and placing an order for the property appraisal (i.e., an MLO cannot directly contact an appraiser/cannot place an order). [See http://www.fdic.gov/regulations/laws/rules/5000-4800.html]

A borrower's ability to qualify for a real estate loan depends on *many* factors related to income, credit history, and assets. There are guidelines for determining what sufficient income for a given housing expense is but it would be wrong to apply these figures too rigidly. **All aspects of the borrower's financial situation must be considered before a loan decision is made.** Quality, quantity, and durability of income are important. A borrower with a higher debt-to-income ratio may still qualify for a loan if he has substantial assets, indicating an ability to manage his financial affairs.

Conversely, strong earnings and substantial assets may not be enough to offset the damage caused by poor credit paying habits. A borrower must be both *able and willing* to pay the housing expense. Past lending experience shows that a borrower who makes large investments in his property is far less likely to default than those with little or no equity.

The Four C's of Underwriting

When evaluating an application for a loan, underwriters or lenders consider the "**4 C's of Underwriting**:"

- **C**redit history of the borrower, which indicates the borrower's willingness to repay debt
- **C**apacity to repay the loan, which includes income and employment history
- **C**ash assets, which are available to close the mortgage
- **C**ollateral, which evaluates the value of the home

Income

Before deciding if a borrower has sufficient income to qualify for a loan, the underwriter must decide what portion of the borrower's total verified earnings are acceptable as a part of the total monthly income. This is accomplished by studying the dependability of the income source(s) and the probability that the income will continue.

Stable monthly income, the *monthly income that can reasonably be expected to continue in the future*, is generally meant to include the **gross** base income of the borrower(s) from a **primary** job(s).

Secondary Sources of Income

Predictable earnings from acceptable secondary sources are considered if a lender's thorough analysis determines they can be substantiated and are durable. Secondary sources of income include, but are not limited to, the following:

- Bonuses
- Commissions above base salary
- Part-time earnings
- Overtime
- Disability payments
- Social Security
- Pensions
- Retirement payments
- Auto allowance
- Foster care
- Capital gains
- Interest-yielding investments

- Rental income
- Alimony
- Child support
- Maintenance
- Unemployment and welfare (if verifiable, continuous, and ongoing)
- Boarder income
- Housing/parsonage allowance
- VA disability compensation

A **quality** source of income is one that is *reasonably reliable,* such as income from an established employer, government agency, interest-yielding investment account, etc. A **durable** source of income can be *expected to continue for a sustained period.* Permanent disability, retirement earnings, and interest on established investments clearly are durable types of income. Temporary unemployment benefits are unlikely to be counted.

Bonuses, Commissions, and Part-Time Earnings

To be considered **durable**, bonus, commission, and part-time earning types of income must be shown to have been a consistent part of the borrower's earnings for *two years. Less than two years* is considered **unstable** but may be used to justify a higher qualifying ratio.

Proof of such consistency can be shown by submitting copies of W-2 forms, pay stubs, or federal income tax returns. Tax returns are reviewed for unreimbursed business expenses (found on IRS Form 2106), which are deducted from income. The lender may send the employer a request for verification of employment earnings and the likelihood of continuance for **at least three years**.

Calculating Inconsistent Income

If sporadic income (commission, self-employed, bonus, overtime, etc.) must be established as durable. If so, follow the table:

The most recent year's income is **higher** than the previous year's income	The current, higher year income is averaged over a 12-month period (**Total income for the year ÷ 12**).
The most recent year's income is **lower** than the previous year's income	The income for both years must be combined and averaged over a 24-month period. **(Previous year income + recent year income) ÷ 24** An explanation of the declining income will likely be required by the underwriter, and if not acceptable, the loan request may be declined.

Overtime

Overtime earnings technically are eligible to count as part of a borrower's qualifying monthly gross income but many underwriters are reluctant to rely on such earnings because their durability is uncertain. When qualifying a buyer, overtime earnings should not be counted unless they show a consistent pattern. If substantiated, refer to the Calculating Inconsistent Income paragraph.

Disability Payments

Disability payments count as income if they are a permanent source of income, but the lender will use caution if they are only for a limited time. If the benefits have a defined expiration date, the remaining term should be **at least three years from the date of the mortgage application.** CFPB Bulletin 2014-03 prohibits a creditor from discriminating against an applicant because of the source of her income, whether part or all of it comes from public assistance. In this bulletin, the CFPB also addresses the documentation requirements for Social Security disability income and Social Security annuity income.

To meet the requirements set by the regulation *not to impose additional income documentation requirements*, the creditor may impose requirements for the continuity for income but may not impose additional documentation requirements for the applicant.

Creditors should review the borrower's disability award letter to determine if the disability income is taxed or non-taxable. Not all disability payments are income tax-free.

Social Security

Social Security income counts as permanent income for a borrower who has reached retirement age. If these payments are the result of a disability or some other condition, the lender treats them like other disability payments and requires no greater amount of documentation than what is imposed on a regular-paid employee.

Pensions and Retirement Benefits

Lenders generally consider pension and retirement benefits as stable income, although they may investigate the source to determine solvency.

Auto Allowance

An **auto allowance** is *an amount an employer gives an employee for the business use of her car.* This amount of reimbursement may be offset by deducting actual expenses from the allowance. The remainder is considered taxable income by the IRS and when averaged for the previous two years is considered income for loan qualification.

Foster Care Income

Qualifying payments for foster care are generally not taxable, according to IRS Publication 525. To be excluded from income, foster care payments must have been received from a state or local government or a qualified placement organization for care provided in the taxpayer's home. The income is considered a reimbursement. To fully document the income for use in loan qualification, an MLO must:

- Obtain a letter from the state agency case worker to substantiate the foster worker's placement and that the placement of children will be ongoing.
- Document receipt of reimbursement for the previous 24 months. Because the income will likely be sporadic and change monthly, use a 24-month average.
- Place a letter in the loan file from the borrower stating he intends to continue with foster care.

Capital Gains

Almost everything owned and used for personal or investment purposes is a capital asset. Examples include a home, personal-use items like household furnishings, and stocks or bonds held as investments. When a capital asset is sold, the difference between the adjusted basis in the asset and the amount realized from the sale is a capital gain or a capital loss. A person who buys a capital asset such as a stock or machinery and then sells the asset at a later date is required to file IRS Form D for recording income and loss from capital gains. The capital gain income should show a monthly average for the previous two years.

Interest-Yielding Investments

When investments are sound and interest payments consistent, lenders will consider this durable income. If investments are a source of down payment, income must be deducted in proportion to what is used for the loan closing. This income will likely be found on the IRS Form Schedule B.

Rental Income

Income from rental properties can be counted if a stable pattern of positive **cash flow** can be verified. **Cash flow** is *money available to an individual on a regular basis after subtracting all expenses*. Rents must cover all expenses and mortgage payments while still leaving excess cash for the owner. Tax returns are used for verifying rental income and expenses. If rental income is not reported on current tax returns, rental leases and PITI documentation must be obtained.

To determine the amount of rental income that may be counted, use the following calculation:

(Gross Rental Income – PITI) * 75% = Net Income

Alimony, Child Support, and Maintenance

Alimony, child support, and/or maintenance can be considered part of the borrower's monthly qualifying income if it's determined they are likely to be made on a consistent basis. Such a determination is dependent on whether the payments are required by written agreement or court decree, the length of time the payments have been received, the age of the child (child support payments generally stop at age 18), the overall financial and credit status of the payer, and the ability of the borrower to compel payment if necessary (e.g., through a court order). They should be expected to continue for a **minimum of three years** to be used in income calculations. They do *not* need to be listed as sources of income if a borrower does not want them considered for the loan, per ECOA.

A copy of the **divorce decree** is generally sufficient to establish the amount and the enforceability of the required payments. To verify receipt of income, the borrower must verify child support payments either by 12 months of cancelled checks or three month's consecutive bank statements showing child support/alimony deposits.

Child support income for:

- **Dependent** children is *not* taxed and, therefore, is not included on tax returns. Such non-taxable income may be grossed up by as much as 125% depending on the loan product type and the lender.
- **Non-dependent** children *is* listed on tax returns as is alimony income.

Unemployment and Welfare

When considering whether income from unemployment or welfare can be counted as stable income, the MLO should ask these questions:

- Is it *verifiable*—can it be proven that the income was received?
- Is it *continuous*—has this income stream been regular for two years?
- Is it *ongoing*—is this income stream likely to continue for at least three more years?

 MLOs may not discriminate against a borrower based on receipt of public assistance.

Case in Point

Borrower A has worked as a groundskeeper for five years at a golf course. Every winter, he is laid off and receives unemployment. He gets a W-2 from the unemployment office each year. His unemployment income should be considered.

Borrower B has a six-year-old son and receives aid for dependent children. This should be considered if the borrower chooses to include it on the application.

Boarder Income

Income from a boarder in the borrower's principal residence or second home is not considered acceptable stable income *except*:

- When a borrower with a disability receives rental income from a live-in personal assistant, whether that individual is a relative of the borrower. The rental payments can be considered as acceptable stable income in an amount up to 30% of the total gross income used to qualify the borrower for the mortgage loan. Personal assistants typically are paid with Medicaid Waiver funds, which also cover room and board from which rental payments are made to the borrower.

- For HomeReady mortgages. Eligibility requirements include an additional exception. See B5-6, HomeReady Mortgage at https://www.fanniemae.com/content/guide/selling/b5/6/02.html.

Housing/Parsonage Allowance

Housing or parsonage income may be considered qualifying income if there is documentation that the income has been received for the most recent 12 months and the allowance is likely to continue for the next three years. The housing allowance may be added to income but may not be used to offset the monthly housing payment.

 This requirement does not apply to military quarters' allowance. For information on military housing, refer to B3-3.1-03, Base Pay (Salary or Hourly), Bonus, and Overtime Income at https://www.fanniemae.com/content/guide/selling/b3/3.1/03.html.

VA Benefits Income

VA education benefits are *not* considered acceptable income as they are offset by education expenses.

Verification of VA Benefits Income

The MLO must document the borrower's receipt of VA benefits via a letter or distribution form from the VA, including verifying that the income can be expected to continue for a minimum of three years from the date of the mortgage application.

Self-Employment Income

To qualify with self-employment income:

- The borrower must own **at least 25% of the business**.
- Self-employed borrowers need to provide personal and entity (corporation, partnership, sole proprietorship) **tax returns** (all schedules) for a **minimum of two years**.
- The lender may also ask to see **financial statements,** which are *documents that show assets and liabilities for an individual or an entity, such as a company for a specific period or point in time.*
- Profit and loss statements and/or balance sheets may also be required.

Secondary market guidelines generally require a self-employed borrower to have operated the business profitably for at least **two years**. If a borrower has been self-employed for *less* than two years, it is difficult to qualify for a loan. However, someone with a shorter history of self-employment (one to two years) may be considered if the borrower's most recent signed federal income tax returns reflect income:

- At the same (or greater) level in a field providing the same products or services as the current business, or
- In an occupation in which the borrower had similar responsibilities to those undertaken in connection with the current business.

In such cases, the lender must give careful consideration to the nature of the borrower's level of experience and the amount of debt the business has.

For this circumstance, an MLO would use the guidelines contained in the section **Calculating Inconsistent Income**.

Considering Nontaxable Income

If a lender can verify that a regular source of a borrower's income is nontaxable—such as child support payments, Social Security benefits, disability retirement payments, workers' compensation benefits, certain types of public assistance payments, and food stamps—and is likely to continue, they may develop an **adjusted gross income** for the borrower by **adding up to 25%** of the nontaxable income to the borrower's income, according to the Fannie Mae Selling Guide (Chapter B3-3.1-04).

This process may be described as "grossing up." The Selling Guide goes on to indicate:

If the actual amount of federal and state taxes that would generally be paid by a wage earner in a similar tax bracket is more than 25% of the borrower's nontaxable income, the lender may use that amount to develop the adjusted gross income, which should be used in calculating the borrower's qualifying ratio.

Caution: Not all disability, workers' comp, and other payments are non-taxable. If they are taxed, they cannot be "grossed-up."

Evaluating Income

Keeping in mind a lender's general guidelines toward certain kinds of income, it's still important to remember that *each type of income is evaluated separately by the underwriter*. When deciding which income counts toward a home mortgage, the underwriter takes each income source and looks at employment history, advancement, and education/training in deciding the strength of each position—particularly for the borrower's primary job.

Employment History

When evaluating the elements of a borrower's income (quantity, quality, and durability), the underwriter analyzes the individual's employment **stability**. A borrower with a history of steady, full-time employment is given more favorable consideration than one who has changed employers frequently unless the changes are properly explained.

Generally, a borrower should have continuous employment for at least **two years** in the same field. However, every borrower is unique and if there is not an established two-year work history, there may be explainable circumstances that would warrant loan approval, such as having recently finished college or being discharged from military service.

Advancement. When a borrower has changed employers frequently for the sake of advancement and/or can show a stable and reliable flow of predictable income, the underwriter will not likely view these changes negatively. On the other hand, persistent job hopping without maintaining income flow or showing advancement usually signifies a problem of some kind; in this case, an underwriter tends to regard the individual's earnings as unstable.

Education and Training. Special education or training that prepares a person for a specific job (such as a nurse or medical doctor) can strengthen a loan application. Such education or training can offset minor weaknesses with respect to earnings or job tenure, especially if the underwriter is convinced of a continuing demand for people, job stability, or opportunity for advancement in this line of work.

Verifying Standard Employment Income

The borrower can substantiate employment and income by providing:

- **W-2 forms** for the previous **two years**.
- **Payroll stubs** for the previous **30-day** period.

Since federal labor regulations promulgated by the Department of Labor (29 C.F.R. § 516.5) and the Equal Employment Opportunity Commission (29 C.F.R. § 1627.3) require employers to keep payroll records for **three years**, if the borrower cannot locate pay stubs or W-2's, it may be possible to get copies directly from the employer.

Pay stubs must identify the borrower, employer, and the borrower's gross earnings for the current pay period *and* year-to-date. Pay stubs may reveal other factors that could impact the mortgage application, such as garnishments or 401K loans.

Verbal employment confirmations are normally completed for each borrower prior to closing. **Verification of Employment (VOE)** forms may also be used to verify income and employment history.

MLOs should caution a borrower at the time of application regarding the complications that might arise if job changes occur during the application process.

IRS Form 4506-T

Underwriters generally require the lender to obtain a completed and signed **Form 4506-T** from the borrower(s) at application. This form *gives the lender permission to request electronic transcripts of federal tax returns from the IRS when documenting the borrower's income.* Under current requirements, the lender determines when to submit the form to the IRS (or designee) to obtain the tax information.

These transcripts are used to validate the borrower's income against their W-2s with the intention of helping to reduce instances of mortgage fraud. Many lenders have some level of quality control audit procedures where a random number of loan files are pulled for review; sometimes this is done prior to close, and sometimes after close. Because the 4506-T form is valid for only 90 days, some MLOs also ask borrowers to sign a second form prior to closing so that tax information may be accessed as part of the quality assurance process, if necessary.

Computing Monthly Income

After determining which income counts, all gross monthly income from those sources is added together to arrive at a total gross monthly income figure. If a borrower earns an hourly wage, it must be converted to a monthly figure. To convert a borrower's hourly wages to monthly earnings:

1. Multiply the hourly wage by the number of hours worked in a week.
2. Multiply by 52 (weeks in a year).
3. Divide by 12 (months in a year).

Case in Point

A borrower makes $19.50 per hour. Assuming the borrower works 40 hours a week:

Weekly Income:	$19.50 x 40 hours = $780
Annual Income:	$780 x 52 weeks = $40,560
Monthly Income:	$40,560 ÷ 12 months = $3,380

Exercise 2.2: Apply Your Knowledge

Directions: Consider the following scenario, and then write your responses.

Scenario: Two months ago, Lisa was honorably discharged from the Air Force where she spent four years training as an airplane mechanic. After discharge, she relocated to take a 40 hour per week apprentice mechanic job with a major airline company where she earns $18 an hour. Last month, her husband Dave, who has worked the past two years as a registered nurse, found a nursing job with a local hospital making $625 per week. They just bought a new car and pay $400 each month on that loan.

1. What is the maximum mortgage payment (PITI) a lender would allow for a conventional loan based on the housing expense ratio?

    _____

    _____

    _____

2. What is Lisa and Dave's total debt-to-income? What is the maximum mortgage amount (PITI) a lender would likely approve?

    _____

    _____

    _____

3. Can Lisa and Dave get approved for a loan, even though they've only been at their jobs a short time? Explain.

    _____

    _____

    _____

Credit History

Credit history is a *record of debt repayment detailing how a person paid credit accounts in the past as a guide to whether she is likely to pay accounts on time and as agreed in the future.*

A **debt** is simply *money owed.* When evaluating a borrower's credit history, however, a debt is generally considered *any secured or unsecured recurring monetary obligation that will not be cancelled until paid in full.*

-   A car lease is considered a debt; so are a student loan or court-ordered child support.

-   Utilities and insurance premiums are *not* considered debts because they can, in theory, be cancelled. Lenders assume borrowers would turn off their phones or cable service before losing their houses.

-   Gray areas can include such things as doctor bills. These are generally not considered to be debt unless there is a payment schedule (e.g., for braces).

Borrowers must inform a lender of *all* debts—even things that may not show up on a credit report.

As part of the loan evaluation, the underwriter analyzes the borrower's (and any co-borrower's) credit history by obtaining a credit report from a national credit reporting company—e.g., Experian, Equifax, and TransUnion. If the credit history shows a slow payment record or other derogatory credit information (lawsuit, judgment, repossession, collection, foreclosure, or bankruptcy), a loan application could be declined or the borrower put into a **high-risk** (B-C credit) category.

In some cases, derogatory ratings don't prevent a borrower from obtaining a loan if the credit problems can be explained. The underwriter must be satisfied that these problems don't represent the borrower's overall attitude toward credit obligations and the circumstances were temporary and no longer exist.

Real Success

If a borrower's credit report is laced with derogatory ratings over a period of years, there's probably little hope for loan approval through a traditional lender. Perpetual credit problems more likely reflect an attitude instead of a circumstance, and it's reasonable for lenders to presume that pattern will continue. All credit problems can be resolved with time, however, so never assume a borrower can't qualify for a loan eventually.

When evaluating a borrower's credit history, lenders use many methods, including objective evaluation methods to ensure compliance with the **Equal Credit Opportunity Act** (ECOA). This Act prohibits discrimination in lending based on age (except minors under 18), sex, race, marital status, color, religion, national origin, or receipt of public assistance.

An MLO must never discourage an applicant from submitting a mortgage application because of his membership in a protected class under ECOA.

Credit Scoring

Credit scoring is an *objective means of determining creditworthiness of potential borrowers based on a number system.*

A **credit score** is *a numeric representation of the borrower's credit profile compiled by assigning specified numerical values to different aspects of the borrower.* These numbers are adjusted up and down based on the strengths and weaknesses of particular qualifications. The numbers are added from all the categories and a credit score based on these various criteria is assigned.

For example, a person with a large line of available credit that is hardly used would likely score higher than a person with lower credit limits but whose credit cards are all maxed out.

Credit scores also play an important role in automated underwriting since Fannie Mae and Freddie Mac have identified a strong correlation between mortgage performance and credit scores.

- The **higher** the score, the *better the credit risk.*
- The **lower** the score, the *higher the risk of default.*

Credit reports and scores are typically obtained from a national credit reporting company. The main credit reporting companies are **Experian, Equifax, and TransUnion.**

Credit Scoring Systems

Credit scores are the result of very complex calculations carried out by a computer that considers every aspect of the borrower's credit file. There are many different names for credit scoring systems. The system that most consumers are likely to be familiar with is **FICO®**, which was developed by Fair, Isaac & Co. Other common names for credit scoring systems include BEACON® (used by Equifax) and EMPERICA® (used by TransUnion).

Items considered by a credit scoring system include:

- Number of open accounts
- Total credit limit
- Types of credit (e.g., credit cards, installment loans)
- Length of credit history (e.g., when opened, latest activity)
- Total amount of debt outstanding
- Number of late payments in the past 30-60-90 days
- Presence of adverse public records (e.g., liens, judgments, bankruptcies)
- Number of recent credit inquiries
- Re-establishment of positive credit history after past payment problems

Credit scoring systems do *not* consider items such as a consumer's race, sex, age, marital status, religion, national origin, salary, or employment history.

Each of the three main credit bureau scores is calculated a little differently. For example, FICO® weighs payment history as 35% of the total score, amounts owed as 30%, length of credit history as 15%, and new credit and types of credit used as 10% each. Regardless of the actual calculation, all credit bureaus produce similar credit scores, which range from about **300 to 850**.

While lenders can't tell you exactly how each credit score is computed, they will disclose what cutoff scores they use in qualifying a borrower for various mortgage loan programs.

Secondary Market

The secondary market has pricing adjustments to the interest rate depending upon credit score and LTV. Fannie Mae and Freddie Mac guidelines generally consider those with credit scores:

- **Above 720** as an *acceptable* credit risk and, therefore, have little interest rate adjustment.
- **Between 620 and 660** as *marginal* and held to a more comprehensive review.
- **Below 620** as *high risk*. Fannie Mae and Freddie Mac do *not* accept these loans except for certain products and programs.

Before making decisions regarding qualification, lenders are encouraged to check the accuracy of credit information.

Explaining Derogatory Credit

Most people try to meet credit obligations on time; when they don't, there's usually a reason. Job loss, hospitalization, prolonged illness, death in the family, or divorce can create financial pressures that affect debt-paying habits. If a few derogatory items appear on a credit report, it may be possible to show that the problems occurred during a specific period of time for understandable reasons and that prior and subsequent credit ratings have been good.

If a borrower refuses to accept responsibility by explaining credit difficulties based on misunderstandings or on the creditors themselves, underwriters may not look favorably upon such explanations. Underwriters reason that a borrower's reluctance to take responsibility for prior credit problems is an indication of what can be expected in the future.

A borrower may have questions regarding his credit score. The Fair Credit Reporting Act, as amended by Section 212(c) of the Fair and Accurate Credit Transactions Act of 2003 (16 C.F.R. Part 602), requires that a **Notice to the Home Loan Applicant Credit Score Information Disclosure** be provided to a borrower. This disclosure must include the score that a credit reporting agency distributed to the lender used in connection with a home loan and the key factors affecting the credit score. This disclosure must include contact information for any credit agency used.

Bankruptcy

Bankruptcy, as established by Title 11 of the U.S. Code, is *a court process that cancels debt and provides some relief for creditors*. There are two basic proceedings for individuals:

- **Chapter 7.** Sometimes called a straight bankruptcy, it is a *liquidation proceeding*. The debtor turns over all non-exempt property to the bankruptcy trustee who then converts it to cash for distribution to the creditors. The debtor receives a discharge of all dischargeable debts, usually within four months. Someone wishing to file Chapter 7 must meet certain tests related to income and debt.

- **Chapter 13.** This is filed by an individual who wants to pay off debt over a period of three to five years. This is preferable to someone who has non-exempt property he wants to keep. It is only an option for an individual with predictable income that is sufficient to pay reasonable expenses with some left over to pay off debts.

According to the Fair Credit Reporting Act (FCRA) (15 U.S.C. 1681c § 605 (a)(1)), consumer reporting agencies may maintain bankruptcy information on a consumer's credit report for **no more than 10 years** from the date of entry of the order for relief or the date of adjudication, whichever the case may be. While credit reporting agencies keep completed Chapter 7 bankruptcies on the credit report for the maximum 10 years, they often keep Chapter 13 bankruptcies on the credit report only for **seven years** after discharge date. This is an incentive for consumers to file under Chapter 13 and repay their debts.

Other Negative Information

According to FICO®, the other types of negative information that remain on a consumer's credit report for **seven years** includes:

- Late payments
- Foreclosures
- Collections (generally depending on the age of the debt being collected)

Also, information that is part of the public record may show for seven years, although unpaid tax liens can remain indefinitely.

Bill Consolidation and Refinancing

Even without derogatory ratings, lenders may find other concerns in a credit report that might indicate the borrower is a marginal credit risk. If an individual's credit pattern is one of continually increasing liabilities and periodically bailing out through bill consolidation (borrowing a larger sum of money to pay off many smaller debts) and refinancing, he may be classified as a marginal risk. This pattern suggests a tendency to live beyond a prudent level. It is a subjective consideration likely to influence the lender's decision if a borrower is weak in other areas, such as income or net worth.

Real Success

Creditors who have a legitimate business need to access a potential borrower's credit report (when a business transaction is initiated by the consumer) may do so if they have authorization from the borrower. While some MLOs require separate written consent from the borrower before obtaining a credit report, Paragraph 6 in Section 6 (Acknowledgements and Agreements) includes language that authorizes the creditor to access the borrower's credit information from any source named in the application or from a consumer reporting agency.

Although credit reports presented by a borrower would not likely be acceptable to lenders, the FCRA (15 U.S.C. 1681b § 604 (b) (2) (B) (IV)) does allow consumers to request one free credit report per year from each of the national credit bureaus—Experian, Equifax, and TransUnion— by visiting www.annualcreditreport.com. A borrower should be encouraged to take advantage of this annually. He is also entitled to a free report:

- If information in a credit report resulted in some sort of adverse action.
- If the consumer was a victim of identity theft and a fraud alert was inserted in a credit file.
- If the credit file contains inaccurate information because of fraud.
- If the consumer is on public assistance or unemployed.

Assets

Assets are simply *items of value*. The underwriter takes the necessary steps to verify the nature and value of assets held by a borrower. If a borrower has a marginal total debt-to-income ratio, above average assets can offset this deficiency. Underwriters know that assets, especially in liquid form such as savings or stocks and bonds, can be used to pay unexpected bills or to support a borrower when there's a temporary interruption in income.

Liquid versus Non-Liquid Assets

Liquid assets are *cash and any other assets—such as stocks or bonds—that can quickly be converted to cash*. Automated underwriting systems (AUSs) generally consider the following assets as liquid and include their value when evaluating a borrower's:

- Checking accounts
- Savings accounts
- Certificates of deposit
- Money market funds
- Mutual funds
- Stocks and bonds
- Retirement accounts
- Trust funds, if the borrower is the beneficiary or settlor and the trust is irrevocable
- Cash value of life insurance

Non-liquid assets include:

- Cash deposits on the sales contract (earnest money)
- Proceeds from the sale of a non-real estate asset
- Proceeds from a property being sold on or before closing of the subject property
- Sweat equity
- Employer assistance
- Rent credit
- Secured borrowed funds
- Trade equity
- Unsecured borrowed funds

Gifts include gift funds from a(n):

- Relative
- Unmarried partner
- Employer
- Religious nonprofit
- Community nonprofit
- Federal, state, or local agency

Evaluating Assets

There are three aspects of a borrower's assets in which lenders and underwriters are interested: Down payment, reserves, and other assets.

Down Payment

It must be determined that the borrower has **sufficient liquid assets** to make the cash down payment and pay the closing costs and other expenses incidental to the purchase of the property. Most loan programs require the borrower to bring at least 5% of the down payment from her personal savings history into the transaction. There are some programs that allow a smaller down payment—mostly government programs or those programs to assist a first-time home buyer. The lender also wants to know the **source** of the borrower's down payment. Savings or sale of a prior home are both acceptable sources of down payment.

Borrowed Funds. Borrowed funds must be secured and the debt considered in the total debt-to-income ratio. Most lenders only allow a secured loan for closing costs to be obtained using the borrower's own personal liquid assets, such as a Roth IRA or a traditional 401K plan.

Gifts. If an applicant lacks the necessary funds to close a transaction, a gift of the required amount is usually acceptable to the underwriter. The gift should be confirmed by means of a **gift letter** signed by the donor. The letter should clearly state that the money represents a gift and *does not have to be repaid*. The gift usually must be from an immediate family member, although rules can vary. In addition to the gift letter, lenders want to verify that the donor has the funds available to provide the gift by seeing a copy of the gift check, a recent bank statement from the donor showing he has the ability to give the gift and a copy of the deposit receipt showing funds have been deposited and are available for closing. In the past, this has been an area of mortgage fraud, so it is important to validate the funds came from the account verified on the gift letter and bank statement provided by the donor.

Fannie Mae and Freddie Mac require a borrower to make at least a 5% down payment from her own funds in addition to the gift, unless the gift equals 20% or more of the purchase price. On conventional loans, a borrower can't use borrowed funds or gifts for the first 5%. There are other special programs that will allow for a gift of the entire down payment, with special qualifications, such as the borrower/buyer being considered a first-time homebuyer.

Reserves

Reserves are *cash on deposit or other highly liquid assets a borrower will have available after the loan funds.* Lenders would like to see enough to cover two months' PITI mortgage payments of principal, interest, taxes, and insurance (and assessments such as condominium association fees, if applicable) after the borrower makes the down payment and pays all closing costs; however, in most cases, this is not required.

For investment properties, six months' PITI payments must be verified for loans on non-owner-occupied property. When a borrower converts a primary residence she has occupied during the past 12 months into investment property, if the equity in the property is less than 30%, she is required to have six months reserves for **both properties**—the investment property and her principal residence—for conventional loans.

Other Assets

Having assets in addition to cash and other liquid assets show that the borrower is able to manage money and has resources, if needed, to handle emergencies and make mortgage payments.

Real estate equity is an important asset to consider. Equity is *the difference between the market value of the property and the sum of the mortgages and other liens against the property.* Equity, less all selling expenses, is what a buyer should receive from the sale of property.

- If the equity from the sale of a home is the source of money for the purchase of the subject property, the underwriter might require evidence that the sale closed and the borrower received the proceeds before making the new loan.

- If the loan is a construction loan and the borrower has owned the lot for 12 months or more, the underwriter treats the borrower's equity in that lot as cash or its equivalent when determining the down payment needed.

Other real estate also counts as an asset, but only the equity in the property—and not its total value—contributes to net worth since it can be converted to cash by selling an interest in or mortgaging the property. Real estate with little or no equity, or investment property with income that's equal to or below expenses, hurts a loan application more than it helps because the property may require cash from the borrower. Of course, a lender must be told of any financial obligations or expense shortfalls not covered by property rents.

Verifying Deposits for Down Payment/Reserves

Documentation of assets includes **one to two months of bank statements** (all pages) to verify available funds. A **Verification of Deposit (VOD)** form may also be used to verify current and average bank statement balances. When the underwriter reviews the bank statements or receives the completed VOD forms, four questions are considered:

1. Does the verified information conform to statements in the loan application?
2. Is there enough money in the bank to pay costs of buying the property?
3. Has the bank account been opened recently (within the last few months)?
4. Is the present balance notably higher than the average balance?

Lenders prefer to see **seasoned funds**, which means *they have been in the account for the entire period covered by the bank statements*. Recently opened accounts or higher-than-normal balances must be explained as these are strong indications the applicant may have borrowed the funds. Also, the source of any large and unusual deposit will need to be documented.

Insurance and Escrow Requirements

Providing funds to a borrower to purchase or refinance a home carries with it a great deal of financial risk for the lender, who is said to have an **insurable interest** in the property. To protect that collateral, therefore, lenders normally require insurance.

Homeowner's Hazard Insurance. A policy that covers loss or damage to the home or property in the event of fire or other disasters such as tornado, snow, and hail damage. Lenders generally:

- Require the policy to be sufficient to replace the home or reimburse the mortgage amount, with the lender being named on the actual policy.

- Have the right to place insurance on the property to cover its interest (the loan value) in the event of a loss if the borrower does not comply with the lender's insurance requirements (force-placed insurance).

- Require borrowers to pay the first year's insurance premium in full *prior* to closing.

- Incorporate the annual insurance cost (along with current property taxes) into an **escrow account,** which is prorated over the next 12 months to determine a monthly insurance and property tax payment amount. This is added to the monthly principal and interest due for loan repayment. Upon payment each month, the insurance and taxes are deposited into the borrower's escrow account. When property taxes and insurance become due, the lender/servicer forwards the payment to the respective recipients on behalf of the property owner.

Flood Insurance. Homeowner's hazard insurance does **not** cover damage caused by the peril of flood. When a property is in a federally-designated special flood hazard area (SFHA), either in *Flood Zone A or Flood Zone V*, the lender for federal loans will require a flood insurance policy for the life of the loan in addition to homeowner's hazard insurance. Flood insurance must be purchased from the **National Flood Insurance Program (NFIP)** or from an insurer participating in the Write Your Own program. In order to buy federal flood insurance, the property must be in a community that is voluntarily participating in the NFIP.

Private Mortgage Insurance (PMI). PMI is offered by private companies to insure a lender against default on a loan by a borrower where there is a loss of collateral value at the time of the default. Prior to the advent of PMI in the early 1970s, lenders would only lend 80% of the value of a property, assuming that the 20% down payment was the incentive needed for the borrower to keep mortgage payments current. Both Fannie Mae and Freddie Mac also require private mortgage insurance (whether lender-paid or third-party) on home loans with less than 20% down. When insuring a loan, the mortgage insurance insurer shares the lender's risk, but only part of the risk. The insurer does not insure the entire loan amount, but rather the upper portion of the loan that exceeds the standard 80% LTV. The amount of coverage can vary, but is typically 20% to 25% of the loan amount.

 After the sale of the security, the proceeds may not be sufficient for the lender to reclaim all the lender's losses from the principal balance, foreclosure, and other costs. The lender may be able to pursue a deficiency judgment against the borrower for any losses, depending on state statutes. This is referred to as **recourse**.

Exercise 2.3: Apply Your Knowledge

Directions: Consider the following scenario, and then write your responses.

Scenario: Sam Able wants to buy a home and it's estimated that an 80% conventional loan will have a mortgage payment of $878. He has an automobile payment of $212 a month with 14 installments remaining. He earns $700 per week. His down payment and closing costs are estimated at $18,400. Sam is selling a home with equity of $14,000. He has a checking and savings account with a local bank and plans to draw on that account to close the transaction. The VOD showed Sam's savings account has an average monthly balance of $1,000 and a current balance of $3,600.

1. What is Sam's housing expense ratio?

2. What is Sam's total debt-to-income ratio?

3. Will Sam have any problems closing this transaction? Explain.

4. Do you see any problems with Sam's VOD? Explain.

Underwriting

There are general steps all lenders take before deciding whether to make a real estate loan and if yes, on what terms. This evaluation process is called **loan underwriting**, where *an underwriter evaluates the documentation, borrower information, and various risk factors associated with a loan in order to make a decision.*

Putting Together a Loan File

To make any decision, however, the underwriter must have all the relevant data. Before submitting a loan file to underwriting, MLOs should review the application one last time before shipping it for the underwriter's review. A good MLO takes ownership of the loan file, ensuring that the information in the submitted application is accurate, that all required documentation in the loan file is included and complete, and that all readily identifiable issues that an underwriter might raise have been addressed. If a loan processor misses something, it's the MLO's job to figure it out and fix it before it goes to the underwriter. The goal of the MLO should be to never have a loan file rejected as "*incomplete*."

Real Success

There is no standardized order in which to assemble the loan file, although lenders may have a preference. Submitting the loan file for final underwriting can usually be accomplished in an email, by courier, or by fax. When submitting a loan file by email or other electronic delivery, use a **secure transmission method** to ensure the information is kept confidential and to prevent identity theft.

Also, it is a good practice to include a "Dear Underwriter" letter and place it on top of the file. If the loan application has potential issues—for example, unusual circumstances, odd letters of explanation, strange income—use the letter to prepare the underwriter for what's coming. Let the underwriter know that *you* know where the issues are; if he finds something strange on his own, he may start doubting the whole package. Do anything you can do to make the process go smoothly. In addition to the negative issues, you can also accent the positive items of the loan file in your "Dear Underwriter" letter.

For the sake of your borrowers, find out how long the file will sit in the review queue and when they can expect a decision. It is stressful waiting to hear—keep your borrowers informed to alleviate their worry. Share with them that during busy times, it may take several weeks for the underwriter to finish. ECOA [12 CFR Part 1022, Subpart B, §1022.9(a)(i)] requires a lender to communicate a credit decision (approval, counteroffer to, or adverse action) within **30 days** of receiving a completed application.

Evaluating a Loan File

When evaluating a loan file, the primary concern throughout the loan underwriting process is determining the **degree of risk** a loan represents. The underwriter attempts to answer several fundame4ntal questions:

- Is there sufficient value in the property pledged as collateral to assure recovery of the loan amount in the event of default? This is determined by an appraisal of the real property.

- Is there a marketable property title that provides the borrower and the lender a good and perfect lien position? This is determined by a title report provided by a title insurance company or an abstract of title.

- Are items regarding the real property considered such as flood zones, environmental issues, and local municipal and regulatory issues that may affect the property?

- Does the borrower's overall financial situation, which is comprised of credit, income, and assets, indicate a reasonable expectation of making the proposed monthly loan payments in a timely manner?

A complete and accurate loan file, therefore, allows the underwriter to make an informed decision.

According to Freddie Mac, "Underwriting mortgage loans is an art, not a science." The underwriting process can be **automated**, where *all information is fed into an AUS*, or **manual**, which is *done by an individual who works for the lender*. Both processes have various qualifying standards applied to the loan information.

Regardless of whether underwriting process is manual or automated, the resulting final decision will be:

1. Reject the loan as applied for (which may be because the borrower or collateral was not a good risk or because the loan application file was incomplete).

2. Make the loan on the terms applied for.

3. Make the loan on different terms (for example, a higher interest rate, a different loan program, additional collateral, etc.).

Automated Underwriting Systems

Automation is used in all facets of the lending process. The purpose of automated underwriting is to reduce the cost of examining a loan application and speed up mortgage approvals. An AUS can provide consistent underwriting decisions using statistical computer models based on traditional underwriting factors and never considers factors such as race, ethnicity, age, or any other characteristic prohibited by law. And with large databases of statistics and information available, the secondary market has increased efforts to manage credit risk by improving loan criteria.

The AUS makes a recommendation to accept a loan for delivery or refers it to an underwriter for further manual review and analysis. Even with an automated approval, an underwriter still must validate the information entered into the AUS, along with the supporting documentation. While lenders may rely on AUSs for a preliminary decision, it generally comes down to a human underwriter to make the final decision.

Both Fannie Mae and Freddie Mac have proprietary AUSs and they charge lenders for the privilege of using them. Fannie Mae's automated underwriting system is **Desktop Underwriter®** (DU®). Freddie Mac has a similar direct AUS called **Loan Prospector®** (LP®).

Chapter 2 Summary

1. The common areas of work for a mortgage professional are MLO, loan processor, underwriter, and servicer. An **MLO** takes applications, pulls credit reports, orders appraisals, and assembles documents for mortgage loans. A **loan processor** works on the file assembled by the originator, verifying the information in the file and coordinating other aspects of the loan and closing. The **underwriter** is responsible for reviewing the file and arriving at a credit decision for the lender or investor based on the credit risk associated with a particular loan. If there are conditions on the loan, they must be satisfied prior to closing. A **servicer** oversees the collection of mortgage payments and pursues late payments on behalf of the mortgagee.

2. **Lender's return** is the total amount a lender or broker makes on a loan's discount points, such as from loan fees. **Points** are 1% of loan amount, increase lender's yield, and are paid for many reasons. **Discount points** are used to buy down the interest rate. **Yield spread premium** (or lender credits) is a tool MLOs can use to reduce a borrower's settlement costs.

3. A borrower can get pre-qualified or pre-approved. **Pre-qualification** is when a mortgage broker or lender reviews a borrower's history to determine if she is likely to get approved for a loan and the approximate amount. Pre-qualification is *not* binding on the lender. **Pre-approval** is when a lender uses an application to determine that a potential borrower can be financed for a certain amount for a specific property. A mortgage broker cannot give a borrower a pre-approval; only a lender can.

4. The loan process consists of four steps: 1. **Consulting** with an MLO; 2. Completing the **application**; 3. **Processing** the application; 4. **Analyzing** the borrower and the property. Common fees include credit report, appraisal, title work, inspections, etc. The loan application asks a number of personal and financial questions, along with information about the property the borrower wishes to purchase. The MLO must document that a borrower is reasonably able to repay the loan.

5. Address and **employment** information must go back two to three years. **Income** should be stable and verifiable. Alimony/child support may be excluded as income if a borrower chooses (if included, it may be grossed up 125%). Those who are self-employed (at least 25% ownership) may need personal and company tax returns and financial statements. **Assets** and **liabilities** must all be disclosed, including alimony and child support, if it's an obligation. **Liquid assets** can be quickly and easily converted to cash. **Net worth** is assets minus liabilities.

6. **Bankruptcy** is a court process that cancels debt and provides some relief for creditors. Chapter 7 bankruptcy is a liquidation proceeding where the debtor receives a discharge of all dischargeable debts. Chapter 13 bankruptcy is filed by an individual who wants to pay off debt over a period of three to five years.

7. The **underwriting** process may evaluate: Capacity (ability to pay), collateral (down payment, home value), credit (good payment history), character (job stability, reserves), and conditions (health of job market, economy). Some elements of the mortgage process may be automated to reduce time and costs for lenders. AUSs offer computerized analysis to recommend accepting the loan or refer it to a human underwriter for further consideration. Fannie Mae's AUS is **Desktop Underwriter**®; Freddie Mac's system is Loan Prospector®.

8. Monthly **income** must show stability, quality, and durability. Bonuses, commission, part-time earnings, and overtime all count if shown to be a consistent part of the borrower's income for the past few years. Lenders do not usually count temporary unemployment, welfare, and other income. **Credit history** is a record of debt repayment. **Credit scoring** is an objective means of evaluating credit. Lenders verify assets and may require financial statements. The three main credit bureaus produce similar credit scores, which range from about **300 to 850.** A **gift letter** can show part of the down payment/closing costs are a non-repayable gift.

9. Conforming loans sold on the secondary market (e.g., Fannie Mae and Freddie Mac) require income ratios of **28%** for housing expense and **36%** for debt-to-income (DTI). The housing expense ratio is the relationship of the borrower's total monthly housing expense, or PITI (principal, interest, taxes, and insurance) to gross monthly income (stable) expressed as a percentage. PITI must also consider required homeowner's association fees. Total debt-to-income ratio is the relationship of the borrower's total monthly debt obligations (including housing and debts that will not be cancelled and that have ten or more payments remaining) to gross monthly income expressed as a percentage. A borrower must qualify under **both** ratios. Fannie Mae, however, focuses on the back-end ratio (DTI).

Chapter 2 Quiz

1. Joe buys a house for $150,000, making a $30,000 down payment and paying three discount points to buy down the interest rate. What is the total cost of the discount points?

   A. $1,500
   B. $3,000
   C. $3,600
   D. $4,500

2. Mary receives a monthly payment from her ex-husband to assist her with their children's expenses. Bob receives a monthly check because of a service-connected injury from his days in the military. John is a minister and receives money every month for living expenses. These payments are examples of

   A. gross up income.
   B. nontaxable income.
   C. public assistance payments.
   D. unemployment compensation.

3. If a borrower is self-employed, he should provide

   A. an average monthly income amount earned over the previous two years.
   B. employment verification from the last employer.
   C. profit and loss statements for the previous six years.
   D. tax returns for the previous two years.

4. Bob and Mary are providing a gift to their daughter, Amy, as down payment for the purchase of her new home. They provide a current bank statement for their account, a copy of their check to Amy, and a copy of the deposit slip into Amy's account. Amy provides a current ledger from her checking account that verifies the deposit was made and the amount of the current balance. What key document is missing?

   A. agreement signed by all parties stating when the gift is to be repaid
   B. copy of the deposit receipt from the settlement agent
   C. gift letter signed by the donor stating no repayment is expected
   D. letter from Amy's bank stating the gift funds have been deposited

5. To be classified as self-employment income, the borrower must own at least what percent of the business used for qualifying?

   A. 5%
   B. 10%
   C. 25%
   D. 50%

6. Loans that are not backed by the full faith and credit of the United States follow the underwriting guidelines of

   A. ECOA.
   B. Fannie Mae and Freddie Mac.
   C. the FHA.
   D. RESPA.

7. When qualifying for a conventional loan, stable gross monthly income can include

   A. alimony received (that a borrower chooses to reveal).
   B. a bonus received for the first time last year.
   C. erratic unemployment earnings.
   D. income from other family members.

8. To combat income-related mortgage fraud, lenders require a review of the income provided to the IRS. What document authorizes the lender to obtain income transcripts from the IRS?

   A. 1003 and Verification of Income
   B. 4506-T
   C. Schedule 15
   D. URAR

9. Joe wants to get a loan to buy a house. When evaluating his credit obligations, which would LEAST LIKELY be considered as debt?

   A. car loan payment
   B. cell phone service payment
   C. child support payment
   D. credit card payment

10. A borrower's stable monthly income is $3,000. He has three monthly debts: $350 car payment, $50 personal loan payment, and $50 credit card payment. What is the maximum monthly mortgage payment he would qualify for on a conforming loan?

    A. $390
    B. $630
    C. $840
    D. $1,080

Finance Instruments

Whether you work for a bank, a mortgage company, a mortgage broker, another type of primary lender, or for an agency that is active in the secondary market, you must be familiar with the various forms, reports, and documents you will encounter in your work. The "instruments" discussed in this chapter focus on the more common legal documents you will encounter as part of real estate transactions that are used to establish the rights and duties of the parties involved. These include legal instruments, such as promissory notes, security instruments, trust deeds, and mortgages. We will also discuss typical clauses found in these instruments.

After completing this chapter, you will be able to:

- Contrast a financing instrument with a security instrument.
- Describe advantages and disadvantages of mortgages and trust deeds.
- Identify typical mortgage clauses.

Key Terms

Acceleration Clause	Foreclosure, Judicial	Power of Sale Clause
Alienation Clause	Foreclosure, Non-judicial	Prepayment Clause
Balloon Payment	Hypothecate	Promissory Note
Collateral	Junior Lien	Reconveyance Clause
Deed of Trust	Legal Title	Senior Lien
Defeasance Clause	Lien Position	Subordination Agreement
Equitable Title	Lis Pendens	
First Mortgage	Mortgage	

Promissory Notes

Promissory notes are *financing instruments that evidence a promise to pay a specific amount of money to a specific person within a specific time frame.* Simply stated, a promissory note is a written promise to pay money. The **payee** is the person or institution lending the money. The maker is also known as the **payor**, who is the person who makes the promise to repay the funds by signing a promissory note. A typical promissory note includes several key items, including:

- Names of the parties
- Amount of the debt, including the interest rate used to amortize the debt, known as the **note rate**
- Signature of the maker

Most promissory notes used in real estate are **negotiable instruments**, which mean they are *freely transferable from one party to another.* When a note is freely transferable, the lender or other creditor can obtain immediate cash by selling the note.

Types of Notes

The four types of notes usually used in real estate transactions are:

1. **Straight Note or Interest-Only Note.** Calls for interest-only payments during the term of the note with a balloon payment at the end of the loan term to pay off the principal amount; usually a short-term loan.

2. **Installment Note.** Calls for payments of principal and/or interest at designated intervals (possibly, a balloon payment may be required).

3. **Partially Amortizing Installment Note** or **Installment Note with Balloon.** Calls for periodic payments of principal and interest during the loan term with a balloon payment at the end of the term to pay off the balance due.

4. **Fully Amortizing Installment Note.** Calls for regular payment of principal and interest calculated to pay off the entire balance by the end of loan term.

Exercise 3.1: Knowledge Check

1. **A note is a borrower's promise to repay a debt.**

   A. true
   B. false

2. **A note should be signed by the payee.**

   A. true
   B. false

NOTE

_____, _____   _____, _____
[Date]   [City]   [State]

_____
[Property Address]

1. BORROWER'S PROMISE TO PAY

In return for a loan that I have received, I promise to pay U.S. $_____ (this amount is called "Principal"), plus interest, to the order of the Lender. The Lender is _____. I will make all payments under this Note in the form of cash, check or money order.

I understand that the Lender may transfer this Note. The Lender or anyone who takes this Note by transfer and who is entitled to receive payments under this Note is called the "Note Holder."

2. INTEREST

Interest will be charged on unpaid principal until the full amount of Principal has been paid. I will pay interest at a yearly rate of _____%.

The interest rate required by this Section 2 is the rate I will pay both before and after any default described in Section 6(B) of this Note.

3. PAYMENTS

(A) Time and Place of Payments

I will pay principal and interest by making a payment every month.

I will make my monthly payment on the _____ day of each month beginning on _____, _____. I will make these payments every month until I have paid all of the principal and interest and any other charges described below that I may owe under this Note. Each monthly payment will be applied as of its scheduled due date and will be applied to interest before Principal. If, on _____, 20____, I still owe amounts under this Note, I will pay those amounts in full on that date, which is called the "Maturity Date."

I will make my monthly payments at _____ or at a different place if required by the Note Holder.

(B) Amount of Monthly Payments

My monthly payment will be in the amount of U.S. $_____.

4. BORROWER'S RIGHT TO PREPAY

I have the right to make payments of Principal at any time before they are due. A payment of Principal only is known as a "Prepayment." When I make a Prepayment, I will tell the Note Holder in writing that I am doing so. I may not designate a payment as a Prepayment if I have not made all the monthly payments due under the Note.

I may make a full Prepayment or partial Prepayments without paying a Prepayment charge. The Note Holder will use my Prepayments to reduce the amount of Principal that I owe under this Note. However, the Note Holder may apply my Prepayment to the accrued and unpaid interest on the Prepayment amount, before applying my Prepayment to reduce the Principal amount of the Note. If I make a partial Prepayment, there will be no changes in the due date or in the amount of my monthly payment unless the Note Holder agrees in writing to those changes.

5. LOAN CHARGES

If a law, which applies to this loan and which sets maximum loan charges, is finally interpreted so that the interest or other loan charges collected or to be collected in connection with this loan exceed the permitted limits, then: (a) any such loan charge shall be reduced by the amount necessary to reduce the charge to the permitted limit; and (b) any sums already collected from me which exceeded permitted limits will be refunded to me. The Note Holder may choose to make this refund by reducing the Principal I owe under this Note or by making a direct payment to me. If a refund reduces Principal, the reduction will be treated as a partial Prepayment.

MULTISTATE FIXED RATE NOTE—Single Family—Fannie Mae/Freddie Mac UNIFORM INSTRUMENT   Form 3200   1/01 *(page 1 of 3 pages)*

6. BORROWER'S FAILURE TO PAY AS REQUIRED

(A) Late Charge for Overdue Payments

If the Note Holder has not received the full amount of any monthly payment by the end of _____ calendar days after the date it is due, I will pay a late charge to the Note Holder. The amount of the charge will be _____ % of my overdue payment of principal and interest. I will pay this late charge promptly but only once on each late payment.

(B) Default

If I do not pay the full amount of each monthly payment on the date it is due, I will be in default.

(C) Notice of Default

If I am in default, the Note Holder may send me a written notice telling me that if I do not pay the overdue amount by a certain date, the Note Holder may require me to pay immediately the full amount of Principal which has not been paid and all the interest that I owe on that amount. That date must be at least 30 days after the date on which the notice is mailed to me or delivered by other means.

(D) No Waiver By Note Holder

Even if, at a time when I am in default, the Note Holder does not require me to pay immediately in full as described above, the Note Holder will still have the right to do so if I am in default at a later time.

(E) Payment of Note Holder's Costs and Expenses

If the Note Holder has required me to pay immediately in full as described above, the Note Holder will have the right to be paid back by me for all of its costs and expenses in enforcing this Note to the extent not prohibited by applicable law. Those expenses include, for example, reasonable attorneys' fees.

7. GIVING OF NOTICES

Unless applicable law requires a different method, any notice that must be given to me under this Note will be given by delivering it or by mailing it by first class mail to me at the Property Address above or at a different address if I give the Note Holder a notice of my different address.

Any notice that must be given to the Note Holder under this Note will be given by delivering it or by mailing it by first class mail to the Note Holder at the address stated in Section 3(A) above or at a different address if I am given a notice of that different address.

8. OBLIGATIONS OF PERSONS UNDER THIS NOTE

If more than one person signs this Note, each person is fully and personally obligated to keep all of the promises made in this Note, including the promise to pay the full amount owed. Any person who is a guarantor, surety or endorser of this Note is also obligated to do these things. Any person who takes over these obligations, including the obligations of a guarantor, surety or endorser of this Note, is also obligated to keep all of the promises made in this Note. The Note Holder may enforce its rights under this Note against each person individually or against all of us together. This means that any one of us may be required to pay all of the amounts owed under this Note.

9. WAIVERS

I and any other person who has obligations under this Note waive the rights of Presentment and Notice of Dishonor. "Presentment" means the right to require the Note Holder to demand payment of amounts due. "Notice of Dishonor" means the right to require the Note Holder to give notice to other persons that amounts due have not been paid.

10. UNIFORM SECURED NOTE

This Note is a uniform instrument with limited variations in some jurisdictions. In addition to the protections given to the Note Holder under this Note, a Mortgage, Deed of Trust, or Security Deed (the "Security Instrument"), dated the same date as this Note, protects the Note Holder from possible losses which might result if I do not keep the promises which I make in this Note. That Security Instrument describes how and under what conditions I may be required to make immediate payment in full of all amounts I owe under this Note. Some of those conditions are described as follows:

> If all or any part of the Property or any Interest in the Property is sold or transferred (or if Borrower is not a natural person and a beneficial interest in Borrower is sold or transferred) without Lender's prior written consent, Lender may require immediate payment in full of all sums secured by this Security Instrument. However, this option shall not be exercised by Lender if such exercise is prohibited by Applicable Law.

MULTISTATE FIXED RATE NOTE—Single Family—**Fannie Mae/Freddie Mac UNIFORM INSTRUMENT**   Form 3200   1/01   *(page 2 of 3 pages)*

If Lender exercises this option, Lender shall give Borrower notice of acceleration. The notice shall provide a period of not less than 30 days from the date the notice is given in accordance with Section 15 within which Borrower must pay all sums secured by this Security Instrument. If Borrower fails to pay these sums prior to the expiration of this period, Lender may invoke any remedies permitted by this Security Instrument without further notice or demand on Borrower.

WITNESS THE HAND(S) AND SEAL(S) OF THE UNDERSIGNED.

_____(Seal)
                                           - Borrower

_____(Seal)
                                           - Borrower

_____(Seal)
                                           - Borrower

[Sign Original Only]

MULTISTATE FIXED RATE NOTE—Single Family—**Fannie Mae/Freddie Mac UNIFORM INSTRUMENT**   Form 3200   **1/01** *(page 3 of 3 pages)*

Security Instruments

In almost all real estate financing transactions, a promissory note is accompanied by a **security instrument**. A security instrument requires a debtor to **hypothecate** his property as a condition of a loan, which means that *a debtor pledges personal or real property as security for a debt, typically without giving up possession of it.*

A security instrument serves as protection for the creditor, and motivation for the debtor, to make sure that the terms of the note are fulfilled and the note is repaid as agreed. When the debt is repaid, the note and the security instrument are canceled.

The two main types of security instruments used in real estate transactions are trust deeds and mortgages.

Trust Deeds

Trust deeds, or deeds of trust, are *instruments placing a specific financial interest in the title to real property into the hands of a disinterested third party as security for the payment of a note.* With a trust deed, the:

- Borrower is called the **trustor.**
- Lender is the **beneficiary** who retains both the note and the deed of trust.
- **Trustee** holds legal title to the security property described in the deed of trust, subject to the terms of the trust for the benefit of the lender.

Who is eligible to be a trustee varies from state to state; it could be an attorney, for example, or a title company that provides trustee services. With a trust deed, the borrower has possession of an **equitable title** to the property. When the loan is paid, the note and the deed of trust are canceled and both legal title and equitable title are then vested in the borrower.

A distinguishing characteristic of trust deeds is that the trustee has the authority under the terms of the trust to commence a **non-judicial foreclosure action** (*foreclosure by a trustee under the power of sale clause in a deed of trust without the involvement of a court*) when the lender has declared the loan to be in default. However, such action would not be taken until after the trustee has notified the borrower of the default and given the borrower the opportunity to cure.

Mortgages

A **mortgage** is a type of security instrument where the borrower (the mortgagor) conveys an interest in property to the lender (the mortgagee) as collateral for the debt, creating a **voluntary lien** on the property. When a borrower defaults on a mortgage, the lender may commence a **judicial foreclosure action**, which is *a lawsuit filed by a lender or other creditor to foreclose on a mortgage or other lien. It can also be a court-ordered sheriff's sale of the property to repay the debt.*

[A sample of a mortgage agreement is available for review (see Appendix G – Sample Mortgage Agreement).]

Lien Theory and Title Theory

Some states follow lien theory, while others follow title theory.

Generally, in **lien theory** states, the *security instrument creates a lien against the property, which must be repaid by the debtor.* The property serves as collateral that is hypothecated to the lender as security for the debt, but the mortgagor holds the title to the property (or equitable title if a deed of trust is used). The lender may be required to go through a judicial foreclosure proceeding to obtain title and possession in the event of default.

In **title theory** states, the *security instrument gives actual title to the property to the lender while the debt is outstanding, with the borrower retaining only equitable title and possession of the land.*

Once the mortgage amount has been repaid, legal title reverts or is conveyed to the borrower. The lender does not have possession or use of the property, and would have to go through a foreclosure proceeding to gain possession in the event of default, although it may be possible to avoid a lengthy judicial foreclosure proceeding and gain possession through non-judicial or strict foreclosure.

Some lien theory states allow only mortgages to be recorded. Some title theory states allow only trust deeds to be recorded. And some states allow either type of security instrument to be recorded. Make certain that you understand how mortgages and deeds of trust are handled in the states in which you practice.

Judicial Foreclosure Procedure

When a borrower is in **default** on a loan, the lender *accelerates the due date of the debt to the present and gives the debtor notice of default, demanding the full loan balance to be paid at once.* If the debtor fails to do so, the lender files a lawsuit, called a **foreclosure action**, in a court of jurisdiction where the land is located.

 There are some differences in how foreclosure proceedings progress depending on the state and county in which the action takes place.

Under a **foreclosure action**, the *court determines whether the lender is rightfully owed the money and whether the debtor is in default.* If the court finds in favor of the creditor, the creditor takes ownership and a judge issues an order of execution directing an officer of the court, usually the county sheriff, to seize the property.

If the creditor chooses to sell:

- The public is notified of the place and date of the sale via advertising that runs for a specified number of weeks in a newspaper circulated in the county.

- The property is sold to the highest bidder, with proceeds used to pay costs of the sale and to pay off the mortgages and liens.

- Any **overages** remaining after all debts, liens, expenses, and costs related to the property are paid to the debtor.

If the property does not bring enough money at the sale to pay off the mortgage, the creditor may be able to obtain a **deficiency judgment**, which is *a court order stating that the debtor owes money to the creditor when the collateral property does not bring enough at a foreclosure sale to cover the entire loan amount, accrued interest, and other costs.*

The deficiency judgment is a personal judgment against the debtor that creates a general, involuntary lien against all real and personal property.

 In today's marketplace, foreclosure procedures are undergoing challenges and modifications by both state governments and federal agencies. Make sure that you stay current with the practices and legal issues in the jurisdictions where you do business.

Redemption

Debtors may be able to redeem (save) their property from the time a *notice of a pending legal action*, called a **lis pendens,** is filed until the confirmation of the foreclosure sale. This is done by paying the court what is due, which may include court costs and attorneys' fees. In some states, this right to *save or redeem the property prior to the confirmation of sale* is called the **equitable right of redemption.**

Some other states use the **statutory right of redemption,** which allows debtors to redeem themselves *after the final sale.* Once the redemption is made, the court will set aside the sale, pay the parties, and the debtor gains title to the property again.

One other option debtors have to avoid foreclosure is to make a voluntary conveyance, also called **deed in lieu of foreclosure.** With this action, *debtors still lose the property, but by conveying it voluntarily before final court action, they avoid having a foreclosure on their credit record.* After confirmation of sale, however, it is too late. Note that a lender is not obligated to accept a deed in lieu of foreclosure as full satisfaction of the debt and could still pursue a deficiency judgment.

Exercise 3.2: Apply Your Knowledge

Match each listed mortgage term on the left with the appropriate description on the right.

Mortgage Terms	Match
1. Balloon Note	____ A. Additional payment at end of term
2. Beneficiary	____ B. Benefits from Deed of Trust
3. Fully Amortizing	____ C. Borrower
4. Hypothecate	____ D. Court decision
5. Judicial	____ E. Evidence of debt
6. Non-Judicial	____ F. Holds title
7. Note	____ G. Interest-only
8. Security Instrument	____ H. Pledge as security
9. Straight Note	____ I. Protects lender
10. Trustee	____ J. Trustee's sale
11. Trustor	____ K. Zero balance due at end of term

Mortgage Lien Position

Lien position establishes the *order in which liens are paid off out of the proceeds of a foreclosure sale.* By law, real estate tax liens always have the highest priority and get paid first, followed by the first recorded lien. Then if there's money left, the second lien gets paid, and so on. Once the funds are exhausted, liens in a later position get nothing.

A **first mortgage** is a *security instrument with a first lien position.* As such, a first mortgage almost always has priority over all other mortgages, meaning the first mortgage holder is paid first in the event of a foreclosure sale.

A **second mortgage** is a *security instrument in a second lien position.* A second mortgage may be used to help buy the property (e.g., small loan from the seller) or might be taken out later to generate additional funds from the owner's accumulated equity in the property (e.g., a home equity loan) for repairs, college tuition, or some other purpose. Although the property is still used as security, the second mortgage lender is in a riskier position because, as we just learned, the first mortgage gets paid first out of foreclosure proceedings. If nothing is left, the second mortgage holder gets nothing.

Generally, *any mortgage in a higher lien position* is said to be a **senior mortgage**; therefore, a first mortgage is always a senior mortgage. A **junior mortgage** is *any mortgage with a lower lien position than another.* Thus, a second mortgage is a junior mortgage to a first mortgage, but a second mortgage is a senior mortgage to a third mortgage.

It's important to note that a mortgage would not necessarily be the first recorded lien on a property. For example, if someone purchases a new home from a builder who did not pay all the subcontractors or suppliers prior to the borrower purchasing the home, any lawsuit for collection from the builder may relate back to when the work was commenced, which puts a mechanic's or materialman's lien ahead of the lender.

Subordination Agreement

In some situations, the parties may desire that a later recorded instrument has priority over an earlier recorded instrument. This is common in construction financing.

For Example

Because of the high-risk nature of construction loans, construction lenders frequently refuse to lend money unless they can be assured of a first lien position. Since in many cases, the developer has already purchased the land on some sort of deferred payment plan, there is often a security instrument (mortgage, trust deed, or land contract) already recorded. For the construction mortgage to take priority over the land mortgage, the first lender would need to file a **subordination agreement** in the public record that permits the second lien holder to be in the first lien position.

Another example is when a property owner has a junior mortgage, such as a home equity line of credit, and wants to refinance his first mortgage but keep the line of credit open. The holder of the junior mortgage would file a subordination agreement that gives the new mortgage priority, even though it was recorded later.

Exercise 3.3: Knowledge Check

A subordination clause is used to place a superior lien in a junior lien position.

A. true

B. false

Typical Clauses in Finance Instruments

Various clauses are used in mortgages to give certain rights to the lender or borrower. Many of these clauses can be found in the promissory note or security instrument, and often appear in both.

Acceleration Clause

An **acceleration clause** *gives the lender the right to declare the entire loan balance due immediately due to borrower default or violation of other contract provisions*. Most promissory notes, mortgages, trust deeds, and land contracts contain acceleration clauses as lenders want to be able to make all payments due without having to file a separate action for each missed payment.

Lenders must wait until payments are delinquent *at least 120 days* before enforcing an acceleration clause that appears in the mortgage or note due to CFPB regulation.

[For more information, see 12 CFR Part 1024, Subpart C, §1024.41(f)(1) Pre-foreclosure review period. Or see 12 CFR Part 1024, Subpart C, §1024.39 Early intervention requirements for certain borrowers.]

Alienation Clause

An **alienation clause** in a contract *gives the lender certain stated rights when there is a transfer of ownership in the property*. It may also be referred to as a **due on sale clause**. It is designed to limit the debtor's right to transfer property without the creditor's permission. Depending on the actual wording of the clause (that's why lawyers are important), alienation may be triggered by a transfer of title, transfer of a significant interest in the property, or even abandonment of the property.

Although FHA and VA loans cannot technically have alienation clauses, they still attempt to restrict transfers in other ways, such as by reserving the right to approve a new debtor who will take over an FHA or VA loan.

Defeasance Clause

A **defeasance clause** is a *clause in a legal document that states that in the event a stated condition has been fulfilled, the document becomes null and void*. This clause can appear in contracts or mortgages. With a mortgage, for example, once the borrower has repaid the debt, the mortgage is canceled and the mortgagor can redeem title to the property. This clause is more likely to be found in title theory states where the title is transferred to the lender until the debt is repaid.

Partial Release, Satisfaction, or Reconveyance Clause

A **partial release, satisfaction, or reconveyance clause** in a contract *obligates the creditor to release part of the property from the lien and convey title to that part back to the debtor once certain provisions of the note or mortgage have been satisfied.* Usually, this occurs after a certain percentage of the mortgage balance has been paid. This is an important clause that appears in many blanket mortgages and some construction mortgages so the developer or builder can sell off completed homes with clear title before having to pay back the entire amount borrowed for the entire development project. Also, if the land is bought with a mortgage, construction financing is much easier to obtain later when the builder owns part of the land free of liens.

Case in Point

A builder bought five acres of land with a contract that had a partial release clause. As per the contract, one acre of land would be released with clear title to the builder for each 25% of the note amount that was paid. This would allow the builder to build a house on this one-acre parcel and sell it free and clear.

Prepayment Clause

A **prepayment clause** in a contract *gives the lender the right to charge the borrower a penalty for paying off the loan early,* such as when refinancing a loan. An example might be a prepayment clause that calls for the debtor to pay an additional 3% of the loan amount if more than 20% of the principal is repaid during the first five years of the loan. This type of clause may be seen in a conventional loan but is prohibited in FHA or VA loans.

Title XIV of Dodd-Frank prohibits prepayment penalties on residential mortgage loans other than qualified mortgages (Dodd-Frank Act §1414).

Other Mortgage Covenants

In addition to the typical clauses discussed that appear frequently in real estate mortgages, there are also a number of covenants. **Covenants**, simply, are *promises.* Covenants can appear in deeds, mortgages, or any other document. Typical covenants can compel or prevent certain actions by the property owner or uses for the property.

Typical covenants in mortgages include provisions protecting the lender's security interests in the property. These covenants include such things as the property owner:

- Promising to keep the property in good condition and repair.
- Not committing waste, which is damaging or diminishing the value of the property in any way.
- Promising to keep fire, hazard, and flood insurance in force on the property.
- Agreeing to pay taxes and other assessments on time.

Failure to keep any of these promises or covenants can be cited in the mortgage or note as causing the borrower to be in default. If a borrower is in default for violating a covenant and the security instrument contains a ***demand clause***, the lender may demand that the default be cured or the note is due and payable immediately.

There are, of course, many other clauses and covenants important to typical mortgages. Borrowers should make sure they understand them and should be encouraged to consult legal counsel before entering into a mortgage.

Chapter Summary

1. Finance instruments are written documents establishing rights and duties of the parties in a transaction. Promissory notes are written promises to pay money. They are negotiable instruments and are freely transferable. There are four common note types: Straight note, installment note, installment note with a balloon, and fully amortizing note. The rate that is used to amortize the mortgage loan and determine the monthly loan payments is known as the note rate.

2. Security instruments give a creditor the right to take ownership of collateral to satisfy the debt if the debtor doesn't pay as agreed. They require a debtor to hypothecate the property, which means to pledge it as collateral without giving up possession. Two types of security instruments are trust deeds and mortgages.

3. Trust deeds (or deeds of trust) place legal title interest in the property into the hands of a third-party as security for the payment of a note; they allow for non-judicial foreclosure in the event of default.

4. Mortgages or deeds of trust create liens against property as security for debt. A debtor has equitable right of redemption to regain property until the confirmation of sale. The order of mortgage is important: A senior mortgage is any mortgage in a higher lien position; a junior mortgage is in a lower lien position. Property tax liens are always senior and paid first.

5. Many clauses are common in real estate financing contracts. An *acceleration clause* allows the lender to call the loan balance due if in default. A *prepayment clause* allows the lender to charge a penalty for paying a loan off early. An *alienation clause* allows the lender some stated rights if the property is transferred (also called due on sale clause). A *defeasance clause* cancels a mortgage when it has been repaid. *Subordination* allows a later recorded mortgage to take priority over an earlier one. A *partial release* occurs when a part of the property is released from the lien upon payment of part of the balance. A *demand clause* allows the lender to demand repayment in full if a borrower defaults on a promise or covenant that was made in the security instrument.

Chapter Quiz

1. A promissory note calling only for payment of interest during its term is a(n)

   A. amortizing note.
   B. installment note.
   C. negotiated note.
   D. straight note.

2. A clause that permits the lender to call the outstanding balance due and payable should the property be sold by the borrower is a(n)

   A. acceleration clause.
   B. alienation clause.
   C. balloon payment clause.
   D. exculpatory clause.

3. Which document accompanies the mortgage?

   A. abstract of title
   B. contract of sale
   C. deed
   D. promissory note

4. To foreclose a mortgage, a creditor

   A. files an attachment in the amount of the debt.
   B. files a court action.
   C. notifies the debtor of the default, waits ten days, publishes a notice of default in the paper, then claims a forfeiture.
   D. notifies the trustee of default.

5. Which term describes the process by which a borrower pledges property as security for a loan without giving up possession of it?

   A. defeasance
   B. hypothecation
   C. redemption
   D. subordination

6. What clause gives a lender the right to declare the entire loan balance due immediately because of borrower default or for violation of other contract provisions?

   A. acceleration clause
   B. alienation clause
   C. defeasance clause
   D. prepayment clause

7. The document that creates a lien against real property as security for the promise to repay a loan is called a(n)

   A. equitable title.
   B. mortgage.
   C. promissory note.
   D. subordination note.

8. The borrower who pledges property to a lender as collateral for a debt is referred to as the

   A. beneficiary.
   B. mortgagee.
   C. mortgagor.
   D. trustee.

Conventional Loans/Financing

This chapter is designed to help the MLO recognize elements of conventional loans and financing. In the chapter, we will review different types of conventional loans, as well as how private mortgage insurance and secondary financing options have expanded the availability of conventional lending.

After completing this chapter, you will be able to:

- Identify the characteristics of a conventional loan.
- Define amortization.
- Identify different types of conventional loans.
- Recognize the use of private mortgage insurance.
- Contrast conforming and nonconforming loans.
- Describe methods of secondary financing.

KEY TERMS

Amortization
Bi-Weekly Payment Plan
Depository Institution
Immediate Family Member
Secondary Financing
Subordinate Financing

Conventional Loans and Financing

Conventional financing refers to real estate that is paid for or financed with a **conventional loan**—one that is usually made by a bank or institutional lender and that is *not insured or guaranteed by a government entity or agency, such as FHA or VA*. However, most conventional loans are written to guidelines set by government-sponsored entities (GSEs), such as Freddie Mac and Fannie Mae, so that they may be sold in the secondary market. When a loan meets the criteria necessary to be sold in the secondary market, it is considered a **conforming** loan. Conventional loans may be conforming loans or nonconforming loans.

Fannie Mae and Freddie Mac are now under the conservatorship of the Federal Housing Finance Agency. Just under half of all residential mortgages are handled as conventional financing. That percentage can certainly change depending on market conditions or consumer trends.

Traditional Conventional Loans

Traditional conventional loans are typically **long-term, fully amortizing, fixed-rate real estate loans**. This is the type of loan with which borrowers are most familiar.

Long-Term

Long-term loans today limit borrowers to terms of a maximum of 30 years.

Fully Amortizing

Amortization is the *reduction of the balance of the loan by paying back some of the principal owed on a regular basis*. Amortizing loans have payments applied to principal and interest (as opposed to interest-only loans with payments only applied to the interest on the loan). A **fully amortizing loan** is one for which *the total payments over the life of a loan pay off the entire balance of principal and interest due at the end of the term*. This is also known as **self-liquidating**.

Regular periodic payments reduce the loan by the end of the term, although different amounts are applied to interest and principal out of each regular payment.

Payment Number	Principal Balance	Total Payment	Interest Portion	Principal Portion	Ending Balance
	Example: $100,000 loan @ 6%, 30-year term (figures approximate)				
1	$100,000.00	$599.55	$500.00	$99.55	$99,900.45
2	$99,900.45	$599.55	$499.50	$100.05	$99,800.40
3	$99,800.40	$599.55	$499.00	$100.55	$99,699.85
4	$99,699.85	$599.55	$498.50	$101.05	$99,598.80
5	$99,598.80	$599.55	$497.99	$101.56	$99,497.24

This partial example of an amortization table demonstrates a very different repayment structure in contrast to how mortgage loans were repaid before FHA when loans were only partially amortizing or non-amortizing.

Negative amortization occurs anytime the monthly payment is not sufficient to cover the accrued interest from the previous month.

Fixed-Rate

Fixed-rate loans have *interest rates, but not necessarily payments, that remain constant for the duration of the loan*. Of course, the biggest advantage is that a borrower does not need to worry that rates will increase.

For example, in an **interest-only payment** mortgage, the borrower had *a period of reduced payments for a specified time, and then the payment would increase to fully amortize the mortgage loan by the end of the term*; however, the interest rate would never increase. Interest-only loans are *prohibited* by regulations implemented by the CFPB. [For further information, refer to http://www.consumerfinance.gov/f/201301_cfpb_ability-to-repay-summary.pdf.]

15-Year Mortgage Loans

Lenders often give a borrower a better interest rate on a 15-year mortgage because the shorter term means less risk for the lender. Over the life of the mortgage, the **total interest** paid on a 15-year, fixed-rate mortgage is about **one-half less** than a 30-year mortgage at the same interest rate. An added benefit is that the borrower can attain full ownership in half the time it takes to pay off a 30-year mortgage.

Of course, there are *disadvantages* to 15-year mortgages:

- Payments are higher.
- Higher payments consume financial resources that might be invested in other ways and earn a higher return than the interest rate paid on the mortgage.
- The borrower's income tax deduction declines more quickly because less interest is paid each year as the principal is paid sooner.

15-YEAR MORTGAGE TO 30-YEAR MORTGAGE COMPARISON OF INTEREST PAID				
Loan Amount	Term (YRS)	Interest Rate	Monthly Payment	Total Interest Paid
$50,000	15	7%	$449.41	$30,893.80
	30	7%	$332.65	$69,754.00
$100,000	15	7%	$898.83	$61,789.40
	30	7%	$665.30	$139,508.00
$150,000	15	7%	$1,348.24	$92,683.20
	30	7%	$997.95	$209,262.00

Note: Typically, a rate for a 15-year mortgage is lower than a rate for a 30-year mortgage. The same rate was used here for both to illustrate a direct comparison of total interest paid.

Bi-Weekly Payment Plan

A mortgage with a bi-weekly payment plan is a version of a fixed-rate mortgage set up like a standard 30-year conventional loan, which calls for regular monthly payments determined by a monthly payment amortization schedule but for which payments are made every two weeks instead of once a month.

Loans with bi-weekly payment structures are usually paid off in about 22 to 26 years instead of 30 years, depending on the interest rate charged. The higher the interest rate, the lower the repayment term of a loan when utilizing a bi-weekly payment plan.

Exercise 4.1: Knowledge Check

1. A conforming loan is a loan that can be sold in the secondary market to FNMA or FHLMC.

   A. true

   B. false

2. A self-liquidating loan requires a balloon payment to be made at the end of the loan term.

   A. true

   B. false

Conforming versus Nonconforming Loans

Conforming loans *meet Fannie Mae/Freddie Mac standards and therefore can be sold on the secondary market.* Conforming conventional financing has traditionally used the following qualifying guidelines:

- **28%** total housing expense ratio

- **36%** total debt-to-income ratio

Remember that a borrower must typically qualify under **both** ratios. In addition, note that borrowers should have **5% of their own funds** for a down payment and **two months of reserves on deposit**. However, for some lenders, these guidelines may be less rigid when automated underwriting is used.

Nonconforming loans, on the other hand, do *not* meet these standards and therefore *cannot be sold to Fannie Mae or Freddie Mac*. However, there are other secondary markets where nonconforming loans can be sold and lenders that have the option of keeping loans in their own portfolio (mostly banks and S & L s) can, within the limits of the law, deviate from the standards set by secondary markets.

There are two main reasons why a loan would be classified as nonconforming:

- **Size of the Loan.** So-called **jumbo loans** *exceed the maximum loan amount established by Fannie Mae and Freddie Mac for conforming mortgage loans.*

- **Credit Quality of Borrower.** MLOs may see a borrower who does not meet the minimum standards established by Fannie Mae/Freddie Mac classified as a **B or C borrower**. This might be someone who has had a credit problem in the past.

A-Minus Conventional Loans

In order to meet the increasing consumer demand and limit the loss of market share to the nonconforming lenders, many lenders instituted an **A-minus conventional loan** program. This loan program *allows a borrower with a less than perfect credit history, limited money for down payments, or a higher debt-to-income ratio to get a loan that could be sold on the secondary market.* It is important to note that final interest rate and fees are determined based on the risk factors present in the loan. This type of loan is, again, rare in today's mortgage market.

Conventional Loan Products

Fannie Mae and Freddie Mac have standardized products for the mortgage loans that they purchase. Among the loan types FNMA or Freddie Mac purchases in the secondary market are:

- Standard fixed-rate mortgages with terms ranging from eight to 30 years and a maximum loan-to-value of 95%. 97% loan-to-value loans are available when certain restrictions are met.

- Adjustable rate mortgages with terms ranging from eight to 30 years with a maximum loan-to-value of 90% for owner-occupied home loans.

- Home Ready (FNMA) or Home Possible (FHLMC) loans that offer relaxed guidelines regarding the borrower's down payment requirements, require homebuyer education, and require the borrowers to meet annual income limits established by the GSEs.

- Home Style Renovation (FNMA) and Renovation Mortgages (FHLMC) loans that are designed for financing the GSE's REOs. These loans offer no appraisal, no MI, and 5% down financing. Freddie Mac's Renovation Mortgages are only available in certain states.

- Home Affordable Refinance Programs (FNMA HARP) offer loans for borrowers who have a consistent mortgage repayment history, but the property has negative equity (mortgage balance exceeds appraised value). Often there is no requirement for an appraisal and income verification of the borrower is limited. **The program for these loans will expire on December 31, 2018**.

- Construction-to-Permanent mortgages loans to retire a construction loan and provide permanent, long-term takeout financing.

[For more information on the loan products purchased in the secondary market by FNMA or Freddie Mac, see https://www.fanniemae.com/singlefamily/originating-underwriting or http://www.freddiemac.com/singlefamily/mortgages/]

Conventional Loan Programs

Conventional loan programs can be classified by the **percentage of down payment** that the borrower pays to acquire the loan. As we review "typical" loan programs and "typical" down payments with private mortgage insurance (PMI), remember that some lenders offer high LTV loans where PMI is not necessary, but fees may be higher or conditions and standards imposed.

80% LTV Conventional Loan

The **loan-to-value ratio** (LTV) refers to *the amount of money borrowed (the loan amount of a first mortgage) compared to the value of the property*. Lenders use LTV to determine how much they are willing to loan on a given property based on its value. The lender will always use the *lower* of the appraised value or the sale price to protect its interest. The lower the LTV, the higher the borrower's down payment, which means the loan is more secure.

For example, for years, the **80% conventional loan** was the standard so, for example, for a house with a sale price of $200,000, the most a borrower could borrow would be:

$$\$200,000 \times 0.8 = \$160,000 \text{ loan amount}$$

Subtracting the loan amount from the sale price indicates that the borrower would need a down payment of $40,000.

Higher LTV Loans

Loans with an LTV higher than 80% are possible because of PMI and secondary financing, which will be next.

The qualifying standards and lender adherence for higher LTV loans tend to be more stringent, even if the loan is insured through PMI. These loans may also have a higher interest rate, call for higher loan origination fees, or impose additional conditions and standards.

Lender and agency requirements determine if the property must be **owner-occupied** as a condition for obtaining the loan. Most conventional loans over 80%, as well as all FHA and VA loans, require the property to be owner-occupied. There may be exceptions to these guidelines for specific programs or investors.

90% Conventional Loan

For a **90% LTV loan**, at least half of the required down payment (10% / 2 = 5%) must be made from personal cash reserves. The remainder of the down payment may be a gift from a family member, equity in other property traded to the seller, or credit for rent already paid under a lease/purchase.

95% Conventional Loan

A **95% LTV loan** requires owner occupancy of the property and the down payment must be made from personal cash reserves, without using secondary (owner) financing or gifts.

97% Conventional Loan

A **97% LTV loan** is offered under "Home Ready (FNMA)" and "Home Possible (FHLMC)" with relaxed underwriting guidelines regarding sources of down payment, income, underwriting, and credit standards. Borrowers utilizing these loan programs do not need to be first-time homebuyers, but they must meet certain income limit requirements. FNMA provides a website (https://homeready-eligibility.fanniemae.com/homeready/) that shows the maximum income limits for a specific property address to assist the originator in offering this loan product to the consumer

Exercise 4.2: Apply Your Knowledge

Directions: Consider the following scenario, then write your responses. Be prepared to present and discuss your responses.

Scenario: Bill wants to buy a house that is selling for $160,000 and the lender has approved him for an 80% conventional loan.

1. How much can Bill borrow? _____

2. What would be the required down payment? _____

3. If the house appraises for $150,000, how much can Bill borrow? _____

4. What other options does he have? _____

Private Mortgage Insurance (PMI)

Private mortgage insurance (PMI) is *offered by private companies to insure a lender against default on a loan by a borrower where there is a loss of collateral value at the time of the default.* Prior to the advent of PMI in the early 1970's, lenders would only lend 80% of the value of a property, assuming that the 20% down payment was the incentive needed for the borrower to keep mortgage payments current. Both Fannie Mae and Freddie Mac also require mortgage insurance—whether lender-paid or third party—on home loans with less than 20% down.

How Private Mortgage Insurance Works

When insuring a loan, the mortgage insurance insurer shares the lender's risk, but only *part of the risk.* The insurer does **not** insure the entire loan amount, but rather the *upper portion of the loan* that exceeds the standard 80% LTV. The amount of coverage can vary but is typically 20% to 25% of the loan amount.

After the sale of the security, the proceeds may not be sufficient for the lender to reclaim all of the lender's losses from the principal balance, foreclosure, and other costs. *The lender may be able to pursue a deficiency judgment against the borrower for any losses, depending on state statutes.* This is referred to as **recourse**.

In this example, $18,000 is the maximum amount a lender can claim as a loss and collect from the PMI insurer. Note that there must be both a borrower default and a loss of collateral value at the time of sale to make a claim for payment against the PMI insurer. If there is a default and a trustee/sheriff's sale but no loss, there is no claim against the PMI insurer.

Example:

20% coverage on a 90% loan

$100,000	Total Sale Price
x .90	LTV
$ 90,000	90% Loan
x .20	Amount of Coverage
$ 18,000	Amount of Policy

T O T A L S A L E P R I C E

10%	Down payment
18%	Coverage (20% of loan amount)
72%	Exposure (80% of loan amount)

PMI Premiums

Fee at Closing and Renewal Premium

The traditional way insurers charge for PMI is with a one-time, non-refundable fee at closing and a *recurring* fee, called a **renewal premium**, added to the borrower's monthly mortgage payment. These charges are often referred to as PMI. Each insurer provides PMI rate cards that are used to determine the monthly premium, as shown in this example.

MONTHLY PMI PREMIUM		FIXED		TEMPORARY BUYDOWNS		ARMs	
		30-yr	15-yr	30-yr	15-yr	30-yr	15-yr
Base LTV	PMI Coverage	1st month and renewal to Yr. 10		1st month and renewal to Yr. 10		1st month and renewal to Yr. 10	
95% to 90.01%	35%	1.06%	0.83%	1.21%	1.10%	1.25%	1.13%
	30%	0.94	0.81	1.04	0.92	1.08	0.95
	25%	0.84	0.70	0.90	0.77	0.94	0.81
90% to 85.01%	30%	0.69	0.54	0.84	0.71	0.89	0.77
	25%	0.62	0.48	0.73	0.60	0.78	0.65
	17%	0.49	0.33	0.56	0.36	0.61	0.44
85% & under	17%	0.43	0.30	0.44	0.30	0.49	0.36
	12%	0.38	0.26	0.39	0.27	0.44	0.31
	6%	0.34	0.24	0.36	0.25	0.40	0.28

Figure 4.1: Sample PMI Rate Card.

One-Time PMI Premium

Some PMI insurers offer a one-time mortgage insurance premium with no renewal fee. Combining the initial premium and renewal premiums into one payment allows the borrower to finance the PMI premium. When the PMI premium is financed, monthly payments may still be lower than if the renewal premiums are added to the regular mortgage payment.

Exercise 4.3: Apply Your Knowledge

Directions: Consider the following scenario, then write your responses. Be prepared to present and discuss your responses.

Scenario: If the sale price of a home is $100,000, on a 90% LTV 30-year fixed-rate mortgage, calculate the PMI using the sample rate card. Use the Fannie Mae/Freddie Mac required 25% coverage at a rate of 0.62%.

1. What is the loan amount? _____

2. What is the fee due at closing? _____

3. How much will be added to the borrower's monthly mortgage payment?

_____

PMI Cancellation

Once the increased risk of loss from borrower default has been reduced (when the loan-to-value ratio is reduced to 80% or less), mortgage insurance has fulfilled its purpose. In the past, many lenders did not cancel PMI, even when the risk was reduced. The **Homeowners Protection Act of 1998 (HPA)** (12 U.S.C. 4901 et seq.) requires lenders to automatically cancel PMI when a home has been paid down to **78% of its original value or has attained 22% equity based on the original value**, assuming the borrower is not delinquent.

The law has some *exceptions*, such as for multi-family units, non-owner-occupied homes, mortgages on second homes, and second mortgages. As is often the case, though, the law sets a minimum, but the market moves the bar higher. For example, Fannie Mae and Freddie Mac:

- Have adopted rules that apply the 78% cancellation rule to *all* of their mortgages, even those closed before HPA's mandated date of July 1999.

- Have expanded the rules to cover investment properties and second homes.

- Will consider the *present value* of the home, not just the original value as required by the law. This effectively cancels PMI more quickly, assuming the home appreciates. Most lenders also now follow these guidelines.

The law also says that for loans closed *after July 29, 1999,* lenders must drop PMI coverage at a borrower's request if these conditions are met:

- A new lender-approved appraisal shows that the loan has been paid down to 80% or less (or attained 20% equity) of the home's original value.

- The borrower shows a history of timely repayment over the past 12 months.

- Certification that the equity of the mortgagor in the residence securing the mortgage is unencumbered by a subordinate lien.

 Fannie Mae and Freddie Mac also apply these rules to all loans, but can require up to five years of seasoning (outstanding age) on the loan before the rules apply.

Whether through automatic or borrower-requested PMI cancellation, the lender terminates the policy and reduces the monthly mortgage payment by the PMI amount. Note that the law and Fannie Mae/Freddie Mac rules do *not* apply to any upfront, government-insured or one-time PMI premium paid.

Underwriting PMI in Declining Markets

In recent years, most PMI insurers have added guidelines for considering the risks of insuring loans in markets where property values are declining. While every company has its own standards, the result is often that the loan is put in jeopardy.

For example, some PMI insurers may simply refuse to offer mortgage insurance in these markets, forcing the borrower to come up with a 20% down payment; or an insurer may raise the premiums for PMI in those markets, which could make the loan too expensive for the borrower.

Secondary Financing

Secondary financing is when *a buyer borrows money from another source to pay part of the purchase price or closing costs.* This is another way a borrower can get a conventional loan without a 20% down payment.

With secondary financing, it may be the **seller who carries the extra financing**. In effect, the seller extends credit to the borrower just as if the money had been borrowed from a lending institution.

When underwriting a loan that will have secondary financing, the primary lender will include that payment as part of the borrower's monthly housing expense and consider the total amount borrowed when determining the combined loan-to-value. The borrower must still make 5% minimum investment from his own funds when obtaining a conventional loan.

It is important to recognize that **subordinate financing** (*debt financing in which the lender is not the first party due to be repaid by the borrower*) can be more than simply a second mortgage. Borrowers may have additional **junior liens**, such as with a down payment assistance program or even a third or fourth mortgage.

Secondary financing may be:

- Fully amortized.
- Partially amortized.
- Interest only.

 An MLO must consider all subordinate financing, not only the primary financing when evaluating a borrower's ability to repay and qualify for loans.

Combined Loan-to-Value (CLTV)

The **combined loan-to-value** (CLTV) is *the percentage of the property value borrowed through a combination of more than one loan,* such as a first mortgage and a second mortgage home equity loan. The CLTV is calculated by adding all loan amounts and dividing by the home's appraised value or purchase price, whichever is lower.

For Example

A buyer purchases a property valued at $100,000 with two loans: A first mortgage for $80,000 and a second for $10,000:

$$\frac{\$80,000 + \$10,000}{\$100,000} = 90\% \text{ CLTV}$$

Remember that the **loan-to-value ratio** considers *only the first mortgage* and, in the example, would be only 80%: $80,000 / $100,000, meaning that this borrower would *not* need to have PMI.

Both loan-to-value (LTV) and combined loan-to-value (CLTV) can be used to determine the amount of home equity. Therefore, a borrower with 90% CLTV has 10% equity in the property.

Secondary Financing Conditions

For conventional loans, the primary lender will often insist on certain conditions with secondary financing from any source. Although individual lenders may impose additional or different specific conditions, the following are typical examples:

- **Down Payment.** The borrower must make a **5%** down payment. The first mortgage cannot exceed 80% LTV.

- **Loan Terms.** The term of the second loan cannot exceed 30 years or be less than five (5) years.

- **Interest Rate.** The interest rate on a second mortgage could be fixed or adjustable. Note, however, that a borrower cannot have an adjustable rate on *both* the first mortgage and the second mortgage.

- **No Prepayment Penalty.** The second mortgage must be payable in full or in part at any time without penalizing the borrower for paying the debt early.

- **Regularly Scheduled Payments.** Although payments must be due on a regular basis, they do not have to be monthly. Secondary finance payments can be monthly, quarterly, semi-annually, or any other regular schedule. Payments can fully or partially amortize the debt, or pay interest only.

- **No Negative Amortization.** Payments on the second mortgage must, at least, equal the interest on the loan. Loan balances cannot grow because of deferred interest.

- **Ability to Qualify.** The borrower must be able to afford payments on the first and second mortgages. This means that the primary lender on the first mortgage will count both mortgages when qualifying the borrower for the mortgage debt.

- **Subordination Clause.** Most primary lenders require secondary financing to have a subordination clause to ensure that the primary lender's lien will take priority, even if the second mortgage is recorded first.

Exercise 4.4: Apply Your Knowledge

Directions: Consider the following scenario about secondary financing, then answer the questions. Be prepared to present and discuss your responses.

Scenario: Review the example below of secondary financing for a $120,000 home:

$90,000	75%	First Mortgage (primary lender)
$18,000	15%	Second Mortgage (from seller)
+ $12,000	10%	Down Payment (from borrower)
$120,000	100%	Total Sales Price

1. What is the loan-to-value (LTV)? _____

2. What is the combined loan-to-value (CLTV)? _____

Chapter Summary

1. Conventional loans are not insured or guaranteed by a government agency. Traditional conventional loans are long-term, fully amortizing, and have a fixed-rate. An amortizing loan has payments that are applied to both principal and interest. A fixed-rate, fully amortizing loan has regular payments that are substantially equal in amount that fully retires the debt at the end of the term.

2. Conventional loans may be 15- or 30-year, conforming or nonconforming. A 15-year loan retires sooner and saves interest, but requires higher payments. A bi-weekly payment structure allows the borrower to the make the equivalent of one extra monthly payment each year, so the balance is paid faster and saves interest.

3. Conforming loans meet Fannie Mae/Freddie Mac standards and can be sold on the secondary market. Qualifying standards are 28% for housing expense and 36% for total debt-to-income. Nonconforming loans do not meet these standards and cannot be sold to Fannie Mae/Freddie Mac, but may be sold on the secondary market to other buyers. Nonconforming can be due to credit quality or loan size (jumbo loans exceed Fannie Mae/Freddie Mac maximum loan amount).

4. An 80% conventional loan means the loan-to-value ratio (LTV) is 80% of the appraised value or sale price of the property, whichever is less. Interest rates and fees may be higher on higher LTVs and PMI is required. Loans with LTV above 80% generally require the property to be owner-occupied.

5. Private mortgage insurance (PMI) insures lenders against borrower default, compensating lenders for a loss of collateral value in the event of default, and shares partial risk (upper part) with the lender. PMI can be a fee paid at closing and as a renewal premium, a one-time PMI premium, or no PMI premium but with a higher interest rate. Federal law says that loans must drop PMI when LTV is 78% of original property value and the borrower is not delinquent, or if the borrower requests and the appraisal is 80% of original property value. Fannie Mae/Freddie Mac rules require a drop of PMI if the LTV is 78% (or a borrower-paid appraisal is 80%) of the property's current value.

6. Secondary financing is when the buyer borrows money for part of the purchase price or closing costs. To determine the combined loan-to-value ratio (CLTV) when there is more than one loan, add all loan amounts and divide by the home's appraised value or purchase price, whichever is lower. Typical conditions for secondary financing include:

   • Borrower must make a 5% down payment

   • Term of the second loan must be five to 30 years

   • No prepayment penalty

   • Scheduled payments due on a regular basis

   • No negative amortization

   • Borrower must be able to afford payments on first and second mortgages

   • Required subordination clause

7. A second mortgage can be fully amortizing, partially amortizing with a balloon payment, or interest-only with a balloon payment. Partial amortization is when payments are scheduled as if the loan term is longer (e.g., 30 years), but the balance is due sooner (e.g., 5 years). Partially amortizing and interest-only loans have smaller payments than fully amortizing loans, so they may help a borrower qualify. Such loans generally have payments that are regular and equal (if fixed) or recomputed regularly (if adjustable) with a final, larger balloon payment at the end of the term that will fully retire the debt. One lender can provide both loans at different interest rates.

Chapter Quiz

1. A loan that is repaid with periodic payments of both principal and interest so that the entire loan amount is paid in full at the end of the loan term is a(n)

    A. annualized loan.

    B. conventional loan.

    C. fully amortizing loan.

    D. partially amortizing loan.

2. Which statement about 15-year mortgages is FALSE?

    A. Higher interest rates are usually charged.

    B. There is an earlier loss of interest deduction for income tax purposes.

    C. They have higher monthly payments.

    D. They result in less interest owed.

3. You are pre-qualifying a buyer for a conventional loan on a house with the purchase price of $160,000. She states she does not want to pay PMI on the loan. In that case, what is the maximum loan amount she can receive (assuming no lender-paid PMI)?

    A. $32,000

    B. $128,000

    C. $136,000

    D. $144,000

4. Which type of mortgage is NOT insured or guaranteed by the government?

    A. conventional mortgage

    B. FHA mortgage

    C. rural home mortgage

    D. VA mortgage

5. When seeking an 80% conventional loan with the seller taking back a second mortgage, the buyer

    A. can expect to pay a higher interest rate than with a 90% loan.

    B. may choose which mortgage (first or second) will have lien priority.

    C. must make at least a 5% down payment from personal funds.

    D. must make at least a 20% down payment from personal funds.

6. PMI must be cancelled

    A. any time the borrower requests it.

    B. only if the lender is satisfied that the borrower is no longer a credit risk.

    C. when a home has been paid down to 78% of its original value and the borrower is current.

    D. whenever a new appraisal is ordered, regardless of the value.

7. Lenders are often willing to charge lower interest rates for 15-year mortgages because the

    A. borrower is always a better risk.

    B. interest rate is fixed for a longer period of time.

    C. loan funds will be repaid more quickly.

    D. loan qualifications are much more stringent.

8. A buyer is paying $200,000 for a house. He makes a $30,000 down payment, gets a first mortgage for $160,000, and a second mortgage to cover the balance. What is his CLTV?

    A. 70%

    B. 75%

    C. 80%

    D. 85%

Government Loan Programs

The federal government provides a number of different programs to insure and protect consumer residential mortgage loans. This chapter presents information about several of the major government mortgage protection programs.

In this chapter, we will review the Federal Housing Administration (FHA) home loan insurance programs and the Veterans Administration (VA) loan guarantee programs for eligible military veterans. We will also discuss the USDA Rural Development Program that provides assistance for farm loans, as well as grants and loans in rural communities for a variety of facilities (e.g., clinics, schools, fire stations).

After completing this chapter, you will be able to:

- Identify basic qualifying standards for FHA-insured loans.
- Define the use of upfront mortgage insurance premiums.
- Recognize different FHA loan programs.
- Identify basic qualifying standards for VA-guaranteed loans.
- Define eligibility and entitlement for veterans.
- Recognize different USDA loan programs.

KEY TERMS

Alienation Clause
Debt-to-Income Ratio
Entitlement
Housing Expense Ratio
Residual Income

FHA-Insured Loans

The Federal Housing Administration (FHA) **insures** loans for single-family and multi-family homes made by approved lenders. Mortgage insurance, you'll recall, provides lenders with protection against losses when borrowers default.

A common misconception about FHA loans is that they are targeted to lower-income borrowers or first-time homebuyers only, but this is not the case. The FHA does *not* have income limits to determine who is eligible for their loans. Anyone who is a U.S. citizen, permanent resident, or non-permanent resident with a qualifying work visa, and who meets the lending guidelines, may qualify for an FHA-insured loan. However, the FHA sets a *maximum mortgage amount* that it will insure.

The FHA is part of the Department of Housing and Urban Development (HUD). Oversight of FHA loan programs is through HUD's Office of Housing, which has three business areas related to real estate transactions:

- Single-family housing
- Multi-family housing
- Regulatory programs, such as the Fair Housing Act

HUD issues regulations and establishes guidelines for approving lenders authorized to make FHA loans. Its regulations have the force and effect of law. The FHA defines the loan programs and sets guidelines for the programs in accordance with HUD's regulations.

Approved Lenders

The purpose of the Direct Endorsement program, as authorized under §203(b) of the National Housing Act (12 USC 1709 (b), (I)), is to simplify and expedite the process by which mortgagees can obtain mortgage insurance endorsements from HUD.

[For more information about Section 203(b), see http://portal.hud.gov/hudportal/HUD?src=/program_offices/housing/sfh/ins/203b--df]

Lending institutions that make FHA-insured loans must first be **approved**. Once approved as an unconditional **FHA Direct Endorsement Lender** (Direct Endorser or DE), the lender is authorized to underwrite and close mortgage loans *without* prior submission for FHA review or approval. This includes all aspects of the mortgage loan application, the property analysis, and borrower underwriting.

HUD Homeownership Centers

Four regional U.S. Homeownership Centers process FHA loans and oversee the selling of HUD-owned homes acquired through foreclosure or through deeds in lieu of foreclosure. Homeownership Centers are organized to serve specific states:

Philadelphia, PA	Connecticut, Delaware, District of Columbia, Maine, Maryland, Massachusetts, Michigan, New Hampshire, New Jersey, New York, Ohio, Pennsylvania, Rhode Island, Vermont, Virginia, West Virginia
Atlanta, GA	Alabama, Florida, Georgia, Kentucky, Illinois, Indiana, Mississippi, North Carolina, South Carolina, Tennessee
Denver, CO	Arkansas, Colorado, Iowa, Kansas, Louisiana, Missouri, Minnesota, Montana, Nebraska, New Mexico, North Dakota, Oklahoma, South Dakota, Texas, Wisconsin, Utah
Santa Ana, CA	Alaska, Arizona, California, Hawaii, Idaho, Nevada, Oregon, Washington

Exercise 5.1: Knowledge Check

The FHA defines income limits to determine who is eligible for FHA loans.

    A. true

    B. false

Limited Denial of Participation (LDP)

A **Limited Denial of Participation** (LDP) is *an action taken by a HUD Field Office or the Deputy Assistant Secretary for Single-Family or Multi-family Housing that excludes a person or company who fails to comply with HUD program standards from further participation in a HUD program area.* Unless otherwise noted, LDPs are effective nationwide and generally expire in one year. Going forward, parties issued an LDP are prevented from new participation in the HUD program.

Therefore, MLOs need to check the LDP list before attempting to process an FHA loan application.

In addition to the LDP list, the General Services Administration's (GSA) provides the **System for Award Management** (SAM) website [see https://www.sam.gov/portal/public/SAM/#1], which is used to determine if individuals or companies are suspended or debarred from further participation in HUD programs.

Underwriting Standards for FHA Loans

When evaluating an application for an FHA loan, underwriters and/or lenders consider FHA's "4 Cs of Underwriting:"

- **C**redit history of the borrower, which indicates the borrower's willingness to repay debt
- **C**apacity to repay the loan, which includes income and employment history
- **C**ash assets available to close the mortgage
- **C**ollateral, which evaluates the value of the home

Although an underwriter likes to see a stellar **credit history**, some prior credit issues might not be a problem. As with other mortgages, however, court-ordered judgments must be paid off first. In addition, a borrower who has defaulted on a student loan or is delinquent or in default on any federal debt would *not* qualify for an FHA loan. This is confirmed through the **Credit Alert Verification Reporting System** (CAIVRS), which is *a federal database of delinquent federal debtors that allows federal agencies to reduce the risk to federal loan and loan guarantee programs.* CAIVRS alerts participating federal lending agencies when an applicant for credit benefits, or for a position of trust in support of the administration of a federal credit program, has a federal lien, judgment, or federal loan that is currently in default or foreclosure, or has had a claim paid by a reporting agency. A borrower who had a claim paid by HUD or the VA on a prior defaulted mortgage loan will also appear on the CAIVRS list. The borrower will be ineligible for an FHA-insured mortgage for *three years after the claim was paid*, regardless of the elapsed time from the date of foreclosure.

FHA is less stringent when it comes to a borrower's level of **income**. While no minimum or maximum income is required for an FHA loan, the borrower must have sufficient income to service the debt on the home mortgage and all other credit obligations. This is determined by housing expense and total debt-to-income ratios, which are slightly more liberal than those allowed for conventional loans.

FHA Underwriting Guidance

HUD Housing handbooks provide detailed underwriting guidance on FHA loan programs. In particular, MLOs making single-family FHA loans will likely become very familiar with the Handbook 4000.1, FHA Single Family Housing Policy Handbook (Handbook 4000.1).

A copy of this handbook is available at https://portal.hud.gov

In addition, HUD regularly publishes **Mortgagee Letters** as a way to communicate program changes, commentary on regulations, and other critical information to lenders and MLOs. Current and past letters, numbered sequentially by year, can be found on the homepage of the 4000.1 HUD Handbook.

Note: Guidelines discussed in this chapter generally apply to standard FHA 203(b) loans on single-family homes. Other FHA loan types may have different guidelines or additional criteria.

FHA TOTAL Mortgage Scorecard

The **Technology Open to Approved Lenders** (TOTAL) Mortgage Scorecard was developed by HUD to evaluate the credit risk of FHA loans that are submitted to an automated underwriting system (e.g., Desktop Underwriter®, Loan Prospector®). TOTAL evaluates the overall creditworthiness of the applicants based on these variables:

- Credit score
- Monthly housing expense
- Number of monthly payments in reserve
- Loan-to-value ratio
- Loan term

When combined with the functionalities of the AUS, TOTAL indicates a recommended level of underwriting and documentation to determine a loan's eligibility for insurance by the FHA as follows:

- **Accept/Approve**, which means that the loan is eligible for the FHA endorsement
- **Refer**, which requires the lender to manually underwrite the loan

It is the FHA's policy that no borrower will be denied an FHA-insured mortgage loan solely based on a risk assessment generated by the TOTAL Mortgage Scorecard.

In cases where mortgage loans cannot be rated by FHA's TOTAL Mortgage Scorecard, the loan is referred by TOTAL or is manually downgraded; the loan must be manually underwritten. When FHA's standard qualifying ratios for total mortgage payment-to-income and total fixed payment-to-income are exceeded, lenders must cite at least one compensating factor.

Exercise 5.2: Knowledge Check

Which of the following is NOT one of FHA's "4 Cs of Underwriting"?

- A. capacity to repay
- B. cash
- C. credit history
- D. current interest rate

Mortgage Payment Expense to Effective Income Ratio

A borrower's **housing expense ratio** is *the relationship of the borrower's total monthly housing expense to income, expressed as a percentage.* The FHA considers a borrower's income adequate for a loan if the proposed total mortgage payment does not exceed **31%** of gross stable monthly income. As with conventional loans, the FHA's maximum mortgage payment includes **principal, interest, taxes, and insurance (PITI)**, as well as any required monthly homeowners association dues or mortgage insurance premiums (MIPs).

When the MLO knows a borrower's stable monthly income, he can multiply that by the housing expense ratio to determine the maximum monthly housing expense the borrower can afford. For example, if a borrower has a stable monthly income of $3,200, the maximum housing expense on an FHA loan is $992 ($3,200 x .31).

Here is another way to use this ratio. When the MLO knows the total housing expense, he can determine whether the borrower's income is sufficient to qualify under the loan guidelines.

Total Debt-to-Income Ratio

A borrower's **total debt-to-income ratio** is *the relationship of the borrower's total monthly debt obligations (including housing and other long-term debts that will not be cancelled) to income, expressed as a percentage.* This back end ratio is given primary consideration by the TOTAL Mortgage Scorecard, ensuring the borrower's total expenses do not exceed **43%** of monthly income.

For manually underwritten loans a maximum front-end ratio and a maximum back-end ratio that may not be exceeded based on the borrower's credit score.

Borrower Credit Score	Maximum Front-End and Maximum Back-End Ratio
No credit score or credit scores below 580	May not exceed the standard 31%/43% ratios
Credit scores of 580 or higher with one compensating factor	May be approved for ratios as high as 37%/47%
Credit scores of 580 or higher with two compensating factors	May be approved for ratios as high as 40%/50%

The HUD Handbook 4000.1 restricts the use of compensating factors to borrowers with credit scores of 580 or higher. Borrowers not meeting this standard are limited to maximum ratios of 31%/43%. [HUD Handbook 4000.1.II.AA.5.d.viii]

Exercise 5.3A: Apply Your Knowledge – (Part 1)

Directions: Consider the following information, then determine the monthly gross income. Be prepared to present and discuss your response.

Information: Mary wants an FHA loan to buy a house. She would have these monthly expenses:

$536.82	Principal and Interest ($100,000 at 5% for 360 months)
$ 53.00	Property Taxes
$ 25.00	Homeowners Insurance
$ 95.83	MIP (FHA Mortgage Insurance Premium based on 96% LTV)
+$ 90.00	Homeowners Association Dues
$800.65	Total Housing Expense (PITI)

What should Mary's required stable monthly gross income be to qualify for this loan?

Exercise 5.3B: Apply Your Knowledge – (Part 2)

Directions: Consider the following information, then determine the monthly gross income. Be prepared to present and discuss your response.

Information: Mary wants an FHA loan to buy a house. She would have these monthly expenses:

$ 800.65	Housing Expense (from previous example)
$ 192.65	Auto Payment
+$ 40.00	Revolving Credit Account
$1,033.30	Total Debt

Based on her debt, what should Mary's required stable monthly gross income be in order to qualify for this loan using the total debt-to-income ratio?

_____

_____

Compensating Factors

For a manually underwritten loan (i.e., loan not using an automated underwriting system), if a loan applicant exceeds either or both of the permissible ratios of 31% / 43%, the lender must document compensating factors that mitigate the risk:

Compensating Factor	Comments
Energy Efficient Homes	For mortgages on new construction, the borrower is eligible for the EEH stretch ratios when the property meets or exceeds the higher of: • The 2006 International Energy Conservation Code • Any successor energy code standard that has been adopted by HUD for its minimum property standard • The applicable IECC year used by the state or local building code For mortgages on existing construction, the borrower is eligible for the EEH stretch ratios when the property meets either of the following conditions: • Homes that currently score a "6" or higher on the Home Energy Score scale • Homes where documented cost-effective energy improvements, as identified in the Home Energy Score Report, would increase a home's score to a "6" or higher are completed prior to closing, or in association with FHA's 203(k), Weatherization, EEM or Solar and Wind programs.
Verified and Documented Cash Reserves	Subject to the following requirements. • Reserves are equal to or exceed three total monthly mortgage payments (one and two units) • Reserves are equal to or exceed six total monthly mortgage payments (three and four units) Reserves are calculated as the borrower's total assets as described in asset requirements less: • The total funds required to close the mortgage • Gifts • Borrowed funds • Cash received at closing in a cash-out refinance transaction or incidental cash received at closing in the mortgage transaction
Minimal Increase in Housing Payment	Subject to the following requirements: • The new total monthly mortgage payment does not exceed the current total monthly housing payment by more than $100 or 5 percent, whichever is less; and • There is a documented 12-month housing payment history with no more than one 30-day late payment. In cash-out transactions all payments on the mortgage being refinanced must have been made within the month due for the previous 12 months. • If the borrower has no current housing payment mortgagees may not cite this compensating factor.

Compensating Factor	Comments
No Discretionary Debt	Subject to the following requirements: • The borrower's housing payment is the only open account with an outstanding balance that is not paid off monthly, • The credit report shows established credit lines in the borrower's name open for at least six months, and • The borrower can document that these accounts have been paid off in full monthly for at least the past six months. Borrowers who have no established credit other than their housing payment, no other credit lines in their own name open for at least six months, or who cannot document that all other accounts are paid off in full monthly for at least the past six months, do not qualify under this criterion. Credit lines not in the borrower's name but for which they are an authorized user do not qualify under this criterion.
Significant Additional Income Not Reflected in Effective Income	Subject to the following: • The mortgagee must verify and document that the borrower has received this income for at least one year, and it will likely continue; and • The income, if it were included in gross effective income, is sufficient to reduce the qualifying ratios to not more than 37/47. Income from non-borrowing spouses or other parties not obligated for the mortgage may not be counted under this criterion. This compensating factor may be cited only in conjunction with another compensating factor when qualifying ratios exceed 37/47 but are not more than 40/50.
Residual Income	Residual income may be cited as a compensating factor provided it can be documented and is at least equal to the applicable amounts for household size and geographic region found on the Table of Residual Incomes By Region in the VA Lenders Handbook (VA Pamphlet 26-7, Chapter 4.9 b, e). The mortgagee must count all members of the household of the occupying borrower without regard to the nature of their relationship and without regard to whether they are joining on title or the note to determine "family size." The mortgagee may omit any individuals from "family size" who are fully supported from a source of verified income which is not included in effective income in the mortgage analysis.

[See HUD Handbook 4000.1.II.A.5.d.ix.A-F]

Property Guidelines for FHA Loans

Among the important property guidelines for FHA loan approval are:

- **Eligibility** of the property.
- **Condition** of the property.
- **Maximum mortgage amount** permitted where the property is located.
- **Occupancy**.

Property Eligibility

Eligible one- to four-family dwellings include:

- Detached or semi-detached dwellings (with additional requirements for dwellings that are not detached)
- Row houses
- Multiplex dwellings
- Individual condominium units (approved)
- Some manufactured housing

Additionally, HUD guidelines indicate that utilities and other facilities should be independent for each unit and must include:

- A continuing supply of safe, potable water
- Sanitary facilities and a safe method of sewage disposal
- Heating adequate for health and comfort
- Domestic hot water
- Conventional electrical source for lighting and equipment

Property Conditions

At a minimum, the site conditions of a property must be free of health and safety hazards. FHA Handbooks provide **minimum property standards** (MPS) for new construction and **minimum property requirements** (MPR) for existing properties. An appraiser will note any issues and make recommendations about the need to engage qualified property inspectors as necessary to ensure that the property complies with FHA's MPR, or MPS, together with the estimated cost to cure. Typical conditions that would require further inspection or testing by qualified individuals or entities include:

- Infestation/evidence of termites
- Inoperative or inadequate plumbing, heating, or electrical systems
- Structural failure in framing members
- Leaking or worn-out roofs
- Cracked masonry or foundation damage
- Drainage problems

The lender determines which repairs for existing properties must be made for the property to be eligible for FHA-insured financing. Required repairs include those that are necessary to:

- Protect the health and **safety** of the occupants.
- Protect the **security** of the property.
- Correct physical deficiencies or conditions affecting **structural integrity**.

Occupancy

Borrowers with FHA loans are required to establish bona fide occupancy of the property as their principal residence **within 60 days** of signing a security instrument (e.g., mortgage, trust deed). Furthermore, they are required to live in the house for **at least one year**. Generally, a borrower may have only one FHA loan at a time, although some exceptions may be made.

 When there is a co-borrower who will not occupy the property as a principal residence, the maximum mortgage is limited to 75% LTV. However, if the non-occupying co-borrower is a family member or someone with documented evidence of a long-standing and substantial relationship separate from the loan transaction, maximum financing is available.

Maximum Mortgage Amount

Although there are no income limits on FHA loans, HUD limits the *maximum loan amount—* sometimes called a **loan ceiling** or **base**—*that may be insured in a given community*. When determining limits, boundaries may be based on county, zip code, or metropolitan statistical areas (MSAs). The loan amounts are reviewed every three years.

For example, the 2018 limits for most single-family homes start at $294,515 (there are different loan ceilings for one-, two-, three-, and four-family dwellings) and go as high as $679,650 for costlier areas of the country.

High cost area limits are subject to a ceiling based on a percent of the Freddie Mac loan limits. Section 214 of the National Housing Act provides that mortgage limits for Alaska, Guam, Hawaii, and the Virgin Islands may be adjusted up to 150 percent of the ceilings.

A current schedule of maximum FHA loan limits may be accessed from the HUD website [see https://www.hud.gov/program_offices/housing/sfh/lender/origination/mortgage_limits].

Loan Regulations

Other important regulations for FHA loans are summarized in the sections that follow.

Required Minimum Investment

A borrower seeking an FHA loan must make a minimum required investment of at least **3.5%** of the home's purchase price or appraised value, *whichever is less* (i.e., maximum LTV of 96.5%), from an acceptable source. This assumes that the borrower has a credit score of **at least 580**. Note that lenders have the ability to sell the mortgages on the secondary markets and may choose to impose higher standards than HUD to protect themselves from losses. This extra protection refers to *creditor's additional requirements over and above FHA guidelines*, commonly known as **lender overlays**.

HUD authorized additional requirement conditions for the following options:

- Borrowers with a minimum decision credit score at or above 580 are eligible for maximum financing.

- Borrowers with a minimum decision credit score between 500 and 579 are limited to 90 percent LTV.

- Borrowers with a minimum decision credit score of less than 500 are not eligible for FHA-insured mortgage financing.

- Borrowers with a nontraditional credit history or insufficient credit are eligible for maximum financing but must meet the underwriting guidance in HUD 4000.1.I.A.5.a.B.1&2.

- Borrowers using 203(h), Mortgage Insurance for Disaster Victims, are eligible for 100 percent financing and no down payment is required, provided that the borrowers have a minimum credit score of 500.

None of the required minimum cash investment can be provided by the seller of the property, any other person, or entity who financially benefits from the transaction, or from any person who is reimbursed by any prohibited source. [For more information, see HUD Handbook 4000.1.1.II.A.2.b.i & ii]

Closing costs (includes closing costs, prepaid expenses, and discount points) may not be used to help meet the required minimum investment. However, a borrower may qualify for a **down payment assistance** grant from a state or municipal agency, non-profit organization, etc. [For more information, see HUD Handbook 4000.1.II.A.4.d.i.A]

Gifts

The entire required minimum investment can be a non-repayable **gift** from a relative, an employer or labor union, a charitable organization, or a close friend with a clearly defined and documented interest in the borrower.

The gift donor may *not* be a person or entity with an interest in the sale of the property, such as the seller, a real estate agent or broker, or a builder/associated entity. Gifts from these sources are considered inducements to purchase and *must be subtracted* from the sales price.

A lender must document any borrower gift funds through a **gift letter**, signed by the donor and borrower, that shows the donor's name and contact information, specifies the dollar amount of the gift and states the nature of the relationship to the borrower and that no repayment is required.

Secondary Financing

The FHA will insure first mortgage transactions that also include secondary financing, subject to certain restrictions. These restrictions can be found in the FHA Single Family Housing Policy Handbook (HUD Handbook 4000.1.IIA.4.d.J.)

It has been found that Section 203(b)(9)(C) of the National Housing Act does not prohibit the FHA from insuring mortgages originated as part of the homeownership programs of federal, state, or local government or their agencies or instrumentalities (hereinafter referred to as "government entities") when the government entities also directly provide funds toward the required minimum cash investment. These funds typically come in the form of silent or disappearing second liens, often from home ownership or government housing agencies. [HUD Handbook 4000.1.IIA.4.d.i.I]

The FHA reserves the right to refuse to insure the first mortgage if there is any secondary financing that does **not** serve the needs of the intended borrower or where the costs to participants outweigh the benefits derived by the borrower.

Seller/Third-Party Contribution Limits

The seller and/or interested third-party may contribute up to **6%** of the *lesser of* the property's sales price or the appraised value toward the buyer's closing costs, prepaid expenses, discount points, and other financing concessions. This limit also includes:

- Third-party payment for permanent and temporary interest rate buydowns and other payment supplements (note that borrowers must qualify at the note rate on temporary buydowns)
- Payments of mortgage interest for fixed-rate mortgages
- Mortgage payment protection insurance
- Payment of the upfront mortgage insurance premium (UFMIP)

Such contributions *cannot* be used to reduce the borrower's required minimum investment.

Payment of real estate commissions or fees, typically paid by the seller under local or state law or local custom, is not considered an interested third-party contribution. Contributions *exceeding* 6% are considered **inducements to purchase**, which requires that each dollar over the 6% limit must be subtracted from the property's sales price before applying the appropriate LTV factor (Handbook 4000.1.II.A.4.d.iii.H).

Loan Assumption

Most FHA loans made *prior to December 15, 1989* are fully assumable—for a nominal handling fee—since they do not have alienation (due on sale) clauses. *The HUD definition of assumption is "**Assumption** refers to the transfer of an existing mortgage obligation from an existing Borrower to the assuming Borrower."* [See HUD Handbook 4000.1.II.A.8.n.i]

Recall that an **alienation clause** *allows the lender to exercise certain rights upon the sale or transfer of an interest in the property;* for example, call the note due, change the interest rate, or charge an assumption fee. However, it is important to note that the original borrower is NOT released from liability *unless* FHA agrees to the assumption.

FHA loans endorsed *on or after December 15, 1989* may include an alienation clause. Such loans may be assumable; however, the lender will require a creditworthiness review of the new borrower as well as a fee. With these loans, assumptions without credit approval may be grounds for acceleration of the mortgage. Therefore, any offers involving mortgage assumptions must be investigated thoroughly with the lender, who must supply a specific release of liability, and perhaps even with legal counsel. [See HUD Handbook 4000.1.II.A.8.iii-vi]

Prepayment Penalties

HUD regulations *prohibit* prepayment penalties on FHA loans. A borrower may prepay a mortgage, in whole or in part, on the first of any month. However, if the payment is received after the first of the month, the lender may, at his discretion, collect the remainder of the month's interest for mortgages made before January 21, 2015. For an FHA-insured mortgage loan closing after this date, the FHA has aligned their former policy with that of the CFPB policy on prepayment penalties, which allows a mortgagee who is receiving a full and final payment to charge interest only through the date of receipt of the payoff funds.

[See FHA Handbook 4000.1 - Transmittal Summary 2 "Deleted Section 'Disclosure Regarding Interest Due Upon Prepayment.'"]

Mortgage Insurance Premium

A **mortgage insurance premium** (MIP)—not to be confused with PMI for conventional loans—*is required for all FHA loans*, regardless of the down payment, which includes an initial premium called the **upfront mortgage insurance premium** (UFMIP and a **monthly premium** based on the annual average outstanding loan balance divided into 12 monthly payments.

The UFMIP on 15- and 30-year purchase and refinance transactions for case numbers assigned *on or after April 9, 2012* is **1.75%** of the loan amount. [See HUD Handbook 4000.1.II.A.2.e.i.a]

The monthly premium reflects the type of loan and loan-to-value.

Annual MIP			
Base Loan Amount	LTV	MIP (bps)	Duration
Mortgage Term of More Than 15 Years			
≤ $625,500	≤ 95.00%	80 bps	11 years
≤ $625,500	> 95.00%	85 bps	Mortgage term
> $625,500	≤ 95.00%	100 bps	11 years
> $625,500	> 95.00%	105 bps	Mortgage term
Mortgage Term of Less Than or Equal to 15 Years			
≤ $625,500	≤ 90.00%	45 bps	11 years
≤ $625,500	> 90.00%	70 bps	Mortgage term
> $625,500	≤ 78.00%	45 bps	11 years
> $625,500	78.01 - 90.00%	70 bps	11 years
> $625,500	> 90.00%	95 bps	Mortgage term

[For more information, see HUD Handbook 4000.1. Appendix 1.0]

Financing MIP

If the UFMIP for a 15-year or 30-year loan is paid in cash at closing, it may be paid by the borrower or by the seller or other third party (within limits); **however, it must all be paid**

in cash or all of the premium must be financed. HERA limits the total FHA-insured first mortgage to 100% of the lesser of the sales price or appraised value, which would include the financing of the upfront mortgage insurance premium (UFMIP) within that limit.

Cancellation

For loans made *after January 1, 2001*, MIP is automatically cancelled when the LTV reaches **78%** of the original value (for 30-year mortgages, the annual MIP must have also been paid for at least five years). Borrowers may be able to make additional or early payments of principal to reduce the LTV to the 78% threshold where MIP is automatically cancelled. **Financed MIP cannot be cancelled.**

For loans made *after June 3, 2013*, FHA will collect the annual MIP for the maximum duration permitted as shown in the chart above. [See HUD Handbook 4000.1. Appendix 1.0]

HUD Handbook 4000.1 states that a mortgagee and a mortgagor may request the Federal Housing Commissioner (Assistant Secretary for Housing, HUD) to terminate the monthly MIP contract. In the event of early termination, the mortgage would no longer be governed by the FHA insurance program's rules and regulations, including FHA's Loss Mitigation requirements. Each borrower must sign a Borrower's Consent to Voluntary Termination of FHA Mortgage Insurance and must acknowledge that the FHA insurance program rules and regulations, including the FHA's Loss Mitigation requirements, will no longer be available to them. (See HUD Handbook 4000.1.III.A.1.l.B)

> ### Real Success
>
> As you review the regulations discussed here or as you encounter others, be aware that laws regulating FHA loans continually evolve. Any changes to program details—for example, product availability, mortgage insurance premiums, seller contribution limits, credit score requirements, down payments, etc.—are communicated through **Mortgagee Letters**. [https://portal.hud.gov]

VA-Guaranteed Loans

VA-guaranteed loans are *guaranteed by the federal government through the Veterans Benefits Administration*, which is part of the **Department of Veterans Affairs (VA)**. The VA's main purpose in guaranteeing loans is to help meet the housing needs of eligible veterans who have served or are currently serving on active duty in the U.S. Armed Forces, which includes the Army, Navy, Air Force, Marine Corps, Coast Guard, Reserves, or National Guard. VA loans are available to eligible veterans for the purchase of *owner-occupied single-family homes and for multi-family dwellings up to four units if the veteran intends to occupy one of the units as the primary residence.*

The VA rarely loans money directly to borrowers. It may do so in isolated rural areas where financing isn't readily available, but usually, a veteran must borrow money from a VA-approved lender.

Lenders may apply to become **Automatic Endorsers**, which gives them the authority to close VA-guaranteed loans without the prior approval of the VA. Automatic Endorsers are *responsible for supervising the entire mortgage process through closing, performing underwriting functions (credit examination, appraisal review, etc.), and then submitting the loan to the VA after closing for guaranty.*

"VA will apply the same standards for all married couples for VA loan guaranties regardless of the sex of spouses. VA is in the process of updating all forms that request marital status and dependent information in order to clarify that same-sex married couples and their dependents are eligible for benefits, including by replacing references to "husband" or "wife" with "spouse" and providing appropriate references to children of same-sex marriages." [https://www.va.gov/opa/marriage/]

The VA offers a variety of benefits and services that depend on a Veteran's marital status, including certain benefits to a veteran's "spouse" or "surviving spouse." The VA will generally accept a claimant's statement that he or she is married, but may investigate further if an assertion appears unreliable. This same procedure applies regardless whether the claimant is in an opposite-sex marriage or a same-sex marriage. [https://www.va.gov/opa/marriage/]

The VA provides access to an online **Lender's Handbook** [http://benefits.va.gov/warms/pam26_7.asp] as well as other valuable resources on its website [www.homeloans.va.gov].

Eligibility

Although the lender will examine the borrower's credit history, amount of income, and other factors before approving the loan, the primary requirement to be approved for a VA loan is the borrower's military **eligibility**, which is based on the borrower's length of continuous active service and other factors, such as when he or she enlisted and whether he or she served during war time. Spouses of veterans who died in active duty from service-related causes or who were MIA or a POW may also be eligible for a VA loan.

A current list of eligibility requirements is available from the VA website [http://benefits.va.gov/HOMELOANS/purchaseco_eligibility.asp].

Documentation

Lenders may not process or close a VA loan without verifying the eligibility of the borrower. This is done through a **Certificate of Eligibility** (COE), which is issued by the VA. The lender or the borrower may apply for a COE online [https://www.ebenefits.va.gov/ebenefits/homepage] or through the mail using VA Form 26-1880, Request for a Certificate of Eligibility.

To receive a COE, the veteran must be able to document his or her service as follows:

- **Discharged veterans who served in a regular component of the Armed Forces.** Certificate of Release or Discharge from Active Duty, or **DD-214**, issued by the Department of Defense to identify the character of service and reason for discharge (honorable, dishonorable, etc.)

- **Discharged members of the Army or Air National Guard never activated.** NGB Form 22 (Report of Separation and Record of Service) or NGB Form 23 (Retirement Points Accounting) and proof of character of service

- **Veterans on active duty or individuals who are still members of the Reserve/Guard.** A statement of service signed by, or by the direction of, the adjutant, personnel office, or commander of the unit or higher headquarters to which they are attached

If a veteran does not possess any discharge/separation documentation, he or she may submit Form 180, which can be obtained from https://www.va.gov/vaforms/form_detail.asp?FormNo=180.

Maximum Loan Limit

The VA doesn't limit the price a veteran can pay for a house (as long as the house appraises for the loan amount), but does limit the amount it will guarantee in the event of default to **25%** of the purchase price or the established reasonable value, whichever is less. A veteran's *maximum guaranty amount*, known as **entitlement**, represents the portion of the loan that the VA guarantees in the event of default by the borrowing veteran. Therefore, veterans can generally purchase a home priced up to **four times** the amount of their entitlement with no down payment.

All eligible veterans receive **$36,000 of basic entitlement**. Since the VA requires a minimum 25% of guaranty to meet secondary market requirements, the maximum loan amount a veteran would be eligible for using just basic entitlement would be $144,000 ($36,000 x 4 = $144,000). However, to account for the rise in the cost of homes, the Veteran's Benefits Improvement Act of 2008 provided that every eligible veteran receive a **bonus entitlement** that equals **25%** of the annual loan limit for single-family homes in the **county where the property is located**.

In 2018, the single-family home loan maximum for most counties is $453,100. With the loan amount of $453,100, the veteran's eligibility for guarantee will be a maximum of **$113,275** ($453,100 x 25%). This limit is significantly higher in some counties; for example, the 2018 loan limit in Marin County, CA, which is just north of San Francisco, is $679,650. A list of VA annual loan limits by county may be accessed from its website at https://www.benefits.va.gov/homeloans/purchaseco_loan_limits.asp.

The veteran's current eligible entitlement will be documented in the **Certificate of Eligibility** (COE). If the veteran's entitlement is insufficient—or if the purchase price/appraised value of the home exceeds the current VA loan limit for that county—the veteran can make a cash down payment so that the combination of entitlement and down payment equals the required guaranty of 25%. (Equity can also contribute to the 25% guaranty requirement for refinance loans.)

Exercise 5.4: Knowledge Check

1. Before closing, the VA requires the lender to confirm the veteran qualifies for a loan with a Certificate of Eligibility.

   A. true
   B. false

2. What two items must accompany every application for a VA-guaranteed mortgage?

   A. Bonus Entitlement Letter from VA
   B. Current Certificate of Eligibility
   C. Current Certificate of Reasonable Value
   D. DD214, NGB22/23, or Statement of Service

Restoring Entitlement

It is possible for a veteran to use some of his or her entitlement on a previous purchase and have partial entitlement available for another purchase. Some or all of a veteran's entitlement previously used in connection with a VA home loan may be restored and used again for another VA loan under either of these circumstances:

- The property, which secured the VA-guaranteed loan, has been sold and that loan has been paid in full.

- An eligible veteran has agreed to assume the outstanding balance on a VA loan and substitute his or her entitlement for the same amount originally used on the loan. The assuming veteran must also meet occupancy, income, and credit requirements.

Case in Point

Let's look at a couple of examples to illustrate. Assume each veteran is buying a home in a county where the current conforming loan limit for a single-family home is $424,100, making the maximum guaranty $106,025 ($424,100 x .25).

Example 1: Veteran Bob has full entitlement available and is purchasing a home for $350,000.

$350,000	Purchase Price
x .25	
$ 87,500	Guaranty Required

Since Bob has his entire entitlement of $106,025 available, he can purchase this house without a down payment. Even though he still has $18,525 in available entitlement, the loan-to-value on this purchase cannot exceed 100%.

Example 2: Veteran Ann wants to buy a house for $320,000. She has already used $27,500 of her entitlement on a prior loan, which has not been restored.

$106,025	Maximum Entitlement
–$ 27,500	Used Entitlement
$78,525	Available Entitlement
$320,000	Purchase Price
x .25	
$80,000	Guaranty Required
– $78,525	Available Entitlement
$ 1,475	Down Payment

If Ann wants to buy this house, she must convince the seller to lower the price, restore some of her entitlement, or make a down payment of $1,475.

Exercise 5.5: Apply Your Knowledge

Directions: Consider the following information, then determine the available entitlement. Be prepared to present and discuss your response.

Information: Veteran Dave wants to buy a house for $480,000. He has his full entitlement of $106,025 available.

What is the cash down payment Dave must make to buy this house?

Borrower Qualifying Standards

Once a veteran's eligibility is confirmed, underwriters making VA loans must qualify the borrower to ensure that he or she is a satisfactory credit risk and has the means to repay the loan. This is accomplished by looking at both the borrower's debt-to-income ratio and the residual income. If legally married, a spouse's income may also be considered for qualification purposes. However, a non-married co-borrower is **not** allowed on a VA-guaranteed loan *unless* he or she is also an eligible veteran who will occupy the home as a primary residence.

Total Debt-to-Income Ratio

One difference from conventional underwriting is that underwriters on VA loans do not generally consider the *housing expense ratio*, also called the **front-end ratio**. Instead, underwriters start with the *total debt-to-income (DTI) ratio*, or **back-end ratio**, when evaluating a potential borrower. In general, they also have more latitude than with conventional loans, generally looking for a total DTI that does not exceed **41%.**

 Tax-free income may be "grossed up" for the purpose of calculating the debt-to-income ratio only, using current income tax withholding tables to determine an appropriate adjustment. Tax-free income generally includes certain military allowances, child support payments, Workers Compensation benefits, disability retirement payments, and certain types of public assistance payments. The amount of "gross up" is typically **no more than 25%** of the tax-free income, in relation to the federal and state income tax liability of the borrower's other income.

Residual Income

In addition to the debt-to-income ratio, an underwriter must ensure that an eligible borrower has the appropriate balance of cash flow remaining for family support. This is determined by looking at **residual income**, which is *the amount of income remaining after subtracting taxes, housing expenses, and all recurring debts and obligations.* Residual income uses **net effective income** in its calculation, not gross income. This analysis also takes the **size of the veteran's family** into consideration when determining whether the residual income meets the VA's minimum requirements.

Property Guidelines for VA Loans

An existing home, which has either been previously owner-occupied or had all onsite and offsite improvements fully completed *for one year or more* is eligible for a VA loan. Newly completed properties (completed *less than one year* and never owner-occupied) are eligible if covered by a one-year VA builder's warranty, enrolled in a HUD-accepted ten-year insured protection plan, or have been built by a veteran, as the general contractor, for his/her own occupancy. Some manufactured homes may also be eligible.

The VA's minimum property requirements (MPRs) provide general acceptability criteria for properties that will become the security for VA-guaranteed loans.

VA Residual Income Calculation Worksheet

Gross monthly income

(Borrower) +$ _____

(Co-borrower)+$ _____

Deductions from Income

Federal Income Tax (from tables) -$ _____   -$ _____
State Income Tax (19% of FIT)   -$ _____   -$ _____
Social Security (7.65% of GMI)   -$ _____   -$ _____

Proposed PITI payment   -$ _____
Total Credit Card Payments   -$ _____   -$ _____
Total Installment Payments   -$ _____   -$ _____

Estimated Utility Expense   -$ _____
(Square ft. of subject x 14¢)

Childcare/Child Support   -$ _____

Net income (Residual) $ _____ $ _____

Balance remaining for family support guidelines (Residual):

Family Size	Table of Residual Incomes by Region For loan amounts of $80,000 and above			
	Northeast	Midwest	South	West
1	$450	$441	$441	$491
2	$755	$738	$738	$823
3	$909	$889	$889	$990
4	$1,025	$1,003	$1,003	$1,117
5	$1062	$1,039	$1,039	$1,158
over 5	Add $80 for each additional member up to a family of seven			

Establishing the Reasonable Value

Every appraisal made for VA purposes must be reviewed either by the lender's VA-authorized staff appraisal reviewer, **known as a SAR**, or by a VA staff appraiser, who then issues a **Notice of Value** (NOV) or a **Certificate of Reasonable Value** (CRV). The SAR typically is employed by the VA-authorized lender to review the appraisal performed by an independent VA-approved appraiser. Every NOV or CRV issued in conjunction with an appraisal review must include a list of any conditions and requirements that must be satisfied for the property to be eligible for VA loan guaranty.

The **established reasonable value** (or the sales price, whichever is less) defines *the maximum mortgage amount a veteran may have on a VA-guaranteed loan for that property*. If the price of the property exceeds the established reasonable value, the veteran must contribute the difference in cash to buy that property. The loan amount **cannot** exceed the established reasonable value, except to finance the required funding fee.

Occupancy

The law requires a veteran obtaining a VA-guaranteed loan to certify that he or she intends to personally occupy the property as his or her home. As of the date of certification, the veteran must either:

- Personally live in the property as his or her home, or

- Intend, upon completion of the loan and acquisition of the dwelling, to personally move into the property and use it as his or her home within a reasonable time, which generally means *within 60 days* after the loan closing.

Single or married service members, while deployed from their permanent duty station, are considered to be in a temporary duty status and able to meet the occupancy requirement.

VA Loan Regulations

Many terms of a VA loan, such as the interest rate, may be negotiated between the veteran borrower and the lender. However, the VA does impose certain requirements and restrictions on loans that it guarantees, some of which are covered here.

Variable Funding Fee

While there are no upfront or monthly mortgage insurance premiums required for VA loans, borrowers must pay a *non-refundable one-time* **variable funding fee** at closing for guaranteeing the loan. The variable funding fee is waived for disabled veterans and surviving spouses of veterans who died in service or from service-connected disabilities.

 The variable funding fee is waived if the veteran has a disability of 10% or more.

The funding fee may be financed or paid in cash. If financed, the funding fee percentage must be applied to the loan amount. The fee is based on the veteran's status, the number of times the veteran has used the program, and the amount of any down payment.

VA Variable Funding Fees			
Type of Veteran	Down Payment	1st Time Use	Subsequent Use
Regular Military	No down payment *	2.15 %	3.30 %
	5% or more (up to 10%)	1.50 %	1.50 %
	10% or more	1.25 %	1.25 %
National Guard and Reservists	No down payment *	2.40 %	3.30 %
	5% or more (up to 10%)	1.75 %	1.75 %
	10% or more	1.50 %	1.50 %

* Also applies to cash-out refinancing loans

Closing Costs

The veteran can pay a maximum of reasonable and customary amounts for any or all of the itemized fees and charges designated by the VA including:

- Flood zone determination
- Recording fees
- Credit report
- Prepaid items
- Hazard insurance

- Appraisal and compliance inspections
- Survey
- Title examination and title insurance
- Special mailing fees for refinancing loans
- Mortgage Electronic Registration System (MERS) fee

The veteran *cannot* be charged for the following fees and charges under VA regulations:

- Attorney's fees
- Brokerage fees

- Prepayment penalties
- Builder's HUD/FHA inspection fees

In addition to the itemized charges, the lender may charge a **flat fee**, *not to exceed 1% of the loan amount*, to cover the lender's costs and services for originating the loan. If the loan does not close for any reason, the lender must refund this 1% flat fee.

[For more information, see VA Lenders Handbook (Pamphlet 26-7): http://www.benefits. va.gov/warms/pam26_7.asp (Chapter 8)]

Seller Concessions

A **seller concession** is *anything of value added to the transaction by the builder or seller for which the buyer pays nothing additional and which the seller is **not** customarily expected or required to pay or provide;* for example:

Considered Seller Concessions and Subject to a 4% Limit	Not Considered as Seller Concessions
Payment of the buyer's VA funding fee	Payment of the buyer's closing costs
Prepayment of the buyer's property taxes and/or insurance	Payment of points as appropriate to the market
Gifts (such as a television or microwave oven)	
Payment of extra points to provide permanent interest rate buydowns	
Provision of escrowed funds to provide temporary interest rate buydowns	
Payoff of credit balances or judgments on behalf of the buyer	

Any seller concession or combination of concessions that *exceeds 4% of the established reasonable value of the property* is considered excessive and unacceptable for VA-guaranteed loans. The reason for this restriction is to prevent concessions from enticing unwary and unqualified veterans into home mortgages they cannot afford.

Secondary Financing

The VA permits secondary financing simultaneous with a VA-guaranteed first loan for a variety of purposes; for example, closing costs or a down payment (unless the down payment is required to cover an excess purchase price beyond the VA's established reasonable value).

Loan Assumption

For VA loans committed and closed *on or after March 1, 1988*, VA loan assumptions are *not* allowed, unless the veteran first has the assumption **approved** by the Department of Veterans Affairs or its authorized agent (i.e., the loan holder). If an assumption is approved by the VA or the loan holder, the original veteran is released from liability in the event the assumer defaults on the loan, resulting in a loss to the VA.

Entitlement associated with an assumption may only be restored to the veteran if these conditions are met:

- The assumer is an eligible veteran.
- The assumption has been approved by the loan holder or the VA.
- The assumer agrees to substitute his or her VA home loan entitlement for the original veteran and occupies the property as his or her principal residence.

Prepayment Penalties

The VA does **not** allow clauses for prepayment penalties to be included in VA loans. (However, the VA may allow these clauses for secondary financing.) VA loans may be paid off early without additional charges or penalties of any kind.

USDA Rural Development Programs

Although one mission of the USDA's Rural Development Agency is to provide financial support to low-income homebuyers in rural communities, the definition of "rural" may be broader than one might think. It can include small towns of up to 35,000 inhabitants, even those in areas that may be in close proximity to larger metropolitan areas. The most recent data from the U.S. Census Bureau is used to determine eligible areas. In addition, the USDA could determine that particular areas are temporarily eligible for their programs in response to certain conditions or natural disasters, such as a flood or hurricane. For this reason, a loan officer needs to verify whether the property is located in a designated area for specific programs. For property eligibility, visit the USDA's Rural Housing Website [see http://eligibility.sc.egov.usda.gov/eligibility/welcomeAction.do].

Section 502 Loans

In the remainder of this chapter, we will look at **Section 502 loans** for single-family homes. The Section 502 loan program either **guarantees loans** made by approved private lenders or **makes direct loans** if no local lender is available.

Section 502 loans can be used to:

- Purchase an existing home.
- Construct a new home.
- Renovate or repair an existing home.
- Relocate an existing home.
- Purchase and prepare a site for a home, including sewage and water facilities.

Under the Section 502 programs, eligible houses must be **modest in size, design, and cost**— defined as *having a market value that does **not** exceed the applicable area loan limit and does not contain certain prohibited features.*

Applicants must:

- Be without decent, safe, and sanitary housing.
- Be unable to obtain a loan from other resources on terms and conditions that they can be reasonably expected to meet.
- Agree to occupy the property as their primary residence.
- Have the legal capacity to incur a loan obligation.
- Meet citizenship or eligible noncitizen requirements.
- Not be suspended or debarred from participation in federal programs.

Properties financed with direct loan funds must:

- Generally be 2,000 square feet or less.
- Not have market value in excess of the applicable area loan limit.
- Not have in-ground swimming pools.
- Not be designed for income producing activities.

Applicants for Section 502 loans—guaranteed and direct—must meet certain income requirements based on the **area median income** (AMI). Assuming that the applicant meets the income eligibility and the house is in an approved area, the borrower may receive **100% financing**, based on the appraised value or acquisition cost, whichever is less. The terms of the loan will be different depending on whether it is a guaranteed loan or a direct loan.

USDA mortgage insurance rates are:

- For all loans, 1.00% upfront fee paid at closing, based on the loan size.
- For all loans, 0.35% annual fee, based on the remaining principal balance.

Note that the annual fee is for the life of the loan. It does not end when the loan-to-value reaches a certain point.

Applicants for Section 502 guaranteed loans may have an income of up to **115%** of the area median income (AMI).

To check property eligibility and income limits for Section 502 Direct and Guaranteed loans, visit the USDA website [see http://eligibility.sc.egov.usda.gov/eligibility/].

Chapter Summary

1. For the purposes of this chapter, government agency financing refers to real estate loans that have been traditionally insured or guaranteed by government programs. Government agency programs include FHA-insured, VA-guaranteed, and USDA Rural Development guaranteed and direct loans.

2. FHA-insured loans are for owner-occupied single family and multi-family dwellings of four or fewer units, made by approved lenders. FHA loans require lower down payments and less stringent qualifying standards than conventional loans. Direct Endorsers can underwrite FHA loans. The FHA sets a maximum mortgage amount, depending on the geographic area.

3. HUD issues regulations for FHA loans, including:

   a) Required minimum investment of 3.5% of the lesser of the purchase price or the appraised value

   b) UFMIP required (1.75% for most purchase and refinance loans, monthly MIP on annual average loan balance up to .85%)

   c) Monthly mortgage insurance payment terms vary with the amount of the down payment and the amortization term of the loan

   d) Assumable only with lender approval for loans on or after December 15, 1989

   e) Prepayment penalty not allowed, but the lender can require payoff be made on the due date or collect an extra month's interest

   f) Items paid by the seller are negotiable, but the seller contribution is limited to six (6) points. MLOs can stay current on FHA loan programs via Mortgagee Letters

4. VA-guaranteed loans help eligible veterans buy homes often with no down payment. The veteran must occupy the home. The VA doesn't limit home price, but limits the guaranty amount that the lender can recover for default to 25% of the maximum loan limit in the county where he property is located.

   The VA loan rules include:

   a) Borrower needs DD-214 (discharge papers) and COE (Certificate of Eligibility)

   b) The VA issues Notice of Value (NOV) or Certificate of Reasonable Value (CRV) based on appraisal; if price exceeds estimate of reasonable value, veteran must make up difference with down payment/equity

   c) Secondary financing may be permitted

   d) Required variable funding fee—paid in cash or financed (waived for disabled veterans); lender flat fee limited to 1% of loan amount

   e) No limit on seller contribution to closing costs; 4% limit on seller concessions

   f) Assumable by eligible veterans only with VA approval (for loans after March 1, 1988)

   g) Prepayment penalty not allowed

   h) Veteran may restore entitlement if loan is paid off, home is sold, and mortgage assumed by eligible veteran

5. Rural Development is an agency under the USDA that offers various assistance programs for both businesses and homebuyers in rural communities, which can include small towns and areas hit by natural disasters. The Rural Development's Housing and Community Facilities Programs Section 502 loans for single-family homes either guarantees loans made by private lenders or makes direct loans if no local lender is available. Eligible borrowers can get 100% financing without any mortgage insurance, but must pay a guarantee fee of 1.00% of the loan amount. Applicants for Section 502 Guaranteed Loans may have an income of up to 115% of the area median income (AMI).

Chapter Quiz

1. An eligible borrower applies for an FHA loan on a house with an appraised value of $100,000 and a purchase price of $96,000. What is the required minimum investment?

   A. $3,000

   B. $3,360

   C. $3,500

   D. $4,800

2. An upfront mortgage insurance premium is required

   A. on all FHA loans.

   B. only when the buyer cannot pay the required down payment in cash.

   C. only when the LTV exceeds 80%.

   D. only when the LTV exceeds 90%.

3. To qualify for an FHA loan, a borrower should have a maximum housing expense ratio of _____ and a total debt-to-income ratio of _____.

   A. 28%; 36%

   B. 29%; 36%

   C. 29%; 41%

   D. 31%; 43%

4. A residual income calculation shows the

   A. amount of cash flow available for maintenance and utilities.

   B. cash flow remaining for family support.

   C. funds remaining for the proposed PITI payment.

   D. true composite debt-to-income ratio.

5. FHA-insured loans are funded by

   A. approved lenders.

   B. the FDIC.

   C. the FHA.

   D. HUD.

6. The annual area median income for a county is $50,000. Using USDA-guaranteed financing, what is the maximum amount of gross annual income that the borrower can earn and qualify?

   A. $50,000

   B. $55,000

   C. $57,500

   D. $62,500

7. What is the maximum flat fee that a lender may charge on a VA loan?

   A. 1%

   B. 2%

   C. 3.5%

   D. There is no limit; the fee is negotiable.

8. Full VA entitlement can generally be restored to a veteran

   A. if any disabled veteran assumes the loan.

   B. if an eligible veteran substitutes his entitlement for the seller's.

   C. under no circumstances.

   D. when the loan is paid down to below 50% LTV.

Nontraditional/ Nonconforming Loans & Financing

This chapter reviews the elements and identifies the characteristics of nontraditional and nonconforming loans. The chapter also reviews the guidelines and the regulations that affect these types of loans.

After completing this chapter, you will be able to:

- Describe the advantages and disadvantages of buydown plans.
- Identify the elements that make up an adjustable rate mortgage.
- Describe the purpose of construction loans, including the three most common disbursement plans.
- Identify the characteristics of a reverse mortgage.
- Identify the factors that define a subprime loan.
- Describe the agency guidelines on lending and subprime loans.
- Contrast the various types of alternative financing.

Key Terms

Adjustable Rate Mortgage (ARM)
Alt-A Loan
Assumption
Boot
Conforming Loan
Conventional Loan
Conversion Option

Cost of Funds Index (COFI)
Equity Exchange
Home Equity Loan
Home Equity Line of Credit (HELOC)
Hybrid Mortgage (ARM)
Land Contract
Lease

Lease/Option
Lease/Purchase
Nontraditional Mortgage Product
Option
Release
Traditional Mortgage Product

Mortgage Products

Just as there are many different goals borrowers might have, there are many financing tools to help them achieve those goals. With the wide variety of nontraditional mortgage products available in today's real estate market, it is important for the MLO to understand how each works to help customers reach their goals.

For example, if the goal is to lower the monthly payment, the borrower can:

- Prepay some of the interest at closing as **discount points** to the lender, which buys down the interest rate and, therefore, lowers the required monthly payment.

- Agree to **assume part of the lender's interest rate risk** with an **adjustable rate mortgage** (ARM). Since the lender is not locked into a fixed-interest rate for the loan term, the lender can offer the borrower a lower interest rate as a start rate.

Jumbo Loans and B and C Borrowers

There are two main reasons why a loan is classified as a nonconforming loan and, thus, is not saleable to FNMA or FHLMC:

- **Size of the Loan.** So-called **jumbo loans** *exceed the maximum loan amount established by Fannie Mae and Freddie Mac for conforming mortgage loans.* . The 2018 single-family home conforming loan maximum is $453,100 ($679,650 for most locations in Alaska, Hawaii, Guam, and U.S. Virgin Islands). In addition, the conforming loan maximum can be even higher in specific counties or metropolitan statistical areas.

 Fannie Mae/Freddie Mac's maximum loan amount changes annually and is published by the Federal Housing Finance Agency (FHFA). [For published rates on the loan limits see, https://www.fanniemae.com/singlefamily/loan-limits]

- **Credit Quality of Borrower.** A borrower who does not meet the minimum standards established by Fannie Mae/Freddie Mac may be classified as a **B or C borrower**. This might be someone who had a credit problem in the past, such as a bankruptcy within the past seven to ten years; someone with late or unpaid medical bills; or someone whose credit scores are low because he owns multiple investment properties or has been self-employed for too short a period of time. Lenders, such as neighborhood banks, may still offer loans to these borrowers, but the loans cannot be sold to Fannie Mae or Freddie Mac.

Alt-A and A-Minus Loans

Alt-A loans, also called alternative documentation loans, are *loans that hold **borrowers with good credit** to different documentation standards than traditional loans.* It is possible that a borrower with excellent credit and a large down payment will not be required to furnish as much documentation as a borrower with average scores and an average down payment. The AUS recognizes a good credit risk and may require a reduced list of documentation; for example, only verbal verification of employment as opposed to two years of W-2s.

A-minus loans, on the other hand, are *for borrowers with **credit record blemishes***, such as being 30 days late one or two times over the past year, having limited funds for a down payment, a high debt-to-income ratio, or a record of bankruptcy and/or foreclosure. A-minus loans are riskier than prime mortgages but not as risky as subprime mortgages. The approval can be obtained through an AUS. Since the loan is riskier, the interest rate is higher.

Buydown Plans

Recall from an earlier chapter that a **point** is simply *one percent of the loan amount.* Points may be charged for a variety of reasons, such as to cover the costs of processing or servicing a loan. **Discount points** are *additional funds paid to a lender at the beginning of a loan to lower the note interest rate and, therefore, the monthly payments.* Such a buydown could make it easier for a borrower to qualify for the loan.

Typically, a borrower pays for a buydown by simply prepaying some interest at closing. Therefore, a buydown in the form of discount points appears on a Loan Estimate as a charge to the borrower.

Advantages to a buydown plan include:

- The borrower's monthly payment is lower.
- The lender may evaluate the borrower for loan qualification based on the reduced payment after the buydown.

While a permanent buydown plan may allow a borrower to lower monthly payments, borrowers must weigh their monthly savings over the life of the loan against what they are paying in upfront points at closing to buy down the interest rate. To determine how many months it would take to recoup those upfront points, divide the payment difference between the two interest rates by the cost of the discount points.

Case in Point

Let's first see how a buydown can provide a **net tangible benefit** to a borrower obtaining a mortgage loan.

- FHA and VA loans (and many conventional lenders) impose a requirement that a refinance loan must provide a benefit to the consumer to avoid loan flipping and predatory lending.
- The VA also requires that the "time to recoup closing costs" is calculated to verify the benefit to a veteran.

Consider an FHA refinance for a mortgage loan originated in 2008 that had a PITI payment of $1924.89 per month for a 30-year fixed term. Six years later, the borrower refinances to a new 30-year term loan with a PITI payment of $1447.09, a reduction of $477.80 per month. If the borrower paid $3000 in closing costs to obtain the new loan, the time to recapture the investment is calculated as follows:

Total Closing Costs ($3000) / Monthly Decrease in Payments ($477.80) = Time to Recoup (Recapture Time) or 6.28 Months

Knowledge Check: Exercise 6.1

Using the Case in Point example, if the borrower remains in the home during the full 30-year term of the new loan, what is the dollar amount of his lifetime savings?

_____

_____

_____

Another option is for the seller or other interested third party, such as a builder/developer or an employer to help facilitate the move of an employee being transferred, to pay discount points to buy down the interest rate for the borrower. While this means less money in the seller's pocket, it may be necessary to make the deal. The lender determines what the buydown amount is and subtracts that amount from the loan proceeds paid to the seller for the property (reflected on the Closing Disclosure as a charge to the seller). The borrower still signs a note for the full amount but receives a lower interest rate over the life of the loan.

Permanent Buydown

A **permanent buydown** is *when points are paid to a lender to reduce the interest rate and loan payments for the entire life of the loan.* When a buyer's interest rate is reduced for the life of the loan, the lender writes that lower interest rate into the promissory note. Thus, the nominal rate (or coupon rate) stated in the note is the actual reduced interest rate.

Temporary Buydown

A buydown paid to reduce the borrower's payments early in the loan is called a **temporary buydown**. Whoever pays for the buydown—often the seller or developer, sometimes the borrower—*deposits funds at closing with the lender that will be used to supplement the borrower's reduced monthly out-of-pocket payment.* The supplemental funds allow the lender to receive the full payment, based on the permanent interest rate, during the months of the temporary buydown when the borrower's monthly payments are less than what is called for in the note according to the permanent interest rate. Once the "deposited" funds run out; in other words, the specified temporary buydown period ends; the borrower must make the full required monthly payment out-of-pocket.

Limits on Interested Party Contributions and Other Considerations

Fannie Mae, Freddie Mac, and the FHA limit points and other **interested party contributions** (IPCs). An interested party may be *anyone other than the buyer who has a financial interest in, or can influence the terms and the sale or transfer of, the subject property.* Limits are placed on these items so buyers aren't induced into a property they cannot afford.

Fannie Mae/Freddie Mac

Fannie Mae and Freddie Mac guidelines impose limits on discounts, buydowns, and other forms of interested party contributions to help buyers get into homes. These other contributions include finance costs, such as prepaid interest, and escrows for property taxes, hazard insurance, and mortgage insurance.

Contributions by sellers or other interested parties are limited to a percentage of the sale price of a property or its appraised value, *whichever is less.* If the contributions *exceed* Fannie Mae and Freddie Mac guidelines, the contribution amount must be *deducted* from the value or sale price of the property before determining the maximum loan amount.

These maximum contributions are based on the type of property and the loan-to-value:

Property Type	LTV/CLTV Ratio	Maximum Contribution
Investment Property	All CLTV ratios	2%
Principal Residence or Second Home	Greater than 90%	3%
	75.01% - 90%	6%
	75% or less	9%

This example reflects FNMA/FHLMC guidelines. Other investors may impose other standards.

 Contributions made by employers or immediate family members usually are not subject to these limits.

FHA and VA Guidelines

FHA guidelines also impose limits on discounts points, buydowns, and other forms of seller/interested party contributions to help buyers purchase homes.

The FHA does **not** permit underwriting at a *temporary buydown rate* on fixed-rate mortgages; it requires the borrower to qualify at the **note rate**. Furthermore, the buydown must *not* result in a reduction of more than two percentage points below the interest rate on the note.

The **FHA** allows *maximum IPCs of 6%* of the lesser of the sale price or appraised value. If the contribution is more than the allowable limit, like Fannie Mae and Freddie Mac, the FHA deducts the excess from the maximum loan amount. For this rule, remember that seller-paid contributions include any items normally paid by the buyer.

The **VA** has *no set limits* on IPCs, although the seller payment of concessions (as defined by the VA Lenders Handbook) is *limited to 4%* of the lesser of the sale price or appraisal.

Exercise 6.2: Knowledge Check

Fannie Mae/Freddie Mac guidelines limit loan purchase contributions by sellers or other interested parties to a percentage of the property sale price or its appraised value, whichever is lower.

A. true
B. false

Exercise 6.3: Apply Your Knowledge

Directions: Consider the following scenario, and then write your responses.

Scenario: A borrower wants to buy a $150,000 home and is going to make a $15,000 down payment. The borrower is seeking a conventional loan but doesn't want to pay more than 6.5% interest. The lender agrees to 6.5% interest based on three discount points and a loan origination fee of 2%.

1. What is the total amount of points (in dollars and percentage) that the lender will receive for making this loan? _____

2. If the seller agrees to pay the discount points, how much will the seller net from the transaction? (Assume the seller pays no other costs.)

_____

_____

_____

3. What will the borrower's note state as the interest rate on the loan? What dollar amount will the note say was borrowed?

_____

_____

_____

4. Can the lender sell this loan to Fannie Mae or Freddie Mac on the secondary market? Why or why not?

_____

_____

_____

Adjustable Rate Mortgages

An **adjustable rate mortgage** (ARM) frees lenders from being locked into a fixed-interest rate for the entire life of a loan as interest rates may adjust, according to the terms in the note, to reflect the current cost of money. ARMs are popular alternative financing tools as they may help borrowers qualify more easily for a home loan or for a more expensive home. Many lenders like ARMs because they can pass the risk of fluctuating interest rates on to borrowers. Lenders may offer multiple types of ARM programs.

Lenders normally charge a lower start rate for an ARM than for a fixed-rate loan because the risk of interest rate fluctuations is shifted. Although most borrowers prefer the security of a fixed rate (provided the rate is not too high), ARMs have maintained a place in the market despite comparatively low mortgage rates. Of course, as interest rates rise, so does ARM popularity.

Terms, rate changes, and many other aspects of ARMs are regulated by several agencies, depending on the type of lender. Any applicable guidelines or requirements of Fannie Mae, Freddie Mac, the FHA, and/or private mortgage insurers must be followed as well.

Components of ARMs

There are several components to an ARM:

- Index
- Margin
- Rate adjustment period
- Interest rate cap/floor (if any)
- Conversion option (if any)

The borrower's interest rate is determined initially by the cost of money when the loan is made.

Index

Once the initial interest rate for the loan is set, the rate of the loan is tied to a widely recognized and published index. The **index** is often referred to as the *cost of money*.

At the time a loan is made, the index preferred by the borrower is selected. Because of market forces, the index fluctuates during the term of the loan, causing the borrower's actual interest rate to increase and decrease. The index moves in step with other short-term interest rate debt instruments. The index should be one that is determined and affected by market conditions and regularly listed in a major publication, such as The Wall Street Journal.

Common indices include:

- Treasury Bill Index (MTA)
- 11th District Cost of Funds Indexes (COFI)
- Constant Maturity Treasury (CMT)
- London Interbank Offered Rate (LIBOR)

Indices have rates that are published. The index is subject to change over time and is, therefore, likely to be different each time there is an adjustment to the loan's interest rate. In general, indices with longer terms offer borrowers more protection from short-term fluctuations in the economy than indices with short terms. For example, a borrower with an ARM that uses a six-month U.S. Treasury bill for the index has less protection from increases in the interest rate than a borrower who uses a three-year Treasury bill as the index.

Margin

A **margin**, which is sometimes referred to as a *spread*, remains fixed or constant for the duration of the loan. The margin is the number of percentage points added to the index and set by the lender. The *index plus the margin* equals the adjustable interest rate or **fully indexed rate** the borrower pays on the loan. The margin can vary greatly between different lenders.

For Example:

4.25%	Current Index Value
+ 2.00%	Margin
6.25%	Fully Indexed Rate

Rate Adjustment Period

The **rate adjustment period** is *the length of time between interest rate changes with ARMs.*

Teaser Rates

When the **initial rate** on an ARM, also known as the *start rate*, is less than the *fully indexed rate*, it is considered a **discounted index rate**, sometimes referred to as a *teaser rate*. Lenders offer teaser rates to make ARMs more attractive to borrowers.

Interest Rate Cap

Interest rate caps are used with ARMs to *limit the number of percentage points an interest rate can be increased during the term of a loan*, helping to eliminate large fluctuations in mortgage payments.

Rate caps are often shown as two numbers; for example, **2/6**, where:

- **2/6** – The first number indicates the maximum amount the interest rate can increase (or potentially decrease) from one adjustment period to the next.

- **2/6** – The second number indicates the maximum amount the interest rate can increase during the life of the loan.

Some ARMs allow for a higher rate change at the first adjustment and then apply a periodic adjustment cap to future adjustments. These ARMs are usually identified with three numbers, where the first number is the interest rate cap for the first adjustment, the second number is the period adjustment cap, and the third number is the lifetime interest rate cap.

For Example

If you see a rate cap described as **5/2/6**, the interest rate cannot increase more than:

- **5%** at the first adjustment.
- **2%** for subsequent adjustment periods.
- **6%** total over the life of the loan.

How an ARM Works

When attempting to understand how an ARM works and how payments adjust, think of an ARM as a set of stair steps. The **floor**, where the ARM begins, is *the period of time subject to the initial, start, or teaser interest rate.* See the chart that follows for further description.

- With 2/6 interest rate caps, we know that the **maximum interest rate** at the first rate change date is the current interest rate (in this case, the start rate of 3.00%) + the rate cap (in this case, 2%). *This formula is used for each successive interest rate adjustment calculation.* This sets the maximum second year (period) rate at 5.00%.

- The second calculation is the **fully indexed rate**. Assume that the current index is 2.125% and the margin is 2.25%. The fully indexed rate is the sum of these two figures or 4.375%.

- The lesser of the maximum interest rate or the fully indexed rate sets the interest rate for the coming year. In this example, the maximum interest rate per the periodic cap is 5.00% and the fully indexed rate is 4.375%. Following the rule of using the lesser rate, the 2nd year interest rate is 4.375%.

Use the same concepts for calculation of the next year's interest rate adjustment. Again, remember the "stairs."

- The first calculation is the maximum interest rate, which is the current rate (4.375%) + the rate cap (2.00%) = 6.375%.

- Next, we calculate the fully indexed rate. For the next year, assume that the index has risen to 5.50%. To calculate the fully indexed rate, add the index (5.50%) to the margin (fixed at 2.25%). The fully indexed rate is 7.75%.

- The lesser of the maximum interest rate or the fully indexed rate in this scenario is the previous rate + rate cap formula, or 6.375%. Remember that the new interest rate is always the lesser of the two calculations that are performed at the time of rate adjustment.

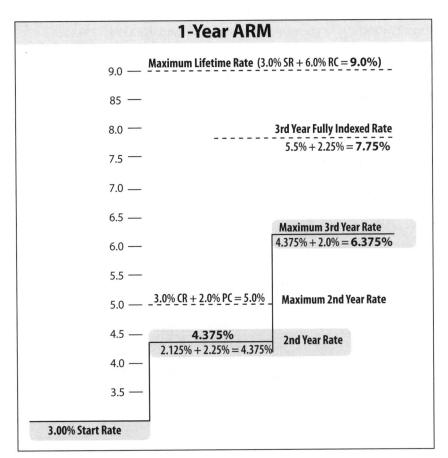

Hybrid ARM

A **hybrid ARM** is *an ARM with an initial fixed-rate period greater than one year (period)*. That is, the loan has a fixed rate for a specified number of years, and then the interest rate adjusts regularly for the remainder of the loan term, according to the terms of the note.

For example, a 3/1 hybrid ARM has an introductory rate period or teaser rate for three years from the date of the loan. Other options include 5/1, 7/1, or 10/1 ARMs, where the fixed period is for five, seven, or ten years and the interest rate adjusts annually for the remainder of the loan term.

MLOs need to be careful about how they discuss these loans so that consumers aren't confused by the term "fixed."

The calculations for the interest rate change at the end of the fixed period (e.g., three years) follow the calculations previously introduced, using the initial rate cap adjustment rather than the periodic cap.

- To find the first interest rate adjustment maximum, add the current interest rate (3.50%) to the initial rate cap (5.00% from the 5/2/6 figure) for a sum of 8.50%.

- The fully indexed rate is then calculated and compared with the first calculation (initial rate adjustment) and the lesser of the two calculations is selected. For the initial rate adjustment, assume the index has risen to 5.50%. To calculate the fully indexed rate, add the index (5.50%) to the margin (fixed at 2.25%). The fully indexed rate is 7.75%.

After the initial interest rate adjustment, the 2/6 caps are the only caps used and the loan and rate adjustments function in the same manner as a standard ARM.

The last number in either example (the "6" in the 5/2/6 or 2/6 adjustment guidelines) denotes *the maximum interest rate that can be charged by the lender during the life of the loan.* This maximum rate is calculated by adding the starting interest rate to the maximum rate cap (6.00%).

- Using the start rate of 3.5% and adding it to the maximum rate cap of 6.0%, the maximum rate would be 9.50%,

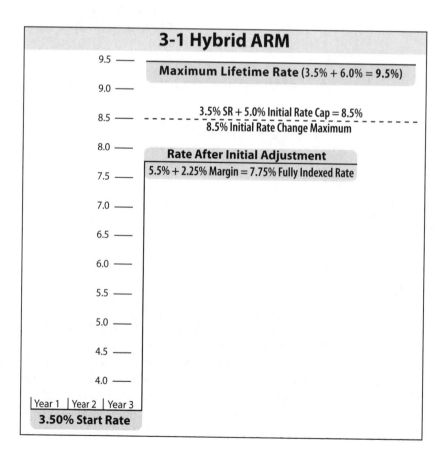

Exercise 6.4: Apply Your Knowledge

Directions: Consider the following information, and then determine the interest rates and complete the table entries for years two through five (i.e., borrower interest rate w/cap).

Information: Assume a borrower gets a 1-year ARM for $100,000 for 30 years. It has a 5/2/6 interest rate cap. The current index rate is 4.5%, the margin is 3%, and the discounted start rate is 4%.

	Start / Year 1	Year 2	Year 3	Year 4	Year 5
Index	4.5%	6.5%	4%	7%	8%
Fully Indexed Rate (Index + 3%)	7.5%	9.5%	7%	10%	11%
Borrower Interest Rate w/Caps	4% (start)				
Monthly Payment (P&I only)	$536.82	$804.62	$665.30	$804.62	$877.57

Conversion Option

A **conversion option** *gives the borrower the right to convert from an ARM to a fixed-rate loan.* ARMs with a conversion option normally identify the following factors in the note:

• Interest rate (often, the initial rate and converted rate are higher)

• Limited time to convert (e.g., between the first and fifth year)

• Conversion fee (typically about 1%)

For Example

A Fannie Mae convertible ARM program may be converted between the 13th and 60th month for a small processing fee paid to the lender.

ARM Standardization

Previously, most lenders underwrote ARMs based on their standards and kept them as portfolio loans. Now, lenders usually follow secondary market guidelines so they can sell ARMs just as they do fixed-rate loans. With uniform ARM underwriting standards, secondary market agencies, such as Freddie Mac, purchase large volumes of ARMs that follow their guidelines.

Loan-to-Value Ratios

ARMs with loan-to-value ratios (LTVs) of 80%, 90%, and 95% may be available, depending on current conditions in the local market. Loans with higher LTVs, though, are often subject to some restrictions. Due to additional default potential that determines qualification for increasing payments, ARMs may be subject to higher underwriting standards such as higher FICO® score requirements, lower loan-to-value ratios, or lower debt-to-income ratios.

ARM Disclosures

Lenders offering residential financing, including ARMs, must comply with federal guidelines under Regulation Z of the Truth in Lending Act that require certain disclosures to borrowers (12 CFR §1026.19).

- A lender is required to give the loan applicant the **Consumer Handbook on Adjustable Rate Mortgages** (CHARM), prepared by the Federal Reserve Board, *within three business days of loan application*.

- The rules also require certain specific disclosures if relevant to the specific ARM program and the disclosure of the APR.

The lender or servicer must comply with all the terms of the loan as indicated in the note, including any changes that occur during the life of the loan to the index, the rate, the payment, etc. The note will also indicate specific requirements for disclosing pending changes to the borrower.

ARM Disclosure Requirements for Interest Rate/Payment Changes

A loan servicer must provide a borrower with an ARM:

- *At least 60 days' notice before* an interest rate change occurs, if that change will result in a new payment amount. The notice is required to alert the borrower that the payment is about to rise.

- An initial interest rate change disclosure *seven to eight months before* the first payment is due at the new rate. The notice will show the new rate and payment or at least an estimate of the new rate and payment.

Real Success

MLOs working with consumers on an ARM should **never** use the term "fixed rate," even when discussing the period between adjustments during which that interest rate remains unchanged. A consumer will hear "fixed," and that perception could create certain expectations about the loan that are false. Complete disclosure of how an ARM works and the impact on the borrower is required by law and is simply the ethical behavior expected from all mortgage professionals.

Annual Percentage Rate

Recall the APR is *the relationship between the cost of borrowing money and the total amount financed, represented as a percentage*. Regulation Z disclosures regarding the APR cannot be made based solely on an ARM's initial rate. For an ARM, the disclosure of the APR on Page 3 "Comparisons" section of the Loan Estimate *must reflect the finance charges and fees as well as the **composite APR***, which is based on the initial payment rate and the fully indexed rate that could exist for the remaining years of the loan term.

For Example

If the initial rate on a 30-year loan is 6% for one year but adjusts to the **Cost of Funds Index** (for illustration purposes, let's say 3%) plus 5% for the initial cap, the lender's disclosed payment schedule should reflect a composite APR based on 6% for 12 payments and 8% (3% + 5%) for the remaining 348 payments. **The main point is that a lender must disclose more than the low initial rate.** A required disclosure under Regulation Z, the APR composite rate is designed to let consumers' comparison shop for rates among lenders, since all lenders must calculate APR the same way.

Exercise 6.5: Apply Your Knowledge

Directions: Consider the following scenario, and then write your responses.

Scenario: A borrower received a 30-year ARM mortgage loan for $200,000. Rate caps are 3/2/6. The start rate is 3.50% and the loan adjusts every 12 months for the life of the mortgage. The index used for this mortgage is LIBOR (for this exercise, 3.00% at the start of the loan, 4.45% at the end of the first year, and 4.50% at the end of the second year). The margin on the loan is 3.00%, which remains the same for the duration of the loan.

1. What is the initial rate (start rate) the borrower will pay during the first year?

   _____

   _____

2. What is the interest rate the borrower will pay after the first rate adjustment? (Hint: Remember to use the "stair step method" for determining the new interest rate.)

   _____

   _____

   _____

3. What is the fully indexed rate after the second year?

   _____

   _____

4. What is the maximum interest rate the borrower will pay during the 30-year term for this loan?

   _____

   _____

5. If the interest rate is at its maximum, what would the LIBOR index have to be to reach the maximum interest rate?

   _____

   _____

Exercise 6.6: Apply Your Knowledge

Identify some of the advantages and disadvantages of ARMs and list them in the appropriate column. Consider items that may not have already been identified.

Advantages	Disadvantages

Construction Loans

Another type of nontraditional loan program is a **construction mortgage,** which is *an interim, or short-term, temporary loan used to finance the construction of improvements and buildings on land.* Generally, an appraiser will value the property for a construction loan by evaluating the building plans and specifications, completing a "subject to" appraisal.

After the loan is approved and funded, the construction funds are set aside in a special account and released to the borrower and builder as "draws" or obligatory advances for the construction of the dwelling. To protect themselves, lenders use plans for **disbursing construction loan proceeds** to guard against overspending by the borrower. Three common disbursement plans are the:

- Fixed Disbursement Plan.
- Voucher System,
- Warrant System,

Fixed Disbursement Plan. A fixed disbursement plan *pays a percentage of funds at a set time.* Called **obligatory advances,** they are paid out at various stages of construction as follows:

- First Release/Draw 10% of Loan - Project 20% complete
- Second Release/Draw 20% of Loan - Project 40% complete
- Third Release/Draw 20% of Loan - Project 60% complete
- Fourth Release/Draw 20% of Loan - Project 80% complete
- Fifth Release/Draw 20% of Loan - Project 100% complete

Lenders often hold the final 10% (or more) of the loan proceeds until the lien period has expired to protect against unpaid mechanic's liens, which could affect the marketability of the property. If a valid mechanic's lien is recorded, the construction loan agreement usually allows lenders to pay it from the part of the loan not disbursed.

Voucher System. The contractor or borrower must pay her own bills, and then submit the receipts to the lender for reimbursement.

Warrant System. The lender directly pays bills presented by the various suppliers and laborers on a project. During construction, the borrower makes an interest-only payment to the lender on the outstanding funds that have been advanced. A lender may collect these payments monthly or "escrow" the interest funds at the closing of the loan.

New construction can take a year or more to complete, depending on the size of the home to be constructed; therefore, some contracts may include extended rate locks. Construction loans can be profitable, but lenders regard them as risky.

Permanent Financing (Take-Out Loan)

When construction is complete, the appraiser verifies that plans and specifications have been met and the original opinion of value is valid; the loan is then replaced by a permanent amortizing loan, often called a take-out loan. A **permanent loan** is *a long-term mortgage loan that "takes out" the interim or construction loan and replaces it with permanent financing, such as a conventional or government-insured loan.*

Subprime Loans

A mortgage loan extended to a borrower who has experienced some form of credit trauma (or currently cannot verify income to repay the loan), thus increasing the risk of the loan, may be considered a **subprime loan**. A subprime mortgage loan does not conform to secondary market standards and, thus, is not considered a prime loan.

These types of loans became popular in the 1990s until the mortgage meltdown of 2008-2009. Borrowers who did not meet the guidelines of the local bank or conform to the government-regulated secondary markets turned to subprime lending as a method of meeting their financial difficulties or goals. Borrowers were willing to accept a mortgage loan with a higher interest rate or other toxic features (as defined by the Qualified Mortgage regulation) in exchange for the lender making a loan that contained a higher amount of risk. Many of the lenders that offered subprime loans were forced into insolvency when the default ratios for these types of loans skyrocketed.

The Characteristics of a Subprime Loan

A basic characteristic of a subprime loan is the allowance for increased risk factors when compared with a standard conventional loan. Subprime loans possess one or more of the following features:

1) High interest rates

2) High debt-to-income ratios

3) Low down payment requirements

4) Little or no verification of ability to repay the mortgage debt

5) Excessive loan fees

6) Lower FICO® scores allowed

7) Hybrid loan features such as a lower initial interest rate for a short time (recall from the ARM section of this chapter that a hybrid ARM can be shown as a 5/1 ARM, with the "5" denoting the initial fixed period of interest and the "1" denoting the subsequent adjustment period.

Interest Rate Components

Leading up to the 2007-2008 mortgage crisis, the cost of a subprime loan was driven primarily by the collateral value, the borrower's equity, and the credit score of the borrower to assess the risk associated with the loan. Today, the borrower's ability to repay the debt is a predominant factor in most subprime loans.

Underwriting Standards

The Interagency Guidance on Nontraditional Mortgage Product Risks indicates that mortgage loan underwriting standards should address the effect of a substantial payment increase on the borrower's capacity to repay a nontraditional mortgage loan when amortization begins.

When *an underwriter identifies more than one risk factor associated with the mortgage loan*, this is referred to as **layering of risk**, including:

- Interest-only loans where no principal payment reduction is made
- **Negative amortization loans** where *the monthly payment made is insufficient to pay the entire amount of interest due*
- ARMs with a short introductory interest rate period
- Low FICO® scores
- Payment delinquencies
- Charge-offs, bankruptcies, foreclosures, or judgments
- Reduced documentation loans
- High loan-to-value
- Secondary financing, which reduces the borrower's equity or down payment
- High debt-to-income ratios
- Lack of employment or job stability
- Significant increase in the borrower's current housing expense in relation to the proposed housing expense

The presence of these, among other, risk factors in a loan raise a red flag and should motivate the underwriter to use caution in considering the loan. When risk factors (or multiple risk factors) are present, compensating factors should be present to offset the risk. **Compensating factors** are *factors that add strength to a mortgage loan file*; i.e., significant down payment, low debt-to-income ratios, low payment shock, etc.

Today's Subprime Loans

Subprime loans are re-emerging as an alternative loan product in today's market, though with a new look and new requirements. The average credit score in the U.S. is 691, yet many consumers still struggle to own a home. Many homeowners who experienced financial trauma in the past due to their credit reports or household income are returning to the market to purchase homes, but still have credit scores in the lower brackets. These "boomerang buyers" still may not meet the criteria for a prime loan, but have sizeable assets for a large down payment towards a property. A subprime loan that is more forgiving of credit situations may provide a suitable resource for the financing of their "boomerang" home.

Subprime lenders are again entering the lending arena but with a different manner of making mortgage loans than what was previously offered. Today's subprime lender:

- Must comply with a variety of laws, including HOEPA (high cost loan) provisions, Qualified Mortgage requirements, and a verification of each borrower's ability to repay (for owner-occupied properties) the mortgage loan they are seeking.

- Must assume a more responsible attitude about the borrower's loan than what was experienced in the past. Lenders, through the implementation of Dodd-Frank, are exercising greater caution in the borrower's loan qualification and have a higher regard for the stability of the loan outcome.

There continues to be a strong market for these loans, despite the greater regulations imposed. Of course, no one can predict the occurrence of life's challenges, but the subprime secondary market can have confidence that today's subprime loans provide greater stability for their investment portfolio and greater protections for the consumer.

Balloon Mortgage Loans

A **balloon mortgage loan**, also known as a partially-amortizing loan, *calls for periodic payments of principal and interest during the loan term with a balloon payment at the end of the term to pay off the balance due.* For example, a balloon loan could be expressed as "360/120".

- The "360" states the term of the loan, such as 360 months.
- The "120" provides the month of the loan that the full payment, or balloon payment, is due.

Home equity loans are often expressed as 30/15, which denotes a 30-year loan term with a balloon payment requirement in 15 years. Balloon mortgage loans were often used in subprime and home equity loans.

Home Equity Loans

A **home equity loan** or **home equity line of credit (HELOC)** is a loan *secured by a mortgage on one's principal residence.*

- A home equity loan is typically a **closed-end** loan that offers a fixed amount of money that can be repaid with regular payments over a fixed term.

- A home equity line of credit is a type of **open-end** loan in which a borrower is granted a specific credit limit from which he can draw and pay back principal only as it is used. As the balance is paid down, the principal is available to be used again.

- HELOCs usually have two phases: A draw period during which borrowers commonly pay interest-only, and a repayment period during which payments are generally amortized.

Usually, these financing vehicles attach a junior mortgage to the property.

Reverse Mortgages

Another type of nontraditional mortgage is the **reverse mortgage**. The purpose of a reverse mortgage is to *provide a vehicle for a borrower who has substantial equity in a property to convert that accumulated equity—at a cost—to cash and additional debt without selling the property and without making payments to the lender.* Seniors can use the equity in their home for any use, including, but not limited to start a small business, pay off credit card debt, health care, home repairs and upkeep, dream vacation, and/or to maintain a lifestyle that is otherwise unaffordable. A reverse mortgage may also be called a reverse equity mortgage or a reverse annuity mortgage. The most popular reverse mortgage program is FHA's **Home Equity Conversion Mortgage** or HECM.

Many mortgage loans that are made today are "forward" or amortizing mortgage loans, where the loan balance falls and the equity increases. With a typical reverse mortgage, the balance of the loan rises as the borrower receives money from the lender and incurs interest to the outstanding loan balance. Since the borrower is not making any payments, by the time a reverse mortgage becomes due, the borrower may have a high loan balance and little to no, or even negative equity. For most reverse mortgages, the amount owed grows and the equity shrinks, which creates a "rising debt, falling equity" scenario.

Eligibility Requirements

Reverse mortgages have some very specific requirements that address the borrower's ability and willingness to continue to pay property charges (property taxes and hazard/flood insurance), and some less stringent requirements that make the qualification for a Home Equity Conversion Mortgage more flexible than conventional or government-insured loans.

HUD Guidelines for Initial Funds Disbursement to a Borrower

HUD initial disbursement guidelines for today's HECM insurance program include:

1. Implementation of a maximum disbursement of either 60% of the principal limit (total proceeds available at loan closing) or the sum of the mandatory obligations (closing costs, mortgage insurance, etc.) plus 10% of the principal limit to the borrower.

For Example

If the principal limit for a HECM is $100,000, a borrower in the first twelve months of the loan may receive the greater of:

- $60,000, or
- The sum of the payoff amount, the mandatory obligations, mortgage insurance, and $10,000.

2. For fixed-interest rate HECM's, with case numbers issued after June 25, 2014, HUD will only insure fixed-rate, single lump sum disbursements that do not provide for future draws by the mortgagor under any circumstances. The HECM borrower continues to be responsible for the payment of taxes and insurance while the HECM loan is outstanding. If the mortgagor fails to pay the property charges, the mortgagee must seek remedies according to Mortgagee Letter 2011-01.

3. Mortgage insurance is charged by HUD on all mortgage loans. Mortgagee Letter 2017-12, effective for all HECM loans originated on or after October 2, 2017 set the mortgage insurance fees as follows:

- **Two percent (2.0%)** Up-front mortgage insurance fee of the Maximum Claim Amount, and

- **One-half of one percent (0.50%)** of the outstanding mortgage balance.

4. Tax and hazard insurance defaults by mortgagors require a heightened need for a financial assessment of a potential mortgagor's financial capacity and willingness to comply with mortgage provisions.

Mortgagees must complete a financial assessment of each prospective mortgagor *prior to loan approval and loan closing*. The purpose of the financial assessment is to evaluate the mortgagor's willingness and capacity to meet his financial obligations and his ability to comply with the mortgage requirements. The financial assessment is also used to determine whether, and under what conditions, the prospective mortgagor meets FHA eligibility criteria.

If a borrower does **not** meet the credit history and cash flow/residual income requirements of the new guidelines, he will be required to allow the lender/servicer to impound from the tenure payments or the line of credit (LOC) an amount equal to the actual cost of property insurance and hazard insurance.

[For more specific information regarding the Home Equity Conversion Mortgage guidelines, review Mortgage Letters 2013-27, 28, & 33, http://portal.hud.gov/hudportal/HUD under "Resources" tab.]

Effective with case numbers assigned on or after March 2, 2015, a Life Expectancy Set-Aside for the payment of property taxes, including special assessments levied by municipalities or state law; hazard insurance premiums; and applicable flood insurance premiums, is required for certain HECMs based on the financial assessment results.

- The **Fully-Funded Life Expectancy Set-Aside** is available for both adjustable and fixed-interest-rate HECMs when required by the mortgagee based on the results of the financial assessment or if the mortgagee does not require a Life Expectancy Set-Aside and the mortgagor elects to have one.

- The **Partially-Funded Life Expectancy Set-Aside** is only available for an adjustable interest rate HECM when required by the mortgagee based on the results of the financial assessment. (Mortgagee Letter 2014-21)

Income

With a traditional mortgage, the income of the borrower is critical in determining the terms of the loan, the amount that can be borrowed, etc. A reverse mortgage, on the other hand, has no income requirements to qualify. However, the lender will consider the borrower's ability to meet continuing obligations to pay property taxes, insurance premiums, and homeowners association fees (if applicable) and to maintain the property.

Age

To qualify for a reverse mortgage, **all persons who have an ownership interest** in the security property must be **at least 62 years of age**. If one of the owners does *not* satisfy this age requirement, one way to secure a reverse mortgage loan on the property is for the younger owner to relinquish all ownership interests in the property. This strategy, while solving the age requirement issue, could create other issues related to ownership and survivorship and so should be taken with caution.

There is a second method used to secure a reverse mortgage when one spouse does not meet the minimum age requirement that has been implemented by HUD that is detailed below.

Successors in Interest to the Property of a Deceased Borrower

Amid extensive controversy and lawsuits (Bennett v. Donovan was heard by the U.S. District Court for the District of Columbia), HUD has reversed itself, somewhat. Since HECMs became available with mortgage insurance provided by HUD in 1989, HUD has enforced the guideline that required a home be sold and the reverse mortgage be paid if the borrower(s) were not able to occupy the secured home for twelve continuous months. Spouses who did not meet the criteria for qualifying for a HECM or chose not to be on the loan were required to comply with the terms of the note signed by the borrower, including the provision that the property is sold to satisfy the outstanding reverse mortgage balance. Many times, qualifying for a new mortgage to purchase the property often proved difficult for these surviving spouses and they were unable to remain in the home.

Mortgagee Letter 2014-07 outlined a new interpretation of the guideline and implemented a provision to allow non-borrowing spouses to remain in the secured home after the death of the obligors to the reverse mortgage if HUD's requirements were met.

- If the mortgage was issued **before August 4, 2014**, the current rules continue to apply, which state that when the borrowing spouse dies or permanently vacates the home for twelve months or more, *the loan must be paid in full.*

- Reverse mortgage loans issued **after August 4, 2014** must contain a statement that *extends the deferral date of the due and payable status* that occurs because of the death of the last surviving mortgagor if a mortgagor was married at the time of closing. To retain occupancy of the home, the non-borrowing spouse must be identified at the time of closing and must be married to the mortgagor at the time of their death.

To *defer the due and payable status of the HECM*, the non-borrowing spouse must:

1. Have been the spouse of a HECM mortgagor at the time of closing and have remained the spouse of the mortgagor for the duration of the HECM mortgagor's lifetime.

2. Have properly disclosed to the mortgagee at the origination and is specially named as a non-borrowing spouse in the HECM documents.

3. Have occupied and continue to occupy the property securing the HECM as the principal residence of the non-borrowing spouse.

If a surviving non-borrowing spouse *fails to comply with the provisions of the deferral* of the due and payable clause:

- The HECM will become immediately due and payable. The mortgagee is not required to obtain approval from HUD at the end of the deferral period to call a loan due and payable.

- The lender may not require immediate payment in full until the end of the deferral period.

- The mortgagor continues to maintain the ability to sell the property for at least the lesser of the sale price or appraised value. The estate always maintains the right to dispose of the property if legally entitled to.

While the loan may be in deferral, the HECM is *not assumable*. Because the loan is not assumable, no proceeds may be disbursed to the non-borrowing spouse. If a Set-Aside for

Repairs was part of the provisions of the HECM loan, those escrowed funds can be disbursed per the terms and conditions of the loan.

If the HECM *mortgagor predeceases the identified non-borrowing spouse and desires to continue to occupy the home*, he must continue to satisfy the following conditions:

1. Establish legal ownership to the secured property within ninety days of the death of the mortgagor

2. Ensure all other conditions contained in the loan documents continue to be satisfied (payment of property taxes, maintaining property insurance, etc.)

3. Ensure that the HECM does not become eligible to be called due and payable for any other reason.

Mortgage Letter 2014-07 further defines the terms of the HECM that must continue to be met by the mortgagor's estate or the non-borrowing spouse, including the following;

1. The note will continue to accrue interest per the terms of the mortgage and loan agreement.

2. The monthly MIP must continue to be paid to HUD by the mortgagee.

3. The mortgagee may continue to collect servicing fees per the terms of the mortgage agreement.

4. The only future disbursements under the agreement may be for Repair Set-Aside that was a part of the original mortgage documents.

To *qualify for the deferral period* after the death of the mortgagor, at the time of application:

- The mortgagor and the non-borrowing spouse must state whether they are legally married and confirm the information at loan closing.

- The MLO must obtain and verify the name and age of any non-borrowing spouse. Non-borrowing spouses do not have to be 62 years of age or older for a qualified mortgagor to obtain a HECM loan.

Lenders are *not required to verify the marital status* of the mortgagor and non-borrowing spouse during the loan process, however:

- Both parties must sign a certification at loan closing verifying the truth and accuracy of the information provided in the application with respect to the mortgagor's marital status.

- Mortgagors who hold themselves out to be married with a non-borrowing spouse must submit a certification annually to the mortgagee.

After the death of the last surviving mortgagor, the mortgagee must obtain the Non-Borrowing Spouse certification within 30 days of receiving notice of the last surviving mortgagor's death and then every year thereafter.

In the event of a divorce between the parties during the term of the reverse mortgage, a mortgagee should obtain a copy of the divorce decree. If the parties are divorced at the time of the mortgagor's death, the protections of the deferral period are no longer available to the non-borrowing spouse.

A married couple seeking a HECM, *with one spouse choosing **not** to be a borrower on the loan*, should follow these guidelines to remain in the home after the principal borrower is no longer residing in the home:

1. Inform the lender that the couple is legally married, make sure the lender confirms the marriage, and file the required forms with HUD annually

2. Remain married to guard your interest in the home

3. Review the loan documents to make sure the non-borrowing spouse is named in the mortgage papers

4. Pay the property taxes and hazard insurance when due to preserve the deferral period for the surviving spouse

5. Continue to occupy the home as a primary residence

6. When the borrowing spouse ceases to be an owner occupant, file the appropriate paperwork to establish legal ownership within 90 days of their departure

Borrowers should always be advised to seek legal advice on such issues.

Eligible Properties

Although the specific type of reverse mortgage may impose different standards, in general, single-family, one-unit dwellings are considered eligible properties for a reverse mortgage. Depending on the program, condominiums, planned unit developments (PUDs), and manufactured homes may be acceptable. Mobile home and cooperative units are **not** generally eligible, although HUD may approve some types of mobile homes.

Insurance

Note that, as with a traditional mortgage, the lender will require that the borrower maintains a **homeowner's insurance** policy that is sufficient to cover the replacement value of the collateral property. This protects the lender's interest in the event of damage that causes a loss of value, such as a fire, tornado, etc.

The lender may also require a separate flood insurance policy.

Since borrowers obtaining a reverse mortgage may have had the same insurance policy in place for years, they are urged to review the policy to ensure that the insurance in place provides adequate coverage.

Ownership

To be eligible for a reverse mortgage, *the home must be the principal residence* and any debt on the home should be paid off. A borrower is not necessarily prevented from getting a reverse mortgage if there is debt on the home since funds from the reverse mortgage may be used to pay off any remaining debt on the home, but the reverse mortgage created must be a first lien.

Meeting with a Counselor

HECM programs impose an additional condition on prospective borrowers by requiring them to participate in a consumer counseling session given by an approved counselor *before* they can apply for the loan. The counselor will explain the costs of the loan and the financial implications as well as provide guidance and advice in selecting a program and/or a lender. **A lender cannot submit an application for an FHA-insured reverse mortgage until the applicant provides proof that the required counseling session occurred.**

This unbiased, independent counselor can help guide the borrower through what can be a confusing process and many difficult decisions. Moreover, at the end of the session, the counselor must provide any required **certification of counseling**. A counselor may even point the homeowner to other programs or assistance that might be a better solution than a reverse mortgage.

In the event of a non-borrowing spouse, counselors are required to:

- Discuss the implications of marital status in states that recognize common law marriage.
- Inform prospective borrowers and non-borrowing spouses about the requirement that a non-borrowing spouse obtain ownership of the property or other legal right to remain upon the death of the last surviving mortgagor.
- Explain that failure to obtain ownership or other legal right to remain in the property will result in the HECM becoming due and payable and no deferral will be issued.

For Your Development

For more information about counseling support and guidance through the mortgage loan process, see the HUD Mortgagee Letters: http://portal.hud.gov/hudportal/HUD?src=/program_offices/administration/hudclips/letters/mortgagee.

Amount Available with a Reverse Mortgage

Many factors determine how much money a homeowner can receive with a reverse mortgage.

- A required appraisal will determine the value of the home, which determines the maximum claim amount, subject to the established lending limits. The more the home is worth, the more cash that can be borrowed with the reverse mortgage.
- Other factors that could impact the amount of money available include the amount of equity that has been built up, the payment options, the interest rates, the program costs, and/or loan financing fees.
- The specific program selected has much to do with determining the impact of these factors. For example, since the FHA's HECM is the major reverse mortgage product, the location of the home is critical, as that will determine the FHA's lending limits. HUD sets a nationwide maximum amount for reverse mortgages annually when forward mortgage limits are defined. The nationwide maximum loan amount for a reverse mortgage is **$636,150**.

Age of the Homeowner

Another important factor that figures into the determination of the amount of money available is the **age** of the homeowner. Typically, an older homeowner would have a higher dollar amount available with a reverse mortgage than a younger homeowner since an older person has a shorter life expectancy and, therefore, the loan would be for a shorter term.

In the event of a non-borrowing spouse who has made full disclosure and is part of the closing, *the lowest age of the borrower or the non-borrowing spouse* will be considered for establishing the maximum claim amount.

Exercise 6.7: Knowledge Check

A property homeowner must be at least 65 years old to qualify for a reverse mortgage.

A. true
B. false

Payment Options

The homeowner who takes out a reverse mortgage generally gets to decide how to receive the money. The payment options include:

- **Fixed monthly payments** for *as long as the homeowner remains in the home*; also called "tenure"
- A **lump sum** payment upfront
- A **fixed monthly payment** for *a certain term* during the lifetime of the borrower
- A **line of credit** that allows the homeowner to have access to funds on an "as-needed" basis

A homeowner may also choose to receive some **combination** of these options. However, the payment option that a homeowner chooses could affect the amount of cash he may be eligible to receive from the loan.

Tax Implications

For the most part, the funds paid out with a reverse mortgage are not considered income by the IRS, so they are not taxed. Unlike a typical mortgage, the interest the lender charges on the reverse mortgage can be deducted *only* at the conclusion of the loan when the loan principal and the interest are repaid. There are exceptions.

Although the funds paid out from a reverse mortgage are *generally* tax-free, homeowners should get advice from a qualified reverse mortgage counselor and/or attorney to determine whether the income received could in any way affect their eligibility for any needs-based public assistance benefits such as Medicaid or Supplemental Social Security.

Repayment

Assuming the borrower upholds the terms of the contract, a typical reverse mortgage becomes due when the last surviving borrower:

- Dies.
- Sells the home.
- Ceases to live in the home for 12 consecutive months.

At that point, the homeowner, or the homeowner's heirs, must repay the total loan amount, which includes the money that was paid out as well as any interest, insurance, closing costs, or other fees as stipulated in the terms of the loan.

Of course, it is often the case that the proceeds from the sale of the home are used to repay the reverse mortgage. Any remaining equity belongs to the estate (in the event of death) or the homeowner (if they sold the home or moved).

Non-Recourse Loans

Generally, a lender cannot force a borrower out of her home during the life of the loan, nor can the lender simply sell the home when a reverse mortgage comes due. Usually, the lender will allow up to 12 months for payment in the event of death. If the home is not sold or is not deeded to the lender, a formal foreclosure process may be started in the county where the home is located, depending on the terms of the note.

A reverse mortgage is considered a "non-recourse" loan, so even in the rare instance that the amount of money distributed over the life of the reverse mortgage exceeds the value of the home, the borrower or the borrower's heirs *cannot owe more than fair market sale price of the home, minus reasonable sales expenses.* The lender has no claims on any other assets that may be held by the borrower or the borrower's heirs.

Accelerating Repayment

As with any mortgage situation, there are some circumstances that might cause the lender to require immediate repayment; for example:

- The homeowner fails to make necessary repairs to the property.
- The property is condemned.
- The homeowner does not pay the mandatory property taxes.
- The homeowner ceases to pay the appropriate homeowner's insurance premiums.
- A government entity claims eminent domain over the property.
- The borrower ceases to live in the property, or it is discovered the property is no longer the borrower's principal residence.

Seller Financing

This section presents a brief overview of seller financing and some other forms of creative financing in use today. While the types of transactions discussed here do *not* require the services of a licensed MLO, an awareness of these financing options can be beneficial for the well-rounded MLO.

The continuing implementation of the Dodd-Frank Act rules on owner-occupied housing has been expanded to include owner financing. With the broad interpretation of the term "mortgage originator," there is an *exemption for property owners who provide financing in connection with the sale of a dwelling.* This exemption does not require the seller (also the financer) to be a licensed MLO, even though negotiation of mortgage rates and terms are involved in the sale negotiations. [For information, see 12 CFR Subpart E, §1026.36, (a)(4) *Seller financers; three properties.* and (a)(5) *Seller financers; one property.*]

Seller Financing Overview

Seller financing is *when a seller extends credit to a buyer to finance the purchase of the property.* This can be instead of, or in addition to, the buyer obtaining a loan from a third party, such as an institutional lender. A seller may help with financing for several reasons; for example, the buyer:

- May be unable to afford the cash necessary for the required down payment for a conventional mortgage.
- May want to take advantage of the low interest rate on the seller's existing mortgage.
- Is not able to qualify for a loan from a lender for various reasons.

Purchase Money Mortgage

The term **purchase money mortgage** may be used to describe a *mortgage given by the buyer to the seller for the purchase of real estate.* This is also referred to as a **seller-held mortgage.** The central advantage of this arrangement is that sellers are not bound by institutional policies regarding loan ratios, interest rates, or qualifying standards.

Assumption

The **assumption** of a loan means *one party agrees to take over payments of another party's debt, with terms of the note staying unchanged.* FHA and VA loans permit assumptions (with a credit check of buyers); some conventional mortgages also allow assumptions because they don't have an enforceable alienation clause (borrowers should always consult the original lender or a lawyer.) The property remains security for the loan, but the buyer becomes primarily liable for repayment.

In the event of foreclosure, the lender may still have recourse against the original party (seller) if the debt isn't fully satisfied. To be relieved of liability, the seller must get a **release**, which is *a document in which a legal right is given up,* from the lender. Here, the lender accepts the buyer as the new mortgagor and releases the seller from all mortgage obligations.

Seller-Sponsored Wraparound Financing

In **seller-sponsored wraparound financing**, *the seller retains an existing loan on the property while giving the buyer a second loan.* This new total loan is treated as one obligation by the buyer, who makes one payment to the seller for the entire (combined) debt. The seller, in turn, pays the original mortgage lender and keeps the excess.

Seller Financing Rules

[See Mortgage Reform and Anti-Predatory Lending Act (Public Law 111-203), Title XIV, §1401(2)(E).]

Seller financing regulations address the loan(s) created by a seller providing financing to a buyer. Two different guidelines were implemented for seller carrybacks, separated by the number of sold and seller-financed properties during the preceding 12 months.

Guidelines for Three-or-Less Seller-Financed Properties in Preceding 12 Months

A seller who provides financing for the sale of *three or fewer properties in any 12-month period* to purchasers of these properties, each of which is owned by the seller and serves as security for the financing, must meet both guidelines:

1. The seller has **not** constructed, or acted as a contractor for the construction of, a residence on the property in the ordinary course of business.

2. The seller financing must meet the following requirements:

   - The financing is fully amortizing.

   - The financing is determined that, in good faith, the consumer has a reasonable ability to repay.

   - The financing has a fixed rate or an adjustable rate that is adjustable after five or more years (5/1 Hybrid ARM), subject to reasonable annual and lifetime limitations on interest rate increases. If the financing agreement has an adjustable rate, the rate is determined by the addition of a margin to an index rate and is subject to reasonable rate adjustment limitations. The index the adjustable rate is based on is a widely available index, such as indices for U.S. Treasury securities or LIBOR.

[See §1401(2)(E)(i)/(ii)/(iii)/(iv)/(v)]

A seller who provides financing for the sale of *one property in any 12-month period* is subject to the following criteria:

1. The natural person, estate, or trust provides seller financing for the sale of only one property in any 12-month period to purchasers of such property, which is owned by the natural person, estate, or trust and serves as security for the financing.

2. The natural person, estate, or trust has *not* constructed, or acted as a contractor for the construction of, a residence on the property in the ordinary course of business of the person.

3. The natural person, estate, or trust provides seller financing that meets the following requirements:

   • The financing has a repayment schedule that does not result in negative amortization.

   • The financing has a fixed rate or an adjustable rate that is adjustable after five or more years (5/1 Hybrid ARM), subject to reasonable annual and lifetime limitations on interest rate increases. If the financing agreement has an adjustable rate, the rate is determined by the addition of a margin to an index rate and is subject to reasonable rate adjustment limitations. The index the adjustable rate is based on is a widely available index, such as indices for U.S. Treasury securities or LIBOR.

Any deviation from these guidelines gives the buyer a *three-year right of rescission* to rescind the sale and demand all the funds paid to be returned.

Any seller financing that *exceeds the three financed properties per year* guideline will require the seller to use an MLO to qualify the buyer of the financed property.

 This section applies to closed-end consumer credit transactions secured by a consumer's principal dwelling.

Alienation Clause

It is imperative that anyone considering any form of seller financing confirm whether any existing mortgage has an **alienation clause**. This clause, sometimes called a **due-on-sale clause**, gives the lender the *right to exercise certain rights upon transfer of the property*. Most alienation clauses are worded so that the borrower's transfer of *any ownership interest* in the property securing the loan without the lender's knowledge or consent would be a **default** under the mortgage. So, for example, the clause would be triggered by the transfer of title or even by transfer of a significant interest in the property, such as with a long-term lease.

Land Contracts

Land contracts are another instrument used to finance the purchase of real estate. A **land contract** is a *real estate installment agreement where the buyer makes payments to the seller in exchange for the right to occupy and use the property, but no deed or title is transferred until all, or a specified portion, of the payments have been made.* Land contracts—also called land installment contracts, installment sales contracts, land sales contracts, real estate contracts, and other names—are different from mortgages or trust deeds where the debtor takes possession of the property while the creditor holds a mortgage or trust deed as a security lien against the property.

Under a land contract, the seller (**vendor**) actually *holds title to the property as security, not just a mortgage lien*. The buyer/debtor (**vendee**) has the right to possess and enjoy the land but is *not the legal owner*. The seller retains legal title to the subject property while the buyer is only an owner in fact, having possession and **equitable title** but no actual title and no deed.

Land contracts usually require the vendor to give the vendee a statement, at least once a year or as requested, showing the amount of payments that have been credited to principal and interest and the balance due under the contract.

For the vendor, the advantage of a land contract is the right to hold title as security. This lack of ownership is, conversely, the main disadvantage for a vendee, since it makes it difficult to later obtain financing based on the equity built up or for improvements, as banks are reluctant to lend to a person without actual legal title to the property.

Other Forms of Creative Financing

These financing alternatives provide additional opportunities for motivated sellers and purchasers to close a transaction.

Lease/Option

A **lease/option** is *when a seller leases property to someone for a specific term, with an option to buy the property at a predetermined price during the lease term*. The lease/option plan is comprised of two elements—a lease and an option. A **lease** is a *contract where one party pays the other rent in exchange for possession of real estate*. An **option** is a *contract giving one party the right to do something within a designated time period without obligation to do so*.

Lease/Purchase

A **lease/purchase** is *when a seller leases property to someone for a specific term, with the tenant agreeing to buy the property at a set price during or following the lease term*. The lease/purchase plan is comprised of two elements: A lease and a purchase contract.

Equity Exchanges

An **equity exchange** is *value in one property being traded for value in another property*. This is also called a tax-deferred exchange, tax-free exchange, like-kind exchange, or Section 1031 (from the section number of IRS law). To make a tax-deferred equity exchange of real estate, the properties must be like-kind property (real estate for real estate) and the properties must be held for use in a trade or business, or held by the party as an investment. When property is exchanged as part of an equity exchange, the seller defers paying taxes until a capital gain (profit) is realized from the transaction; usually, this means when the property is sold in the future. If the transaction does qualify for tax-free exchange treatment, any gain that is purely a result of the exchange is deferred. **Professional tax advice and legal counsel should always be consulted for any deal involving equity exchanges or tax deferral.**

Homebuyer Assistance Programs

Homebuyer assistance programs can include down payment assistance programs (sometimes referred to collectively as DAP programs), subsidized mortgage interest rates, help with closing costs, or a combination. These programs may be offered by government or non-profit organizations to promote homeownership or by lenders as part of their obligation under the Community Reinvestment Act.

These programs may be offered by cities, counties, or states and the money may be targeted to specific neighborhoods. Often a portion or all the required down payment is paid on behalf of the buyer. Money for these programs is usually limited and administered on a first-come, first-serve basis. Various bond issues or levies may replenish the funding for these programs, but it is hard to predict when money will become available. Some non-profit organizations also provide grants, gifts, or otherwise arrange money for down payment assistance.

Interest rate subsidies may also be obtained from a variety of sources. Bond money is available from time to time, whereby the state issues bonds and uses the funds to subsidize the interest rate paid on mortgages by low-income families. Underwriting requirements may be the same as for FHA loans, but the interest rate is lower than an FHA loan because of the subsidy. Some such programs may even offer both down payment assistance and interest rate subsidies through various agencies.

Chapter Summary

1. Nontraditional mortgage products are defined by the SAFE Act as anything *other than* 30-year fixed rate loans. The Interagency Guidance on Nontraditional Mortgage Product Risks defines nontraditional mortgage products as mortgage products that allow borrowers to defer principal and, sometimes, interest.

2. Buydowns are additional money (discount points) paid to the lender at the start of a loan to lower the interest rate and payments. Discount points are paid to the lender to make up the difference between the market interest rate and the rate a borrower gets in the note. A permanent buydown (for the life of a loan) has a reduced rate stated in the note. A temporary buydown (early in a loan) can be level payment or graduated payment. With buydowns, the lowest rate a buyer can qualify for is 2% below market rate. The FHA requires buyers to qualify at the note rate, not the buydown rate. Fannie Mae, Freddie Mac, and the FHA limit points and other IPCs that can be paid.

3. ARMs have interest rates that may adjust up or down, according to the terms of the note. Borrowers select an index (statistical report reflecting the cost of money), lenders add a margin (spread), and this is the fully indexed rate paid on the loan. Caps keep loans from growing out of control. Conversion options allow buyers to convert to a fixed rate. MLOs must provide the CHARM booklet to borrowers in addition to other mandated disclosures, including the APR. For ARMs, the APR is a composite rate that reflects a lower rate for a certain number of years and a higher rate for later years. Lenders cannot disclose only initial low rates.

4. A construction mortgage is a temporary loan used to finance the construction of improvements and buildings on the land. Three common disbursement plans are the fixed disbursement plan, voucher system, and warrant system.

5. Proceeds from a reverse mortgage may be disbursed to eligible borrowers aged 62 or older as a monthly payment, a lump sum of cash, or a line of credit, based on the equity in their homes. Among the events that trigger loan repayment is when the borrower dies, moves out of the house for 12 consecutive months, or sells the house.

6. A HECM is a reverse mortgage insured by the FHA. A reverse mortgage borrower may only draw 60% of the principal limit (or 10% above the principal limit plus mandatory obligations and payoffs) as determined by many factors, including appraised value, the age of borrowers, type of payment received, etc.

7. Up-front mortgage insurance for HECMs is 2% of the maximum claim amount (MCA). The annual MIP is now 0.5% of outstanding balance.

8. A reverse mortgage borrower must pay for the property charges (such as the property taxes, property insurance, and HOA fees). A senior borrower must meet the requirements of the HECM Financial Assessment and Property Charge Guide. If he fails to meet the guidelines, the mortgagee is required to "set aside" funds for property charges.

9. A HECM requires a borrower analysis to determine if property taxes and insurance should be required in an escrow account. Mortgage insurance is determined by the percentage of the maximum claim amount taken by the borrower at the initial disbursement at closing.

10. If a borrower is married at the time of the HECM application and the spouse will not be on the reverse loan, she is known as a non-borrowing spouse. HUD allows this spouse to remain in the home after the borrower can no longer occupy the home as a primary residence if the non-borrowing spouse adheres to certain requirements. While the non-borrowing spouse continues to live in the home; interest continues to accrue, monthly MIP is required to be paid to HUD by the servicer, and any future disbursements cease to be paid.

11. Subprime loans (B-C loans, low-doc, SISA, NINA) have more risk than what is allowed by the conventional market. Borrower risk factors determine the interest rate and terms. A-minus loans are riskier than prime loans but less risky than subprime loans.

12. Seller financing is when the seller extends credit to a buyer to finance the purchase of property. A seller can extend all or partial credit. This can help a buyer who doesn't have enough cash to buy a property, who can't qualify for a conventional loan, or who wants or needs a lower-than-market interest rate. The seller gets the benefit of a home that's easier to sell and often a better price by offering terms. A purchase money mortgage or seller-held mortgage is given by a buyer to a seller to secure part or all the money borrowed to purchase the property. Unencumbered property with no liens is best for this transaction; encumbered property with liens needs assumption or wraparound. Assumption has the buyer take responsibility for the mortgage, but the seller must get a release from the lender. A seller-wraparound mortgage has the seller retain the existing mortgage (the buyer makes one larger payment; the seller pays the lender and keeps the difference).

13. The CFPB regulates seller financing of owner-occupied homes within 12 months. A seller may provide financing for one home every 12 months without verifying the borrower's ability to repay the loan.

14. A land contract is a real estate installment agreement. The buyer makes payments to the seller for the right to occupy the land, but no title is transferred until all, or part of, the payments are made. The buyer has an equitable title under a land contract. States differ in how they treat land contracts.

15. Problems for the buyer include difficulty in borrowing against equity with a land contract and protecting equity if the land contract is not recorded. A lender may consent to the deal using an estoppel letter.

16. A lease/option has the seller lease to a tenant who has the right (but no obligation) to buy the property at a set price within a certain time. An option can be used for profit, speculation, investment, comparison, or to give the optionor time to acquire cash, to qualify, or credit rent toward the purchase price. A lease/purchase combines a lease with a purchase contract. An equity exchange is property traded for value in other property. Properties must be exchanged (or delayed exchange), like kind, and held for trade, business, or investment. Capital gains tax is deferred.

17. Homebuyer assistance programs can be down payment assistance programs (DAP), subsidized mortgage interest rates, help with closing costs, or a combination. Programs can be offered by government or non-profit groups, or by lenders.

Chapter Quiz

1. **Which statement is true about interest rate buydowns on FHA loans?**

   A. A borrower may qualify at the buydown rate.

   B. A borrower must qualify at the note rate.

   C. The FHA does not allow builder-paid buydowns.

   D. The FHA does not allow seller-paid buydowns.

2. **What is the adjustable number used to compute the interest rate on an ARM?**

   A. cap

   B. index

   C. margin

   D. prepayment

3. **With an ARM, the index is added to the _____ to determine the _____.**

   A. APR/cost of funds

   B. home value/amount borrowed

   C. margin/interest rate charged

   D. qualifying ratio/maximum monthly mortgage payment

4. **Negative amortization occurs when**

   A. a borrower suffers payment shock.

   B. each mortgage payment is adjusted more frequently than a typical interest rate allows.

   C. a loan decreases in value.

   D. the payment made does not cover the interest due for that period.

5. **Subprime loans are different from conforming loans because they**

   A. allow for lower interest rates.

   B. allow for more risk.

   C. are only offered by banks.

   D. are sold in the secondary market.

6. **Which scenario BEST describes a land contract?**

   A. A buyer makes payments to the seller in exchange for the right to occupy, use, and enjoy the property, but no deed or title transfers until a specified portion of payments have been made.

   B. A buyer takes over primary liability for the loan of a seller, usually implying no change in loan terms.

   C. A seller keeps the existing loan and continues to pay on it while giving the buyer another loan.

   D. A seller leases the property with the provision that part of the rent payments be applied to the sale price if the tenant decides to purchase before the lease expires.

7. **The type of mortgage where a borrower receives a monthly check rather than making scheduled payments to a lender is known as a**

   A. budget mortgage.

   B. forward mortgage loan.

   C. fully amortizing loan.

   D. reverse mortgage.

8. **Increased risk factors for subprime loans include all of the following features EXCEPT**

   A. excessive loan fees.

   B. high-interest rates.

   C. higher FICO® scores required.

   D. low down payment requirements.

Federal Financial Disclosure Laws

Federal financial disclosure laws specify a variety of disclosure requirements that must be fulfilled by MLOs and other parties involved in mortgage lending transactions and activities. This chapter provides information about many of these requirements that affect the mortgage lending industry.

This chapter reviews the rules and requirements of Regulation X (RESPA). The chapter covers Regulation Z (TILA) and related federal laws about disclosure, updates, and advertising. The chapter also reviews the Mortgage Disclosure Improvement Act and Homeowners Protection Act regulations.

After completing this chapter, you will be able to:

- Identify RESPA and the regulation on payment of kickbacks and unearned fees.
- Recognize the responsibilities of mortgage loan servicers and the documentation they must provide according to Section 10 of RESPA.
- Describe disclosure provisions of federal laws related to mortgage lending.
- Describe the disclosures implemented by Regulation Z: The Loan Estimate and the Closing Disclosure.

KEY TERMS

Appraisal Management Company
Assets
Closing
Debt
Finance Charge
Liabilities
Mortgage Servicer

Referral
Rescind
Residential Mortgage
Servicing
Single-Family Dwelling
Thing of Value

Real Estate Settlement Procedures Act (RESPA) – Regulation X

[For more information, see http://www.ecfr.gov]

The Real Estate Settlement Procedures Act of 1974 (RESPA) became effective on June 20, 1975. The U.S. Department of Housing and Urban Development (HUD) promulgated Regulation X [see 12 CFR Part 1024], which is now implemented by the Consumer Financial Protection Bureau (CFPB). The purpose of RESPA is to help consumers become better shoppers for settlement services and to eliminate unnecessary increases in the costs of certain settlement services due to kickbacks and referral fees.

There are four sections to RESPA that impact and guide the mortgage industry in protecting borrowers from abuses.

- Section 6—Protects homeowners against abuses in loan servicing

- Section 8—Prohibits kickbacks, fee-splitting, and unearned fees

- Section 9—States a seller cannot require the use of a particular title company

- Section 10—Identifies the amounts that can be charged to maintain escrow accounts

Settlement Services

Regulation X (12 CFR §1024.2) defines **settlement services** as *any service provided in connection with a prospective or actual settlement*, including, but not limited to, any one or more of the following:

- Origination of a federally-related mortgage loan (including, but not limited to, the taking of loan applications, loan processing, and the underwriting and funding of such loans)

- Services by a mortgage broker (including counseling, taking of applications, obtaining verifications and appraisals, other loan processing and origination services, and communicating with the borrower and lender)

- Any services related to the origination, processing, or funding of a federally-related mortgage loan

- Title services, including title searches, title examinations, abstract preparation, insurability determinations, and the issuance of title commitments and title insurance policies

The following service providers are *not* regulated by RESPA or subject to RESPA rules,- provided they are not active in the mortgage loan origination process prior to settlement. These would be considered post-settlement service providers:

- Building/remodeling contractors

- Service and repair contractors

- Moving companies

- Landscaping companies

- Home improvement or design companies

Covered Transactions

Regulation X (12 CFR §1024.05), which addresses RESPA, applies **to any federally-related mortgage loan secured by a first or subordinate lien on a residential real property designed for one-to-four families**. The rules and regulations of RESPA apply to:

- Conventional loans.
- FHA, VA, and other government-sponsored loans.
- Purchase loans.
- Reverse mortgages.
- Assumptions.
- Refinances.
- Property improvement loans.
- Equity lines of credit.

The following types of transactions are **not** covered:

- All-cash sale
- Sale where the individual home seller takes back the mortgage
- Rental property transaction
- Temporary construction loans
- Other business purpose transaction
- Property of 25 acres or more
- Vacant or unimproved property, unless a dwelling will be constructed or moved onto the property within two years

Exercise 7.1: Knowledge Check

1. When you think about RESPA rules and regulations, all of the following fulfill the purpose of the rules and regulations EXCEPT to help consumers

   A. become better-informed borrowers.
   B. compare available options.
   C. obtain the lowest interest rate.
   D. shop for settlement services.

2. According to RESPA, all of the following are considered settlement service providers EXCEPT

   A. appraisers.
   B. attorneys who prepares loan documents.
   C. escrow agents.
   D. landscaping companies.

RESPA Mortgage Servicing Final Rules

The Regulation X final rule implements Dodd-Frank Act sections addressing servicers' obligations to correct errors asserted by mortgage loan borrowers and other duties prescribed by the Consumer Financial Protection Bureau.

Mortgage servicers received much publicity in the past during the nationwide housing decline. A **mortgage servicer** is *the company that collects monthly mortgage payments, pays taxes, insurance, and other items as they come due, and notifies the borrower of late payments*. The mortgage servicer is supposed to work with homeowners if they have trouble making their mortgage payments.

There have been numerous settlements paid by the nation's largest mortgage servicers to individuals and states in connection with the servicing of mortgage loans. Accusations of excessive foreclosure or modification fees, foreclosing without the proper paperwork, or failing to help people stay in their homes were leveled at mortgage servicers. The amendments to Regulations X and Z by the Consumer Financial Protection Bureau were made to alleviate these practices by mortgage servicers.

Kickbacks, Fee-Splitting, and Unearned Fees

Section 8 of the Real Estate Settlement and Procedures Act (12 U.S.C. 2607*):*

- Prohibits giving or accepting a fee, kickback, or any thing of value in exchange for referrals of settlement service business involving a federally-related mortgage loan (allows an item **of minimal value** used for promotional purposes, such as pens, mementos, coffee cups, hats, etc.)

- According to Regulation X, a **referral** is *any oral or written action directed to a person, which has the effect of affirmatively influencing the selection by any person of a provider of a settlement service or business.* [See 12 CFR Part 1024, Subpart B, §1024.14 Prohibition against kickbacks and unearned fees.]

- Defines prohibited **thing of value** to include, without limitation, monies, things, discounts, salaries, commissions, fees, duplicate payments of a charge, stock, dividends, distributions of partnership profits, franchise royalties, credits representing monies that may be paid at a future date, the opportunity to participate in a money-making program, retained or increased earnings, increased equity in a parent or subsidiary entity, special bank deposits or accounts, special or unusual banking terms, services of all types at special or free rates, sales or rentals at special prices or rates, lease or rental payments based in whole or in part on the amount of business referred, trips and payment of another person's expenses, or reduction in credit against an existing obligation

- Prohibits fee-splitting and receiving unearned fees or a percentage of any charge made or received for services not actually performed

- Prohibits a "required use" of specific settlement service providers, except in cases where a lender refers a borrower to an attorney, credit reporting agency, or real estate appraiser to represent the lender's interest in the transaction

- Does **not** prohibit the payment of fees to attorneys, title companies, or agents for service actually performed, the payment of a bona fide salary or compensation to a person for goods or products actually furnished or services actually performed in the making of a loan, and payments pursuant to cooperative brokerage and referral arrangements or agreements between real estate agents and brokers

- Allows legitimate discounts on services to consumers if a combination of settlement services is offered at a total price lower than the sum of the individual settlement services, as long as:

  - The use of any such combination is optional to the purchaser, and

  - The lower price for the combination is not made up by higher costs elsewhere in the settlement process

- Subjects violators to criminal and civil penalties, including:

  - Fines up to $10,000

  - Imprisonment up to one year

  - Liability up to three times the amount of the charge paid for the service (civil lawsuit)

Under RESPA, a referring party (such as a lender) may **not** accept any thing of value from a settlement service provider (such as a title agency or credit agency) in exchange for referrals of settlement business.

What exactly does any "thing of value" include? The term is very broad in its interpretation and includes any payment, advance, fund, loan, service, or other consideration offered in exchange for business referrals.

Case Study:
Consent Order for Prospect Mortgage and the CFPB

Directions: In this discussion activity, you will apply your knowledge of the Real Estate and Settlement Procedures Act (RESPA) relating to Section 8, which addresses kickbacks in exchange for referrals of future business.

Review the summary below of the Consent Order between Prospect Mortgage and the Consumer Financial Protection Bureau, which was filed on January 30, 2017.

Note: The full case is located in *Administrative Proceeding File No. 2017-CFPB-0006* and can be reviewed at https://www.consumerfinance.gov/policy-compliance/enforcement/actions/prospect-mortgage-llc/ . The author chose significant portions of the twenty-six-page consent order that are relevant for the understanding of RESPA's prohibition of kickbacks for referrals.

Description

Prospect Mortgage, LLC.'s marketing services agreements, lead agreements, desk license agreements, and co-marketing arrangements with real estate brokers and servicers were reviewed by the Consumer Financial Privacy Bureau, which identified the following violations:

1. Prospect entered into hundreds of such agreements that it sued to funnel payments to real estate brokers and others in exchange for mortgage referrals.

2. Prospect's partners to these agreements then took various steps to steer consumers to Prospect, often with Prospect's encouragement. For example, some of Prospect's partners:

    a) Required all consumers to apply for and obtain Preapprovals with Prospect before allowing them to submit an offer on the property; (A preapproval means the initial screening process that Prospect performed for potential buyers to help establish their credit-worthiness for mortgage financing when submitting offers on real estate)

    b) Paid their agents cash or a cash equivalent bonus, each time the agent steered a consumer to Prospect;

    c) Selectively imposed economic measures to coerce consumers into using Prospect, or credits that would be given only if the consumer used Prospect; and

    d) Directly referred consumers to Prospect.

3. Prospect therefore violated Section 8(a) of the Real Estate Settlement Procedures Act's prohibition on the payment of kickbacks in exchange for referrals of federally-related mortgage loans, 12 U.S.C. § 2607(a), and its implement regulation, Regulation X, 12 C.F.R. part 1024 (collectively RESPA.

Selected Background Findings and Conclusions

6. Buying a house is one of the most significant financial transactions in a typical consumer's life. Many consumers rely on real estate agents to guide them through this process.

9. Brokers and agents often make recommendations to their clients for various services, such as mortgage lending, title insurance, or home inspections. In part to prevent exploitation of consumers" reliance on their brokers or ages in this respect, RESPA Section 8(a) prohibits making payments or giving kickbacks to anyone, including real estate brokers and agents, in return for referring consumers to particular real estate settlement service providers. 12 U.S.C. § 2607(a).

10. But despite RESPA's prohibition, Prospect paid many brokers, as well as a mortgage servicer, form mortgage origination referrals.

Findings and Conclusions Relating to Prospect's violation of RESPA's Prohibition of Paying Referral Fees

11. **Prospect entered into lead agreements with more than 200 different counterparties**. Most of these counterparties were real estate brokers.

12. Under these agreements, **Prospect paid the counterparty for each lead it received.** A lead general consisted of a prospective buyer's name, address, email address, and phone number.

13. But the counterparties who received Prospect's lead fees went well beyond simply transferring information about prospective buyers. They also actively referred prospective buyers to Prospects loan officers.

14. **Most of Prospect's lead agreements included an exclusivity provision.** This provision prohibited the counterparty from sharing the prospective buyer's information with Prospect's competitors, and discouraged the counterparty from promoting other lenders to those prospective buyers.

15. To maximize the number of leads they provide to Prospect's loan officer—and their resulting revenue streams from these agreements—**many real estate brokers provided incentives for their agents to steer buyers and sellers t**o Prospect's loan officer. Some brokers paid their agents each time the agent referred a consumer to Prospect.

16. For example, Prospect paid one broker anywhere from $25 to $500 per lead, depending on the time period and the type of lead. This typically totaled $2000--$3000 per month for this broker. The broker, in turn, passed some of the spoils on to its agents. **During the broker's monthly meetings with its agents, the broker would physically hand out $20 bills** to their agents, one for each consumer that the agent directed to one of Prospect's loan officers.

17. Another broker, Willamette Legacy, LLC, dba Keller Williams Mid-Willamette (KW Mid-Willamette), also paid a portion of Prospect's lead fees to its agents. KW Mid-Willamette received at least $145,000 in lead fess from Prospect between 2012 and 2015.

18. The agents could use the credit to offset (in whole or in part) the monthly fees they paid to affiliate with KW Mid-Willamette. **The amount KW Mid-Willamette paid to its brokers increased with the volume of referrals,** with some agents receiving more than $500 in a given month.

20. One of Prospect's regional sales managers sent an email to a broker on September 26, 2012, which include suggested language for the broker to send to its agents. The message read, in part, **"in order to promote our relationship with Prospect, the broker will pay each agent $100 for each Qualified Buyer Lead that we send to Prospect."**

Findings and Conclusions …by Using MSAs to Pay Brokers for Referrals

23. Prospect paid real estate brokers a fixed amount of money per month under these MSAs, ranging from a few hundred dollars to over $20,000 a month. In return for the monthly payments, the brokers purportedly performed marketing services for Prospect.

24. **Prospect, however, managed these MSA's to encourage referrals. Prospect based its payments on referral levels, not marketing efforts.** And Prospect tracked these referral levels as a percentage of the counterparty's overall business. Prospect labeled this figure its "capture rate" of the counterparty's business.

Findings and Conclusions…by Using Desk Licensing Agreements to Pay Brokers for Referrals.

29. **Prospect entered desk licensing agreements with more than 100 different counterparties.**

30. Under these desk licensing agreements, **Prospect paid various real estate brokers to locate its loan officers onsite with the broker.** But these agreements were not just payment for renting office space. **The broker also promised to "promote Prospect as a preferred lender"** and "endorse the use of Prospect's services to its employees, agents, and the visiting public."

32. Prospect analyzed the value of these desk licensing agreements in **terms of the number of referrals they produced per office, rather than whether they were paying market rates for the cost of renting office space in a particular area.**

33. The payments that Prospect made and that the brokers and others received for these desk licensing agreements were therefore actually, at least in part, payments for referrals.

Findings and Conclusions...to Require Buyers to Obtain Preapprovals with Prospect's Loan Officers

36. **There are numerous lenders** is each geographic area in which Prospect does business from **which any buyer may choose to seek and obtain preapproval**. There is rarely any special expertise possess by only one lender in a given area that precludes other lenders in that same area from offering equally reliable preapprovals.

37. Prospect sometimes incorporated this scheme directly into its lead agreements. For example, one lead agreement required the broker to "**educate and train" its agents on the need for consumers to seek Preapproval with Prospect**, and that the broker would only earn lead fees for those listings "in which Prospect has been designated as the preferred lender such that the listing agent is required to have all customers who desire to submit an offer on the property receive a Prospect Mortgage pre-qualification."

41. The listing agents who worked for a broker receiving lead fees or MSA fees from Prospect often inserted the Preapproval requirement into the agent-only remarks section of the MLS, which the general public could not see. **These instructions required the buyers' agent to inform their buyers that they needed to obtain Preapproval with one of Prospect's loan officers before submitting offers on the seller's properties if they wanted their offers to be considered by the sellers.**

42. For example, one of the broker's listings stated that "**All buyers MUST be pre-qualified with no obligation or cost with [Prospect's loan officers]."**

43. **This tactic steered consumers to Prospect.**

45. For example, one of Prospects regional sales mangers suggested that a broker and the brokers agents could generate more leads—and receive more lead fees—if they would "**add a requirement to the listing agreements and on the MLS that all buyers need to be pre-approved by Prospect Mortgage."**

46. Some brokers that engage in the "writing-in" practice even **required prospective buyers who had already obtained preapproval with another lender to also obtain Preapproval with Prospect.** Prospect and the brokers call this a "double application or double app" which referred to the idea that such buyers would have to Preapprove a second time. Broker's sometimes Brokers would even force all-cash buyers to obtain Preapproval with one of Prospect's loan officers.

Findings and Conclusions...By Using a Third-Party's Website Ads to Pay for Referrals

51. Prospect exited MSAs and lead agreements in late 2015. But they continued to employ co-marketing agreements with provided another means for it to continue to pay for referrals.

56. There is also a check box in the advertisement that says: "**I want financing information."** **This box was hyperlinked to provide the agent information who then sent the consumer information directly to Prospect.**

Findings and Conclusions...by Encouraging Brokers to Use Fees and Credits to Pressure Consumers into Using Prospect

59. **Prospect pressured the real estate brokers it worked with to send customers its way as part of the quid pro quo for receiving Respondent's payments.**

60. One listing agent made a seller's credit—essentially a discount on the sales price—conditional on using Prospect for the mortgage: "they must use Prospect to get the credit." Similarly, other listing agents included per diem fees—a penalty imposed on the buyer for each day closing is delayed, if they used a competing lender for their financing.

Conduct Provisions

64. Prospect Mortgage must not now or anytime in the future:

   a) Agree to purchase or pay for any service in exchange for referrals

   b) Enter into marketing service agreements, lead agreements or co-,marketing agreements with any real estate broker or agent.

   c) Enter into any desk license agreement with any broker or agent that will require influencing prospective home buyers to use Prospect Mortgage.

   d) Give or accept any fee, kickback, or thing of value pursuant to any agreement or understanding that requires referrals to Prospect.

Order to Pay Civil Money Penalties

71. Pay $3,500,000 to the Bureau.

Exercise 7.2: Apply Your Knowledge

Review the following questions concerning Prospect Mortgage Company and the Consent Order with the Consumer Financial Protection Bureau. Consider how federal regulations, most notably RESPA are the subject of the violations that occurred as a result of marketing agreements and referral fees paid. Discuss each question as a group and write down your answers in the space provided. Have your group spokesperson be prepared to share and discuss the group's opinions. Feel free to express your opinions and answers in the classroom also.

1. **What right of a prospective mortgage borrower is taken away when Section 8 of the Real Estate Settlement Procedures Act is violated?**

    _____

    _____

    _____

2. **List several of the methods that Prospect urged real estate agents to use to steer mortgage business to them:** _____

    _____

    _____

3. **How were the brokers and agents paid for their referrals?** _____

    _____

    _____

4. **What concepts and ideals can you learn from this recent case?** _____

    _____

    _____

Affiliated Business Arrangements (AfBA)

While kickbacks from referrals are prohibited, Regulation X does recognize the legitimacy of affiliated business arrangements involving real estate settlement services for federally-related mortgage loans (12 CFR §1024.15). An **affiliated business arrangement** is *a situation where a person in a position to refer settlement services—or an associate of that person—has either an affiliate relationship with or a direct or beneficial ownership interest of more than 1% in a provider of settlement services and who then refers business to that provider or in some way influences the selection of that provider.*

Seller-Required Title Insurance

Section 9 of RESPA (12 U.S.C. §2608) prohibits a seller from requiring the home buyer to use a particular title insurance company, either directly or indirectly, as a condition of sale. Buyers may sue a seller who violates this provision for an amount equal to **three times** all charges made for the title insurance [for more information, see Regulation X, 12 CFR Part 1024, Subpart B, §1024.16 Title companies].

Limits on Escrow Accounts

Section 10 of RESPA (12 U.S.C. §2609) sets limits on the amounts a lender may require a borrower to put into an escrow account. An **escrow account** *holds money (e.g., for purposes of paying taxes, hazard insurance, and other charges related to the property) that some mortgage lenders collect every month along with a mortgage payment* [for more information, see Regulation X, 12 CFR Part 1024, Subpart B, §1024.17(c) Limits on payments to escrow accounts].

RESPA does **not** require lenders to impose an escrow account on borrowers; however, certain loan programs may require escrow accounts as a condition of the loan in order to better protect lenders and insurers. For example:

- A mortgage loan that includes mortgage insurance generally requires an escrow account.
- All government-insured or guaranteed loans require an escrow account.
- A loan that meets the TILA definition of a "higher-priced" loan is required to have a lender-imposed escrow account for *at least 60 months.*
- Lenders are required to collect monthly escrow payments for certain other mortgage loans for at least the first five years of the mortgage.

During the course of the loan, RESPA prohibits a lender from charging excessive amounts for the escrow account. Each month, the lender may require a borrower to pay into the escrow account no more than **1/12th of the total of all disbursements payable during the year** (one month), plus an amount necessary to pay for any shortage in the account. In addition, the lender may require a cushion not to exceed an amount equal to **1/6th of the total disbursements for the year** (two months).

The lender must perform an escrow account analysis *once during the year* and notify borrowers of any shortage. Any **excess of $50 or more** in the escrow account must be returned to the borrower, assuming the borrower is not delinquent with payments. In that case, the lender is not required to return any excess escrow.

Effective June 2013, the rules for escrow accounts only affect certain "higher-priced" mortgage loans that have a rate based on interest, points, and other loan terms that are higher than levels set in the rule.

APPENDIX D TO PART 1024—AFFILIATED BUSINESS ARRANGEMENT DISCLOSURE STATEMENT FORMAT NOTICE

To:_____

From:_____

    (Entity Making Statement)

Property:_____

Date:_____

This is to give you notice that [*referring party*] has a business relationship with [*settlement services provider(s)*]. [Describe the nature of the relationship between the referring party and the provider(s), including percentage of ownership interest, if applicable.] Because of this relationship, this referral may provide [*referring party*] a financial or other benefit.

[A.] Set forth below is the estimated charge or range of charges for the settlement services listed. You are NOT required to use the listed provider(s) as a condition for [settlement of your loan on] [or] [purchase, sale, or refinance of] the subject property. THERE ARE FREQUENTLY OTHER SETTLEMENT SERVICE PROVIDERS AVAILABLE WITH SIMILAR SERVICES. YOU ARE FREE TO SHOP AROUND TO DETERMINE THAT YOU ARE RECEIVING THE BEST SERVICES AND THE BEST RATE FOR THESE SERVICES.

[*provider and settlement service*]_____

_____

_____

[*charge or range of charges*]_____

_____

_____

[B.] Set forth below is the estimated charge or range of charges for the settlement services of an attorney, credit reporting agency, or real estate appraiser that we, as your lender, will require you to use, as a condition of your loan on this property, to represent our interests in the transaction.

[*provider and settlement service*]_____

_____

[*charge or range of charges*]_____

_____

_____

ACKNOWLEDGMENT

I/we have read this disclosure form, and understand that *referring party* is referring me/us to purchase the above-described settlement service(s) and may receive a financial or other benefit as the result of this referral.

_____

Signature

[INSTRUCTIONS TO PREPARER:] [Use paragraph A for referrals other than those by a lender to an attorney, a credit reporting agency, or a real estate appraiser that a lender is requiring a borrower to use to represent the lender's interests in the transaction. Use paragraph B for those referrals to an attorney, credit reporting agency, or real estate appraiser that a lender is requiring a borrower to use to represent the lender's interests in the transaction. When applicable, use both paragraphs. Specific timing rules for delivery of the affiliated business disclosure statement are set forth in 12 CFR 1024.15(b)(1) of Regulation X). These INSTRUCTIONS TO PREPARER should not appear on the statement.]

Source: http://www.ecfr.gov/cgi-bin/text-idx?SID=97a08eabe556ccb664ea605b3506c7

b5&mc=true&node=ap12.8.1024_141.d&rgn=div9

Prohibition on Certain Fees

Federal law requires that consumers of credit be provided with specific disclosures. The Real Estate Settlement Procedures Act and the Truth in Lending Act prohibit lenders and servicers from charging a fee for the preparation of the Loan Estimate (LE) or other disclosures required by the Truth in Lending Act or disclosures and statements required, such as the Loan Estimate (LE), Closing Disclosure (CD), or annual escrow account statements.

Required Disclosures

RESPA requires and regulates various types of disclosures that lenders must deliver at particular times during the loan process. We will examine these disclosures and how this timely information is necessary for a borrower to make better-informed choices and decisions.

Disclosure Timing

To comply with RESPA and other regulations, it is important to understand *what* is required and *when* it is required. Required disclosures regarding settlement services must be provided to the borrower:

- At the time of loan application.
- Before settlement.
- At settlement.
- After settlement.

 The words "settlement" and "closing" are two terms used to refer to the same time period; these terms are used interchangeably in this textbook.

The table that follows identifies each disclosure and the applicable timing when the disclosure is required:

Timing of Required Disclosures	
When	**Which Disclosure**
At or Within 3 Business Days of Application	Home Loan Toolkit (RESPA and TILA) Loan Estimate (TRID) List of HUD-Approved Home Counselors (RESPA) Affiliated Business Arrangement (AfBA) Disclosure (if affiliated services are required by the lender.)
Before Settlement	Affiliated Business Arrangement (AfBA) Disclosure: The AfBA must be given at or before the time of referral Closing Disclosure: 3 days prior to consummation (TRID)
At Settlement	Finalized Closing Disclosure (TRID) Initial Escrow Statement (RESPA) - (within 45 days of closing)
After Settlement	Annual Escrow Statement (RESPA) Servicing Transfer Statement (RESPA)

Note: TRID stands for the TILA-RESPA Integrated Disclosure Rule. The Special Information Booklet was redesigned by the CFPB into the Your Home Loan Toolkit. TILA and RESPA both require this disclosure.

Until the Loan Estimate disclosure and other required disclosures are delivered to the borrower, an MLO may charge the borrower a fee *only* for the actual cost of obtaining a credit report.

 In cases where a Social Security number (SSN) is not the unique identifier used to pull a credit report to assess a potential borrower's credit history, another unique identifier such as a tax ID number (TIN) may be used.

Disclosures Within 3 Business Days of Completed Application

When consumers complete an application—or provide the information sufficient to complete an application—MLOs must give them certain disclosures. **If a borrower does not receive these disclosures at the time of application,** the MLO must provide them **within three business days** of receiving the completed application. (http://files.consumerfinance. gov/f/201311_cfpb_final-rule_integrated-mortgage-disclosures.pdf page 5)

If the applicant withdraws the application or the lender turns down the loan before the end of the three-business-day period, RESPA does **not** require the MLO to provide these documents.

The TILA-RESPA Integrated Disclosures

Overview of Truth in Lending Act (TILA)

The Truth in Lending Act (TILA) is administered by the CFPB. The specific provisions of the Act, which are contained in Title I of the Consumer Credit Protection Act as amended (15 U.S.C. 1601 et seq.), are implemented by **Regulation Z** [see Regulation Z, 12 CFR Part 1026]. TILA has been amended numerous times: By the Housing and Economic Recovery Act of 2008; the Mortgage Disclosure Improvement Act (MDIA), which went into effect in 2009; and the Dodd-Frank Wall Street Reform and Consumer Protection Act of 2010.

While Regulation Z does not set limits on interest rates or other finance charges imposed by lenders, it does regulate the disclosure of these items [see Regulation Z, 12 CFR Part 1026, Subpart C – Closed-End Credit, §1026.17 General disclosure requirements.]. Prior to the 1968 passage of the Truth in Lending Act, there were no federal laws requiring the disclosure of consumer credit costs expressed as a percentage. Specifically, the Act requires all creditors who deal with consumers to make certain disclosures concerning all finance charges and related aspects of credit transactions (including disclosing finance charges expressed as an annual percentage rate) [see Regulation Z, 12 CFR Part 1026, Subpart C – Closed-End Credit, §1026.18 Content of disclosures.]. The Act also establishes a three- business- day right of rescission in certain transactions.

Your Home Loan Toolkit

Information that guides the consumer about a mortgage loan is provided in a new format with the integration of the Know Before You Owe Disclosures. The *"Your Home Loan Toolkit"* must be provided to the primary borrower within **three business days** after receipt of a completed application. Creditors must provide the Toolkit, referred to in the TILA-RESPA Integrated Disclosure (TRID) rule as the Special Information Booklet, to mortgage applicants as a part of the application process.

The Toolkit is designed to be used in connection with the Loan Estimate and Closing Disclosure forms. Creditors must provide the Toolkit to mortgage applicants as part of the application process. Other industry participants, including real estate professionals, are encouraged to provide it to potential homebuyers.

The CFPB also provides an electronic version complete with fillable text fields and interactive checkboxes so consumers can save and print their progress as they work through the Toolkit. The electronic version meets federal accessibility standards to ensure that all consumers, including those with disabilities, can use the resource. The CFPB encourages lenders to keep this level of accessibility when delivering the PDF to consumers.

Your Home Loan Toolkit (designed for web posting and interactivity) is available at: http://files.consumerfinance.gov/f/201503_cfpb_your-home-loan-toolkit-web.pdf

[*See "CFPB Announces New 'Know Before You Owe' Mortgage Shopping Toolkit," Consumer Financial Protection Bureau, March 31, 2015, http://www.consumerfinance.gov/newsroom/cfpb-announces-new-know-before-you-owe-mortgage-shopping-toolkit/*]

Truth in Lending Required Disclosures – Regulation Z and HOEPA Regulations

1. Lenders are required by TILA to provide a list of homeownership counseling organizations to consumers *within three business days* after they apply for a mortgage loan, with the exclusion of reverse mortgages and mortgage loans secured by a timeshare. [*See 12 CFR, § 1024.20(a)(1), List of Homeownership Counseling Organizations.*] The rule requires the lender to obtain the list from either a website that will be developed by the CFPB, data that will be made available by the CFPB, or HUD for compliance with this requirement.

2. TILA also requires that creditors must obtain confirmation that a first-time borrower has received homeownership counseling from a federally-certified or approved homeownership counselor or counseling organization before making a loan that provides for or permits negative amortization to the borrower. [*See 12 CFR, § 1024.36(k)(1), Negative Amortization Counseling.*]

The **Mortgage Servicing Disclosure Statement** provides information to the borrower regarding whether the lender intends to service the loan, sell, or transfer servicing to another lender. The **servicing of a mortgage loan** is defined *as the continued maintenance of a mortgage loan, including accepting escrow payments and paying these charges when due.*

- If the lender, table funding mortgage broker, or dealer in a first lien dealer loan **will engage** in the servicing of the mortgage loan for which the applicant has applied, the disclosure may consist of a statement that the entity will service such loan and does not intend to sell, transfer, or assign the servicing of the loan.

- If the lender, table funding mortgage broker, or dealer in a first lien dealer loan **will not engage** in the servicing of the mortgage loan for which the applicant has applied, the disclosure may consist of a statement that such entity intends to assign, sell, or transfer servicing of such mortgage loan before the first payment is due [see 12 CFR §1024.33(a) 3].

- In all other instances, the disclosure must state that the servicing of the loan may be assigned, sold, or transferred while the loan is outstanding.

[12 CFR §1024.33 Mortgage servicing transfers.]

Exercise 7.3: Knowledge Check

A Mortgage Servicing Disclosure Statement states all of the following EXCEPT

- A. if the lender will engage in the servicing of the mortgage loan for which the applicant has applied.
- B. the process for resolution of a servicing complaint.
- C. a statement that such entity intends to assign, sell, or transfer servicing of such mortgage loan before the first payment is due.
- D. whether the servicing of the loan may be assigned, sold, or transferred.

SERVICING DISCLOSURE STATEMENT

Lender: **Florida Mortgage Corporation**
           2420 Enterprise Road #105
           Clearwater , FL 33763

NOTICE TO FIRST LIEN   MORTGAGE LOAN APPLICANTS: THE RIGHT TO COLLECT YOUR MORTGAGE LOAN PAYMENTS MAY BE TRANSFERRED. FEDERAL LAW GIVES YOU CERTAIN RELATED RIGHTS.   IF YOUR LOAN IS MADE,   SAVE THIS STATEMENT WITH YOUR LOAN DOCUMENTS. SIGN THE ACKNOWLEDGMENT AT THE END OF THIS STATEMENT ONLY IF YOU UNDERSTAND ITS CONTENTS.

Because you are applying for a mortgage loan covered by the Real Estate Settlement Procedures Act (RESPA) (12 U.S.C. Section 2601 et seq.) you have certain rights under that Federal law.

This statement tells you about those rights. It also tells you what the chances are that the servicing for this loan may be transferred to a different loan servicer.   "Servicing" refers to collecting your principal, interest and escrow account payments, if any.   If your loan servicer changes, there are certain procedures that must be followed.   This statement generally explains those procedures.

Transfer practices and requirements

If the servicing of your loan is assigned, sold, or transferred to a new servicer, you must be given written notice of that transfer.   The present loan servicer must send you notice in writing of the assignment, sale or transfer of the servicing not less than 15 days before the effective date of the transfer.   The new loan servicer must also send you notice within 15 days after the effective date of the transfer.   The present servicer and the new servicer may combine this information in one notice, so long as the notice is sent to you 15 days before the effective date of transfer.   The 15 day period is not applicable if a notice of prospective transfer is provided to you at settlement.   The law allows a delay in the time (not more than 30 days after a transfer) for servicers to notify you, upon the occurrence of certain business emergencies.

Notices must contain certain information.   They must contain the effective date of the transfer of the servicing of your loan to the new servicer, and the name, address, and toll-free or collect call telephone number of the new servicer, and toll-free or collect call telephone numbers of a person or department for both your present servicer and your new servicer to answer your questions.   During the 60 day period following the effective date of the transfer of the loan servicing, a loan payment received by your old servicer before its due date may not be treated by the new loan servicer as late, and a late fee may not be imposed on you.

Complaint Resolution

Section 6 of RESPA (12 U.S.C. Section 2605) gives you certain consumer rights, whether or not your loan servicing is transferred.   If you send a "qualified written request" to your servicer, then your servicer must provide you with a written acknowledgment within 20 Business Days of receipt of your request.   A "qualified written request" is a written correspondence, other than notice on a payment coupon or other payment medium supplied by the servicer, which includes your name and account number, and the information regarding your request.   Not later than 60 Business Days after receiving your request, your servicer must make any appropriate corrections to your account, or must provide you with a written clarification regarding any dispute.   During this 60 Business Day period, your servicer may not provide information to a consumer reporting agency concerning any overdue payment related to such period or qualified written request.

A Business Day is any day in which the offices of the business entity are open to the public for carrying on substantially all of its business functions.

Damages and Costs

Section 6 of RESPA also provides for damages and costs for individuals or classes of individuals in circumstances where servicers are shown to have violated the requirements of that Section.

Servicing Transfer Estimates

1. The following is the best estimate of what will happen to the servicing of your mortgage loan:

   A. ☐ We may assign, sell or transfer the servicing of your loan while the loan is outstanding.

      We are able to service your loan, and we
      ☐ will service your loan.
      ☐ will not service your loan.
      ☐ haven't decided whether to service your loan.

   B. ☑ We do not service mortgage loans ☑ and we have not serviced mortgage loans in the past three years.
      We presently intend to assign, sell or transfer the servicing of your mortgage loan. You will be informed about your servicer.

2. For all mortgage loans that we make in the 12 month period after your mortgage loan is funded, we estimate that the percentage of such loans for which we will transfer servicing is between:

   _____ 0 to 25%   _____ 26 to 50%   _____ 51 to 75%   _____ 76 to 100%

   This estimate ☐ does ☐ does not   include assignments, sales or transfers to affiliates or subsidiaries.

   This is only our best estimate and it is not binding. Business conditions or other circumstances may affect our future transferring decisions.

3. A. ☐ We have previously assigned, sold, or transferred the servicing of mortgage loans.

   B. ☐ This is our record of transferring the servicing of mortgage loans we have made in:

Year	Percentage of Loans Transferred
	%
	%
	%

   This information ☐ does ☐ does not   include assignments, sales or transfers to affiliates or subsidiaries.

Acknowledgment of Mortgage Loan Applicant(s)

I/We have read and understood the disclosure; and understand that the disclosure is a required part of the mortgage application as evidenced by my/our signature(s) below;

_____   _____   _____   _____
Applicant   Date   Applicant   Date

_____   _____   _____   _____
Applicant   Date   Applicant   Date

CALYX Form Sds2.frm 2/99   Page 2 of 2

Disclosures Before Settlement Occurs

RESPA and TILA mandate additional disclosures before settlement—or closing—occurs:

Affiliated Business Arrangement (AfBA or ABA) Disclosure. The referring party must give the AfBA disclosure to the consumer **at or prior** *to the time of referral*. The referring party may not require the consumer to use the particular provider being referred. Required when the creditor owns more than 1% interest in the referred third party settlement service provided.

The Closing Disclosure (Preliminary Closing Disclosure). The TILA-RESPA Integrated Disclosure rules require a Closing Disclosure be delivered to the borrower within **three business days** *prior to loan consummation*. This disclosure provides the consumer information about the loan terms and settlement service provider charges incurred in an easy to read and understand format. It gives the borrower an opportunity to question loan terms or settlement charges before settlement.

Disclosures at Settlement

The Closing Disclosure (Final Closing Disclosure). This document shows the actual finalized loan terms and settlement costs of the loan transaction. Separate forms may be prepared for the borrower and the seller. Where it is not the practice that the borrower and the seller both attend the settlement, the Closing Disclosure should be mailed or delivered to the borrowers within **three business days** *of loan consummation*.

Initial Escrow Statement. Itemizes the estimated taxes, insurance premiums, and other charges anticipated to be paid from the escrow account during the first 12 months of the loan. It lists the escrow payment amount and any required impound account cushion. Although the statement is usually given at settlement, the lender has *45 days* from settlement to deliver it.

Disclosures After Settlement

RESPA requirements continue even after the loan closes:

Annual Escrow Statement. Must be delivered to borrowers by loan servicers **once a year**. This statement summarizes all escrow account deposits and payments during the servicer's 12-month computation year. It also notifies the borrower of any shortages or surpluses in the account and advises the borrower about the course of action being taken.

Servicing Transfer Statement. Required if the loan servicer sells or assigns the **servicing rights** to a borrower's loan to another loan servicer. Generally, the loan servicer must notify the borrower **15 days** before the effective date of a servicing transfer. As long the borrower makes a timely payment to the previous servicer **within 60 days** of the servicing transfer, the borrower cannot be penalized. The notice must include the name and address of the new servicer, toll-free telephone numbers, and the date the new servicer will begin accepting payments.

Note that a *bona fide* transfer of ownership of a loan into the secondary market without a corresponding transfer of servicing rights is **not** covered under this provision of RESPA and, therefore, does not require a servicing transfer statement to the borrower.

Exercise 7.4: Knowledge Check

The TILA-RESPA Integrated Disclosures were implemented to
- A. help consumers become better and more informed shoppers.
- B. provide a new format for reverse mortgages.
- C. provide new forms that will yield higher-cost loans.
- D. save the MLO document preparation time.

The Loan Estimate

Please turn to Page 171 to review a sample Loan Estimate form. The Loan Estimate provides the borrower information about the following:

- An interest rate lock is disclosed.

- Payments are compared during the years that mortgage insurance is in place with the remaining years after mortgage insurance is cancelled, showing the borrower the difference in payments.

- Provides comparisons of payments made and the principal reduction of the loan in the **first five years**.

- Estimated Closing Costs are calculated, but new to the disclosure is the provision for Lender Credits to be deducted from the Estimated Closing Costs.

- Estimated Cash to Close is disclosed. The earnest money deposit is shown and deducted from the Cash to Close total so the borrower has a clear picture of the funds required at closing.

- **Total Interest Percentage (TIP),** which *informs the borrower of the total amount of interest the borrower will pay over the loan term as a percentage of the loan amount,* is shown.

- Information on the servicing of the loan is included.

- Information about the delivery of the appraisal to the borrower is included.

- Disclosure about the likelihood of future refinance transactions of the subject loan is made.

- A designated place for borrowers to sign and confirm they have received the Loan Estimate if the creditor chooses to offer this option.

The Loan Estimate holds a mortgage broker or creditor to the same standards regarding the collection of advance fees and disclosure as previously followed. No fee (with the exception of a bona fide and reasonable credit report fee) may be received by the MLO or creditor *until the borrower has received the*:

- Loan Estimate.
- List of HUD Approved Housing Counselors.
- Your Home Loan Toolkit.

These disclosures must be delivered to the borrower within **three business days** of receipt of a complete application or placed in the mail within **three business days** of receipt of a **complete application**. An MLO may *not* obtain a credit/debit card number to pay for appraisal fees, application fees, or any other fee until the disclosures have been delivered to the borrowers and the borrowers acknowledge their intent to proceed with the mortgage loan.

The definition of a **complete application** has changed to *the initial six items of information that an MLO receives and no more.* The items necessary for a creditor to make a credit decision are:

1. Name(s) of borrower
2. Social Security number for each borrower
3. Gross monthly income of borrower(s)
4. Loan amount sought
5. Address of subject property
6. Estimate of property value

FICUS BANK

4321 Random Boulevard • Somecity, ST 12340

Save this Loan Estimate to compare with your Closing Disclosure.

Loan Estimate

DATE ISSUED	2/15/2013
APPLICANTS	Michael Jones and Mary Stone
	123 Anywhere Street
	Anytown, ST 12345
PROPERTY	456 Somewhere Avenue
	Anytown, ST 12345
SALE PRICE	$180,000

LOAN TERM	30 years
PURPOSE	Purchase
PRODUCT	Fixed Rate
LOAN TYPE	☒ Conventional ☐ FHA ☐ VA ☐ _____
LOAN ID #	123456789
RATE LOCK	☐ NO ☒ YES, until 4/16/2013 at 5:00 p.m. EDT

*Before closing, your interest rate, points, and lender credits can change unless you lock the interest rate. All other estimated closing costs expire on **3/4/2013** at 5:00 p.m. EDT*

Loan Terms

		Can this amount increase after closing?
Loan Amount	$162,000	**NO**
Interest Rate	3.875%	**NO**
Monthly Principal & Interest *See Projected Payments below for your Estimated Total Monthly Payment*	$761.78	**NO**

		Does the loan have these features?
Prepayment Penalty		**YES** • **As high as $3,240** if you pay off the loan during the first 2 years
Balloon Payment		**NO**

Projected Payments

Payment Calculation	Years 1-7	Years 8-30
Principal & Interest	$761.78	$761.78
Mortgage Insurance	+ 82	+ —
Estimated Escrow *Amount can increase over time*	+ 206	+ 206
Estimated Total Monthly Payment	**$1,050**	**$968**

		This estimate includes	In escrow?
Estimated Taxes, Insurance & Assessments *Amount can increase over time*	**$206** a month	☒ Property Taxes	**YES**
		☒ Homeowner's Insurance	**YES**
		☐ Other:	

See Section G on page 2 for escrowed property costs. You must pay for other property costs separately.

Costs at Closing

Estimated Closing Costs	$8,054	Includes $5,672 in Loan Costs + $2,382 in Other Costs – $0 in Lender Credits. *See page 2 for details.*
Estimated Cash to Close	$16,054	Includes Closing Costs. *See Calculating Cash to Close on page 2 for details.*

Visit **www.consumerfinance.gov/mortgage-estimate** for general information and tools.

Closing Cost Details

Loan Costs

A. Origination Charges	$1,802
.25 % of Loan Amount (Points)	$405
Application Fee	$300
Underwriting Fee	$1,097

B. Services You Cannot Shop For	$672
Appraisal Fee	$405
Credit Report Fee	$30
Flood Determination Fee	$20
Flood Monitoring Fee	$32
Tax Monitoring Fee	$75
Tax Status Research Fee	$110

C. Services You Can Shop For	$3,198
Pest Inspection Fee	$135
Survey Fee	$65
Title – Insurance Binder	$700
Title – Lender's Title Policy	$535
Title – Settlement Agent Fee	$502
Title – Title Search	$1,261

D. TOTAL LOAN COSTS (A + B + C)	$5,672

Other Costs

E. Taxes and Other Government Fees	$85
Recording Fees and Other Taxes	$85
Transfer Taxes	

F. Prepaids	$867
Homeowner's Insurance Premium (6 months)	$605
Mortgage Insurance Premium (months)	
Prepaid Interest ($17.44 per day for 15 days @ 3.875%)	$262
Property Taxes (months)	

G. Initial Escrow Payment at Closing		$413
Homeowner's Insurance	$100.83 per month for 2 mo.	$202
Mortgage Insurance	per month for mo.	
Property Taxes	$105.30 per month for 2 mo.	$211

H. Other	$1,017
Title – Owner's Title Policy (optional)	$1,017

I. TOTAL OTHER COSTS (E + F + G + H)	$2,382

J. TOTAL CLOSING COSTS	$8,054
D + I	$8,054
Lender Credits	

Calculating Cash to Close

Total Closing Costs (J)	$8,054
Closing Costs Financed (Paid from your Loan Amount)	$0
Down Payment/Funds from Borrower	$18,000
Deposit	– $10,000
Funds for Borrower	$0
Seller Credits	$0
Adjustments and Other Credits	$0
Estimated Cash to Close	$16,054

Additional Information About This Loan

LENDER	Ficus Bank	**MORTGAGE BROKER**
NMLS/__ LICENSE ID		**NMLS/__ LICENSE ID**
LOAN OFFICER	Joe Smith	**LOAN OFFICER**
NMLS/__ LICENSE ID	12345	**NMLS/__ LICENSE ID**
EMAIL	joesmith@ficusbank.com	**EMAIL**
PHONE	123-456-7890	**PHONE**

Comparisons — Use these measures to compare this loan with other loans.

In 5 Years	$56,582	Total you will have paid in principal, interest, mortgage insurance, and loan costs.
	$15,773	Principal you will have paid off.
Annual Percentage Rate (APR)	4.274%	Your costs over the loan term expressed as a rate. This is not your interest rate.
Total Interest Percentage (TIP)	69.45%	The total amount of interest that you will pay over the loan term as a percentage of your loan amount.

Other Considerations

Appraisal

We may order an appraisal to determine the property's value and charge you for this appraisal. We will promptly give you a copy of any appraisal, even if your loan does not close. You can pay for an additional appraisal for your own use at your own cost.

Assumption

If you sell or transfer this property to another person, we
☐ will allow, under certain conditions, this person to assume this loan on the original terms.
☒ will not allow assumption of this loan on the original terms.

Homeowner's Insurance

This loan requires homeowner's insurance on the property, which you may obtain from a company of your choice that we find acceptable.

Late Payment

If your payment is more than *15* days late, we will charge a late fee of *5% of the monthly principal and interest payment.*

Refinance

Refinancing this loan will depend on your future financial situation, the property value, and market conditions. You may not be able to refinance this loan.

Servicing

We intend
☐ to service your loan. If so, you will make your payments to us.
☒ to transfer servicing of your loan.

Confirm Receipt

By signing, you are only confirming that you have received this form. You do not have to accept this loan because you have signed or received this form.

_____   _____   _____   _____
Applicant Signature   Date   Co-Applicant Signature   Date

LOAN ESTIMATE   PAGE 3 OF 3 • LOAN ID #123456789

If a consumer receives a written estimate of loan terms or an itemized closing cost statement, the top of the first page must contain the statement:

"Your actual rate, payment, and costs could be higher. Get an official Loan Estimate before choosing a loan."

 Caution! This statement must be in 12-point type and must be noticeable to the borrower. A creditor or MLO *cannot* require a borrower submission of documents that verify the information related to the application before providing the Loan Estimate.

[*For more information, see Regulation Z, 12 CFR §1026.19(e)(2)(ii) Written Information Provided to Consumer.*]

The Loan Estimate *does not* apply to all real estate loans. Exemptions include:

- Home equity lines of credit
- Reverse mortgages
- Loans to secure a fractional interest in real estate (timeshares)
- Loans for mobile homes or dwellings not affixed to real property
- Loans made by a person or entity that makes **five or fewer** mortgages in a calendar year. This is a federal exemption from compliance and state laws and regulations may impose different requirements.
- Loans made to a non-natural person (business entity)

[*For more information, see Regulation Z, 12 CFR §1026.2(a)(17) Creditor.*]

The new regulation *does* apply to:

- Vacant land or land consisting of .
- Loans made to certain trusts utilized for tax and estate planning purposes.
- Construction-only loans.

If a **mortgage broker**, *one who places a loan submission with a wholesale lender to underwrite and fund the loan*, receives a complete loan application, either the lender or the mortgage broker may make the initial disclosures. If the mortgage broker completes the Loan Estimate, the wholesale lender's name (if known) must be used. If it is not known the space must be left blank. The creditor has the ultimate responsibility for correct and timely delivery of disclosures to the consumer.

A lender may not use the term "N/A" on the Loan Estimate. A creditor should leave the space blank rather than using "N/A."

Availability of Terms

The estimate of the charges and terms for all settlement services must be available for at least **10 business days** from when the Loan Estimate is provided, but may remain available longer if the MLO extends the period of availability. This expiration period is located on Page 1 of the Loan Estimate, in the Rate Lock section. However, this 10-business-day provision does **not** apply to the interest rate, charges, and terms dependent upon the interest rate—which includes the charge or credit for the interest rate chosen—the adjusted origination charges, and per diem interest. Because of this, borrowers and lenders frequently agree to a **rate lock** for a pre-determined period of time.

Timing and Delivery Requirements for the Loan Estimate	
After the Loan Estimate is...	**And borrower has indicated the intent to proceed, other fees may be collected ...**
Hand-delivered to the borrower	That day.
Emailed to the borrower with the borrower's permission	The next day after a send receipt is returned as evidence that the email was received.
Faxed to the borrower	The next day after a signed document evidencing receipt of the Loan Estimate is faxed back.
Mailed to the borrower	Three business days after the Loan Estimate is mailed.

Once the Closing Disclosure has been provided to the borrowers, a revised Loan Estimate may not be given to the borrower. If a new Loan Estimate is required because of a changed circumstance, it must be disclosed and received by the borrower *four days prior to consummation of the loan.*

A revised Loan Estimate is considered received by the consumer on the day it is provided. If it is mailed or delivered electronically (email, fax, etc.), the consumer is considered to have received it *three business days after the disclosures are mailed or transmitted.* If the creditor can provide evidence that a consumer received the disclosures sent by mail or electronically earlier than the three-business-day guideline, then the disclosures will be considered as received by the consumer on that date.

[See Regulation Z, 12 CFR §1026.19(e)(1)(iii-iv) Timing – Receipt of Early Disclosures.]

Two different definitions of a business day are applicable with the Integrated Disclosures. For the purpose of:

- **Providing a new disclosure of the Loan Estimate to the borrower**, a business day is defined as *any day the creditor's offices are open to the public for the purpose of transacting substantially all of the creditor's business.*

For example, a bank, mortgage broker, or banker that is open Monday through Friday for regular business would not be allowed to count Saturday as a business day for the purpose of fulfilling the required disclosure period of three business days.

- **The four-business-day period for redisclosure of the Loan Estimate due to a valid changed circumstance** (which must be delivered one day before the delivery of the Closing Disclosure), a business day is considered to be *all calendar days except Sundays and legal public holidays, as defined by Regulation Z.*

[See Regulation Z, 12 CFR §1026.2(a)(6).Business Day; see also 5 U.S.C. §6103(a) Holidays.]

Regulation Z also states that "*revised disclosures may not be delivered at the same time as the Closing Disclosure.*" If a changed circumstance:

- Exists *prior to loan consummation*, a creditor may **not** provide a revised Loan Estimate to a consumer within four (4) business days of loan consummation.

- Occurs *too close to loan closing*, the valid changed circumstances may be revised on the Closing Disclosure.

Upon redisclosure of a corrected Loan Estimate, the borrower receives a *new* three-business-day period to review the disclosures, prior to consummation.

[See Regulation Z, 12 CFR §1026.19(e)(4)(ii) Provision and Receipt of Revised Disclosures.]

Tolerance Guidelines for the Loan Estimate

The Loan Estimate is designed to provide an accurate estimate of all settlement provider charges the borrower can expect to incur during the course of the loan and at loan consumption. Whether the Loan Estimate is made in good faith is determined by the difference of the initial cost estimate and the final costs charged at loan closing.

If the closing costs on the Closing Disclosure are:

- **Greater** than what was disclosed initially on the Loan Estimate, the Loan Estimate is considered to *not be made in good faith*.

- **Less** than the Loan Estimate, the originator is considered to have *acted in good faith* when making the initial Loan Estimate.

Even if a Loan Estimate is provided to the borrower in good faith, settlement charges can change at loan consummation unexpectedly. There are regulations regarding what settlement service provider costs may change, may change by a limited amount, or may not change from the original Loan Estimate. These variations are permitted by the TILA-RESPA rule, subject to tolerance limits. Regulation Z states, "*Changed circumstances permit a revised Loan Estimate or a Closing Disclosure that permits the charge to be changed.*"

[*For more information, see Regulation Z, 12 CFR (§ 1026.19(e)(3) Good Faith Determination for Estimates of Closing Costs.]*

Valid Changed Circumstances

With the Loan Estimate, there must be a valid "changed circumstance" affecting the Loan Estimate or the Closing Disclosure. A **changed circumstance,** for purposes of a Loan Estimate, can be any of the following:

- An event that is beyond the control of the creditor or the borrower that occurs, such as a natural disaster in the property's community, which results in increased settlement costs.

- Information that was known or provided at the time of the application changed subsequent to the application and caused a change in the initial loan terms, interest rates, or settlement service provider charges; i.e., a third-party provider ceases to be in business and the creditor is forced to seek services from another source that charges an increased fee.

- New information regarding the borrower or the loan that the creditor did not rely on when supplying the Loan Estimate, as in a borrower becoming unemployed prior to closing during the course of the loan.

[*For more information, see Regulation Z, 12 CFR (§ 1026.19(e)(3)(iv)(A) Changed Circumstance Affecting Settlement Charges.]*

A valid changed circumstance also includes a *borrower-requested change to the interest rate or loan terms*. An example of this occurrence would include a borrower requesting a cash out loan at a higher loan-to-value as a result of a higher than anticipated appraised value. The increase in loan-to-value and the increased loan risk due to the cash out refinance request may result in an increase in interest rate or discount points due to risk-based pricing guidelines. This increase would affect the Loan Estimate fees, but because the change is *borrower-initiated*, a valid changed circumstance exists.

Another valid changed circumstance occurs when the borrower does not initially lock an interest rate, but does so *after* the Loan Estimate is initially delivered. The CFPB guidance allows a lender up to **three business days** to issue a new Loan Estimate after the borrower locks the loan's interest rate.

If a consumer obtains a Loan Estimate from a mortgage loan originator and does not provide an *intent to proceed*, the creditor may issue a revised Loan Estimate if the borrower returns after the expiration date of the Loan Estimate. Regulation Z states:

*"Creditors also may use a revised **Loan Estimate** where the transaction involves financing of new construction and the creditor reasonably expects that settlement will occur more than 60 calendar days after the original **Loan Estimate** has been provided."*

[*See Regulation Z, 12 CFR § 1026.19(e)(3)(iv)(C-F) Revisions Requested by the Consumer – Delayed Settlement Date on a Construction Loan.*]

Lender Tolerance Cures

The settlement service provider charges provided on the Loan Estimate are subject to **tolerance limits** at closing that are regulated by TILA. These tolerance limits include:

1. Charges that can change by any amount. These may include:

    i.   Prepaid interest, property insurance premiums, amounts deposited in reserve with the lender for property charges (such as property taxes), homeowner's insurance, flood insurance, condo interior insurance, etc.

    ii. Charges that the creditor allows the borrower to shop for if the borrower selects a settlement service provider that is not on the creditor list of settlement service providers (provided to the borrower at the time the Loan Estimate). An example would include a creditor estimating charges on the Loan Estimate for title services from Provider "A," but the borrower chooses to obtain the title services from Provider "B." As long as provider "A" was identified on a Settlement Service Provider List delivered at the time of the Loan Estimate, the creditor would not be held to the specific charges quoted from Provider "A" for the title company charges.

    iii. Charges for optional services that are not required by the lender to obtain the mortgage loan.

2. "Charges for third-party services and recording fees paid by or imposed on the consumer are grouped together and subject to a **10% cumulative tolerance**. This means the creditor may charge the consumer more than the amount disclosed on the Loan Estimate for any of these charges so long as the total sum of the charges added together does not exceed the sum of all such charges disclosed on the Loan Estimate by more than 10%."

    i.   **Third-party charges** are *fees that are paid to any party other than the creditor or their affiliates*. This includes fees for services that the borrower is allowed to choose, such as title and closing agent fees, owner's title insurance premiums, pest inspection report, location survey, etc., and recording fees.

    ii. If a creditor discloses a charge for a settlement service and the service is not obtained or provided by loan consummation, the charge for the service must be *removed from the calculation of the 10% variance*. For example, if the borrower is quoted $200 for a termite report and no termite report is required or performed, the $200 charge for the termite report must be *removed* from the aggregate calculation prior to analyzing the amount for a 10% variance.

[*See Regulation Z, 12 CFR § 1026.19(e)(3-5) Good Faith Determination for Estimates of Closing Costs – No Fee.*]

3. Charges that may *not* change on the Closing Disclosure by any amount from the amounts disclosed on the Loan Estimate.

    i.   Any charge paid to the creditor, mortgage broker, or affiliate of the creditor or mortgage broker for the origination, processing, and closing of a mortgage loan

    ii. Any charge paid to a non-affiliate for a settlement service that the borrower is not permitted to shop for

    iii. Fees paid to an unaffiliated third party if the borrower is not allowed to shop for the third-party service

    iv. Transfer taxes

[*See Regulation Z, 12 CFR § 1026.19(e)(3)(ii) Limited Increases Permitted for Certain Charges.*]

The regulation states that if the amounts paid by the consumer at closing exceed the amounts disclosed on the Loan Estimate beyond the **applicable tolerance threshold**, the creditor must refund the excess to the consumer no later than **60 calendar days after consummation**.

- For charges subject to **zero tolerance**, any amount charged beyond the amount disclosed on the Loan Estimate must be refunded to the consumer.

- For charges subject to a **10% cumulative tolerance** to the extent the total sum of the charges added together exceeds the sum of all such charges disclosed on the Loan Estimate by *more than 10%,* the difference must be refunded to the consumer.

[*See Regulation Z, 12 CFR § 1026.19(e)(3)(i-ii) General Rule – Limited Increases Permitted for Certain Charges.*]

Exercise 7.5: Apply Your Knowledge

An MLO needs to issue a new Loan Estimate. He must have a valid changed circumstance. Review the following scenarios and determine which are allowable and which are not. Be prepared to discuss your answers.

1. The appraisal comes in and shows the borrowers to have more equity than originally thought when they applied for their rate and term refinance. They request a change to a cash out loan.

2. The loan originator neglected to disclose the review appraisal fee when the underwriter conditioned for it.

3. The appraisal was received, but the value was less than anticipated. The loan-to-value now exceeds 80%.

4. The borrowers qualify for and decide they can afford a 15-year fixed-rate mortgage rather than the 30-year fixed-rate mortgage for which they originally applied.

_____

_____

Exercise 7.6: Knowledge Check

1. If a revised Loan Estimate is emailed to the borrower (with his permission), it is considered received

   A. the day the email is sent.

   B. the next business day after the disclosure is emailed.

   C. three business days after the email is sent, if not informed of receipt by the borrower sooner.

   D. the seventh business day after the email is sent.

2. When a Loan Estimate is provided to a borrower, it is considered to be provided in good faith when the actual closing costs are lower as shown on the

   A. Closing Addendum.

   B. Closing Disclosure.

   C. Good Faith Estimate.

   D. HUD-1 Settlement Statement.

3. With a revised Loan Estimate, a valid changed circumstance must exist. A valid change circumstance is considered to be all of the following EXCEPT

   A. a borrower-requested change.

   B. an event that is beyond the control of the borrower.

   C. information known at the time of application but subsequently changed.

   D. an MLO neglected to charge an origination fee initially.

4. Third-party fees, shown on the Loan Estimate, include all of the following EXCEPT

   A. a credit report fee.

   B. a flood cert fee.

   C. hazard insurance premiums.

   D. a lock-in fee.

The Closing Disclosure

For loans that require a Loan Estimate and that proceed to the closing, creditors must provide a new final disclosure reflecting the actual terms of the transaction called the **Closing Disclosure**.

[*For more information, see Regulation Z, 12 CFR § 1026.19(f) Mortgage Loans Secured by Real Property—Final Disclosures.*]

The Closing Disclosure generally must contain the actual terms and costs of the transaction. Creditors may estimate disclosures using the best information reasonably available when the actual term or cost is not *reasonably available* to the creditor at the time the disclosure is made. However, creditors must act in good faith and use due diligence in obtaining the information. The creditor normally may rely on the representations of other parties in obtaining the information, including, for example, the settlement agent. The creditor is required to provide corrected disclosures containing the actual terms of the transaction **at or before consummation.**

[*See Regulation Z, 12 CFR § 1026.19(f)(1)(i-ii) Provision of Disclosures – Timing.*]

If costs vary from the original Closing Disclosure prior to consummation, the creditor must make a **new** disclosure to the consumer of the changed costs. Only those costs that are *valid changed costs* may be changed on the revised Closing Disclosure. If a new Closing Disclosure is delivered to the borrower, the borrower is given *a new **three business day** waiting period* prior to loan consummation.

The term consummation differs from the term closing. **Consummation** is defined as *the date when the consumer becomes contractually obligated to the creditor on the loan.* This may not be the same day that the borrower is obligated to the seller in a purchase money transaction. Creditors and closing agents should verify the applicable state law to comply with the state's statutes regarding the date of consummation.

[*See Regulation Z, 12 CFR § 1026.2(a)(13) Consummation.*]

The use of the Loan Estimate and the Closing Disclosure for federally-regulated mortgages is **mandatory and the forms may not be altered**.

The creditor is responsible for providing the Closing Disclosure to the borrower and ensuring that the con-tent, delivery, and timing requirements set by the Consumer Financial Protection Bureau are met. The settlement agent is responsible for providing the seller with the Closing Disclosure that discloses the actual terms of the transaction to the seller. The settlement agent may provide a copy of the borrower's Closing Disclosure to the seller if the terms of the seller's transaction are shown on the buyer's form. If the settlement agent provides the seller a form that *differs* from the buyer's form, then the settlement agent is required to provide a copy of the seller's form to the creditor.

[*For more information see Regulation Z, 12 CFR § 1026.19(f)(4) Transactions Involving a Seller, 12 CFR § 1026.19(f)(1)(ii)(A) Timing: In General, see also 12 CFR §1026.38(t)(5)(v-vi) Separation of Consumer and Seller Information – Modified Version of the Form for a Seller or Third-Party.*]

Creditors can share the responsibility for completion and accuracy of the Closing Disclosure with the settlement agent. The settlement agent can complete part or all of the statement for the creditor. The creditor must, of course, maintain communication with the settlement agent to ensure timely delivery of the Closing Disclosure. However, even if the Closing Disclosure is prepared and delivered by the settlement agent, the creditor *still maintains the responsibility* for the accuracy and delivery of the disclosure.

[*For more information, see Regulation Z, 12 CFR § 1026.19(f)(1)(v) Settlement Agent.*]

To ensure the consumer receives the Closing Disclosure within the **three business day requirement** that is imposed, creditors must deliver the Closing Disclosure either:

* In person directly to the borrower.
* By mailing or by other methods, including email.

Creditors must make certain the borrower receives the Closing Disclosure at least **three business days** prior to consummation. If the Closing Disclosure is:

* Delivered in person, it is considered delivered the day it is provided.
* Mailed or delivered electronically, the consumer is considered to have received the Closing Disclosure three (3) business days after it is placed in the mail or delivered electronically.

If it can be documented that the borrower received the Closing Disclosure *prior* to the expiration of the three-day period, the transaction may proceed. If a transaction is subject to the period of rescission provided by TILA provisions, the Closing Disclosure must be given to each consumer who has the right to rescind the mortgage transaction. In a transaction not subject to the rescission provisions, any consumer who has primary liability for the mortgage loan must receive a Closing Disclosure.

[*For more information, see Regulation Z, 12 CFR § 1026.19(b) Certain Variable-Rate Transactions, see also 12 CFR § 1026.19(f)(1)(ii-iii) Timing – Receipt of Disclosures.*]

The Closing Disclosure Form

Please turn to Page 182 to review a sample Closing Disclosure form. This Integrated Disclosure provides the borrower with two major items:

1. Final statement of closing costs the borrower will incur

2. Final Truth in Lending Statement that discloses the APR

Some notable information contained in the Closing Disclosure includes:

- Page 1 of the Closing Disclosure when compared with Page 1 of the Loan Estimate appears very similar.

- Page 2 itemizes and discloses the closing costs paid by the borrower, the seller, or by others. The columns for the borrower and the seller are divided into two parts:

    1. Items paid *at closing*

    2. Items paid *before closing*

- The top portion of Page 3 calculates the Cash to Close for the borrower, providing information regarding the amount of closing costs disclosed to the borrower on the Loan Estimate and the Closing Disclosure. The borrower is also informed if there was a change from the disclosure by the Loan Estimate and the Closing Disclosure.

- The bottom portion of Page 3 summarizes the transaction details.

- Page 4 of the Closing Disclosure makes further disclosures to the borrower regarding:

    1. Assumption of the loan

    2. Demand features

    3. Late payment information

    4. Negative amortization features

    5. Partial payments

    6. Description of the security for the loan (property address)

    7. Escrow account information

- Page 5 of the Closing Disclosure discloses information from the "Federal Box" of the Truth In Lending Statement. The Total Interest Percentage (TIP) is re-disclosed on the Closing Disclosure.

- Other disclosures made to the borrower on Page 5 include:

    1. Appraisal

    2. Details about the note and security instrument

    3. Any liability for any deficiency judgment resulting from a foreclosure on the property securing the note

    4. Disclosure regarding the probability of a potential refinance at a later date of the note and security instrument

    5. Contact information for the lender, mortgage broker, real estate agents, and the settlement agent

Closing Disclosure

This form is a statement of final loan terms and closing costs. Compare this document with your Loan Estimate.

Closing Information

Date Issued	4/15/2013
Closing Date	4/15/2013
Disbursement Date	4/15/2013
Settlement Agent	Epsilon Title Co.
File #	12-3456
Property	456 Somewhere Ave
	Anytown, ST 12345
Sale Price	$180,000

Transaction Information

Borrower	Michael Jones and Mary Stone
	123 Anywhere Street
	Anytown, ST 12345
Seller	Steve Cole and Amy Doe
	321 Somewhere Drive
	Anytown, ST 12345
Lender	Ficus Bank

Loan Information

Loan Term	30 years
Purpose	Purchase
Product	Fixed Rate
Loan Type	☒ Conventional ☐ FHA ☐ VA ☐ _____
Loan ID #	123456789
MIC #	000654321

Loan Terms

		Can this amount increase after closing?
Loan Amount	$162,000	**NO**
Interest Rate	3.875%	**NO**
Monthly Principal & Interest *See Projected Payments below for your Estimated Total Monthly Payment*	$761.78	**NO**
		Does the loan have these features?
Prepayment Penalty		**YES** • **As high as $3,240** if you pay off the loan during the first 2 years
Balloon Payment		**NO**

Projected Payments

Payment Calculation		Years 1-7		Years 8-30
Principal & Interest		$761.78		$761.78
Mortgage Insurance	+	82.35	+	—
Estimated Escrow *Amount can increase over time*	+	206.13	+	206.13
Estimated Total Monthly Payment		**$1,050.26**		**$967.91**

		This estimate includes	In escrow?
Estimated Taxes, Insurance & Assessments *Amount can increase over time* *See page 4 for details*	**$356.13** a month	☒ Property Taxes	YES
		☒ Homeowner's Insurance	YES
		☒ Other: Homeowner's Association Dues	NO
		See Escrow Account on page 4 for details. You must pay for other property costs separately.	

Costs at Closing

Closing Costs	$9,712.10	Includes $4,694.05 in Loan Costs + $5,018.05 in Other Costs – $0 in Lender Credits. *See page 2 for details.*
Cash to Close	$14,147.26	Includes Closing Costs. *See Calculating Cash to Close on page 3 for details.*

Closing Cost Details

Loan Costs		Borrower-Paid		Seller-Paid		Paid by Others
		At Closing	Before Closing	At Closing	Before Closing	
A. Origination Charges		**$1,802.00**				
01 0.25 % of Loan Amount (Points)		$405.00				
02 Application Fee		$300.00				
03 Underwriting Fee		$1,097.00				
04						
05						
06						
07						
08						
B. Services Borrower Did Not Shop For		**$236.55**				
01 Appraisal Fee	to John Smith Appraisers Inc.					$405.00
02 Credit Report Fee	to Information Inc.		$29.80			
03 Flood Determination Fee	to Info Co.	$20.00				
04 Flood Monitoring Fee	to Info Co.	$31.75				
05 Tax Monitoring Fee	to Info Co.	$75.00				
06 Tax Status Research Fee	to Info Co.	$80.00				
07						
08						
09						
10						
C. Services Borrower Did Shop For		**$2,655.50**				
01 Pest Inspection Fee	to Pests Co.	$120.50				
02 Survey Fee	to Surveys Co.	$85.00				
03 Title – Insurance Binder	to Epsilon Title Co.	$650.00				
04 Title – Lender's Title Insurance	to Epsilon Title Co.	$500.00				
05 Title – Settlement Agent Fee	to Epsilon Title Co.	$500.00				
06 Title – Title Search	to Epsilon Title Co.	$800.00				
07						
08						
D. TOTAL LOAN COSTS (Borrower-Paid)		**$4,694.05**				
Loan Costs Subtotals (A + B + C)		$4,664.25	$29.80			

Other Costs						
E. Taxes and Other Government Fees		**$85.00**				
01 Recording Fees	Deed: $40.00 Mortgage: $45.00	$85.00				
02 Transfer Tax	to Any State			$950.00		
F. Prepaids		**$2,120.80**				
01 Homeowner's Insurance Premium (12 mo.) to Insurance Co.		$1,209.96				
02 Mortgage Insurance Premium (mo.)						
03 Prepaid Interest ($17.44 per day from 4/15/13 to 5/1/13)		$279.04				
04 Property Taxes (6 mo.) to Any County USA		$631.80				
05						
G. Initial Escrow Payment at Closing		**$412.25**				
01 Homeowner's Insurance $100.83 per month for 2 mo.		$201.66				
02 Mortgage Insurance per month for mo.						
03 Property Taxes $105.30 per month for 2 mo.		$210.60				
04						
05						
06						
07						
08 Aggregate Adjustment		– 0.01				
H. Other		**$2,400.00**				
01 HOA Capital Contribution	to HOA Acre Inc.	$500.00				
02 HOA Processing Fee	to HOA Acre Inc.	$150.00				
03 Home Inspection Fee	to Engineers Inc.	$750.00			$750.00	
04 Home Warranty Fee	to XYZ Warranty Inc.			$450.00		
05 Real Estate Commission	to Alpha Real Estate Broker			$5,700.00		
06 Real Estate Commission	to Omega Real Estate Broker			$5,700.00		
07 Title – Owner's Title Insurance (optional) to Epsilon Title Co.		$1,000.00				
08						
I. TOTAL OTHER COSTS (Borrower-Paid)		**$5,018.05**				
Other Costs Subtotals (E + F + G + H)		$5,018.05				
J. TOTAL CLOSING COSTS (Borrower-Paid)		**$9,712.10**				
Closing Costs Subtotals (D + I)		$9,682.30	$29.80	$12,800.00	$750.00	$405.00
Lender Credits						

Calculating Cash to Close

Use this table to see what has changed from your Loan Estimate.

	Loan Estimate	Final	Did this change?
Total Closing Costs (J)	$8,054.00	$9,712.10	**YES** · See **Total Loan Costs (D)** and **Total Other Costs (I)**
Closing Costs Paid Before Closing	$0	− $29.80	**YES** · You paid these Closing Costs **before closing**
Closing Costs Financed (Paid from your Loan Amount)	$0	$0	**NO**
Down Payment/Funds from Borrower	$18,000.00	$18,000.00	**NO**
Deposit	− $10,000.00	− $10,000.00	**NO**
Funds for Borrower	$0	$0	**NO**
Seller Credits	$0	− $2,500.00	**YES** · See Seller Credits in **Section L**
Adjustments and Other Credits	$0	− $1,035.04	**YES** · See details in **Sections K and L**
Cash to Close	$16,054.00	$14,147.26	

Summaries of Transactions

Use this table to see a summary of your transaction.

BORROWER'S TRANSACTION

K. Due from Borrower at Closing	$189,762.30
01 Sale Price of Property	$180,000.00
02 Sale Price of Any Personal Property Included in Sale	
03 Closing Costs Paid at Closing (J)	$9,682.30
04	
Adjustments	
05	
06	
07	
Adjustments for Items Paid by Seller in Advance	
08 City/Town Taxes to	
09 County Taxes to	
10 Assessments to	
11 HOA Dues 4/15/13 to 4/30/13	$80.00
12	
13	
14	
15	

L. Paid Already by or on Behalf of Borrower at Closing	$175,615.04
01 Deposit	$10,000.00
02 Loan Amount	$162,000.00
03 Existing Loan(s) Assumed or Taken Subject to	
04	
05 Seller Credit	$2,500.00
Other Credits	
06 Rebate from Epsilon Title Co.	$750.00
07	
Adjustments	
08	
09	
10	
11	
Adjustments for Items Unpaid by Seller	
12 City/Town Taxes 1/1/13 to 4/14/13	$365.04
13 County Taxes to	
14 Assessments to	
15	
16	
17	

CALCULATION	
Total Due from Borrower at Closing (K)	$189,762.30
Total Paid Already by or on Behalf of Borrower at Closing (L)	− $175,615.04
Cash to Close ☒ From ☐ To Borrower	**$14,147.26**

SELLER'S TRANSACTION

M. Due to Seller at Closing	$180,080.00
01 Sale Price of Property	$180,000.00
02 Sale Price of Any Personal Property Included in Sale	
03	
04	
05	
06	
07	
08	
Adjustments for Items Paid by Seller in Advance	
09 City/Town Taxes to	
10 County Taxes to	
11 Assessments to	
12 HOA Dues 4/15/13 to 4/30/13	$80.00
13	
14	
15	
16	

N. Due from Seller at Closing	$115,665.04
01 Excess Deposit	
02 Closing Costs Paid at Closing (J)	$12,800.00
03 Existing Loan(s) Assumed or Taken Subject to	
04 Payoff of First Mortgage Loan	$100,000.00
05 Payoff of Second Mortgage Loan	
06	
07	
08 Seller Credit	$2,500.00
09	
10	
11	
12	
13	
Adjustments for Items Unpaid by Seller	
14 City/Town Taxes 1/1/13 to 4/14/13	$365.04
15 County Taxes to	
16 Assessments to	
17	
18	
19	

CALCULATION	
Total Due to Seller at Closing (M)	$180,080.00
Total Due from Seller at Closing (N)	− $115,665.04
Cash ☐ From ☒ To Seller	**$64,414.96**

Additional Information About This Loan

Loan Disclosures

Assumption

If you sell or transfer this property to another person, your lender

☐ will allow, under certain conditions, this person to assume this loan on the original terms.

☒ will not allow assumption of this loan on the original terms.

Demand Feature

Your loan

☐ has a demand feature, which permits your lender to require early repayment of the loan. You should review your note for details.

☒ does not have a demand feature.

Late Payment

If your payment is more than *15 days* late, your lender will charge a late fee of *5% of the monthly principal and interest payment.*

Negative Amortization (Increase in Loan Amount)

Under your loan terms, you

☐ are scheduled to make monthly payments that do not pay all of the interest due that month. As a result, your loan amount will increase (negatively amortize), and your loan amount will likely become larger than your original loan amount. Increases in your loan amount lower the equity you have in this property.

☐ may have monthly payments that do not pay all of the interest due that month. If you do, your loan amount will increase (negatively amortize), and, as a result, your loan amount may become larger than your original loan amount. Increases in your loan amount lower the equity you have in this property.

☒ do not have a negative amortization feature.

Partial Payments

Your lender

☒ may accept payments that are less than the full amount due (partial payments) and apply them to your loan.

☐ may hold them in a separate account until you pay the rest of the payment, and then apply the full payment to your loan.

☐ does not accept any partial payments.

If this loan is sold, your new lender may have a different policy.

Security Interest

You are granting a security interest in
456 Somewhere Ave., Anytown, ST 12345

You may lose this property if you do not make your payments or satisfy other obligations for this loan.

Escrow Account

For now, your loan

☒ will have an escrow account (also called an "impound" or "trust" account) to pay the property costs listed below. Without an escrow account, you would pay them directly, possibly in one or two large payments a year. Your lender may be liable for penalties and interest for failing to make a payment.

Escrow		
Escrowed Property Costs over Year 1	$2,473.56	Estimated total amount over year 1 for your escrowed property costs: *Homeowner's Insurance Property Taxes*
Non-Escrowed Property Costs over Year 1	$1,800.00	Estimated total amount over year 1 for your non-escrowed property costs: *Homeowner's Association Dues* You may have other property costs.
Initial Escrow Payment	$412.25	A cushion for the escrow account you pay at closing. See Section G on page 2.
Monthly Escrow Payment	$206.13	The amount included in your total monthly payment.

☐ will not have an escrow account because ☐ you declined it ☐ your lender does not offer one. You must directly pay your property costs, such as taxes and homeowner's insurance. Contact your lender to ask if your loan can have an escrow account.

No Escrow	
Estimated Property Costs over Year 1	Estimated total amount over year 1. You must pay these costs directly, possibly in one or two large payments a year.
Escrow Waiver Fee	

In the future,

Your property costs may change and, as a result, your escrow payment may change. You may be able to cancel your escrow account, but if you do, you must pay your property costs directly. If you fail to pay your property taxes, your state or local government may (1) impose fines and penalties or (2) place a tax lien on this property. If you fail to pay any of your property costs, your lender may (1) add the amounts to your loan balance, (2) add an escrow account to your loan, or (3) require you to pay for property insurance that the lender buys on your behalf, which likely would cost more and provide fewer benefits than what you could buy on your own.

Loan Calculations

Total of Payments. Total you will have paid after you make all payments of principal, interest, mortgage insurance, and loan costs, as scheduled.	$285,803.36
Finance Charge. The dollar amount the loan will cost you.	$118,830.27
Amount Financed. The loan amount available after paying your upfront finance charge.	$162,000.00
Annual Percentage Rate (APR). Your costs over the loan term expressed as a rate. This is not your interest rate.	4.174%
Total Interest Percentage (TIP). The total amount of interest that you will pay over the loan term as a percentage of your loan amount.	69.46%

 Questions? If you have questions about the loan terms or costs on this form, use the contact information below. To get more information or make a complaint, contact the Consumer Financial Protection Bureau at **www.consumerfinance.gov/mortgage-closing**

Other Disclosures

Appraisal
If the property was appraised for your loan, your lender is required to give you a copy at no additional cost at least 3 days before closing. If you have not yet received it, please contact your lender at the information listed below.

Contract Details
See your note and security instrument for information about
- what happens if you fail to make your payments,
- what is a default on the loan,
- situations in which your lender can require early repayment of the loan, and
- the rules for making payments before they are due.

Liability after Foreclosure
If your lender forecloses on this property and the foreclosure does not cover the amount of unpaid balance on this loan,

☒ state law may protect you from liability for the unpaid balance. If you refinance or take on any additional debt on this property, you may lose this protection and have to pay any debt remaining even after foreclosure. You may want to consult a lawyer for more information.

☐ state law does not protect you from liability for the unpaid balance.

Refinance
Refinancing this loan will depend on your future financial situation, the property value, and market conditions. You may not be able to refinance this loan.

Tax Deductions
If you borrow more than this property is worth, the interest on the loan amount above this property's fair market value is not deductible from your federal income taxes. You should consult a tax advisor for more information.

Contact Information

	Lender	Mortgage Broker	Real Estate Broker (B)	Real Estate Broker (S)	Settlement Agent
Name	Ficus Bank		Omega Real Estate Broker Inc.	Alpha Real Estate Broker Co.	Epsilon Title Co.
Address	4321 Random Blvd. Somecity, ST 12340		789 Local Lane Sometown, ST 12345	987 Suburb Ct. Someplace, ST 12340	123 Commerce Pl. Somecity, ST 12344
NMLS ID					
ST License ID			Z765416	Z61456	Z61616
Contact	Joe Smith		Samuel Green	Joseph Cain	Sarah Arnold
Contact NMLS ID	12345				
Contact ST License ID			P16415	P51461	PT1234
Email	joesmith@ ficusbank.com		sam@omegare.biz	joe@alphare.biz	sarah@ epsilontitle.com
Phone	123-456-7890		123-555-1717	321-555-7171	987-555-4321

Confirm Receipt

By signing, you are only confirming that you have received this form. You do not have to accept this loan because you have signed or received this form.

_____   _____   _____   _____
Applicant Signature   Date   Co-Applicant Signature   Date

All borrowers responsible for repayment of the loan must sign the Closing Disclosure.

Closing Disclosure Requirements

- The guidelines a creditor to provide the Closing Disclosure and the consumer must receive the disclosure **three business days prior to loan consummation**.

A creditor is also responsible for ensuring that the Closing Disclosure meets the content, delivery, and timing requirements. The delivery requirements can include:

- Providing the disclosures to the borrower in person
- Mailing or other delivery methods, including email or fax

[*For more information, see Regulation Z, 12 CFR §1026.19(f) Mortgage Loans Secured by Real Property-Final Disclosures, see also 12 CFR §1026.38 Content of Disclosures for Certain Mortgage Transactions (Closing Disclosure).*]

[*See Regulation Z, 12 CFR §1026.38(t)(3)(iii) Form.*]

The Closing Disclosure is considered received by the consumer:

- If provided in person, as of that day.
- If mailed or delivered by electronic methods three business days after it is delivered or placed in the mail.
- If a creditor has documented evidence of earlier receipt of the disclosures by the borrower, as of that date.

[*For more information, see Regulation Z, 12 CFR §1026.19(f)(1)(ii-iii) Scope – Timing.*]

The **creditor** has the *responsibility for the delivery of the Closing Disclosure to the borrower.* The creditor:

- May contract with the settlement agent to have the agent either assist the creditor in the preparation of the Closing Disclosure or take the full responsibility for preparation and delivery of the Closing Disclosure to the borrower.
- Must maintain communication with the settlement agent to ensure that the Closing Disclosure and its delivery meet the requirements set by the CFPB.

In short, the creditor remains responsible for all compliance and delivery requirements of the Closing Disclosure.

[*For more information, see Regulation Z, 12 CFR §1026.19(f)(1)(v) Settlement Agent.*]

The **settlement agent** does, however, have the *responsibility for the delivery of the Closing Disclosure that accurately reflects the costs of the transaction.* He may:

- Deliver a copy of the borrower's disclosure to the seller, *if the disclosure contains the seller charges and costs also.*
- Provide a Closing Disclosure to the seller that contains *information applicable to the seller's transaction.*

If the seller is provided with a separate document for signature, a copy of the executed Closing Disclosure is required to be provided to the creditor by the settlement agent.

[*For more information, see Regulation Z, 12 CFR §1026.38(t)(5)(v-vi) Closing Cost Details – Separation of Consumer and Seller Information, see also, 12 CFR §1026.19(f)(4) Transactions Involving a Seller.*]

If there are multiple borrowers in a transaction that is rescindable under the Truth in Lending Act, the Closing Disclosure must be delivered to *each* borrower who has the right to rescind the transaction. Adjustable rate mortgage disclosures required to be signed at closing need only be provided to a borrower who expresses an interest in receiving a copy. If the transaction is not rescindable, the Closing Disclosure may be provided to *any consumer* with primary liability for the loan.

[*For more information, see Regulation Z, 12 CFR §1026.17(d) Multiple Creditors; Multiple Consumers, see also 12 CFR 1026.38(t)(5)(v-vi) Separation of Consumer and Seller Information – Modified Version of the Form for a Seller or Third-Party.*]

With a timeshare transaction, the creditor must ensure that the Closing Disclosure is received by the consumer on the **day of loan consummation**.

There is a **three-business-day waiting period** prohibiting the loan from being consummated less than three business days after the Closing Disclosure is received by the consumer. If a settlement is scheduled during the waiting period, the creditor must generally postpone the settlement, *unless* the settlement is within the waiting period necessary to meet a bona fide personal financial emergency.

Consumers may waive or modify the three-business-day waiting period when:

- The extension of credit is needed for a bona fide personal financial emergency.

- The consumer has received the Closing Disclosure.

- The consumer (a) gives the creditor a dated written statement that describes the emergency, (b) specifically modifies or waives the waiting period, and (c) bears the signature of all consumers who are primarily liable for the mortgage.

The CFBP provided guidance regarding a bona fide financial emergency, which would include *"the imminent sale of the consumer's home at foreclosure, where the foreclosure sale will proceed unless loan proceeds are made available to the consumer during the waiting period, may be considered a bona fide personal financial emergency."*

The borrower requesting the waiver must sign a handwritten statement along with any other primary obligors.

[*For more information, see Regulation Z, 12 CFR §1026.19(f)(1)(iv) Consumer's Waiver of Waiting Period Before Consummation.*]

Revisions and Corrections to the Closing Disclosures

The general rule to be remembered is the creditor *must* deliver or place in the mail the revised Loan Estimate to the consumer no later than **three business days** after receiving the information sufficient to establish that one of the reasons for the revision has occurred.

After the creditor provides the Closing Disclosure, a revised Loan Estimate **may not** be issued. The creditor must make sure that the revised Loan Estimate is received at least **four (4) business days** prior to the consummation of the mortgage loan.

For example, if the creditor places the revised Loan Estimate in the mail and relies on the **three-business-day rule** pertaining to the receipt of documents that are mailed, the creditor must mail the disclosures **seven business days** prior to the consummation of the mortgage loan to allow for the three-business-day receipt rule.

[*For more information, see Regulation Z, 12 CFR § 1026.19(e)(4) Provision and Receipt of Revised Disclosures.*]

Changed Circumstances Prior to Loan Consummation

If sufficient time between the changed circumstance and the issuance of the Loan Estimate does not exist because the Closing Disclosure has been issued, a mortgage loan originator or creditor may *not* issue a revised Loan Estimate. The Closing Disclosure may be amended and re-disclosed with the approved changes if the consumer receives the revised charges on the Closing Disclosure **three business days** prior to consummation.

- If the borrower has received the first Closing Disclosure (within the three-business-day waiting period), the creditor **may** issue revised changes on the Closing Disclosure prior to loan consummation. The consumer may then compare the amounts charged for the purposes of determining good faith and tolerance.

[*See Regulation Z, 12 CFR § 1026.19(e)(4)(ii) Relationship to Disclosures Required Under § 1026.19(f)(1)(i).*]

Changes to Correct or Revise Closing Disclosures

"The **three-business-day waiting period** requirement applies to a corrected **Closing Disclosure** that is provided when:

- There are changes to the loan's APR.
- There are changes to the loan product.
- The prepayment penalty is added.

If other types of changes occur, creditors must ensure that the consumer receives a corrected *Closing Disclosure* at or before **consummation**."

[*See Regulation Z, 12 CFR §1026.19(f)(2)(i-ii) Changes Before Consummation Not Requiring a New Waiting Period – Changes Before Consummation Requiring a New Waiting Period.*]

Changes that occur to the APR before consummation that require a new three-business-day waiting period include the disclosed APR on a closed-end transaction accurate for either:

- **Regular** transactions (which include any single advance transaction with equal payments and equal payment periods, or an irregular first payment period and/or a first or last irregular payment) if it is *within one-eighth of one percentage point* of the APR calculated under.

- **Irregular** transactions (which include multiple advance transactions and other transactions not considered regular) if it is *within one-quarter of one percentage point* of the APR calculated under.

For *any other changes before consummation* that do not fall under the categories above (i.e., related to the APR, loan product, or the addition of a prepayment penalty), the creditor still must provide a corrected **Closing Disclosure** with any terms or costs that have changed, and ensure that the consumer receives it.

For these changes, there is **no** additional three-business-day waiting period required. The creditor must ensure only that the consumer receives the revised Closing Disclosure **at or before consummation**.

A consumer has the right to inspect the Closing Disclosure during the business day before consummation.

[*For more information, see Regulation Z, 12 CFR § 1026.19 Certain Mortgage and Variable-Rate Transactions, 12 CFR § 1026.19(f)(2)(i) Charges Before Consummation Not Requiring a New Waiting Period, see also 12 CFR §1026.22(a)(2-3) Accuracy of Annual Percentage Rate.*]

Timing of Revisions and Redisclosure of the Closing Disclosure

When a Closing Disclosure is discovered to have an inaccuracy, whether numerical or clerical, a redisclosure must be made. The consumer may receive a corrected Closing Disclosure **after consummation** that:

- Corrects a numerical error.

- May include proceeds for a lender tolerance cure.

- Corrects a non-numerical clerical error that corrects the inaccuracy.

A seller may also receive a corrected Closing Disclosure for the same errors. Lenders must follow the timelines shown below by delivering the required disclosure and possibly additional funds.

Deliver or Mail within	
30 days	**60 days**
Closing Disclosure becomes inaccurate and results in a change to the amount paid by the consumer that was originally disclosed.	Non-numerical clerical errors and refunds for tolerance violations.
Closing Disclosure becomes inaccurate and results in a change to the amount paid by the seller that was originally disclosed.	If a creditor cures a tolerance violation and provides a refund to the consumer.

[*See Regulation Z, 12 CFR § 1026.19(f) Mortgage Loans Secured by Real Property—Final Disclosures.*]

Disclosures that May Be Required at Loan Consummation

Three other disclosures exist that may be provided to the borrower after loan consummation:

1. Escrow Closing Notice

2. Partial Payment Policy Disclosure

3. Servicing Transfer Disclosure Statement

The Escrow Closing Notice

The **Escrow Closing Notice** must be provided by the creditor *prior to cancelling an escrow account* for any consumers who had one established by the creditor. There are select exemptions to the rule that do not require the disclosure.

- The creditor is required to provide this notification to the borrower *when the consumer requests cancellation*. The servicer must ensure the borrower receives the Escrow Closing Notice no later than **three business days** before the consumer's escrow/impound account is closed.

- If the escrow is closed *for any other reason*, the creditor is required to provide the notice within **30 business days** of cancelling the consumer's escrow account.

If the Escrow Closing Notice is not delivered to the consumer in person, the consumer is considered to have received the disclosure three business days after it is delivered electronically or placed in the mail.

[*See Regulation Z, 12 CFR § 1026.20(e)(5) Timing.*]

Partial Payment Policy Disclosure

The Closing Disclosure includes disclosure regarding the acceptance of a partial mortgage payment by the loan servicer. This disclosure *informs the consumer about the policy of the mortgage servicer/creditor* and the acceptance of a payment less that the full amount due under the note. The creditor must provide information about the likelihood that partial mortgage payments will be accepted in the event of a hardship of the borrower.

The Closing Disclosure contains the following disclosure on Page 4:

Your lender:

- *May accept payments that are less than the full amount due (partial payments) and apply them to your loan*

- *May hold them in a separate account until you pay the rest of the payment, and then apply the full payment to your loan*

- *Does not accept any partial payments*

If this loan is sold, a new lender may have a different policy. A mortgage broker should know the policies of each wholesale lender he may broker loans to so he can complete this form accurately for the applicant.

Servicing Transfer Disclosure Statement

The Servicing Transfer Disclosure Statement informs the consumer of the sale, transfer, or reassignment of the mortgage loan. The Disclosure Statement (in addition to identifying the mortgage loan sold) must contain:

1. *The name, address, and telephone number of the covered person*

2. *The date of transfer*

3. *The name, address, and telephone number of an agent or party authorized to receive notice of the right to rescind and resolve issues concerning the consumer's payments on the loan*

4. *Where transfer of ownership of the debt to the covered person is or may be recorded in public records*

5. *The partial payment policy*

This disclosure is required to be mailed or delivered to the consumer within **30 calendars days** following the date of transfer of the loan.

[See Regulation Z, 12 CFR § 1026.39(d) Content of Required Disclosures.]

The Consumer Financial Protection Bureau is an excellent source of information regarding these changes. A very useful guidebook can be found on the CFPB website by searching for "TILA-RESPA Integrated Disclosure Rule Implementation."

Applying TILA Regulations to MLO Practices

MLOs should ask themselves three questions to make sure they protect themselves and their employees from any disciplinary actions:

1. Are the disclosures that are provided to the consumers on the correct form?

2. Are the disclosures provided to the consumers within the timeframes required by the new TILA regulations?

3. Are the allowable tolerances complied with on the Loan Estimate and Closing Disclosure forms or is there a potential for redisclosure and lender tolerance fees?

For failure to properly provide certain disclosures in an accurate manner, statutory penalties may be imposed. The CFPB has enforcement jurisdiction for both TILA and RESPA, which include the ability to impose fines and penalties up to **$25,000 per day** for violations.

MLOs need to communicate clearly to borrowers about the need to provide information in a *timely manner* and encourage them to either be available for in-person disclosure or utilize electronic delivery methods to ensure a smooth and compliant process. Borrowers who still desire to utilize the "paper" process will need to understand the delays this method will present.

Exercise 7.7: Knowledge Check

1. When a changed circumstance has occurred to the loan product and the Closing Disclosure has been delivered to the borrower, the creditor must

    A. call the borrower and inform him of the fee change.
    B. complete a valid changed circumstance form and have the borrower sign it.
    C. deliver a revised Closing Disclosure and apply a new three-day waiting period before consummation.
    D. make redisclosure.

2. When a numerical error has occurred to Closing Disclosure and the initial Closing Disclosure has been delivered to the borrower, the creditor must

    A. call the borrower and inform him of the fee change.
    B. complete a valid changed circumstance form and have the borrower sign it.
    C. deliver a revised Closing Disclosure and apply a new three-day waiting period before consummation.
    D. make redisclosure.

Exercise 7.8: Apply Your Knowledge

Directions: In this discussion activity, you will apply your knowledge of the Loan Estimate and the Closing Disclosure involving decisions related to their use.

Review the scenario, sample Closing Disclosure, and the information presented about it.

Description: A borrower applies for a $200,000 refinance loan. He uses the services of a mortgage broker who charges a 1% origination fee and a $600 processing fee. The broker intends to broker the loan to a wholesale lender who charges a $1,000 administration fee.

Discussion Questions:

1. What dollar amount must be shown on the Loan Estimate on Page 2, Section A "Origination Charges"?

   _____

   _____

   _____

   _____

2. If the mortgage broker is unsuccessful at obtaining approval with the first lender and submits the loan file to a second lender whose administration fee is $1,200, what can the broker do about the fee increase?

   _____

   _____

   _____

   _____

3. If the dollar amount shown on Closing Disclosure for items listed on Page 2, Section B of the "Services You Cannot Shop For" totals $4,625, what is the maximum amount the borrower can be charged on the final Closing Disclosure?

   _____

   _____

   _____

   _____

4. If the actual fees charged on the Closing Disclosure for items listed on page 2, Section B of the "Loan Costs" total $6,000, what must the mortgage broker do?

   _____

   _____

   _____

   _____

Truth in Lending Act – Regulation Z

Truth in Lending Act Provisions

TILA is administered by the CFPB. The specific provisions of the Act, which are contained in Title I of the Consumer Credit Protection Act as amended (15 U.S.C. 1601 et seq.), are implemented by **Regulation Z** [see Regulation Z, 12 CFR Part 1026]. TILA has been amended numerous times, most recently by the Housing and Economic Recovery Act of 2008; the Mortgage Disclosure Improvement Act (MDIA), which went into effect in 2009; and the Dodd-Frank Wall Street Reform and Consumer Protection Act of 2010.

While Regulation Z does not set limits on interest rates or other finance charges imposed by lenders, it does regulate the disclosure of these items [see Regulation Z, 12 CFR Part 1026, Subpart C – Closed-End Credit, §1026.17 General disclosure requirements.]. Prior to the 1968 passage of the **Truth in Lending Act**, there were no federal laws requiring the disclosure of consumer credit costs expressed as a percentage. Specifically, the Act requires all creditors who deal with consumers to make certain disclosures concerning all finance charges and related aspects of credit transactions (including disclosing finance charges expressed as an annual percentage rate) [see Regulation Z, 12 CFR Part 1026, Subpart C – Closed-End Credit, §1026.18 Content of disclosures.]. The Act also establishes a three-business-day right of rescission in certain transactions.

TILA's provisions apply to each creditor who offers or extends credit to consumers in the ordinary course of business, primarily for personal, family, or household purposes. The credit offered must be subject to a finance charge or payable by written agreement in **more than four installments** [see Regulation Z, 12 CFR Part 1026, Subpart A – General, §1026.1(c)(iii) Authority, purpose, coverage, organization, enforcement, and liability.]. Under the Act, the definition of **credit** includes *all real estate loans made to consumers—no matter what the amount—if the loan is **for other than business or commercial purposes***.

Business or commercial purposes is further defined by *12 CFR §1026.3.a* as "*an extension of credit, primarily for a business, commercial, or agricultural use.*" This could include a non-owner-occupied home when credit is extended to purchase, refinance, or rehabilitate the non-owner occupied property. The test of an owner occupancy or business purpose loan is the *number of days* that an owner occupies the property. If an owner will occupy the home for **more than 14 days**, the exemption from TILA regulations for the property is **not** applicable.

For example, if a borrower purchases a cabin in the mountains and will occupy the home during the summer months, the exemption for complying with TILA *does not apply*.

[*See Regulation Z, 12 CFR §1026.3 Exempt Transactions.*]

 One exemption from coverage is credit of more than $25,000 that is not secured by real property.

Disclosures

Disclosures are required in two general areas:

- **When creditors offer credit but before the transaction is consummated**. Regulation Z requires disclosures be made clearly, conspicuously, *in writing*, and in a form the consumer may keep and read prior to the loan closing. If the disclosures are incorporated into the loan agreement, they must be separated from all other loan details; for example, they may be placed in a boxed section on the form or be separated by bold print dividing lines.

Creditors cannot impose any fees on a consumer before the party has received applicable disclosures about such fees and their conditions.

[See Regulation Z, 12 CFR Part 1026, Subpart C – Closed-End Credit, §1026.17(a)(b) General disclosure requirements, see Regulation Z, 12 CFR Part 1026, Subpart C – Closed-End Credit, §1026.19(a)(ii) Imposition of fees.]

- **When credit terms are advertised to potential customers** Advertisers of consumer credit must clearly and conspicuously provide certain information if they use specific triggering terms in their credit ads. The credit terms advertised must actually be available.

 [See Regulation Z, 12 CFR Part 1026, Subpart C – Closed-End Credit, §1026.16 Advertising.]

The following are specific disclosures required by Regulation Z:

- The Loan Estimate and the Closing Disclosure,
- Consumer Handbook on Adjustable Rate Mortgages (CHARM booklet) and adjustable rate mortgage (ARM) loan program details *(only for ARM loans)*
- When Your Home is on the Line *(only for home equity installment loans and home equity lines of credit)*

Regulation Z disclosure requirements include post-consummation events that address the coverage, timing, and format of:

- Rate adjustments with a corresponding change in payment
- Initial rate adjustment

A creditor must retain evidence of compliance with these disclosure requirements for at least two years after the disclosures were required to be made.

[See Regulation Z, 12 CFR Part 1026, Subpart C – Closed-End Credit, §1026.20(c)(d) Disclosure Requirements Regarding Post-Consummation Events, see Regulation Z, 12 CFR Part 1026, Subpart D – Miscellaneous, §1026.25 Record Retention]

Annual Percentage Rate (APR)

For residential mortgages, the disclosure of the **annual percentage rate** (APR) is very important. [See Regulation Z, 12 CFR Part 1026, Subpart B – Open-End Credit, §1026.14 Determination of annual percentage rate.] The APR tells a borrower *the total cost of financing a loan in percentage terms, as a relationship of the total finance charges to the total amount financed*. The APR is *not* simply the interest rate that appears in the promissory note, known as the **note rate**. Rather, it reflects certain **finance charges** associated with the loan, spread out over the life of the loan. Therefore, the APR is generally higher than the note rate.

Points to Remember

The most important concept to remember about the federal Truth In Lending Act is the requirement of disclosures to provide a uniform method of finance charge disclosure. This method is expressing the true cost of credit over the term of the loan as a percentage, not a dollar amount (as is the RESPA requirement).

It can be a challenge to explain closing costs and fees to consumers, especially to define those fees that are considered finance charges for the purpose of calculating the APR. Regulation Z defines the **finance charge** [see Regulation Z, 12 CFR Part 1026, Subpart A – General, §1026.4 Finance charge.] as the *cost of consumer credit as a dollar amount*. It includes any charge payable directly or indirectly by the consumer and imposed directly or indirectly by the creditor as an incident to or a condition of the extension of credit. It does not include any charge of a type payable in a comparable cash transaction.

Fees charged by a mortgage broker (including fees paid by the consumer directly to the broker or to the creditor for delivery to the broker) are finance charges, even if the creditor does not require the consumer to use a mortgage broker and even if the creditor does not retain any portion of the charge.

Charges Included in the Finance Charge

According to Regulation Z [see Regulation Z, 12 CFR Part 1026, Subpart A – General, §1026.4(b) Finance charge.], the following are examples of finance charges:

- Interest, time price differential, and any amount payable under an add-on or discount system of additional charges

- Service, transaction, activity, and carrying charges, including any charge imposed on a checking or other transaction account to the extent that the charge exceeds the charge for a similar account without a credit feature

- Points, loan fees, assumption fees, finder's fees, and similar charges

Charges Excluded from the Finance Charge

According to Regulation Z [see Regulation Z, 12 CFR Part 1026, Subpart A – General, §1026.4(c) (d)(e) Finance charge], the following are **excluded** from the finance charge:

- Seller's points

- Interest forfeited as a result of an interest reduction required by law on a time deposit used as security for an extension of credit

- Fees in a transaction secured by real property or in a residential mortgage transaction, if bona fide and a reasonable amount, including:

  - Fees for title examination, abstract of title, title insurance, property survey, and similar purposes

  - Fees for preparing loan-related documents, such as deeds, mortgages, and reconveyance or settlement documents

  - Notary and credit report fees

  - Property appraisal fees or fees for inspections to assess the value or condition of the property if the service is performed prior to closing, including fees related to pest infestation or flood hazard determinations

  - Amounts required to be paid into escrow or trustee accounts if the amounts would not otherwise be included in the finance charge

Exercise 7.9: Apply Your Knowledge

Directions: In this discussion activity, you will apply your knowledge of TILA disclosure requirements and determining Annual Percentage Rates (APR).

Description: Two borrowers each apply for a mortgage loan of $125,000. Their closing costs are $3,500 for each loan and the interest rate charged is 4.25%. The first borrower receives a 30-year fixed-rate mortgage and the second borrower secures a 15-year fixed-rate mortgage.

Discussion Questions:

1. Which borrower is quoted the highest Annual Percentage Rate?

   _____

   _____

2. Which borrower will pay the higher finance charges imposed on the loan?

   _____

   _____

3. Which borrower will pay more in principal repayment?

   _____

   _____

Real Success

Whenever you quote an interest rate to a consumer—including advertisements, websites, etc.—the APR must also be disclosed. When a potential borrower inquires about the cost of credit orally, only the APR is required to be stated. If you cannot determine the APR in advance, other cost information for the consumer's specific transaction may be given, as well as:

- For open-end credit, the corresponding APR must be stated.
- For closed-end credit, the APR for a sample transaction must be stated.

As a general rule to assist you with determining what closing costs are included in the APR, consider this: If a borrower is purchasing a home for cash, there are certain closing costs that he would not incur, such as an application fee, credit report fee, underwriting fee, mortgage insurance, and interest. These are generally the same costs that are included in the APR calculation.

APR Accuracy and Redisclosure

According to Regulation Z [see 12 CFR Part 1026, §1026.22], the annual percentage rate is generally considered accurate if it does not vary above or below the APR initially disclosed by more than:

- 1/8% (.125) for a regular transaction
- 1/4% (.25) for an irregular transaction

An **irregular** transaction is defined as one that includes *one or more* of the following features:

- Multiple advances
- Irregular payment periods
- Irregular payment amounts (other than an irregular first period or irregular first and final payment)

If a change renders the APR inaccurate prior to loan consummation, TILA requires that the borrower is given a corrected disclosure of all terms. The consumer must receive the corrected Closing Disclosure no later than **three days prior to loan consummation** or the corrected Loan Estimate **no later than four business days** prior to loan consummation. If the corrected disclosures are mailed or delivered by some method other than in person, the consumer is considered to have received them three (3) business days after they were mailed [see 12 CFR Part 1026, §1026.19(a)(2)(ii)].

The loan generally cannot be consummated until both waiting periods have expired. However, a borrower *may* be able to **waive** the waiting periods and expedite the closing if there is a **bona fide personal financial emergency**, such as to avoid foreclosure. This requires a dated written statement from the borrower with the details of the emergency [see 12 CFR Part 1026, §1026.19(a)(3)].

Also, remember that consumers are **not** required to continue with the loan during these waiting periods simply because the creditor provided these disclosures.

The Mortgage Disclosure Improvement Act or the 3/7/3 Rule

Remember these disclosure requirements as the 3/7/3 Rule [see 12 CFR Part 1026, §1026.19 Certain mortgage and variable-rate transactions.]:

- The initial disclosure must be given (or placed in the mail) within **three business days** of receipt of a completed application.
- The earliest a loan may be consummated is on the **seventh business day** after disclosures are delivered/mailed.
- Any corrected APR, as shown on the Loan Estimate or Closing Disclosure, that exceeds the tolerance threshold must be received by the consumer at least **three business days** before the loan is consummated.

This means that in order to comply with the Mortgage Disclosure Improvement Act, the earliest a loan may close is the **seventh business day** after the initial disclosures are delivered or placed in the mail [see Regulation Z, 12 CFR Part 1026, Subpart C – Closed-End Credit, §1026.19(a)(2)(i)].

When considering these waiting periods, Regulation Z defines a **business day** to be *all calendar days **except** Sundays and the legal public holidays specified in 5 U.S.C. 6103(a), such as New Year's Day, the birthday of Martin Luther King, Jr., Washington's Birthday, Memorial Day, Independence Day, Labor Day, Columbus Day, Veterans Day, Thanksgiving Day, and Christmas Day [see 12 CFR Part 1026, §1026.2(a)(6)].*

For Example

Example 1: The creditor takes an application for a fixed-rate loan on Tuesday, May 1 and mails the Loan Estimate the next day, Wednesday, May 2. The earliest the loan can close—assuming the APR on the Closing Disclosure is within the tolerance—is the following Thursday, May 10, the seventh business day after mailing the initial disclosure (assuming no legal federal holidays occur during the waiting period).

Example 2: Same situation as above, but on Friday, May 4, the interest rate goes up, causing the APR to increase by more than .125 percent. The creditor mails a revised Loan Estimate on Saturday, May 5. The consumer is assumed to have received it three business days later (Wednesday, May 9). The three-business-day waiting period then begins Thursday. Since the next day after the three-business-day waiting period is a Sunday, the earliest this loan will close is Monday, May 14 (assuming no legal federal holidays occur during the waiting period).

Qualified Mortgage (QM)

The Dodd-Frank Act provides that **qualified mortgages**, which *must meet certain requirements that prohibit or limit the risky features that harmed consumers in the recent mortgage crisis*, are entitled to a presumption that the creditor making the loan satisfied the Ability-To-Repay requirements.

Originally, the Act did not specify whether the presumption of compliance is conclusive (i.e., creates a safe harbor, which is a provision of a statute or a regulation that specifies that certain conduct will be deemed not to violate a given rule (Peter Swire, Safe Harbors and a Proposal to Improve the Community Reinvestment Act, 79 Va. L. Rev. 349, 372 (1993)) or is rebuttable.

The final rule provides a safe harbor for loans that satisfy the definition of a qualified mortgage and are not "higher-priced," as generally defined by the Board's 2008 rule. The final rule also provides a rebuttable presumption for higher-priced mortgage loans. The line the CFPB draws is one that has long been recognized as a rule of thumb to separate prime loans from subprime loans. Indeed, under the existing regulations that were adopted by the Board in 2008, only higher-priced mortgage loans are subject to an Ability-to-Repay requirement and a rebuttable presumption of compliance if creditors follow certain requirements. The new rule strengthens the requirements needed to qualify for a rebuttable presumption for subprime loans and defines more clearly the grounds for rebutting the presumption.

The Bureau granted limited legal protection to creditors in return for implementation of the new regulations. Prior to the $25 billion settlement with various mortgage lenders, the litigious climate in our court system (when many lender lawsuits were filed) was unsettling to the mortgage industry. The lenders were found to have committed a wide range of mortgage abuses, including falsifying foreclosure documents, executing those documents without review (automatic or robo signing), and falsifying mortgage loan documents (CBS News, February 9, 2012).

In order to lessen their liability and culpability in a court of law, lenders will be presumed to have complied with the Ability-to-Repay rule if they issue qualified mortgages (QM).

Specifically, the final rule provides that consumers may show a violation with regard to a subprime qualified mortgage by showing that, at the time the loan was originated, the consumer's income and debt obligations left insufficient residual income or assets to meet living expenses. The analysis would consider the consumer's monthly payments on the loan, loan-related obligations, and any simultaneous loans of which the creditor was aware, as well as any recurring, material living expenses of which the creditor was aware. Guidance accompanying the rule notes that the longer the period of time that the consumer has demonstrated actual ability to repay the loan by making timely payments, without modification or accommodation, after consummation or, for an adjustable-rate mortgage, after recast, the less likely the consumer will be able to rebut the presumption based on insufficient residual income.

With respect to prime loans, if a prime loan satisfies the qualified mortgage criteria, it will be presumed that the creditor made a good faith and reasonable determination of the consumer's ability to repay.

The rule excludes open-end credit plans, timeshare plans, reverse mortgages, or certain temporary loans.

Ability-to-Repay and Qualified Mortgage Rule

[For more information, see 12 CFR §1026.43 (as amended) Minimum standards for transactions secured by a dwelling (Regulation Z)]

A creditor must generally consider eight types of information when establishing the borrower's ability to repay a mortgage loan:

1. Current income or assets
2. Current employment status
3. Borrower's credit history
4. Monthly payment for the mortgage
5. Borrower's monthly payments on other simultaneous mortgage loans
6. Monthly payments for other mortgage-related expenses (such as property taxes, hazard insurance, private mortgage insurance)
7. Other debts of the borrower
8. Monthly debt payments, including the mortgage, compared to the borrower's monthly income (debt-to-income ratio)

Borrower Must Have Sufficient Assets or Income to Pay Back Loan

Lenders must evaluate and conclude that the borrower can repay the loan. For example, lenders may look at the consumer's **debt-to-income ratio** –*total monthly debt divided by their total monthly gross income*. Knowing how much money a consumer earns and is expected to earn and knowing how much they already owe helps a lender determine how much more debt a consumer can take on.

Teaser Rates Cannot Mask True Cost of Mortgage

Lenders cannot base their evaluation of a consumer's ability to repay on teaser rates. *Lenders must determine the consumer's ability to repay both the principal and the interest over the long term* – not just during an introductory period when the rate may be lower.

If a lender complies with the clear criteria of a qualified mortgage, consumers will have greater assurance that they can pay back the loan.

Features of Qualified Mortgages (QM)

- **No excess upfront points and fees:** Limits points and fees, including those used to compensate loan originators, such as loan officers and brokers. A loan generally *cannot* be considered a qualified mortgage *if the points and fees paid by the consumer exceed three percent (3%) of the total loan amount,* although certain bona fide discount points are excluded for prime loans. See chart for 2018 trigger amounts.

For a loan amount greater than or equal to $105,158	3 percent of the total loan amount
For a loan amount greater than or equal to $63,095 but less than $105,158	$3,155
For loans greater than or equal to $21,032 but less than $63,095	5 percent of the total loan amount
For a loan amount greater than or equal to $13,145 but less than $21,032	$1,052
For loans less than $13,145	8 percent of the total loan amount

- **No toxic loan features:** *Cannot* have risky loan features, such as:
  - Terms that exceed 30 years
  - Interest-only payments
  - Negative amortization payments where the principal amount increases.
- **Cap on how much income can go toward debt:** Qualified mortgages generally will be provided to people who have *debt-to-income ratios less than or equal to 43 percent.* This requirement helps ensure consumers are only getting what they can likely afford. For a temporary, transitional period, loans that do not have a 43 percent debt-to-income ratio but meet government affordability or other standards – such as that they are eligible for purchase by Fannie Mae or Freddie Mac will be considered qualified mortgages.
- **No-doc loans not eligible:** So-called no-doc loans where the creditor does not verify income or assets cannot be qualified mortgages.
- **Prepayment penalties prohibited:** Prepayment penalties are generally prohibited, except for certain fixed-rate, qualified loans.

Additional Provisions of the Rule

The final rule provides for a:

- Second *temporary* category of qualified mortgages that have more flexible underwriting requirements if they satisfy the general product feature prerequisites for a qualified mortgage and also satisfy the underwriting requirements of, and are therefore eligible to be purchased, guaranteed, or insured by either the GSEs while they operate under federal conservatorship or receivership; or the U.S. Department of Housing and Urban Development, Department of Veterans Affairs, or Department of Agriculture or Rural Housing Service.

 This temporary provision is scheduled to end in January of 2021, as the various Federal agencies issue their own qualified mortgage rules and if GSE conservatorship ends. This category ends after seven years.

- The record retention requirements to demonstrate compliance for lenders and creditors is *three years*.

In addition to the foregoing Ability-to-Repay provisions, the Dodd-Frank Act established other new standards concerning a wide range of mortgage lending practices, including compensation of mortgage originators, federal mortgage disclosures, and mortgage servicing.

Exercise 7.10: Knowledge Check

1. **The purpose of the Ability-to-Repay regulation is to (select all correct responses)**

   A. allow a borrower to obtain a stated income loan

   B. allow a borrower to sue the lender in Federal District Court to cancel the loan.

   C. allow a presumption that the lender followed the Ability-to-Repay guidelines if certain requirements are made.

   D. protect the borrower from a loan he may not be able to afford.

2. **A Qualified Mortgage, according to the Dodd-Frank Act, defines a mortgage loan's**

   A. minimum loan amount.

   B. minimum loan term.

   C. maximum loan amount.

   D. maximum loan term.

Right of Rescission

Under Regulation Z (§1026.15 and §1026.23), consumers have the right to rescind certain credit transactions. **Rescind** means to *take back or withdraw an offer or contract*. The right of rescission as discussed in these sections of Regulation Z applies to any credit transaction involving the establishment of a security interest (for example, a mortgage or deed of trust) in a **principal residence**, such as:

- Home equity loans

- Home improvement loans

- Refinances

- Home equity lines of credit

There are additional rescission rights associated with high cost and higher-priced loans.

This right of rescission does **not** apply to the following:

- Purchase loans (which protect sellers who may have entered into another contract or purchased a home contingent on the buyers purchasing their present home)

- Construction loans (which protect builders who may have performed services based on the buyer's commitment)

- Commercial loans

- Loans on vacation or second homes

- Refinancing or consolidation by the same creditor of an extension of credit already secured by the consumer's principal dwelling *unless* the new amount financed exceeds the unpaid principal balance, any earned unpaid finance charge on the existing debt, and amounts attributed solely to the costs of the transaction.

- Transactions in which a state agency is a creditor.

Points to remember:

- When more than one consumer has the right to rescind, the exercise of the right by one consumer is effective for **all** consumers.

- If a consumer chooses to exercise the right to rescind, the mortgage is void and the creditor must return any money collected related to the loan **within 20 calendar days**. The consumer has no liability for the loan, including finance charges.

- Consumers may exercise the right to rescind the credit transaction **until midnight of the third business day** following loan consummation, delivery of the required rescission notice, or delivery of all material disclosures, **whichever occurs last**.

Note that for the purposes of rescission, the term **consumer** is expanded to include any *"natural person in whose principal dwelling a security interest is or will be retained or acquired, if that person's ownership interest in the dwelling is or will be subject to the security interest"* (§1026.2 (a)(11)).

Case in Point

Loan papers for a refinance are signed on Wednesday. The consumer can consider the paperwork and disclosures and decide if she will proceed with the mortgage closing on Thursday (Day 1), Friday (Day 2), and Saturday (Day 3). Under Regulation Z's provisions for rescission, Saturdays are included in the rescission period, but Sundays and federal holidays are not included in the three-business-day calculation. The mortgage can be recorded and money disbursed the next business day, Monday (assuming Monday is not a legal federal holiday).

Wednesday	Thursday	Friday	Saturday	Sunday	Monday
Loan Consummation	Day 1	Day 2	Day 3	--	$$ Disbursed

Notice of Right to Rescind

Creditors must inform consumers of their right to rescind by providing **two copies** of a **Notice of Right to Rescind** document to *each consumer entitled to rescind*. The Notice of Right to Rescind must be in a separate document from the sale or credit document, and must identify the transaction or occurrence and conspicuously disclose the following:

- Retention or acquisition of a security interest in the consumer's principal dwelling

- Consumer's right to rescind

- How to exercise the right of rescission, with a form to use that designates the address of the creditor's place of business

- Effects of rescission

- Date on which the rescission period ends

Extended Right of Rescission

Consumers may have the right to an extended rescission period of up to **three years** under these circumstances:

- The creditor fails to properly notify consumers of the right to rescind.

- The creditor does not provide the consumer with the required material disclosures (or the required corrected redisclosures). **Material** refers to *the annual percentage rate, finance charge, amount financed, total payments, or payment schedule within the acceptable tolerances.*

Additional Rescission Considerations for Foreclosures

After the initiation of foreclosure on the consumer's principal dwelling that secures the credit obligation, the consumer shall have the right to rescind the transaction if:

- A mortgage broker fee that should have been included in the finance charge was not included.

- The creditor did not provide the properly completed Notice of Rescission.

Tolerance for disclosures. After the initiation of foreclosure on the consumer's principal dwelling that secures the credit obligation, the finance charge and other disclosures affected by the finance charge (such as the amount financed and the annual percentage rate) shall be considered accurate if the disclosed finance charge is:

- Understated by no more than $35; or

- Greater than the amount required to be disclosed.

Advertising Disclosures

Prior to the passage of the Truth in Lending Act, an advertiser might have disclosed only the most attractive credit terms, distorting the true cost of financing. For example, the ad could have included the low monthly payment (e.g., $275 a month) without indicating the large down payment necessary to qualify for that payment level. Advertisers did not have to disclose the APR or whether the transaction was a credit sale or lease.

The Act requires the advertiser to tell the whole story and to tell it **clearly** and **conspicuously**. Here's a critical point: When discussing an adjustable rate mortgage that has a fixed term, the word "**fixed**" must be accompanied by an equally prominent and closely proximate statement of the fixed time period and the fact that the rate may vary or the payment may increase after that period.

Anyone who places advertising that references consumer credit is required to follow the advertising provisions of the Truth in Lending Act. In addition, if specific loan terms are shown in an ad, those terms must be **actually available**.

Triggering Terms Requiring Disclosure

If an advertisement is for credit secured by a dwelling, the advertisement may *not* state any other rate, except that a simple annual rate that is applied to an unpaid balance may be stated in conjunction with, but not more conspicuously than, the annual percentage rate.

If an advertisement contains any one of the triggering terms about the loan as specified in the Truth in Lending Act, that advertisement must also include the required disclosures. Examples of triggering terms in advertisements include:

- Amount of the down payment (e.g., "20% down")

- Amount of any payment (e.g., "Pay only $700 per month")

- Number of payments (e.g., "Only 360 monthly payments")

- Period of repayment (e.g., "30-year financing available")

- Amount of any finance charge (e.g., "1% finance charge")

The common element in the above examples is the quoting of a "specific" number. When creating any form of advertisement, the mortgage company or loan originator must refer to the Truth In Lending Act for guidance in making full disclosure to the consumer who will view the advertisement. Pay attention to the placement of "specific" numbers in the advertisement and the requirements they implement.

Exercise 7.11: Knowledge Check

A mortgage broker or banker who is writing an advertisement for the local newspaper, which will also be published on an Internet website, should consider which regulation to create a compliant ad?

A. Fair Housing Act

B. Regulation B

C. Regulation X

D. Regulation Z

Required Advertising Disclosures

If any triggering terms are used in an ad, **all** of these disclosures must be made:

- Amount or percentage of down payment

- Terms of repayment; e.g., payment schedule, including any balloon payments

- Annual percentage rate, using that term spelled out in full or APR; if the rate may increase (e.g., for ARMs), that fact must also be disclosed

 If an ad discloses only the APR, the additional disclosures are not required.

Terms That Do NOT Trigger Disclosure

Examples of terms that do *not* trigger required disclosures include:

- "5% Annual Percentage Rate loan available here."

- "Easy monthly payments."

- "FHA financing available." or "100% VA financing available."

- "Terms to fit your budget."

Advertising Closed-End Credit

A **closed-end** credit transaction is *one in which the balance is expected to be repaid—along with any interest and finance changes—by a specified future date*. Most real estate loans are closed-end. Additional advertising provisions in Regulation Z *(*§1026.24) related to these loans include:

Rate. If an advertisement states a simple annual rate of interest and more than one rate applies over the term of the loan, the advertisement must also disclose—with equal prominence and in close proximity to the advertised rate:

- Each simple annual rate of interest that will apply; if a variable-rate, a reasonably current index and margin must be used.

- The period of time during which each simple annual rate of interest applies.

- The APR for the loan.

Payment Amount. If the advertisement states the amount of any payment, it must also disclose—with equal prominence and in close proximity to the payment:

- The amount of each payment that applies over the term of the loan, including any balloon payment; if a variable-rate, a reasonably current index and margin must be used.

- The period of time during which each payment applies.

 When the ad for a first lien mortgage loan states the amount of any payment, it must also state prominently (but not with equal prominence) and in close proximity to the advertised payment that the payments do not include amounts for taxes and insurance, if applicable, and that the actual payment amount will be higher.

Payment and Rate Comparisons. Advertisements may not compare actual or hypothetical payments or rates and a "teaser" payment or simple annual rate available for the advertised product *unless* the ad includes a clear and conspicuous comparison to the terms required to be disclosed (APR, term, payments, etc.). If advertising a variable rate transaction where the payment or simple annual rate is based on the index and margin used to make subsequent rate or payment adjustments, the advertisement must include an equally prominent statement, in close proximity, that the payment or rate is subject to adjustment, as well as the time period when the first adjustment will occur.

Use of the Term "Fixed." If an advertisement references **both variable and non-variable rate** loans, the terms "adjustable rate mortgage," "variable rate mortgage," or "ARM" must appear with equal prominence as any use of the term "fixed" or "fixed-rate mortgage." Also, the term "fixed" must clearly refer *only* to the transactions with fixed rates. If referring to a payment or to a variable rate, it must also include the time period for which the rate or payment is fixed and a statement that the rate can vary and the payment can increase after that.

If an advertisement references a **variable rate** loan, the phrase "adjustable rate mortgage," "variable rate mortgage," or "ARM" must appear *before* the first use of the term "fixed" and must be at least as conspicuous as the word "fixed." In addition, the ad must clearly indicate the time period for which the rate or payment is fixed, and the fact that the rate may vary or the payment may increase after that period.

If the ad references a **non-variable rate** loan where the payment amount increases, the use of the word "fixed" must state the fact that the rate may vary or the payment may increase after that period.

Catalogs, Multiple-Page Ads, Electronic Ads. If a catalog or other multiple-page advertisement, or an electronic advertisement (such as an advertisement appearing on an Internet website), gives information in a table or schedule in sufficient detail that includes triggering terms requiring additional disclosure, it would be considered a single advertisement under the following circumstances:

- The table or schedule is clearly and conspicuously set forth, and

- Any statement of the triggering credit terms appearing anywhere else in the catalog or advertisement clearly refers to the page or location where the table or schedule begins.

The table or schedule of terms must include all appropriate disclosures for a representative scale of amounts up to the level of the more commonly sold higher-priced property or services offered.

Advertising Open-End Credit

Regulation Z was amended to comply with the Mortgage Disclosure Improvement Act of 2009 (§1026.16) to address the unique challenges in advertising open-end credit plans secured by the borrower's dwelling.

Remember, **open-end** credit refers to *a loan where credit is extended to the borrower during the term and the creditor may impose a finance charge on the outstanding unpaid balance*, such as a home equity line of credit (HELOC). It's critical that ads for these loans not use misleading terms, such as "free money."

These loans are also subject to the disclosure provisions previously discussed as well these additional provisions:

Additional Disclosures. If any of the triggering terms are used or the payment terms of the plan are set forth, affirmatively or negatively, in an advertisement, the ad must also clearly and conspicuously state the following:

- Any **loan fee** that is a percentage of the credit limit under the plan and an estimate of any other fees imposed for opening the plan, expressed as a single dollar amount or a reasonable range
- Any **periodic rate** used to compute the finance charge, expressed as an annual percentage rate
- The **maximum annual percentage rate** that may be imposed in a variable-rate plan

Further, if an advertisement states an initial APR that is **not** based on the index and margin used to make later rate adjustments in a variable-rate plan, the ad must also clearly indicate the period of time such initial rate is in effect and a reasonably current APR that would have been in effect using the index and margin.

Balloon Payments. In an ad that states a minimum payment and it's possible that a balloon payment would result if only the minimum periodic payment is made, that fact must be stated with equal prominence and close proximity.

Promotional Rates and Payment. If a HELOC advertisement states a promotional rate and/or a promotional payment, the ad must disclose—in a clear and conspicuous manner and with equal prominence and in close proximity to each listing of the promotional rate or payment—**all** of the following:

- The period of time during which the promotional rate or payment applies
- If a promotional **rate**, any APR that applies (if a variable rate, the APR must be disclosed within established accuracy standards)
- If a promotional **payment**, the amounts and time periods of any payments that will apply under the plan (if the payment is based on the application of a variable index and margin, it must be disclosed based on a reasonable current index and margin)

If an ad stating a promotional rate is broadcast on radio or television, in lieu of stating these disclosures, a toll-free telephone number (or one that allows consumers to reverse charges) from which to get additional cost information must be indicated.

 These provisions do not apply to an envelope in which an application or solicitation is mailed, nor to a banner advertisement or pop-up advertisement linked to an application or solicitation provided electronically.

Other General Provisions

Tax Implications. Care must be taken to ensure that an advertisement that states any tax implications—such as whether interest is tax-deductible—is not misleading. There are additional requirements imposed on ads distributed in paper form or through the Internet, rather than broadcast on radio or television:

- If the ad states the advertised extension of credit may exceed the fair market value of the dwelling, it must also clearly and conspicuously state that the interest on that portion of the loan is not tax deductible for federal income tax purposes.

- The consumer must be advised to consult a tax adviser about the deductibility of interest and charges.

Misrepresentations. Regulation Z prohibits:

- Misrepresentations about a loan product being government endorsed.

- Misleading use of the current lender's name in the advertisement or claims of debt elimination.

- Using the term "counselor" in any advertisement to refer to a for-profit mortgage broker or lender.

- In a foreign language advertisement, providing information about some trigger terms or required disclosures in a foreign language, while providing information about other trigger terms or required disclosures only in English.

Clear and Conspicuous Standard. When considering **oral advertisements** for credit secured by a dwelling, including alternative disclosures as provided for by §1026.24(g), a **clear and conspicuous disclosure**, whether by radio, television, or other medium, means *that the required disclosures are given at a speed and volume sufficient for a consumer to hear and comprehend them.*

For example, information stated very rapidly at a low volume in a radio or television advertisement would not meet the clear and conspicuous standard if consumers cannot hear and comprehend the information required to be disclosed.

Other Prohibited Practices

Regulation Z was amended to comply with the Mortgage Disclosure Improvement Act of 2009 (§1026.42) to specifically address perceived abuses in the mortgage industry. The following prohibitions apply to any **closed-end mortgage** loan that is subject to TILA and secured by the consumer's **principal dwelling**, regardless of pricing or loan purpose.

Appraisal

Creditors, mortgage brokers, and their affiliates are prohibited from coercing, influencing, or encouraging an appraiser to misstate the value of the dwelling. The law specifically prohibits:

- Implying to an appraiser that current or future retention of the appraiser depends on the amount at which the appraiser values a consumer's principal dwelling.

- Excluding an appraiser from consideration for future engagement because the appraiser reports a value of a consumer's principal dwelling that does not meet or exceed a minimum threshold.

- Telling an appraiser a minimum reported value of a consumer's principal dwelling that is needed to approve the loan.

- Failing to compensate an appraiser because the appraiser does not value a consumer's principal dwelling at or above a certain amount.

- Conditioning an appraiser's compensation on loan consummation.

In addition, a creditor cannot extend credit, if the creditor knows at or before closing, that improper coercion has occurred by anyone *unless* the creditor can document that it has acted with reasonable diligence to determine that the appraisal does not materially misstate or misrepresent the dwelling's value.

The following practices are *not* prohibited:

- Asking an appraiser to consider additional information about the dwelling or comparable properties.

- Asking an appraiser to correct factual errors

- Obtaining multiple appraisals of a consumer's principal dwelling, as long as the creditor adheres to a policy of selecting the most reliable appraisal, rather than the appraisal that states the highest value

- Withholding compensation from an appraiser for breach of contract or substandard performance of services as provided by contract

Homeowners Protection Act

The federal **Homeowners Protection Act** of 1998, or HPA, (Pub. L. No. 105-216, 112 Stat. 897) [see 12 USC, Ch. 49, Homeowners Protection Act, §4901-§4910] requires lenders or servicers:

- To provide certain disclosures and notifications concerning **private mortgage insurance** (PMI) on residential mortgage transactions [see 12 USC, Ch. 49, Homeowners Protection Act, §4903 Disclosure requirements].

- That refinance or service home mortgages to comply with its terms.

 Most provisions of the Act do not apply to home loans made before July 29, 1999.

Exclusions

The HPA does *not* cover loans that do not have private mortgage insurance or loans secured by second or multi-family homes. Nor does it apply to:

- Veterans Affairs (VA) or Federal Housing Administration (FHA) loans.

- Loans with lender-paid PMI, although these loans do require an upfront disclosure to the borrower [see 12 USC, Ch. 49, Homeowners Protection Act, §4905(b) Disclosure requirements for lender paid mortgage insurance].

Disclosure Provisions of the HPA

[See Consumer Compliance Handbook, Cancellation and Termination of PMI: Non-High-Risk Residential Mortgage Transactions (p. 2): http://www.federalreserve.gov/boarddocs/supmanual/cch/hpa.pdf.]

The HPA requires that lenders provide an **initial written disclosure** regarding PMI cancellation—and **annual reminders** of this right—to residential mortgage borrowers. The written notice must include these disclosures:

- **Borrower Cancellation.** The borrower's right to request cancellation of PMI when a mortgage has been paid down to **80%** of its original appraised value or purchase price, whichever is less. Additionally, a borrower requesting PMI cancellation must have:
    - o   A good history of payment,
    - o   Not taken out any other loans on the property, and
    - o   Not experienced a decline in the value of the home.
- **Automatic Termination.** The automatic cancellation of PMI by the lender when a mortgage has been paid down to **78%** of the property's original value, assuming the borrower is current with payments.
- **Prepayment.** The borrower's right to accelerate the cancellation date by making additional payments that bring the loan-to-value ratio to 80%.

The Act requires written disclosure for both adjustable rate and fixed-rate mortgages on primary residences. Disclosure requirements, however, vary depending on how the mortgage accrues interest:

- **Fixed-Rate Mortgages.** At the loan closing for a fixed rate mortgage, lenders must provide an initial amortization schedule with a written notice stating both the cancellation date that the borrower may seek to cancel PMI based on the amortization schedule and the automatic termination date.
- **Adjustable Rate Mortgages.** For ARMs, an amortization schedule would *not* be provided at closing, but the lender must inform the borrower when the LTV reaches 80%.

A **final disclosure** must be sent to the borrower *after the PMI coverage has been terminated or cancelled* to notify the borrower that the borrower is no longer covered by PMI and that the borrower is not required to pay PMI premiums any longer.

High-Risk Loans

[See Consumer Compliance Handbook, Exceptions to Cancellation and Termination of PMI: High-Risk Residential Mortgage Transactions (page 3): http://www.federalreserve.gov/boarddocs/supmanual/cch/hpa.pdf.]

Additional disclosures are required for so-called high-risk loans. The borrower-requested cancellation of PMI at 80% LTV and the automatic termination at 78% LTV requirements do *not* apply to high-risk loans. However, high-risk loans are subject to final termination and are divided into two categories: Conforming and nonconforming:

Conforming. *Conforming loans are loans that have an original principal balance not exceeding Fannie Mae and Freddie Mac's limit for conforming loans.* PMI on a conforming high-risk loan must be terminated:

- By the first day of the month following the date that is **the midpoint of the loan's initial amortization schedule** (in the case of a fixed-rate loan) or amortization schedules (in the case of an adjustable rate loan) if, on that date, the borrower is current on the loan. If the borrower is not current on that date, PMI must be terminated when the borrower becomes current.

Nonconforming. *Nonconforming loans are residential mortgage transactions that have an original principal balance exceeding Freddie Mac's and Fannie Mae's conforming loan limit.* If a residential mortgage transaction is a lender-defined high-risk loan, PMI must be terminated:

- On the date on which the principal balance of the mortgage—based solely on the initial amortization schedule (in the case of a fixed-rate loan) or the amortization schedules (in the case of an adjustable rate loan) for that mortgage—is **first scheduled to reach 77% of the original value of the property securing the loan**, regardless of the outstanding balance for that mortgage on that date.

Disclosure

[See 12 USC, Ch. 49, Homeowners Protection Act, §4902(a)(b)(c) Termination of private mortgage insurance.]

When PMI is required for high-risk residential mortgage transactions, the lender must provide to the borrower *a written notice* stating that PMI will not be required beyond the date that is the midpoint of the loan's amortization schedule if, on that date, the borrower is current on the payments as required by the terms of the loan. The lender must provide this notice at consummation.

The lender need not provide disclosure of the termination at 77% LTV for lender-defined high-risk mortgages.

Real Success

Property values can change over time for a variety of reasons—for example, due to an overall increase in a neighborhood's property values or significant home improvements. Borrowers whose PMI payments are included in their mortgage may assume that the equity in their homes should trigger the automatic cancellation of PMI. Although the Homeowners Protection Act does *not* require a mortgage servicer to consider the current property value, borrowers may contact the lender or servicer to determine if they have internal policies and procedures for the early cancellation of PMI because of increased values. For example, a servicer might consider:

- A minimum amount of time (years) before a borrower can request cancellation.

- A good payment history for at least a minimum amount of years.

- Documentation of home improvements to demonstrate the higher property value, which could include a new appraisal.

Chapter Summary

1. The regulations and guidelines that are in place in today's mortgage industry are a result of events that occurred in the last several decades. These regulations and guidelines mandated the following:

   - Disclosure of settlement costs expressed as a dollar figure

   - Disclosure of financial interests in a transaction

   - Disclosure of final settlement costs

   - Disclosure of closing costs and interest rates in a uniform manner

   - Disclosure of loan terms in advertising

   - Improved document review times for consumers

   - Elimination of PMI insurance at certain thresholds

2. A goal of RESPA is to help consumers become better-informed borrowers and to be able to compare available options and shop for settlement services. Therefore, RESPA requires and regulates various types of disclosures that lenders must deliver at particular times during the loan process. The required disclosures required by RESPA are in written format expressed as dollar amounts. This is one of the important concepts for a new MLO to comprehend.

3. Until the Loan Estimate disclosure, the Home Loan Toolkit, and other required disclosures are delivered to the borrower, an MLO may charge the borrower a fee only for the actual cost of obtaining a credit report.

4. A lender is held to the settlement terms specified and charges listed on the Loan Estimate delivered to the borrower at the time of application. The Loan Estimate shows the borrower which charges are:

   - Origination charges and services a borrower is not permitted to shop for, which cannot change at loan consummation (Page 2, Section A and B)

   - Services they can shop for, which could vary by up to 10% of the total (Page 2, Section C)

   - Services that can vary by any amount at loan consummation (Page 2, Section F, G, and H)

5. The Home Loan Toolkit is intended to help persons borrowing money to finance the purchase of residential real estate better understand the nature and costs of real estate settlement services. The CFPB requires lenders to distribute this information to borrowers *at the time of loan application or within three business days.*

6. The Mortgage Servicing Disclosure Statement is the standard form used to disclose to the borrower whether the lender intends to retain the mortgage servicing for the loan. This form is delivered to the borrower within three business days of a completed application.

7. The four sections of RESPA that impact and guide the mortgage industry in protecting borrowers from abuses include:

   - Section 6—Protects homeowners against abuses in loan servicing

   - Section 8—Prohibits kickbacks, fee-splitting, and unearned fees

   - Section 9—States a seller cannot require the use of particular title company

   - Section 10—Lists amounts that can be charged to maintain escrow accounts

8. Regulation X (12 CFR §1024.05), which addresses RESPA, applies to any federally-related mortgage loan secured by a first or subordinate lien on a residential real property designed for one-to-four families.

9. Regulation X prohibits giving or accepting a fee, kickback, or any thing of value in exchange for referrals of settlement service business involving a federally-related mortgage loan (allows an item of minimal value used for promotional purposes, such as pens, mementos, coffee cups, hats, etc.)

10. When it is necessary to provide a revised Loan Estimate, MLOs must do so *within three (3) business days* of receiving information sufficient to establish changed circumstances. MLOs must document the reason for the revised Loan Estimate, and then retain that documentation for *no less than three (3) years* after settlement.

11. The Truth in Lending Act is administered by the CFPB. The specific provisions of the Act are implemented by Regulation Z. TILA has been amended numerous times, most recently by the Housing and Economic Recovery Act of 2008, the Mortgage Disclosure Improvement Act (MDIA), which went into effect in 2009, and the Dodd-Frank Wall Street Reform and Consumer Protection Act of 2010.

12. For residential mortgages, disclosure of the APR is very important. The APR is not simply the interest rate that appears in the promissory note, known as the note rate. Rather, it reflects certain finance charges associated with the loan, spread out over the life of the loan. Therefore, the APR is generally higher than the note rate.

13. The most important concept to remember about the Truth in Lending Act is the requirement of disclosures to provide a uniform method of finance charge disclosure. This method expresses the true cost of credit over the term of the loan as a percentage, not a dollar amount (as is the requirement of RESPA).

14. According to Regulation Z (12 CFR §1026.22), the annual percentage rate is generally considered accurate if it does not vary above or below the APR initially disclosed by more than:

    - 1/8% (.125) for a regular transaction.

    - 1/4% (.25) for an irregular transaction.

15. The Mortgage Disclosure Improvement Act or the 3/7/3 Rule mandates:

    - Initial disclosures must be given to mortgage borrowers (or placed in the mail) *within three business days* of receipt of a completed application.

    - The earliest a loan may be consummated is on the *seventh business day* after disclosures are delivered/mailed.

    - Any corrected APR redisclosures must be received by the consumer at least *three business days* before the loan is consummated.

16. The right of rescission as discussed in Regulation Z applies to any credit transaction involving the establishment of a security interest in the principal residence. Creditors must inform consumers of their right to rescind by providing two copies of a Notice of Right to Rescind document to each consumer entitled to rescind.

17. Anyone who places advertising that references consumer credit is required to follow the advertising provisions of the Truth in Lending Act. If specific loan terms are shown in an ad, those terms must be actually available. If an advertisement is for credit secured by a dwelling, the advertisement may not state any other rate, except that a simple annual rate that is applied to an unpaid balance may be stated in conjunction with, but not more conspicuously than, the annual percentage rate. If an advertisement contains any

one of the triggering terms about the loan as specified in the Truth in Lending Act, that advertisement must also include the required disclosures. When creating any form of advertisement, the mortgage company or loan originator must refer to the Truth in Lending Act for guidance in making full disclosure to the consumer who will view the advertisement.

18. The federal Homeowners Protection Act of 1998, or HPA (Pub. L. No. 105-216, 112 Stat. 897), requires lenders or servicers to provide certain disclosures and notifications concerning private mortgage insurance (PMI) on residential mortgage transactions.

Chapter Quiz

1. **Which law requires MLOs to provide borrowers with a Loan Estimate of closing costs?**

   A. FCRA

   B. HMDA

   C. RESPA

   D. TILA

2. **The TILA-RESPA Integrated Disclosures are designed to help consumers**

   A. become better and more informed shoppers for consumer loans.

   B. know the methods available to file a consumer complaint.

   C. understand property appraisals.

   D. understand the right of rescission on a purchase.

3. **How many business days after closing does the consumer have the right to rescind a refinance of his personal residence?**

   A. 2

   B. 3

   C. 5

   D. There is no right of rescission.

4. **If an advertisement discloses only the APR, what additional disclosures are required?**

   A. amount of any finance charges

   B. percentage of down payment

   C. terms of repayment

   D. no additional disclosures are required

5. **Under what circumstances does RESPA allow a sale to be conditioned on the use of a particular title company chosen by the seller?**

   A. if full disclosure is made

   B. if no kickbacks are involved

   C. if no unearned fees are involved

   D. under no circumstances

6. **Which regulation mandates the use of the Closing Disclosure?**

   A. Regulation B

   B. Regulation C

   C. Regulation Z

   D. Regulation X

7. **According to the Homeowners Protection Act, borrowers may request cancellation of their mortgage insurance premiums when the borrower's equity reaches**

   A. 20%.

   B. 22%.

   C. 78%.

   D. 80%.

8. **Which fee can be collected prior to delivery of the Loan Estimate?**

   A. appraisal fee

   B. credit report fee

   C. origination fee

   D. No fees can be collected prior to delivery of the Loan Estimate.

9. The APR on a Loan Estimate for a 30-year-fixed rate loan is 6.25%, and the APR on the Closing Disclosure is 6.5%. After redisclosure, how long must the borrower wait to close the loan?

   A. one business day
   B. three business days
   C. seven business days
   D. There is no waiting required since the difference is within the acceptable tolerance.

10. Which statement about loan origination fees on a Loan Estimate is FALSE?

    A. The fee cannot change unless there is a changed circumstance.
    B. The fee includes services performed by or on behalf of the MLO.
    C. Lender and mortgage broker fees for the same transaction must be itemized.
    D. Origination fees must be expressed as a lump sum.

11. Which of these circumstances would NOT be an acceptable reason to provide a revised Loan Estimate to a borrower?

    A. The borrower lost the income from a part-time job and as a result was no longer eligible for the specific loan terms identified in the Loan Estimate.
    B. The borrower requested to change the loan term from 15 to 30 years.
    C. The MLO regretted overlooking certain liabilities in order to qualify the borrower for a better interest rate.
    D. The title company discovered a junior lien on the property that was not considered when preparing the Loan Estimate.

12. For purposes of initial disclosures, the day on which the offices of the business entity are open to the public for carrying on substantially all the entity's business functions is known as a

    A. business day.
    B. legal holiday.
    C. rescission day.
    D. work day.

13. The definition of a "Complete Application" includes all of the following EXCEPT the

    A. address of the subject property.
    B. gross monthly income.
    C. most recent two months of bank statements.
    D. name of the borrower.

14. The Loan Estimate does not apply to all real estate loans. All of the following loan types are exempt from the disclosures EXCEPT

    A. home equity lines of credit.
    B. home equity loans.
    C. reverse mortgages.
    D. timeshare loans.

15. A lender may NOT use _____ on the Loan Estimate.

    A. N/A
    B. POD
    C. TBD
    D. UNK

16. The Closing Disclosure discloses the settlement service provider charges the borrower will pay and all of the following EXCEPT

    A. assumption of the mortgage loan.
    B. escrow account information.
    C. negative amortization features.
    D. rate lock in information.

17. The total amount of interest a consumer will pay over the loan term as a percentage of the loan amount is referred to as the

    A. annual percentage rate.
    B. interest plus PMI charges.
    C. total finance charge.
    D. total interest percentage.

18. When providing the initial Loan Estimate, a business day is considered to be

    A. all calendar days except Sundays.
    B. all calendar days except Sundays and legal public holidays.
    C. the day a business entity is open for business to the public for the purpose of transacting substantially of the entity's business.
    D. the day the Loan Estimate is prepared.

19. **When providing the revised Loan Estimate prior to the delivery of the Closing Disclosure, a business day is considered to be**

    A. all calendar days except Sundays.

    B. all calendar days except Sundays and legal public holidays.

    C. the day a business entity is open for business to the public for the purpose of transacting substantially of the entity's business.

    D. the day the Loan Estimate is prepared.

20. **If a changed circumstance exists prior to loan consummation, a creditor may NOT provide a revised Loan Estimate to a consumer within ____ business day(s) of loan consummation.**

    A. 1

    B. 2

    C. 3

    D. 4

21. **Delivering the Closing Disclosure to the borrower is the responsibility of the**

    A. creditor.

    B. MLO.

    C. mortgage broker.

    D. settlement agent.

22. **Delivering the Closing Disclosure to the seller is the responsibility of the**

    A. creditor.

    B. MLO.

    C. mortgage broker.

    D. settlement agent.

23. **With a mortgage loan that is rescindable under the Truth In Lending Act, the Closing Disclosure must be delivered to**

    A. all borrowers who have the right to rescind.

    B. the borrower(s) with the primary responsibility for the mortgage loan.

    C. co-signers for the mortgage loan.

    D. the settlement agent for notarization.

24. **Adjustable rate disclosures that are required to be signed at closing need only be provided to the borrower who**

    A. expresses an interest in receiving a copy.

    B. has primary responsibility for the mortgage loan.

    C. has the right to rescind.

    D. is a co-signer for the mortgage loan.

25. **Loan consummation is the day that the**

    A. borrower becomes contractually obligated on the credit transaction.

    B. borrower becomes contractually obligated to the seller to perform on the sales contract.

    C. mortgage loan funds.

    D. refinance loan documents are fully executed.

26. **A Loan Estimate that is made in good faith is determined by the closing costs quoted on the Loan Estimate and on the Closing Disclosure. For a Loan Estimate to be made in good faith, the costs on the Loan Estimate should be**

    A. disclosed on a changed circumstance form.

    B. higher than what is charged on the Closing Disclosure.

    C. lower than what is charged on the Closing Disclosure.

    D. redisclosed on a revised Loan Estimate delivered to the borrower at least one business day before loan consummation.

27. **A changed circumstance for the purpose of the Loan Estimate can be any of the following EXCEPT**

    A. an event that is beyond the control of the creditor or borrower.

    B. information that was known or provided at the time of application but changed after the application, altering the interest rate of the loan.

    C. the MLO neglected to inform the borrower of the additional cost and necessity of a review appraisal when requested.

    D. new information regarding the borrower or the loan that the creditor did not rely on when providing the original Loan Estimate.

28. A borrower completes a loan application/ disclosures, but instead of locking the interest rate at the time of application, he locks the rate at a later date. The lender has _____ business days to redisclose the terms of the locked loan.

    A. There is no requirement to disclose.
    B. 1
    C. 2
    D. 3

29. Items on the Loan Estimate that have no tolerance restrictions for change include all of the following EXCEPT

    A. hazard insurance.
    B. periodic interest.
    C. private mortgage insurance.
    D. property taxes.

30. Charges for third-party services paid by or imposed on the consumer are grouped together and subject to a 10% cumulative tolerance. These fees can include all of the following EXCEPT the

    A. lender processing fee.
    B. location survey.
    C. recording fees.
    D. termite inspection.

31. If a borrower is quoted $200 for a termite report and no termite report is required or performed, what must be done?

    A. The fee is charged and then credited to the borrower for payment of other settlement costs.
    B. The fee is deducted from the aggregate amount for the 10% tolerance calculation prior to analyzing the amount for a 10% variance.
    C. The fee remains as a part of the aggregate amount for the 10% tolerance calculation and is included in the analysis for a 10% variance.
    D. The fee reverts to the creditor issuing the Closing Disclosure.

32. If the amounts paid by the consumer at closing exceed the prescribed tolerance thresholds, a creditor must refund the excess to the consumer no later than

    A. at closing.
    B. within five calendar days of loan closing.
    C. within 30 calendar days of closing.
    D. within 60 calendar days after consummation.

33. A creditor must deliver to the consumer, or place in the mail, the revised Loan Estimate no later than _____ business day(s) after receiving information regarding a fee that qualifies as a changed circumstance.

    A. 1
    B. 3
    C. 5
    D. 30

34. A creditor is generally required to ensure that the consumer receives the Closing Disclosure no later than ___ business day(s) before loan consummation.

    A. 0
    B. 1
    C. 3
    D. 5

35. The three-business-day waiting period requirement applies to a corrected Closing Disclosure when all of the following occur EXCEPT

    A. the addition of a pre-payment penalty to the loan.
    B. changes to the loan product.
    C. changes to the loan's APR.
    D. clerical errors made to the Closing Disclosure.

36. **The partial payment disclosure, located in the Closing Disclosure, contains all the following disclosures EXCEPT**

    A. the lender does not accept any partial payments.

    B. the lender may accept partial payments and apply them to the loan.

    C. the lender may hold partial payments in a separate account until a full payment is made.

    D. the lender will only accept partial payments after foreclosure proceedings have been initiated.

37. **According to the Truth in Lending Act, an advertising term that WOULD NOT trigger additional required dis-closures includes:**

    A. 5% APR loan available here.

    B. 20% down.

    C. 25-year financing available.

    D. pay only $650 a month.

38. **A qualified mortgage may contain all of the following terms EXCEPT**

    A. a 40-year term loan.

    B. the ability to repay the mortgage debt.

    C. debt-to-income ratios of 43% or less.

    D good standing on current income or assets.

Federal Privacy Protection and Consumer Identification Laws

8

Federal laws call for MLOs, and others involved in the mortgage lending industry to protect consumer privacy and identification. These regulations were adopted to ensure consumers have access to their financial credit information, the information remains private, and consumers can limit contact from others about this data.

This chapter reviews federal regulations regarding fair credit reporting and the limitations on mortgage loan originators/lenders. The chapter also reviews privacy protections and record requirements that protect against fraud or illegal contact under federal laws such as the Do Not Call Registry and USA PATRIOT Act.

After completing this chapter, you will be able to:

- Identify procedures to protect the privacy of consumers.
- Recognize limitations on lenders'/MLOs' use of consumer credit information.
- Describe control of credit reporting information.
- Describe requirements for recording consumer credit information.

KEY TERMS

Adverse Action

Consumer

Consumer Financial Protection Bureau (CFPB)

Credit Freeze

Customer

Fraud Alert

Fair Credit Reporting Act (FCRA) – Regulation V

Regulation V implements the **Fair Credit Reporting Act** [see Fair Credit Reporting Act (Regulation V) 12 CFR §1022: http://www.ecfr.gov/cgi-bin/text-idx?SID=edb045e637658b3ee 6e0ece3ae020540&node=12:8.0.2.8.16&rgn=div5], a *federal law dealing with the granting of credit, access to credit information, the rights of debtors, and the responsibilities of creditors.* A **creditor** is defined as "*a person who regularly extends consumer credit that is subject to a finance charge, or is paid by written agreement in more than four installments, and to whom the obligation is originally payable* (12 CFR § 1026.2(a)(16)(ii). The Fair Credit Reporting Act, implemented in 1970, was the first legislation to address credit reporting. It is important to remember that when this legislation was enacted, the nation had not yet fallen victim to identity theft. Americans were less concerned about their identity being stolen and more concerned about access to their personal credit information.

Consumer Rights

The Fair Credit Reporting Act provides consumers with the rights to:

- An adverse action notice.
- A copy of the consumer credit report.
- Request their credit score.
- Dispute incomplete or inaccurate information.
- Limit prescreened offers.

Credit Scores, and Credit Reports

The Consumer Financial Protection Bureau defines the difference between a credit report and a credit score.

A **credit report** is *a statement that has information about your credit activity and current credit situation such as loan paying history and the status of your credit accounts.* Credit reports often include:

- Personal information
- Current and historical credit accounts, including the type of account (mortgage, installment, revolving, etc.)
- Public records
- Inquiries

A **credit score** *predicts how likely you are to pay back a loan on time.* A scoring model uses information from your credit report to create a credit score. Some factors that make up a typical credit score include:

- Bill-paying history
- Current unpaid debt
- Number and type of loan accounts you have
- Length of time loan accounts are open
- Available credit currently utilized
- New applications for credit
- Debt sent to collection, foreclosure, or bankruptcy (and when this event occurred)

[See *"What is a Credit Report?"* Consumer Financial Protection Bureau, https://www.consumerfinance.gov/ask-cfpb/what-is-a-credit-report-en-309/ ; see also *"What is a Credit Score?"* Consumer Financial Protection Bureau, https://www.consumerfinance.gov/ask-cfpb/what-is-a-credit-score-en-315/]

Adverse Action Notice

Any entity that uses a credit report or another type of consumer report to deny an application for credit, insurance, or employment—or to take another adverse action—must provide the consumer with the name, address, and phone number of the agency that provided the information. The requirements under the FCRA differ somewhat from those under the Equal Credit Opportunity Act, although both laws can be satisfied with a single adverse action notice. [For more information, see Consumer Compliance Outlook (2nd Q 2013, Federal Reserve publication), *"Adverse Action Notice Requirements Under the ECOA and the FCRA"* http://www.philadelphiafed.org/bank-resources/publications/consumer-compliance-outlook/2013/second-quarter/adverse-action-notice-requirements-under-ecoa-fcra.cfm]

Title X of the Dodd-Frank Wall Street Reform and Consumer Protection Act, §1100F, amended the Fair Credit Reporting Act to require a creditor to provide a consumer with a written or electronic disclosure of the numeric credit score used in taking any adverse action, including a risk-based pricing notice.

Dispute Incomplete or Inaccurate Information

Consumers have the right to dispute any incomplete or inaccurate information found in their credit report. The consumer reporting agency must correct or delete inaccurate, incomplete, or unverifiable information. The act of disputing a trade line does not require its removal, only its investigation. [See Consumer Credit Protection, Ch. 41 (15 U.S.C. §1681g(c)), Subch. III Credit Reporting Agencies: http://www.gpo.gov/fdsys/pkg/USCODE-2012-title15/html/USCODE-2012-title15-chap41-subchapIII.htm]

Limit Prescreened Offers

[See Commercial Practices, 16 CFR §642, Prescreen opt-out notice: http://www.ecfr.gov/cgi-bin/text-idx?SID=202f9404499156c4e6ee2f027c873a8b&node=16:1.0.1.6.76&rgn=div5]

Consumers may choose to limit "prescreened" offers of credit and insurance based on information in their credit report. Unsolicited prescreened offers for credit and insurance must include a toll-free phone number to be removed from the lists on which these offers are based.

Exercise 8.1: Knowledge Check

The Fair Credit Reporting Act entitles consumers access to the same credit information that lenders use in making their credit decisions.

A. true
B. false

Adverse Action Notice

Applicant(s):	William A Sample
Loan Amount:	$ 150,000
Interest Rate:	6.000 %
Term:	360 months

Date Denied:	May 1, 2011
Noticed Mailed:	May 5, 2011

In compliance with Regulation B (Equal Credit Opportunity Act), you are advised that your recent application for an extension of credit has been declined. The decision to deny your application was based on the following reason(s):

- Delinquent credit obligations
- Temporary employment
- Insufficient stability of income
- Stable monthly income insufficient to make monthly mortgage payments

Our decision was based in whole or in part on information that has been obtained from the consumer reporting agency checked below. You have a right under the Fair Credit Reporting Act to know the information contained in your credit file at the consumer reporting agency. The reporting agency played no part in our decision and is therefore unable to supply specific reasons for the credit decision.

☐ Agency #1: Experian, Toll Free: 888-397-3742, P.O. Box 2002, Allen, TX 75013
☐ Agency #2: Equifax, Toll Free: 800-685-1111, P.O. Box 740241, Atlanta, GA 30374
☒ Agency #3: TransUnion, Toll Free: 800-888-4213, P.O. Box 1000, Chester, PA 19022

You also have a right to a free copy of your report from the reporting agency, if you request it no later than 60 days after you receive this notice. If you find that any information contained in the report you receive is inaccurate or incomplete, you have the right to dispute the matter with the reporting agency.

If you have any questions regarding this notice or if you have additional information that might assist us in further evaluating your loan application, please contact:

ABC SAVINGS AND LOAN *[INSERT COMPANY NAME/ADDRESS]*
123 Main Street
Anytown, USA 00011
1-800-555-9999

NOTICE
The Federal Equal Credit Opportunity Act prohibits creditors from discrimination against credit applicants on the basis of race, color, religion, national origin, sex, marital status, or age (provided the applicant has the capacity to enter into a binding contract); because all or part of the applicant's income derives from any public assistance program; or because the applicant has in good faith exercised any right under the Consumer Credit Protection Act. The Federal Agency that administers compliance with this law concerning this creditor is the Office of Thrift Supervision *[INSERT APPROPRIATE AGENCY HERE]*.

Consumer Reporting Agency Obligations

[See Consumer Credit Protection, Ch. 41 (15 U.S.C. Subchapter III Credit Reporting Agencies): http://www.gpo.gov/fdsys/pkg/USCODE-2012-title15/html/USCODE-2012-title15-chap41-subchapIII.htm]

Under the Fair Credit Reporting Act, consumer reporting agencies:

- **May not report outdated negative information.** In most cases, a consumer reporting agency may not report negative credit information that is more than **seven years old** or bankruptcies that are more than **ten years old**. There is no time limit on the reporting of criminal convictions [see 15 U.S.C. §1681c].

- **Must limit access to a credit report.** A consumer reporting agency may provide information to people with a legitimate business need—usually to consider an application with a creditor, insurer, employer, landlord, or other business. The FCRA specifies those with a valid need for access [see 15 U.S.C. §1681d].

- **May not give out consumer credit information** to an employer, or a potential employer, without written consent given by the consumer [see 15 U.S.C. §1681b].

Exercise 8.2: Knowledge Check

1. According to the FCRA, all of the following would have a business need for access to credit reports EXCEPT a(n)

    A. "buy here, pay here" automobile dealer.

    B. doctor's office

    C. employer performing a background check for a potential employee.

    D. mortgage loan originator.

2. The consumer reporting agency must correct or delete any data EXCEPT information that is

    A. disputed.

    B. inaccurate.

    C. incomplete.

    D. unverifiable.

Para informacion en espanol, visite www.ftc.gov/credit o escribe a la FTC Consumer Response Center, Room 130-A 600 Pennsylvania Ave. N.W., Washington, D.C. 20580.

A Summary of Your Rights Under the Fair Credit Reporting Act

The federal Fair Credit Reporting Act (FCRA) promotes the accuracy, fairness, and privacy of information in the files of consumer reporting agencies. There are many types of consumer reporting agencies, including credit bureaus and specialty agencies (such as agencies that sell information about check writing histories, medical records, and rental history records). Here is a summary of your major rights under the FCRA. **For more information, including information about additional rights, go to www.ftc.gov/credit or write to: Consumer Response Center, Room 130-A, Federal Trade Commission, 600 Pennsylvania Ave. N.W., Washington, D.C. 20580.**

- **You must be told if information in your file has been used against you.** Anyone who uses a credit report or another type of consumer report to deny your application for credit, insurance, or employment – or to take another adverse action against you – must tell you, and must give you the name, address, and phone number of the agency that provided the information.

- **You have the right to know what is in your file.** You may request and obtain all the information about you in the files of a consumer reporting agency (your "file disclosure"). You will be required to provide proper identification, which may include your Social Security number. In many cases, the disclosure will be free. You are entitled to a free file disclosure if:

  - a person has taken adverse action against you because of information in your credit report;
  - you are the victim of identify theft and place a fraud alert in your file;
  - your file contains inaccurate information as a result of fraud;
  - you are on public assistance;
  - you are unemployed but expect to apply for employment within 60 days.

  In addition, by September 2005 all consumers will be entitled to one free disclosure every 12 months upon request from each nationwide credit bureau and from nationwide specialty consumer reporting agencies. See www.ftc.gov/credit for additional information.

- **You have the right to ask for a credit score.** Credit scores are numerical summaries of your credit-worthiness based on information from credit bureaus. You may request a credit score from consumer reporting agencies that create scores or distribute scores used in residential real property loans, but you will have to pay for it. In some mortgage transactions, you will receive credit score information for free from the mortgage lender.

- **You have the right to dispute incomplete or inaccurate information.** If you identify information in your file that is incomplete or inaccurate, and report it to the consumer reporting agency, the agency must investigate unless your dispute is frivolous. See www.ftc.gov/credit for an explanation of dispute procedures.

- **Consumer reporting agencies must correct or delete inaccurate, incomplete, or unverifiable information.** Inaccurate, incomplete or unverifiable information must be removed or corrected, usually within 30 days. However, a consumer reporting agency may continue to report information it has verified as accurate.

- **Consumer reporting agencies may not report outdated negative information.** In most cases, a consumer reporting agency may not report negative information that is more than seven years old, or bankruptcies that are more than 10 years old.

- **Access to your file is limited.** A consumer reporting agency may provide information about you only to people with a valid need – usually to consider an application with a creditor, insurer, employer, landlord, or other business. The FCRA specifies those with a valid need for access.

- **You must give your consent for reports to be provided to employers.** A consumer reporting agency may not give out information about you to your employer, or a potential employer, without your written consent given to the employer. Written consent generally is not required in the trucking industry. For more information, go to www.ftc.gov/credit.

- **You may limit "prescreened" offers of credit and insurance you get based on information in your credit report.** Unsolicited "prescreened" offers for credit and insurance must include a toll-free phone number you can call if you choose to remove your name and address from the lists these offers are based on. You may opt-out with the nationwide credit bureaus at 1-888-5-OPTOUT (1-888-567-8688).

- **You may seek damages from violators.** If a consumer reporting agency, or, in some cases, a user of consumer reports or a furnisher of information to a consumer reporting agency violates the FCRA, you may be able to sue in state or federal court.

- **Identity theft victims and active duty military personnel have additional rights.** For more information, visit www.ftc.gov/credit.

States may enforce the FCRA, and many states have their own consumer reporting laws. In some cases, you may have more rights under state law. For more information, contact your state or local consumer protection agency or your state Attorney General. Federal enforcers are:

TYPE OF BUSINESS:	CONTACT:
Consumer reporting agencies, creditors and others not listed below	Federal Trade Commission: Consumer Response Center - FCRA Washington, DC 20580 1-877-382-4357
National banks, federal branches/agencies of foreign banks (word "National" or initials "N.A." appear in or after bank's name)	Office of the Comptroller of the Currency Compliance Management, Mail Stop 6-6 Washington, DC 20219 800-613-6743
Federal Reserve System member banks (except national banks, and federal branches/agencies of foreign banks)	Federal Reserve Consumer Help (FRCH) P O Box 1200 Minneapolis, MN 55480 Telephone: 888-851-1920 Website Address: www.federalreserveconsumerhelp.gov Email Address: ConsumerHelp@FederalReserve.gov
Savings associations and federally chartered savings banks (word "Federal" or initials "F.S.B." appear in federal institution's name)	Office of Thrift Supervision Consumer Complaints Washington, DC 20552 800-842-6929
Federal credit unions (words "Federal Credit Union" appear in institution's name)	National Credit Union Administration 1775 Duke Street Alexandria, VA 22314 703-519-4600
State-chartered banks that are not members of the Federal Reserve System	Federal Deposit Insurance Corporation Consumer Response Center, 2345 Grand Avenue, Suite 100 Kansas City, Missouri 64108-2638 1-877-275-3342
Air, surface, or rail common carriers regulated by former Civil Aeronautics Board or Interstate Commerce Commission	Department of Transportation , Office of Financial Management Washington, DC 20590 202-366-1306
Activities subject to the Packers and Stockyards Act, 1921	Department of Agriculture Office of Deputy Administrator - GIPSA Washington, DC 20250 202-720-7051

Fair and Accurate Credit Transactions Act (FACTA)

[See Consumer Credit Protection, Ch. 41 (15 U.S.C. Subchapter III Credit Reporting Agencies), §1681-§1681x: http://www.gpo.gov/fdsys/pkg/USCODE-2012-title15/html/USCODE-2012-title15-chap41-subchapIII.htm]

The **Fair and Accurate Credit Transactions Act** of 2003 [see Pub.L. 108-159, http://www.gpo.gov/fdsys/pkg/PLAW-108publ159/pdf/PLAW-108publ159.pdf], sometimes referred to as either the FACT Act or simply FACTA, amended the federal Fair Credit Reporting Act and is intended primarily to *help consumers fight the growing crime of identity theft*. The FACT Act was passed in 2003, during a time in which identity theft was an ever-increasing problem for consumers and creditors. Thus, the law focused on accuracy, privacy, limits on information sharing, and new consumer rights to disclosure.

Provisions of the FACT Act

The FACT Act contains seven major titles:

- Identity Theft Prevention and Credit History Restoration
- Improvements in Use of and Consumer Access to Credit Information
- Enhancing the Accuracy of Consumer Report Information
- Limiting the Use and Sharing of Medical Information in the Financial System
- Financial Literacy and Education Improvement
- Protecting Employee Misconduct Investigations
- Relation to State Laws

Access to Credit Reports

[See Consumer Credit Protection, Ch. 41 (15 U.S.C. Subchapter III Credit Reporting Agencies), §1681j. Charges for certain disclosures: http://www.gpo.gov/fdsys/pkg/USCODE-2012-title15/html/USCODE-2012-title15-chap41-subchapIII.htm]

The FCRA gave consumers the right to ask for a credit score from any consumer reporting agencies that create or distribute scores used in residential real property loans, but permitted reporting agencies to charge a fee for the score. Prior to the passage of the FACT Act, consumers had to pay to get a copy of their credit report from each of the three national credit bureaus: Equifax, Experian, and TransUnion. The FCRA only allowed consumers a free copy of their **credit report** from a consumer credit reporting agency under these circumstances:

- The information in a credit report resulted in adverse action.
- The consumer was a victim of identity theft and a fraud alert was inserted in the credit report.
- The credit report contains inaccurate information as a result of fraud.
- The consumer is on public assistance or is unemployed.

[See Fair Credit Reporting Act (Regulation V), Subpart N, 12 CFR §1022.130-1022.139: http://www.ecfr.gov/cgi-bin/text-idx?SID=f773d2c0460837d6c5db710ad47779ac&node=12:8.0.2.8.16&rgn=div5#12:8.0.2.8.16.12]

One of the major provisions of the FACT Act is to allow consumers easier **access to their credit reports** as a way to *spot possible identity theft and to allow dispute of inaccurate information.* With the passage of the FACT Act, consumers applying for home loans are now required to receive the **Home Loan Applicant Credit Score Information Disclosure** notice, which explains their rights. The FACT Act allows consumers to request and obtain a free copy of their credit report **once every 12 months** from each of these credit bureaus by contacting a centralized website, maintained in cooperation with the Federal Trade Commission [see www.annualcreditreport.com] or by calling 877-322-8228.

Fraud Alerts and Freezes

[See Consumer Credit Protection, Ch. 41 (15 U.S.C. Subchapter III Credit Reporting Agencies), §1681c. Identity theft prevention; fraud alerts and active duty alerts: http://www.gpo.gov/fdsys/pkg/USCODE-2012-title15/html/USCODE-2012-title15-chap41-subchapIII.htm]

If a consumer believes he has been a victim of identity theft, the FACT Act allows the consumer to contact the credit bureau and place a **fraud alert**.

 If an MLO is running a credit report and sees a fraud alert, he must contact the person whose name is on the account at the number provided to the credit bureau or take other reasonable steps to ensure that the person applying for a mortgage loan is not really an identity thief.

The FACT Act also allows consumers to place a **credit freeze** to prevent the information from showing on a credit report. When applying for a loan, the consumer may then temporarily "thaw" the credit report by contacting the credit bureau that is "freezing" the report to obtain a temporary password, which allows a credit reporting agency to access the report.

Finally, the Act allows members of the military who are deploying overseas to place a credit freeze, thereby making fraudulent applications for credit more difficult.

Truncation of Credit and Debit Card Numbers

[See Consumer Credit Protection, Ch. 41 (15 U.S.C. Subchapter III Credit Reporting Agencies), §1681g(a). Information on file; sources; report recipients: http://www.gpo.gov/fdsys/pkg/USCODE-2012-title15/html/USCODE-2012-title15-chap41-subchapIII.htm.]

The FACT Act prohibits businesses from printing *more than five digits* of any customer's credit/debit card number or expiration date on any receipt provided to the cardholder at the point of sale or transaction. The provision excludes handwritten or imprinted receipts if that is the only method of recording the card number.

Security and Disposal

[See Consumer Credit Protection, Ch. 41 (15 U.S.C. Subchapter III Credit Reporting Agencies), §1681w. Disposal of records: http://www.gpo.gov/fdsys/pkg/USCODE-2012-title15/html/USCODE-2012-title15-chap41-subchapIII.htm.]

To further protect the privacy of consumer financial information, the FACT Act requires businesses to take measures to responsibly **secure and dispose** of sensitive personal information found in a consumer's credit report. Reasonable methods for security and disposal include:

- Burning or shredding papers that contain consumer report information so that information cannot be reconstructed.

- Destroying or erasing electronic files or media so that information cannot be recovered or reconstructed.

- Placing all pending loan documents in locked desks, cabinets, or storage rooms at the end of the workday.

Fact Act Credit Score Disclosure

Refer to a copy of your credit report (consumer report) to view the credit scores that were generated at the specific request of the Lender. These scores reflect the original credit information obtained from the three (3) credit bureaus listed below:

Equifax
PO Box 740256   800-685-1111
Atlanta, GA 30374   www.equifax.com

Experian
475 Anton Boulevard   888-397-3742
Costa Mesa, CA 92626   www.experian.com

TransUnion
PO Box 2000   800-916-8800
Chester, PA 19022   www.transunion.com

In addition to the scores, you will find the key factors that adversely affect your credit scores in the models used, together with a brief explanation of what each factor means, the date the credit scores were created, and the range of possible credit scores under the models used.

Risk Based Pricing

Your Loan may contain credit terms that are materially less favorable than the most favorable terms available to a substantial proportion of borrowers based in whole or in part on a consumer report (credit report) obtained from a consumer-reporting agency. The terms offered to you are based on information from a consumer report.

Your Loan Officer can provide specific information about how the pricing of your loan may be affected by your credit scores. You may obtain a copy of your consumer report without charge from either the Lender or Loan Officer.

I/We have received a copy of this disclosure.

_____   _____   _____   _____
(Borrower)   (Date)   (Borrower)   (Date)

_____   _____   _____   _____
(Borrower)   (Date)   (Borrower)   (Date)

Exercise 8.3: Knowledge Check

1. The primary focus of the Fair and Accurate Credit Transactions Act (FACT Act) is to ensure that consumers' credit information is accurately maintained and recorded.

    A. true
    B. false

2. To properly dispose of a consumer's loan file, the FACT Act requires that paper files be burned or shredded after the loan closes.

    A. true
    B. false

Red Flags Rules

[See Consumer Credit Protection, Ch. 41 (15 U.S.C. Subchapter III Credit Reporting Agencies), §1681m(e). Red flag guidelines and regulations required: http://www.gpo.gov/fdsys/pkg/USCODE-2012-title15/html/USCODE-2012-title15-chap41-subchapIII-sec1681m.htm]

As Congress went into final hearings on FCRA amendments, several widely reported surveys on the number of identity theft victims were released. A September 2003 Federal Trade Commission report estimated approximately 10 million people were victims of identity theft in 2002 alone. This resulted in **Section 114** of the FACT Act [See Fair and Accurate Credit Transactions Act of 2003 (Pub.L. 108-159), Sect. 114. Establishment of Procedures for the Identification of Possible Instances of Identity Theft: http://www.gpo.gov/fdsys/pkg/PLAW-108publ159/pdf/PLAW-108publ159.pdf (page 1960)], known as the **Red Flags Rules**, which require:

- Financial institutions and creditors to implement a written identity theft prevention program.

- Card issuers to assess the validity of change of address requests.

- Users of consumer reports to reasonably verify the identity of the subject of a consumer report in the event of a notice of address discrepancy.

Section 114 applies to federal and state-chartered banks and credit unions, non-bank lenders, mortgage brokers, any person who regularly participates in a credit decision—including setting the terms of credit, and any person who requests a consumer report. Every organization has the flexibility to define a program that is appropriate to the size and operation of their particular business.

Exercise 8.4: Knowledge Check

1. According to Regulation V, a creditor is defined as

   A. the agency that maintains, gathers, and scores information for credit reports.
   B. someone who grants credit.
   C. someone who is obtaining credit.
   D. the title insurance agency.

2. An MLO hired a third-party independent processing company to perform processing functions on their loan files. Loan files for applicants who were not approved were disposed of in a dumpster at the back of the processing company's office. The processing company violated

   A. ECOA.
   B. FACTA.
   C. HMDA.
   D. RESPA.

Gramm-Leach-Bliley Act (GLB Act)

[See Gramm-Leach-Bliley Act (Pub.L. 106-102): http://www.gpo.gov/fdsys/pkg/PLAW-106publ102/pdf/PLAW-106publ102.pdf]

The **Financial Services Modernization Act of 1999**, also known as the **Gramm-Leach-Bliley Act** (Pub.L. 106-102), includes provisions in **Title V – Privacy** [See Gramm-Leach-Bliley Act, Privacy of Consumer Financial Information (Regulation P), 12 CFR §1016: http://www.ecfr.gov/cgi-bin/text-idx?SID=202f9404499156c4e6ee2f027c873a8b&node=12:8.0.2.8.15&rgn=div5] to *protect and regulate the disclosure of consumers' personal financial information.* There are three principal parts to the privacy requirements: The Financial Privacy Rule, the Safeguards Rule, and Pretexting Provisions.

The GLB Act gives authority to eight federal agencies and the states to administer and enforce **Title V – Privacy**. These regulations apply to financial institutions, which include not only banks, securities firms, and insurance companies, but also companies providing many other types of financial products and services to consumers, such as:

- Lending, brokering, or servicing any type of consumer loan
- Transferring or safeguarding money
- Preparing individual tax returns
- Providing financial advice or credit counseling
- Providing residential real estate settlement services
- Collecting consumer debts

Financial Privacy Rule

[see Privacy, Ch. 94 (15 U.S.C. §6801-6809), Subch. I – Disclosure of Nonpublic Personal Information: http://www.gpo.gov/fdsys/pkg/USCODE-2012-title15/html/USCODE-2012-title15-chap94-subchapI.htm]

Information that many would consider private—including bank balances and account numbers—is regularly bought and sold by banks, credit card companies, and other financial institutions. The **Financial Privacy Rule** governs the collection and disclosure of customers' personal financial information—known as **nonpublic personal information**—restricting when and under what circumstances such information may be disclosed to affiliates and to nonaffiliated third parties. Nonpublic personal information could include the following types of information:

- What a consumer or customer puts on an application

- Data about the individual from another source, such as a credit bureau

- Transactions between the individual and the company, such as an account balance, payment history, or credit/debit card purchase information

- Whether an individual is a consumer or customer of a particular financial institution

These restrictions are based on a required **Consumer Privacy Policy** notice provided to the consumer, explaining the lender's information collection procedures and information sharing and transfer practices. A financial institution must disclose its policy to consumers **before** they disclose personal information, disclose the policy **annually** for customers throughout the financial relationship, and provide the consumer instructions on how to **opt-out** of having this information shared.

Even if a consumer does **not** opt-out, financial institutions are prohibited from disclosing—other than to a consumer reporting agency—access codes or account numbers to any nonaffiliated third party for use in telemarketing, direct mail marketing, or other marketing through electronic mail. Creditors are responsible for validating any other entity to which they transfer custody of private consumer data.

Consumer or Customer?

A company's obligations under the GLB Act depend on whether the company has consumers or customers who obtain its services:

- A **consumer** is *an individual who obtains, or has obtained, a financial product or service from a financial institution for personal, family, or household reasons, usually with a one-time transaction.*

- A **customer** is *a consumer with a continuing relationship with a financial institution.* Generally, if the relationship between the financial institution and the individual is significant and/or long-term, the individual is a customer of the institution. In the mortgage industry, the loan servicer is typically the servicer of the mortgage loan.

For example, a person who gets a mortgage from a lender or hires a broker to get a personal loan is considered a customer of the lender or the broker, while a person who uses a check-cashing service is a consumer of that service.

Under the GLB Act, **customers** must receive a financial institution's privacy notice *every year for as long as the customer relationship lasts.* **Consumers**, on the other hand, are entitled to receive a privacy notice from a financial institution *only if the company shares the consumer's information with companies not affiliated with it,* with some exceptions.

Safeguards Rule

[See Privacy, Ch. 94 (15 U.S.C. §6801), Protection of nonpublic personal information: http://www.gpo.gov/fdsys/pkg/USCODE-2012-title15/html/USCODE-2012-title15-chap94-subchapI.htm]

The **Safeguards Rule** requires all financial institutions to design, implement, and maintain safeguards to protect customer information while it is in the custody and control of the institution and its agents. This rule applies not only to financial institutions that collect information from their customers, but also to any institution—such as a credit reporting agency or even an educational institution—that receives customer information from other financial institutions. A written Safeguards Policy must include provisions that:

- Ensure the security and confidentiality of customer records.
- Protect against any anticipated threats or hazards to the security of such records.
- Protect against the unauthorized access or use of such records or information in ways that could result in substantial harm or inconvenience to customers.

Pretexting Provisions

This provision [see 15 U.S.C. §6821–6827] protects consumers from individuals and companies that obtain their personal financial information under false, fictitious, or fraudulent pretenses.

Exercise 8.5: Apply Your Knowledge

Directions: Review the following scenario, then fill-in the blanks by choosing from among the following regulations.

  A. Fair and Accurate Credit Transactions Act (FACTA)
  B. Fair Credit Reporting Act (FCRA)
  C. Gramm-Leach-Bliley Act (GLB)

Which regulation is it?

Borrower Frank makes an application for a mortgage loan with ABC Mortgage Brokers. According to (1) _____, Frank is considered a consumer. When MLO Kerry reviews the credit report, he notices an alert for an address mismatch. Kerry is required to assess the validity of the address discrepancy to comply with (2) _____. On the report, Kerry notices a Chapter 7 bankruptcy that was discharged eight years ago. This credit entry remains on the report for ten years, according to (3) _____. Frank notices a delinquent auto loan payment that is an error. According to (4) _____, Frank can dispute this item with the credit bureaus and if it is found to be inaccurate, it will be corrected. Frank's credit score is 562, and he receives an adverse action notice that is required by (5) _____. Frank also receives the credit reporting agency information that is provided according to (6) _____. Frank's paper loan file is then shredded by Kerry to comply with (7) _____.

USA PATRIOT Act

[See USA PATRIOT Act (Pub.L. 107-56): http://www.gpo.gov/fdsys/pkg/PLAW-107publ56/pdf/PLAW-107publ56.pdf]

The Uniting and Strengthening America by Providing Appropriate Tools Required to Intercept and Obstruct Terrorism Act (Pub.L. 107-56), more commonly known as the USA PATRIOT Act, was enacted in October 2001 in response to the September 11, 2001 terrorist attacks. The Act:

- Increases the ability of law enforcement agencies to search telephone, e-mail, medical, financial, and other records.
- Eases restrictions on foreign intelligence gathering within the United States.
- Expands the Secretary of the Treasury's authority to regulate financial transactions, particularly those involving foreign individuals and entities.
- Enhances the discretion of law enforcement and immigration authorities in detaining and deporting immigrants suspected of terrorism-related acts.

Title III of the USA PATRIOT Act, designated the International Money Laundering Abatement and Financial Anti-Terrorism Act of 2001, requires lenders and banks to create and maintain **customer identification programs** (CIPs) to prevent financing of terrorist operations and money laundering (§ 326). CIPs require covered institutions to verify the identity of customers who are entering into a "formal relationship," such as taking out a loan or a credit account. These requirements are more clearly defined in the Bank Secrecy Act/Anti Money Laundering regulations.

Minimum Data Required

A covered institution must obtain from all customers opening a new account, *at a minimum*, the following:

- Name
- Date of birth
- Residential or work address for individuals, or physical location address for legal entities
- For U.S. citizens or legal entities organized under state law: A tax identification number (TIN)
- For lawful permanent residents or non-immigrants: A TIN, passport number and country of issuance, alien identification card number, or number and country of issuance of any other government-issued document evidencing nationality or residence and bearing a photo
- For non-U.S. legal entities with no TIN: A government-issued certificate of existence or good standing

 If a lender is extending credit to the borrower using a mortgage broker as its agent, it must ensure the broker is performing the bank's CIP.

PATRIOT ACT
INFORMATION DISCLOSURE

Applicant Name   _____

Co-Applicant Name   _____

Present Address   _____

Mailing Address   _____

_____

To help the government fight the funding of terrorism and money laundering activities, Federal law requires all financial institutions to obtain, verify, and record information that identifies each person who opens an account.

What this means for you: When you open an account, we will ask for your name, address, date of birth, and other information that will allow us to identify you. We may also ask to see your driver's license or other identifying documents.

I/we acknowledge that I/we received a copy of this disclosure.

_____   _____

Applicant   Date

_____   _____

Applicant   Date

Patriot Act Information Disclosure: *31 C.F.R. §1020.220*
http://www.fdic.gov/regulations/laws/rules/8000-1600.html

Exercise 8.6: Knowledge Check

The USA PATRIOT Act requires lenders and banks to create and maintain programs that verify their customers' identity.

A. true
B. false

National Do Not Call Registry

[See Telemarketing Sales Rule, Part 310, Abusive telemarketing acts or practices, 16 CFR §310.4(b) Pattern of calls: http://www.ecfr.gov/cgi-bin/text-idx?SID=64ba8def2f0c5d34d58b3 a974e75fc1a&node=16:1.0.1.3.34&rgn=div5#16:1.0.1.3.34.0.32.4]

A provision of the federal Telemarketing Sales Rule (16 C.F.R. Part 310), the National Do Not Call (DNC) Registry, is managed by the **Federal Trade Commission** (FTC), the nation's consumer protection agency, and enforced by the FTC, the Federal Communications Commission (FCC), and state law enforcement officials.

The National Do Not Call Registry applies to any plan, program, or campaign to sell goods or services through *interstate* phone calls. This includes telemarketers who solicit consumers, often on behalf of third party sellers. It also includes sellers who provide, offer to provide, or arrange to provide goods or services to consumers in exchange for payment. The National Do Not Call Registry does *not* limit calls by political organizations, charities, or telephone surveyors. However, note that it is a violation of the Telemarketing Sales Rule to make outbound telemarketing calls to the person's home outside the hours of 8 a.m. and 9 p.m. local time.

To keep from violating National Do Not Call regulations, a company must maintain national and internal lists of customers and prospects and keep them updated regularly. The national DNC list must be updated *every three months*, and the internal DNC list must be updated *every 30 days*.

A consumer who receives a telemarketing call despite being on the registry is able to file a complaint with the FTC. Violators could be fined up to **$16,000 per incident**.

[See 16 CFR §310.4(c) Calling Time Restrictions.]

Established Business Relationship (EBR)

[See Fair Credit Reporting Act (Regulation V), Subpart C, 12 CFR §1022.21(c) Exceptions: http://www.ecfr.gov/cgi-bin/text-idx?SID=f773d2c0460837d6c5db710ad47779ac&node=12:8. 0.2.8.16&rgn=div5#12:8.0.2.8.16.3.1.2]

A telemarketer or seller may call a consumer with whom it has an **established business relationship** (EBR) for up to **18 months** after the consumer's last purchase, delivery, or payment, *even if* the consumer's number is on the National Do Not Call Registry. In addition, a company may call a consumer for up to **three months** after the consumer makes an inquiry or submits an application to the company. Obtaining the name, phone number, and **signature** from a consumer provides written consent that does not expire until rescinded.

One warning: If a consumer has asked to be put on the company's internal Do Not Call list, the company may *not* call, even if there is an EBR. This prohibition is *only* against solicitation of new business. Calls may be made to consumers in reference to a current relationship, such as a creditor making a collection call.

Exercise 8.7: Knowledge Check

The National Do Not Call Registry regulations require companies to update their national customer lists every 30 days.

    A. true

    B. false

Chapter Summary

1. **Regulation V** implements the **Fair Credit Reporting Act** (12 CFR §1022), also known as the FCRA, which is a federal law dealing with the granting of credit, access to credit information, the rights of debtors, and the responsibilities of creditors.

2. The FCRA provides consumers with the right to; an **adverse action notice** in the event of a loan decline, request a copy of their consumer credit report, request their credit score, dispute incomplete or inaccurate information, and limit prescreened offers.

3. Under the FCRA, consumer reporting agencies: **May not report outdated negative information**—in most cases, information that is more than seven years old or bankruptcies that are more than ten years old; there is no time limit on reporting of criminal convictions; **must limit access to a credit report**—may provide information to people with a legitimate business need—usually to consider an application with a creditor, insurer, employer, landlord, or other business; and **may not give out consumer credit information** to an employer, or a potential employer, without written consent given to the employer by the consumer. The FCRA specifies those with a valid need for access.

4. The **Fair and Accurate Credit Transactions Act** of 2003 (Pub.L. 108-159), sometimes referred to as either the **FACT Act** or simply **FACTA**, amended the federal Fair Credit Reporting Act and is intended primarily to help consumers fight the growing crime of identity theft.

5. One of the major provisions of the FACT Act is to allow consumers easier access to their credit reports as a way to spot possible identity theft and to allow dispute of inaccurate information. The Act requires that consumers applying for home loans receive the **Home Loan Applicant Credit Score Information Disclosure Notice**, which explains their rights.

6. If a consumer believes he or she has been a victim of identity theft, the FACT Act allows the consumer to contact the credit bureau and place a fraud alert.

7. The FACT Act also allows consumers to place a credit freeze in order to prevent the information from showing on a credit report.

8. The FACT Act prohibits businesses from printing more than five digits of any customer's credit/debit card number or expiration date on any receipt provided to the cardholder at the point of sale or transaction.

9. The FACT Act requires businesses to take measures to responsibly secure and dispose of sensitive personal information found in a consumer's credit report, such as shredding the consumer's documents, placing them in a locked storage area when not in use, and taking steps to protect information stored on electronic media.

10. Section 114 of the FACT Act, known as the **Red Flags Rules**, requires: Financial institutions and creditors to implement a written identity theft prevention program; card issuers to assess the validity of change of address requests; and users of consumer reports to reasonably verify the identity of the subject of a consumer report in the event of a notice of address discrepancy.

11. The Financial Services Modernization Act of 1999, also known as the **Gramm-Leach-Bliley Act** (Pub.L. 106-102), includes provisions to protect and regulate the disclosure of consumers' personal financial information. There are three principal parts to the privacy requirements: The Financial Privacy Rule, Safeguards Rule, and Pretexting Provisions.

12. A company's obligations under the **GLB Act** depend on whether the company has consumers (i.e., people who obtain or have obtained a financial product or service from a financial institution) or customers (i.e., people who have a continuing relationship with a financial institution). Generally, if the relationship between the financial institution and an individual is significant and/or long-term, the individual is a customer of the institution. In the mortgage industry, the loan servicer is typically the servicer of the mortgage loan.

13. The **USA PATRIOT Act** increases the ability of law enforcement agencies to search telephone, e-mail, medical, financial, and other records; eases restrictions on foreign intelligence gathering within the United States; expands the Secretary of the Treasury's authority to regulate financial transactions, particularly those involving foreign individuals and entities; and enhances the discretion of law enforcement and immigration authorities in detaining and deporting immigrants suspected of terrorism-related acts.

14. The **National Do Not Call Registry** applies to any plan, program, or campaign to sell goods or services through interstate phone calls, including telemarketers who solicit consumers, often on behalf of third party sellers and sellers who provide, offer to provide, or arrange to provide goods/services to consumers in exchange for payment.

15. A loan originator may call a consumer with whom it has an established business relationship (EBR) for up to 18 months after the consumer's last purchase, delivery, or payment, even if the consumer's number is on the National Do Not Call Registry. In addition, a company may call a consumer for up to three months after the consumer makes an inquiry or submits an application to the company.

Chapter Quiz

1. For how many months after a loan closes may a mortgage loan originator call to solicit new business from a customer whose phone number is on the National Do Not Call Registry?

    A. 3 months

    B. 6 months

    C. 18 months

    D. No calls can be made to a number on the Registry.

2. Which law includes Red Flags Rules that require financial institutions and creditors to implement procedures to protect customer identity?

    A. Fair and Accurate Credit Transactions Act

    B. Fair Credit Reporting Act

    C. Gramm-Leach-Bliley Act (The Financial Privacy Act)

    D. Homeowners Protection Act

3. The Fair Credit Reporting Act allows a consumer to request a

    A. credit score disclosure statement from a creditor.

    B. dispute of inaccurate or incomplete information of a report.

    C. fraud alert in the event of stolen identity.

    D. freeze on a credit report.

4. The FCRA mandates that a credit reporting bureau remove a consumer's Chapter 7 bankruptcy record after

    A. credit has been re-established for over five years.

    B. 7 years.

    C. 10 years.

    D. dismissal of the case by a Federal Bankruptcy Court.

5. The Fair and Accurate Credit Transactions Act regulates all of the following EXCEPT

    A. an adverse action notice to the borrower who is turned down for a loan.

    B. a credit freeze registered with a credit bureau.

    C. fraud alerts placed on a credit report.

    D. truncation of credit card numbers on a credit card receipt.

6. The Red Flags Rules are also known as

    A. advertising triggering terms.

    B. Chapter 8 of Regulation X.

    C. Section 32.

    D. Section 114.

7. According to the GLB Act, a person who completes a single transaction with a creditor is known as a(n)

    A. applicant.

    B. consumer.

    C. creditor.

    D. customer.

8. The penalty per occurrence per day for violating the National Do Not Call regulations is

    A. $5,000.

    B. $10,000.

    C. $11,000.

    D. $16,000.

Federal Prohibition of Predatory Lending

9

Federal laws protect consumers and prohibit MLOs, lenders, and others involved in the mortgage lending industry from predatory lending practices. Regulations were established to prevent consumers from paying excessive fees or becoming victims of fraud throughout the mortgage lending process.

This chapter reviews federal regulations that enforce Truth in Lending requirements and home equity protections. The chapter also reviews rules governing MLO compensation.

After completing this chapter, you will be able to:

- Describe regulations designed to address predatory lending.
- Describe the rules for compensation for an MLO and a registered MLO.
- Discuss the rules regarding seller financing of owner-occupied residences.

KEY TERMS

Average Prime Offer Rate
Demand Clause
High Cost Loans
Higher-Priced Loan
Negative Amortization
Prepayment Penalty
Steering
Yield Spread Premium (YSP)

Home Ownership and Equity Protection Act (HOEPA)

The **Home Ownership and Equity Protection Act** (HOEPA), a 1994 amendment to the Truth in Lending Act, *establishes disclosure requirements and prohibits deceptive and unfair practices in lending.* HOEPA also establishes requirements loans with high interest rates and/or fees. The rules for these loans are contained in Regulation Z, which implements the Truth in Lending Act. [see 12 CFR, Part 1026, Subpart E, §1026.32 Requirements for certain closed-end home mortgages]

This Act is enforced by the Federal Trade Commission for non-depository lenders and by each state's attorney general. The CFPB enforces the Act for federally-regulated depository institutions. The Rule Making and Enforcement Authority for TILA and HOEPA were transferred to the CFPB in July 2011. HOEPA also gives the Federal Reserve Board broad regulatory authority to prohibit additional practices it finds to be unfair or deceptive, not just for HOEPA loans, but **all** consumer mortgage loans. A lender who violates HOEPA may be sued by the consumer, who may be able to recover statutory and actual damages, court costs, and attorney's fees. In addition, a violation of HOEPA may enable a consumer to rescind the loan for *up to three years.*

High Cost Loans

[See http://www.consumerfinance.gov/regulations/high-cost-mortgage-and-homeownership-counseling-amendments-to-regulation-z-and-homeownership-counseling-amendments-to-regulation-x/, *High-Cost Mortgage and Homeownership Counseling Amendments to the Truth in Lending Act (Regulation Z) and Homeownership Counseling Amendments to the Real Estate Settlement Procedures Act (Regulation X) Summary* (PDF, pages 3, 84).]

HOEPA provisions must be complied with after the triggers for a "high cost loan" have been met. A **high cost loan**, according to HOEPA, is *a closed-end loan secured by a borrower's principal residence.* The rules primarily affect **refinancing** and **home equity installment loans** that also meet the definition of high-rate or high-fee loans. Under the rules, most types of mortgage loans secured by a consumer's principal dwelling, including purchase money mortgage loans, refinances, closed-end home-equity loans, and open-end credit plans (i.e., home-equity lines of credit, HELOCs) are potentially subject to HOEPA coverage.

A loan is a HOEPA loan if:

• The original mortgage on the property, as the APR exceeds the value of the APOR Index (as of the loan lock-in date) by more than 6.5 percentage points.

• A second mortgage, as the APR exceeds the value of the APOR Index (as of the loan lock-in date) by more than 8.5 percentage points.

- For HOEPA loans, the adjusted total loan amount threshold for high-cost mortgages in 2018 will be $21,032. The adjusted points and fees dollar trigger for high-cost mortgages in 2018 will be $1,052. When the total loan amount for a transaction is $21,032 or more, and the points and fees amount exceeds 5 percent of the total loan amount, the transaction is a high-cost mortgage. When the total loan amount for a transaction is less than $21,032, and the points and fees amount exceeds the lesser of the adjusted points and fees dollar trigger of $1,052 or 8 percent of the total loan amount, the transaction is a high-cost mortgage.

[See 12 CFR, Part 1026, Truth in Lending – Regulation Z §1026.32(a)(1)]

HOEPA does **not** regulate construction loans or reverse mortgages.

 The **average prime offer rate** (APOR) is defined as *the annual percentage rate derived from average annual percentage rates currently offered to consumers by a representative sample of lenders for prime mortgage transactions.* A representative example of the prime offer rate tables follow.

2016
PRIMARY MORTGAGE MARKET SURVEY®
Summary page with all rate types - U.S. averages

Week	U.S. 30 yr FRM	30 yr fees & points	U.S. 15 yr FRM	15 yr fees & points	U.S. 5/1 ARM	5/1 ARM fees & points	5/1 ARM margin	U.S. 30 yr FRM/ 5/1 ARM spread
5/5	3.61	0.6	2.86	0.5	2.80	0.5	2.73	0.81
5/12	3.57	0.5	2.81	0.5	2.78	0.5	2.74	0.79
5/19	3.58	0.6	2.81	0.5	2.80	0.5	2.74	0.78
5/26	3.64	0.5	2.89	0.5	2.87	0.5	2.75	0.77
6/2	3.66	0.5	2.92	0.5	2.88	0.5	2.74	0.78
6/9	3.60	0.5	2.87	0.5	2.82	0.5	2.74	0.78
6/16	3.54	0.5	2.81	0.5	2.74	0.5	2.74	0.80
6/23	3.56	0.6	2.83	0.5	2.74	0.5	2.74	0.82
6/30	3.48	0.5	2.78	0.4	2.70	0.5	2.74	0.78
7/7	3.41	0.5	2.74	0.4	2.68	0.5	2.75	0.73
7/14	3.42	0.5	2.72	0.5	2.76	0.4	2.74	0.66
7/21	3.45	0.5	2.75	0.5	2.78	0.5	2.74	0.67
7/28	3.48	0.5	2.78	0.5	2.78	0.5	2.74	0.70
8/4	3.43	0.5	2.74	0.5	2.73	0.5	2.74	0.70
8/11	3.45	0.5	2.76	0.5	2.74	0.5	2.74	0.71
8/18	3.43	0.5	2.74	0.5	2.76	0.4	2.74	0.67
8/25	3.43	0.6	2.74	0.5	2.75	0.4	2.74	0.68
9/1	3.46	0.5	2.77	0.5	2.83	0.4	2.74	0.63
9/8	3.44	0.6	2.76	0.5	2.81	0.4	2.74	0.63
9/15	3.5	0.5	2.77	0.5	2.82	0.4	2.74	0.68
9/22	3.48	0.6	2.76	0.5	2.80	0.5	2.74	0.68
9/29	3.42	0.5	2.72	0.5	2.81	0.4	2.74	0.61
10/6	3.42	0.5	2.72	0.5	2.80	0.4	2.74	0.62
10/13	3.47	0.6	2.76	0.6	2.82	0.4	2.74	0.65
10/20	3.52	0.5	2.79	0.5	2.85	0.4	2.74	0.67
10/27	3.47	0.6	2.78	0.5	2.84	0.4	2.74	0.63
11/3	3.54	0.5	2.84	0.5	2.87	0.4	2.74	0.67
11/10	3.57	0.5	2.88	0.5	2.88	0.4	2.74	0.69
11/17	3.94	0.5	3.14	0.5	3.07	0.4	2.74	0.87
11/23	4.03	0.5	3.25	0.5	3.12	0.4	2.74	0.91
12/1	4.08	0.5	3.34	0.5	3.15	0.4	2.74	0.93
12/8	4.13	0.5	3.36	0.5	3.17	0.5	2.74	0.96
12/15	4.16	0.5	3.37	0.5	3.19	0.4	2.74	0.97
12/22	4.3	0.5	3.52	0.5	3.32	0.4	2.74	0.98
12/29	4.32	0.5	3.55	0.5	3.30	0.5	2.74	1.02

2017
PRIMARY MORTGAGE MARKET SURVEY®
Summary page with all rate types - U.S. averages

Week	U.S. 30 yr FRM	30 yr fees & points	U.S. 15 yr FRM	15 yr fees & points	U.S. 5/1 ARM	5/1 ARM fees & points	5/1 ARM margin	U.S. 30 yr FRM/ 5/1 ARM spread
1/5	4.20	0.5	3.44	0.5	3.33	0.4	2.74	0.87
1/12	4.12	0.5	3.37	0.5	3.23	0.5	2.74	0.89
1/19	4.09	0.5	3.34	0.5	3.21	0.4	2.74	0.88
1/26	4.19	0.4	3.40	0.4	3.20	0.4	2.74	0.99
2/2	4.19	0.5	3.41	0.5	3.23	0.4	2.74	0.96
2/9	4.17	0.4	3.39	0.4	3.21	0.4	2.74	0.96
2/16	4.15	0.5	3.35	0.5	3.18	0.4	2.74	0.97
2/23	4.16	0.5	3.37	0.5	3.16	0.4	2.74	1.00
3/2	4.10	0.5	3.32	0.5	3.14	0.4	2.74	0.96
3/9	4.21	0.5	3.42	0.5	3.23	0.4	2.74	0.98
3/16	4.30	0.5	3.50	0.5	3.28	0.4	2.74	1.02
3/23	4.23	0.5	3.44	0.5	3.24	0.4	2.74	0.99
3/30	4.14	0.5	3.39	0.4	3.18	0.4	2.74	0.96
4/6	4.10	0.5	3.36	0.5	3.19	0.4	2.74	0.91
4/13	4.08	0.5	3.34	0.5	3.18	0.4	2.74	0.90
4/20	3.97	0.5	3.23	0.5	3.10	0.4	2.74	0.87
4/27	4.03	0.5	3.27	0.4	3.12	0.4	2.74	0.91
5/4	4.02	0.5	3.27	0.5	3.13	0.5	2.74	0.89
5/11	4.05	0.5	3.29	0.5	3.14	0.5	2.74	0.91
5/18	4.02	0.5	3.27	0.5	3.13	0.5	2.74	0.89

Although Freddie Mac attempts to provide reliable, useful information in this document, Freddie Mac does not guarantee that the information is accurate, current or suitable for any particular purpose. Estimates contained in this document are those of Freddie Mac currently and are subject to change without notice.

Information from this document may be used with proper attribution. Alteration of this document is strictly prohibited. © 2017 by Freddie Mac.

Source: http://www.freddiemac.com/pmms/archive.html

Required Disclosures

Creditors granting loans meeting HOEPA criteria must disclose certain facts about the loan as part of the loan package at least *three business days* prior to consummation of a mortgage transaction.

This notice is intended to protect consumers from pressure tactics that imply the consumer is already locked into the agreement, or that canceling will be prohibitively complex or expensive.

In addition, the creditor must disclose:

- The APR.

- The regular payment amount (including any balloon payment where the law permits balloon payments).

- The loan amount (when the amount borrowed includes credit insurance premiums).

- For variable rate loans, the amount of the maximum monthly payment and the fact that the rate and monthly payment may increase.

- For a mortgage refinancing, the total amount borrowed as reflected by the face amount of the note. When the amount borrowed includes premiums or other charges for optional credit insurance or debt-cancellation coverage, that fact must also be stated. To be considered accurate, the amount disclosed *cannot vary by more than $100 above or below the amount required to be disclosed.*

These disclosures are *in addition to* the other required Truth in Lending disclosures.

A sample of the required HOEPA disclosure language follows (the disclosure statements in brackets are provided to the consumer only when applicable):

Disclosure Form

You are not required to complete this agreement merely because you have received these disclosures or signed a loan application.

If you obtain this loan, the lender will have a mortgage on your home.

You could lose your home, and any money you have put into it, if you do not meet your obligations under the loan.

You are borrowing $ _____ .

[Optional credit insurance __ is __ is not included in this amount.]

The annual percentage rate on your loan will be _____ %.

Your regular <u>frequency</u> payment will be $_____.

[At the end of the loan, you will still owe us $<u> balloon amount</u> .]

[Your interest rate may rise. Increases in the interest rate could raise your payment. The highest amount your payment could increase is to $ _____ .]

Source: http://www.freddiemac.com/pmms/archive.html

Higher-Priced Loans

[See 12 CFR §1026.35 Prohibited acts or practices in connection with higher-priced mortgage loans (TILA Regulation Z)].

 This chapter uses this regulation and citations from the CFPB.

Regulation Z has been amended with rules that affect **higher-priced loans**, which were part of the Housing and Economic Recovery Act of 2008, which amended Regulation Z and the Truth In Lending Act. Regulation Z [see 12 CFR, part 1026, Subpart E, §1026.35] sets forth the specific requirements for higher-priced loans.

Higher-priced mortgage loans (HPML) are closed-end mortgage loans that are secured by the borrower's principal dwelling. A **higher-priced loan** is defined *as a loan where the APR of a mortgage loan exceeds the average prime offer rate by:*

1. 1.5% for a first mortgage lien
2. 2.5% for a first lien jumbo loan (loan amount over $453,100)
3. 3.5% for a subordinate mortgage lien

A loan originator may verify if a prospective loan is a HOEPA or higher-priced loan by determining the loan APR and entering the data at the FFIEC Rate Spread Calculator website [see http://www.ffiec.gov/ratespread/newcalc.aspx]. The APR calculation is based on the locked interest rate of the prospective loan. This site will calculate the rate spread between the APR and the APOR in effect.

If the loan being made is a higher-priced loan, the originator must establish:

a. The borrower's ability to repay the mortgage loan, and
b. An escrow account for property taxes, homeowner's insurance, private mortgage insurance, etc. for a five-year term.

Exercise 9.1: Knowledge Check

An example of a higher-priced loan is a first mortgage loan that exceeds the yield on the applicable corresponding Treasury Bill by 2%.

    A. true

    B. false

Prohibited Loan Terms

A loan that is subject to HOEPA may **not** include:

- A payment schedule that provides for regular periodic payments that do not fully amortize and result in a **balloon payment** on HOEPA loans having terms of *less than five years*, unless it is a bridge loan of less than one year used by consumers to buy or build a home.

- **Negative amortization**, which involves monthly *payments that do not fully pay the interest due on the loan and that cause an increase in the borrower's total principal debt*. Any interest rate changes and payment schedule caps must be coordinated to avoid this situation.

- A **repayment schedule** that consolidates more than two periodic payments that are to be paid in advance from the proceeds of the loan. The borrower should get the maximum use of the funds and have a legitimate opportunity to use the loan proceeds.

- **Default interest rates** that are higher than pre-default note rates and increase due to a default of the borrower.

- **Rebating,** a refund calculated by a method less favorable than the actuarial method for rebates of interest arising from a loan acceleration due to default.

- **Prepayment penalties**, although there are exceptions. Prepayment penalties are allowed if limited to the *first two years* of the loan or if the source of the prepayment funds is a refinancing by the lender or lender affiliate. They are also allowed if the amount of the periodic payment of principal, interest, or both will not change at any time during the *first four years* of the loan. Prepayment penalties may also be allowed in cases where the borrower's debt-to-income ratio does not exceed 50%.

- **Demand clauses**, including *any provision that enables the creditor to call the loan before maturity*. Only certain behavior of the consumer would permit the lender to call the loan; for example, fraud, material misrepresentation, default, or damage to the security property.

[see 12 CFR, Part 1026, Truth in Lending – Regulation Z §1026.32(d) Limitations]

Prohibited Acts and Practices

Additionally, according to Regulation Z [see 12 CFR, Part 1026, Truth in Lending – Regulation Z §1026.34(a) Prohibited acts or practices for high-cost mortgages], creditors granting loans meeting HOEPA criteria may **not**:

- Grant loans solely on the collateral value of the borrower's property without regard to the borrower's ability to repay the loan.

- Disburse proceeds from home improvement loans to anyone other than the borrower, jointly to the borrower and the home improvement contractor, or, in some instances, to a third-party escrow agent as established by written agreement between the borrower, the creditor, and the contractor.

- Sell or otherwise assign the loan without furnishing the following statement to the purchaser or assignee:

  "Notice: This is a mortgage subject to special rules under the federal Truth in Lending Act. Purchasers or assignees of this mortgage could be liable for all claims and defenses with respect to the mortgage that the borrower could assert against the creditor."

- Refinance a HOEPA loan into another HOEPA loan *within the first 12 months* of origination unless the new loan is in the borrower's best interest. The prohibition also applies to assignees holding or servicing the loan.

Verifying Repayment Ability

[See 12 CFR, Part 1026, Truth in Lending – Regulation Z §1026.43(c)(4) Verification of income or assets.]

Creditors may **not** grant loans solely based on the collateral value of the borrower's property without regard to the borrower's ability to repay the loan, including the consumer's current and reasonably expected income, employment, assets other than the collateral, current obligations, and mortgage-related obligations, which include expected property taxes, premiums for mortgage-related insurance required by the creditor, and similar expenses. Income and assets can include:

- Expected income or assets
- Tax returns and W-2s
- Payroll receipts
- Financial institution records
- Other third-party documents that provide reasonably reliable evidence of the consumer's income or assets

The amounts the creditor uses to verify the repayment ability *cannot be materially greater* than the amounts the creditor could have verified when the loan was consummated.

Furthermore, the lender must determine the borrower's repayment ability using the largest payment of principal and interest scheduled in the *first five years* following consummation [see 12 CFR, Part 1026, Truth in Lending – Regulation Z §1026.43(e)(2)(iv)(A)]. The creditor must also consider the current obligations and mortgage-related obligations and assess the borrower's repayment ability, taking into account at least one of the following:

- The ratio of total debt obligations to income
- The income the consumer will have after paying debt obligations

A creditor is not presumed to be in compliance if the regular periodic payments *for the first five years* of the transaction would cause the principal balance to increase or if the term of the loan is *less than five years* and the regular periodic payments when aggregated do not fully amortize the outstanding principal balance.

The requirement to prove ability to repay does **not** apply to temporary or "bridge" loans *with terms of 12 months or less*, such as a loan to purchase a new dwelling where the borrower plans to sell a current dwelling within 12 months [see 12 CFR, Part 1026, Truth in Lending – Regulation Z §1026.43(a)(3)(ii)].

Escrow Account Restriction

Regulation Z imposes the following restriction on loans that meet the definition of a *higher-priced mortgage loan*:

Escrow Account – The rule requires the originating lender to establish and maintain an escrow (impound) account for property taxes and insurance (hazard, flood, mortgage, etc.) *for a minimum of five years* [see 12 CFR, Part 1026, Truth in Lending – Regulation Z §1026.35(b)(3) Cancellation]. Unless creditors meet certain exemptions, the rule applies to all higher-priced loans as defined under HOEPA regulations [see https://www.federalregister.gov/articles/2013/01/22/2013-00734/escrow-requirements-under-the-truth-in-lending-act-regulation-z].

Escrow Requirements for Jumbo Loans

In response to the Dodd-Frank Act (Pub.L. 111-203, H.R. 4173), the Federal Reserve Board adopted a final rule related to escrow requirements on next first lien loans that exceed Freddie Mac's conforming loan limit (jumbo loans). The rule relates to a 2008 rule implementing HOEPA, which prohibits a creditor from extending such a next mortgage loan unless an escrow account is established for payment of required property taxes and premiums for related insurance, including any required mortgage insurance premiums and homeowner's hazard insurance. If property hazard insurance is paid through a homeowners' association, as may be the case with a condominium, it would be excluded from the escrow requirement. Similarly, if the property taxes for a cooperative are paid by the corporation and collected through cooperative association fees, property taxes would be excluded from these escrow requirements.

This rule, which became effective April 1, 2011, revised §1026.35(b)(3) of Regulation Z, to provide a higher APR threshold for determining whether jumbo mortgage loans secured by a first lien on a consumer's principal dwelling are next mortgage loans for which an escrow account must be established.

As revised, the threshold for coverage of the escrow requirement for jumbo loans is 2.5 percentage points (rather than 1.5 percentage points) in excess of the average prime offer rate for a comparable transaction, as of the date the transaction's rate is set. Raising the APR threshold applicable to jumbo loans eliminates the mandatory escrow requirement for loans with an APR above the existing threshold but below the new threshold. Creditors may, at their option, elect to continue to use the 1.5 percentage point threshold for these loans.

Appraisal Requirements for Certain Higher-Priced Mortgage Loans (HPML)

[See Consumer Financial Protection Bureau website: http://www.consumerfinance.gov/regulations/appraisals-for-higher-priced-mortgage-loans/, *Appraisals for Higher-Priced Mortgage Loans Summary* (PDF, page 10).]

For higher-priced mortgage loans, the rule requires creditors to:

- Use a licensed or certified appraiser who prepares a written appraisal report based on a physical inspection of the interior of the property [see 12 CFR, Part 1026, Truth in Lending – Regulation Z §1026.35(c)(3)]. The rule is designed to help make sure that a homebuyer does not borrow more than the home is worth and that the lender is using an accurate value when determining whether to lend money and at what rate.

- Disclose to applicants information about the purpose of the appraisal and provide consumers with a free copy of any appraisal report. The creditor has the right to be reimbursed for the bona fide cost of the appraisal and must provide the borrower a copy of the appraisal a *minimum of three (3) days* prior to close of escrow [see 12 CFR, Part 1026, Truth in Lending – Regulation Z §1026.35(c)(5)].

- If the seller acquired the property for a lower price *during the prior six months*, this is considered a "flip" sale. A second appraisal may be required at *no cost* to the consumer [see 12 CFR, Part 1026, Truth in Lending – Regulation Z §1026.35(c)(4)(6)].

- If the price difference exceeds **10%** of the seller's original acquisition cost *during the first ninety days* or **20%** of the original cost *during the first six months*, creditors are *required* to obtain a second appraisal [see 12 CFR, Part 1026, Truth in Lending – Regulation Z §1026.35(c)(4)(A)(B)]. This requirement for next home purchase mortgage loans is intended to address fraudulent property flipping by seeking to ensure that the value of the property legitimately increased. The borrower cannot pay for the cost of the second appraisal report.

Exemptions

The rule exempts several types of loans, such as qualified mortgages, temporary bridge loans and construction loans (*12-month term or less*), loans for new manufactured homes, and loans for mobile homes, trailers, and boats that are dwellings.

The rule also has exemptions from the second appraisal requirement to facilitate loans in rural areas and other transactions.

Balloon Payments, Late Fees, and Other Loan Terms

The Dodd-Frank Act has certain restrictions and requirements concerning loan terms and origination practices for mortgages that fall within HOEPA's coverage test.

For Example:

- Balloon payments are generally banned, unless they are to account for the seasonal or irregular income of the borrower, are part of a short-term bridge loan, or are made by creditors meeting specified criteria, including operating predominantly in rural or underserved areas.

- Late fees are restricted to *four percent* of the payment that is past due, fees for providing payoff statements are restricted, and fees for loan modification or payment deferral are banned. The four percent rule, while it conforms with government-insured mortgage loans, reduces the late fee on conventional conforming loans from *five percent*.

- Most fees for obtaining a payoff statement from the current mortgagee will be banned.

- Fees for loan modifications, if a borrower has trouble and cannot pay the mortgage, will **not** be allowed.

- Creditors or brokers are restricted from advising homeowners refinancing into a high cost mortgage not to make their payments on an existing loan. It has never been a sound business practice to advise someone not to pay scheduled payments, no matter what type of loan they have.

[See http://www.consumerfinance.gov/regulations/high-cost-mortgage-and-homeownership-counseling-amendments-to-regulation-z-and-homeownership-counseling-amendments-to-regulation-x/. See Preamble, *High-Cost Mortgage and Homeownership Counseling Amendments to the Truth in Lending Act (Regulation Z) and Homeownership Counseling Amendments to the Real Estate Settlement Procedures Act (Regulation X)*: http://files.consumerfinance.gov/f/201301_cfpb_final-rule_high-cost-mortgages-preamble.pdf (pages 4, 5).]

Exercise 9.2: Knowledge Check

When a seller owns a property that is to be resold during the first 90 days, a second appraisal is required for a conventional loan if the increase in price is

A. 5%.

B. 6.5%.

C. 9.99%.

D. 12.5%.

Loan Originator Compensation Rule

[See CFPB website: http://www.consumerfinance.gov/regulations/loan-originator-compensation-requirements-under-the-truth-in-lending-act-regulation-z/, Loan Originator Compensation Requirements under the Truth in Lending Act (Regulation Z).]

After the national mortgage meltdown, the Federal Reserve implemented the Loan Officer Compensation Rule that took effect April 1, 2011. The Dodd-Frank Act expanded on previous efforts by lawmakers and regulators to strengthen loan originator qualification requirements and regulate industry compensation practices.

One of the objectives of the Dodd-Frank Act (Pub.L. 111-203, H.R. 4173) was to address perceived unfair practices by MLOs related to **compensation** paid by consumers.

This rule applies to transactions involving closed-end extensions of credit secured by a consumer's principal dwelling and must be followed by all persons who originate loans, including mortgage brokers and their employees, as well as mortgage loan officers employed by depository institutions and other lenders. For the purposes of this rule, **loan originator** is defined in Regulation Z §1026.36(a) as:

> … *a person who for compensation or other monetary gain, or in expectation of compensation or other monetary gain, arranges, negotiates, or otherwise obtains an extension of consumer credit for another person. The term "loan originator" includes an employee of the creditor if the employee meets this definition. The term "loan originator" includes the creditor only if the creditor does not provide the funds for the transaction at consummation out of the creditor's own resources, including drawing on a bona fide warehouse line of credit, or out of deposits held by the creditor.*

The rule prohibits creditors from compensating MLOs based on the loan's interest rate or other terms or conditions—such as the APR, loan-to-value, loan program, or provisions (such as a prepayment penalty) selected. Therefore, a loan originator offering a loan of the same dollar amount utilizing different loan programs (i.e., FHA-insured, conventional, VA, fixed-rate, ARM) receives the same compensation – **no matter which program the borrower chooses**.

This prohibition also applies to compensation from a mortgage broker to an employee who originates loans. For example, a mortgage broker *cannot* pay an employee more for a transaction with a 6% interest rate than a 5% interest rate. Compensation can be based on any of the following triggers:

- Flat fee fixed in advance

- Hourly rate for time worked

- Overall loan volume

- Long-term loan performance
- Existing/new customer
- "Pull-through" rate; i.e., quality of loan files

Creditors can also set a minimum and a maximum compensation—such as paying 1% for **all loans** the MLO originates, with a minimum of $1,000 and a maximum of $5,000—as long as the amount is the same for every transaction.

Note that "compensation" does not include any amounts an MLO receives as payment for bona fide and reasonable non-affiliated third-party charges, such as an appraisal fee, escrow fees, or insurance premiums. However, fees that are paid to affiliated third-parties would be considered part of MLO compensation.

Prohibition Against Dual Compensation

When a loan originator receives compensation directly from a consumer in connection with a mortgage loan, Regulation Z provides that no loan originator may receive compensation from *another person in connection with the same transaction*. The Dodd-Frank Act codifies this prohibition, which was designed to address consumer confusion over mortgage broker loyalties in which brokers were receiving payments from the consumer and the creditor. The final rule implements this restriction, but provides an exception to allow mortgage brokers to pay their employees or contractors commissions, although the commissions cannot be based on the terms of the loans they originate [see http://files.consumerfinance.gov/f/201301_cfpb_loan-originator-compensation-rule_summary.pdf].

The rule does not prohibit a consumer from accepting *a higher interest rate in return for reducing closing costs*, known as **yield spread premium** (YSP). This shows as a credit to the borrower on the Loan Estimate and is not considered compensation paid by the consumer to the MLO.

The final rule also requires creditors to retain evidence of compliance with the rule *for three (3) years* after a covered loan is consummated.

To prevent evasion, the final rule also *prohibits* compensation:

- **Based on a proxy for a term of a transaction.** The rule also further clarifies the definition of a proxy to focus on whether: (1) the factor consistently varies with a transaction term over a significant number of transactions; and (2) the loan originator has the ability, directly or indirectly, to add, drop, or change the factor in originating the transaction. If a loan originator's compensation is based in whole or in part on a factor that is a proxy for a term of a transaction, the loan originator's compensation is based on a term of a transaction. A factor that is not itself a term of a transaction is a proxy for a term of the transaction if the factor consistently varies with that term over a significant number of transactions, and the loan originator has the ability, directly or indirectly, to add, drop, or change the factor in originating the transaction.

- **From being reduced to offset the cost of a change in transaction terms (often called a "pricing concession").** However, the final rule allows loan originators to reduce their compensation to defray certain unexpected increases in estimated settlement costs.

- **From the mortgage entity organization for referring a borrower to a service provider.** This typically is regulated by Chapter 8 of RESPA, but the CFPB made it very clear that if a mortgage entity owns any interest in another settlement service provider and a loan originator refers a borrower to the provider, the loan originator may not receive additional compensation for the referral.

- **Based upon the profitability of a transaction or a pool of transactions.** Lenders are prohibited from establishing "point banks or pools" under this regulation. However, the final rule clarifies the application of this prohibition to various kinds of retirement and profit-sharing plans. For example, mortgage-related business profits can be used to contribute to certain tax-advantaged retirement plans, such as a 401(k) plan, and to make bonuses and contributions to other plans that do not exceed ten percent of the individual loan originator's total compensation.

Originators may not be paid by the consumer and another person or entity in connection with a mortgage loan closing, *except* **an MLO may receive compensation from the loan originator organization.** Consumers may pay bona fide discount points and creditors may pay an overage for higher note yield, but none of these additional fees may be paid to the loan originator.

Bonus Compensation and Non-Deferred Compensation Plans

Mortgage-related business profits can be used to contribute to certain tax-advantaged retirement plans, such as a 401(k) plan, as well as to make bonuses and contributions to other plans that *do not exceed ten (10) percent* of the individual loan originator's total compensation.

If compensation is paid through a profits-based compensation plan that is not based on profits from a mort-gage-related business, this compensation is *not* considered to be based on terms of multiple transactions conducted by multiple loan originators.

Using mortgage-related business profits as described above would still be prohibited, however, if it other-wise violates the rule, such as where the amount of money that is paid to a loan originator depends on the transaction terms originated by that loan originator. Thus, even if a profits-based bonus is unrelated to prof-its on mortgage loans, the bonus *must not vary based on whether the loan originator is making higher-rate mortgage loans.*

[*See Regulation Z § 1026.36(d)(1)(i) Payments Based on a Term of a Transaction.*]

Tax-Advantaged Deferred Compensation

A loan originator organization may structure tax-advantaged deferred compensation that is based on mortgage-related profits in two ways:

1. As a contribution to a defined contribution plan that is a designated tax-advantaged plan

2. As a benefit under a defined benefit plan that is a designated tax-advantaged plan

If an employer contributes to a defined contribution plan for an individual loan originator, they may not base the contribution on the terms of that originator's transactions.

Defined Contribution and Defined Benefit Plan

A **defined contribution plan** is *a plan which provides for an individual account for each participant and for benefits based solely on the amount contributed to the participant's account, and any income, expenses, gains and losses, and forfeitures of accounts of other participants which may be allocated to such participant's account.*

[*See Internal Revenue Code Section 414(i), 26 U.S.C. 414(i) Defined Contribution Plan.*]

A **defined benefit plan** is *defined, in the Internal Revenue Code Section 414(j), 26 U.S.C. 414(j) Defined Benefit Plan, as any plan which is not a defined contribution plan.*

An easy way to think of the difference between the two plans follows:

- A **contribution plan** is based on *contributions made by the employee*, and possibly by the employer (as a company matching contribution) and the plan is *controlled by the employee.*

- A **defined benefit plan** is a pension plan with *sole contributions and control coming from the employer.*

Compensation Direct Payment

A **non-deferred profits-based compensation plan** is *any non-deferred compensation arrangement where an individual loan originator may be paid variable, additional compensation based in whole or in part on the mortgage-related business profits of the person paying the compensation, any affiliate, or a business unit in the person's or the affiliate's organization.*

[See Regulation Z, 12 CFR §1026.36(d)(1)-3.ii.]

Non-deferred profits-based compensation plans include, but are not limited to, the following types of compensation if they are determined based on the mortgage-related profits of the person paying the compensation, its business unit, or its affiliate:

- Bonus pools
- Bonus plans
- Profits pools
- Profit-sharing plans
- Awards of merchandise, services, trips, or similar prizes or incentives

[See Regulation Z, 12 CFR §1026.36(d)(1)-3.ii.]

For example, if you are a creditor, you have appropriately set up a non-deferred profits-based compensation plan if you pay your individual loan originators bonuses at the end of a calendar year based on your average net return on assets for the calendar year.

Note that this compensation **cannot** be paid directly to the loan originator *unless:*

- The bonus **does not exceed 10%** of the originator's gross pay for the previous year, or

- The individual loan originator was a loan originator for **ten or fewer transactions**, subject to this paragraph, consummated during the 12-month period preceding the date of the compensation determination

The bonus may only be **10%** of the originator's total compensation, including the amount of the bonus. For example, if the loan originator receives $80,000 in compensation and the employer makes a contribution to a tax-advantaged retirement plan in the amount of $10,000, the employer may only pay a $10,000 cash bo-nus to the originator. The total compensation to the originator for the year is $100,000, with 80% coming from loan originator functions, 10% to the tax advantaged plan, and 10% from an employer-paid cash bonus.

 The common requirement of either a bonus, tax-deferred, or direct plan is the bonus cannot be based on the loan originator's transactions.

[See Regulation Z, 12 CFR §1026.36 (d)(1) (iii). See also "2013 Loan Originator Rule: Small Entity Com-pliance Guide," January 13, 2014, Page 47, http://files.consumerfinance. gov/f/201401_cfpb_complaince-guide_loan-originator.pdf.]

Exercise 9.3: Knowledge Check

1. **An MLO may be compensated**

    A. additional basis points for closing a government-insured loan.
    B. based on the interest rate offered to the consumer.
    C. based on the loan amount.
    D. with a bonus for steering a consumer to an affiliate for a settlement service.

Steering and Safe Harbor

To further protect the interests of the consumer, Regulation Z §1026.36 (e) prohibits MLOs from "**steering**"—*influencing, advising, counseling, directing*—consumers to accept the terms offered by a particular creditor in order to receive greater compensation than might be available from a different creditor, unless the loan is actually in the borrower's interest. However, for such actions to constitute steering, the consumer must actually consummate the transaction in question.

In order to facilitate compliance, the rule creates what is referred to as a **safe harbor** by setting specific requirements for providing loan options to consumers. Although not a guarantee, if an MLO meets the requirements for providing loan options, it is generally recognized that the loan conditions are legitimate, not likely subject to legal disputes, and protect the consumer's interests – establish a "safe harbor." In short, under safe harbor, there is greater confidence that the consumer will be able to repay the loan, which lowers risk to the lender.

To stay within the safe harbor, an MLO must obtain loan options from a significant number of the creditors—three or more—with which the originator regularly does business, and the MLO must have a good faith belief that the options presented to the consumer are loans for which the consumer likely qualifies. For each type of transaction in which the consumer has expressed an interest, an MLO must present loan options that include the following:

* Lowest interest rate
* Lowest interest rate without risky features; i.e., prepayment penalties, negative amortization, interest-only payments, balloon payments in the first seven years of the loan, a demand feature, shared equity or shared appreciation; or, in the case of a reverse mortgage, a loan without a prepayment penalty or shared equity or appreciation
* Lowest total dollar amount for origination fees and discount points

The term "type of transaction" refers to the following types of loans:

* A loan with an APR that cannot increase after consummation
* A loan with an APR that may increase after consummation
* A reverse mortgage

It does **not** apply to a home equity line of credit or a loan secured by a consumer's interest in a timeshare plan.

For each type of transaction, if an MLO presents to the consumer *more than three loans*, the MLO must highlight the loans that satisfy the criteria specified in the rule. The MLO can present *fewer than three loans* and satisfy the safe harbor if the loan(s) otherwise meets the criteria in the rule.

A violation of this steering prohibition may provide a borrower with an affirmative defense in a foreclosure proceeding. The Dodd-Frank Act ensures that such a defense is not subject to the statute of limitations that normally impact private action for damages.

[For more information, see Title 12: Banks and Banking, Part 1026 Regulation Z, Supplement I to Part 1026—Official Staff Interpretations at: https://www.gpo.gov/fdsys/search/home.action].

Exercise 9.4: Knowledge Check

MLOs **CANNOT** receive compensation based on the type or terms of a loan.

A. true
B. false

Guidelines for Registered Loan Originators

The Loan Officer Compensation Rule also addresses the qualifications for licensed and registered MLOs. Guidelines require that a loan originator organization that is **not** a government agency or state housing agency must:

1. Comply with all state law requirements for legal existence.

2. Ensure that each individual loan originator is licensed or registered as required under the SAFE Act [see 12 CFR, Part 1008, S.A.F.E. Mortgage Licensing Act (Regulation H) §1008.103].

3. Provide [see 12 CFR, Part 1008, S.A.F.E. Mortgage Licensing Act (Regulation H) §1008.105]:

   • A criminal background check through the NMLS.

   • A credit report from a consumer reporting agency.

   • A check for information from the Nationwide Mortgage Licensing System and Registry (NMLSR) about any administrative, civil, or criminal findings by any government jurisdiction.

   • Information that the MLO has not been convicted of, or pleaded guilty or nolo contendere, to a felony in a domestic or military court in the preceding seven-year period or in the case of a felony involving an act of fraud, dishonesty, a breach of trust, or money laundering at any time.

   • Information to demonstrate financial responsibility, character, and general fitness to warrant that the individual loan originator will operate honestly, fairly, and efficiently.

4. Provide periodic training covering federal and state law requirements that apply to the individual loan originator's loan origination activities [see 12 CFR, Part 1008, S.A.F.E. Mortgage Licensing Act (Regulation H) §1008.107].

Written Policies and Procedures

A depository institution must establish and maintain written policies and procedures to ensure and monitor the compliance of the institution, its employees, its subsidiaries and the subsidiaries' employees with the requirements of the Loan Officer Compensation Rules [see 12 CFR, Part 1026, Truth in Lending (Regulation Z) §1026.36(j)]. In addition to MLOs engaged by depository institutions, all mortgage lenders and brokers actively engaged in mortgage lending activities in other roles must comply with the Loan Officer Compensation Rules.

Exercise 9.5: Apply Your Knowledge

Introduction: In this discussion activity, you will apply your knowledge of higher priced and high cost loans. Review the following scenario.

Description: A borrower is seeking an FHA insured loan. He will put the minimum 3.5% down payment and pay the upfront mortgage insurance fee of 1.75%. He will pay the annual mortgage insurance fee of .85% for the life of the loan. His interest rate is 5%, the APOR (as of the date the loan interest rate is locked) is 4.672%, and his APR for this loan is 6.474%.

1. Is this a higher-priced loan? Explain your answer.

   _____

   _____

   _____

2. If this loan is a higher-priced loan, what must be done?

   _____

   _____

   _____

3. Is this a high cost loan? Explain your answer.

   _____

   _____

   _____

4. If the finance charge includes two points origination, two discount points, and 1.5 percent of the loan amount as closing costs, using the provided information, is this a high cost loan if it was refinance transaction? Explain your answer.

   _____

   _____

   _____

5. If the loan is a high cost loan, what must be done?

   _____

   _____

   _____

Chapter Summary

1. The Home Ownership and Equity Protection Act (HOEPA) was implemented to prevent deceptive practices and predatory lending in the mortgage industry.

2. Higher-priced mortgage loans reference the average prime offer rate, which is added to a set percentage to determine if a loan is an HPML.

3. There are certain aspects of a mortgage loan that are prohibited, such as balloon payments (within the first five years of the loan), negative amortization, demand clauses, etc.

4. A lender must verify that a borrower has the ability to repay a mortgage debt using one of several approaches.

5. An HPML requires an escrow account be established for a minimum of five years.

6. An appraiser must make a physical inspection of the interior and exterior of the subject property. A copy of the appraisal (if the borrower has paid the lender for the appraisal) must be given to the borrower within three business days prior to loan closing. A second appraisal is required if the property is sold within 180 days at a specified profit above the acquisition cost of the seller.

7. High cost loans apply to owner-occupied refinance loans and second mortgage loans. The average prime offer rate is the index used to calculate when a loan is considered high cost.

8. High cost loans require an additional disclosure to be signed by the borrower prior to signing loan documents. This also gives the borrower an additional three-day rescission period.

9. A loan originator may never be compensated for loan origination activities based on any other term other than the loan amount. The interest rate or program type of the loan must never be a basis for compensating an MLO.

10. A borrower may accept a higher interest rate resulting in a yield spread premium/lender credit to offset closing costs.

11. A creditor may compensate an MLO by contributing to a tax-advantage plan in an amount no greater than 10% of the MLO's total gross income for the previous year.

Chapter Quiz

1. The Home Ownership and Equity Protection Act amends which regulation?

   A. Regulation B

   B. Regulation C

   C. Regulation X

   D. Regulation Z

2. A pension plan with sole employer control of contributions is considered a(n)

   A. defined benefit plan.

   B. defined contribution plan.

   C. employee benefit plan.

   D. employer contribution plan.

3. A higher-priced loan is one that

   A. has an APR greater than 6.5%.

   B. includes finance charges greater than 5% of the loan amount.

   C. is also known as a Section 32 loan.

   D. uses the average prime offer rate as an index.

4. The borrower's ability to repay a mortgage loan may be based on

   A. anticipated earnings from projected overtime pay.

   B. current or expected income.

   C. the equity in the subject property.

   D. sporadic bonus income.

5. If a seller sells a home within three to six months after purchasing the home, a second appraisal is required if the sale price exceeds the seller's acquisition costs by more than

   A. 5%.

   B. 10%.

   C. 20%.

   D. 50%.

6. A high cost loan is one that is defined as a mortgage loan (first lien) where the APR exceeds the average prime offer rate by

   A. 4.0%.

   B. 5.0%.

   C. 6.5%.

   D. 8.5%.

7. Creditors must provide borrowers a copy of the appraisal used for their mortgage loan _____ day(s) before loan closing.

   A. 1

   B. 2

   C. 3

   D. 5

The SAFE Act

The focus of the Housing and Economic Recovery Act of 2008 (HERA) is to help in the recovery and revitalization of America's residential housing market. One of the primary elements of HERA is , the or **SAFE Act**.

This chapter reviews the primary elements of the SAFE Act. The chapter also reviews national educational and licensing requirements for MLOs.

After completing this chapter, you will be able to:

- Identify licensing requirements and procedures for mortgage loan professionals.
- Recognize education requirements for MLOs.

KEY TERMS

Nontraditional Mortgage Product
Registered Loan Originator
Residential Mortgage Loan
Residential Real Estate
State-Licensed Mortgage Loan Originator
Unique Identifier

The SAFE Act – Introduction

The **Housing and Economic Recovery Act (HERA)** is a major housing law (Pub.L. 110-289) that serves multiple purposes: The modernization of the Federal Housing Administration, foreclosure prevention, and the enhancement of consumer protections.

Title V, the **Secure and Fair Enforcement for Mortgage Licensing Act** or **SAFE Act**, is a key component of HERA. It is designed to enhance consumer protection and reduce fraud by requiring national minimum standards for mortgage training, including prelicensing education and annual continuing education. Furthermore, under the SAFE Act, all mortgage loan originators must be either state-licensed or federally-registered. All mortgage loan originators seeking state licensure—or currently holding a state license—are required to pass the SAFE Mortgage Loan Originator Test, which includes a national component, the Uniform State Test (UST) component for participating states, and may include a state-specific component. [See S.A.F.E. Mortgage Licensing Act – State Compliance and Bureau Registration System (Regulation H), 12 CFR 1008: http://www.ecfr.gov/cgi-bin/text-idx?SID=ee95b4601c6 b02fba152d96a1076733a&node=12:8.0.2.8.7&rgn=div5].

The SAFE Act requires all states to implement an MLO licensing process that meets certain standards through the **Nationwide Mortgage Licensing System & Registry (NMLS)**. The NMLS, which began in January 2008 by the Conference of State Bank Supervisors (CSBS) and the American Association of Residential Mortgage Regulators (AARMR), is responsible for providing a centralized and standardized system for mortgage licensing that accommodates both the regulatory agencies and the mortgage industry. The NMLS website [see http://mortgage.nationwidelicensingsystem.org/Pages/default.aspx] contains valuable comprehensive information for all MLOs, including specific details about the steps necessary to set up an account, schedule a test appointment, and access state-specific requirements.

Objectives of the SAFE Act

Among the objectives of the SAFE Act are to:

- Provide uniform license applications and reporting requirements for state-licensed MLOs.
- Provide a comprehensive licensing and supervisory database.
- Aggregate and improve the flow of information to and between regulators.
- Provide increased accountability and tracking of MLOs.
- Streamline the licensing process and reduce regulatory burden.
- Enhance consumer protections and support anti-fraud measures.
- Provide consumers with free, easy-to-access information about an MLO's employment history and any public disciplinary and enforcement actions.
- Establish a means by which residential MLOs are required to act in the best interests of the consumer.
- Facilitate responsible behavior in the subprime mortgage market place.
- Provide comprehensive training and examination requirements related to nontraditional mortgage products.
- Facilitate the collection and disbursement of consumer complaints on behalf of state mortgage regulators.

SAFE Act Mandates for States

With the enactment of the SAFE Act, the **CSBS** and the **AARMR** worked with HUD to fulfill the mandates of the Act, including the requirements that states establish minimum standards for the licensing or registration of all MLOs. The CSBS and AARMR developed a model state law that met the minimum standards in the SAFE Act, including definitions, education and testing requirements, and financial responsibility and criminal background standards for MLOs. HUD reviewed the model legislation and determined that it met the SAFE Act requirements. Therefore, any state legislation that follows the model also met the applicable minimum requirements of the SAFE Act. [See State Model Language for Implementation of P.L. 110-289, Title V—SAFE Mortgage Licensing Act MSL]

Loan Originator Definition

The SAFE Act defines a **loan originator** (Sec. 1503) as an individual who:

- Takes a residential mortgage loan application.
- Offers or negotiates terms of a residential mortgage loan for compensation or gain.

An individual "assists a consumer in obtaining or applying to obtain a residential mortgage loan" by, among other things, advising on loan terms (including rates, fees, and other costs), preparing loan packages, or collecting information on behalf of the consumer with regard to a residential mortgage loan.

The definition does *not* include:

- Any individual who performs purely administrative or clerical tasks on behalf of a licensee.
- A person or entity that only performs real estate brokerage activities and is licensed or registered in accordance with applicable state law, unless the person or entity is compensated by a lender, a mortgage broker, or other mortgage loan originator or by any agent of such lender, mortgage broker, or other mortgage loan originator.
- A person or entity solely involved in extensions of credit relating to timeshare plans.

A **loan processor** or **underwriter** who does **not** represent to the public, through advertising or other means of communicating or providing information (including the use of business cards, stationery, brochures, signs, rate lists, or other promotional items), that he or she can or will perform any of the activities of a loan originator shall *not* be required to be a state-licensed mortgage loan originator.

An **independent contractor** may **not** engage in residential mortgage loan origination activities as a loan processor or underwriter *unless* such independent contractor is a state-licensed mortgage loan originator.

The SAFE Act requires all residential mortgage loan originators to be identified by a unique NMLS identifier number as either:

- **Federally-registered**—Any mortgage loan originator employed by a depository institution, a subsidiary that is owned and controlled by a depository institution and regulated by a federal banking agency, or an institution regulated by the Farm Credit Administration.
- **State-licensed**—All other MLOs, without exception.

Exercise 10.1: Knowledge Check

A loan originator takes a mortgage loan application with the expectation of compensation.

A. true
B. false

Other Definitions

Administrative or Clerical Tasks. The receipt, collection, and distribution of information common for the processing or underwriting of a loan in the mortgage industry and communication with a consumer to obtain information necessary for the processing or underwriting of a residential mortgage loan.

Depository Institution. Has the same meaning as in Section 3 of the Federal Deposit Insurance Act (i.e., any bank or savings association) and includes any credit union.

Federal Banking Agencies. The Board of Governors of the Federal Reserve System, the Comptroller of the Currency, the Director of the Office of Thrift Supervision, the National Credit Union Administration, and the Federal Deposit Insurance Corporation.

Loan Processor or Underwriter. In general, an individual who performs clerical or support duties at the direction of and subject to the supervision and instruction of:

- A state-licensed mortgage loan originator; or

- A registered mortgage loan originator.

"Clerical or support duties" may include:

- The receipt, collection, distribution, and analysis of information common for the processing or underwriting of a residential mortgage loan; and

- Communicating with a consumer to obtain the information necessary for the processing or underwriting of a loan to the extent that such communication does not include offering or negotiating loan rates or terms, or counseling consumers about residential mortgage loan rates or terms.

Nontraditional Mortgage Product. Any mortgage product other than a 30-year fixed-rate mortgage.

Real Estate Brokerage Activity. Any activity that involves offering or providing real estate brokerage services to the public, including:

- Acting as a real estate agent or real estate broker for a buyer, seller, lessor, or lessee of real property.

- Bringing together parties interested in the sale, purchase, lease, rental, or exchange of real property.

- Negotiating, on behalf of any party, any portion of a contract relating to the sale, purchase, lease, rental, or exchange of real property (other than in connection with providing financing with respect to any such transaction).

- Engaging in any activity for which a person engaged in the activity is required to be registered or licensed as a real estate agent or real estate broker under any applicable law.

- Offering to engage in any activity, or act in any capacity described above.

Registered Loan Originator. Any individual who:

A. Meets the definition of loan originator and is an employee of:

    1. A depository institution.

    2. A subsidiary that is:

        a) Owned and controlled by a depository institution; and

        b) Regulated by a federal banking agency.

    3. An institution regulated by the Farm Credit Administration.

B. Is registered with, and maintains a unique identifier through the Nationwide Mortgage Licensing System and Registry.

Residential Mortgage Loan. Any loan primarily for personal, family, or household use that is secured by a mortgage, deed of trust, or other equivalent consensual security interest on a dwelling (as defined in Section 103(v) of the Truth in Lending Act) or residential real estate upon which is constructed or intended to be constructed a dwelling (as so defined).

State. The term "state" means any state of the United States, the District of Columbia, any territory of the United States, Puerto Rico, Guam, American Samoa, the Trust Territory of the Pacific Islands, the Virgin Islands, and the Northern Mariana Islands.(12 USC § 5102.11 State)

State-Licensed Loan Originator. Any individual who:

A. Is a loan originator.

B. Is not an employee of:

    1. A depository institution.

    2. A subsidiary that is:

        a) Owned and controlled by a depository institution; and

        b) Regulated by a federal banking agency.

    3. An institution regulated by the Farm Credit Administration.

C. Is licensed by a state or by the Secretary under Section 1508 and registered as a loan originator with, and maintains a unique identifier through, the Nationwide Mortgage Licensing System and Registry.

Unique Identifier. In general, a number or other identifier that:

- Permanently identifies a loan originator.

- Is assigned by protocols established by the Nationwide Mortgage Licensing System and Registry and the federal banking agencies to facilitate electronic tracking of loan originators and uniform identification of, and public access to, the employment history of and the publicly adjudicated disciplinary and enforcement actions against loan originators.

- Shall not be used for purposes other than those set forth under the SAFE Act.

- To the greatest extent possible and to accomplish the purpose of the SAFE Act, states shall use unique identifiers in lieu of Social Security numbers.

The NMLS unique identifier is required on all marketing materials, applications, required disclosures, and business cards. If the marketing materials reference the company only, the company's unique identifier must be used. If the marketing materials and business cards are issued in the name of the mortgage loan originator, then the marketing materials and business cards require the MLO's unique identifier. All disclosures require the MLO's unique identifier.

MLO Prelicensing Education Requirements

[See S.A.F.E. Mortgage Licensing Act – State Compliance and Bureau Registration System (Regulation H), 12 CFR 1008, §1008.105(d) Minimum loan originator license requirements.]

To become a state-licensed MLO, an applicant must complete **at least twenty (20) hours** of approved prelicensing education, which includes:

- Federal law and regulation (3 hours)
- Ethics, including fraud, consumer protection, and fair lending (3 hours)
- Nontraditional mortgage products, which the SAFE Act defines as anything other than 30-year fixed rate loan (2 hours)
- Elective topics (12 hours)

 It is up to each state to determine whether to also require state-specific topics, either *as part of* the 12 hours of electives or *in addition to* the 20 hours required.

Mortgage Loan Originator Test

[See S.A.F.E. Mortgage Licensing Act – State Compliance and Bureau Registration System (Regulation H), 12 CFR 1008, §1008.105(e)(1) Minimum loan originator license requirements.]

In order to meet the written test requirement as defined by the state, an individual must pass, in accordance with the standards established under this subsection, a qualified written test developed by the NMLS and administered by a test provider approved by the NMLS based upon reasonable standards.

All state-licensed MLOs must pass the national component of the SAFE Mortgage Loan Originator Test. Passing the Uniform State Content (UST) component of the national test qualifies an MLO to apply for licensure in a participating state, subject to any additional state requirements.

The national component covers the following topics:

- Federal mortgage-related laws (23%)
- General mortgage knowledge (23%)
- Mortgage loan origination activities (25%)
- Ethics (16%)
- Uniform State Content (13%)

Note that not all states have adopted the UST test component and may still require the passage of a separate state examination.

[*See "SAFE Mortgage Loan Originator Test: National Component with Uniform State Test Content Outline," http://mortgage.nationwidelicensingsystem.org/profreq/testing/Pages/TestContentOutline.aspx*]

Minimum Competence

[See S.A.F.E. Mortgage Licensing Act – State Compliance and Bureau Registration System (Regulation H), 12 CFR 1008, §1008.105(e)(1) Minimum loan originator license requirements.]

An individual shall *not* be considered to have passed a qualified written test unless the individual achieves a test score of *not* less than **75 percent** correct answers to questions. The national component of the SAFE Mortgage Loan Originator Test with Uniform State Content allows for a total of 190 minutes for the student to complete the test.

Resource Assistance

The NMLS website provides many resources, including information regarding the SAFE Mortgage Loan Originator Test. Each test appointment includes an additional 30-35 minutes for completing a tutorial and an optional candidate survey. Test enrollment fees are non-refundable and non-transferable. A detailed guide for the entire testing process (from creating an enrollment and scheduling a testing appointment to what to expect at the testing center, etc.) is available at *http://mortgage.nationwidelicensingsystem.org/profreq/testing/Documents/MLO%20Handbook.pdf.*

Retaking the Exam

[See S.A.F.E. Mortgage Licensing Act – State Compliance and Bureau Registration System (Regulation H), 12 CFR 1008, §1008.105(e)(2) Minimum loan originator license requirements.]

According to the HUD final rule implementing the SAFE Act, any candidate may only take and fail the national component of the SAFE Mortgage Loan Originator Test with Uniform State Content **three consecutive times**, which are separated by 30-day waiting periods. After the third failure, that candidate must wait at least **six (6) months** before taking the test again. The same timeframes also apply to failing and retaking non-UST state components, for those states that do not participate in the UST program.

License Maintenance Requirements

[See S.A.F.E. Mortgage Licensing Act – State Compliance and Bureau Registration System (Regulation H), 12 CFR 1008, §1008.107 Minimum annual license renewal requirements.]

The *minimum* standards for license renewal for MLOs shall include the following:

- The MLO continues to meet the **standards for license issuance as defined by the state**.
- The MLO has satisfied the **annual continuing education requirements as defined by the state**.
- The MLO has paid all required fees for renewal of the license.

Failure to Satisfy Minimum Standards

[See S.A.F.E. Mortgage Licensing Act – State Compliance and Bureau Registration System (Regulation H), 12 CFR 1008, §1008.105(e)(3) Minimum loan originator license requirements.]

The license of an MLO failing to satisfy the *minimum* standards for license renewal shall expire. When an MLO's license is allowed to lapse, he must fulfill all licensing requirements to obtain the license again.

Continuing Education for Mortgage Loan Originators

[See S.A.F.E. Mortgage Licensing Act – State Compliance and Bureau Registration System (Regulation H), 12 CFR 1008, §1008.107(a)(2) Minimum annual license renewal requirements.]

State-licensed MLOs must complete **at least eight (8) hours** of continuing education every year, including these topics:

- Federal law and regulation (3 hours)
- Ethics, including fraud, consumer protection, and fair lending (2 hours)
- Nontraditional mortgage products (2 hours)
- Elective (1 hour)

Each jurisdiction may impose additional continuing education requirements. The one hour of elective content may present as required content under a state licensing authority.

Approved Courses

[See Secure and Fair Enforcement for Mortgage Licensing, 12 U.S.C. Chapter 51, §5104(c)(2)/(3). State license and registration application and issuance; http://www.gpo.gov/fdsys/pkg/USCODE-2012-title12/html/USCODE-2012-title12-chap51-sec5104.htm]

Continuing education courses shall be reviewed and approved by the NMLS based upon reasonable standards. Review and approval of a continuing education course shall include review and approval of the course provider.

Employer and Affiliate Educational Courses

[See State Model Language for Implementation of Public Law 110-289, Title V – S.A.F.E. Mortgage Licensing Act, Pre-Licensing and Re-Licensing Education of Loan Originators: https://portal.hud.gov/hudportal/documents/huddoc?id=DOC_19674.pdf (*Approval of Employer and Affiliate Educational Courses*, (3), page 7).]

Nothing in the SAFE Act shall preclude any education course, as approved by the NMLS, which is provided by the employer of the MLO, or an entity that is affiliated with the mortgage loan originator, by an agency contract, or any subsidiary or affiliate of such employer or entity.

Educational Offerings

[See State Model Language for Implementation of Public Law 110-289, Title V – S.A.F.E. Mortgage Licensing Act, Pre-Licensing and Re-Licensing Education of Loan Originators: https://portal.hud.gov/hudportal/documents/huddoc?id=DOC_19674.pdf (Venue of Education, (4), page 9).]

Continuing education may be offered either in a classroom, online, or by any other means approved by the NMLS. All educational materials must be approved by the NMLS prior to publication.

Continuing Education Credits

[See S.A.F.E. Mortgage Licensing Act – State Compliance and Bureau Registration System (Regulation H), 12 CFR 1008, §1008.107(b) Minimum annual license renewal requirements.]

A licensed MLO may only receive credit for a continuing education course in the year in which the course is taken, and may *not* take the same approved course in the same or successive years to meet the annual requirements for continuing education. This is known as the **Successive Year Rule.**

Reciprocity of Education

[See State Model Language for Implementation of Public Law 110-289, Title V – S.A.F.E. Mortgage Licensing Act, Pre-Licensing and Re-Licensing Education of Loan Originators: https://portal.hud.gov/hudportal/documents/huddoc?id=DOC_19674.pdf (*Reciprocity of Education*, (5), page 9).]

A person having successfully completed the education requirements approved by the Nationwide Mortgage Licensing System and Registry in subsections (1)(a), (b) and (c) of this section for any state shall be accepted as credit towards completion of continuing education requirements in any other state.

Lapse in License

[See State Model Language for Implementation of Public Law 110-289, Title V – S.A.F.E. Mortgage Licensing Act, Pre-Licensing and Re-Licensing Education of Loan Originators: https://portal.hud.gov/hudportal/documents/huddoc?id=DOC_19674.pdf *(Re-licensing Education Requirements*, (8), page 9).]

A licensed MLO who subsequently becomes unlicensed must complete the continuing education requirements for *the last year in which the license was held* prior to issuance of a new or renewed license.

Make-Up of Continuing Education

[See State Model Language for Implementation of Public Law 110-289, Title V – S.A.F.E. Mortgage Licensing Act, Continuing Education for Mortgage Loan Originators: https://portal.hud.gov/hudportal/documents/huddoc?id=DOC_19674.pdf *(Make Up of Continuing Education*, (9), page 9).]

A person meeting the requirements as defined by the state may make up any deficiency in continuing education as established by rule or regulation of the state regulatory authority.

SAFE Act Licensing Requirements

[See S.A.F.E. Mortgage Licensing Act – State Compliance and Bureau Registration System (Regulation H), 12 CFR 1008, §1008.105 Minimum loan originator license requirements.]

To meet its objectives, the SAFE Act requires that applicants for an MLO license must:

- Submit to a background check (including fingerprints, state, and national criminal check).

- Provide personal history and experience.

- Provide authorization to obtain an independent credit report, and information relative to any administrative, civil, or criminal findings.

- Never have had an MLO license revoked in any government jurisdiction (a subsequent formal vacating of such revocation is not considered a revocation).

- Not have been convicted of or pled guilty or nolo contendere to a felony in a domestic, foreign, or military court during **the seven-year period preceding** the date of the application for licensing and registration or at **any time preceding** such date of application, if such felony involved an act of fraud, dishonesty, or a breach of trust, or money laundering (any pardon of a conviction is not considered a conviction).

- Meet these requirements according to revisions to §1026.36 (prohibited acts or practices and certain requirements for credit secured by a dwelling) as an employee of a depository institution.

Exercise 10.2: Apply Your Knowledge

Match each MLO license-related term with the general description.

MLO License Term	Description
___ 1. Continuing Education	A. 3/1 Adjustable Rate Mortgage
___ 2. Registered MLO	B. Clerical/Administrative Duties
___ 3. Loan Originator	C. Depository Institution
___ 4. Loan Processor	D. HERA
___ 5. Nontraditional	E. NMLS #
___ 6. Prelicensing	F. Takes a Loan Application
___ 7. SAFE Act	G. Twenty Hours of Education
___ 8. Unique Identifier Number	H. Two Hours of Ethics Education
___ 9. UST	I. Uniform State Test

Character and Fitness

[See S.A.F.E. Mortgage Licensing Act – State Compliance and Bureau Registration System (Regulation H), 12 CFR 1008, §1008.105(c) Minimum loan originator license requirements.]

The model state language of the SAFE Act indicates that an applicant must demonstrate financial responsibility, character, and general fitness such as to command the confidence of the community and to warrant a determination that the MLO will operate honestly, fairly, and efficiently within the purposes of this Act.

A person has shown that he is **not** financially responsible when he has shown a disregard in the management of his own financial condition. A determination that an individual has not shown financial responsibility may include, but not be limited to:

- Current outstanding judgments, except judgments solely as a result of medical expenses.
- Current outstanding tax liens or other government liens and filings.
- Foreclosures within the past three years.
- A pattern of seriously delinquent accounts within the past three years.

State Requirements

A state must maintain a loan originator licensing, supervisory, and oversight authority that provides effective supervision and enforcement, in accordance with the minimum standards. A supervisory authority must have the legal authority and mechanisms to suspend, terminate, and refuse renewal of a loan originator license for violation of state or Federal law and to impose civil money penalties for individuals acting as mortgage loan originators. [See 12 CFR § 1008.111 Other Minimum Requirements for State Licensing Systems.]

Exercise 10.3: Knowledge Check

If an individual fails the national component of the SAFE Mortgage Loan Originator Test with Uniform State Content, he can repeat taking the test up to two more times as part of the same enrollment.

A. true
B. false

Chapter Summary

1. In response to a failed economy, HERA was passed into law. A significant part of the Act was Title V, which is known as the Secure and Fair Enforcement for Mortgage Licensing Act or SAFE Act.

2. The SAFE Act implemented nationwide testing, prelicensing education, and annual continuing education for all state-licensed mortgage loan originators.

3. The SAFE Act required states to implement the use of the Nationwide Mortgage Licensing System and Registry (NMLSR) to provide a centralized and standardized system for mortgage licensing and registration of all mortgage loan originators. All requirements and functions of an MLO are accomplished through this website.

4. A mortgage loan originator is defined as an individual who takes a residential mortgage loan application or offers or negotiates terms of a residential mortgage loan for compensation or gain.

5. Employees of a mortgage company are not required to be licensed if they perform only clerical or administrative functions subsequent to the taking of a mortgage loan.

6. A registered mortgage loan originator is an individual who is employed by a depository institution, which is regulated by a federal banking agency. A registered mortgage loan originator must meet the requirements imposed on a state-licensed loan originator, such as background checks, fingerprints, credit report verification, felony conviction regulation, etc.

7. An MLO who is not a registered mortgage loan originator must be a state-licensed mortgage loan originator.

8. The unique identifier is issued on a nationwide basis and serves as a means to identify an MLO. The NMLS number issued to the MLO must be on every form of advertisement and communication from the MLO.

9. State-licensed MLOs must pass a National Test with a score of 75% or better. States that do not participate in the UST program may also require a separate state component to be passed.

10. An MLO may take and fail the test three times, separated by a 30-day waiting period, before being required to wait a six-month period prior to retaking the test.

11. MLOs must take 20 hours of approved education prior to licensing, and then must take eight hours of education annually to maintain their license. The SAFE Act mandates a specific number of education hours be provided on federal law, ethics, and nontraditional loan products. If a loan originator allows his license to lapse, he must complete the entire licensing process from the beginning.

12. An MLO must pass a background check, have good character and financial fitness, provide personal and employment history, have his credit report reviewed, never had an MLO license revoked, and never been convicted of a felony involving a financial crime. There is no felony of any type allowed in the first seven years prior to license application.

Chapter Quiz

1. According to the SAFE Act, which incident from 10 years ago would NOT automatically disqualify an applicant for a mortgage loan originator license?

   A. conviction for felony assault

   B. conviction for felony fraud

   C. conviction for felony money laundering

   D. revocation by the state of a mortgage broker's license

2. The SAFE Act requires state-licensed loan originators to have a minimum of how many hours of approved prelicensing education?

   A. 8

   B. 12

   C. 20

   D. 24

3. An MLO applying for a state license must provide all of the following EXCEPT

   A. employment history.

   B. evidence of completion of the mandatory eight-hour education requirement.

   C. a passed background check.

   D. a personal residence and employment history.

4. The SAFE Act defines a loan originator as a natural person who

   A. offers or negotiates terms of a residential mortgage.

   B. processes a mortgage loan under the direction of a mortgage banker.

   C. takes a residential mortgage loan application.

   D. both A & C

5. Which of the following is NOT a required continuing education topic under the SAFE Act?

   A. ethics

   B. federal mortgage laws

   C. nontraditional mortgage loans

   D. property taxes

6. A former director/manager of a mortgage company moves to another state. The company he left had its license revoked due to one of the principal's conviction of fraud. Will he be granted a license in the new state?

   A. No, because he was in active management of the firm, but not an active MLO.

   B. No, because the state authority has the power to investigate and issue or deny a license, and he was a principal of the firm that lost its license.

   C. Yes, because his personal MLO license was not revoked.

   D. Yes, a state cannot hold an applicant responsible for something that happened in a different state.

Ethics in Mortgage Lending

11

Ethical behavior is more than simply complying with the letter of the law. Ethical behavior requires understanding and respecting the spirit of the law. It requires adhering to a set of moral principles, to rules, and to standards of conduct. These standards may be informal and implied, or they may be formally codified into laws.

Ethics in mortgage lending involves applying fundamental principles. All mortgage loan professionals should strive to understand ethical decision-making and to demonstrate ethical behavior in their practice. This chapter reviews the purpose and nature of ethical behavior. It identifies ethical advertising practices. The chapter also reviews issues associated with mortgage fraud and predatory lending.

After completing this chapter, you will be able to:

- Define ethics and discuss the purpose of the codes of ethics.
- Recognize material facts in an advertisement.
- Define the bait and switch advertising strategy.
- List classes that are protected from illegal discrimination.
- Identify scenarios that violate RESPA's prohibition against kickbacks.
- Recognize indicators of mortgage fraud.
- Identify the participants and their roles in mortgage fraud schemes.
- Identify predatory lending practices.

Key Terms

Abusive Act	Disparate Impact	Referral
Advertisement	Dower or Curtesy Rights	Thing of Value
Bona Fide Offer.	Exclusionary Zoning Laws	
Consumer Financial Protection Bureau (CFPB)	Identity Theft	

Ethical and Legal Considerations

Ethics in the mortgage industry may seem like a complex issue, but it really boils down to a few simple points:

- Serve the mortgage lending needs of the public in an ethical manner.
- Treat everyone equally.
- Be honest.
- Give full disclosure about all terms and conditions of the mortgage loan.
- Don't use your knowledge to take advantage of people.
- Keep good documentation.
- Adhere to a code of ethics from a professional organization.

The code of ethics forming the standard for the mortgage industry is presented by the National Association of Mortgage Brokers (NAMB). The following ideals are found in NAMB's code of ethics:

- *Honesty and Integrity: NAMB members shall conduct business in a manner reflecting honesty, integrity, and honor.*
- *Professional Conduct NAMB members shall conduct their business activities in a professional manner. Members shall not pressure any provider of services, goods, or facilities to circumvent industry professional standards. Equally, members shall not respond to any such pressure placed upon them.*
- *Honesty in Advertising: NAMB members shall provide accurate information in all advertisements and solicitations.*
- *Confidentiality: NAMB members shall not disclose unauthorized confidential information*
- *Compliance with Law: NAMB members shall conduct their business in compliance with all applicable laws and regulations.*
- *Disclosure of Financial Interests: NAMB members shall disclose any equity or financial interest they may have in the collateral being offered to secure a loan.*

[*see "National Association of Mortgage Brokers: Code of Ethics," http://www.namb.org/*]

In 2008, NAMB instituted the Lending Integrity Seal of Approval for its members. To qualify to use and advertise the seal, MLOs undergo a rigorous validation process and must meet NAMB's high national standard for ethics, professionalism, integrity, and service. This seal is the nation's first national standard for licensed MLOs. In addition to character investigation, annual education requirements must be met, with courses requiring study in ethics, integrity, and other topics that raise the professionalism level of the MLO.

[*See "Lending Integrity Seal of Approval," The National Association of Mortgage Brokers, https://www.namb.org/lending_integrity.php*]

By participating in and adhering to the standards implemented by NAMB, MLOs are working to improve themselves and the mortgage industry. Membership is open to anyone in the mortgage or affiliated industries. By developing ethical behavior, practicing professionalism, and promoting integrity, MLOs can help to ensure the reputation of their profession. To accomplish this, it takes every licensee and registered originator to follow the professional standards set for them.

Penalties for Unethical Behavior

When an MLO behaves in an unethical manner or otherwise breaches his professional obligations, there are several possible consequences:

- Action by the state licensing authority
- Civil lawsuits filed by injured parties
- Disciplinary action by professional associations
- Filing of criminal charges (in very serious cases)

Ethics in Advertising

An MLO spends hours every day dealing with the details of the industry; however, most consumers are significantly less informed and buying or refinancing a home is usually a stressful and confusing undertaking. According to the Better Business Bureau (BBB), many consumers begin their search for a mortgage by reviewing printed advertisements in newspapers or magazines. Television and radio commercials—as well as the Internet—are also used more frequently as a means of advertising mortgages and other loan products. According to Regulation Z, an **advertisement** is a *commercial message in any medium that promotes, directly or indirectly, a credit transaction.* [See Truth in Lending (Regulation Z), 12 CFR §1026.2(a)(2) Advertisement.] The Truth In Lending Act (Regulation Z) is the federal regulation that has the primary responsibility of overseeing advertising.

While there are obviously many laws in place to protect consumers, customers generally rely on the honesty and integrity of those mortgage professionals with whom they deal.

The **Federal Trade Commission** has the authority to act in the interest of all consumers to prevent deceptive and unfair acts or practices. Section 5 of the Federal Trade Commission Act (Title 15 USC §41-58) prohibits unfair or deceptive practices of *any kind*, which includes advertising in any medium. Therefore, advertising must tell the truth and not mislead consumers. A claim can be misleading if relevant information is left out or if it implies something that is not true. For example, an advertisement for a loan that promotes "$0 Down" may be misleading if significant and undisclosed charges are due at closing.

To comply with the mandate to be truthful and fair, advertising should **not**:

- Misrepresent **material facts** or make **false promises** likely to influence, persuade, or induce an applicant for a mortgage loan or mortgagor to take a mortgage loan.

- **Conceal** any material factors, terms, or conditions of a transaction to which the MLO is a party, including the receipt of payment from a third party, pertinent to an applicant for a mortgage loan or a mortgagor.

Regulation N: Prohibited Representations

The CFPB adopted additional rules under Regulation N – Prohibited Representations [see Appendix F, Mortgage Acts and Practices—Advertising (Regulation N), 12 CFR §1014.3 *Prohibited representations*].

Mortgage Acts and Practices

The Mortgage Acts and Practices (MAP) rules provide guidance for the commercial communication of any message or statement using any medium, including written or oral statements, telemarketing scripts, the Internet, cellular networks, promotional materials, and web pages. These rules, which can be researched at 12 CFR Parts 1014, provide a defined list of prohibited acts and advertising prohibitions. Enforcement of the MAP rules is delegated to the states for enforcement. Advertisers are required to keep all commercial communication of the mortgage credit product for a minimum of 24 months from the date of the last advertisement.

Misrepresentation and Material Facts

Misrepresentation is more than mere "**puffing**," which *is an opinion that is not necessarily intended as a representation of fact*, such as "best customer service in town!" When a misrepresentation is made to a consumer with the intent to deceive, it is a form a fraud and can result in prosecution. Note that written disclosures or fine print in an ad may not be sufficient to correct a misleading representation.

Sometimes, a misrepresentation may be made unintentionally or through **negligence**. While not necessarily actionable fraud, obviously, a mortgage professional has an obligation to consumers to be factually accurate *in all communication*. Either way, misrepresentation is serious, especially when it involves material facts.

When claiming fraud or deception, it may not be necessary to prove that the person to which the deliberate misstatement, misrepresentation, or omission was made was harmed financially in the transaction or relied upon such misstatement, misrepresentation, or omission to make a decision in the transaction. This brings us to the next key concept: What is a "material fact?" A **material fact** is generally defined as *a fact that, if known, might have caused a reasonable consumer to make a different decision*. For example, when offering a mortgage loan, material facts may include the loan's:

- Annual percentage rate
- Length of loan term
- Fixed or adjustable interest rate
- Origination fees or other closing costs
- Prepayment penalties

From a legal perspective, the misrepresentation of a material fact *could possibly* give a consumer grounds to rescind a contract. Because the terms of a mortgage loan constitute material facts, however, federal law requires significant disclosures that inform and protect the consumer.

Bait and Switch

When discussing advertising, one may hear the term **bait and switch.** This is *a tactic of luring consumers in with promises of low rates and specific products, and then* **steering** *otherwise qualified buyers to other terms so that the MLO can earn a higher fee*. The Federal Trade Commission Act addresses the practice of bait and switch in Title 16, Part 238. According to §238.0:

> *"Bait advertising is an alluring but insincere offer to sell a product or service which the advertiser in truth does not intend or want to sell. Its purpose is to switch consumers from buying the advertised merchandise, in order to sell something else, usually at a higher price or on a basis more advantageous to the advertiser. The primary aim of a bait advertisement is to obtain leads as to persons interested in buying merchandise of the type so advertised."*

Bona Fide Offer

It is a violation of 16 CFR 238 to *discourage* the purchase of the advertised merchandise as part of a bait scheme to sell other merchandise. When determining whether the initial offer was **bona fide** (i.e., an *offer made in good faith*), these points would be considered:

- The refusal of the advertiser to show, demonstrate, or sell the product offered in accordance with the terms of the offer

- The disparagement by acts or words of the advertised product or the disparagement of the guarantee, credit terms, availability of service, repairs or parts, or in any other respect, in connection with it

- The failure to have available, at all outlets listed in the advertisement, a sufficient quantity of the advertised product to meet reasonably anticipated demands, unless the advertisement clearly and adequately discloses that supply is limited and/or the merchandise is available only at designated outlets

- The refusal to take orders for the advertised merchandise to be delivered within a reasonable period of time

- The showing or demonstrating of a product which is defective, unusable, or impractical for the purpose represented or implied in the advertisement

- Use of a sales plan or method of compensation for salespersons or penalizing of salespersons, designed to prevent or discourage them from selling the advertised product

While some of these points may seem more relevant to personal property, such as appliances or automobiles, they could apply to mortgage products and services as well.

Switch After Sale

Section 238.4 of the FTC Act indicates that no practice should be pursued by an advertiser, in the event of a sale of the advertised product, of "unselling" with the intent and purpose of selling other merchandise in its stead. Included among acts or practices that will be considered in determining if the initial sale was in good faith and not a stratagem to sell other merchandise, are:

- Accepting a deposit for the advertised product, then switching the purchaser to a higher-priced product.

- Failure to make delivery of the advertised product within a reasonable time or to make a refund.

- Disparagement by acts or words of the advertised product, or the disparagement of the guarantee, credit terms, availability of service, repairs, or in any other respect, in connection with it.

- The delivery of the advertised product which is defective, unusable, or impractical for the purpose represented or implied in the advertisement.

What if the consumer decided to accept different terms and apply for the loan anyway? According to 16 CFR Part 238, even though the facts are subsequently made known to the buyer, the law is violated if the first contact or interview is secured by deception.

Exercise 11.1: Knowledge Check

MLO Jack advertises refinance loans with 0 points and 3.8% APR just to get prospective borrowers in the door and then tells them that such terms are not available because of their debt, income, or another factor. In reality, Jack did not intend to originate any loan with those terms. Jack is guilty of bait and switch advertising.

A. true
B. false

Exercise 11.2: Apply Your Knowledge

Directions: Consider the following scenarios, then write your responses.

Scenario 1: MLO Jane advertises what she calls "5 for 5" mortgage loans: 5% down and 5% fixed-rate interest for 30 years. A qualified borrower arrives and starts the loan process, paying for a credit report, and completing a loan application. However, Jane does not lock in that interest rate. She knows that rates are going up, so she sits on the application for an extra week, and then tells the borrower that the best she can do is 5 3/4%.

Would this be considered an example of a bait and switch tactic? Why or why not?

_____

_____

_____

_____

Scenario 2: MLO Alex advertises that he will close loans in 14 business days, even though he knows that his average close takes 47 days. His ad brings in 100 new customers, and he works hard to close a few of those loans in 14 days so that his advertisement remains legitimate.

Would this be considered an example of a bait and switch tactic? Why or why not?

_____

_____

_____

_____

Unfair and Deceptive Practice

When determining whether an advertisement or practice is likely to be deceptive, the FTC will examine it from the perspective of a consumer acting reasonably under the circumstances, examining the entire advertisement, transaction, or course of dealing. Rather than focusing on certain words, the FTC will look at the ad in context—including words, phrases, and images—to determine what it conveys to consumers.

The CFPB has issued guidance on unfair and deceptive practices and established a standard of items that constitute what is an unfair and deceptive act.

Unfair Practices

It is considered **unfair** if:

1. The act causes or is likely to cause substantial injury (monetary harm) to consumers.

2. The injury is not reasonably avoided by consumers.

3. The injury is not outweighed by countervailing benefits to the consumers or to competition.

Deceptive Practices

According to the CFPB, an act is considered **deceptive** if:

1. The representation, omission, act, or practice misleads or is likely to mislead the consumer.

2. The consumer's interpretation of the representation, omission, act, or practice is reasonable under the circumstances.

3. The misleading representation, omission, act, or practice is material.

Abusive Practices

The CFPB further goes on to define **abusive** acts, which are acts that:

1. Materially interfere with the ability on the part of the consumer to understand a term or condition of a consumer financial product or service, or

2. Reasonably take advantage of a lack of understanding on the part of the consumer of the material risks, costs, or conditions of the product or service; the inability of the consumer to protect its interests in selecting or using a consumer financial product or service; or the reasonable reliance by the consumer on a covered person to act in the interests of the consumer.

 While an act or practice may be all three types (unfair, deceptive, and abusive), be aware that there are three different legal tests, one for each type.

Examining Advertisements

If the representation or practice affects or is directed primarily to a particular group, such as the elderly, the FTC examines reasonableness from the perspective of that group.

For example, think about the advertisements on television for reverse mortgages, which are marketed for homeowners age 62 or older to take advantage of the equity in their homes. These ads often employ well-known actors telling potential borrowers about the benefits of a particular loan product, but do not necessarily explain all the details. While there are certainly many regulations in place to protect elderly borrowers—such as required counseling—when considering advertisements, the FTC would examine the ad's message from the perspective of an elderly homeowner.

To assist consumers in determining whether advertisements for mortgage products are fair, the FTC distributed a consumer alert entitled **Deceptive Mortgage Ads: What They Say; What They Leave Out**. [For more information, see: http://www.consumer.ftc.gov/articles/0087-deceptive-mortgage-ads]

The main points are summarized below:

- Consumers should be able to understand all the terms and conditions of a proposed loan. They are advised to learn to read what's between the lines as well as what's emphatically stated in the ad.
- Some ads—whether Internet, television, paper, fax, or mail—may look tempting, but are flawed if they don't disclose the true terms.
- The APR is a critical factor in comparing mortgage offers from different lenders; sometimes the APR is hidden in the fine print or buried deep in a website.
- Important payment information is often excluded from an ad. Consumers should be prepared to ask about payments, terms, escrow, penalties, etc.
- Consumers are advised to consider shopping with several lenders to compare all the fees they charge and encouraged to ask MLOs to see a list of mortgage rates.
- Consumers are reminded that negotiating is acceptable.

Evaluating Buzzwords

The FTC consumer alert on mortgage advertising also advises consumers to look for certain **buzzwords** that often appear in ads. Though these are not deceptive in and of themselves, when preparing an advertisement, the MLO should *consider whether the use of such words or terms is fair, accurate, and complete within the context of an advertisement.* Taking time to evaluate such language will help the MLO remain in compliance with state and federal laws prohibiting deception. Look at these examples:

- **Low "Fixed" Rate.** If an ad indicates the availability of a "fixed" rate, it should also indicate how long it will be fixed.
- **Very Low Rates.** Is the ad referring to a low "payment" rate or a low-interest rate? There is a big difference, and it should be clear to the consumer. Does the rate or payment apply only for an introductory period? Ads with teaser rates don't often disclose that. Consumers must be informed of *all the details* to avoid payment shock when the rate and payment increase dramatically.
- **Very Low Payment Amounts.** Such ads should tell the whole story. Is it an interest-only loan? Does it cover the interest due? Is it an adjustable rate loan?

The FTC alert also provides examples of solicitation and advertising tactics that are intended to deceive consumers, such as a mailer that has information about their mortgage that is not actually from their lender, or mailings with official-looking stamps, envelopes, forms, etc., that appear to be from a government agency. Sadly, *there are people and organizations willing to walk a fine line when it comes to deceptive advertising; consumers must be on their guard.*

Internet Advertising

As members of the mortgage business community, MLOs advertise, provide guidance and counseling, and accept loan applications electronically via the Internet. The Internet has become indispensable, and its power to reach potential consumers for products and services seems virtually limitless. It's critical to understand, though, that *the same laws that regulate print and broadcast media apply equally to advertising, promotion, and marketing on the Internet.* Briefly:

- Advertising must be truthful and not misleading.
- Advertisers must have evidence to back up their claims.
- Advertisements cannot be unfair.

An unfair or deceptive message will be unfair or deceptive wherever the consumer views or hears it. Additionally, required disclosures are as important online as anywhere else, and the MLO must comply with all laws related to disclosures. The mandate that disclosures be "clear and conspicuous" applies here as well.

When considering the idea of clear and conspicuous disclosures in online ads, placement and proximity are critical. The FTC's **.Com Disclosures: Information about Online Advertising** paper [for more information, see: https://www.ftc.gov/sites/default/files/attachments/press-releases/ftc-staff-revises-online-advertising-disclosure-guidelines/130312dotcomdisclosures.pdf] provides valuable guidance on making disclosures clear and conspicuous:

- Place disclosures **near**, and when possible, on the same screen as the triggering claim.
- Use text or visual **cues** to encourage consumers to scroll down a web page when it is necessary to view a disclosure.
- If hyperlinking to disclosures, make the links **obvious**, label the hyperlinks appropriately to convey the importance of the information they lead to, and take consumers directly to the disclosures (note that buying disclosures in a link may result in a disclosure that is NOT clear and conspicuous).
- **Prominently** display disclosures so they are noticeable to consumers, and evaluate the size, color, and graphic treatment of the disclosure in relation to other parts of the page.
- Review the entire ad to ensure that other elements—text, graphics, hyperlinks or sound—**do not distract** consumers' attention from the disclosure.
- **Repeat** disclosures, as needed, on lengthy websites and in connection with repeated claims.
- Display visual disclosures for a **duration** sufficient for consumers to notice, read, and understand them.
- Use **clear language** and syntax so that consumers understand the disclosures.

With the advent of social media technology, such as Facebook, LinkedIn, and Twitter, the need for clear and conspicuous disclosure to avoid even unintentional deception is an ongoing challenge.

Better Business Bureau Advertising Guidance

The BBB also offers general guidance related to advertising ethics, which includes considering these questions:

- Does your advertising result in satisfied customers? Your advertising is just another outlet through which you can promote good will and customer loyalty.
- Do you avoid impossible promises and guarantees? When using the term "guarantee," you should include a statement that explains complete details are available at the office or, in the case of mail or telephone sales, are freely available upon written request.
- Is the advertised merchandise or program readily available? When advertising to consumers, the merchandise or program must actually be available to distribute to consumers responding to the advertisement.
- Is it your intent to sell what is advertised? Avoid **bait and switch** tactics that involve advertising a low-priced item to attract customers, then persuading them to buy similar but higher-priced items.
- Do you avoid using misleading inferences? Misleading advertising is considered a questionable business practice that should be avoided.

- Do advertised terms agree with the facts? An advertisement may be misleading, even if every sentence separately considered is literally true.

- Is the advertisement easy to understand (e.g., without asterisks and fine print)? Asterisks used as a means of contradicting or substantially changing the meaning of an advertising statement should be avoided.

- Do you agree with your comparatives? You should be able to substantiate all claims made in the ad.

- Are you attracted by your ad? If it is not attractive to you, it most likely will not be attractive to your customers.

Finally, MLOs must follow all laws and regulations (federal and state) related to advertising, such as the requirements to include the NMLS unique identifier and Equal Housing Lender logo/slogan, as applicable, and the disclosure requirements found in the Truth in Lending Act and Regulation Z.

Exercise 11.3: Apply Your Knowledge

Directions: Determine if these examples of advertising ideas, terms, and slogans might be considered deceptive to the public.

Discussion Questions:

1. "We have loans with an APR of 4.607%." Deceptive or not? Why?

_____

_____

_____

_____

2. "Interest rates from 2.00%." Deceptive or not? Why?

_____

_____

_____

_____

3. "Very Low Monthly Payments." Deceptive or not? Why?

_____

_____

_____

_____

4. An Internet advertisement contains a hyperlink that directs the consumer to a disclosure page with the details of the advertised loan. Deceptive or not? Why?

_____

_____

_____

_____

5. A licensed MLO has a Facebook "fan page" where he describes various loan programs as well as a range of interest rates available, but does not display his NMLS unique identifier number or his employing broker information. Deceptive or not? Why?

_____

_____

_____

_____

Civil Rights Act of 1866

The **Civil Rights Act of 1866**, codified in Title 42, Section 1981(a) of the U.S. Code, prohibits public and private racial discrimination in any property transaction in the United States. The Act states:

> *"All citizens of the United States shall have the same right, in every State and Territory, as is enjoyed by white citizens thereof to inherit, purchase, lease, sell, hold, and convey real and personal property."*

The 1866 Civil Rights Act applies to all property—real or personal, residential or commercial, improved or unimproved. The Act prohibits any discrimination based on race or ancestry and was upheld in 1968 by the United States Supreme Court in the landmark case of *Jones v. Mayer*. The court ruled that the 1866 federal law "prohibits all racial discrimination, private or public, in the sale and rental of property" and is constitutionally based on the 13th Amendment to the U.S. Constitution, which prohibits slavery.

Enforcement

A person who has been unlawfully discriminated against under the 1866 Act can sue *only* in federal district court. The court fashions the remedies it finds necessary, which may include **injunctions** (*court orders requiring the defendant to do or refrain from doing a particular act*), **compensatory damages** (*reimbursement for expenses caused by the discrimination and/or for emotional distress*), or **punitive damages** (*to punish the wrongdoer if the acts are deliberate or malicious*). Depending on the circumstances, these remedies may be instead of or in addition to those available to parties under other federal and state statutes. There is **never** any exemption to discrimination under the Civil Rights Act of 1866.

Fair Housing Act

Title VIII of the Civil Rights Act of 1968 is commonly called the **Fair Housing Act**. The Fair Housing Act expanded the 1866 Act, making it illegal to discriminate in the sale or lease of residential property, including vacant land intended for residential housing. The Act has been amended several times and extends protection against discrimination based on:

- Race
- Color
- Religion
- Sex
- National origin
- Disability
- Familial status

Although the Fair Housing Act prohibits discrimination in housing against the disabled, Congress further expanded protection with the more comprehensive **Americans with Disabilities (ADA) Act**, which was signed into law in 1990.

Fair Housing Act Exemptions

The Fair Housing Act covers most residential transactions in the U.S., although there are specific exemptions:

- The rental of a room or unit in a dwelling of no more than four independent units, provided the owner occupies one unit as a residence
- Single-family home sold or rented by a private owner without the use of a broker
- Housing operated by organizations
- Housing operated by private clubs

Fair Housing Violations

The following discriminatory practices and activities violate the Fair Housing Act (42 USC §3604-3605) if they are based on a person's membership in a protected class:

Violation	Example
Refusing to rent or sell residential property after receiving a good faith offer	A homeowner declines an offer after learning the buyer is of a different religion.
Refusing to negotiate for the sale or rental of residential property	A listing agent follows his seller's instructions not to show the house to anyone of a different race.
Taking any action that would otherwise make residential property unavailable or deny it to any person	A minority couple tells an agent what they're looking for in a home. Six listings in the MLS match their criteria, but the agent tells them only about three that are in neighborhoods with a high population of minorities.
Using discriminatory advertising or any other notice that indicates a limitation or preference or intent to make any limitation, preference, or discrimination	A landlord includes the phrase "no children" in an advertisement for an apartment.
Making any representation that property is not available for inspection, sale, or rent when it is, in fact, available	A landlord tells a potential tenant who has a foreign accent that the apartment is already rented, but shows the unit to someone who does not sound foreign.
Coercing, intimidating, threatening, or interfering with anyone because of his enjoyment, attempt to enjoy, or encouragement and assistance to others in their enjoyment of the rights granted by the Fair Housing Act	A landlord threatens to evict a tenant who files a fair housing complaint.
Discriminating in the terms or conditions of any sale or rental of residential property or in providing any services or facilities in connection with such property	A landlord advises female applicants to include deposits with their rental applications but does not tell male applicants to ensure their applications are not processed.

In addition, it is illegal for anyone to threaten, coerce, intimidate, or interfere with anyone exercising a fair housing right or assisting others who exercise that right.

Exercise 11.4: Knowledge Check

1. A lender may decline to make a mortgage loan in a particular neighborhood if the

    A. area is largely a commercial district.
    B. foreclosure rate in the area is higher than 50%.
    C. property is in a declining market area and no protected class is singled out.
    D. racial demographics of the neighborhood indicate a high percentage of minority borrowers.

2. The Fair Housing Act prohibits discrimination against all the following EXCEPT

    A. age.
    B. familial status.
    C. religion.
    D. sex.

Discrimination in Mortgage Lending

From the perspective of a mortgage professional, no one may take any of the following actions if the actions are based on a person's membership in a **protected class**:

- Refusing to make a mortgage loan

- Refusing to provide information regarding loans

- Imposing different terms or conditions on a loan, such as different interest rates, points, or fees

- Discriminating in the appraisal of property

- Refusing to purchase a loan

- Setting different terms or conditions for purchasing a loan; for example, a bank charging a higher interest rate to a creditworthy borrower who wants to buy a house in a minority neighborhood than is charged for an equally creditworthy borrower in a different neighborhood.

Discriminatory Practices

The Fair Housing Act prohibits redlining, blockbusting, and steering in any real estate or mortgage credit transaction. Most discussions on fair housing include these illegal acts:

- **Blockbusting.** Blockbusting is *trying to induce owners to sell their homes by suggesting that the ethnic or racial composition of the neighborhood is changing, with the implication that property values will decline.* This practice is also called **panic selling**. The person making the prediction buys the properties from the owners and then resells them for a profit.

- **Steering.** Steering is *channeling prospective real estate buyers or tenants to particular neighborhoods based on their race, religion, or ethnic background.* Any such attempt to maintain or change the character of those neighborhoods is prohibited.

- **Redlining.** Redlining is *a refusal to make loans—or making loans on less favorable terms— on property located in a particular neighborhood for discriminatory reasons.* In the past, many lenders assumed that an integrated or predominantly minority neighborhood was automatically a place where property values declined. Based on that assumption, they refused to make loans in those neighborhoods. Since it was almost impossible to obtain purchase or renovation loans, it was extremely difficult to market, maintain, or improve homes, which caused neighborhood values to decline even further, a cycle from which few neighborhoods could recover.

Lenders may still deny loans in neighborhoods where property values are declining, but this must be based on objective criteria regarding the condition and value of the property or area. A lender may not simply equate integrated or minority neighborhoods with declining property values.

Advertising Provisions

The Fair Housing Act also prohibits discrimination in advertising, real estate brokerage, lending, and other services associated with residential transactions. To comply with this Act, lenders are required to:

- Include the "Equal Housing Lender" slogan in any broadcast advertisement.
- Display the Equal Housing Opportunity poster in every branch where mortgage loans are made.
- Display the Equal Housing Opportunity logo on all printed promotional material.

Enforcement

A person who has been discriminated against in violation of the Fair Housing Act may file a written complaint to the nearest HUD office within **one year** of the alleged violation (42 USC §3610). Complaints are investigated by the Office of Fair Housing and Equal Opportunity (FHEO). HUD may investigate the incident or refer the complaint to the state or local agency that has similar responsibilities (for example, a state civil rights commission). HUD tries to obtain voluntary compliance with the Fair Housing Act.

The parties involved in the discrimination may choose to have the dispute decided in a civil lawsuit instead, in U.S. District Court or another court that has jurisdiction. The court may grant an injunction, compensatory damages, punitive damages, and attorney's fees. In addition, the U.S. Attorney General may bring a civil suit in federal district court against anyone engaged in an ongoing pattern or practice of discriminatory activities, referred to as a "pattern or practice lawsuit."

Discrimination and Same-Sex Marriage

The United States Supreme Court, in Case No. 14-556 (Obergefell Et Al. V. Hodges, Director, Ohio Department of Health, Et Al. Certiorari to The United States Court of Appeals for the Sixth Circuit) decided June 26, 2015, provided that same-sex couples have the same right to marry as opposite-sex couples and cannot be discriminated against due to sexual preference. With this decision, any prohibition against same-sex married borrowers was made void. A mortgage lender may not discriminate against married same-sex couples for any loan program.

THE HOUSING FINANCIAL DISCRIMINATION ACT OF 1977
FAIR LENDING NOTICE

DATE: COMPANY: *[INSERT COMPANY NAME]*
APPLICATION NO: *[INSERT ADDRESS]*
PROPERTY ADDRESS:

It is illegal to discriminate in the provisions of or in the availability of financial assistance because of the consideration of:

1. Trends, characteristics or conditions in the neighborhood or geographic area surrounding a housing accommodation, unless the financial institution can demonstrate in the particular case that such consideration is required to avoid am unsafe and unsound business practice; or

2. Race, color, religion, sex, marital status, national origin or ancestry.

It is illegal to consider the racial ethnic, religious or national origin composition of a neighborhood or geographic area surrounding a housing accommodation or whether or not such composition is undergoing change, or is expected to undergo change, in appraising a housing accommodation or in determining whether or not, or under what terms and conditions, to provide financial assistance.

These provisions govern financial assistance for the purpose of the purchase, construction, rehabilitation or refinancing of a one-to-four unit family residence occupied by the owner and for the purpose of the home improvement of any one-to-four unit family residence.

If you have any questions about your rights, or if you wish to file a complaint, contact the management of this financial institution or the agency noted below:

[INSERT APPROPRIATE ENFORCEMENT AGENCY NAME/ADDRESS HERE]

I/We received a copy of this notice

_____   _____
                    (Date)   (Date)

The Equal Credit Opportunity Act

The **Equal Credit Opportunity Act (ECOA)** [see Equal Credit Opportunity Act (Regulation B), 12 CFR §1002] is a federal law that *ensures that all consumers are given an equal chance to obtain credit*. ECOA requires anyone who grants credit or sets the terms of that credit must never discriminate based on:

- Race
- Color
- Religion
- National origin
- Age (provided the applicant has the capacity to contract; i.e., 18 years old)
- Sex
- Marital status
- Receipt of income from public assistance programs
- Exercised rights under the Consumer Credit Protection Act

The law also indicates that someone cannot be **discouraged from applying for credit** based on any of these factors.

The law protects a borrower against any creditor who regularly extends credit, including banks, small loan and finance companies, retail and department stores, credit card companies, and credit unions. Anyone involved in granting credit, such as real estate brokers and mortgage brokers who arrange financing, is covered by the law. Businesses applying for credit also are protected by the law. ECOA, implemented by **Regulation B** of the CFPB, must be followed when:

- Taking loan applications.
- Evaluating an application.
- Approving or denying a loan.

The law was originally passed in 1974 to prohibit lending discrimination based on sex or marital status. This law led to, among other things, the requirement that credit bureaus maintain separate credit files for married spouses, if so requested. The law ensured that women received the same consideration by lenders when applying for credit.

The law was expanded in 1976 to include the protected classes listed above. Most notable among the law's revisions is prohibiting the discrimination against a potential borrower on public assistance.

If the borrower's income from public assistance is stable (or permanent), the lender or mortgage broker must consider this income as valid as any other qualifying income. *The adequacy and stability of a borrower's income should be considered and **not** its source.* Lenders and mortgage brokers must, therefore:

- Consider reliable public assistance income the same as other income.
- Consider reliable income from part-time employment, Social Security, pensions, and annuities.
- Consider reliable alimony, child support, or separate maintenance payments if the borrower chooses to provide this information (lenders may ask for proof).
- Accept someone other than a spouse as a co-signer, if needed.

While ECOA clearly indicates that a lender or mortgage broker must consider reliable alimony, child support, or separate maintenance payments as income, the applicant is **not required to disclose** such income. Furthermore, an MLO may **not** discriminate against an applicant who exercises her good faith rights of nondisclosure of those sources of income.

EQUAL CREDIT OPPORTUNITY ACT

APPLICATION NO:

PROPERTY ADDRESS:

The Federal Equal Credit Opportunity Act prohibits creditors from discriminating against credit applicants on the basis of race, color, religion, national origin, sex, marital status, age (provided the applicant has the capacity to enter into a binding contract); because all or part of the applicant's income derives from any public assistance program; or because the applicant has in good faith exercised any right under the Consumer Credit Protection Act. The Federal Agency that administers compliance with this law concerning the company is *[INSERT APPROPRIATE FEDERAL AGENCY HERE].*

We are required to disclose to you that you need not disclose income from alimony, child support or separate maintenance payment if you choose not to do so.

Having made this disclosure to you, we are permitted to inquire of any of the income shown on your application is derived from such a source and to consider the likelihood of consistent payment as we do with any income on which you are relying to qualify for the loan for which you are applying.

(Applicant) (Date)	(Applicant) (Date)
(Applicant) (Date)	(Applicant) (Date)

Real Success

To comply with ECOA, an MLO usually *may not* inquire about an interested borrower's marital status. Nor can he ask about a spouse *unless* it is for a joint application and the spouse will use the account or be contractually liable, or if the applicant is relying on a spouse's income, or alimony or child support from a former spouse, to qualify for the loan. When the loan is secured by property—as with a mortgage—the MLO *may* ask about a spouse, since in many states, certain rights and benefits exist for spouses. If, for example, a lender must foreclose on a property, it may be necessary for the spouse to legally relinquish those rights.

However, when permitted to ask about marital status, an MLO may *not* ask if the applicant is widowed or divorced.

The MLO may use only these terms (12 CFR §1002.2(u)):

- Married
- Unmarried (which includes single, divorced, or widowed)
- Separated

Additionally, he *cannot* ask an applicant about any plans for having or raising children but *can* ask questions about expenses related to any dependents.

In states that recognize **dower or curtesy rights** of spouses, which is *interest in the real estate of a deceased spouse given by law to the surviving partner*, it is acceptable to ask about marital status even if only one person is applying for the loan. In such states, the non-borrowing spouse must consent, since the non-borrowing spouse has an interest in the security instrument.

Considering Income

[See Equal Credit Opportunity Act (Regulation B), 12 CFR §1002.6(b)(5) Rules concerning evaluation of applications.]

When evaluating a potential borrower's gross income, a creditor may consider the amount and probability of any income continuing. A creditor may **not**:

- Refuse to consider public assistance income the same way as other income.
- Discount income because of sex or marital status.
- Discount or refuse to consider income because it comes from part-time employment or pension, annuity, or retirement benefits programs.
- Refuse to consider regular alimony, child support, or separate maintenance payments.

While ECOA clearly indicates a lender must consider reliable alimony, child support, or separate maintenance payments as income, the applicant is **not** required to disclose such income. Furthermore, an MLO may **not** discriminate against applicants who exercise their good faith rights of nondisclosure of those sources of income.

Age of Applicant

[See Equal Credit Opportunity Act (Regulation B), 12 CFR §1002.6(b)(2) Rules concerning evaluation of applications.]

Creditors can consider the age of an applicant for credit under these circumstances:

- The applicant is too young to sign contracts, generally under age 18.
- The creditor would favor applicants age 62 and older.
- It is used to determine the meaning of other factors important to creditworthiness, such as to determine if an applicant's income might drop because of pending retirement.
- It may be used in a valid credit scoring system that favors applicants depending on their age.

Citizenship Status and ECOA

"The creditor may inquire about the applicant's permanent residence and immigration status in the United States in determining creditworthiness." (12 CFR 1002.5(e))

Credit Decisions

A creditor has 30 days after the receipt of a "complete application" to provide a credit decision to the applicant. (12 CFR 1002.9) If the credit decision is adverse:

- A notification must be in writing and must contain certain information, including the name and address of the creditor and the nature of the action that was taken.
- The creditor must provide an ECOA notice that includes the identity of the federal agency responsible for enforcing compliance with the act for that creditor. This notice is generally included in the notification of adverse action.
- The creditor must also provide the applicant with the specific principal reason for the action taken or disclose that the applicant has the right to request the reason(s) for denial within 60 days of receipt of the creditor's notification, along with the name, address, and telephone number of the person who can provide the specific reason(s) for the adverse action. The reason may be given orally if the creditor also advises the applicant of the right to obtain the reason in writing upon request.

(12 CFR 1002.9(a)(2))

Loan Application: Home Mortgage Disclosure Act Reporting Requirement

Under the Home Mortgage Disclosure Act (HMDA) [see Regulation C, 12 CFR §1003 Home Mortgage Disclosure], it is permissible to ask an applicant (for a loan to purchase or to refinance a principal residence) for certain information for the federal government's use in monitoring lender compliance with equal credit and equal housing laws. The information that is required to comply with HMDA is in Section 7 of the URLA or the 1003. To follow the mandates of the Dodd-Frank Act, information must be collected to reveal any patterns of discriminatory practices by the creditor.

The three areas of concern for compliance with anti-discrimination laws are **ethnicity, sex, and race**. It is critical that the MLO has a polished presentation when inquiring about the sex, race, and ethnicity of the borrower, and co-borrower, as the inquiry at many times will seem invasive or appear unnecessary to the consumer. An MLO must stress the importance of collecting the information to comply with federal regulations.

On a mortgage loan application, if a borrower identifies as:

- **Hispanic/Latino**, he is further asked to identify whether he is:

  o Mexican   o Cuban

  o Puerto Rican   o And Other Central American countries

- **American Indian** or **Alaska Native**, he is further asked to provide the name of the principal tribe he is a member of.

- **Asian**, he is further asked to identify whether he is:

  o Asian Indian   o Asian Filipino

  o Asian Chinese   o Other Asian,
                                               where he can provide additional details about his heritage.

- **Native Hawaiian** or **Other Pacific Islander**, he is further asked whether he is:

  o Samoan   o Tongan

  o Fijian

Caution! If a borrower declines to provide this information, there can be no pressure to complete the inquiry. The borrower cannot be discriminated against because he does not complete these information sections.

"If a financial institution accepts an application through electronic media with a video component, it must treat the application as taken in person. However, if a financial institution accepts an application through electronic media without a video component, it must treat the application as accepted by mail."

[See "Home Mortgage Disclosure (Regulation C): Small Entity Compliance Guide," Consumer Financial Protection Bureau, December 2015, https://s3.amazonaws.com/files. consumerfinance.gov/f/documents/201512_cfpb_hmda_small-entity-compliance-guide.pdf]

Data transparency helps to ensure that financial institutions are not engaging in discriminatory lending or failing to meet the credit needs of the entire community, including low- and moderate-income neighborhoods. The gathering of information that can detect a creditor's discriminatory patterns is at the heart of HMDA. By stipulating a review of the data of a lender's origination business, the Fair Housing Act and ECOA have a greater opportunity for ensuring compliance and borrower receipt of equal consideration when requesting a credit decision.

As the name implies, HMDA is a disclosure law that relies upon public scrutiny for its effectiveness. It does not prohibit any specific activity of lenders and it does not establish a quota system of mortgage loans to be made in any metropolitan statistical area (MSA) or other geographic area as defined by the Office of Management and Budget.

The HMDA provisions affect applications for residential loans, including:

- Home purchase   • Refinancing

- Home improvement   • Subordinate financing

 These provisions do **not** apply to loans on vacant land, new construction, or loans that are sold as part of a pool for servicing.

Enforcement

[See Home Mortgage Disclosure (Regulation C), 12 CFR §1003.6 Enforcement.]

ECOA is enforced by the CFPB; however, each financial institution further falls under the authority of its respective regulatory agency. Consumers who apply for credit and feel they have been unjustly discriminated against may file a complaint with the same bodies as for other types of discrimination claims.

Any creditor that fails to comply with a requirement imposed by ECOA is subject to civil liability for actual and punitive damages in individual or class actions. Liability for **punitive damages** can apply only to nongovernmental entities and is limited to $10,000 in individual actions and the lesser of $500,000 or 1% of the creditor's net worth in class actions. A **civil action** may be brought in the appropriate United States district court within **two years** after the date of the occurrence of the violation.

Community Reinvestment Act (CRA)

Congress enacted the **Community Reinvestment Act** (12 USC §2901 et seq.) in 1977 to encourage financial institutions to help meet the credit needs of the communities in which they operate, including low- and moderate-income neighborhoods, consistent with safe and sound lending practices.

The CRA requires that each insured depository institution's record in helping meet these needs of its entire community be evaluated periodically.

That record is taken into account when considering an institution's application for deposit facilities, including mergers and acquisitions. CRA examinations are conducted by the federal agencies that are responsible for supervising depository institutions.

In some states, the requirements of CRA have been extended to mortgage lenders. **Make sure you know the laws of the states in which you conduct business.**

Exercise 11.5: Apply Your Knowledge

Match each listed protected class/condition with the regulation(s) that implements and regulates it. Some protected classes/conditions may match with more than one regulation.

Regulation	Protected Class or Condition
1. ECOA	_____ Age
2. Civil Rights Act of 1866	_____ Color
3. Fair Housing Act	_____ Disability
4. None	_____ Familial status
5. All	_____ Income from public assistance
	_____ Marital status
	_____ National origin/ethnicity
	_____ Race
	_____ Religion
	_____ Separate credit reports
	_____ Sex

Other Types of Discrimination

Blatant discrimination still exists but it is less common today, although, there are subtler ways—both intentional and unintentional—that may amount to discrimination. If an MLO is ever in doubt about what qualifies as discrimination, she should talk with her broker or an experienced mortgage professional.

Discrimination in Municipal Actions

Exclusionary zoning laws are defined as *any laws that have the effect of denying housing to minorities or other protected classes.* The clause "make otherwise unavailable or deny" in anti-discrimination legislation has been interpreted to prohibit such exclusionary zoning. Since it is currently unlikely that a municipality would enact an openly racist ordinance, these cases usually involve arguments based on the concept of **disparate impact.** A law with disparate impact *may be neutral on its face, but it has a discriminatory effect since it has a greater adverse impact on one group than on others.*

Exclusionary zoning cases usually involve ordinances that prohibit or unreasonably restrict multi-family or low-income housing. Statistics show that in comparison to the white population, members of minority groups are more likely to be considered low-income. As a result, it has been successfully argued in a number of cases that ordinances limiting low-cost housing have a disparate impact on minority groups; in effect, excluding them from certain communities.

Discrimination in Advertising

Words carry great power. The use of certain words can influence, inform, and sometimes, mislead consumers, and the misuse of words, even if unintentional, can create problems. For example, certain phrases used in residential mortgage advertising could convey either overt or tacit discriminatory preferences or limitations.

In addition to outlawing discrimination in housing, the Fair Housing Act restricts the publication of any real estate advertising that indicates a limitation, preference, or intent to discriminate based on race or other protected class. Specifically, §804(c) of the Fair Housing Act states that it is:

> *"… unlawful to make, print, or publish, or cause to be made, printed, or published, any notice, statement, or advertisement, with respect to the sale or rental of a dwelling, that indicates any preference, limitation, or discrimination because of race, color, religion, sex, handicap, familial status, or national origin, or an intention to make any such preference, limitation, or discrimination. However, the prohibitions of the Act regarding familial status do not apply with respect to housing for older persons…"*

These provisions apply to advertisements for residential mortgage loans as well. Under certain circumstances, even the newspapers chosen for advertising may be held to have the effect of racial steering. MLOs should choose their words very carefully and should measure whether advertising content could be construed as being in violation of the Fair Housing Act.

And it's not just the words. An appendix to the Fair Housing Act indicates that human models in photographs, drawings, or other graphic techniques may not be used to indicate exclusiveness because of race, color, religion, sex, handicap, familial status, or national origin. If models are used in display advertising campaigns, the models should be clearly definable as reasonably representing majority and minority groups in the metropolitan area, both sexes, and, when appropriate, families with children. Models, if used, should portray persons in an equal social setting and indicate to the general public that the housing is open to all without regard to race, color, religion, sex, handicap, familial status, or national origin, and is not for the exclusive use of one such group.

Real Success

All mortgage industry professionals are required to observe these federal laws, as well as the anti-discrimination statutes and laws passed by their state and local governments. If you are accepting a mortgage application and the property is in another state other than where you normally do business, it is your responsibility to research any specific laws and regulations for that state. Also, know the licensing requirements in that state.

Kickbacks and Referral Fees

Recall that the **Real Estate Settlement Procedures Act (RESPA)** of 1974 requires mortgage lenders, mortgage brokers, or servicers of home loans to *provide borrowers with pertinent and timely disclosures of the nature and costs of the real estate settlement process*. Its purpose is to regulate settlement and closing procedures and to protect borrowers.

Section 8 of RESPA [see Real Estate Settlement Procedures Act (Regulation X), 12 CFR §1024.14 Prohibition against kickbacks and unearned fees.] prohibits anyone from giving or accepting a fee, kickback, or anything of value in exchange for referrals of settlement service providers involving a federally-related mortgage loan. RESPA also prohibits fee splitting and receiving unearned fees for settlement services not actually performed.

Key terms related to these provisions include "thing of value" and "referral." RESPA defines a **thing of value** to include *any payment, advance, funds, loan, service, or other consideration*. A **referral** includes *any oral or written action directed to a person which has the effect of affirmatively influencing the selection of a settlement services provider* (12 CFR §1024.14(f)). A referral also occurs when a borrower is required to use a particular provider of settlement services.

Allowable Fees

Fees, salaries, compensation, or other payments for services *actually rendered* and that are *not based on a referral* do **not** violate RESPA. [See 12 CFR §1024.14(g) Fees, salaries, compensation, or other payments] These include:

- A payment to an attorney at law for services actually rendered
- A payment by a title company to its duly appointed agent for services actually performed in the issuance of a policy of title insurance
- A payment by a lender to its duly appointed agent or contractor for services actually performed in the origination, processing, or funding of a loan
- A payment to any person of a *bona fide* salary or compensation or other payment for goods or facilities actually furnished or for services actually performed
- A payment pursuant to a cooperative brokerage and referral arrangements or agreements between real estate agents and real estate brokers (this does **not** apply to any fee arrangements between real estate brokers and mortgage brokers or between mortgage brokers)
- Normal promotional and educational activities that are not conditioned on the referral of business and that do not involve the defraying of expenses that otherwise would be incurred by persons in a position to refer settlement services or business
- An employer's payment to its own employees for any referral activities

Multiple Services

When a person in a position to refer settlement service providers—such as an attorney, MLO, real estate broker or agent, or developer or builder—receives a payment for providing additional settlement services as part of a real estate transaction, such payment must be for services that are *actual*, *necessary*, and *distinct* from the primary services provided by such person.

Required Use

According to RESPA definitions, a **required use** occurs *when a consumer paying for a settlement service is required to use a particular provider of that settlement service* (12 CFR §1024.2(b)). While RESPA makes clear that the use of both economic incentives and disincentives to improperly influence a consumer's choice of settlement service providers are prohibited, this provision does not prohibit **legitimate** discounts on services to consumers.

RESPA provides that settlement service providers can offer **legitimate discounts** to consumers by offering **a combination of settlement services** at a total price lower than the sum of the individual settlement services. This combination of services will **not** be considered a prohibited "required use" if:

1. The use of any such combination is *optional* to the purchaser, and
2. The lower price for the combination is not made up by higher costs elsewhere in the settlement process.

Violations

Violations of Section 8's anti-kickback, referral fees, and unearned fees provisions of RESPA are subject to criminal and civil penalties.

- In a *criminal* case, a person who violates Section 8 may be fined **up to $10,000** and/or be imprisoned **up to one year**.
- In a *civil* lawsuit, a person who violates Section 8 may be liable to the person charged for the settlement service an amount **equal to three times** the amount of the charge paid for the service.

[See 12 U.S.C. 2607(d) Penalties for violations.]

Exercise 11.6: Apply Your Knowledge:

Directions: Consider the following scenario, and then write your responses.

Scenario: XYZ Mortgage encourages their borrowers to employ attorney Bob to perform title searches and related settlement services in connection with their transaction. XYZ and Bob have an understanding that in return for the referral of this business, Bob provides legal services to XYZ's officers or employees at abnormally low rates or for no charge.

Since the borrower is not required to use the attorney, is anyone in violation of RESPA?

_____

_____

_____

Mortgage Fraud

Being honest with everyone requires the MLO to avoid fraud—intentional or unintentional—at all times. Either may lead to civil and even criminal penalties. **Negligence** is *an unintentional breach of a legal duty*. It's a tort if it causes harm, though, and the MLO can be sued for it. **Fraud** is *intentional or negligent misrepresentation or concealment of material facts,* which can include failing to disclose required information, actively concealing information, and making false or misleading statements.

- **Actual Fraud.** Actual fraud is *an intentional misrepresentation or concealment of a material fact*. Actual fraud occurs when a person actively hides information or makes statements known to be false or misleading. When any of these are done with intent to deceive, they constitute actual fraud. (This is also called deceit or intentional misrepresentation).

- **Constructive Fraud.** Constructive fraud is *a negligent misrepresentation or concealment of a material fact*. When information is not disclosed or false statements are made unintentionally, it may be considered constructive fraud. Here, the false statements or failures to disclose are the result of carelessness or negligence, rather than an intent to deceive. (This is also called negligent misrepresentation.)

Mortgage fraud involves any misrepresentation or concealment used in an attempt to obtain a mortgage loan. It can generally be divided into two main categories: **Fraud for profit**, which is *usually perpetrated by industry insiders*, and **fraud for property**, which is *usually perpetrated by borrowers*. This is a serious federal crime when done for any federally-related loan (which includes most loans, since HUD, Fannie Mae, or a federally-chartered bank is involved at some point in the process).

Common ways in which fraud may be committed include:

- Material misrepresentations, such as altered paycheck stubs and tax returns

- Material misstatements, such as the intent to occupy a home as a primary residence when it really is intended to be used as a rental

- Omission, such as failing to mention the borrower is taking an early retirement in six weeks

The fraud can be perpetrated by borrowers who lie on applications, by an appraiser who provides an inflated property value, or by a mortgage broker who ignores derogatory information to get a loan approved. This also includes not reporting all items on the HUD closing statement accurately, creating phantom documents for verification, or concealing the true nature of a borrower's down payment.

Fraud Participants

Since many people are involved in the process of making loans for property, the opportunity for fraud exists on several levels. A fraud scheme could be simply the initiative of a desperate borrower, or it could involve the participation of multiple industry insiders.

Borrowers—Fraud for Property

When a borrower commits mortgage fraud, it is typically to obtain ownership to a property under false or fictitious pretenses. For example, a borrower may make the statement that he will "occupy the property as his primary residence" when he intends to acquire the property and use it as a rental. Or, a borrower may knowingly supply false documents, such as verification of employment (VOEs), forged W-2s, or false information on the loan application, thereby committing mortgage fraud, whether or not he is working in partnership with any mortgage professionals. The borrower usually plans to make regular payments and has no plans to default. The purpose of the fraud is to make the mortgage loan happen at desirable terms for the borrower, not to enter into foreclosure or flip a property for profit.

A borrower might also act as a **straw buyer**, which is *someone who allows his name and personal details to be used to obtain a mortgage loan for a property he has no intention of inhabiting*. Sometimes, straw buyers are paid for their participation in the scheme and other times, straw buyers have no idea that their personal information was used.

Borrowers can also get involved in **credit enhancement** schemes. To show the necessary assets or credit to qualify for a loan, borrowers may look for fraudulent ways to enhance their financial situation. For example, they may add their names to the bank accounts of friends or family to show that they have sufficient assets on deposit. Another scheme is where friends, family, or even builders or MLOs temporarily park assets into a borrower's account until the underwriter qualifies the borrower and the loan closes. This type of fraud can be very sophisticated, even to the point of borrowers "buying" seasoned credit account lines and creating fraudulent retailer relationships to improve the borrower's credit history and credit scores.

If home values fall, some homeowners might find themselves **underwater** with their mortgage—*owing more than the property is worth*. This could lead to foreclosure, as well as homeowners with little or no equity in the property walking away from their house and the loan. Such a situation might lead to "creative" schemes by borrowers to get out from under an unsustainable mortgage payment, including:

- **Buy and Bail.** Homeowners apply for a mortgage to purchase a similar home that, because of the market, sells for less money. The homeowner may claim that he is renting the original property, perhaps engaging a family member or friend who claims to be the renter and even supplying a fake lease. After getting the new property, the borrower simply walks away from the first home and bails on that mortgage.

- **Short Sale Fraud.** With a **short sale**, *the lender agrees to allow the sale of the property to a third party for less than the balance owed and release its lien on the collateral property*. Although a short sale does not bring a sufficient amount to pay the lender in full, the lender avoids foreclosure, including the need to acquire title and market the property, while getting the nonperforming loan off its books. Some lenders even agree to forgive any deficiency between the sale and the balance owed. A short sale is not necessarily fraudulent; however, if a borrower intentionally stops making mortgage payments to force default and then enlists the assistance of someone else—e.g., straw buyer—to purchase the property at a reduced price, fraud has most likely occurred.

- **Arson.** Some homeowners may resort to the crime of arson and file fraudulent insurance claims to obtain cash back or payment of the current property liens.

Lenders and Brokers

Lenders and mortgage brokers commit mortgage fraud by falsifying loan documents, making loans to straw buyers, illegally flipping properties, and other schemes. Lenders benefit by making loans that should never have been made and by selling them to the secondary market as quickly as possible. Mortgage brokers benefit by collecting fees and yield spread premiums for creating fraudulent mortgage packages. Dishonest lenders and mortgage brokers see the opportunity to make a loan that results in a commission with high profitability. Often, these loans are knowingly made to unqualified buyers or even straw buyers who will never make a payment on the loan, resulting in foreclosure.

Appraisers

Appraisals are a critical aspect of mortgage lending. An appraisal with inaccurate information—whether completed because of fraud or negligence—can have a serious impact. An **inflated appraisal** scheme occurs *when a property is intentionally appraised with a higher-than-market value by an appraiser acting in collusion with a real estate agent, mortgage broker, or lender*. Unscrupulous lenders hire only those appraisers who agree to "hit the number," regardless of the appraisal's relationship to actual market value. When these mortgages are part of sales transactions, continued inflation of values in the same neighborhood creates a vicious cycle that results in appraisals at higher-than-market values than appear justified. Even unsuspecting appraisers are caught when they unknowingly use the inflated sale prices as comparables.

Appraisers subscribe to a set of rules and guidelines known as the Uniform Standards of Professional Appraisal Practice (USPAP). The appraiser is required by law and professional standards to act ***independently, impartially and objectively*** when performing the work he is engaged in. An appraiser must *never* accept an assignment that requires him to "hit a specific number" or bring the value in keeping with the client's demands.

While inflated appraisals may be more common, deliberately **understating** the value of a property, for example, to allow someone to purchase a foreclosed home or short sale at a lower price, is also fraud. Understated appraisals may also occur with a loan modification to ensure more favorable terms from a lender.

Appraisal Practices Prohibited by Regulation Z

Regulation Z [see 12 CFR §1026.42 Valuation independence] was amended in 2009 to specifically address perceived abuses in the mortgage industry. Lenders, mortgage brokers, and their affiliates are prohibited from coercing, influencing, or encouraging an appraiser to misstate the value of the dwelling. For example, the law specifically prohibits these practices:

- Implying to an appraiser that current or future retention of the appraiser depends on the amount at which the appraiser values a consumer's principal dwelling

- Excluding an appraiser from consideration for future engagement because the appraiser reports a value of a consumer's principal dwelling that does not meet or exceed a minimum threshold

- Telling an appraiser a minimum reported value of a consumer's principal dwelling that is needed to approve the loan

- Failing to compensate an appraiser because the appraiser does not value a consumer's principal dwelling at or above a certain amount

- Conditioning an appraiser's compensation on loan consummation

In addition, a lender cannot extend credit if the lender knows, at or before closing, that improper coercion has occurred by anyone unless the lender can document that it has acted with reasonable diligence to determine that the appraisal does not materially misstate or misrepresent the dwelling's value.

The following practices are **not** prohibited:

- Asking an appraiser to consider additional information about the dwelling or comparable properties or to correct factual errors

- Obtaining multiple appraisals of a consumer's principal dwelling, unless the creditor adheres to a policy of selecting the most reliable appraisal, rather than the appraisal that states the highest value

- Withholding compensation from an appraiser for breach of contract or substandard performance of services as provided by contract

Other Industry Insiders

- **Attorneys** may prepare bogus deeds and get them duly recorded in public records with the participation of government workers.

- **Accountants** may falsify tax returns, profit and loss statements, and other documentation required by lenders to qualify loans.

- **Title companies** may charge borrower's fees for services never provided at the closing or may complete incorrect title reports that omit valid liens or that create false chains of title.

- **Government workers** may falsify deeds and other records.

- **Real estate agents** may assist in the preparation of false documentation, such as sales contracts or property inspections, and in finding straw buyers for a property. Real estate brokers and agents collude in flipping schemes by finding borrowers for scams and by raising listing prices of homes to make an over-inflated appraisal value appear valid. Unscrupulous real estate agents may also steer borrowers to a specific lender in exchange for kickbacks or other consideration.

- **Rehabbers** and **FSBO (For Sale By Owner) flippers** may use sub-par material, removing materials or fixtures after an appraisal, providing straw buyers, and improperly influencing appraisers, loan officers, and title companies.

- **Investment property owners** may falsify occupancy rates on their rent rolls or otherwise misrepresent the condition of rental units or incomplete renovations.

Flipping

One of the most common and well-known mortgage fraud schemes is **property flipping.** Many people are confused by the term "flipping" as it has long been understood to mean that an investor has remodeled a property and quickly sold it for a profit. *If the investor bought the property below market and remodeling has brought it up to true market value, this is the good side of flipping and is completely legal.* It also serves the public well as it increases property values, improves neighborhoods, and provides housing that otherwise might not be available.

Illegal flipping is something else entirely. Illegal property flipping generally requires collusion between the seller, buyer, appraiser, and lender/broker. An illegal property-flipping scheme occurs *when a property is purchased at a low price, appraised at an inflated value without any valid reason for the increase, and then resold at a much higher price.* It may involve a series of sales and quick resales, with one property and a group of sellers and buyers changing ownership among them.

A home in an illegal flipping scheme is typically resold at a new, higher price fairly soon after its initial purchase. Statistics show that the criminals involved in these schemes do not wait long time periods to sell, often only weeks or perhaps a few months at most.

Exercise 11.7: Knowledge Check

If a real estate agent accepted flyers from a mortgage company (containing marketing information about the real estate agent and the MLO) and distributed them at an open house,

    A. only the MLO is violating RESPA.

    B. only the real estate agent is violating RESPA.

    C. both are violating RESPA.

    D. neither are violating RESPA.

Attributes of Flipping Schemes

Typically, flipping schemes are more prevalent in **mixed-value areas** where *higher-priced homes are located near lower-priced homes in poor repair* and home values fluctuate extremely. These neighborhoods often include rental properties and tend to have higher rates of crime, which can adversely affect property values.

Homes involved in flipping schemes are often purchased at low prices because they are in poor condition. The distressed nature of these properties can include broken pipes, no electrical wiring, or other items in disrepair. When repairs are made after the purchase, they are generally cosmetic or exterior-only repairs.

Another common attribute of illegal flipping is that perpetrators rarely use local entities to handle the loan. As a result, the underwriter who reviews the loan is not based locally and is unfamiliar with the property and neighborhood.

FHA Response to Flipping Schemes

The FHA requires sellers to own a property for at least **three (3) months** prior to a new sale. For resales ranging from 91-180 days, the FHA may impose additional requirements, assuming that criminals interested in quick resales are not willing to wait. FHA rules include:

- The FHA will not insure any resale properties unless the owner of record is the seller. This prevents thieves from flipping properties without ever having legally owned them.

- Resales that take place 91–180 days after the initial sale can be FHA-insured **only if there is a second appraisal that matches a resale threshold percentage established by HUD**. The second appraisal may *not* be paid for by the borrower.

Recall that higher-priced loans state that if the price difference exceeds 10% of the seller's original acquisition cost during the first 90 days or 20% of the original cost during the first six months, creditors are required to obtain a second appraisal [see 12 CFR, Part 1026, Truth in Lending – Regulation Z §1026.35(c)(4)(A)(B)]. This requirement for new home purchase mortgage loans is intended to address fraudulent property flipping by seeking to ensure that the value of the property legitimately increased. The borrower **cannot** pay for the cost of the second appraisal report.

Other Types of Mortgage Fraud

Air Loan

An **air loan scam** involves *loans made on non-existent properties*. For example, a broker enlists or creates a straw buyer, identifies fictional properties, opens accounts for payments, and maintains custodial accounts for escrow payments. A bank of telephones in an office may even be set up, with one phone line used for the employer, one for the appraiser, etc., for verification purposes.

Deed Scam

In a **deed scam**, *the seller's signature on the deed is forged, meaning the real homeowner is not even aware the property is being fraudulently transferred. The deed is recorded; the thief mortgages the property with cash-out refinancing, and then pockets the money and walks away without making a payment*. Once again, the owner has no idea the property has even been transferred! This scheme typically takes place for properties that are paid in full, vacant, or when the owners are having trouble making their mortgage payments.

Double Sold Loans

Double sold loans are instigated in various ways. One method involves *the primary mortgage holder who sells the loan on the secondary market*. In this instance, the loan is sold to a fraudulent company that, supposedly, will service the loan (and receive the mortgage payments). However, when a payment is received, the fraudulent company simply steals the money. The property eventually goes into foreclosure due to nonpayment.

Another method of devising a double sold loan is when *a borrower signs multiple copies of the same documents and the MLO submits each "set" of the loan papers to different lenders*. When the loan is approved by more than one lender, the MLO forges a duplicate set of closing documents, delivers them to a second lender, and keeps the proceeds.

Unrecorded or Silent Second

In a down market, it's not unusual for a seller to make concessions to entice a buyer. These concessions could even include financing some of the purchase price for the buyer. For example, let's say that the buyer applies for a 75% first mortgage, agrees to pay 5% down, and gives the seller a second mortgage at 20% of the sale price. *This second mortgage will not be recorded so the lender will think the buyer is putting 25% down.*

The buyer may have every intention of paying the seller, but this **unrecorded second**—also called a **silent second**—is a type of mortgage fraud, and it could be quite a risk for the seller. If the buyer does not pay the second mortgage loan, the seller will not be able to foreclose to get the property back. Even if the seller does, at some point, record the mortgage, there may be other liens by that time against the property or the property owner that would have priority over the second mortgage.

Disappearing Second

A more common variation on this scheme is when the buyer has *no intention of paying* the second mortgage. For example, schemers find uninformed buyers willing to sign a sales contract beyond market price with an enticement such as "seller will help finance." In these cases, the seller holds a second mortgage and presents it to the lender as if it were an actual mortgage to induce the bank to loan a higher amount. Once the transaction closes, the seller destroys the mortgage, sometimes even gives it back to the buyer immediately. This is called a **disappearing second**. The lender thinks it has an 80% LTV loan; for example, when it may actually be 100% LTV.

Email/Mail Scams

In **e-mail or mail scams**, *e-mail messages or letters promise to eliminate mortgage loans or get rid of credit card debt in return for paying a fee*. The consumer pays the money but gets nothing in return. Consumers desperate to eliminate their crushing debt are most vulnerable to these schemes. The e-mail messages or letters often offer credit counseling or are sent under a name like "American Credit Counseling," implying a legitimate business performing a public service.

Identity Theft

A **false identity** *is when someone uses another person's identity on a loan application without the knowledge of the rightful property owner*. This is also known as **identity theft**. An identity can be stolen in a variety of ways, including such common scenarios as applying for a job or from discarded documents.

Many times, a thief needs only one piece of information—a Social Security number—to steal an identity. Today, counterfeit Social Security numbers are relatively easy to obtain. Thieves use retired numbers (due to death), numbers issued to someone else, stolen numbers, or numbers issued before the borrower's birth year. Thieves also use altered employment records, bank statements, and pay stubs to commit identity theft. With this information, they are able to impersonate homebuyers and sellers using actual, verifiable identities that give the mortgage transactions the appearance of legitimacy.

When suspicious of the validity of a Social Security number provided in connection with an application for a mortgage loan, MLOs should continue the application and gather as much information on the borrower as possible. There are many services that investigate the validity of a Social Security number. If a fraudulent use of a Social Security number is discovered, it should be reported the FTC, who investigates number theft, or the IRS Service if there are issues involving taxes. [See https://faq.ssa.gov/link/portal/34011/34019/Article/3792/What-should-I-do-if-I-think-someone-is-using-my-Social-Security-number]

Exercise 11.8: Knowledge Check

1. **Illegal property flipping could involve all the following EXCEPT the seller**

    A. cosmetically remodeling the home only so it looks good to prospective buyers.

    B. obtaining a higher than market appraised value.

    C. purchasing the home at below market price.

    D. selling the property at market value.

2. **The FHA will insure a flipped home under all the following conditions EXCEPT**

    A. the buyer must pay the lender for the second appraisal.

    B. the flipped home requires a second appraisal.

    C. the seller must be the owner of record.

    D. the transaction must be an arm's length transaction.

3. **Identity theft consists of all the following EXCEPT**

    A. altering the bank statement of another person to acquire access to the account.

    B. co-signing an auto loan for a relative.

    C. using another's credit card without permission to purchase a flat screen television.

    D. using a deceased person's Social Security number for personal gain.

Red Flags of Mortgage Fraud

A red flag is a situation that requires additional scrutiny. According to the **Federal Financial Institutions Examination Council** (FFIEC), one red flag by itself may not be significant, however, multiple red flags may indicate an operating environment that is conducive to fraud, including:

- **Steering Buyers to a Specific Lender.** Buyers may choose any lender they want for a purchase transaction. However, it is not unusual for real estate agents to recommend the use of a certain lending institution. Lenders often solicit loans through these real estate agents by forming alliances with them. If a transaction will close only if a certain lender is used, ask questions because it is unlikely that only one lender would offer a buyer certain favorable terms. Unfortunately, in many mortgage fraud scams, the buyer is unsophisticated in seeking financing and may have credit issues that make lending more challenging. The buyer may be told this loan is the only chance for a home purchase when, in fact, it is a scam.

- **Stated Income.** Since the inception of no-doc or low-doc loans, the documentation required for the loan may be limited. These loans—rare in today's market—allow the borrower to provide, *without verification*, employment history, income, and debt. Be suspicious if a borrower only had to produce minimal documentation to qualify for the loan.

- **No Money Due at Closing.** If a buyer is not required to pay anything at closing, questions should be asked. What this means is the buyer has been able to get around down payment requirements, and the seller is paying all the points and closing costs involved with the buyer's loan. In theory, the sales price may have been inflated to cover these costs. Even with less stringent lending guidelines and requirements, it is unusual for a buyer to need no money for a closing.

- **Sale Subject to the Seller Acquiring Title.** A huge red flag in a transaction is when the seller in the purchase contract is not the owner of record. There could be legitimate reasons for this, like the seller could be the buyer of the property via land contract or the seller could have recently purchased the property at a sheriff's sale and will not gain title until confirmation of the sale. Participants in the sale should ask why the seller is not the owner of record and verify that the reason is legitimate.

- **Difference in Sale Price.** The sales contract is supposed to guide the title agency or closing agent to the terms of the Closing Disclosure, and there should be no discrepancies. Buyers have the right to review their Closing Disclosure **three (3) business days** before closing. They should compare this document to the purchase contract and to the Loan Estimate received from the lender.

- **Sale Price Changes to Fit Appraisal.** To carry out this scheme, an appraisal is ordered and completed. The appraiser is then contacted regarding alterations or addendums to the purchase contract, typically made after the lender is told the appraised amount. The new, altered contract now matches the appraisal value. These schemes enable the lender to profit more from the transaction because additional money was available through a higher-than-expected appraisal.

- **Related Parties Involved.** Certainly, there is no law against a mother selling her property to her son or daughter, even at a discounted price. However, mortgage fraud scams often involve family members. So, when the transaction is *not* an arm's length transaction, full disclosure is imperative. Cases of mortgage fraud involving entire families have been reported. Many times, the straw buyer in a scam is a family member. Purchase contracts between family members should specifically state their relationships so it does not appear intentionally hidden.

- **Funds Paid to Undisclosed Third Parties.** In certain mortgage fraud schemes, unknown third parties who appear to have no relevance to the transaction are paid out of the funds received at the closing. The implication, of course, is there may be debt not revealed in the closing statements. Once again, a closing statement that is not followed to the letter is a red flag to the borrower. It may be prudent to have legal representation to review all the closing paperwork before signing any documents.

- **Cash Paid to Seller Outside of Escrow.** The seller receives cash from the sale of the property; however, it is not stated in the Closing Disclosure or in the purchase contract. The motive, of course, is unstated profits. No paper trail exists to show the payment.

- **Cash Paid to Borrower.** The borrower receives cash when purchasing the property. Usually, in these cases, the borrower does not have a down payment and the purchase contract calls for the seller to pay all loan costs. Although seller-paid costs are becoming more typical in today's economy, schemes in which the borrower receives money from the transaction are not.

Elder Abuse

Another common example of mortgage fraud is when elderly homeowners are required to apply for and obtain mortgage loans they do not want. Oftentimes, a child or caregiver brings the elderly consumer to an application appointment for a home mortgage loan. If the senior homeowner appears confused or does not appear to be a willing participant in the loan process, the other party may be exercising coercion, causing the elderly consumer to be under duress. If an MLO is presented with this situation, he should take the consumer's application, but before actively proceeding with the loan request, a conversation should be conducted one-on-one with the senior borrower to determine if he is being forced to obtain a loan he does not want.

Fraud Enforcement

The **Fraud Enforcement and Recovery Act** of 2009 (Pub.L. 111-21), or **FERA,** makes it a felony to falsify loan documents submitted to a broad range of financial institutions, including mortgage lending businesses. It also includes any other person "that makes in whole or in part a federally-related mortgage loan." The amendments assure that private mortgage brokers and companies are held accountable under federal fraud laws. Without these amendments, for example, the financial institution bribery statute would not extend beyond traditional banks and financial institutions.

FBI and Suspicious Activity Reports

The FBI tracks mortgage fraud through **Suspicious Activity Reports** (SARs) filed by federally-insured financial institutions and others, and from reports from the Department of Housing and Urban Development's Office of the Inspector General.

One way you can participate in combating fraud and protecting your reputation is by staying current with the industry. For example, **Mortgage Asset Research Institute** (MARI) is a private subscription service that gives members access to a database of all fraud and suspected fraud cases as reported by its members and state and federal regulatory agencies, as well as the actions taken. The service allows those in the industry to check credentials of companies and individuals with whom they work.

 There are also many free websites that document various mortgage fraud scams and the consequences to the participants. It would be a good practice to bookmark some of those sites and make a point of visiting them regularly.

MORTGAGE FRAUD IS INVESTIGATED BY THE FBI

Mortgage Fraud is investigated by the Federal Bureau of Investigation and is punishable by up to 30 years in federal prison or $1,000,000 fine, or both. It is illegal for a person to make any false statement regarding income, assets, debt, or matters of identification, or to willfully overvalue any land or property, in a loan and credit application for the purpose of influencing in any way the action of a financial institution.

Some of the applicable Federal criminal statutes which may be charged in connection with Mortgage Fraud include:

18 U.S.C. § 1001 - Statements or entries generally
18 U.S.C. § 1010 - HUD and Federal Housing Administration Transactions
18 U.S.C. § 1014 - Loan and credit applications generally
18 U.S.C. § 1028 - Fraud and related activity in connection with identification documents
18 U.S.C. § 1341 - Frauds and swindles by Mail
18 U.S.C. § 1342 - Fictitious name or address
18 U.S.C. § 1343 - Fraud by wire
18 U.S.C. § 1344 - Bank Fraud
42 U.S.C. § 408(a) - False Social Security Number

Unauthorized use of the FBI seal, name, and initials is subject to prosecution under Sections 701, 709, and 712 of Title 18 of the United States Code. This advisement may not be changed or altered without the specific written consent of the Federal Bureau of Investigation, and is not an endorsement of any product or service.

Exercise 11.9: Apply Your Knowledge

Directions: Consider the following scenarios, and then write your responses.

Scenario 1: Young couple June and Bud really wanted to buy a home, but their debt ratio was too high and they didn't have enough for a down payment. June's dad, Jack, decided to help them by applying for an FHA loan himself, with the understanding that June and Bud would make the mortgage payments. Within a year of moving in, they were well behind in their monthly payments, and the lender called Jack. Jack said he had no intention of making the payments, so the lender started foreclosure procedures, and June and Bud moved into Jack's basement.

What are the fraud scheme(s) or legal violations for which Jack is potentially at risk?

_____

_____

_____

_____

Scenario 2: MLO Stu is working with Emily, who is planning on buying her cousin Doug's house. Emily is putting 10% down and Doug is willing to hold a 10% purchase money mortgage so Emily can avoid paying private mortgage insurance. As he's consulting with Doug and Emily to put the deal together, Doug asks Stu if he can just tear the mortgage up after closing, since he doesn't really expect Emily to pay him back.

What are the fraud scheme(s) or legal violations for which Stu is potentially at risk?

_____

_____

_____

_____

Scenario 3: Patrick is behind on his mortgage payments and has been threatened with foreclosure. He has his house on the market and a few people are showing interest in purchasing the property. Patrick contacts his lender and asks if they would consider agreeing to a short sale. Patrick has several offers but does not submit the highest offer to the lender. Instead, he convinces his friend Joe to purchase the property. The lender agrees to the sale and once the lien is released, Joe sells the property at market value to the other prospective buyer, then he and Patrick split the $30,000 profit.

What are the fraud scheme(s) or legal violations for which Patrick is potentially at risk?

_____

_____

_____

_____

Penalties for Mortgage Fraud

The penalties for mortgage fraud, either buyer or industry insider fraud, are stated in 18 U.S. Code § 1344:

Whoever knowingly executes, or attempts to execute, a scheme or artifice:

(1) To defraud a financial institution; or

(2) To obtain any of the moneys, funds, credits, assets, securities, or other property owned by, or under the custody or control of, a financial institution, by means of false or fraudulent pretenses, representations, or promises;

*shall be fined **not more than $1,000,000 or imprisoned not more than 30 years, or both**.*

Predatory Lending

Along with the advantages of subprime lending, which extends credit to people who might not otherwise qualify for a home mortgage, come some of the inevitable negative by-products—lenders taking advantage of borrowers. **Predatory lending** involves loans that *take advantage of ill-informed consumers through excessively high fees, misrepresented loan terms, frequent refinancing that does not benefit the borrower, and other prohibited acts.* Predatory lending targets borrowers with little knowledge of, or defense against, these practices. New regulations require that complete and clear disclosures be made to borrowers and specifically prohibits certain practices, including:

- Packing a loan with credit insurance and other extra fees

- Extending credit to people with little or no income and who have little chance of repaying the loan (the lender forecloses on the property and keeps the excess equity to cover costs)

- Refinancing the lender's own high-cost loan with another fee-rich loan in less than a year's time (unless a lender can show that the new loan benefits the borrower)

The motive for predatory lending is profit. The goal of a predatory lender is to take the property or strip its equity, or to profit from the exorbitant fees charged. Undoubtedly, the lender claims to help borrowers achieve the dream of homeownership. Predatory loans are approved without regard for the borrower's ability to repay. Interest rates are higher than the level of risk justifies. And, lenders may bundle unrelated products—such as a life insurance policy—into the mortgage loan to further their profit.

Predatory Lending Regulations

TILA is implemented by the Bureau's Regulation Z [see 12 CFR part 1026], and historically by the Board of Governors of the Federal Reserve System [see Regulation Z, 12 CFR part 226]. Most notably, the Board's 2010 Loan Originator Final Rule substantially restricted payments creating incentives for MLOs to steer consumers to more expensive loans. Under this Rule, creditors *may not base a loan originator's compensation on the transaction's terms or conditions, other than the mortgage loan amount.*

Title XIV of the Dodd-Frank Act of 2010, designated as the **Mortgage Reform and Anti-Predatory Lending Act** [see Dodd-Frank Act, Title XIV (Pub. L. 111-203)], gave the CFPB authority to *prohibit MLOs from steering borrowers to any loan that the borrower lacks the* *ability to repay or that has predatory characteristics*, such as equity stripping, excessive fees, or abusive terms. Final rules on these steering provisions amended Regulation Z (§1026.36 (e)) on January 1, 2014.

The Dodd-Frank Act Section 1414 added TILA Section 129C(d), which generally *prohibits a creditor from financing any premiums or fees for credit insurance in connection with any residential mortgage loan* or with any extension of credit under an open-end consumer credit plan secured by the consumer's principal dwelling. The prohibition:

- Applies to credit life, credit disability, credit unemployment, credit property insurance, and other similar products.

- Does *not* apply to credit insurance for which premiums or fees are calculated and paid in full on a monthly basis.

- Does *not* apply to credit unemployment insurance for which the premiums are reasonable, the creditor receives no compensation, and the premiums are paid pursuant to a separate insurance contract and are not paid to the creditor's affiliate.

Subprime Lenders and Predatory Lending

Legitimate subprime lenders offer loans to low-income and risky borrowers and must charge higher interest rates to accommodate the risk. The higher-than-typical closing and processing fees allow them to take on that risk. Without these lenders, riskier borrowers could not tap into their home equity or even own a home. Subprime lenders may be mainstream lenders who also offer conventional loans to borrowers or mortgage brokers specializing in working with the "credit impaired" or with borrowers who are unable or unwilling to meet other criteria—such as verification of income or assets—required for a conventional loan.

These lenders usually do not make government-backed loans and, therefore, often operate outside of some federally-related loan guidelines.

While many instances of predatory lending involve subprime loans, not all subprime lenders are predatory lenders. It may be difficult for potential borrowers to discern who are legitimate subprime lenders.

Excessive Fees

Predatory lending costs the borrower in many ways. Although it is understandable that a higher-risk borrower would pay higher interest rates than someone with good credit, it still forces borrowers to pay more than they would for a typical transaction. If the terms are difficult to understand, the borrower may be paying exorbitant loan origination, settlement, and servicing fees.

- Total fees *greater than 4-5%* of the loan amount may be considered *higher than normal* and may be a red flag for **junk fees**—*multiple fees under a variety of names alleging services done on the borrower's behalf.*

- Exorbitant **prepayment penalties** may lock borrowers into abusive loans that cannot be easily refinanced when credit scores improve. Prepayment penalties may be tens of thousands of dollars and be enforced for many years into the loan. The reason? To discourage payoff of the highly profitable loan. In reality, the majority of lenders do not charge prepayment penalties or, if they do, only in the first years of the loan.

Documentation

For many borrowers, particularly those who are uninformed, loan documents may be difficult to understand. Legal jargon, small print, and page after page of confusing documentation may be presented for immediate signature. Often, the pressure is on finishing the closing with no time allowed to read the documents carefully. What is the solution for the borrower? Borrowers should be advised to have an attorney, credit counselor, or other expert to review all documents before signing.

Equity Skimming

Equity skimming involves lenders making various types of loans knowing the borrowers will not be able to make the monthly payments and thus setting them up for foreclosure. The borrower loses everything—the home and the equity in it. Some common types of equity skimming schemes include:

- **Loans Exceeding Ability to Repay.** Borrowers typically rely on a lender's advice regarding debt-to-income ratio, believing there are reasonable limits in place on what they can borrow. Equity skimming schemes may falsify loan documents so the borrower does not realize the amount being borrowed is too much with a monthly payment amount that is too high. The lender makes the loan, knowing the borrower will not be able to make those monthly payments, setting them up for foreclosure. The borrower loses everything—the home and the equity in it. [For more information about lender's legal responsibility, see Regulation Z, Minimum standards for transactions secured by a dwelling. 12 CFR 1026.43(c) Repayment ability.]

- **Home Improvement Scams.** A contractor working in conjunction with a predatory lender recommends repairs to the home or property that may or may not actually need to be done. The quote for the work is typically extremely high, and the contractor indicates arrangements for financing are available. Enter the lender—offering a loan that will strip the equity out of the home, again resulting in possible foreclosure.

- **Loan Flipping.** This involves refinancing repeatedly, usually with minimal to no net tangible benefit to the borrower in terms of lowering the interest rate or saving fees. The borrower is promised benefits that never materialize. Since the lender profits every time a loan is made, there is no incentive for the lender to recommend otherwise. Often, the refinancing raises the interest rate to the borrower! With higher monthly payments, the borrower may wind up defaulting on the loan, undergoing foreclosure, or being forced to refinance into even more unfavorable terms. Once again, the high-risk borrower takes a hit financially—a price he can ill afford to pay!

- **Extreme Lending.** Some borrowers fall victim to extreme lending. Borrowers with extremely high debt to income are targets. With typical lending guidelines restricting borrowers to around 30% of income toward the mortgage payment, this extreme lending—often as much as 50% or more of income going toward the mortgage payment—puts borrowers at risk. If the borrower is laid off, loses a job, or experiences unanticipated expenses due to injury or illness, the risk for foreclosure is great.

Foreclosure Rescue Scams

The FTC warns borrowers about certain schemes regarding unscrupulous individuals trying to take advantage of homeowners facing foreclosure, including:

- **Phony Counseling or Phantom Help**. A scam artist tells homeowners that he can negotiate a deal with their lender to save their homes for an upfront fee. Homeowners may be told not to contact their lenders, lawyers, or credit counselors and to let the scam artist handle all the details. Once they pay the fee, the scam artist takes off with their money. Sometimes, the scam artist insists that homeowners make all mortgage payments directly to him while he negotiates with the lender. In this instance, the scammer may collect a few months of payments before disappearing.

- **Rent-to-Buy Scheme**. A homeowner is told to surrender the title as part of a deal that allows him to remain in the home as a renter with the intention of buying it back during the next few years. The schemer may tell the homeowner that surrendering the title will permit a different borrower with a better credit rating to secure new financing and prevent the loss of the home. But the terms of these deals usually are so burdensome that buying back the home becomes impossible. The homeowner loses the

home, and the scam artist walks off with all or most of the home's equity. Worse yet, when the new borrower defaults on the loan, the original homeowner is evicted. In a variation, the scam artist raises the rent over time to the point that the former homeowner can't afford it. After missing several rent payments, the renter—the former homeowner—is evicted, leaving the "rescuer" free to sell the house.

- **Bait and Switch Scheme**. Recall that bait and switch usually refers to an advertising tactic where a consumer is enticed with what sounds like a great deal, and then is sold something else either more expensive or somehow less advantageous to the consumer. Similarly, a rescue scam artist will provide borrowers with loan documents to sign to make their mortgage current, but buried in the stack of documents is one that surrenders title to the scammer [see http://www.ftc.gov/bcp/edu/pubs/consumer/credit/cre42.shtm].

To combat these schemes, the FTC issued Regulation 0, 12 CFR Part 1015, which contains provisions against advance fees prior to a written offer that is acceptable to the homeowner, who can reject the offer free of charge, added disclosures, and prohibited claims.

Indicators of Predatory Lending

Changing loan terms at closing was historically one of the most common predatory lending schemes. Borrowers discovered closing documents did not reflect the loan terms and fees originally stated in the Loan Estimate, and often felt as though they had no choice but to go through with the loan. A difference between the sale price on the Closing Disclosure and the price on the sales contract is a red flag. Of course, it could be an honest mistake, but as the sales contract is supposed to guide the title agency or closing agent to the terms of the Closing Disclosure, there should be no discrepancies. The 3/7/3 Rule introduced with the Mortgage Disclosure Improvement Act amendments to TILA that requires an *additional waiting period of three business days after disclosing changed loan terms* helps to address this situation (12 CFR §1026.19 (a)(2)(ii)).

HUD identifies several other predatory schemes used by unscrupulous MLOs, including:

- Encouraging borrowers to lie about their income, expenses, or cash available for down payments to get a loan.

- Knowingly lending more money than a borrower can afford to repay.

- Charging high-interest rates to borrowers based on their race or national origin and not on their credit history.

- Charging fees for unnecessary or nonexistent products and services.

- Pressuring borrowers to accept higher-risk loans such as balloon loans, interest-only payments, and steep prepayment penalties.

- Targeting vulnerable borrowers to cash-out refinances offers when they know borrowers need cash due to medical, unemployment, or debt problems.

- Stripping homeowners' equity from their homes by convincing them to refinance again and again when there is no benefit to the borrower.

HUD indicates that borrowers should be aware of the following red flags that could indicate predatory tactics:

- Lenders tell borrowers that they are the borrower's only chance of getting a loan or owning a home. Borrowers should be able to take their time to shop around and compare prices and houses.

- The house the borrower is buying costs a lot more than other homes in the neighborhood but isn't any bigger or better.

- Borrowers are asked to sign a sales contract or loan documents that are blank or that contain information which is false.

- Borrowers are told that FHA insurance protects them against property defects or loan fraud when it does not.

- The cost or loan terms at closing are not what the borrower agreed to.

- Borrowers are told that refinancing can solve their credit or money problems.

[see: https://www.hudexchange.info/resources/documents/11-tips-for-smart-consumers-fact-sheet.pdf].

Exercise 11.10: Apply Your Knowledge

Directions: Consider the following scenarios and determine if they are examples of predatory lending, then write your responses.

Scenario 1: Allen faces possible foreclosure and contacts a mortgage lender whose ad promises to save his home. At closing, Allen sees that the lender changed the terms of the loan that they had agreed to, but he felt he had no choice but to go ahead with the loan or lose the house. Is this a case of predatory lending? Why or why not?

_____

_____

_____

_____

_____

Scenario 2: Bill takes an application for a cash-out loan from a woman on a fixed income so she can pay her real estate taxes. Bill does not advise her to make sure the new loan collects for real estate taxes, hoping in a few years she will need to get a new loan for the same reason. Is this a case of predatory lending? Why or why not?

_____

_____

_____

_____

_____

Scenario 3: Kara has some credit issues and is trying to bounce back from a recent bankruptcy. Still, she is interested in buying a home. She finds a mortgage broker who can secure a loan for her, but only if she pays 20% down and consents to an interest rate that is higher than that offered to consumers with perfect credit. Is this a case of predatory lending? Why or why not?

_____

_____

_____

_____

Scenario 4: Pamela has applied for a loan with XYZ Mortgage Company. The MLO tells her that because she is a single woman, she can only be approved for the loan if she takes out a credit insurance policy to cover the mortgage in the event of her death. The insurance policy requires a significant one-time fee at closing. Is this a case of predatory lending? Why or why not?

_____

_____

_____

_____

Exercise 11.11: Apply Your Knowledge

Directions: Consider the following scenario and decide how you would handle it, then write your responses.

Scenario, Part 1: Velma, a 59-year-old minority woman who works as a teacher, contacts you about getting a loan to purchase a condominium. As you're chatting, she indicates that she's hoping to retire from teaching in three years. You take her financial and personal information and see that you should be able to get her the amount she needs to purchase the home, and now you need to discuss terms. You share some loan options with her and she insists that she's only interested in an adjustable rate mortgage, because she wants the lower monthly payments to start and is convinced the interest rates will stay low or go down even further.

What should you share with Velma about an ARM loan given her situation? Are you obligated to help her apply for the loan she wants?

_____

_____

_____

_____

_____

_____

Scenario, Part 2: Suppose you decide that you will not submit an application for an ARM due to Velma's intention to retire in three years, about the time the monthly payments on the loan could jump beyond her ability to pay on a fixed income. You don't want to seem as though you are pushing through an inappropriate loan. Velma is very unhappy and accuses you of refusing to help her because she's a woman and a minority.

It seems as though your choice is between risking accusations of discrimination or accusations of predatory lending. Now, what do you do?

_____

_____

_____

_____

_____

_____

Chapter Summary

1. Outlined laws are the minimum duty required of an MLO. However, MLOs should strive to fulfill not only the letter of the law but also its intent. There are many sources from which an MLO can obtain ethical guidance. The BBB and state attorney general's office can provide guidance. The National Association of Mortgage Brokers (NAMB) has created and adopted a Code of Ethics.

2. **Bait and switch** advertising is an alluring but insincere offer to sell a product or service that the advertiser, in truth, does not intend or want to sell in order to switch consumers from buying the advertised merchandise. Every advertisement should be a bona fide offer to sell. An advertisement is a **commercial message in *any medium* that promotes, directly or indirectly, a credit transaction.**

3. **Misrepresentation** is simply false or misleading information that could include documents, misstatements, or omission. A **material fact** is one that, if known, might have caused a reasonable consumer to make a different decision. **The FTC Act** [see FTC Act, 15 U.S.C. §41-58] states that advertisements must be truthful and nondeceptive, that advertisers must have evidence to back up their claims, and that advertisements cannot be unfair. An ad is **unfair** if it causes or is likely to cause substantial consumer injury, which a consumer could not reasonably avoid, and it is not outweighed by the benefit to consumers. An ad is **deceptive** if it contains a statement—or omits information—that is likely to mislead consumers acting reasonably under the circumstances and is material to a consumer's decision to buy or use the product. The same laws that regulate print and broadcast media apply equally to advertising, promotion, and marketing on the Internet.

4. Treating everyone equally helps avoid violations of the **Civil Rights Act of 1866** [see Civil Rights Act of 1866, 14 Stat. §27] and the federal **Fair Housing Act of 1968** (Title VIII) [see Fair Housing Act of 1968, 42 U.S.C. §800-820]. It is illegal to discriminate based on race, color, religion, sex, national origin, disability, or familial status. **Redlining** is illegally refusing to make loans on property located in a particular neighborhood for discriminatory reasons.

5. The **Home Mortgage Disclosure Act** (HMDA) [see Home Mortgage Disclosure Act (Regulation C), 12 CFR §1003] helps enforce compliance of redlining by requiring certain lenders and mortgage brokers to file an annual report categorizing the location of loans made so cases of redlining can be spotted. Exclusionary zoning laws are also discriminatory, especially if they have a disparate impact on a minority group. The courts can step in to remedy these situations. Advertising must also be fair and neutral in its language.

6. The **Equal Credit Opportunity Act** [see Equal Credit Opportunity Act (Regulation B), 12 CFR §1002] prohibits discrimination in granting credit to people based on sex, age (if at least 18), marital status, race, color, religion, national origin, receipt of public assistance, or exercised rights under the Consumer Credit Protection Act.

7. **RESPA** [see Real Estate Settlement Procedures Act (Regulation X), 12 CFR §1024] regulates settlement and closing procedures and requires lenders, mortgage brokers, or servicers of home loans to provide borrowers with pertinent and timely disclosures. Among RESPA requirements is Section 8, which prohibits kickbacks and unearned fees.

8. Appraisers subscribe to a set of rules and guidelines known as USPAP. The appraiser is required by law and professional standards to act independently, impartially, and objectively when performing his work. An appraiser must never accept an assignment that requires him to "hit a specific number" or bring the value in keeping with the client's demands.

9. Illegal property flipping generally requires collusion between the seller, buyer, appraiser, and lender/broker. An illegal property flipping scheme occurs when a property is purchased at a low price, appraised at an inflated value without any valid reason for the increase, and then resold at a much higher price.

10. Loan flipping involves refinancing repeatedly, usually with minimal to no net tangible benefit to the borrower in terms of lowering the interest rate or saving fees.

11. Being honest with everyone involves avoiding **fraud**, which is intentional misrepresentation or concealment of a material fact. Mortgage professionals must also steer clear of any situation that can be construed as mortgage fraud because it is a serious crime. The fraud can be perpetrated by borrowers who lie on applications, by an appraiser who provides an inflated property value, or by an MLO who ignores derogatory information to get a loan approved. Mortgage fraud also includes not reporting all items on the Closing Disclosure accurately, creating phantom documents for verification, or concealing the true nature of the borrower's down payment.

12. **Predatory lending** involves loans that take advantage of ill-informed consumers through excessively high fees, misrepresented loan terms, frequent refinancing that does not benefit the borrower, and other prohibited acts. Predatory lending targets borrowers with little knowledge of, or defense against, these practices. Laws such as the **Mortgage Disclosure Improvement Act (MDIA)** [see Mortgage Disclosure Improvement Act, 12 CFR Part 226], and the **Mortgage Reform and Anti-Predatory Lending Act** (Title XIV of the Dodd-Frank Act of 2010) [see Dodd-Frank Act, Title XIV (Pub. L. 111-203)] establish disclosure requirements and prohibit equity stripping and other abusive practices.

Chapter Quiz

1. **The Civil Rights Act of 1866 prohibits what type of discrimination in property transactions?**
   A. familial status
   B. race
   C. religion
   D. sex

2. **The Fair Housing Act prohibits discrimination based on race, color, religion, sex,**
   A. age, disability/handicap, familial status, or national origin.
   B. disability/ handicap, familial status, marital status, or national origin.
   C. disability/handicap, familial status, or national origin.
   D. disability, national origin, or sexual orientation.

3. **Which law requires lenders to document how they are serving the lending needs within the communities in which they do business?**
   A. Equal Credit Opportunity Act
   B. Fair Credit Reporting Act
   C. Fair Housing Act
   D. Home Mortgage Disclosure Act

4. **Which act specifically prohibits redlining?**
   A. Civil Rights Act of 1866
   B. Equal Credit Opportunity Act
   C. Fair Housing Act
   D. Home Mortgage Disclosure Act

5. **As MLO Sam creates an ad to attract new customers, what law should he be most concerned about?**
   A. FACT Act
   B. GLBA
   C. RESPA
   D. TILA

6. **Mortgage fraud can be committed by**
   A. any party to a mortgage loan.
   B. appraisers only.
   C. borrowers only.
   D. lenders and brokers only.

7. **Which law prohibits kickbacks?**
   A. Fair Credit Reporting Act
   B. Gramm-Leach-Bliley Act
   C. Regulation Z
   D. RESPA

8. **Predatory lending involves all of the following EXCEPT**
   A. forcing the borrower to refinance a loan with inferior terms.
   B. misrepresenting the loan terms by the lender.
   C. requiring excessively high fees, such as for credit life insurance.
   D. requiring private mortgage insurance.

9. **Which situation is LEAST likely to be an example of predatory lending?**
   A. ABC Mortgage Co. offers a subprime loan to Mark, who is coming out of bankruptcy.
   B. Dave shows up at closing and finds that the lender has changed the terms of the loan.
   C. Ellie was 12 days late paying her mortgage and the lender raised the interest rate 1/4%.
   D. Frank paid off his mortgage loan early with lottery winnings and the lender charged a $12,000 prepayment penalty.

10. **Which situation does NOT involve a straw buyer?**
    A. Ann revises her pay stubs so she can qualify for a loan to buy her dream house.
    B. Bob uses his twin brother's Social Security number and credit information to apply for a loan.
    C. Dave agrees to secure a loan under his name, even though only his sister with bad credit will live in the house.
    D. Tina tells Rob, who is facing foreclosure, that if he deeds the property to her, she will refinance on good terms and let him stay in the house.

11. Cindy's customer, Tom, purposely does not tell her that he just co-signed his nephew's auto loan. The credit report shows neither that loan nor a credit inquiry, and so that debt is not considered when the lender preapproves him for a larger mortgage than he should have. Did Cindy do anything wrong?

    A. No, she can't be held responsible if a client withholds information that does not show on Tom's credit report.

    B. Yes, she colluded with Tom to withhold material information.

    C. Yes, she committed actual fraud by approving a purposely false application.

    D. Yes, she committed constructive fraud by not confirming Tom's debts.

12. Which of the following is NOT an indicator of predatory lending?

    A. charging excessive prepayment penalties

    B. falsifying loan documents

    C. increasing interest charges on late loan payments

    D. requiring mortgage insurance

13. If an ad mentions the interest rate on a specific loan product, that interest rate must be

    A. available for at least 10 business days.

    B. given to every applicant.

    C. locked in without a lock-in fee.

    D. made available to a reasonable number of qualified applicants.

14. An MLO takes an application and suspects that a Social Security number provided by the consumer may not be valid. What should the MLO do?

    A. approve the mortgage loan for the consumer if the middle credit score is 680 or above

    B. report the fraudulent number to the CFPB

    C. stop the application and inform the consumer that he cannot obtain a mortgage loan

    D. take the application and verify the validity of the Social Security number

Uniform
State Test

This chapter provides mortgage industry professionals with an overview and background information about the Uniform State Test (UST). The chapter reviews elements addressed by the UST, including mortgage regulatory authority of federal and state entities, licensing laws and requirements adopted by federal and state entities, and compliance conditions that affect mortgage industry professionals.

After completing this chapter, you will be able to:

- Identify the elements that affect the Uniform State Test.
- Recognize the regulatory authority of federal and state mortgage entities.
- Recognize the definitions of components and concepts in the mortgage industry.
- Identify licensing laws and requirements that regulate MLOs and other mortgage professionals.
- Describe compliance conditions and practices that apply to the mortgage industry.

KEY TERMS

Depository Institution
Dwelling
Individual
Loan Processor or Underwriter
Person

HERA and the SAFE Act

The Housing and Economic Recovery Act (HERA) of 2008, signed into law on July 30, 2008 (Public Law 110-289) , constitutes a major housing law designed to assist with the recovery and revitalization of America's residential housing market – from modernization of the Federal Housing Administration, to foreclosure prevention, to enhancing consumer protections. The SAFE Act is a key component of HERA.

The SAFE Act is designed to enhance consumer protection and reduce fraud by encouraging states to establish minimum standards for the licensing and registration of state-licensed mortgage loan originators. **It also called for the Conference of State Bank Supervisors (CSBS) and the American Association of Residential Mortgage Regulators (AARMR) to establish and maintain a nationwide mortgage licensing system and registry for the residential mortgage industry**. The objectives and other information about the legislation are available for review [see https://portal.hud.gov/hudportal/HUD?src=/program_offices/housing/rmra/safe/sfea].

The SAFE Act required states to have the licensing and registration system in place by: (1) July 31, 2009 for states whose legislatures meet annually; and (2) July 31, 2010 for states whose legislatures meet biennially.

The CSBS and AARMR spent considerable time reaching out to states and the financial services industry regarding the development of the Nationwide Mortgage Licensing System and Registry (NMLSR) and the development of legislation to meet the requirements of the SAFE Act. The CSBS and AARMR developed a model state law (MSL) designed to assist and facilitate states in the enactment of legislation on MLO licensing that complies with the SAFE Act under the deadlines imposed by the SAFE Act.

State Regulatory Authority

Title V—SAFE Act

The SAFE Act is a federal law that has jurisdiction in all states, the District of Columbia, as well as the U.S. territories of Puerto Rico, U.S. Virgin Islands, and Guam [see 12 CFR, Part 1026, Truth in Lending – Regulation Z §1026.2(a)(26) State].

Mandates of Public Law 110-289:

- **Industry**: All residential MLOs must be either state-licensed or federally registered.

- **States**: All states are required to have a system of licensing in place for residential MLOs that meets national definitions and minimum standards, including among other things: Criminal history and credit background checks, pre-licensure education, pre-licensure testing, continuing education, net worth, and surety bond or recovery fund.

- All states must license MLOs through the NMLS.

 The term "state" means any state of the United States, the District of Columbia, any territory of the United States, Puerto Rico, Guam, American Samoa, the Trust Territory of the Pacific Islands, the Virgin Islands, and the Northern Mariana Islands. (12 USC § 5102.11 State)

Exercise 12.1: Knowledge Check

1. The SAFE Act requires all MLOs to be federally registered with the NMLS.

    A. true
    B. false

2. The SAFE Act establishes national minimum standards for pre-licensing education and annual continuing education of MLOs.

    A. true
    B. false

State Regulatory Authority Agencies

The regulatory authority agency for each state may be referred to by a name similar to one of the following examples:

- Department of Financial Institutions
- Mortgage Regulatory Commission
- Division of Banking

State Regulatory Authority Responsibilities

Under the SAFE Act, the *minimum* requirements for each state's MLO regulatory authority include:

- Must provide effective ***supervision and enforcement of the law***, including the suspension, termination, or nonrenewal of a license for a violation of any state or federal law [see 12 CFR Part 1008, Subpart B, §1008.111(a)].

- Must ensure that all state-licensed MLOs operating in the state are ***registered*** with the NMLS [see 12 CFR Part 1008, Subpart B, §1008.111(c)].

- Must regularly ***report violations, as well as enforcement actions*** and other relevant information, to the NMLS [see 12 CFR Part 1008, Subpart B, §1008.111(d)].

- Must have a process in place for challenging information contained in the NMLS [see 12 CFR Part 1008, Subpart B, §1008.111(e)].

- Must have an established mechanism to ***assess civil money penalties*** for individuals acting as MLOs in the state without a valid license or registration [see 12 CFR Part 1008, Subpart B, §1008.111(b)(6)].

- Must have one of these protection options in place: An established ***minimum net worth or surety bonding requirement*** that reflects the dollar amount of loans originated by a residential MLO, or have an established ***recovery fund*** paid into by MLOs [see 12 CFR Part 1008, Subpart B, §1008.105(f)].

Exercise 12.2: Knowledge Check

1. Under the SAFE Act, the state regulatory authority is responsible for ensuring the proper and legal control of MLO licensing within the state.

   A. true

   B. false

2. Which of the following is NOT a financial protection method required of states by the SAFE Act?

   A. federal fund

   B. minimum net worth

   C. state fund

   D. surety fund

Broad Administrative Authority

The state regulatory authority must have broad administrative authority to administer, interpret, and enforce the SAFE Act, and to make the rules or regulations implementing the Act known, in order to carry out the intentions of the legislature [see 12 CFR Part 1008, Subpart B, §1008.111(b)].

State Examination Authority

In addition to any authority allowed under state law, a state-licensing agency must have the authority to conduct investigations and examinations [see 12 CFR Part 1008, Subpart B, §1008.111(a)(4)].

Authority to Access Information

For purposes of initial licensing and license maintenance, the state shall have access to all MLO or mortgage entity records [see 12 CFR Part 1008, Subpart B, §1008.111(b)(1)].

 It is prohibited to destroy or alter these records.

Investigation, Examination and Subpoena Authority

The state regulatory authority may review, investigate, or examine any licensee, individual, or person subject to the SAFE Act, *as often as necessary in order to carry out (i.e., audit records) the purposes of the Act* [see 12 CFR Part 1008, Subpart B, §1008.111(b)(2)].

Reports and Other Information

Each licensee, individual, or person subject to the SAFE Act shall make or compile reports or prepare other information as directed by the state regulatory authority in order to carry out the purposes of the Act [see 12 CFR Part 1008, Subpart B, §1008.111(b)(2)].

Mortgage Call Reports

Each mortgage licensee shall submit to the NMLS reports of condition, which shall be in such form and shall contain such information as the NMLS may require. The **Mortgage Call Report** contains two (2) report areas that are required to be submitted on a quarterly basis.

These two reports include:

1. **Residential Mortgage Loan Activity (RMLA)** - This component collects application, closed loan, individual MLO, line of credit, servicing, and repurchase information by state.

2. **Financial Condition (FC)** – This component collects financial information at the company level. It does not have to be completed by the state.

 For further information and requirements of mortgage call reports, visit:
http://mortgage.nationwidelicensingsystem.org/slr/common/mcr/Pages/default.aspx

Control of and Access to Records

In making any examination or investigation authorized by the SAFE Act, the state regulatory authority may control access to any documents and records of the licensee or person under examination or investigation.

Additional Authority

In order to carry out the purposes of the SAFE Act, the state regulatory authority may retain attorneys, accountants, or other professionals and specialists as examiners, auditors, or investigators to conduct or assist in the conduct of examinations or investigations.

Penalties

The state regulatory authority may impose a civil penalty on an MLO or person subject to the SAFE Act, if the state regulatory authority finds, after notice and opportunity for hearing, that such MLO or person subject to the Act, violated or failed to comply with any requirement of the SAFE Act, or any regulation prescribed by the state regulatory authority under the Act, or order issued under authority of the Act [see 12 CFR Part 1008, Subpart B, §1008.113(a)(3)].

*The **maximum** amount of penalty for each act or omission shall be $25,000.*

Each violation or failure to comply with any directive or order of the state regulatory authority is a **separate and distinct** violation or failure.

State Department Obligations

The state regulatory authority:

- Must establish a process whereby MLOs may challenge information entered into the NMLS.

- May be responsible for setting, or resetting as necessary, renewal or reporting dates.

- Must establish requirements for amending, transferring, or surrendering a license or any other license status change the state regulatory authority deems necessary for participation in the NMLS.

Fees to apply for or renew licenses may be remitted through the NMLS.

Exercise 12.3: Knowledge Check

The SAFE Act requires each state to control the mortgage lending industry by a system that issues, suspends, denies, or revokes the licenses of parties covered by the Act.

A. true
B. false

Regulatory Authority Limitations

State and federal regulating authorities do **not** have the authority, nor are they empowered, to impose a prison sentence.

MLOs, processors, and underwriters employed by credit unions and depository institutions (local, state, and federal banks and savings associations) are **not** required to be state-licensed under the SAFE Act. The exception requires that the employees of these institutions be registered through the NMLS and have an NMLS Unique Identifier [see 12 CFR Part 1008, Subpart B, §1008.103(e)(5)(6)].

CFPB Examinations

Any appointed examiner shall have power, on behalf of the CFPB (Bureau), to make any examination of any MLO, operating at any time, in any state, which is subject to a licensing system established by the Bureau, whenever the Bureau determines that an examination of any MLO is necessary to determine the compliance by the MLO with minimum requirements of the SAFE Act.

The cost of conducting any examination of any MLO operating in any state shall be assessed by the Bureau and may have to be paid by the MLO or the employing entity, or both.

Fees

The CSBS, AARMR, or the Bureau, as applicable, may charge reasonable fees to cover the costs of maintaining and providing access to information from the NMLS.

Compliance

Prohibited Conduct and Practices

It is a violation of the SAFE Act for a person or individual subject to the SAFE Act to:

- Directly or indirectly employ any scheme, device, or artifice to defraud or mislead borrowers or lenders or to defraud any person.
- Engage in any unfair or deceptive practice toward any person.
- Obtain property by fraud or misrepresentation.
- Solicit or enter into a contract with a borrower that provides in substance that the person or individual subject to this Act may earn a fee or commission through "best efforts" to obtain a loan, even though no loan is actually obtained for the borrower.
- Solicit, advertise, or enter into a contract for specific interest rates, points, or other financing terms, unless the terms are actually available at the time of soliciting, advertising, or contracting.
- Conduct any business covered by the SAFE Act without holding a valid license as required under the Act, or assist or aid and abet any person in the conduct of business under the SAFE Act without a valid license as required under the Act.
- Fail to make disclosures as required by the SAFE Act and any other applicable state or federal law, including regulations thereunder.
- Fail to comply with the rules or regulations promulgated under the SAFE Act, or fail to comply with any other state or federal law, including the rules and regulations thereunder, applicable to any business authorized or conducted under the SAFE Act.

- Make, in any manner, any false or deceptive statement or representation, or optional add-on, including, with regard to the rates, points, or other financing terms or conditions for a residential mortgage loan, or engage in bait and switch advertising.

- Negligently make any false statement or knowingly and willfully make any omission of material fact in connection with any information or reports filed with a governmental agency or the NMLS or in connection with any investigation conducted by the Commissioner or another governmental agency.

- Make any payment, threat, or promise, directly or indirectly, to any person for the purposes of influencing the independent judgment of the person in connection with a residential mortgage loan, or make any payment, threat, or promise, directly or indirectly, to any appraiser of a property, for the purposes of influencing the independent judgment of the appraiser with respect to the value of the property.

- Collect, charge, attempt to collect, or charge or use or propose any agreement purporting to collect or charge any fee prohibited by the SAFE Act.

- Cause or require a borrower to obtain property insurance coverage in an amount that exceeds the replacement cost of the improvements as established by the property insurer.

- Fail to truthfully account for monies belonging to a party to a residential mortgage loan transaction.

Required Conduct

The following conduct and activities would require an individual to be licensed as an MLO through the SAFE Act [see 12 CFR Part 1008, Subpart B, §1008.103(b)]:

- Taking a loan application

- Offering or negotiating loan terms

- Receiving any "thing of value" for compensation or gain when performing as an MLO

- Engaging in the business of an MLO with habitualness or repetition

- Performing as a loan processor or underwriter who is engaged in the business of an MLO while employed as an independent contractor

- Functioning as an attorney who is engaged in the business of an MLO

Exercise 12.4: Apply Your Knowledge

Identify whether an MLO's professional standing calls for License Required (**LR**) or No License Required (**NLR**) for the following tasks:

1.	Pass a federal test with a 75% score	LR	NLR
2.	Receive an application in the mail and forward the information without reviewing it	LR	NLR
3.	Provide a set of fingerprints with a license application	LR	NLR
4.	Explain contents of an application to a borrower	LR	NLR
5.	Describe loan application process to a borrower	LR	NLR
6.	Demonstrate financial responsibility	LR	NLR
7.	Arrange closing and other aspects of the mortgage process	LR	NLR
8.	Seller who provides financing to homebuyers for three or fewer properties in a year	LR	NLR
9.	Provide the borrowers an interest rate quote	LR	NLR

Taking a Loan Application

The SAFE Act is implemented through Regulation H, Part 1008 – SAFE Mortgage Licensing Act – State Compliance and Bureau Registration System, which is under Title 12, Banks and Banking, of the Code of Federal Regulations (CFR).

Taking a residential mortgage loan application, within the meaning of Section 1008.103(c)(1), means:

> *Receipt by an individual, for the purpose of facilitating a decision whether to extend an offer of loan terms to a borrower or prospective borrower, of an application as defined in Section 1008.23 (a request in any form for an offer, or a response to a solicitation of an offer, of residential mortgage loan terms, and the information about the borrower or prospective borrower that is customary or necessary in a decision whether to make such an offer).*

Taking a Loan Application: Example #1

An individual "**takes a residential mortgage loan application**," even if the individual:

- Has received the borrower's or prospective borrower's request or information **indirectly**. Section 1008.103(c)(1) provides that an individual takes an application, whether he receives it "**directly or indirectly**" from the borrower or prospective borrower.

This means that an individual who **offers or negotiates residential mortgage loan terms for compensation or gain** cannot avoid licensing requirements simply by having another person *physically* receive the application from the prospective borrower and then pass the application to the individual.

Taking a Loan Application: Example #2

An individual "**takes a residential mortgage loan application**," even if the individual:

- Is **not** responsible for verifying information. An individual who takes application information from a borrower or prospective borrower and is not responsible for verifying that information still takes the loan application.

This example highlights the fact that just because an individual is a mortgage broker who collects and sends information to a lender who makes the ultimate lending decision, that does not mean that the individual who receives the information is not taking an application.

Taking a Loan Application: Example #3

An individual "**takes a residential mortgage loan application**," even if the individual:

- Only inputs the information into an online application or other automated system, or
- Is **not** involved in approval of the loan, including determining whether the consumer qualifies for the loan.

Similar to an individual who is *not* responsible for verification, an individual can still "take a residential mortgage loan application" even if she is *not* ultimately responsible for approving the loan. For example, a mortgage broker can take a residential mortgage loan application, even though it is passed on to a lender for a decision on whether the borrower qualifies for the loan and for the ultimate loan approval. Therefore, she must be licensed.

Exempt Activities – Taking a Loan Application

Let's compare some examples of activities that do **not** constitute "taking a loan application" and would **not** require an MLO to be state-licensed.

Not Taking a Loan Application

An individual does **not** take a loan application merely because the individual:

- Receives a loan application through the mail and forwards it, without review, to loan approval personnel.

 The CFPB interprets the term "takes a residential mortgage loan application" to exclude an individual whose only role with respect to the application is physically handling a completed application form, or transmitting a completed form to a lender on behalf of a borrower or prospective borrower (i.e., administrative or clerical role) [see 12 CFR, Part 1008, Subpart B, §1008.103(e)(3)(4)].

Not Taking a Loan Application: Other Examples

An individual does **not** take a loan application merely because the individual assists a borrower, or prospective borrower, who is filling out an application by:

- **Explaining the contents** of the application and where particular borrower information is to be provided on the application.
- **Generally describing** the loan application process without a discussion of particular loan products.

An individual also does **not** take a loan application merely because the individual:

- **Responds to an inquiry** regarding a prequalified offer that a borrower, or prospective borrower, has received from a lender.
- **Collects only basic identifying information** about the borrower or prospective borrower on behalf of that lender.

Required Conduct: Offering or Negotiating the Terms of a Loan

The following examples are designed to illustrate when **an individual offers or negotiates terms of a loan** within the meaning of Section 1008.103(c)(2) and would require state licensing.

Presenting Particular Loan Terms: Example #1

Offering or negotiating the terms of a loan includes the following elements:

- Presenting for consideration by a borrower or prospective borrower particular loan terms, whether verbally, in writing, or otherwise, even if:
  - Further verification of information is necessary.
  - The offer is conditional.
  - Other individuals must complete the loan process.
  - The individual lacks authority to negotiate the interest rate or other loan terms.
  - The individual lacks authority to bind the person who is the source of the prospective financing.

Communicating a Mutual Understanding of Terms: Example #2

Communicating directly or indirectly with a borrower or prospective borrower for the purpose of reaching a mutual understanding about prospective residential mortgage loan terms, including responding to a borrower's or prospective borrower's request for a different rate or different fees on a pending loan application by presenting to the borrower or prospective borrower a revised loan offer, even if a mutual understanding is not subsequently achieved.

Exempt Activities – Offering or Negotiating Loan Terms

The following examples are designed to illustrate what does **not** constitute offering or negotiating terms of a loan within the meaning of Section 1008.103(c)(2):

- Providing general explanations or descriptions in response to consumer queries, such as explaining loan terminology (e.g., debt-to-income ratio) or lending policies (e.g., loan-to-value ratio policy of the lender), or describing product-related services
- Arranging the loan closing or other aspects of the loan process, including communicating with a borrower or prospective borrower about those arrangements, provided that any communication that includes a discussion about loan terms only verifies terms already agreed to by the borrower or prospective borrower
- Providing a borrower or prospective borrower with information unrelated to loan terms, such as the best days of the month for scheduling loan closings at the bank

- Making an underwriting decision about whether the borrower or prospective borrower qualifies for a loan
- Explaining or describing the steps that a borrower or prospective borrower would need to take in order to obtain a loan offer, including providing general guidance about qualifications or criteria that would need to be met that are not specific to that borrower or prospective borrower's circumstances
- Communicating on behalf of an MLO that a written offer has been sent to a borrower or prospective borrower without providing any details of that offer
- Offering or negotiating loan terms solely through a third-party licensed MLO, so long as the non-licensed individual does *not* represent to the public that he can or will perform covered activities and does *not* communicate with the borrower or potential borrower

Examples

- A seller who provides financing to a purchaser of a dwelling owned by that seller in which the offer and negotiation of loan terms with the borrower, or prospective borrower, is conducted exclusively by a third-party licensed MLO
- An individual who works solely for a lender, when the individual offers loan terms exclusively to third-party licensed MLOs and not to borrowers or potential borrowers

Required Conduct: For Compensation or Gain

An individual acts **"for compensation or gain"** within the meaning of Section 1008.103(c)(2)(ii) if the individual receives or expects to receive, in connection with the individual's activities, any **"thing of value,"** including, but not limited to, payment of a salary, bonus, or commission. The concept any "thing of value" is interpreted broadly and is not limited only to payments that are contingent upon the closing of a loan.

Exempt Activities – Not for Compensation or Gain

An individual does **not** act "for compensation or gain" if the individual acts as a volunteer without receiving, or expecting to receive, a "thing of value" in connection with the individual's activities.

Required Conduct: Engaging in the Business of an MLO

An individual who acts (or holds himself out as acting) as an MLO in a **commercial context** and with some degree of **habitualness** or **repetition** is considered to be "engaged in the business of an MLO."

Commercial Context

An individual who acts as an MLO does so in a **commercial context** if the individual acts for the purpose of obtaining anything of value for himself, or for an entity, or individual.

Habitualness or Repetition

The **habitualness** or **repetition** of the origination activities that is needed to "engage in the business of an MLO" may be met either if the individual who acts as an MLO does so with a degree of habitualness or repetition, or if the source of the prospective financing provides mortgage financing or performs other origination activities with a degree of habitualness or repetition.

Exempt Activities – Engaging in Business of MLO

The following examples illustrate when an individual generally does **not** "engage in the business of an MLO:"

1. An individual who acts as an MLO in providing financing for the sale of that individual's own residence, provided that the individual does not act as an MLO or provide financing for such sales so frequently and under such circumstances that it constitutes a habitual and commercial activity [Subject to 12 CFR 1026, §1026.36 as issued by the CFPB.]

2. An individual who acts as an MLO in providing financing for the sale of a property owned by that individual, provided that such individual does not engage in such activity with habitualness

3. A parent who acts as an MLO in providing loan financing to her child

4. An employee of a government entity who acts as an MLO only pursuant to her official duties as an employee of that government entity if all applicable conditions in Section 1008.103(e)(6) of this part are met

5. If all applicable conditions in Section 1008.103(e)(7) of this part are met, an employee of a nonprofit organization that has been determined to be a bona fide nonprofit organization by the state supervisory authority, when the employee acts as an MLO pursuant to her duties as an employee of that organization

6. An individual who does not act as an MLO habitually or repeatedly, if the source of prospective financing does not provide mortgage financing or perform other loan origination activities habitually or repeatedly

Loan Processing/Underwriting Activities that Require Licensing

An individual who is a **loan processor** or **underwriter** that must obtain and maintain a state MLO license includes any individual who:

- Engages in the business of an MLO as defined in the SAFE Act

- Performs clerical or support duties and who is an independent contractor, as those terms are defined in the SAFE Act

- Collects, receives, distributes, or analyzes information in connection with the making of a credit decision and who is an independent contractor, as defined in the SAFE Act

- Communicates with a consumer to obtain information necessary for making a credit decision and who is an independent contractor, as that term is defined in the SAFE Act

Loan Processing/Underwriting Activities that Do Not Require Licensing

A state is **not** required to impose SAFE Act licensing requirements on any individual loan processor or underwriter who:

- Performs only clerical or support duties (i.e., the loan processor's or underwriter's activities do not include, e.g., offering or negotiating loan rates or terms, or counseling borrowers or prospective borrowers about loan rates or terms) and who performs those clerical or support duties at the direction of and subject to the supervision and instruction of an individual who either:

  - Is licensed and registered in accordance with Section 1008.103(a) (state licensing of MLOs), or

- Is not required to be licensed because he is excluded from the licensing requirement pursuant to Section 1008.103(e)(2) (timeshare exclusion), (e)(5)(federally registered MLO), (e)(6) (government employees exclusion), or (e)(7) (nonprofit exclusion).

- Performs only clerical or support duties as an employee of a mortgage lender or mortgage brokerage firm, and who performs those duties at the direction of and subject to the supervision and instruction of an individual who is employed by the same employer and who is licensed in accordance with Section 1008.103(a) (state licensing of MLOs).

- Is an employee of a loan processing or underwriting company that provides loan processing or underwriting services to one or more mortgage lenders or mortgage brokerage firms under a contract between the loan processing or underwriting company and the mortgage lender or mortgage brokerage firms, provided the employee performs only clerical or support duties and performs those duties only at the direction of and subject to the supervision and instruction of a licensed MLO employee of the same loan processing and underwriting company.

- Is an individual who does not otherwise perform the activities of an MLO and is not involved in the receipt, collection, distribution, or analysis of information common for the processing or underwriting of a residential mortgage loan, nor is in communication with the consumer to obtain such information.

Actual Nexus

In order to conclude that an individual who performs clerical or support duties is doing so at the direction of and subject to the supervision and instruction of an MLO who is licensed or registered in accordance with Section 1008.103 (or, as applicable, an individual who is excluded from the licensing and registration requirements under Section 1008.103(e)(2), (e)(6), or (e)(7)), there must be an **actual nexus** (i.e., direct link) between the licensed or registered MLO's (or excluded individual's) direction, supervision, and instruction and the loan processor or underwriter's activities.

This actual nexus must be more than a nominal relationship on an organizational chart. For example, there is an actual nexus when:

1. The supervisory licensed or registered MLO assigns, authorizes, and monitors the loan processor or underwriter employee's performance of clerical and support duties.

2. The supervisory licensed or registered MLO exercises traditional supervisory responsibilities, including, but not limited to, the training, mentoring, and evaluation of the loan processor or underwriter employee.

Exercise 12.5: Knowledge Check

An individual who acts as an MLO in providing financing for the sale of her own residence would NOT require licensing as long as it is not a habitual and frequent activity.

A. true

B. false

Other Circumstances That Require a State MLO License

SAFE Act compliant licensing is required for a licensed attorney if the individual is engaged in the business of an MLO as defined in the SAFE Act [see 12 CFR, Part 1008, Subpart E, Appendix D(a)].

Other Circumstances That Do Not Require a State MLO License

SAFE Act compliant licensing is *not* required for a licensed attorney performing activities that come within the definition of an MLO [see 12 CFR, Part 1008, Subpart E, Appendix D(b)], if such activities are:

- Considered by the state's court of last resort (or other state governing body responsible for regulating the practice of law) to be part of the authorized practice of law within the state.

- Carried out within an attorney-client relationship.

- Accomplished by the attorney in compliance with all applicable laws, rules, ethics, and standards.

Advertising

The unique identifier of any person originating a residential mortgage loan shall be clearly shown on **all** residential mortgage loan application forms, solicitations, or advertisements, including business cards or websites, and any other documents as established by rule, regulation, or order of the state regulatory authority.

Prohibited Advertising Practices

It is **prohibited** for an MLO to:

- Solicit, advertise, or enter into a contract for specific interest rates, points, or other financing terms *unless* the terms are actually available at the time of soliciting, advertising, or contracting.

- Make, in any manner, any false or deceptive statement or representation, or optional add-on, including with regard to the rates, points, or other financing terms or conditions for a residential mortgage loan, or engage in bait and switch advertising.

Chapter Summary

1. The SAFE Act established national minimum standards for pre-licensing education and annual continuing education of MLOs.

2. The SAFE Act provides that all residential MLOs must be either state-licensed or federally registered.

3. The regulatory authority agency for each state may be referred to by a name similar to one of the following examples: Department of Financial Institutions, Mortgage Regulatory Commission, or the Division of Banking.

4. *Minimum* requirements for each state MLO regulatory authority under the SAFE Act include:

   - *Supervising and enforcing the law*, including the suspension, termination, or nonrenewal of a license for a violation of any state or federal law

   - Ensuring state loan originators are *registered* with (NMLS)

   - *Reporting violations, as well as enforcement actions* to the NMLS

   - Having an appeals process

   - Establishing a process for assessing civil money penalties and establishing a fund to compensate consumers injured by the actions of licensed MLO's

5. The state regulatory authority may issue orders or directives and order or direct persons subject to the SAFE Act to cease and desist from conducting business, including immediate temporary orders to cease and desist.

6. The state regulatory authority may impose a civil penalty on an MLO or mortgage licensee after proper notice and opportunity for an appeal hearing. The maximum amount of penalty for each act or omission shall be $25,000.

7. The state regulatory authority may set the date of renewal or reporting dates and establish requirements for amending, transferring, or surrendering a license, or any other license status change the state regulatory authority deems necessary.

8. An individual acts **"for compensation or gain"** within the meaning of Section 1008.103(c)(2)(ii) if the individual receives or expects to receive, in connection with the individual's activities, any **"thing of value,"** including, but not limited to, payment of a salary, bonus, or commission. The concept "any thing of value" is interpreted broadly and is not limited only to payments that are contingent upon the closing of a loan.

9. The unique identifier of any person originating a residential mortgage loan shall be clearly shown on **all** residential mortgage loan application forms, solicitations, or advertisements, including business cards or websites, and any other documents as established by rule, regulation, or order of the state regulatory authority.

10. SAFE Act compliant licensing is not required for a licensed attorney performing activities that come within the definition of an MLO if the work is ancillary to her legal practice.

11. It is prohibited for an MLO to solicit or advertise, or enter into a contract for specific interest rates, points, or other terms unless the terms are available at the time of soliciting, advertising, or contracting.

12. An MLO must not advertise or engage in bait and switch advertising.

Chapter Quiz

1. Under the SAFE Act, the state regulatory authority is responsible for the following minimum requirements EXCEPT

   A. enforcement of SAFE Act regulations.

   B. establishment of a monetary assessment penalty process for individuals who practice as MLOs without a license.

   C. maintenance of records and enforcement of violations for public access.

   D. registration of all MLOs with the NMLS.

2. To prove an individual performs only clerical duties under MLO supervision, which of the following provides an acceptable actual nexus?

   A. individual's employment contract

   B. MLO assigns and monitors the individual's clerical tasks

   C. MLO's title is manager and the individual's title is secretary

   D. organizational chart

3. Which of the following penalties is the state regulatory authority NOT authorized to administer?

   A. civil sanction

   B. license revocation

   C. monetary payment

   D. prison sentence

4. An individual's act is "for compensation or gain" when that individual

   A. achieves a profit (capital gain) from the transaction.

   B. has ownership interest in the transaction.

   C. is a W-2 employee.

   D. receives something of value.

5. Performing which task requires MLO licensing?

   A. analyzing a loan application that is received from a consumer

   B. communicating details of a loan closing arrangement

   C. making an underwriting decision

   D. offering or negotiating loan terms

6. Which is an example of "offering or negotiating the terms of a loan?"

   A. communicating details of loan closing arrangements

   B. communicating directly or indirectly with a borrower in order to reach a mutual understanding about prospective residential mortgage loan terms

   C. describing the steps that a borrower or prospective borrower would need to take in order to obtain a loan offer

   D. providing general explanations or responses to consumer inquiries about loan programs

Selected Consumer Protection Regulations

13

This chapter helps the loan originator recognize additional elements regarding the prohibition of kickbacks and related activities. The chapter reviews regulations that offer safeguards for consumer information, as well as recordkeeping and anti-money laundering requirements by financial institutions. It addresses additional points on other federal regulations that protect consumers' interests. Finally, the chapter identifies references for reviewing additional information about prohibiting illegal and illicit mortgage lending practices.

After completing this chapter, you will be able to:

- Identify regulations that prohibit illicit mortgage lending practices.
- Recognize federal requirements for anti-money laundering and recordkeeping by financial institutions.
- Recognize regulations that address mortgage assistance programs and financial records.

KEY TERMS

Dual Tracking
Loan Workout
Money Laundering
Mortgage Servicing

RESPA

As you learned earlier, RESPA is a consumer protection law that includes provisions to prohibit certain practices.

Mortgage Servicing

[See Consumer Financial Protection Bureau website: http://www.consumerfinance.gov/regulations/2013-real-estate-settlement-procedures-act-regulation-x-and-truth-in-lending-act-regulation-z-mortgage-servicing-final-rules/, *2013 Real Estate Settlement Procedures Act (Regulation X) and Truth in Lending Act (Regulation Z) Mortgage Servicing Final Rules*]

Mortgage servicers are required to provide a monthly billing statement to borrowers that detail:

- What is owed on the current bill and how much, if any, will be applied to principal, interest, and escrow. If the mortgage loan has multiple payment options, the statement must show whether the principal balance will increase, decrease, or stay the same for each option listed.
- Payments made since the last statement.
- How previous payments were applied.
- Transaction activity (including any fees or charges to the borrower's account).
- Contact information for the borrower's servicer.
- How to contact a housing counselor for help.
- Late payment information (if delinquent on payments).

Mortgage servicers must promptly credit mortgage payments when received [see 12 CFR Part 1026, Subpart C, §1026.36(c)]. Servicers must give a borrower credit for the full payment *as of the day the payment is received*. If only a partial payment is made, the servicer may hold the partial payment(s) in a special account. The servicer must disclose this on the monthly statement. When that special account collects enough money to make a full payment of principal, interest, and any escrow, the servicer must credit that payment to the borrower's account.

A mortgage servicer must respond to a payoff request *within seven (7) business days of receipt of the request.*

Mortgage servicers must set up their business so they can:

- Access correct information about a borrower's loan.
- Respond promptly and correctly to a borrower's problems.
- Pass along correct information about a mortgage account when the servicer sells a borrower's loan servicing to another company.
- Properly evaluate an application for relief when a borrower is having difficulties paying a mortgage loan.
- Keep records for *at least one year* after a mortgage loan is paid in full.

[See 12 CFR Part 1024, Subpart C, §1024.38 General servicing policies, procedures, and requirements.]

Force-Placed Insurance

[See 12 CFR Part 1024, Subpart C, §1024.37 Force-placed insurance.]

When a homeowner fails to keep his home insured, the lender has the right to buy and charge for *insurance to cover the lender's interest in the home*. This insurance is called **force-placed insurance**. Force-placed insurance is usually more expensive than a regular homeowner insurance policy, and it generally *only protects the lender*, not the homeowner or his possessions.

The rule says the servicer must:

- Alert a homeowner *at least 45 days* before it charges for a force-placed insurance policy.

- Warn the owner again *at least 30 days later* if he still hasn't provided proof of purchasing the needed insurance.

- Continue to accept the existing insurance policy, rather than buy force-placed insurance, if there is an escrow/impound account from which the servicer pays the insurance bill.

- Bill the homeowner only the bona fide cost of the force-placed insurance coverage.

A mortgage servicer must quickly resolve any consumer requests for information or complaints *in writing within 30-45 business days* [see 12 CFR Part 1024, Subpart C, §1024.36(d)(2)]. They are required to correct errors, provide borrower-requested information, or explain *in writing* the reason the creditor feels that no errors were made. An example of a mortgage servicer error may include:

- Failure to apply a payment correctly

- Charging improper fees

- Starting a foreclosure sale in violation of regulations

- Making an error in the servicing of a mortgage loan

- Failing to properly credit a payment when proof of receipt is provided

A mortgage servicer is required to implement and maintain good customer service policies and procedures [see 12 CFR Part 1024, Subpart C, §1024.36(d)]. They must provide access to correct information about a borrower's mortgage loan *within five business days*, respond promptly and correctly to consumer complaints, transfer correct information to any purchaser of a borrower's mortgage, and promptly evaluate a mortgagor's request for relief in the event a borrower is having difficulty making a mortgage payment.

Foreclosures/Modifications

[See 12 CFR, Part 1024, Subpart C, 1024.39 Early intervention requirements for certain borrowers.]

Part of the amendment to Regulation X implemented rules regarding home foreclosures and requests for modifications. A mortgage servicer is required to:

- Try to establish contact with the borrower *no later than 36 days* after a missed mortgage payment.

- Provide mortgage workout options to the borrower that may be available to him *within 45 days* after a missed payment.

Loan Workout

[For more information, see 12 CFR Part 1024, Subpart C, 1024.41(c)(d)(e).]

If a borrower is experiencing difficulty making payments, he can apply to the mortgage servicer for assistance in a **loan workout**, which involves *establishing new payment terms that are mutually agreed upon between the lender and delinquent borrower to get payments back on schedule.*

1. The borrower is required to submit an application and supporting documentation for help.

2. The lender, upon receipt of the application, has a *five-day window* to request additional information from the borrower.

3. Within *30 days after submission of a complete loan workout application*, the mortgage servicer must inform the borrower if there is an option to save the home.

After a loan workout request is received, one of the following will take place:

1. The servicer decides a borrower does not qualify for a loan workout, or

2. The borrower rejects the workout options that are offered by the mortgage servicer.

If both parties agree to the conditions, the new terms are implemented. Many times, there is a trial period before the new terms become permanent.

If a borrower submits an application for assistance *at least 90 days prior to a foreclosure sale*, the borrower may seek an independent review (appeal) of the mortgage servicer's workout decision. The servicer may not commence any action during this 90-day timeframe.

If a borrower has not submitted an application for assistance, a mortgage servicer must wait *120 days* before he is allowed to file for foreclosure or trustee's sale.

 If the foreclosure has commenced, the borrower may still have an opportunity to apply for a loan workout. If a borrower submits an application for assistance more than 37 days prior to the scheduled foreclosure sale, the loan servicer generally must address the request for help before proceeding with the repossession of the security.

Dual tracking is the term used *when servicers move forward on a foreclosure at the same time the mortgage servicer is working with a borrower on a workout plan.* Many consumers have discovered too late in the loan modification process that the lender had closed on a foreclosure sale during the modification process. **A foreclosure is not allowed unless all alternatives to foreclosure have been pursued**.

Exercise 13.1: Knowledge Check

1. **A mortgage servicer is required to respond to a payoff request within five (5) days.**
   A. true
   B. false

2. **A mortgage servicer may NOT contact a homeowner who misses a payment for at least 45 days from the date of the missed payment.**
   A. true
   B. false

Mortgage Assistance Relief Services (MARS)

Mortgage Assistance Relief Services (MARS) implements rules to address mortgage relief scams, which take advantage of distressed homeowners. The MARS administration is under CFPB authority. The following are part of the provisions of the Final Rule [for more information, see 12 CFR Part 1015, Mortgage Assistance Relief Services (Regulation O), http://www.ftc.gov/opa/2011/02/mars.shtm]:

- Ban on mortgage foreclosure rescue and loan modification servicers from collecting fees until *after* homeowners have a written offer from their lender or servicer that they decide is acceptable

- Requirement that mortgage relief companies disclose key information to consumers (e.g., company's fee, the fact that the company is not associated with the government, that the consumer has the right to discontinue doing business with the company at any time) to protect consumers from being misled and to help them make better-informed purchasing decisions

- Prohibition against making any false or misleading claims about their mortgage relief services; for example, any guarantees or the amount of money consumers will save

- Prohibition barring mortgage relief companies from advising consumers to discontinue communication with their lenders

- Requirement to retain certain records for at least **two years** from the date documents are created, generated, or received

Exercise 13.2: Knowledge Check

The MARS Rule requires financial institutions to disclose information to help consumers make informed decisions and prevent consumers from receiving misleading information.

- A. true
- B. false

FTC Safeguards Rule

[For more information about the Safeguards Rule, see http://business.ftc.gov/documents/bus54-financial-institutions-and-customer-information-complying-safeguards-rule]

The FTC adopted the Safeguards Rule to protect the security, confidentiality, and integrity of customer information by establishing standards for developing, implementing, and maintaining reasonable administrative, technical, and physical safeguards. The regulation applies to individuals or organizations that are significantly engaged in providing financial products or services to consumers.

Provisions

The following standards for protecting customer information are stated in federal regulations:

(a) Information security program. You shall develop, implement, and maintain a comprehensive information security program that is written in one or more readily accessible parts and contains administrative, technical, and physical safeguards that are appropriate to your size and complexity, the nature and scope of your activities, and the sensitivity of any customer information at issue. Such safeguards shall include the elements set forth in §314.4 and shall be reasonably designed to achieve the objectives of this part, as set forth in paragraph (b) of this section.

(b) Objectives. The objectives of section 501(b) of the Act, and of this part, are to:

(1) Insure the security and confidentiality of customer information;

(2) Protect against any anticipated threats or hazards to the security or integrity of such information; and

(3) Protect against unauthorized access to or use of such information that could result in substantial harm or inconvenience to any customer.

[See 16 CFR Part 314, §314.3 Standards for Safeguarding Customer Information, http://www.ecfr.gov/cgi-bin/retrieveECFR?gp=&SID=26159b913c45cadae826119820ba55c1&r=PART&n=16y1.0.1.3.38#16:1.0.1.3.38.0.32.3]

Definition of Consumer and Customer

The following information describing consumers and customers is stated in federal regulations [see http://www.ftc.gov/privacy/glbact/glboutline.htm].

A *"**consumer**" is an individual who obtains or has obtained a financial product or service from a financial institution that is to be used primarily for personal, family, or household purposes, or that individual's legal representative.* [See 16 CFR, Part 313, §313.3(e)(1).]

A *"**customer**" is a consumer who has a "customer relationship" with a financial institution. A "customer relationship" is a continuing relationship with a consumer.* [See 16 CFR, Part 313, §313.3(h).]

Examples of Establishing a Customer Relationship:

- *Opening a credit card account with a financial institution*
- *Entering into an automobile lease (on a non-operating basis for an initial lease term of at least 90 days) with an automobile dealer*
- *Providing personally identifiable financial information to a broker in order to obtain a mortgage loan*
- *Obtaining a loan from a mortgage lender*
- *Agreeing to obtain tax preparation or credit counseling services*

"Special Rule" for Loans:

- *The customer relationship travels with ownership of the servicing rights.*
- *A financial institution establishes a customer relationship with a consumer when it originates a loan.*
- *If it subsequently sells the loan and retains the servicing rights, it continues to have a customer relationship with the consumer.*
- *If it subsequently transfers the servicing rights, the entity that acquires servicing has a customer relationship with the consumer.*
- *Those with an ownership interest in the loan but without servicing rights have consumers.*

Bank Secrecy Act (BSA)

[For information about the Bank Secrecy Act, see https://www.fdic.gov/regulations/examinations/bsa/]

The **Financial Recordkeeping and Reporting of Currency and Foreign Transactions Act of 1970** (31 USC 1051) is known as the **Bank Secrecy Act (BSA)**. It requires financial institutions to maintain appropriate records and file reports for use in criminal, tax, or regulatory investigations or proceedings. Originally, the Act targeted criminal activities, such as money laundering and income tax evasion. It is also used to investigate financial transactions related to potential terrorist activities. The regulation (31 CFR §103) is issued by the Department of the Treasury.

 Under Treasury Department definitions, financial institutions include a variety of entities such as banks, securities dealers, money services businesses, casinos, commodities brokers, mutual funds, or persons under supervision of any state or federal bank supervisory authority [see 31 CFR, Part 1010, Subpart A, §1010.100(t) Financial institution.].

The BSA consists of two parts:

- **Title I - Financial Recordkeeping**: Requires insured financial institutions to maintain certain records.
- **Title II - Reports of Currency and Foreign Transactions**: Requires reporting of certain transactions greater than $10,000 by and through financial institutions into, out of, and within the United States.

Application to Banking/Mortgage Industry

The following information describing the purpose and scope of Suspicious Activity Reports (SARs) is stated in federal regulations [see 12 CFR Part 353 – Suspicious Activity Reports, http://www.ecfr.gov/cgi-bin/text-idx?SID=96ebf09a3be1d5456720b7978d7b59e7&node=12:5.0.1.2.42&rgn=div5#12:5.0.1.2.42.0.3.1].

§353.1 Purpose and Scope.

The purpose of this part is to ensure that an insured state nonmember bank files a Suspicious Activity Report when it detects a known or suspected criminal violation of federal law or a suspicious transaction related to a money laundering activity or a violation of the Bank Secrecy Act. This part applies to all insured state nonmember banks as well as any insured, state-licensed branches of foreign banks.

Requirements for Reporting

The reporting and recordkeeping provisions of the Bank Secrecy Act apply to depository institutions and other money service businesses (referred to as "non-banks"). Money service businesses are commonly referred to as "MSBs". MSBs that are required to register must prepare a list of their agents every January 1st. (Money Laundering Prevention, a Money Services Business Guide, US Department of the Treasury).

§353.31 Reports and Records.

(a) Suspicious activity reports required. A bank shall file a suspicious activity report with the appropriate federal law enforcement agencies and the Department of the Treasury, in accordance with the form's instructions, by sending a completed suspicious activity report to FinCEN in the following circumstances:

(1) Insider abuse involving any amount.

(2) Transactions aggregating $5,000 or more where a suspect can be identified.

(3) Transactions aggregating $25,000 or more regardless of potential suspects.

(4) Transactions aggregating $5,000 or more that involve potential money laundering or violations of the Bank Secrecy Act

The USA PATRIOT Act placed these additional record keeping requirements on many financial institutions, requiring them to record the total amounts of cash processed *worldwide* in areas where money laundering is a concern for the United States and where it is prevalent in that particular country. The Act also fostered the sharing of certain information between financial institutions to prevent undetected money laundering. Requirements for increased client identification measures were also required and implemented by the USA PATRIOT Act.

[See "USA PATRIOT Act," Financial Crimes Enforcement Network, https://www.fincen.gov/ resources/statutes-regulations/usa-patriot-act]

What is "Suspicious Activity?"

Suspicious activity is *any conducted or attempted transaction or pattern of transactions that you know, suspect, or have reason to suspect, meets any of the following conditions*:

1. Involves money from criminal activity.

2. Is designed to evade Bank Secrecy Act requirements, whether through structuring or other means.

3. Appears to serve no business or other legal purpose and for which available facts provide no reasonable explanation.

4. Involves use of a money services business to facilitate criminal activity.

Examples of Possible Suspicious Activity

1. A customer uses a false ID or multiple IDs on different occasions (name, address, or identification number may be different).

2. Two or more customers use the same or similar IDs (photo or name may be different).

Timing of Suspicious Activity Reports

1. A SAR must be filed within 30 days of detection of the suspicious transaction, although some activity may require an immediate reporting action.

2. It is illegal to tell any person involved in a transaction that a SAR has been filed. Maintaining the confidentiality of SARs prevents suspected individuals involved in criminal activity from structuring their activity to evade detection by law enforcement.

3. If an MSB determines that a Suspicious Activity Report should be filed, a SAR must be filed and a copy of the SAR retained for a minimum of five (5) years.

How to Report Suspicious Activity

1. Record relevant information on a Suspicious Activity Report by MSB (SAR-MSB) form, available at www. msb.gov or by calling the IRS Forms Distribution Center: 1-800-829-3676.

2. Submit the completed SAR to:

   Detroit Computing Center

   Attn: SAR-MSB

   P.O. Box 33117

   Detroit, MI 48232-5980

3. Keep a copy of the report and any supporting documentation for five years from the date of filing the report.

[For more information, see http://www.fincen.gov/ statutes_regs/guidance/pdf/msbsar_quickrefguide. pdf]

Additional Resources to Prevent Money Laundering

There are numerous resources that provide guidance for anti-money laundering laws. A loan originator can learn more about SARs and FinCen at https://www. fincen.gov/. The Office of Foreign Assets Control issues the Specially Designated Nationals and Blocked Entities List (SDN List), which identifies the assets of targeted countries, terrorists, drug cartels, and other specially designated persons. For these lists and compliance regulations, refer to the OFAC website at https://www. treasury.gov/about/organizational-structure/offices/ Pages/Office-of-Foreign-Assets-Control.aspx.

Exercise 13.3: Knowledge Check

The BSA requires financial institutions to maintain specified financial records and report financial transactions larger than $25,000.

    A. true

    B. false

Anti-Money Laundering (AML)

[For more information about anti-money laundering, check the following:

- For the USA PATRIOT Act, see: http://www.fincen.gov/statutes_regs/files/hr3162.pdf

- For the Financial Industry Regulatory Authority (FINRA) – Anti-Money Laundering Compliance Program, see: http://finra.complinet.com/en/display/display. html?rbid=2403&record_id=11859&element_id=8656

- For the Financial Crimes Enforcement Network (FinCEN), Anti-Money Laundering Programs for Financial Institutions – Federal Register /Vol. 67, No. 215 /Wednesday, November 6, 2002 /Rules and Regulations, p.67547, see: http://www.fincen.gov/statutes_regs/frn/ pdf/352tolling.pdf

Money laundering is the *process of concealing illicit sources of money to make it appear to be legitimate money.* Therefore, anti-money laundering activities are practices/regulations adopted by government and financial entities to prevent or control money laundering.

All MSBs are required to develop and implement an Anti-Money Laundering (BSA/AML) Compliance Program, as required by Section 352 of the USA PATRIOT Act and implemented at 31 CFR 1022.210:

- MSBs should file all BSA reports in an accurate and timely manner.

- All BSA reports must be retained for a period of **five years** and must be filed or stored in such a way as to be accessible within a reasonable period of time.

- The MSB should maintain records for the required time period and establish and maintain compliance programs.

AML Information

Money laundering involves three steps:

1. **Placement**: Illegitimate funds are furtively introduced into the legitimate financial system.

2. **Layering**: Money is moved around to create confusion, sometimes by wiring or transferring through numerous accounts.

3. **Integration**: The money is integrated into the financial system through additional transactions until the "dirty money" appears "clean."

Money laundering can facilitate crimes such as drug trafficking and terrorism, and can adversely impact the global economy.

In its mission to "safeguard the financial system from the abuses of financial crime, including terrorist financing, money laundering, and other illicit activity," the FinCEN acts as the designated administrator of the BSA. Since its creation, numerous other laws have enhanced and amended the BSA to provide law enforcement and regulatory agencies with the most effective tools to combat money laundering.

Money Laundering – Why Are You Required to Keep Records and File Reports?

Every year, money launderers try to cover up the illegal source of their money by funneling hundreds of millions of dollars through financial institutions, including money services businesses. Money laundering is most likely to be successful when criminals avoid leaving a "paper trail" of transactions linking the money back to their crime.

Law enforcement can follow the "paper trail" created from reports and records of financial institutions. By following federal recordkeeping and reporting requirements, financial institutions can help law enforcement prevent criminals from getting away with – and profiting from – their crimes.

[For more information, see http://www.fincen.gov/financial_institutions/msb/]

Red flags that may indicate that a MSB has been a party to criminal activity may include:

- Customer provides false or fraudulent identification

- Two or more customers use similar identification

- Customer alters the transaction when learning that he must provide identification

- Customer alters the spelling or order of his last name to avoid detection

[Further information regarding this topic may be accessed at https://www.fincen.gov/sites/default/files/guidance/msb_prevention_guide.pdf]

Exercise 13.4: Knowledge Check

The U.S.A. PATRIOT Act and the Financial Industry Regulatory Authority adopted regulations that enforce anti-money laundering requirements affecting financial institutions and brokerage firms in the United States.

A. true

B. false

Chapter Summary

1. A mortgage servicer is defined as the ongoing relationship with a mortgage borrower and the entity that accepts the borrower's payments, pays taxes and insurance (if escrowed), and works with the borrower in the event of loan default. A mortgage servicer must provide the borrower a monthly statement giving the borrower information on details of the payments she makes and other items. Mortgage servicing is regulated by RESPA, Section 10. Payments must be posted promptly when received. If there is a lapse in the homeowner's insurance coverage, servicers may purchase force-placed insurance, but must alert a homeowner at least 45 days before it charges for a force-placed insurance policy and remind the owner again at least 30 days later if he still hasn't provided proof of purchasing the needed insurance prior to billing the borrower. Servicer's must wait at least 15 days after the reminder notice before assessing the charge. If a borrower misses a payment, a servicer is required to contact her within 36 days of the missed payment. Workout options must be presented within 45 days of the missed payment. A mortgage servicer must wait 120 days after the date of default before taking legal action to repossess the security for the loan.

2. The Mortgage Assistance Relief Services regulation prohibits the collection of advance fees, making a false or misleading statement about services, or advising clients to discontinue communication with the current lender. In addition, it requires servicers to disclose key information to consumers. No fee may be accepted until a trial modification is delivered in writing to the borrower and accepted.

3. The FTC Safeguards Rules protect the security, confidentiality, and integrity of customer information. A consumer is an individual who obtained a product or service from a financial institution, such as a mortgage loan where the servicing is released to another entity. A customer is a consumer who has an ongoing relationship with a financial institution.

4. The Bank Secrecy Act requires financial institutions to maintain appropriate records and file reports for investigations or proceedings. The regulation is issued by the Treasury Department. There are two parts to the BSA: Financial recordkeeping and reports of currency and foreign transactions.

5. Money laundering is the process of concealing illicit sources of money in a transaction to make it appear legitimate. The Anti-Money Laundering regulations prohibit this process.

Chapter Quiz

1. **Mortgage servicers must do all of the following EXCEPT**

   A. credit mortgage payments promptly when received.

   B. provide a monthly billing statement with specific information.

   C. wait 120 days before taking legal action in the event of default.

   D. waive a late payment penalty fee when requested by the borrower.

2. **Force-placed insurance is**

   A. coverage for the borrower's furnishings when purchased.

   B. full coverage insurance purchased at closing by the buyer.

   C. insurance to pay the lender for a loss in the event of default.

   D. purchased by a lender when the borrower's insurance lapses.

3. **If a borrower misses a mortgage payment and applies to the servicer for assistance or modification, the servicer must wait _____ days before taking legal action.**

   A. 30

   B. 45

   C. 90

   D. 120

4. **The Mortgage Assistance Relief Services regulation applies to**

   A. down payment assistance programs.

   B. loan modification requests.

   C. new borrower loan originations.

   D. providing services for potential homebuyers in obtaining a new mortgage.

5. **A customer, according to the FTC, is an individual who**

   A. applies for a mortgage loan but does not consummate the mortgage.

   B. calls and inquires about interest rates offered by a firm.

   C. has an on-going relationship with a financial institution.

   D. obtains a service or product from a financial institution.

6. **BSA/AML regulations are implemented to**

   A. facilitate the opening of a checking or savings account.

   B. license and regulate mortgage loan originators.

   C. oversee credit reporting acts.

   D. prevent money laundering.

Financials and Calculations Review

This chapter reviews different types of financial payments associated with mortgages. It identifies loan-to-value conditions affecting mortgages. The chapter also presents information about mortgage closing costs and prepaid items.

After completing this chapter, you will be able to:

- Identify different types of financial payments.
- Recognize mortgage loan-to-value conditions.
- Determine mortgage closing costs and prepaid items.

KEY TERMS

Acquisition Cost

Buydown, Permanent

Buydown, Temporary

Closing Costs

Debt-to-Income Ratio

Down Payment

Fully Indexed Rate

Hazard Insurance

Housing Expense Ratio

Loan-to-Value (LTV)

Periodic/Prepaid Interest

Prepaid Expenses

Private Mortgage Insurance (PMI)

Qualifying Ratios

Periodic Interest

When performing proration calculations, expenses may be prorated using:

- A 360-day year, 12 months of 30 days each.
- A 365-day year, counting the exact number of days in each month (taking leap years into account).

It is best to consult with the lender to determine whether to use a 360- or a 365-day calendar.

To calculate **periodic or per diem (per paid) interest**, you must determine the amount of daily interest. This is done by multiplying the loan amount by the note rate. The result will be the annual interest charge. To calculate the daily interest, divide this product by either 360 or 365.

For Example

Assume a loan amount of $235,000 with a note rate of 6.25%:

$ 235,000	Loan amount
x .0625	Interest rate
$14,687.50	Annual interest
/ 365	Days per year
$40.2397	Per diem interest charge

If a borrower's loan funds on September 13 and September has 30 days in the month, there would be 18 days from the day of funding to October 1.

The prepaid interest charge, which is charged to the borrower, would be $40.2397 x 18 days = $724.32.

Prepaid Expenses

Prepaid expenses are the *items on a Closing Disclosure the seller has already paid;* for example, condominium association fees or property tax in counties where it is paid in advance. In some cases, prepaid expenses are paid by the borrower (e.g., in a refinance, the borrower may have to pay property taxes in advance at the close of escrow). Usually, prepaid expenses are prorated on the Closing Disclosure as a credit to the seller and a debit to the buyer. Whichever party is responsible for making the payment receives the credit; the other party receives the debit.

Often, local custom dictates which factor is used. Either way, the steps to calculate the adjustment are similar:

1. Determine if the expense is accrued or prepaid.
2. Divide the expense by the appropriate period to find a monthly (daily) rate.
3. Determine how many months (days) are affected by the expense.
4. Multiply the monthly (daily) rate by the number of affected months (days).
5. Determine which party is credited and which is debited.

Credit for items, such as taxes, HOA fees, etc., that have been prepaid by the seller are calculated from the date of settlement to the date the items are paid through. These items will show on the Closing Disclosure as a credit to the sellers.

Items not paid by the seller, but due to be paid, are shown as a credit to the borrower/buyer and a debit to the seller, therefore reducing their cash proceeds. Examples of these items could include unpaid property taxes, unpaid property assessments, etc. These items will show on the closing disclosure.

The method of calculating pro-rated items for a credit to the borrower or seller uses the same method of proration as shown above for calculating prepaid interest.

Payments

To calculate an **interest-only payment**, the loan amount is multiplied by the contract or note rate and divided by 12.

For Example

Assume a loan amount of $235,000 with a note rate of 6.25%:

$ 235,000	Loan amount
x .0625	Interest rate
$14,687.50	Annual interest charge
/ 12	Number of months in a year
$1,223.96	**Interest only payment per month**

To calculate **monthly property taxes (or improvement district assessments),** assume that property taxes are reported as $1,500 per half year. Taxes per month would be calculated as:

$1,500	Property taxes per half year
/ 6	Number of months in one-half year
$250	**Per month property tax payment**

To calculate monthly insurance (hazard, condominium or flood), assume that the homeowner's insurance is reported to cost $636 per year. Monthly cost for the HOI is calculated as follows:

$636	Annual homeowner's insurance premium
/ 12	Number of months in one year
$53	**Per month homeowner's (e.g., hazard) insurance payment**

To calculate **monthly private mortgage insurance (PMI),** assume that DU underwriting requires the loan amount to carry 25% coverage with a PMI factor of .52%. To calculate the monthly charge for private mortgage insurance, use the following calculations:

$235,000	Loan amount
x .0052	PMI factor expressed as a decimal
$ 1,222	**Annual PMI payment**
/ 12	Number of months in a year
$101.83	**Per month PMI charge**

The total monthly payment would be:

Housing expense payment	$1,223.96
Monthly property tax payment	250.00
Monthly hazard insurance payment	53.00
Monthly PMI charge	+ 101.83
Total monthly housing expense	**$1,628.79**

Exercise 14.1 : Knowledge Check

When the initial loan amount is multiplied by the note rate, the result is known as the

- A. annual interest charge.
- B. monthly interest-only payment.
- C. monthly PMI payment.
- D. total housing expense.

PITI Payments

Remember, a monthly mortgage payment is commonly referred to as **PITI** (principal, interest, taxes, and insurance). *This payment represents the combination of the four basic elements of a typical monthly mortgage payment.* Principal and interest payments go toward repaying the mortgage loan. Amounts covering property taxes, homeowner's insurance, and mortgage insurance (if applicable) may go into an escrow account (if required or chosen) to be paid as they come due. PITI is generally used in conjunction with gross income to determine whether maximum debt ratios allowed by loan programs have been exceeded.

[See "What is PITI?" Consumer Financial Protection Bureau, February 24, 2017, https://www.consumerfinance.gov/ask-cfpb/what-is-piti-en-152/]

Down Payment

To calculate a down payment for a home purchase, an MLO first must know the minimum requirements for down payment of each individual loan type. For example, a conventional conforming loan requires a 5% down payments (from the borrower's own funds), an FHA insured loan requires a 3.5% down payment (can be a gift), and VA and USDA guaranteed loans do *not* require a down payment.

For Example

If a property has a sale price of $187,000 and appraised value of $190,000, a conventional conforming loan with a down payment of 5.00% will require a cash down payment of $9,350.

$187,000	**Lesser of sale price or appraised value**
x .05	**Down payment requirement expressed as a decimal**
$ 9,350	**Cash down payment requirement**

If a property has a sale price of $190,000 and an appraised value of $187,000, an FHA-insured loan requires 3.5% down payment and a cash down payment of $6,545.

$187,000	**Lesser of sale price or appraised value**
x .035	**Down payment required expressed as a decimal**
$ 6,545	

 Remember to *always* base the loan amount and/or the down payment amount on the lesser of the sale price or the appraised value.

Loan-to-Value

The loan-to-value is expressed as the proposed or unpaid loan balance, which is in a first lien position, divided by the lesser of the sale price or appraised value.

For Example

If a property has a sale price of $187,000 and appraised value of $190,000 with a loan amount of $142,100, calculate the loan-to-value as follows:

$142,100	**Proposed loan amount**
/ $187,000	**Lesser of sale price or appraised value**
75.99%	**Loan-to-value**

Combined Loan-to-Value

The combined loan-to-value (CLTV) is expressed as the combined total of all lien balances of a property, divided by the lesser of the sale price or appraised value.

For Example

IIn the previous scenario, there was a first lien of $142,100 and an appraised value of $187,000. If the borrower obtained secondary financing (or applied for a HELOC or second equity loan) for $15,000, the combined loan-to-value would be calculated as follows:

$157,100	**Total of all liens ($142,100 (first lien) + $15,000 (subordinate lien))**
/ $187,000	**Lesser of sale price or appraised value**
84.01%	**Combined loan-to-value**

Exercise 14.2: Knowledge Check

When the initial loan amount is divided by the lesser of the sale price or the current appraised value, the result is known as the

A. annual interest charge.
B. combined loan-to-value.
C. housing ratio.
D. loan-to-value.

Income Calculations

The income a borrower can use for loan qualification must be stable and consistent and may be required to be received for a certain time period.

 When calculating a borrower's income, always use the gross monthly income before any deductions are made to the borrower's pay.

To calculate income for a borrower, use the following methods:

Hourly Wage

For a borrower who receives an **hourly wage**:

Hourly Wage x # Hours Worked per Week x 52 (Weeks per Year) ÷ 12 (Number of Months in a Year)

For Example

A borrower, who is paid $14.50 per hour and works 30 hours per week, receives monthly pay of $1,885 per month.

$14.50 x 30 x 52 = $22,620 ÷12 = $1,885 income per month

Bi-Weekly Salary

For a borrower who receives a **bi-weekly fixed salary**:

Bi-Weekly Pay x 26 (# of Paydays per Year) ÷ 12 (Number of Months in a Year)

For Example

A borrower who is paid $1,000 bi-weekly receives a monthly pay of $2,166.67 per month.

$1,000 x 26 = $26,000 ÷ 12 = $2,166.67 income per month

Semi-Monthly Salary

For a borrower who receives a **semi-monthly fixed salary** (twice per month):

Gross Pay x 2 (# of Paydays per Month) = Gross Monthly Income

For Example

A borrower who is paid $1,000 semi-monthly (twice per month) receives a monthly pay of $2,000 per month.

$1,000 x 2 (Paydays per Month) = $2,000 income per month

Debt-to-Income Ratios

The debt-to-income ratios vary by the type of loan the borrower obtains. The MLO should know the debt-to-income ratio guidelines for each loan program and how to correctly calculate the ratios. The **housing expense ratio** (also called front-end ratio) is *the relationship of a borrower's total monthly housing expense (PITI) to gross monthly income, expressed as a percentage (Housing Expense ÷ Income = Ratio %)*. Conventional/conforming qualifying guidelines allow a housing expense ratio of **28%** and a total debt-to-income ratio of **36%**. Remember, FHA loan guidelines allow a **31%** front-end ratio and **43%** back-end ratio. VA loans have no front-end ratio and a **41%** back-end ratio.

In the previous example (see Payments, *"Calculate monthly private mortgage insurance"*), we calculated a monthly housing payment as follows:

Housing expense payment	$1,223.96
Monthly property tax payment	250.00
Monthly hazard insurance payment	53.00
Monthly PMI charge	+ 101.83
Total monthly housing expense	**$1,628.79**

For a borrower who earns an annual salary of $84,000 per year, his gross monthly income is $7,000 per month ($84,000 per year/12 months).

Calculation of his total housing expense is:

$1,628.79 ÷ $7,000 = **23.27% housing debt-to-income ratio**

Assume the borrower had the following monthly debt:

Monthly Payment Amount	Outstanding Balance
Auto = $200	$3,600
Child support = $300	15 years remaining
VISA = $50	$350
Cell phone = $120	3 months left on contract
Student loan = $50	$375

The auto payment, the child support payment, and the VISA card payment, which total $550, are the only debt payments required to be used in the calculation. Since the cell phone and student loan payments have than 10 payments remaining at the time of loan closing, they are not counted.

Calculation of the total debt-to-income ratio is as follows:

PITI payment + other required debt payments ÷ Gross monthly income = DTI

$1,628.79 + $550 = $2,178.79 ÷ $7,000 = **31.13% total debt-to-income ratio**

Exercise 14.3 : Apply Your Knowledge

Directions: Review the following information, and then complete the calculations.

Borrower's Payment:

A borrower earns $15.75 per hour and works 40 hours per week. He wants to be prequalified for FHA home financing with a PITI payment of no more than his current rental payment of $1,000 per month. He has a truck payment of $250 per month and a credit card payment of $25 per month. He intends to obtain a loan from his 401K account for the 3.5% down payment.

What is the maximum payment amount for which the borrower can qualify?

_____

_____

_____

Exercise 14.4 : Knowledge Check

When the PITI payment is divided by the gross monthly income, the result is known as the

A. annual debt payment ratio.
B. back ratio.
C. gross monthly interest-only payment.
D. housing expense ratio.

Temporary and Fixed Interest Rate Buydown – Discount Points

A buydown may be *temporary (for a defined time period during the loan)* or permanent *(for the life of the entire loan)*. Either calculation of the cost for the interest rate buydown is **always based** on the loan amount.

If a property has a sale price of $187,000 and appraised value of $190,000, with a loan amount of $142,100 and a cost of two points, the cost of the buydown would be calculated as follows:

$142,100 (loan amount) x .02 (discount points) = $2,842 (buydown cost)

Temporary buydowns can take two forms:

1. **Level payment buydown** - A plan with the *payment reduction remaining constant throughout the buydown period.*

2. **Graduated payment buydown** - A plan for which *payment subsidies in the early years keep pay-ments low, but payments increase each year as indicated in the note.*

For example, a **2-1 buydown** is a graduated payment buydown with the payments subsidized for only two years—for example, 2.5% below the interest rate in the first year and 1.5% the second year. By the third year, the borrower is paying the fully-indexed interest rate,

Acquisition Cost

The **acquisition cost** is defined as *the total amount needed to purchase property, including down payment, loan amount, and any allowable buyer-paid closing costs.*

Assume that the sale price is $187,000, the loan amount is $142,100, and the closing costs are $5,500, including two discount points to buy down the interest rate to a permanent rate of 6.25%. The acquisition cost is calculated as follows:

Purchase price	$187,000
Borrower-paid closing costs	+ $5,500
Total acquisition cost	**$192,500**

 In this problem, the loan amount and the interest rate are not pertinent to the calculation of the acquisition cost.

If the seller agreed to pay two discount points, the acquisition costs would be as follows:

Purchase price	$187,000
Borrower-paid closing costs	+ $5,500
Seller-paid points	– $2,842 (2% of $142,100 loan)
Total acquisition cost	$189,658

Closing Costs

Closing costs are defined as *expenses incurred in the transfer of real estate in addition to the purchase price* (e.g., appraisal fee, title insurance premiums, broker's commission, transfer tax)

In the previous scenario, the buyer's total closing costs were $5,500. This fee included all of the costs of acquiring the property, including the appraisal fee, title insurance company fees, lender costs, etc.

To calculate the borrower cash required to close the transaction, the following computation is required:

Sale price	$187,000
Loan amount	– $142,100
Down payment required	$44,900
Closing costs	+ $5,500
Total cash required to close	$50,400

If the seller paid two discount points (or $2,842), this amount would be subtracted from the cash required to close and the resulting cash needed would be $47,558.

Total cash required to close	$50,400
Discount points (2)	– $2,842
Net cash required to close	$47,558

ARMs – Fully Indexed Rate

In an adjustable rate mortgage, the **fully indexed rate** is defined as *the sum of the current numerical value of the index value used and the margin, as defined in the note.*

A borrower has a one-year adjustable rate mortgage. The start rate is 3.5% and the margin is 2.5%. The index is the One Year Treasury Constant Maturity (TCM), whose index was 1.5% when the loan was closed. At the time of the first rate adjustment, the index is 2.25%.

To calculate the fully indexed rate at the time of the first adjustment, perform the following computation:

Index value	2.25%
Margin	+ 2.5%
Fully indexed rate	4.75%

Chapter Summary

1. On the Closing Disclosure, items are prorated to compensate the buyer or the seller for unpaid or prepaid expenses.

2. Prepaid interest is the charge a lender makes for the use of the asset from the date of funding to the first day of the next month. To calculate prepaid interest, the MLO must take the annual interest charge and divide it by the number of days in the year (360 or 365) that the lender requires. This product is multiplied by the number of days from closing through the end of the month of closing.

3. To calculate an interest-only payment, the initial loan amount is multiplied by the note rate (expressed as a decimal) and divided by 12 (months per year).

4. Property taxes, property improvement assessments, homeowner's association fees, assessments, and all forms of insurance premiums are converted to monthly payments and are included as a part of the PITI payment.

5. The down payment is the lesser of the sale price or appraised value minus the sum of the loan amounts being obtained for a property.

6. The loan-to-value is known as the first mortgage loan amount shown in relation to the lesser of the sale price or appraised value.

7. The combined loan-to-value is the sum of all outstanding liens on a subject property shown in relation to the lesser of the sale price or appraised value.

8. In calculating a borrower's qualifying income, only stable and continuous income may be used. The annual income that is calculated must be converted to a monthly income in order to accurately assess the borrower's debt-to-income ratios. Use only the borrower's gross monthly income before any deductions from income are made.

9. The cost of discount points, whether paid to temporarily or permanently lower the interest rate, is based on the loan amount.

10. The acquisition cost is the purchase price of a property plus any closing costs the borrower is responsible for paying. This is the amount the buyer pays to the closing agent to consummate the purchase.

11. The closing costs are the expenses incurred when a property is sold or refinanced. They include lender costs, taxes, all types of insurance, transfer taxes, appraisal fees, and escrow/title insurance fees.

12. When the down payment required is added to the closing costs, this amount is known as the cash to close.

13. The fully indexed rate of an adjustable rate loan is the sum of the current index value and the margin, as specified in the note.

Chapter Quiz

1. Bob is buying a house that was appraised at $236,000, the sales price is $228,000, and the loan amount is $216,800. To buydown his interest rate, Bob is willing to pay two points in addition to the one point in loan origination fees. What is the price of Bob's discount points?

   A. $4,336
   B. $4,720
   C. $6,840
   D. $7,080

2. A borrower has a stable monthly gross income of $3,200 and recurring monthly debts of $370. What is the maximum amount of money available to him for monthly housing expenses to qualify for a conforming loan?

   A. $782
   B. $896
   C. $928
   D. $1,152

3. If $90,000 is the loan amount on a $100,000 home with a Fannie Mae/Freddie Mac coverage rate of 0.62%, what is the monthly PMI cost?

   A. $18.75
   B. $46.50
   C. $90.00
   D. $108.00

4. A borrower offers to purchase a home for $120,000. His first mortgage amount is $90,000 and the seller is providing a second mortgage of 15% of the sale price. The borrower provides the balance as a cash down payment. What are the LTV and CLTV?

   A. 70% / 85%
   B. 75% / 15%
   C. 75% / 90%
   D. 80% / 90%

5. A potential borrower is applying for a conventional loan to purchase a primary residence. Currently, he pays $500 in rent, $420 for an auto loan, $170 toward his VISA bill, and $300 on a student loan each month. His gross monthly income totals $4,900 and his take-home pay after taxes is $3,700. What is the maximum housing payment for which he can qualify?

   A. $701
   B. $874
   C. $1,036
   D. $1,372

6. Borrower Stu wants to get an FHA loan for a home priced at $253,500 and appraised for $257,000. The monthly PITI payment on this house would be $1,780. He has a 680 credit score, gross monthly income of $6,850, other monthly recurring debts of $850, and a $75 monthly electric bill. Stu will finance the 1.75% UFMIP into the loan amount. What is Stu's minimum down payment for the home purchase?

   A. $0
   B. $8,872.50
   C. $8,995.00
   D. $9,027.77

7. A borrower purchases a property for $200,000 and pays 20% of the sale price as a down payment. The owner provides a purchase money mortgage at 6% per annum, interest-only monthly payments with a balloon payment in 60 months. In the 40th month, the borrower is approached to sell the property for $240,000. How much equity does the borrower have and what will his sale proceeds be (without any other closing costs)?

   A. $40,000
   B. $72,000
   C. $80,000
   D. $240,000

8. A borrower earns $4,500 weekly and the co-borrower earns $2,400 bi-weekly. If they wish to obtain a conforming loan, what is the maximum PITI payment they qualify for?

   A. $6,384

   B. $6,804

   C. $6,916

   D. $100,464

9. If a borrower pays $695.20 per month for principal and interest on a $110,000 loan for a 30-year term and the interest rate is 5.25%, what is the amount of interest the borrower will pay over the life of the loan?

   A. $90,856

   B. $107,750

   C. $140,272

   D. $250,272

The Successful Mortgage Loan Closing

15

This chapter introduces the MLO to the loan closing process and explores the requirements and components of a successful mortgage loan closing. The MLO will learn the basics of the appraisal process, how an appraiser develops a value for a particular type of real estate, and how the final conclusion and appraised value is derived. Also discussed are the requirements and details of homeowner's or hazard insurance, flood insurance, PMI, and title insurance.

This chapter also describes some of the challenges an MLO may face in working with clients, including how to avoid client complaints as well as how to handle a complaint when one is received.

After completing this chapter, you will be able to:

- Identify the components and requirements of a successful loan closing.
- Describe appropriate and effective methods of dealing with challenging scenarios in the MLO's daily routine.

Key Terms

Accrued Expenses	Easement	Prepaid Expenses
Acquisition Cost	Encumbrance	Proration
Chain of Title	Lien	Settlement Agent
Closing	Lis Pendens	Title Insurance
Cloud on the Title	Marketable Title	

Real Estate Appraisals

An **appraisal** is *an estimate or opinion of value as of a certain date that is supported by objective data from the marketplace.* There are several important concepts in that short definition.

- An appraisal is only an estimate or opinion; it is not a guarantee of value. While it is an opinion of value, however, it must be supportable and based on facts.

- The estimate of value is as of a certain date. As change is constantly occurring, the value is also subject to constant change. Therefore, an appraisal is only valid as of its effective date, which establishes terms, conditions, and economic circumstances upon which the value is estimated.

The appraisal industry is a regulated industry, as prescribed by Congress in 1989 with the passing of the H.R.1278 - Financial Institutions Reform, Recovery, and Enforcement Act of 1989, commonly known as **FIRREA**. In this bill, the certification and licensing of appraisers for all federally-related transactions were implemented. Appraisal requirements continue to mandate this requirement.

"Title XI: Real Estate Appraisal Reform Amendments - Amends the Federal Financial Institutions Examination Council Act of 1978 to establish the Appraisal Subcommittee to monitor: (1) State and Federal certification and licensing of appraisers involved in federally-related transactions; and (2) the procedures and activities of the Appraisal Foundation. Requires the Subcommittee to submit an annual status report to the Congress and to maintain a national registry of State-licensed appraisers eligible to perform appraisals in federally-related transactions. Mandates that each State whose appraiser certification and licensing program complies with this Act transmit to such Subcommittee an annual roster of appraisers eligible to conduct federally-related transactions.

Directs the appraisal Subcommittee to report to the Congress the results of studies regarding: (1) the sufficiency of real estate data to permit appraisers to estimate property values properly in federally-related transactions; and (2) the feasibility of extending the appraisal provisions of this Act to personal property relating to Federal financial and public policy interests."

[See H.R.1278 - Financial Institutions Reform, Recovery, and Enforcement Act of 1989, https://www.congress.gov/bill/101st-congress/house-bill/1278]

An appraisal is developed by a certified and licensed appraiser. There are education and apprenticeship requirements to become a certified and licensed appraiser. All appraisals are ordered, usually by the loan processing staff, through an **appraisal management company** (AMC) to maintain the appraisal independence that is required for a federally-regulated loan transaction. The AMC:

a) "Administers an appraiser panel of independent contract appraisers to perform real property appraisal services in this state for clients.

b) Receives requests for real property appraisal services from clients and, for a fee paid by the client, enters into an agreement with one or more independent appraisers to perform the real property appraisal services contained in the request.

c) Otherwise serves as a third-party liaison of appraisal management services between clients and appraisers."

[See https://boa.az.gov/directories/amc]

Appraisal Approaches

Appraisers value properties using three different approaches. Each approach is independent of the others and is performed separately to arrive at an opinion of value. Many factors can drive the appraiser's choice in the application of the approaches, such as the type of property being appraised and the type and extent of research and analysis needed in an assignment. As a result, the appraiser could elect to use one, two, or all three approaches.

Sales Comparison Approach. Develops an opinion of value of real property by comparing the property being appraised with other similar properties, called comparables or comps, which have sold recently in the same market area as the subject property. This approach is most often used in evaluating residential real property. **The sales comparison approach is considered the most useful and accurate of the three appraisal methods because it is rooted in actual market activity.** This is implied in the Fannie Mae definition of market value as the most probable price that a property should bring in a competitive and open market. With a truly objective appraisal, another buyer should agree with the value and be willing to pay the same price for the property. By looking at enough comparable sales, the assumption is made that the resulting appraisal analysis reflects the actions of typical real estate buyers in the marketplace.

Cost Approach. Develops an opinion of value for a property by calculating the cost of the land, site improvements, the cost to build the structure on the land, and the cost of any depreciation to the property to reproduce the property. **The cost approach is best used for relatively new construction or for unusual or special purpose properties that have few or no comparables and do not produce income, such as hospitals, schools, or churches.**

Income Approach. Sometimes called the capitalization approach, the income approach estimates the value of real estate by analyzing the revenue, or income, the property currently generates or could generate, often comparing it to similar properties. **This approach is most widely used with commercial or investment properties.**

Reconciliation

Opinions of value from all fully-developed approaches are reconciled to arrive at the best estimate of value. Rarely, if ever, are the value estimates from these three approaches equal. The estimates from each of the three approaches are never merely averaged. This is where the appraiser's knowledge and experience are invaluable. **Reconciliation** involves *giving each method an appropriate weight depending on the type of property being analyzed and the amount and accuracy of data available.*

Updating or Recertifying an Appraisal

Sometimes it may be necessary to readdress an appraisal, such as when a new lender evaluates a loan application. While it may seem to be a simple request from a lender's perspective, an appraiser is obligated to consider a request to readdress—or update—an appraisal as a new assignment. This makes sense when you recall that an appraiser's opinion of value is technically valid only as of the date of the appraisal, so if the lender is looking for a more current value, a new appraisal is required.

A **recertification of value (recert)** or a **442 recertification of value** may be necessary to confirm whether certain conditions in the original appraisal have been met, such as when the property was "subject to" some repair or renovation or when the appraisal was performed on a property under construction. A **recert** *verifies that the "subject to" conditions of the original* *appraisal have been met and that the original opinion of value is valid*. Note that a recert, also called a completion report, does not change the effective date of the valuation.

If significant time has passed between an original appraisal that was "subject to" some condition and the actual completion of the improvements, it may be necessary to have both a recertification to remove the condition and an update to get a more current date for the value.

Property Insurance

Property insurance is *coverage that indemnifies a person with an interest in the property for a loss caused to the property by a covered peril*. Standard homeowner's insurance policies require the insured to carry an amount sufficient to cover the cost to replace the structure as the minimum amount of insurance on the property. Homeowner's insurance will most likely have a deductible amount that the borrower must first pay in the event of any loss. The lender has guidelines for the maximum deductible amount also.

The borrower is free to choose a home insurance company of his choice, but the company must meet the lender requirements. It is a good idea to provide the new homeowner, especially a first-time buyer, with the lender requirements for property insurance early in the loan process so there will be no confusion at closing.

A new homeowner may also receive a discount for insuring her automobile and other articles with the hazard insurance provider.

Lender's Interest

The lender has an insurable interest in the property used as collateral for a loan. Lenders, therefore, generally require a mortgage clause be added to the buyer's property policy to cover the lender's interest in preservation and reconstruction of the property after a loss.

Most lenders also require the buyer to pay the first year's insurance premium in full prior to closing. This charge will be found in the Loan Estimate.

- The lender incorporates the premium, along with the current property taxes, into an escrow account. The lender is allowed to maintain a two-month cushion (or 1/6 of a year) for all escrowed items. (Page 2, Section F)

- The insurance cost and property taxes are then prorated over the next twelve months to determine a monthly insurance and property tax payment amount that is then added to the monthly principal and interest due for loan repayment. (Page 2, Section G)

- On payment of the amount due each month, the insurance and tax portion of the payment is deposited into the client's escrow account.

- When property taxes and insurance become due, the lender forwards these amounts to the respective recipients.

If the buyer does not comply with the lender's insurance requirements, the lender has the right to place insurance on the property to cover its interest in the event of a loss. This **force-placed insurance** by the lender *covers only the lender's loan value in case of a covered loss to the structure*. It does not provide for any contents or personal property coverage for the buyer. It also will not provide any liability protection in case of a lawsuit against the buyer.

Flood Insurance

Flood insurance is designed to reduce the cost of national emergencies. When communities enforce and participate in the **National Flood Insurance Program**, the cost of natural disasters due to flooding is minimized.

Flood insurance considers the lowest point at which a flood is likely to occur and dwellings located below that elevation point are considered to be in a flood zone. The risk of flood potential is considered and properties are identified as residing in a Special Flood Hazard Area.

A **Special Flood Hazard Area (SFHA)** is defined as *the area that will be inundated by the flood event having a 1-percent chance of being equaled or exceeded in any given year*. The 1-percent annual chance flood is also referred to as the base flood or **100-year flood**.

- Properties in **Zone A or V** are considered "high risk" and **require mandatory flood insurance to be obtained from the NFIP**. Zones A, AO, AE, V or VE are some of the high-risk flood zone designations.

- Moderate flood hazard areas, labeled **Zone B or Zone X,** are the areas between the limits of the base flood and the 0.2-percent-annual-chance (or 500-year) flood. **Flood insurance is optional in these areas**.

- The areas of minimal flood hazard, which are the areas outside the SFHA and higher than the elevation of the 0.2-percent-annual-chance flood, are labeled **Zone C or Zone X. No flood insurance is required in these areas**.

[See https://www.fema.gov/flood-zones]

Flood insurance coverage is required to be maintained until the loan obligation is satisfied. A standard flood insurance policy only insures the home and not the homeowner's contents, unless the owner purchases an additional policy for personal property protection. Flood insurance often requires a high deductible before paying for any covered loss.

If flood insurance is not obtained by the borrower, the lender will obtain force-place insurance to protect its investment from the perils of a flood.

Private Mortgage Insurance

Private mortgage insurance (PMI) is *offered by private companies to insure a lender against default on a loan by a borrower where there is loss of collateral value at the time of the default.*

The insurer shares the lender's risk, but only part of the risk. The insurer does not insure the entire loan amount, but rather the upper portion of the loan that exceeds the standard 80% LTV. The amount of coverage can vary, but is typically 20% to 25% of the loan amount. After the sale of the security, the proceeds may not be sufficient for the lender to reclaim all the lender's losses from the principal balance, foreclosure, and other costs. The lender may be able to pursue a deficiency judgment against the borrower for any losses, depending on state statutes. This is referred to as **recourse**.

PMI Cancellation

Once the increased risk of loss from borrower default has been reduced (when the loan-to-value ratio is reduced to 80% or less), mortgage insurance has fulfilled its purpose. In the past, many lenders did not cancel PMI, even when the risk was reduced. The Homeowners Protection Act of 1998 (HPA) (12 U.S.C. 4901 et seq.) *requires lenders to automatically cancel PMI when a home has been paid down to 78% of its original value or attained 22% equity based on the original value, assuming the borrower is not delinquent.*

The law has some exceptions, such as for multi-family units, non-owner-occupied homes, mortgages on second homes, and second mortgages.

Title Insurance

When conveying real property, the seller is generally expected to deliver a **marketable title**; that is, *a title that is free and clear from undisclosed encumbrances or other defects that would expose a purchaser to litigation or impede a purchaser's ability to enjoy the property or to later sell the property easily*. A **title search** of the public records, also known as a title examination, is necessary to determine ownership and the quality of the title prior to conveyance. The title search, usually performed by an abstractor or a title company, starts with the chain of title and results in the creation of an **abstract of title**, which is *a complete historical summary of title to a piece of property*.

Chain of Title

The **chain of title** is *a clear and unbroken chronological record of the ownership of a specific piece of property*. Tracing the chain of title simply means tracing the successive conveyances of title, starting with the current deed and going back a suitable number of years. Each owner is linked to the previous owner and the subsequent owner through deeds, forming a chain of title as disclosed in the public records.

Lenders require a 24-month chain of title to appear on the preliminary title report. This provides the ownership of the property and dates of ownership as a method to make sure the property is not being illegally flipped.

A gap or flaw in the chain of title creates uncertainty, which is referred to as a **cloud on the title**. A cloud on the title could be something simple. For example, Sue Jones buys a house; she gets married and is now Sue Smith. When she sells the house, the grantor name on the deed is Sue Smith. This creates an ambiguity in the title.

 Caution: If a marketable title cannot be produced, a closing may have to be postponed.

The abstract, chain of title, and any pertinent documents are examined by the title company to identify any encumbrances, which are non-possessory interests in real property that encumber (or burden) a real property owner's title. Common encumbrances include:

- **Easements.** An easement is *a right to use another person's real property for a particular purpose*. An easement creates limited rights for the easement holder related to the land surface, its airspace, or subsurface. An easement that grants access to property is commonly referred to as a right of way (ROW) and is typically transferred to the new owner.

- **Liens.** A lien is not only a financial interest in property; it is also a financial encumbrance. Liens are typically *security for a debt that gives the creditor, or lien holder, the right to foreclose on the debtor's property if the debt is not paid*. In foreclosure, the property is sold and the lien holder collects the amount of the debt from the proceeds of the foreclosure sale. A mortgage is a **voluntary** lien. **Involuntary** liens include *tax liens, mechanic's liens* (placed by someone hired to build or improve property), and *judgment liens* (attached through court action).

Liens against a property don't prevent its transfer, but the liens still exist. The buyer takes the property subject to the liens. This means that the buyer takes the property along with the liens, but without being personally liable. The buyer must keep paying the liens to retain the property, but only loses equity in the event of default. The creditor can't go after the new owner personally for these debts because the new owner did not assume the debts. In most real estate transactions, however, the seller must clear the title of liens at closing by paying off the debts.

It is important for the MLO to review the preliminary title report for undisclosed liens and encumbrances or property flipping when the report is received. An experienced MLO will review the report for accuracy of all details, including the seller's and borrower's names, the address of the property, sale price, and loan amount.

The amount of property taxes for the property will be disclosed on the report as well as any homeowner association and property assessments that may be required to be paid.

A review of the legal description of the property is essential to verify the property type.

- If the legal description describes the property as "**Lot** 1234", then the properly is owned in fee simple.

- If the legal description uses the word "**Unit** 1234" to describe the property, then the property is most likely a condominium.

The financing options are different for each of these property types.

A **continuation**, or continuance, is *used to bring down the title report from its preliminary issuance to the current date of the settlement to account for any new defects or clouds.*

Title Insurance

The preliminary title report not only provides information about encumbrances, legal descriptions and other items, but is the document that informs the homeowner and the lender of the items that will be covered by title insurance and the items that will be exempt from coverage.

Title insurance protects:

- Lenders (and sometimes property owners) against loss due to disputes over ownership of a property and defects in the title not found in the search of the public record.

- Lenders and property owners from claimants not listed in the insurance policy, including defects in the public record such as forged documents, improper deeds, undisclosed heirs, errors in a property's legal description, and other mistakes.

Title insurance does not generally cure defects, although a title company could potentially purchase the property and fix the problem. More commonly, it simply *insures against losses (up to the coverage amount specified in the policy) due to title defects other than those specifically excluded.* It may require the title company to go to court, if necessary, and defend its policyholder against any claim against the ownership of the land.

A title insurance policy, generally paid for with a one-time premium, may have different insured parties, such as the homeowner and the lender.

Mortgagee's Policies

The **mortgagee's (lender) policy** *protects its interests in the property.* Sometimes called a lender's loan policy, the mortgagee's policy is for the loan amount outstanding at the time a claim is paid. The owner's policies and the mortgagee's policies typically coincide, so the title insurance issuer is not paying twice on the same claim. The existence of a mortgagee's policy helps facilitate the sale of the mortgage to the secondary market.

Owner's Policies

Owner's fee title insurance policies are issued in the name of the property owner. It may be paid for by the buyer or seller as indicated in the sales contract.

An owner's policy:

- Insures that the title to the property is free from liens, encumbrances, and defects except for those listed as exceptions.
- Generally covers losses and damages if the title is unmarketable or if there is no right of access to the property (this does not necessarily mean simply vehicular access; it could include pedestrian access, water access, etc.).

Coverage runs from the time of purchase for as long as the policyholder owns the property, usually with no additional premium. When the property is sold, the new buyer must purchase a new policy and be named beneficiary to collect on a claim from a title defect. An owner's policy does continue to protect the owner who has given a warranty deed to a subsequent owner.

Closing

After the loan is approved by underwriting and all "prior to doc" conditions are met—for example, the lender may request to see a closing statement from the sale of the borrower's previous home, a final inspection report, or property insurance policy—the *lender issues a clear to close* the loan and the necessary documents are prepared for closing.

Closing or funding:

- Completes the process of granting a loan, as funds are disbursed to the settlement agent in accordance with the Closing Disclosure.
- Involves transfer (i.e., recording) of ownership of real property from seller to buyer, according to the terms and conditions of the sales contract or escrow agreement if the transaction involves the sale of real property.

The final stages of a real estate transaction occur when the seller receives value for property (funding – cash, mortgage, etc.) and the buyer receives title, usually via a deed that is recorded in the public record.

Closing Procedures

The closing process may also be referred to as settlement or loan consummation. The mechanics of closing are the responsibility of either an escrow/title/settlement agent or an attorney. This settlement agent may be the lender's in-house escrow department, an independent escrow company, or a title insurance company.

With a sales transaction, the settlement agent simultaneously follows the instructions of both the borrower and seller, as per the sales contract, agreement, or a separate set of escrow instructions (a copy of the sales contract or escrow instructions must be provided to the settlement agent, the title company, and the lender).

The settlement agent:

- Gathers all necessary documents.
- Calculates the various prorations, adjustments, and fees charged to each party.
- Compares the Loan Estimate of closing costs to the Closing Disclosure to verify the proper tolerance with disclosed fees.

Each party receives a Closing Disclosure that complies with TILA. Under TILA, the creditor is responsible for providing a copy of the Closing Disclosure to the borrower three business days in advance of the closing. The settlement agent has the responsibility to provide the Closing Disclosure to the seller in advance of closing.

In addition to the Closing Disclosure, lenders must provide borrowers with an initial escrow statement within 45 days of closing. To review, this disclosure itemizes the estimated taxes, insurance premiums, and other charges anticipated to be paid from the escrow account during the first 12 months of the loan. [See 12 CFR §1024 and 1026].

IRS Form 4506-T

Underwriters require the lender to obtain a completed and signed Form 4506-T from all borrowers at both application and closing. This form gives the lender permission to request electronic transcripts of federal tax returns from the IRS. Under current requirements, the lender determines when to submit the form to the IRS (or designee) to obtain the tax information. These transcripts are used to verify the borrower's income with the intention of helping to reduce instances of mortgage fraud.

At the Closing

The lender wants to ensure that there are no unforeseen problems during closing, that the loan papers (e.g., promissory note, mortgage, deed) are signed, and then makes one final check to ensure everything is in order. *If a borrower is not able to appear in person to execute the loan documents, he may designate a person to execute the legal documents in his place.* This is called a **power of attorney (POA)**. A person designated as a POA may not be a party to the transaction, such as the real estate agent or loan officer, and is oftentimes a close family member.

Once the necessary documents have been recorded, loan funds may then be disbursed to the proper parties, according to the sales contract or escrow instructions.

Exercise 15.1: Apply Your Knowledge

Prioritize the following events as steps of a mortgage loan sequence, indicating the first event with a #1, the second event with a #2, and so on.

Event	Step
Analyze application information	
Appraise the property	
Complete an application	
Consult with the MLO	
Disburse funding	
Process an application	
Record legal documents	
Loan settlement	

Real Success

Closing procedures may be different from state to state—or even from one part of a state to another. For example, in some states, an attorney is required to close the loan. Other states allow a title agent to perform the loan closing. Closings may be conducted in escrow, which means they are handled by a disinterested third party, or roundtable, where all parties are present. A borrower who cannot attend a closing may be able to use a power of attorney (if one exists specific to the property being transferred), subject to lender approval.

Another important point to keep in mind is that settlement costs may also differ from region to region.

For example, in some areas, the seller traditionally pays fees related to the title while in other areas, the buyer pays title fees. Regardless of local practices, the determination of who pays certain fees may be negotiated during the sales process and documented in the purchase contract.

When an MLO takes an application for a state with which he is unfamiliar, the MLO must research the mortgage regulations and laws in that state. Licensing requirements may also be different. An MLO cannot originate a mortgage loan in a state where he is not licensed per the SAFE Act.

 Caution: Note that not only must an individual MLO be licensed to do business in that state, but the MLO's employing company generally must also be licensed in that state.

Closing Disclosure Reconciliation

The responsibility for disclosure and settlement of real estate closings are implemented by the TILA-RESPA Integrated Disclosures (or TRID) that sets forth procedures and guidelines for disclosing settlement costs utilizing the Closing Disclosure.

An MLO must be familiar with the concept of borrower-paid and seller-paid to understand the final distribution of money involved in a transaction as detailed in the Closing Disclosure.

Borrower-paid items are typically *sums of money owed*. A borrower-paid item could be a payment of title fees, loan origination charges, or property taxes that are deposited with the lender that are disclosed and itemized on the Closing Disclosure. These items are shown as either paid at closing or before closing.

Seller-paid items are those *items that have been paid by the seller at closing or before closing*.

On the Summaries of Transactions, shown on Page 3 of the Closing Disclosure, the borrower- and seller-paid items are used in the final calculation of the cash to close for the borrower and the cash proceeds for the seller. Adjustments are made in the Summary for accrued taxes and other property charges, prepaid HOA fees, and other items, credits from interested third parties, and other credits, including a lender tolerance cure.

The mortgage amount shows as a credit to the borrower, since it is the lender who brings that money to closing. If the borrower decides to accept a higher interest rate in return for lender assistance with the payment of the closing costs, this will show as a credit to the buyer on the Closing Disclosure as well.

The details on a settlement statement allow a buyer to see the **acquisition cost**, which is *a total of the amount of money necessary to purchase the property*, since it shows the sales price as well as the charges necessary to close the loan.

Proration

Proration is *the division of expenses between buyer and seller in proportion to the actual usage of the item represented by a particular expense as of the day the loan is funded*. To adjust a cost shared by both buyer and seller, it's necessary to determine whether the expense is accrued or prepaid.

Accrued expenses are the *items on a Closing Disclosure for which the cost has been incurred, but the expense has not yet been paid*; for example, property taxes. Accrued expenses are prorated on the settlement statement as a debit to the seller and a credit to the buyer.

Prepaid expenses are the *items on a Closing Disclosure the seller has already paid*; for example, condominium association fees or homeowner's association fees. Prepaid expenses are prorated on the Closing Disclosure as a credit to the seller and a debit to the buyer.

When performing proration calculations, expenses may be prorated using:

- A 360-day year, 12 months of 30 days each.
- A 365-day year, counting the exact number of days in each month (taking leap years into account).

Often, local custom dictates which factor is used.

Mortgage Interest Payment

An item that may show up on only the borrower's side of the settlement statement is a mortgage interest proration. When a borrower closes a new mortgage loan at settlement, the first payment is not due until the first of the month after the next full month.

For example, the settlement is on May 17. The first mortgage payment is not due until July 1. Mortgage interest is paid in arrears, and so the July payment covers the interest for June. The lender, however, will want to collect the interest from the date of settlement (May 17) until June 1. To find the daily interest rate:

- Step 1: Determine the annual interest (loan amount x interest rate).
- Step 2: Divide annual interest by 360 (using a statutory year, or 365 using a calendar year) to find the daily interest.
- Step 3: Multiply the daily interest by the number of affected days to find the interest proration to be debited from the borrower.

Exercise 15.2: Apply Your Knowledge

Directions: Consider the following scenario, then write your responses.

Scenario: Buyer Bill is obtaining a $200,000 mortgage at 5% interest. The annual interest is $10,000 ($200,000 x 0.05).

1. What is the daily interest?

_____

_____

_____

2. How much must Bill bring to closing to cover the required mortgage interest for May, if escrow closes on May 17?

_____

_____

_____

Mortgage Loan Originator Challenges

Handling the day-to-day challenges of the job can be extremely rewarding or can result in stress and discomfort for the MLO. The keys to a rewarding career include conducting business ethically, efficiently, and embracing consumer-related challenges.

In a mortgage transaction, interaction with a customer is ongoing and crucial to relationship building.

- When an MLO treats a customer in a pleasant, informative, and professional manner that results in a smooth and successful closing, he is likely to have found a "customer for life" as well as positive referrals.

- However, when a customer is not satisfied with the loan process and closing, the MLO's reputation may be damaged due to negative feedback and lack of referrals.

While there is no substitute for on the job training and experience, the following section provides opportunities to gain additional insight into common scenarios an MLO may encounter in working with customers as well as suggestions for how to address these problems.

These scenarios are suggestive only and are not to be construed as legal advice. If an MLO encounters a challenge, he is advised to seek the advice of legal counsel through his management.

Borrower Advice and MLO Liability

While an experienced MLO has a wealth of knowledge about the mortgage industry, loan products, and other pertinent information, he should exercise caution when providing unsolicited advice. An MLO must be very cautious with his words and what he shares with the public to avoid civil liability.

In addition, an MLO may receive unsolicited inquiries for information that are above and beyond his area of expertise. For instance, a consumer may ask an MLO if she should:

- Stop making mortgage payments when default is likely.
- Deduct certain loan expenses on federal income tax returns.
- File for a bankruptcy.
- Short sale her home.

An MLO must remember that he is liable for the advice provided to a consumer, whether he is a customer or not. When advice is followed by the consumer, the MLO is exposed to civil liability. For example, a consumer calls and states she is considering a loan modification and wants to know if she should cease making her mortgage payments to get the loan modification approved. If the MLO advises the consumer to cease making her payments (without a thorough explanation of the potential consequences) and the consumer follows the MLO's advice, the damage could be significant, including:

- Damage to the consumer's credit report
- Loss of the consumer's home
- Violation of the MARS (Mortgage Assistance Relief Services) Regulation that prevents this form of advice without explaining the consequences

It is always best for the MLO to refer the consumer to an attorney, a tax advisor, or a professional who can assist with her questions. An MLO should NEVER provide advice that exceeds his education or qualifications.

Consumer Information and Communication Protocols

Meeting a client face-to-face to take a mortgage loan application is becoming a rare occurrence. Most often, loan application packages (consisting of the 1003, Loan Estimate, and many other disclosures) are delivered to a consumer's e-mail. It is the MLO's responsibility to:

- **Ask for a preferred method of communication**. Today, an MLO can text, email, Skype, call, or communicate with the consumer in other ways. The MLO should address the client's preferred method of communication *at the very first meeting*. Some clients may have hearing loss and prefer written communication. Others may find texting difficult or may enjoy the interaction of a telephone call. Make sure you determine the client's preference for an effortless transaction.

- **Provide a minimum of three loan options**, per the MLO Compensation Rule. For each type of transaction in which the consumer has expressed an interest, an MLO must present loan options that include:

  o Lowest interest rate

  o Lowest interest rate without risky features; i.e., prepayment penalties, negative amortization, interest-only payments, balloon payments in the first seven years of the loan, a demand feature, shared equity or shared appreciation, or, in the case of a reverse mortgage, a loan without a prepayment penalty, shared equity, or appreciation

  o Lowest total dollar amount for origination fees and discount points

Borrowers are often requested to e-sign documents. If an MLO does not have a face-to-face meeting with a client, he should deliver options to review and follow-up with the borrower to discuss:

- Loan options
- Required minimum down payment for each loan program
- Required down payment or equity (in the case of a refinance) to avoid paying mortgage insurance (or lessen the term of the mortgage insurance)
- For a standard or hybrid ARM, a thorough discussion about the introductory interest rate, the rate adjustments, the lifetime maximum interest rate, and other relevant information to make an informed decision

For initial disclosures delivered via a method other than a personal meeting with the consumer, the MLO should have a thorough discussion of the items on the initial Loan Estimate, most particularly the cash to close requirement at the bottom of the first page of the LE. Borrowers who are utilizing electronic signatures for signing often fail to thoroughly read the documents they are signing and do not print a copy of the disclosures for their records and review. An MLO who does not have a verbal discussion with the borrower regarding the cash to close requirement may find the borrower short of funds at closing because the borrower was not adequately informed initially.

MLO Conflict of Interest

RESPA requires that a borrower be informed of any ownership of a settlement service provider if a referral is made to that provider by the mortgage company or MLO. A written disclosure of any interest by the MLO or mortgage company *must be disclosed* to the consumer.

For example, a conflict might exist if the MLO is also the real estate agent in the purchase of the home or the MLO is an owner of the home being purchased by the borrower.

Mortgage Fraud Scenarios

An MLO must avoid fraud—intentional or unintentional—at all times. Regardless of intent, fraud may lead to civil and criminal penalties.

Fraud is *intentional or negligent misrepresentation or concealment of material facts.*

- **Actual Fraud.** *Actual fraud is an intentional misrepresentation or concealment of a material fact.* Actual fraud occurs when a person actively and with the intent to deceive, hides information, or makes statements known to be false or misleading. This is also called **deceit** or **intentional misrepresentation.**
- **Constructive Fraud.** Constructive fraud is *a negligent misrepresentation or concealment of a material fact.* When information is not disclosed or false statements are made unintentionally due to carelessness or negligence rather than an intent to deceive, the act is considered constructive fraud. This is also called **negligent misrepresentation**.
- **Negligence.** Negligence is *an unintentional breach of a legal duty.* A **tort** occurs if *negligence causes harm* and an MLO can be sued for tort.

Mortgage fraud involves any misrepresentation or concealment used to obtain a mortgage loan and is a serious federal crime when committed for any federally-related loan. Mortgage fraud is generally divided into two main categories:

1. **Fraud for profit**: Fraud that is usually perpetrated by *industry insiders*.
2. **Fraud for property**: Fraud that is usually perpetrated by *borrowers*.

Common ways in which fraud may be committed include:

- **Material misrepresentations**, such as altered paycheck stubs and tax returns
- **Material misstatements**, such as the intent to occupy a home as a primary residence when it really is intended to be used as a rental
- **Omission**, such as failing to mention the borrower is taking an early retirement in six weeks

Fraud can be perpetrated by borrowers who lie on applications, by appraisers who provide inflated property values, or by mortgage brokers who ignore derogatory information to get a loan approved. This also includes not reporting all items on the HUD Closing Disclosure accurately, creating phantom documents for verification, or concealing the true nature of a borrower's down payment.

Falsification of Information on Behalf of the Borrower

Lenders and mortgage employees can commit mortgage fraud by falsifying loan documents, making loans to straw buyers, illegally flipping properties, etc.

- Lenders benefit by making loans that should never have been made and selling them to the secondary market as quickly as possible.
- Mortgage brokers benefit by collecting fees and yield spread premiums for putting together fraudulent mortgage packages.

In this form of mortgage fraud, loans are knowingly made to unqualified buyers or even straw buyers who will never make a payment on the loan, resulting in foreclosure.

If an MLO participates in a fraud for profit scheme, the penalty applies to the MLO in addition to any participating consumer. In the absence of federal intervention, states also make it illegal to participate in these profit schemes and are most likely to prosecute any participant.

A fee gained by making and closing a fraudulent loan cannot begin to repair the damage a fraudulent loan causes to family, employers, and the MLO's future.

Borrower Information Fraud

If a borrower provides false information on a loan application or to the MLO, this is a red flag. There are several items an MLO must consider before rushing to judge the borrower:

- Understand honest mistakes are not fraud. For fraud to exist, there must be the intent to deceive. If a borrower overstates his income on the 1003 or provides an asset amount larger than what really exists, do not confront the borrower immediately. If the MLO confronts a borrower without an overwhelming amount of evidence of fraud, she subjects herself and her employer to civil liability.
- Never confront the consumer without checking all the facts.
- If a fraud or mistake is apparent while taking the loan application (face-to-face), the MLO should complete the application process without incident and before placing the loan file in processing, work to verify the questionable information.
- Consult with the manager/owner about the loan file. An MLO should never act on her own, or without the direction of senior management when addressing suspected fraud.
- The penalty for actual (with intent to deceive) mortgage fraud on the federal level can result in a maximum sentence of 30 years in prison, $1,000,000 fine, and ordered restitution.

Addressing Large Deposits that are Not Consistent with the Borrower's Income

A general guideline of loan qualification mandates that all deposits on the borrower's bank statement (typically, the previous two to three months) must be sourced and seasoned. This requires the explanation and documentation of all large deposits from a verifiable and reasonable source. *Deposits that cannot be verified may not be used as cash to close.*

If a borrower cannot or will not explain the source of the deposits, an MLO should review the credit inquiries to see if a loan has been obtained by the borrower.

- If there is a **new loan**, this will impact the borrower's ability to repay the debt and may disqualify the borrower from qualifying for the mortgage loan.
- If **no credit inquiries** are present, then the borrower should provide the source of the funds.

The presence of large, undocumented deposits is a red flag. The MLO should refer the loan file to be addressed by underwriting or management for further review and for a loan decision.

Addressing a Borrower's Undisclosed Income

A borrower is required to disclose all liabilities and income on a loan application. If a borrower fails to disclose income that is received, a check of the income tax transcripts (obtained by the borrower signing IRS Form 4506-T and allowing the lender to obtain a transcript of the tax returns) may show the undisclosed income.

- If a borrower does not claim the income on his IRS Form 1040, it generally cannot be used for qualifying purposes (an exception is made for child support and non-taxable disability payments).
- If the borrower fails to disclose income on the application, the income should be explained, including the source of the income and the reason for non-disclosure on the application.

Addressing the Receipt of a Gift by the Borrower

A conversation with the borrower regarding cash to close should be part of the initial loan application process if the required funds to close cannot be established using the borrower's personal assets. If the amount shown on the bottom of Page 1 of the Loan Estimate cannot be produced, an MLO must ask the borrower the source of the necessary closing funds. If the borrower states that a gift will be given, the MLO then educates the borrower on the proper procedure for the donation and receipt of a gift to purchase the home.

The entire required minimum investment for a mortgage can be a non-repayable **gift** from a relative, an employer or labor union, a charitable organization, or a close friend with a clearly defined and documented interest in the borrower.

The gift donor may *not* be a person or entity with an interest in the sale of the property, such as the seller, a real estate agent or broker, or a builder/associated entity. Gifts from these sources are considered inducements to purchase and *must be subtracted* from the sales price.

A lender must document any borrower gift funds through a **gift letter**, signed by the donor and borrower, that:

- Shows the donor's name and contact information.

- Specifies the dollar amount of the gift.

- States the nature of the relationship to the borrower and that no repayment is required.

If the gift has already been received prior to meeting with the MLO, the MLO must provide the necessary documentation required for a gift along with a reasonable explanation of the pre-application of the gift. Receiving the gift funds in advance of consulting with an MLO will not prevent the borrower from closing on the home, but it will require additional effort from the MLO to properly document the gift. If the gift has been seasoned, the gift documentation is *not* required.

Borrower Applying with Other Mortgage Companies Simultaneously

The non-disclosure of a borrower of other mortgages being sought on the property for which the MLO has taken an application presents a problem. MLOs are prohibited from discouraging a borrower from shopping for the best program or settlement service provider, but the borrower must make disclosure of his actions.

If an MLO is informed or has reason to believe a borrower is applying for financing at another mortgage company, either for the same loan that is being processed by the MLO's firm or for additional financing, such as a subordinate mortgage, the MLO has the duty to have the credit inquiries explained.

An MLO may want to obtain a second, up-to-date credit report (a single bureau will suffice) and note any additional inquiries that have occurred since the first credit report the MLO obtained on the borrower.

- Any new inquiries must be addressed by the borrower and the MLO has an obligation to request this information from the borrower.

- A credit inquiry letter should be written and signed by the borrower, with each new inquiry addressed.

- The borrower must state if any new credit obligation was obtained from the inquiry.

- If new credit has been extended to the borrower, a copy of the terms and payment should be obtained by the MLO and a correct debt-to-income ratio should be analyzed to ensure the borrower's ability to repay the mortgage loan.

Changes to the Application During the Loan Process

A borrower's loan application must be accurate and up-to-date through the date of closing. Any change to the borrower's status (employment, income, assets, credit, etc.) should be immediately brought to the attention of the person who has control of the loan file; for example, if the loan has not been submitted to underwriting, the loan processor will likely have the loan file and should be informed of the change in the borrower status.

Handling Third-Party Inquiries

In the mortgage loan process, there are many parties to the transaction. There are escrow and title company employees, appraisers, and real estate agents. These individuals may seek information from the MLO regarding the status of the loan application, whether closing/consummation will occur on the contract date, or other information that might seem harmless to provide.

An MLO has a duty, per case law, to *deal fairly with all parties* to the real estate contract. Most often, a listing or selling agent will inquire about the status of the loan to make sure everything is being done to provide a smooth and timely close. Great care must be taken when an MLO responds to such requests for information. While the MLO has a duty to be honest and informative, she also has a duty to protect her client's personal, non-public information.

Remember, the FCRA requires the MLO only to provide information to those individuals with a legitimate business need. Two provisions of the FCRA state that a creditor:

1. Must limit access to a credit file. A consumer reporting agency may provide information to those with a legitimate business need (specified by the FCRA) —usually to consider an application with a creditor, insurer, employer, landlord, or other business.

2. May not give out consumer credit information to an employer, or a potential employer, without written consent given to the employer by the consumer.

[See 15 U.S.C. §1681(b) and (d)]

The Gramm-Leach-Bliley Act contains the Financial Privacy Rule that applies to the disclosure of a borrower's information. The Financial Privacy Rule governs the collection and disclosure of customer personal financial information—known as *nonpublic personal information*—restricting when and under what circumstances such information may be disclosed to affiliates and to nonaffiliated third parties. Nonpublic personal information could include:

* Information a consumer/customer puts on an application

* Data about the individual from another source, such as a credit bureau

* Transactions between the individual and the company, such as an account balance, payment history, or credit/debit card purchase

* Whether an individual is a consumer or customer of a particular financial institution

An MLO should be cautious of what information she discloses to these third parties. For example, stating " there are challenges with the loan file that the MLO and the lender are working to overcome; these challenges may delay or cancel the real estate closing" is an acceptable way to inform real estate agents that a loan may not close.

By making such a general statement, the MLO is not inferring that the challenges are borrower-related or providing derogatory information about the borrower. Also, by stating that the closing may be delayed or canceled, the MLO is not concealing facts that are pertinent to the transaction. If a real estate agent presses an MLO for further information, the MLO should decline to provide further information. Sufficient information is considered to have been provided using the response stated.

Handling a Borrower's Personal Information

Remember that the disclosure of a borrower's personal information is protected by:

* FCRA: Providing information only to those with a legitimate business need

* Gramm-Leach-Bliley (GLB) Act: Providing guidance in the sharing of a consumer's personal, non-public information

Another regulation that addresses the consumer's information is the Fair and Accurate Credit Transaction Act (FACTA). This Act requires businesses to take measures to responsibly secure and dispose of sensitive personal information found in a consumer's credit report. Reasonable methods for security and disposal so that information cannot be recovered or reconstructed include:

- Burning or shredding papers that contain consumer report information
- Destroying or erasing electronic files or media
- Placing all pending loan documents in locked desks, cabinets, or storage rooms at the end of the workday

An MLO must exercise great caution when a consumer's information is in his hands and *extreme caution* when disposing of a consumer's information (credit report, bank statements, W-2's, etc.) after a loan closes or cancels. After the MLO is finished with the paper copies of the borrower's information, he cannot simply toss the loan paperwork in a dumpster behind his office or discard the file without taking proper methods to securely dispose of the borrower's information. Employer-provided shredding bins or other employer disposal methods *must be utilized*.

Permissible Acts Regarding a Client's Property Appraisal

According to Regulation Z regarding a client's property appraisal, an MLO is prohibited from:

- Asking an appraiser to consider additional information about the dwelling or comparable properties.
- Asking an appraiser to correct factual errors.
- Obtaining multiple appraisals of a consumer's principal dwelling if the creditor adheres to a policy of selecting the most reliable appraisal rather than the appraisal that states the highest value.
- Withholding compensation from an appraiser for breach of contract or substandard performance of services as provided by contract.

It is an accepted practice for the MLO to have *very limited contact with the appraiser*. As a result, an appraisal request may need to be made by a processor or manager whose income remains relatively unchanged regardless of the outcome of the mortgage loan.

Utilizing a Power of Attorney

A borrower's ability to personally attend the closing should be addressed by the MLO at the beginning of a transaction. A borrower should be informed about the closing date and the need to be personally present, if possible, for the closing.

- If this advance inquiry is made, the borrower may disclose to the MLO the need for a POA to execute loan documents in his absence.
- A POA must be approved by the lender in advance and the lender may limit the person who can be the POA to only immediate family members, such as a spouse or parent/child.

Remember, *a POA may **never** be a party to the transaction*, such as the real estate agent or the MLO.

Chapter Summary

1. An appraisal is an opinion of value of property, as of a specified date, supportable by objective data. Appraisers follow a well-defined process to value properties using three different methods: Sales comparison approach, cost approach, and income approach. Reconciliation is the process of analyzing values derived from different appraisal approaches to arrive at a final opinion of value. Values of the different approaches are never averaged to reach a final value. A recertification of value (recert) may be necessary to confirm whether certain conditions in the original appraisal have been met without changing the effective date of the valuation.

2. Lenders have an insurable interest in the property used as collateral for a loan and, therefore, generally require borrowers to carry property insurance and perhaps flood insurance. The cost for insurance policies may be maintained in an escrow account, and the lender forwards payments to the appropriate third parties to ensure coverage. Most lenders also require the buyer to pay the first year's insurance premium in full *prior* to closing. Flood insurance protects dwellings at risk from flood hazards. Flood Zones A and V require flood insurance coverage. Flood Zones B or X represent less risk and flood insurance is not mandatory

3. An encumbrance is any claim or liability that affects or limits the transfer of title to real property. Easements are a non-possessory right to use another's land for a certain purpose. Liens are also non-possessory interests, which are financial encumbrances. The most common liens are mortgages, tax liens, mechanics' liens, and judgment liens.

4. Title insurance protects lenders and sometimes property owners against loss up to the coverage amount in the policy due to disputes over ownership of a property and defects in the title not found in a public record search. It protects both the buyer (owner's policies) and the lender (mortgagee or lender's title policies). It does not cure defects but insures against losses due to title defects other than those specifically excluded.

5. The lender issues the clear-to-close to the settlement agent. A power of attorney may be used to sign on behalf of the borrower when he cannot be present at closing. Closing, also called settlement, is the culmination of the loan process where papers are signed and funds disbursed. In a real estate sales transaction, it is also the transfer of ownership of real estate from a seller to a buyer per the terms of the sales contract. Proration is the division of expenses between buyer and seller in proportion to the actual usage of the item represented by a particular expense as of the day the loan is funded.

6. Focusing on ethics, the law, and the proper business care of the consumer will provide the MLO with an exciting and rewarding career in the real estate mortgage industry.

Chapter Quiz

1. Which appraisal approach is BEST described as assessing the value of a property by determining the amount it would cost to replicate the structure in its existing condition on a similar parcel of land?

   A. cost approach

   B. income approach

   C. market data approach

   D. sales comparison approach

2. Properties that have the highest risk potential for flooding are referred to as Flood Zone _____ properties.

   A. A

   B. B

   C. O

   D. X

3. A recert does NOT

   A. address issues in a "subject to" appraisal.

   B. change the effective date of the valuation.

   C. confirm the validity of the original opinion of value.

   D. verify that conditions stated in the original appraisal have been met.

4. An appraiser has been contracted to determine the value of a large apartment building for a potential investor. Which appraisal method is probably the most useful for this situation?

   A. competitive market analysis

   B. cost approach

   C. income approach

   D. sales comparison approach

5. What type of lien is voluntary?

   A. judgment lien

   B. mechanic's lien

   C. mortgage lien

   D. property tax lien

6. What should be brought to closing to itemize any changes in a property's title since the preliminary title report was issued?

   A. abstract of title

   B. chain of title

   C. continuation

   D. title policy

Appendix

Appendix A – CFPB Rules and Prior Agency Rules

Federal Law	CFPB Republished Rule	Prior Agency / Rule	
Equal Credit Opportunity Act (ECOA)	Reg B – 12 CFR 1002	Fed	Reg B – 12 CFR 202
Home Mortgage Disclosure Act (HMDA)	Reg C – 12 CFR 1003	Fed	Reg C – 12 CFR 203
Electronic Fund Transfers	Reg E – 12 CFR 1005	Fed	Reg E – 12 CFR 205
Fair Debt Collection Practices Act	Reg F – 12 CFR 1006	FTC	16 CFR 901
SAFE Mortgage Licensing Act – Federal Registration of Mortgage Loan Origination	Reg G – 12 CFR 1007	Interagency regulations, including:	
		OCC	12 CFR 34
		Fed	12 12 CFR 208 & 211
		FDIC	12 CFR 365
		OTS	12 CFR 563
		FCA	12 CFR 610
		NCUA	12 CFR 741 & 761
SAFE Mortgage Licensing Act – State Compliance and Bureau Registration System	Reg H – 12 CFR 1008	Interagency regulations, including:	
		HUD	24 CFR 3400
Federal Deposit Insurance Act	Reg I – 12 CFR 1009	FTC	16 CFR 320
Interstate Land Sales Registration Program	Reg J – 12 CFR 1010	HUD / 24 CFR 1710	
	Reg K – 12 CFR 1011	HUD / 24 CFR 1715	
	Reg L – 12 CFR 1012	HUD / 24 CFR 1720	
Consumer Leasing	Reg M – 12 CFR 1013	Fed	Reg M – 12 CFR 213
Omnibus Appropriations Act, 2009 – Mortgage Acts and Practices – Advertising Rule	Reg N – 12 CFR 1014	FTC	16 CFR 321
Omnibus Appropriations Act, 2009 – Mortgage Assistance Relief – Services Rule	Reg O – 12 CFR 1015	FTC	16 CFR 322
Privacy of Consumer Financial Information	Reg P – 12 CFR 1016	Interagency regulations, including:	
		Fed	12 CFR 216
		FDIC	12 CFR 332
		FTC	16 CFR 313
		NCUA	12 CFR 716 & 741
		OTS	12 CFR 573
		SEC	17 CFR 248
		CFTC	CFTC / 17 CFR 160
Fair Credit Reporting Act	Reg V – 12 CFR 1022	Interagency regulations, including:	
		Fed	12 CFR 222
		FDIC	12 CFR 334
		FTC	16 CFR 600
		OCC	12 CFR 41
		NCUA	12 CFR 717
		OTS	12 CFR 571
Real Estate Settlement Procedures Act (RESPA)	Reg X – 12 CFR 1024	HUD	Reg X – 24 CFR 3500
Truth in Lending Act (TILA)	Reg Z – 12 CFR 1026	Fed	Reg Z – 12 CFR 226
Truth in Savings	Reg DD – 12 CFR 1030	Interagency regulations, including:	
		Fed	Reg DD – 12 CFR 230
		NCUA	12 CFR 707

Appendix B – Financial Disclosure Laws & Regulations

Requiring Financial Disclosures		
Federal Law	**Highlights**	**Disclosures/Notices**
Truth in Lending Act (**Regulation Z**, 12 CFR Part 1026 et seq TILA) 1968; amended by Mortgage Disclosure Improvement Act (**MDIA**) 2009 Enforced by Consumer Financial Protection Bureau	• Promotes the informed use of credit by disclosing finance charges in a uniform manner using the Annual Percentage Rate (APR) • Applies to loans with more than four installments • Provides right of rescission for three business days after loan consummation on refinance of owner-occupied property • Completed application requires use of 3-page Loan Estimate, which discloses settlement service provider costs, the initial Annual Percentage Rate of the loan, Estimated Cash to Close the transaction, and other loan features. • Completed application requires providing information to the consumer regarding the Home Loan Toolkit disclosure within three (3) business days of receipt of a completed loan application. • Imposes a prescribed tolerance between TIL APR and final APR • 3/7/3 Rule – initial disclosure within 3 business days; earliest close 7th business day after initial disclosure; 3 business-day waiting period before consummation if redisclosure required • Requires lenders to verify a borrower's Ability to Repay the loan based on 8 underwriting factors • Provides an alternative to the ATR with the Qualified Mortgage which contains features that must be met • Provides a temporary category for seven years of Qualified Mortgages that are eligible to be purchase, guaranteed or insured by either of the GSE's or FHA, VA or USRDA. • Mandates certain procedures and practices regarding real property appraisals • Requires the delivery of the five (5) page Closing Disclosure, which contains the final terms of the mortgage loan, loan costs, and various loan disclosures three (3) days prior to loan consummation. The Closing Disclosure combines the HUD 1 Settlement Statement and the Final Truth in Lending disclosures.	Within 3 Business Days of Completed Application: • Loan Estimate • The Home Loan Toolkit Disclosure • When Home is on the Line (*home equity loans*) • CHARM Booklet (*ARM loans*) At Settlement (for loans on primary residence): • The Closing Disclosure to be received by the consumer three (3) business days prior to loan consummation • Notice of Right to Rescind (2 copies) General • Disclosure of APR in advertising with certain triggering terms
Home Mortgage Disclosure Act (HMDA) – **Regulation C** (12 CFR §1003) Enforced by Consumer Financial Protection Bureau	• Determines if financial institutions are serving the housing needs of their communities. • Applies to financial institutions and non-depository institutions with assets in excess of $10 million or who originate more than 100 loans/year • Identifies possible discriminatory lending patterns through the collection and disclosure of data about applicant and borrower characteristics	Regulation C requires financial institutions to submit a report—called a Loan/Application Register (LAR)—to their supervisory agencies on a loan-by-loan and application-by-application basis every March.

Requiring Financial Disclosures

Federal Law	Highlights	Disclosures/Notices
Real Estate Settlement Procedures Act (Regulation X, 12 CFR Part 1024) **RESPA**) 1974 Enforced by Consumer Financial Protection Bureau	• Helps consumers compare settlement services and eliminate unnecessary increases in the costs of certain settlement services expressed as a dollar amount • Covers loans secured with a mortgage placed on a one- to four-family residential property • Prohibits kickbacks, fee-splitting, and unearned fees • Sets limits on escrow accounts • Prohibits sellers from requiring homebuyers to use a particular title insurance company • Mandates a creditor provide a monthly statement to a consumer • States that creditors must promptly post a payment the day it is received • Requires creditors to respond to a payoff request within seven (7) business days • Calls for creditors to set up their business so they may access the borrower's information readily • Requires creditors to make disclosure to the consumer 30 and 45 days prior to billing for force-placed insurance • States that creditors resolve written consumer complaints within 30-45 days of receipt • A creditor must attempt to establish live contact within 36 days with a borrower who has missed a mortgage payment • A creditor must provide mortgage workout options to the borrower within 45 days of a missed payment • A creditor must notify a borrower within 30 days after submission of a complete loan workout application if there is an option to save the home. • A creditor may not seek judicial foreclosure or a trustee's sale action for at least 90 days for a borrower who requests a loan workout • A creditor may not seek judicial foreclosure or a trustee's sale actions for at least 120 days if there is no borrower request for assistance • Dual tracking is prohibited	**Within 3 Business Days of Completed Application:** • Mortgage Servicing Disclosure Statement • Provide a list of HUD-approved home ownership counseling organizations obtained from the CFPB or HUD. **Before Settlement:** • Affiliated Business Arrangement Disclosure (delivered at the time of referral) **At Settlement:** • Initial Escrow Statement or within 45 days of closing **After Settlement:** • Annual Escrow Statement • Servicing Transfer Statement
Homeowners Protection Act (**HPA**) 1998 Enforced by Consumer Financial Protection Bureau	• Applies to single-family residential dwellings, owner occupied and non-government insured mortgage loans • Allows borrowers to request PMI cancellation when LTV reaches 80% • Automatically terminates PMI when LTV reaches 78% if borrower is not delinquent • Allows borrowers to accelerate the cancellation date by making additional payments that bring the LTV to 80%	• Initial disclosure of HPA provisions with annual reminders • Disclosure of cancellation and automatic termination dates for fixed rate loans

Requiring Financial Disclosures

Federal Law	Highlights	Disclosures/Notices

Equal Credit Opportunity Act (ECOA) – **Regulation B** (12 CFR §1002)
 	
Enforced by Consumer Financial Protection Bureau
	Federal law that ensures all consumers are given an equal chance to obtain credit.
	
	• Prohibits discrimination in granting credit to people based on sex, age (if at least 18), marital status, race, color, religion, national origin, receipt of public assistance, or exercised rights under the Consumer Credit Protection Act
	• Prohibits creditors from refusing to consider or discounting income from alimony, child support, maintenance if borrower chooses to disclose it
	• Creditors are required to render a credit decision within thirty (30) days of receipt of a completed application from the borrower. The decision can be either:
	  A. Approve
	  B. Counter offer or incomplete loan file
	  C. Adverse action (decline)
	• There are six (6) items that meet the minimum items needed for a complete application. They are:
	  A. Name of borrower
	  B. Social Security number of borrower to have the ability to obtain a credit report
	  C. The gross monthly income of the borrower
	  D. The property address that is being purchase or refinanced Y
	  E. The initial loan amount
	  F. Estimated property value
		• Regulation B also contains disclosure provisions, the primary one being the creditor's lending decision.
		• When adverse action is taken—an application has been denied, the applicant was offered less favorable terms than those applied for, or there was a change in terms of an existing credit agreement—the creditor must either provide notice of the *specific reasons* for the decision or inform the applicant of his right to request specific reasons for the decision within 60 days. This notice, called a Statement of Adverse Action, must be in writing
		• Creditors must also disclose to consumers what their rights are under ECOA, including a notice to the applicant of their right to receive a copy of any appraisal report on the property (one- to four-family dwelling) that was used in the decision-making process within three days of receipt by the lender but in no case later than three business days prior to the closing of the loan, whichever occurs first.

Appendix C – Privacy Protection and Consumer Identification Laws & Regulations

Privacy and Consumer Identification

Federal Law	Highlights	Disclosures/Notices
Fair Credit Reporting Act (**Regulation V**, FCRA, 12 CFR Part 1022) 1968 Enforced by Consumer Financial Protection Bureau	• Gives consumers access to the same information about themselves that lenders use when making credit decisions • Entitles consumers to free credit report upon adverse action or identity theft • Allows consumers to dispute credit report • Provides additional rights for identity theft victims and active duty military personnel	• One-time written notice of derogatory information, separate from Truth in Lending disclosures

Privacy and Consumer Identification

Federal Law	Highlights	Disclosures/Notices
Fair and Accurate Credit Transaction Act of 2003 (**FACT Act**) Enforced by Consumer Financial Protection Bureau	• Amends the Fair Credit Reporting Act to help consumers fight identity theft • Mandates limits on information sharing • Entitles consumers to annual free credit report • Allows consumers to place fraud alerts and credit freezes • Requires businesses to truncate credit/debit card numbers on receipts • Mandates businesses to secure and properly dispose of sensitive personal information in a consumer's credit report • Red Flag Rules require financial institutions and creditors to implement a written identity theft prevention program and verify the validity of an address change request	When Applying for Credit: • Home Loan Applicant Credit Score Information Disclosure
Gramm-Leach-Bliley Act or Financial Services Modernization Act of 1999 (The Privacy Act) Privacy of Consumer Financial Information (Reg P) provisions enforced by Consumer Financial Protection Bureau	Financial Privacy Rule: • Restricts when and under what circumstances personal financial information may be disclosed to non-affiliated third parties • Allows customers to opt out of allowing information to be shared Safeguards Rule: • Requires all financial institutions to design, implement, and maintain safeguards to protect customer information while it is in the custody and control of the institution and its agents and in the transfer of such information Pretexting Provisions: • Protects consumers from those who obtain personal information under false, fictitious, or fraudulent pretenses	Before Disclosing Information to Non-Affiliated Third Parties: • Consumer Privacy Policy (and annually to customers as long as the relationship continues) • Must provide an opt-out opportunity to customers annually
National Do Not Call Registry Enforced by Federal Trade Commission	• Allows consumers to put phone numbers on a national Do Not Call list • Applies to any plan, program, or campaign to sell goods or services through interstate phone calls • Requires companies to maintain national and internal lists of customers and prospects and keep them updated regularly • Allows business to call a consumer with whom it has an established business relationship (EBR) for up to 18 months after the consumer's last purchase, delivery, or payment; or up to 90 days after an inquiry, if not listed on the internal DNC list. • Imposes fines of up to $16,000 per violation	None
U.S. Patriot Act (Uniting and Strengthening America by Providing Appropriate Tools Required to Intercept and Obstruct Terrorism Act) 2001	• Requires lenders and banks to create and maintain customer identification programs (CIPs) to verify identity of customers entering into a "formal relationship" • Mortgage brokers must also perform the lender's CIP • Created to prohibit money laundering (Chapter 3 of the AML) and the financing of terrorists	Patriot Act Information Disclosure

Appendix D – Laws & Regulations Prohibiting Discrimination

Prohibiting Discrimination		
Federal Law	**Highlights**	**Disclosures/Notices**
Civil Rights Act 1866	• Prohibits all racial discrimination, private or public, in the sale and rental of property • Allows someone claiming unlawful discrimination to sue only in federal district court	None
Fair Housing Act 1968	• Prohibits any discrimination in the sale, lease, or loan terms for residential property based on race, color, religion, sex, national origin, disability, or familial status • Allows someone claiming discrimination to file a written complaint to the nearest HUD office within one year of the alleged violation	• Fair/Equal Housing/Lending posters and logos • Post availability of information in lobby (depository institutions)
Equal Credit Opportunity Act (**Regulation B**, ECOA, 12 CFR Part 1002 et. Seq) 1974 Enforced by Consumer Financial Protection Bureau	• Prohibits discrimination in granting credit to people based on sex, age (if at least 18), marital status, race, color, religion, national origin, receipt of public assistance, or exercised rights under the Consumer Credit Protection Act • Requires credit bureaus to keep separate files on married spouses, if requested • Prohibits creditors from refusing to consider or discounting income from alimony, child support, or maintenance if borrower chooses to disclose it • Allows borrowers to request in writing a reason for adverse action within 60 days of notification • Borrowers must be given a copy of the property appraisal within 3 business days of receipt of the report or within 3 days of loan closing, whichever occurs first.	• ECOA Statement of Rights, including right to receive a copy of appraisal report • Notification of credit decision within 30 days of application (statement of adverse action if declined, incomplete, or change of terms offered)
Home Mortgage Disclosure Act (Federal Reserve Board's **Regulation C**, HMDA, 12 CFR Part 1003 et. Seq) 1975 Enforced by Consumer Financial Protection Bureau	• Requires completion of Section X of the loan application, indicating the borrower's race, ethnicity and sex • Determines if financial institutions are serving the housing needs of their communities • Applies to financial institutions and non-depository institutions with assets in excess of $10 million or who originate more than 100 loans/year • Identifies possible discriminatory lending patterns through the collection and disclosure of data about applicant and borrower characteristics	Loan/Application Register (LAR): Report to supervisory agencies on a loan-by-loan and application-by-application basis every March
Community Reinvestment Act (**CRA**) 1977	• Encourage financial institutions to help meet the credit needs of the communities in which they operate • Requires periodic examinations by federal agencies responsible for supervising depository institutions	None

Appendix E – Laws & Regulations Prohibiting Predatory Lending

Prohibit Predatory Lending		
Federal Law	**Highlights**	**Disclosures/Notices**
Secure and Fair Enforcement for Mortgage Licensing Act (**SAFE Act**) Enforced by Consumer Financial Protection Bureau	• Establishes minimum standards for the licensing of state-licensed mortgage loan originators and registered mortgage loan originators • Provides for the establishment and maintenance of a Nationwide Mortgage Licensing System and Registry for the residential mortgage industry • Requires 20 hours of prelicensing education for state-licensed MLO applicants • Requires background checks for applicants • Requires passage of National MLO Exam with UST with a minimum score of 75% Requires 8 hours of continuing education for state licensed MLO's *Note*: Selected states may require an additional state or territory-specific test component • Requires independent contractor loan processors and underwriters to have MLO license	• Display of license • Use of NMLS unique ID on applications and other documents
Home Ownership and Equity Protection Act (**HOEPA**) 1994 [*Note*: HOEPA regulations require financial disclosures and prohibit predatory lending.] Enforced by Consumer Financial Protection Bureau	• Amends Regulation Z, Section 32 (12 CFR Part 1026 et. Seq) to prohibit deceptive and unfair practices in lending • Establishes additional disclosure requirements for high cost loans • Defines high cost loan as: The APR exceeds the rates on the Average Prime Offer Rate by more than six and one half (6.5%) percentage points for a first mortgage or more than eight and one-half percentage points (8.5%) for a second mortgage; or the total points and fees exceed five (5%) percent of the loan amount [See Regulation Z (12 CFR Part 1026, APR coverage test (§1026.32(a)(1)(i) and comments 32(a)(1)(i)-1 through 3 and 32(a)(1)(i)(B)-1).] • Uses some different criteria to define total finance charges (e.g., counts optional credit insurance premiums) • Prohibits balloon payments (on loans of less than 5 years), negative amortization, fees for providing payoff statements or loan modifications by a lender and demand clauses • Limits prepayment penalties • Allows three business-day right of rescission for HOEPA loans	Creditors granting loans meeting HOEPA criteria must disclose certain facts about the loan as part of the loan package at least three business days prior to consummation of a mortgage transaction. Section 32 disclosures include: • Notice that consumer is not required to complete the transaction • Warning that the lender will have a mortgage on the home and the borrower could lose it and equity if in default • The annual percentage rate (APR) • The regular payment amount (including any balloon payment where the law permits balloon payments) • The loan amount • Credit insurance premiums, if applicable • For variable rate loans, the amount of the maximum monthly payment and the fact that the rate and monthly payment may increase

Prohibit Predatory Lending		
Federal Law	**Highlights**	**Disclosures/Notices**
Higher-Priced Loans – **Regulation Z** §1026.35 as amended by Housing and Economic Recovery Act of 2008 (HERA) Enforced by Consumer Financial Protection Bureau	• Closed-end mortgage loan secured by borrower's principal dwelling where APR exceeds applicable average prime offer rate by at least 1.5% for first lien loans, 2.5% for jumbo loans and 3.5% for junior lien loans • Creditors obligated to verify repayment ability • Prepayment penalties generally prohibited • Escrow account must be established for property taxes and mortgage-related insurance premiums required by creditor for a minimum of 5 years	None
MLO Compensation Rule – **Regulation Z** §1026.36 Enforced by Consumer Financial Protection Bureau	• Amends Regulation Z (12 C.F.R. §1026.36) • Prohibits compensation based on loan interest rates or other terms/conditions other than loan amount • Prohibits steering consumers to specific lenders to gain greater compensation, unless loan is in borrower's interest • Sets safe harbor rules for presenting loan options to consumers • Provides that no MLO may be compensated by the consumer and another person in connection with the transaction • Generally may not reduce MLO compensation to offer a reduction in closing costs (pricing reductions) • A MLO may not be compensated for referrals of settlement services to a provider owned by the lender • May not be compensated based on the profitability of a transaction or pool of transactions • MLOs may receive a bonus from the employing creditor subject to certain guidelines and conditions • Registered loan originators (employed by a federal depository institution) must comply with the same guidelines and requirements that pertain for a state licensed originator • Implements rules for seller financing of residential properties • Prohibits a mandatory requirement for consumers to submit to arbitration in the event of a dispute • Prohibits a creditor from financing, directly or indirectly, any premiums or fees for credit insurance on a transaction secured by a dwelling.	Present loan options from significant number of creditors

Prohibit Predatory Lending		
Federal Law	**Highlights**	**Disclosures/Notices**
Ability to Repay – **Regulation Z** §1026.43 Enforced by Consumer Financial Protection Bureau	• Amends Regulation Z (12 C.F.R. §1026.43) • Creditors must make a reasonable, good faith effort to verify borrowers' repayment ability • Independent third party documentation is used to verify borrowers' income, assets, residual, and other criteria • For an Adjustable Rate loan, the creditor must use the highest payment possible during the loan term to establish the ATR	
Qualified Mortgage – **Regulation Z** §1026.43 Enforced by Consumer Financial Protection Bureau	• Amends Regulation Z (12 C.F.R. §1026.43) • Creditors are presumed to meet ATR requirements if they make a Qualified Mortgage • Features of a Qualified Mortgage are: No "interest only" period, no negative amortization, no balloon payments, debt to income ratio of 43% or less and a loan term of more than 30 years	

Appendix F – Regulation N: Prohibited Representations

The CFPB adopted the following additional rules under Regulation N – Prohibited Representations:

It is a violation of this part for any person to make any material misrepresentation, expressly or by implication, in any commercial communication, regarding any term of any mortgage credit product, including but not limited to misrepresentations about:

(a) *The interest charged for the mortgage credit product, including but not limited to misrepresentations concerning:*

    (1) *The amount of interest that the consumer owes each month that is included in the consumer's payments, loan amount, or total amount due, or*

    (2) *Whether the difference between the interest owed and the interest paid is added to the total amount due from the consumer;*

(b) *The annual percentage rate, simple annual rate, periodic rate, or any other rate;*

(c) *The existence, nature, or amount of fees or costs to the consumer associated with the mortgage credit product, including but not limited to misrepresentations that no fees are charged;*

(d) *The existence, cost, payment terms, or other terms associated with any additional product or feature that is or may be sold in conjunction with the mortgage credit product, including but not limited to credit insurance or credit disability insurance;*

(e) *The terms, amounts, payments, or other requirements relating to taxes or insurance associated with the mortgage credit product, including but not limited to misrepresentations about:*

    (1) *Whether separate payment of taxes or insurance is required; or*

    (2) *The extent to which payment for taxes or insurance is included in the loan payments, loan amount, or total amount due from the consumer;*

(f) *Any prepayment penalty associated with the mortgage credit product, including but not limited to misrepresentations concerning the existence, nature, amount, or terms of such penalty;*

(g) *The variability of interest, payments, or other terms of the mortgage credit product, including but not limited to misrepresentations using the word "fixed";*

(h) *Any comparison between:*

    (1) *Any rate or payment that will be available for a period less than the full length of the mortgage credit product; and*

    (2) *Any actual or hypothetical rate or payment;*

(i) *The type of mortgage credit product, including but not limited to misrepresentations that the product is or involves a fully amortizing mortgage;*

(j) *The amount of the obligation, or the existence, nature, or amount of cash or credit available to the consumer in connection with the mortgage credit product, including but not limited to misrepresentations that the consumer will receive a certain amount of cash or credit as part of a mortgage credit transaction;*

(k) *The existence, number, amount, or timing of any minimum or required payments, including but not limited to misrepresentations about any payments or that no payments are required in a reverse mort-gage or other mortgage credit product;*

(l) The potential for default under the mortgage credit product, including but not limited to misrepresentations concerning the circumstances under which the consumer could default for nonpayment of taxes, insurance, or maintenance, or for failure to meet other obligations;

(m) The effectiveness of the mortgage credit product in helping the consumer resolve difficulties in paying debts, including but not limited to misrepresentations that any mortgage credit product can reduce, eliminate, or restructure debt or result in a waiver or forgiveness, in whole or in part, of the consumer's existing obligation with any person;

(n) The association of the mortgage credit product or any provider of such product with any other person or program, including but not limited to misrepresentations that:

(1) The provider is, or is affiliated with, any governmental entity or other organization; or

(2) The product is or relates to a government benefit, or is endorsed, sponsored by, or affiliated with any government or other program, including but not limited to through the use of formats, symbols, or logos that resemble those of such entity, organization, or program;

(o) The source of any commercial communication, including but not limited to misrepresentations that a commercial communication is made by or on behalf of the consumer's current mortgage lender or servicer;

(p) The right of the consumer to reside in the dwelling that is the subject of the mortgage credit product, or the duration of such right, including but not limited to misrepresentations concerning how long or under what conditions a consumer with a reverse mortgage can stay in the dwelling;

(q) The consumer's ability or likelihood to obtain any mortgage credit product or term, including but not limited to misrepresentations concerning whether the consumer has been preapproved or guaranteed for any such product or term;

(r) The consumer's ability or likelihood to obtain a refinancing or modification of any mortgage credit product or term, including but not limited to misrepresentations concerning whether the consumer has been preapproved or guaranteed for any such refinancing or modification; and

(s) The availability, nature, or substance of counseling services or any other expert advice offered to the consumer regarding any mortgage credit product or term, including but not limited to the qualifications of those offering the services or advice.

These rules cannot be waived. Additionally, they require the retention of commercial communications for a period of 24 months from the last date of commercial communications.

Appendix G – Sample Mortgage Agreement

After Recording Return To:

_____

_____

_____

_____

_____ **[Space Above This Line For Recording Data]** _____

MORTGAGE

DEFINITIONS

Words used in multiple sections of this document are defined below and other words are defined in Sections 3, 11, 13, 18, 20 and 21. Certain rules regarding the usage of words used in this document are also provided in Section 16.

(A) "Security Instrument" means this document, which is dated _____, _____, together with all Riders to this document.

(B) "Borrower" is _____. Borrower is the mortgagor under this Security Instrument.

(C) "Lender" is _____. Lender is a _____ organized and existing under the laws of _____. Lender's address is _____. Lender is the mortgagee under this Security Instrument.

(D) "Note" means the promissory note signed by Borrower and dated _____, _____. The Note states that Borrower owes Lender _____ Dollars (U.S. $_____) plus interest. Borrower has promised to pay this debt in regular Periodic Payments and to pay the debt in full not later than _____.

(E) "Property" means the property that is described below under the heading "Transfer of Rights in the Property."

(F) "Loan" means the debt evidenced by the Note, plus interest, any prepayment charges and late charges due under the Note, and all sums due under this Security Instrument, plus interest.

(G) "Riders" means all Riders to this Security Instrument that are executed by Borrower. The following Riders are to be executed by Borrower [check box as applicable]:

☐ Adjustable Rate Rider ☐ Condominium Rider ☐ Second Home Rider
☐ Balloon Rider ☐ Planned Unit Development Rider ☐ Other(s) [specify] _____
☐ 1-4 Family Rider ☐ Biweekly Payment Rider

OHIO--Single Family--**Fannie Mae/Freddie Mac UNIFORM INSTRUMENT** **Form 3036** **1/01** (page 1 of 16 pages)

(H) "Applicable Law" means all controlling applicable federal, state and local statutes, regulations, ordinances and administrative rules and orders (that have the effect of law) as well as all applicable final, non-appealable judicial opinions.

(I) "Community Association Dues, Fees, and Assessments" means all dues, fees, assessments and other charges that are imposed on Borrower or the Property by a condominium association, homeowners association or similar organization.

(J) "Electronic Funds Transfer" means any transfer of funds, other than a transaction originated by check, draft, or similar paper instrument, which is initiated through an electronic terminal, telephonic instrument, computer, or magnetic tape so as to order, instruct, or authorize a financial institution to debit or credit an account. Such term includes, but is not limited to, point-of-sale transfers, automated teller machine transactions, transfers initiated by telephone, wire transfers, and automated clearinghouse transfers.

(K) "Escrow Items" means those items that are described in Section 3.

(L) "Miscellaneous Proceeds" means any compensation, settlement, award of damages, or proceeds paid by any third party (other than insurance proceeds paid under the coverages described in Section 5) for: (i) damage to, or destruction of, the Property; (ii) condemnation or other taking of all or any part of the Property; (iii) conveyance in lieu of condemnation; or (iv) misrepresentations of, or omissions as to, the value and/or condition of the Property.

(M) "Mortgage Insurance" means insurance protecting Lender against the nonpayment of, or default on, the Loan.

(N) "Periodic Payment" means the regularly scheduled amount due for (i) principal and interest under the Note, plus (ii) any amounts under Section 3 of this Security Instrument.

(O) "RESPA" means the Real Estate Settlement Procedures Act (12 U.S.C. §2601 et seq.) and its implementing regulation, Regulation X (24 C.F.R. Part 3500), as they might be amended from time to time, or any additional or successor legislation or regulation that governs the same subject matter. As used in this Security Instrument, "RESPA" refers to all requirements and restrictions that are imposed in regard to a "federally related mortgage loan" even if the Loan does not qualify as a "federally related mortgage loan" under RESPA.

(P) "Successor in Interest of Borrower" means any party that has taken title to the Property, whether or not that party has assumed Borrower's obligations under the Note and/or this Security Instrument.

TRANSFER OF RIGHTS IN THE PROPERTY

This Security Instrument secures to Lender: (i) the repayment of the Loan, and all renewals, extensions and modifications of the Note; and (ii) the performance of Borrower's covenants and agreements under this Security Instrument and the Note. For this purpose, Borrower does hereby

OHIO--Single Family--**Fannie Mae/Freddie Mac UNIFORM INSTRUMENT** Form 3036 1/01 *(page 2 of 16 pages)*

mortgage, grant and convey to Lender the following described property located in the
_____ of _____:
[Type of Recording Jurisdiction]   [Name of Recording Jurisdiction]

which currently has the address of _____
                                            [Street]
_____, Ohio _____("Property Address"):
        [City]   [Zip Code]

TOGETHER WITH all the improvements now or hereafter erected on the property, and all easements, appurtenances, and fixtures now or hereafter a part of the property. All replacements and additions shall also be covered by this Security Instrument. All of the foregoing is referred to in this Security Instrument as the "Property."

BORROWER COVENANTS that Borrower is lawfully seised of the estate hereby conveyed and has the right to mortgage, grant and convey the Property and that the Property is unencumbered, except for encumbrances of record. Borrower warrants and will defend generally the title to the Property against all claims and demands, subject to any encumbrances of record.

THIS SECURITY INSTRUMENT combines uniform covenants for national use and non-uniform covenants with limited variations by jurisdiction to constitute a uniform security instrument covering real property.

UNIFORM COVENANTS. Borrower and Lender covenant and agree as follows:

1. Payment of Principal, Interest, Escrow Items, Prepayment Charges, and Late Charges. Borrower shall pay when due the principal of, and interest on, the debt evidenced by the Note and any prepayment charges and late charges due under the Note. Borrower shall also pay funds for Escrow Items pursuant to Section 3. Payments due under the Note and this Security Instrument shall be made in U.S. currency. However, if any check or other instrument received by Lender as payment under the Note or this Security Instrument is returned to Lender unpaid, Lender may require that any or all subsequent payments due under the Note and this Security Instrument be made in one or more of the following forms, as selected by Lender: (a) cash; (b) money order; (c) certified check, bank check, treasurer's check or cashier's check, provided any such check is

OHIO--Single Family--**Fannie Mae/Freddie Mac UNIFORM INSTRUMENT**   Form 3036 1/01 *(page 3 of 16 pages)*

drawn upon an institution whose deposits are insured by a federal agency, instrumentality, or entity; or (d) Electronic Funds Transfer.

Payments are deemed received by Lender when received at the location designated in the Note or at such other location as may be designated by Lender in accordance with the notice provisions in Section 15. Lender may return any payment or partial payment if the payment or partial payments are insufficient to bring the Loan current. Lender may accept any payment or partial payment insufficient to bring the Loan current, without waiver of any rights hereunder or prejudice to its rights to refuse such payment or partial payments in the future, but Lender is not obligated to apply such payments at the time such payments are accepted. If each Periodic Payment is applied as of its scheduled due date, then Lender need not pay interest on unapplied funds. Lender may hold such unapplied funds until Borrower makes payment to bring the Loan current. If Borrower does not do so within a reasonable period of time, Lender shall either apply such funds or return them to Borrower. If not applied earlier, such funds will be applied to the outstanding principal balance under the Note immediately prior to foreclosure. No offset or claim which Borrower might have now or in the future against Lender shall relieve Borrower from making payments due under the Note and this Security Instrument or performing the covenants and agreements secured by this Security Instrument.

2. Application of Payments or Proceeds. Except as otherwise described in this Section 2, all payments accepted and applied by Lender shall be applied in the following order of priority: (a) interest due under the Note; (b) principal due under the Note; (c) amounts due under Section 3. Such payments shall be applied to each Periodic Payment in the order in which it became due. Any remaining amounts shall be applied first to late charges, second to any other amounts due under this Security Instrument, and then to reduce the principal balance of the Note.

If Lender receives a payment from Borrower for a delinquent Periodic Payment which includes a sufficient amount to pay any late charge due, the payment may be applied to the delinquent payment and the late charge. If more than one Periodic Payment is outstanding, Lender may apply any payment received from Borrower to the repayment of the Periodic Payments if, and to the extent that, each payment can be paid in full. To the extent that any excess exists after the payment is applied to the full payment of one or more Periodic Payments, such excess may be applied to any late charges due. Voluntary prepayments shall be applied first to any prepayment charges and then as described in the Note.

Any application of payments, insurance proceeds, or Miscellaneous Proceeds to principal due under the Note shall not extend or postpone the due date, or change the amount, of the Periodic Payments.

3. Funds for Escrow Items. Borrower shall pay to Lender on the day Periodic Payments are due under the Note, until the Note is paid in full, a sum (the "Funds") to provide for payment of amounts due for: (a) taxes and assessments and other items which can attain priority over this Security Instrument as a lien or encumbrance on the Property; (b) leasehold payments or ground rents on the Property, if any; (c) premiums for any and all insurance required by Lender under Section 5; and (d) Mortgage Insurance premiums, if any, or any sums payable by Borrower to Lender in lieu of the payment of Mortgage Insurance premiums in accordance with the provisions of Section 10. These items are called "Escrow Items." At origination or at any time during the term of the Loan, Lender may require that Community Association Dues, Fees, and Assessments, if any,

OHIO--Single Family--**Fannie Mae/Freddie Mac UNIFORM INSTRUMENT**　　　　Form 3036　1/01 *(page 4 of 16 pages)*

be escrowed by Borrower, and such dues, fees and assessments shall be an Escrow Item. Borrower shall promptly furnish to Lender all notices of amounts to be paid under this Section. Borrower shall pay Lender the Funds for Escrow Items unless Lender waives Borrower's obligation to pay the Funds for any or all Escrow Items. Lender may waive Borrower's obligation to pay to Lender Funds for any or all Escrow Items at any time. Any such waiver may only be in writing. In the event of such waiver, Borrower shall pay directly, when and where payable, the amounts due for any Escrow Items for which payment of Funds has been waived by Lender and, if Lender requires, shall furnish to Lender receipts evidencing such payment within such time period as Lender may require. Borrower's obligation to make such payments and to provide receipts shall for all purposes be deemed to be a covenant and agreement contained in this Security Instrument, as the phrase "covenant and agreement" is used in Section 9. If Borrower is obligated to pay Escrow Items directly, pursuant to a waiver, and Borrower fails to pay the amount due for an Escrow Item, Lender may exercise its rights under Section 9 and pay such amount and Borrower shall then be obligated under Section 9 to repay to Lender any such amount. Lender may revoke the waiver as to any or all Escrow Items at any time by a notice given in accordance with Section 15 and, upon such revocation, Borrower shall pay to Lender all Funds, and in such amounts, that are then required under this Section 3.

Lender may, at any time, collect and hold Funds in an amount (a) sufficient to permit Lender to apply the Funds at the time specified under RESPA, and (b) not to exceed the maximum amount a lender can require under RESPA. Lender shall estimate the amount of Funds due on the basis of current data and reasonable estimates of expenditures of future Escrow Items or otherwise in accordance with Applicable Law.

The Funds shall be held in an institution whose deposits are insured by a federal agency, instrumentality, or entity (including Lender, if Lender is an institution whose deposits are so insured) or in any Federal Home Loan Bank. Lender shall apply the Funds to pay the Escrow Items no later than the time specified under RESPA. Lender shall not charge Borrower for holding and applying the Funds, annually analyzing the escrow account, or verifying the Escrow Items, unless Lender pays Borrower interest on the Funds and Applicable Law permits Lender to make such a charge. Unless an agreement is made in writing or Applicable Law requires interest to be paid on the Funds, Lender shall not be required to pay Borrower any interest or earnings on the Funds. Borrower and Lender can agree in writing, however, that interest shall be paid on the Funds. Lender shall give to Borrower, without charge, an annual accounting of the Funds as required by RESPA.

If there is a surplus of Funds held in escrow, as defined under RESPA, Lender shall account to Borrower for the excess funds in accordance with RESPA. If there is a shortage of Funds held in escrow, as defined under RESPA, Lender shall notify Borrower as required by RESPA, and Borrower shall pay to Lender the amount necessary to make up the shortage in accordance with RESPA, but in no more than 12 monthly payments. If there is a deficiency of Funds held in escrow, as defined under RESPA, Lender shall notify Borrower as required by RESPA, and Borrower shall pay to Lender the amount necessary to make up the deficiency in accordance with RESPA, but in no more than 12 monthly payments.

Upon payment in full of all sums secured by this Security Instrument, Lender shall promptly refund to Borrower any Funds held by Lender.

OHIO--Single Family--**Fannie Mae/Freddie Mac UNIFORM INSTRUMENT**   Form 3036   1/01   *(page 5 of 16 pages)*

4. Charges; Liens. Borrower shall pay all taxes, assessments, charges, fines, and impositions attributable to the Property which can attain priority over this Security Instrument, leasehold payments or ground rents on the Property, if any, and Community Association Dues, Fees, and Assessments, if any. To the extent that these items are Escrow Items, Borrower shall pay them in the manner provided in Section 3.

Borrower shall promptly discharge any lien which has priority over this Security Instrument unless Borrower: (a) agrees in writing to the payment of the obligation secured by the lien in a manner acceptable to Lender, but only so long as Borrower is performing such agreement; (b) contests the lien in good faith by, or defends against enforcement of the lien in, legal proceedings which in Lender's opinion operate to prevent the enforcement of the lien while those proceedings are pending, but only until such proceedings are concluded; or (c) secures from the holder of the lien an agreement satisfactory to Lender subordinating the lien to this Security Instrument. If Lender determines that any part of the Property is subject to a lien which can attain priority over this Security Instrument, Lender may give Borrower a notice identifying the lien. Within 10 days of the date on which that notice is given, Borrower shall satisfy the lien or take one or more of the actions set forth above in this Section 4.

Lender may require Borrower to pay a one-time charge for a real estate tax verification and/or reporting service used by Lender in connection with this Loan.

5. Property Insurance. Borrower shall keep the improvements now existing or hereafter erected on the Property insured against loss by fire, hazards included within the term "extended coverage," and any other hazards including, but not limited to, earthquakes and floods, for which Lender requires insurance. This insurance shall be maintained in the amounts (including deductible levels) and for the periods that Lender requires. What Lender requires pursuant to the preceding sentences can change during the term of the Loan. The insurance carrier providing the insurance shall be chosen by Borrower subject to Lender's right to disapprove Borrower's choice, which right shall not be exercised unreasonably. Lender may require Borrower to pay, in connection with this Loan, either: (a) a one-time charge for flood zone determination, certification and tracking services; or (b) a one-time charge for flood zone determination and certification services and subsequent charges each time remappings or similar changes occur which reasonably might affect such determination or certification. Borrower shall also be responsible for the payment of any fees imposed by the Federal Emergency Management Agency in connection with the review of any flood zone determination resulting from an objection by Borrower.

If Borrower fails to maintain any of the coverages described above, Lender may obtain insurance coverage, at Lender's option and Borrower's expense. Lender is under no obligation to purchase any particular type or amount of coverage. Therefore, such coverage shall cover Lender, but might or might not protect Borrower, Borrower's equity in the Property, or the contents of the Property, against any risk, hazard or liability and might provide greater or lesser coverage than was previously in effect. Borrower acknowledges that the cost of the insurance coverage so obtained might significantly exceed the cost of insurance that Borrower could have obtained. Any amounts disbursed by Lender under this Section 5 shall become additional debt of Borrower secured by this Security Instrument. These amounts shall bear interest at the Note rate from the date of disbursement and shall be payable, with such interest, upon notice from Lender to Borrower requesting payment.

OHIO--Single Family--**Fannie Mae/Freddie Mac UNIFORM INSTRUMENT**   Form 3036   1/01   *(page 6 of 16 pages)*

All insurance policies required by Lender and renewals of such policies shall be subject to Lender's right to disapprove such policies, shall include a standard mortgage clause, and shall name Lender as mortgagee and/or as an additional loss payee. Lender shall have the right to hold the policies and renewal certificates. If Lender requires, Borrower shall promptly give to Lender all receipts of paid premiums and renewal notices. If Borrower obtains any form of insurance coverage, not otherwise required by Lender, for damage to, or destruction of, the Property, such policy shall include a standard mortgage clause and shall name Lender as mortgagee and/or as an additional loss payee.

In the event of loss, Borrower shall give prompt notice to the insurance carrier and Lender. Lender may make proof of loss if not made promptly by Borrower. Unless Lender and Borrower otherwise agree in writing, any insurance proceeds, whether or not the underlying insurance was required by Lender, shall be applied to restoration or repair of the Property, if the restoration or repair is economically feasible and Lender's security is not lessened. During such repair and restoration period, Lender shall have the right to hold such insurance proceeds until Lender has had an opportunity to inspect such Property to ensure the work has been completed to Lender's satisfaction, provided that such inspection shall be undertaken promptly. Lender may disburse proceeds for the repairs and restoration in a single payment or in a series of progress payments as the work is completed. Unless an agreement is made in writing or Applicable Law requires interest to be paid on such insurance proceeds, Lender shall not be required to pay Borrower any interest or earnings on such proceeds. Fees for public adjusters, or other third parties, retained by Borrower shall not be paid out of the insurance proceeds and shall be the sole obligation of Borrower. If the restoration or repair is not economically feasible or Lender's security would be lessened, the insurance proceeds shall be applied to the sums secured by this Security Instrument, whether or not then due, with the excess, if any, paid to Borrower. Such insurance proceeds shall be applied in the order provided for in Section 2.

If Borrower abandons the Property, Lender may file, negotiate and settle any available insurance claim and related matters. If Borrower does not respond within 30 days to a notice from Lender that the insurance carrier has offered to settle a claim, then Lender may negotiate and settle the claim. The 30-day period will begin when the notice is given. In either event, or if Lender acquires the Property under Section 22 or otherwise, Borrower hereby assigns to Lender (a) Borrower's rights to any insurance proceeds in an amount not to exceed the amounts unpaid under the Note or this Security Instrument, and (b) any other of Borrower's rights (other than the right to any refund of unearned premiums paid by Borrower) under all insurance policies covering the Property, insofar as such rights are applicable to the coverage of the Property. Lender may use the insurance proceeds either to repair or restore the Property or to pay amounts unpaid under the Note or this Security Instrument, whether or not then due.

6. Occupancy. Borrower shall occupy, establish, and use the Property as Borrower's principal residence within 60 days after the execution of this Security Instrument and shall continue to occupy the Property as Borrower's principal residence for at least one year after the date of occupancy, unless Lender otherwise agrees in writing, which consent shall not be unreasonably withheld, or unless extenuating circumstances exist which are beyond Borrower's control.

7. Preservation, Maintenance and Protection of the Property; Inspections. Borrower shall not destroy, damage or impair the Property, allow the Property to deteriorate or commit waste

OHIO--Single Family--**Fannie Mae/Freddie Mac UNIFORM INSTRUMENT** Form 3036 1/01 *(page 7 of 16 pages)*

on the Property. Whether or not Borrower is residing in the Property, Borrower shall maintain the Property in order to prevent the Property from deteriorating or decreasing in value due to its condition. Unless it is determined pursuant to Section 5 that repair or restoration is not economically feasible, Borrower shall promptly repair the Property if damaged to avoid further deterioration or damage. If insurance or condemnation proceeds are paid in connection with damage to, or the taking of, the Property, Borrower shall be responsible for repairing or restoring the Property only if Lender has released proceeds for such purposes. Lender may disburse proceeds for the repairs and restoration in a single payment or in a series of progress payments as the work is completed. If the insurance or condemnation proceeds are not sufficient to repair or restore the Property, Borrower is not relieved of Borrower's obligation for the completion of such repair or restoration.

Lender or its agent may make reasonable entries upon and inspections of the Property. If it has reasonable cause, Lender may inspect the interior of the improvements on the Property. Lender shall give Borrower notice at the time of or prior to such an interior inspection specifying such reasonable cause.

8. Borrower's Loan Application. Borrower shall be in default if, during the Loan application process, Borrower or any persons or entities acting at the direction of Borrower or with Borrower's knowledge or consent gave materially false, misleading, or inaccurate information or statements to Lender (or failed to provide Lender with material information) in connection with the Loan. Material representations include, but are not limited to, representations concerning Borrower's occupancy of the Property as Borrower's principal residence.

9. Protection of Lender's Interest in the Property and Rights Under this Security Instrument. If (a) Borrower fails to perform the covenants and agreements contained in this Security Instrument, (b) there is a legal proceeding that might significantly affect Lender's interest in the Property and/or rights under this Security Instrument (such as a proceeding in bankruptcy, probate, for condemnation or forfeiture, for enforcement of a lien which may attain priority over this Security Instrument or to enforce laws or regulations), or (c) Borrower has abandoned the Property, then Lender may do and pay for whatever is reasonable or appropriate to protect Lender's interest in the Property and rights under this Security Instrument, including protecting and/or assessing the value of the Property, and securing and/or repairing the Property. Lender's actions can include, but are not limited to: (a) paying any sums secured by a lien which has priority over this Security Instrument; (b) appearing in court; and (c) paying reasonable attorneys' fees to protect its interest in the Property and/or rights under this Security Instrument, including its secured position in a bankruptcy proceeding. Securing the Property includes, but is not limited to, entering the Property to make repairs, change locks, replace or board up doors and windows, drain water from pipes, eliminate building or other code violations or dangerous conditions, and have utilities turned on or off. Although Lender may take action under this Section 9, Lender does not have to do so and is not under any duty or obligation to do so. It is agreed that Lender incurs no liability for not taking any or all actions authorized under this Section 9.

Any amounts disbursed by Lender under this Section 9 shall become additional debt of Borrower secured by this Security Instrument. These amounts shall bear interest at the Note rate from the date of disbursement and shall be payable, with such interest, upon notice from Lender to Borrower requesting payment.

OHIO--Single Family--**Fannie Mae/Freddie Mac UNIFORM INSTRUMENT**   Form 3036   1/01   *(page 8 of 16 pages)*

If this Security Instrument is on a leasehold, Borrower shall comply with all the provisions of the lease. If Borrower acquires fee title to the Property, the leasehold and the fee title shall not merge unless Lender agrees to the merger in writing.

10. Mortgage Insurance. If Lender required Mortgage Insurance as a condition of making the Loan, Borrower shall pay the premiums required to maintain the Mortgage Insurance in effect. If, for any reason, the Mortgage Insurance coverage required by Lender ceases to be available from the mortgage insurer that previously provided such insurance and Borrower was required to make separately designated payments toward the premiums for Mortgage Insurance, Borrower shall pay the premiums required to obtain coverage substantially equivalent to the Mortgage Insurance previously in effect, at a cost substantially equivalent to the cost to Borrower of the Mortgage Insurance previously in effect, from an alternate mortgage insurer selected by Lender. If substantially equivalent Mortgage Insurance coverage is not available, Borrower shall continue to pay to Lender the amount of the separately designated payments that were due when the insurance coverage ceased to be in effect. Lender will accept, use and retain these payments as a non-refundable loss reserve in lieu of Mortgage Insurance. Such loss reserve shall be non-refundable, notwithstanding the fact that the Loan is ultimately paid in full, and Lender shall not be required to pay Borrower any interest or earnings on such loss reserve. Lender can no longer require loss reserve payments if Mortgage Insurance coverage (in the amount and for the period that Lender requires) provided by an insurer selected by Lender again becomes available, is obtained, and Lender requires separately designated payments toward the premiums for Mortgage Insurance. If Lender required Mortgage Insurance as a condition of making the Loan and Borrower was required to make separately designated payments toward the premiums for Mortgage Insurance, Borrower shall pay the premiums required to maintain Mortgage Insurance in effect, or to provide a non-refundable loss reserve, until Lender's requirement for Mortgage Insurance ends in accordance with any written agreement between Borrower and Lender providing for such termination or until termination is required by Applicable Law. Nothing in this Section 10 affects Borrower's obligation to pay interest at the rate provided in the Note.

Mortgage Insurance reimburses Lender (or any entity that purchases the Note) for certain losses it may incur if Borrower does not repay the Loan as agreed. Borrower is not a party to the Mortgage Insurance.

Mortgage insurers evaluate their total risk on all such insurance in force from time to time, and may enter into agreements with other parties that share or modify their risk, or reduce losses. These agreements are on terms and conditions that are satisfactory to the mortgage insurer and the other party (or parties) to these agreements. These agreements may require the mortgage insurer to make payments using any source of funds that the mortgage insurer may have available (which may include funds obtained from Mortgage Insurance premiums).

As a result of these agreements, Lender, any purchaser of the Note, another insurer, any reinsurer, any other entity, or any affiliate of any of the foregoing, may receive (directly or indirectly) amounts that derive from (or might be characterized as) a portion of Borrower's payments for Mortgage Insurance, in exchange for sharing or modifying the mortgage insurer's risk, or reducing losses. If such agreement provides that an affiliate of Lender takes a share of the insurer's risk in exchange for a share of the premiums paid to the insurer, the arrangement is often termed "captive reinsurance." Further:

(a) Any such agreements will not affect the amounts that Borrower has agreed to pay for Mortgage Insurance, or any other terms of the Loan. Such agreements will not increase

OHIO--Single Family--**Fannie Mae/Freddie Mac UNIFORM INSTRUMENT**   Form 3036   1/01   *(page 9 of 16 pages)*

the amount Borrower will owe for Mortgage Insurance, and they will not entitle Borrower to any refund.

(b) Any such agreements will not affect the rights Borrower has – if any – with respect to the Mortgage Insurance under the Homeowners Protection Act of 1998 or any other law. These rights may include the right to receive certain disclosures, to request and obtain cancellation of the Mortgage Insurance, to have the Mortgage Insurance terminated automatically, and/or to receive a refund of any Mortgage Insurance premiums that were unearned at the time of such cancellation or termination.

11. Assignment of Miscellaneous Proceeds; Forfeiture. All Miscellaneous Proceeds are hereby assigned to and shall be paid to Lender.

If the Property is damaged, such Miscellaneous Proceeds shall be applied to restoration or repair of the Property, if the restoration or repair is economically feasible and Lender's security is not lessened. During such repair and restoration period, Lender shall have the right to hold such Miscellaneous Proceeds until Lender has had an opportunity to inspect such Property to ensure the work has been completed to Lender's satisfaction, provided that such inspection shall be undertaken promptly. Lender may pay for the repairs and restoration in a single disbursement or in a series of progress payments as the work is completed. Unless an agreement is made in writing or Applicable Law requires interest to be paid on such Miscellaneous Proceeds, Lender shall not be required to pay Borrower any interest or earnings on such Miscellaneous Proceeds. If the restoration or repair is not economically feasible or Lender's security would be lessened, the Miscellaneous Proceeds shall be applied to the sums secured by this Security Instrument, whether or not then due, with the excess, if any, paid to Borrower. Such Miscellaneous Proceeds shall be applied in the order provided for in Section 2.

In the event of a total taking, destruction, or loss in value of the Property, the Miscellaneous Proceeds shall be applied to the sums secured by this Security Instrument, whether or not then due, with the excess, if any, paid to Borrower.

In the event of a partial taking, destruction, or loss in value of the Property in which the fair market value of the Property immediately before the partial taking, destruction, or loss in value is equal to or greater than the amount of the sums secured by this Security Instrument immediately before the partial taking, destruction, or loss in value, unless Borrower and Lender otherwise agree in writing, the sums secured by this Security Instrument shall be reduced by the amount of the Miscellaneous Proceeds multiplied by the following fraction: (a) the total amount of the sums secured immediately before the partial taking, destruction, or loss in value divided by (b) the fair market value of the Property immediately before the partial taking, destruction, or loss in value. Any balance shall be paid to Borrower.

In the event of a partial taking, destruction, or loss in value of the Property in which the fair market value of the Property immediately before the partial taking, destruction, or loss in value is less than the amount of the sums secured immediately before the partial taking, destruction, or loss in value, unless Borrower and Lender otherwise agree in writing, the Miscellaneous Proceeds shall be applied to the sums secured by this Security Instrument whether or not the sums are then due.

If the Property is abandoned by Borrower, or if, after notice by Lender to Borrower that the Opposing Party (as defined in the next sentence) offers to make an award to settle a claim for damages, Borrower fails to respond to Lender within 30 days after the date the notice is given, Lender is authorized to collect and apply the Miscellaneous Proceeds either to restoration or repair of the Property or to the sums secured by this Security Instrument, whether or not then due. "Opposing Party" means the third party that owes Borrower Miscellaneous Proceeds or the party against whom Borrower has a right of action in regard to Miscellaneous Proceeds.

Borrower shall be in default if any action or proceeding, whether civil or criminal, is begun that, in Lender's judgment, could result in forfeiture of the Property or other material impairment of Lender's interest in the Property or rights under this Security Instrument. Borrower can cure such a default and, if acceleration has occurred, reinstate as provided in Section 19, by causing the action or proceeding to be dismissed with a ruling that, in Lender's judgment, precludes forfeiture of the Property or other material impairment of Lender's interest in the Property or rights under this Security Instrument. The proceeds of any award or claim for damages that are attributable to the impairment of Lender's interest in the Property are hereby assigned and shall be paid to Lender.

All Miscellaneous Proceeds that are not applied to restoration or repair of the Property shall be applied in the order provided for in Section 2.

12. Borrower Not Released; Forbearance By Lender Not a Waiver. Extension of the time for payment or modification of amortization of the sums secured by this Security Instrument granted by Lender to Borrower or any Successor in Interest of Borrower shall not operate to release the liability of Borrower or any Successors in Interest of Borrower. Lender shall not be required to commence proceedings against any Successor in Interest of Borrower or to refuse to extend time for payment or otherwise modify amortization of the sums secured by this Security Instrument by reason of any demand made by the original Borrower or any Successors in Interest of Borrower. Any forbearance by Lender in exercising any right or remedy including, without limitation, Lender's acceptance of payments from third persons, entities or Successors in Interest of Borrower or in amounts less than the amount then due, shall not be a waiver of or preclude the exercise of any right or remedy.

13. Joint and Several Liability; Co-signers; Successors and Assigns Bound. Borrower covenants and agrees that Borrower's obligations and liability shall be joint and several. However, any Borrower who co-signs this Security Instrument but does not execute the Note (a "co-signer"): (a) is co-signing this Security Instrument only to mortgage, grant and convey the co-signer's interest in the Property under the terms of this Security Instrument; (b) is not personally obligated to pay the sums secured by this Security Instrument; and (c) agrees that Lender and any other Borrower can agree to extend, modify, forbear or make any accommodations with regard to the terms of this Security Instrument or the Note without the co-signer's consent.

Subject to the provisions of Section 18, any Successor in Interest of Borrower who assumes Borrower's obligations under this Security Instrument in writing, and is approved by Lender, shall obtain all of Borrower's rights and benefits under this Security Instrument. Borrower shall not be released from Borrower's obligations and liability under this Security Instrument unless Lender agrees to such release in writing. The covenants and agreements of this Security Instrument shall bind (except as provided in Section 20) and benefit the successors and assigns of Lender.

14. Loan Charges. Lender may charge Borrower fees for services performed in connection with Borrower's default, for the purpose of protecting Lender's interest in the Property and rights under this Security Instrument, including, but not limited to, attorneys' fees, property inspection and valuation fees. In regard to any other fees, the absence of express authority in this Security Instrument to charge a specific fee to Borrower shall not be construed as a prohibition on the charging of such fee. Lender may not charge fees that are expressly prohibited by this Security Instrument or by Applicable Law.

If the Loan is subject to a law which sets maximum loan charges, and that law is finally interpreted so that the interest or other loan charges collected or to be collected in connection with the Loan exceed the permitted limits, then: (a) any such loan charge shall be reduced by the amount necessary to reduce the charge to the permitted limit; and (b) any sums already collected from Borrower which exceeded permitted limits will be refunded to Borrower. Lender may choose to make this refund by reducing the principal owed under the Note or by making a direct payment to Borrower. If a refund reduces principal, the reduction will be treated as a partial prepayment without any prepayment charge (whether or not a prepayment charge is provided for under the Note). Borrower's acceptance of any such refund made by direct payment to Borrower will constitute a waiver of any right of action Borrower might have arising out of such overcharge.

15. Notices. All notices given by Borrower or Lender in connection with this Security Instrument must be in writing. Any notice to Borrower in connection with this Security Instrument shall be deemed to have been given to Borrower when mailed by first class mail or when actually delivered to Borrower's notice address if sent by other means. Notice to any one Borrower shall constitute notice to all Borrowers unless Applicable Law expressly requires otherwise. The notice address shall be the Property Address unless Borrower has designated a substitute notice address by notice to Lender. Borrower shall promptly notify Lender of Borrower's change of address. If Lender specifies a procedure for reporting Borrower's change of address, then Borrower shall only report a change of address through that specified procedure. There may be only one designated notice address under this Security Instrument at any one time. Any notice to Lender shall be given by delivering it or by mailing it by first class mail to Lender's address stated herein unless Lender has designated another address by notice to Borrower. Any notice in connection with this Security Instrument shall not be deemed to have been given to Lender until actually received by Lender. If any notice required by this Security Instrument is also required under Applicable Law, the Applicable Law requirement will satisfy the corresponding requirement under this Security Instrument.

16. Governing Law; Severability; Rules of Construction. This Security Instrument shall be governed by federal law and the law of the jurisdiction in which the Property is located. All rights and obligations contained in this Security Instrument are subject to any requirements and limitations of Applicable Law. Applicable Law might explicitly or implicitly allow the parties to agree by contract or it might be silent, but such silence shall not be construed as a prohibition against agreement by contract. In the event that any provision or clause of this Security Instrument or the Note conflicts with Applicable Law, such conflict shall not affect other provisions of this Security Instrument or the Note which can be given effect without the conflicting provision.

As used in this Security Instrument: (a) words of the masculine gender shall mean and include corresponding neuter words or words of the feminine gender; (b) words in the singular shall mean and include the plural and vice versa; and (c) the word "may" gives sole discretion without any obligation to take any action.

17. Borrower's Copy. Borrower shall be given one copy of the Note and of this Security Instrument.

18. Transfer of the Property or a Beneficial Interest in Borrower. As used in this Section 18, "Interest in the Property" means any legal or beneficial interest in the Property, including, but not

OHIO--Single Family--**Fannie Mae/Freddie Mac UNIFORM INSTRUMENT**   Form 3036   1/01 *(page 12 of 16 pages)*

limited to, those beneficial interests transferred in a bond for deed, contract for deed, installment sales contract or escrow agreement, the intent of which is the transfer of title by Borrower at a future date to a purchaser.

If all or any part of the Property or any Interest in the Property is sold or transferred (or if Borrower is not a natural person and a beneficial interest in Borrower is sold or transferred) without Lender's prior written consent, Lender may require immediate payment in full of all sums secured by this Security Instrument. However, this option shall not be exercised by Lender if such exercise is prohibited by Applicable Law.

If Lender exercises this option, Lender shall give Borrower notice of acceleration. The notice shall provide a period of not less than 30 days from the date the notice is given in accordance with Section 15 within which Borrower must pay all sums secured by this Security Instrument. If Borrower fails to pay these sums prior to the expiration of this period, Lender may invoke any remedies permitted by this Security Instrument without further notice or demand on Borrower.

19. Borrower's Right to Reinstate After Acceleration. If Borrower meets certain conditions, Borrower shall have the right to have enforcement of this Security Instrument discontinued at any time prior to the earliest of: (a) five days before sale of the Property pursuant to any power of sale contained in this Security Instrument; (b) such other period as Applicable Law might specify for the termination of Borrower's right to reinstate; or (c) entry of a judgment enforcing this Security Instrument. Those conditions are that Borrower: (a) pays Lender all sums which then would be due under this Security Instrument and the Note as if no acceleration had occurred; (b) cures any default of any other covenants or agreements; (c) pays all expenses incurred in enforcing this Security Instrument, including, but not limited to, reasonable attorneys' fees, property inspection and valuation fees, and other fees incurred for the purpose of protecting Lender's interest in the Property and rights under this Security Instrument; and (d) takes such action as Lender may reasonably require to assure that Lender's interest in the Property and rights under this Security Instrument, and Borrower's obligation to pay the sums secured by this Security Instrument, shall continue unchanged. Lender may require that Borrower pay such reinstatement sums and expenses in one or more of the following forms, as selected by Lender: (a) cash; (b) money order; (c) certified check, bank check, treasurer's check or cashier's check, provided any such check is drawn upon an institution whose deposits are insured by a federal agency, instrumentality or entity; or (d) Electronic Funds Transfer. Upon reinstatement by Borrower, this Security Instrument and obligations secured hereby shall remain fully effective as if no acceleration had occurred. However, this right to reinstate shall not apply in the case of acceleration under Section 18.

20. Sale of Note; Change of Loan Servicer; Notice of Grievance. The Note or a partial interest in the Note (together with this Security Instrument) can be sold one or more times without prior notice to Borrower. A sale might result in a change in the entity (known as the "Loan Servicer") that collects Periodic Payments due under the Note and this Security Instrument and performs other mortgage loan servicing obligations under the Note, this Security Instrument, and Applicable Law. There also might be one or more changes of the Loan Servicer unrelated to a sale of the Note. If there is a change of the Loan Servicer, Borrower will be given written notice of the change which will state the name and address of the new Loan Servicer, the address to which payments should be made and any other information RESPA requires in connection with a notice of transfer of servicing. If the Note is sold and thereafter the Loan is serviced by a Loan Servicer other than the purchaser of the Note, the mortgage loan servicing obligations to Borrower will remain with the Loan Servicer or be transferred to a successor Loan Servicer and are not assumed by the Note purchaser unless otherwise provided by the Note purchaser.

Neither Borrower nor Lender may commence, join, or be joined to any judicial action (as either an individual litigant or the member of a class) that arises from the other party's actions pursuant to this Security Instrument or that alleges that the other party has breached any provision of, or any duty owed by reason of, this Security Instrument, until such Borrower or Lender has notified the other party (with such notice given in compliance with the requirements of Section 15) of such alleged breach and afforded the other party hereto a reasonable period after the giving of such notice to take corrective action. If Applicable Law provides a time period which must elapse before certain action can be taken, that time period will be deemed to be reasonable for purposes of this paragraph. The notice of acceleration and opportunity to cure given to Borrower pursuant to Section 22 and the notice of acceleration given to Borrower pursuant to Section 18 shall be deemed to satisfy the notice and opportunity to take corrective action provisions of this Section 20.

21. Hazardous Substances. As used in this Section 21: (a) "Hazardous Substances" are those substances defined as toxic or hazardous substances, pollutants, or wastes by Environmental Law and the following substances: gasoline, kerosene, other flammable or toxic petroleum products, toxic pesticides and herbicides, volatile solvents, materials containing asbestos or formaldehyde, and radioactive materials; (b) "Environmental Law" means federal laws and laws of the jurisdiction where the Property is located that relate to health, safety or environmental protection; (c) "Environmental Cleanup" includes any response action, remedial action, or removal action, as defined in Environmental Law; and (d) an "Environmental Condition" means a condition that can cause, contribute to, or otherwise trigger an Environmental Cleanup.

Borrower shall not cause or permit the presence, use, disposal, storage, or release of any Hazardous Substances, or threaten to release any Hazardous Substances, on or in the Property. Borrower shall not do, nor allow anyone else to do, anything affecting the Property (a) that is in violation of any Environmental Law, (b) which creates an Environmental Condition, or (c) which, due to the presence, use, or release of a Hazardous Substance, creates a condition that adversely affects the value of the Property. The preceding two sentences shall not apply to the presence, use, or storage on the Property of small quantities of Hazardous Substances that are generally recognized to be appropriate to normal residential uses and to maintenance of the Property (including, but not limited to, hazardous substances in consumer products).

Borrower shall promptly give Lender written notice of (a) any investigation, claim, demand, lawsuit or other action by any governmental or regulatory agency or private party involving the Property and any Hazardous Substance or Environmental Law of which Borrower has actual knowledge, (b) any Environmental Condition, including but not limited to, any spilling, leaking, discharge, release or threat of release of any Hazardous Substance, and (c) any condition caused by the presence, use or release of a Hazardous Substance which adversely affects the value of the Property. If Borrower learns, or is notified by any governmental or regulatory authority, or any private party, that any removal or other remediation of any Hazardous Substance affecting the Property is necessary, Borrower shall promptly take all necessary remedial actions in accordance with Environmental Law. Nothing herein shall create any obligation on Lender for an Environmental Cleanup.

NON-UNIFORM COVENANTS. Borrower and Lender further covenant and agree as follows:

OHIO--Single Family--**Fannie Mae/Freddie Mac UNIFORM INSTRUMENT**　　　　Form 3036 1/01 *(page 14 of 16 pages)*

22. Acceleration; Remedies. Lender shall give notice to Borrower prior to acceleration following Borrower's breach of any covenant or agreement in this Security Instrument (but not prior to acceleration under Section 18 unless Applicable Law provides otherwise). The notice shall specify: (a) the default; (b) the action required to cure the default; (c) a date, not less than 30 days from the date the notice is given to Borrower, by which the default must be cured; and (d) that failure to cure the default on or before the date specified in the notice may result in acceleration of the sums secured by this Security Instrument, foreclosure by judicial proceeding and sale of the Property. The notice shall further inform Borrower of the right to reinstate after acceleration and the right to assert in the foreclosure proceeding the non-existence of a default or any other defense of Borrower to acceleration and foreclosure. If the default is not cured on or before the date specified in the notice, Lender at its option may require immediate payment in full of all sums secured by this Security Instrument without further demand and may foreclose this Security Instrument by judicial proceeding. Lender shall be entitled to collect all expenses incurred in pursuing the remedies provided in this Section 22, including, but not limited to, costs of title evidence.

23. Release. Upon payment of all sums secured by this Security Instrument, Lender shall discharge this Security Instrument. Borrower shall pay any recordation costs. Lender may charge Borrower a fee for releasing this Security Instrument, but only if the fee is paid to a third party for services rendered and the charging of the fee is permitted under Applicable Law.

24. Certain Other Advances. In addition to any other sum secured hereby, this Security Instrument shall also secure the unpaid principal balance of, plus accrued interest on, any amount of money loaned, advanced or paid by Lender to or for the account and benefit of Borrower, after this Security Instrument is delivered to and filed with the Recorder's Office, _____ County, Ohio, for recording. Lender may make such advances in order to pay any real estate taxes and assessments, insurance premiums plus all other costs and expenses incurred in connection with the operation, protection or preservation of the Property, including to cure Borrower's defaults by making any such payments which Borrower should have paid as provided in this Security Instrument, it being intended by this Section 24 to acknowledge, affirm and comply with the provision of § 5301.233 of the Revised Code of Ohio.

BY SIGNING BELOW, Borrower accepts and agrees to the terms and covenants contained in this Security Instrument and in any Rider executed by Borrower and recorded with it.

OHIO--Single Family--**Fannie Mae/Freddie Mac UNIFORM INSTRUMENT**   Form 3036   1/01   *(page 15 of 16 pages)*

Witnesses:

_____   _____(Seal)
                                                                  - Borrower

_____   _____(Seal)
                                                                  - Borrower

_____ **[Space Below This Line For Acknowledgment]** _____

SAMPLE

Appendix H – UST Adoption Table

State Adoption of Uniform State Test

States which have adopted the UST	States which have not adopted the UST

State Regulatory Registry LLC, last updated 9/18/2017

As of September 18, 2017, 57 state mortgage agencies have adopted the Uniform State Test (UST). The other 2 agencies may elect to adopt the UST at a future date, but are not required to do so. Candidates will need to pass the state-specific test component up until the actual date that state agency adopts the UST.

Have adopted the UST				Have not adopted
Alabama	Illinois	Nevada	South Dakota	West Virginia
Alaska	Indiana DFI	New Hampshire	Tennessee	Minnesota
Arizona	Indiana SOS	New Jersey	Texas OCCC	
Arkansas	Iowa	New Mexico	Texas SML	
California BRE	Kansas	New York	Utah DFI	
California DBO	Kentucky	North Carolina	Utah DRE	
Colorado	Louisiana	North Dakota	Vermont	
Connecticut	Maine	Ohio	Virgin Islands	
Delaware	Maryland	Oklahoma	Virginia	
District of Columbia	Massachusetts	Oregon	Washington	
Florida	Michigan	Pennsylvania	Wisconsin	
Georgia	Mississippi	Puerto Rico	Wyoming	
Guam	Missouri	Rhode Island		
Hawaii	Montana	South Carolina BFI		
Idaho	Nebraska	South Carolina DCA		

Notes:

CHAPTER ANSWER KEYS

Chapter 1

Exercise 1.1: Apply Your Knowledge

A. FDIC - **2. Insures bank deposits**

B. FHA - **3. Largest mortgage loan insurer**

C. Fully Amortizing - **4. Level loan payments**

D. Jumbo Loans - **5. Non-conforming loan**

E. Mortgage Insurance - **1. Covers loss due to default and property value decline**

Exercise 1.2: Knowledge Check

Federal Deposit Insurance Corporation. The FDIC was created in 1933 as part of the New Deal, to insure commercial bank deposits against bank failures and bank runs.

Exercise 1.3: Knowledge Check

1. **C. the primary market.** - When borrowers and lenders negotiate mortgage terms and close mortgage loans, they are acting in the primary market.

2. **C. hedge funds.** - The mortgage banker, as a correspondent, closes the loan with internally generated funds in its own name or with funds borrowed from a warehouse lender.

Exercise 1.4: Knowledge Check

1. **C. the FNMA.** - FNMA (Fannie Mae) creates national underwriting criteria, which is the guideline to the loan characteristics that it will purchase in the secondary market.

2. **D. pooling the loan with other loans and selling on the secondary market.** - The servicing of a mortgage loan is defined as the process of collecting payments, keeping records, and handling defaults for loans.

3. **D. replenish the funds used to make mortgage loans.** - When mortgage lenders sell their mortgage loans to secondary market participants, the source of money used to fund the sold loans is replenished and becomes available to make loans to new consumers.

Exercise 1.5: Knowledge Check

1. **A. true** - Section 1011 of Subtitle A of Title X under the Dodd-Frank Act created the Consumer Financial Protection Bureau whose task is to enforce consumer financial protection laws.

2. **A. true** - The Mortgage Reform and Anti-Predatory Lending Act addresses abusive or predatory lending practices in the mortgage industry. For example, Subtitle B of Title XIV requires MLOs to apply minimum qualifying standards and defines a new category of "qualified" loans.

Chapter 1 Quiz

1. **C. serve as a depository for consumer assets** - Secondary markets are non-depository entities that purchase closed loans, which conform to the guidelines set by the secondary market. They are not depository institutions and cannot accept consumer deposits.

2. **A. Dodd-Frank Act.** - The Dodd-Frank Act established the CFPB.

3. **A. act as intermediaries between borrowers and lenders.** - A lender is a financial institution that makes loans directly to you. A broker does not lend money. A broker finds a lender. A broker may work with many lenders.

4. **A. Federal Home Loan Banks** - Created by Congress, the Federal Home Loan Banks have been the largest source of funding for mortgage lending for nearly eight decades and were established in 1932 as a cooperative to finance housing in local communities.

5. **B. insurance companies** - Insurance companies are not primary lenders of residential mortgages.

6. **B. Ginnie Mae guarantees mortgage-backed securities.** - Ginnie Mae guarantees investors the timely payment of principal

and interest on MBSs backed by federally-insured or guaranteed loans — mainly loans insured by the FHA or guaranteed by the VA.

7. **A. Department of Commerce.** - The Consumer Financial Protection Act consolidated consumer protection responsibilities previously handled by the Office of the Comptroller of the Currency, Office of Thrift Supervision, Federal Deposit Insurance Corporation, Federal Reserve, National Credit Union

Administration, the Department of Housing and Urban Development, and Federal Trade Commission under the CFPB.

8. **C. Federal National Mortgage Association** - The Federal National Mortgage Association (FNMA/Fannie Mae) is the nation's largest investor in residential mortgages. Fannie Mae was originally chartered as a GSE by Congress in 1938 to provide liquidity and stability to the U.S. housing and mortgage markets, primarily as a place for lenders to sell their FHA-insured loans.

Chapter 2

Exercise 2.1: Apply Your Knowledge

1. The maximum monthly mortgage payment Mary can qualify for is $807. Remember, when both ratios are used, Mary must qualify under both ratios, so the lower figure is the most she can afford. The $807 number represents the maximum payment for principal, interest, taxes, and insurance (PITI) plus any other housing obligations, such as Homeowner's Association dues.

Housing expense ratio: 28%

$3,200	Monthly Gross Income
x 0.28	Income Ratio
$ 896	Maximum Mortgage PITI Payment

Total debt-to-income ratio: 36%

$3,200	Monthly Gross Income
x 0.36	Income Ratio
$1,152	Maximum Debt
- $220	Car Payment
- $ 75	Personal Loan Payment
- $ 50	Revolving Charge Card Payment
$ 807	Maximum Mortgage PITI Payment

2. If Mary could pay off some of her installment debts and reduce her total long-term monthly obligations, she could improve her debt-to-income ratio and would be able to qualify for a larger mortgage payment.

Exercise 2.2: Apply Your Knowledge

1. Lisa's monthly income = $18 hourly wage x 40 hours/week x 52 weeks = $37,440 annual income; $37,440 annual income ÷ 12 months = $3,120

Dave's monthly income = $625 weekly income x 52 weeks = $32,500 annual income; $32,500 annual income ÷ 12 months = $2,708.33

Total stable monthly income = $3,120 + $2,708.33 = $5,828.33

Maximum housing expense = $5,828.33 x 0.28 = **$1,631.93**

2. Maximum debt-to-income allowed = $5,828.33 x 0.36 = $2,098.20

Maximum housing expense = $2,098.20 - $400 (car loan) = **$1,698.20**

Remember to use the lower monthly payment allowable, which is $1,631.93.

3. Yes. Although Lisa and Dave have only been at their jobs a short time, Lisa had special training in the Air Force and Dave is a vocational nurse, which also implies special training.

Exercise 2.3: Apply Your Knowledge

1. $700 weekly income x 52 weeks = $36,400 annual income

$36,400 annual income ÷ 12 months = $3,033.33 monthly income

$878 mortgage payment ÷ $3,033.33 monthly income = **0.29 (29% housing expense ratio)**

2. $878 mortgage payment + $212 auto payment = $1,090 total debt service

$1,090 total debt service ÷ $3,033.33 monthly income = **0.36 (36% total debt-to-income ratio)**

3. Yes, Mr. Able will have a few problems closing this transaction. The equity in his home ($14,000) plus money in the bank ($3,600) equals only $17,600, but his down payment plus estimated closing costs = $18,400. He needs to show two additional months of cash reserves. His housing expense ratio of 29% exceeds guidelines.

4. Yes, Mr. Able's VOD is a problem because his current balance of $3,600 is significantly higher than his average balance of $1,000. He will need to have a good explanation of where the funds came from so the lender knows that he did not borrow the down payment.

Chapter 2 Quiz

1. **C. $3,600** - A point is 1% of the loan amount. Since Joe made a $30,000 down payment, the loan amount is $120,000. One point on this loan equals $1,200 ($120,000 x 0.01), so three points is $3,600.

2. **B. nontaxable income.** - A regular source of a borrower's income may be nontaxable—such as child support payments, Social Security benefits, a minister's housing allowance, disability retirement payments, workers' compensation benefits, certain types of public assistance payments, and food stamps.

3. **D. tax returns for the previous two years.** - For self-employment income to be used for qualifying, self-employed borrowers need to provide personal and entity (corporation, partnership, sole proprietorship) tax returns (all schedules) for a minimum of two years.

4. **C. gift letter signed by the donor stating no repayment is expected** - If an applicant lacks the necessary funds to close a transaction, a gift of the required amount may be acceptable. The gift should be confirmed by means of a gift letter signed by the donor. The letter should clearly state that the money represents a gift and does not have to be repaid. In addition to the gift letter, lenders want to verify that the donor has the funds available to provide the gift

by seeing a copy of the gift check, a recent bank statement from the donors showing they have the ability to give the gift and a copy of the deposit receipt showing funds have been deposited and are available for closing.

5. **C. 25%** - To be classified as self-employment income, the borrower must own at least 25% of the business.

6. **B. Fannie Mae and Freddie Mac.** - Loans that are not backed by the full faith and credit of the United States follow the underwriting guidelines of Fannie Mae and Freddie Mac.

7. **A. alimony received (that a borrower chooses to reveal).** - Alimony received can be considered part of the borrower's stable monthly qualifying income if it's determined it's likely to be made on a consistent basis. Alimony should be expected to continue for a minimum of three years in order to be used in income calculations. It does not need to be listed as a source of income if a borrower does not want it considered.

8. **B. 4506-T** - Underwriters generally require the lender to obtain a completed and signed Form 4506-T from a borrower(s) at application. This form gives the lender permission to request electronic transcripts of federal tax returns from the IRS when documenting the borrower's income to prevent mortgage fraud.

9. **B. cell phone service payment** - Utilities and insurance premiums are not considered debts because they can, in theory, be cancelled. Lenders assume borrowers would turn off their phones or cable service before losing their houses.

10. **B. $630** - The housing expense (front-end) ratio for a conventional conforming loan in 28%. $3,000 (income) x 0.28 = $840. The debt-to-income (back-end) ratio is 36%. Looking at the debt-to-income ratio: $3,000 (income) x 0.36, = $1,080. From there, subtract his monthly debts: $1,080 - ($350 +$50+ $50) = $630. The lender will consider the lower number.

Chapter 3

Exercise 3.1: Knowledge Check

1. **A. True** - A note is a document that gives notice of evidence of a debt. While the note is not required to be a matter of public record, it is a document that states the existence of a debt, the amount, etc.

2. **B. False** - The payee is the person or institution lending the money. The maker is also known as the payor, who is the person who makes the promise to repay the funds by signing a promissory note.

Exercise 3.2: Apply Your Knowledge

Mortgage Terms	
1. Balloon Note	**A. Additional payment at end of term**
2. Beneficiary	**B. Benefits from Deed of Trust**
3. Fully Amortizing	**K. Zero balance due at end of term**
4. Hypothecate	**H. Pledge as security**
5. Judicial	**D. Court decision**
6. Non-Judicial	**J. Trustee's sale**
7. Note	**E. Evidence of debt**
8. Security Instrument	**I. Protects lender**
9. Straight Note	**G. Interest-only**
10. Trustee	**F. Holds title**
11. Trustor	**C. Borrower**

Exercise 3.3: Knowledge Check

A. True - An agreement or clause in a security instrument that keeps a lien in a subordinate or junior position is called a subordination clause. A subordination agreement is a written agreement between lienholders on a property that changes the priority of mortgages, judgments, and other liens.

Chapter 3 Quiz

1. **D. straight note.** - A straight note is a note where interest-only payments are made for a specified period of time and a balloon payment is required at the end of the term to retire the note.

2. **B. alienation clause.** - The alienation clause (also called the "due on sale" clause) states that in the event an entire or partial interest is transferred by a borrower, the lender may call the entire balance of the loan due.

3. **D. promissory note** - The promissory note provides the evidence of debt and the mortgage provides the creditor security for the note.

4. **B. files a court action.** - A mortgage requires judicial foreclosure. To begin the judicial foreclosure process, a lender must file an action in court.

5. **B. hypothecation** - Hypothecation is the pledging of security for a note or loan without giving up possession or use of the property.

6. **A. acceleration clause** - An acceleration clause gives the lender the right to declare the entire loan balance due immediately because of borrower default or for violation of other contract provisions. This is sometimes referred to as "calling the note."

7. **B. mortgage.** - A mortgage creates a lien against real property as security for the payment of a note. The mortgage is a type of security instrument where the borrower (mortgagor) pledges the property to the lender (mortgagee) as collateral for the debt.

8. **C. mortgagor.** - The borrower who pledges property as collateral for a debt is called the mortgagor. The lender is called the mortgagee.

Chapter 4

Exercise 4.1: Knowledge Check

1. **A. True** - A conforming loan, a loan that conforms to the standards of FNMA or FHLMC, can be sold on the secondary market.

2. **B. False** - A self-liquidating loan is one where the borrower's monthly payments reduce the principal balance of the loan over the term of the loan.

Exercise 4.2: Apply Your Knowledge

1. Bill can borrow $128,000 for an 80% conventional loan.

2. Bill needs to make a 20% down payment of $32,000.

3. Bill can borrow only $120,000 (80%) if the house is appraised at $150,000.

4. Bill could offer the seller the appraised value of $150,000 or he needs to come up with an additional $8,000 as part of his down payment.

Exercise 4.3: Apply Your Knowledge

1. $90,000 (90% LTV)

2. $558 (0.0062 rate card factor x $90,000)

3. $46.50 ($558.00 ÷ 12 = $46.50)

Exercise 4.4: Apply Your Knowledge

1. **75%.** LTV is the first mortgage loan amount divided by the lesser of the sale price or appraisal.

2. **90%.** CLTV is the sum of all mortgage amounts divided by the lesser of the sale price or appraisal.

Chapter 4 Quiz

1. **C. fully amortizing loan.** - When a mortgage loan has periodic payments that pay both principal and interest payment so that the loan is paid in full at the end of the term, it is known as a fully amortizing loan.

2. **A. Higher interest rates are usually charged.** - A shorter-term loan, such as a 15-year loan, poses less of a risk to a lender. Therefore, because the risk is lower, lenders charge a lower interest rate for these loans.

3. **B. $128,000** - A loan without PMI requires an LTV of 80% or a down payment of 20%. With a sale price of $160,000 and a loan to value of 80%, the loan amount will be $128,000.

4. **A. conventional mortgage** - A loan that is not government insured or guaranteed is known as a conventional mortgage loan.

5. **C. must make at least a 5% down payment from personal funds.** - FNMA and FHLMC both require a 5% investment from the borrower's own funds before any secondary financing or gift funds may be applied to the transaction.

6. **C. when a home has been paid down to 78% of its original value and the borrower is current.** - The Homeowner's Protection Act requires a mortgage lender to cancel PMI when the loan-to-value reaches 78% of the original value of the mortgaged property.

7. **C. loan funds will be repaid more quickly.** - A shorter-term mortgage loan will have a lower interest rate charge because the lender will have their funds returned sooner.

8. **D. 85%** - The first mortgage amount is $160,000. The second mortgage amount is the sale price minus the first mortgage and the down payment amounts: $200,000 – $190,000 ($160,000 first mortgage + $30,000 down payment) = $10,000. $160,000 + $10,000 = $170,000, which is the sum of all liens on the property. $170,000 ÷ $200,000 (sale price) = 85% CLTV.

Chapter 5

Exercise 5.1: Knowledge Check

B. False - Anyone who is a U.S. citizen, permanent resident, or non-permanent resident with a qualifying work visa, and who meets the lending guidelines, can qualify for an FHA-insured loan.

Exercise 5.2: Knowledge Check

D. current interest rate - Current interest rates are not used as a basis for underwriting by the FHA; collateral, which identifies the property value, is the 4th C used by the FHA.

Exercise 5.3A: Apply Your Knowledge – (Part 1)

Dividing the total housing expense by 31%, this loan requires a stable monthly income of $2,582.74 ($800.65 ÷ .31 = $2,582.74).

Exercise 5.3B: Apply Your Knowledge – (Part 2)

FHA allows a maximum total debt-to-income ratio of 43% so $1,033.30 ÷ 0.43 = $2,403.02, the minimum monthly income needed. Remember, though, a borrower must qualify under both ratios so $2,403.02 is the minimum monthly income Mary would need to buy this home (barring other offsetting factors).

Exercise 5.4: Knowledge Check

A. True - The lender cannot process a VA-approved loan until the veteran can document his or her military service.

Exercise 5.5: Knowledge Check

B. Current Certificate of Eligibility

D. DD214, NGB22/23, or Statement of Service

The current certificate of eligibility that shows the amount of guarantee the veteran is eligible for and the DD214, NG 22/23, or Statement of Service showing the veteran's status are both required at the time of application.

Exercise 5.6: Apply Your Knowledge

If Dave wants to buy this house, he must make a cash down payment of $13,975 so that the guaranty amount is 25% of the loan amount.

$480,000	Purchase Price
x .25	
$120,000	Guaranty Required
− $106,025	Available Entitlement
$13,975	Down Payment

Chapter 5 Quiz

1. **B. $3,360** - The minimum down payment (3.5%) for FHA-insured loans is calculated using the lower of the sale price or appraised value. $96,000 x .035 = $3,360.

2. **A. on all FHA loans.** - The upfront mortgage insurance premium is required on all FHA loans, regardless of the loan program or LTV.

3. **D. 31%; 43%.** - According to the 4155.1, FHA's underwriting manual, the debt-to-income ratios for an FHA insured loan are 31% for the housing ratio and 43% for the total debt-to-income ratio.

4. **B. cash flow remaining for family support.** - When the residual is calculated, the amount of cash flow remaining for the veteran to pay for family support (e.g., auto insurance, clothing, food, entertainment, and other debt) is computed. This amount is compared with the residual table to ensure the veteran will have ample monies for the items needed.

5. **A. approved lenders.** - FHA-insured loans are funded by lenders that are approved by the FHA. The loans are insured by the FHA.

6. **C. $57,500** - A borrower using USDA financing can earn no more that 115% of the area median income that is established in the area where the borrower wishes to purchase.

7. **A. 1%** - The VA considers a 1% flat fee to be the maximum a lender can charge the veteran for origination services, including processing, document preparation fee, etc. These fees are typically charged to the

seller and are not considered part of the 1% flat fee if the seller or interested third party pays the costs.

8. **B. if an eligible veteran substitutes his entitlement for the seller's.** - If a seller has an existing VA loan, a buyer with a sufficient amount of entitlement may assume the existing loan on its original terms, with the approval of VA or the lender. When the assumption is approved, the buyer's eligibility is substituted for the selling veteran's eligibility, and the seller's entitlement used for the purchase is restored.

Chapter 6

Exercise 6.1: Knowledge Check

The borrower will save $477.80 per month for 360 months (30-year term x 12 months/year). This equates to a gross savings of $172,008. The borrower paid $3000 in closing costs (escrow, doc prep, etc.) so the net savings is $169,008.

Exercise 6.2: Knowledge Check

A. True - The limits are in place to determine whether the buyer can afford to make the monthly loan payments.

Exercise 6.3: Apply Your Knowledge

1. Points are based on the loan amount of $135,000 ($150,000 – $15,000 down payment). The lender is charging a total of 5 points, or 5% of the loan. Discount points total $4,050 ($135,000 x .03) and the loan origination fee is $2,700 ($135,000 x .02). The total the lender will receive in points is $6,750 ($4,050 + $2,700).

2. The seller net is the sale price minus any seller-paid points, so the seller will net $145,950 ($150,000 – $4,050).

3. The loan note rate will be 6.500% since this is not a temporary buydown. The amount on the note equals the loan amount, not the sale price, and does not reflect the seller-paid points, so it's $135,000 ($150,000 – $15,000).

4. Yes, the lender should be able to sell this loan to Fannie Mae/Freddie Mac on the secondary market because with a 90% LTV, it has less than the 6% seller assistance limit that their programs allow.

Exercise 6.4: Apply Your Knowledge

	Start / Year 1	Year 2	Year 3	Year 4	Year 5
Borrower Interest Rate w/Caps	4% (start)	9%	7%	9%	10%

Exercise 6.5: Apply Your Knowledge

1. The start rate or initial rate is 3.50.

2. The borrower will pay 6.50%, which is the sum of the previous rate (3.50%) + the initial adjustment cap (3.00%). The fully indexed rate is 7.45% (4.45% (LIBOR index) + 3.00% (margin)) and the borrower always receives the lower of the two calculated interest rates.

3. The fully indexed rate **after** the second year is 7.50%. The fully indexed rate is the sum of the current index and the margin. The index is 4.50% and the margin remains constant at 3.00%, which equals a fully indexed rate of 7.50%.

4. The maximum interest rate that the borrower will pay during the term of the loan is the sum of the start rate (3.50%) plus the lifetime cap (6.00%) which sets the maximum lifetime rate at 9.50%.

5. If the maximum interest rate is 9.50%, using the formula of FIR = Index + Margin the LIBOR index would need to reach 6.50%:

9.50% (maximum rate) = ? (LIBOR index) + 3.00% (margin)
9.50% (maximum rate) – 3.00% (margin) = 6.50% (LIBOR index)

Exercise 6.6: Apply Your Knowledge

Possible responses:

Advantages	Disadvantages
• Lower initial interest rate and payments	• No interest rate guarantees
• May be easier to qualify for loan	• No payment guarantees
• Leverage buyer into a higher-priced home	• Buyer's financial situation may change
• Payments may decrease over time	• Buyer may over-leverage
• May be converted to a fixed-rate loan	• Possibility of negative amortization
• Good in times of low inflation or for short-term ownership	• May have to pay a fee to convert even if the borrower chooses not to convert

Note: These are just representative; there may be others.

Exercise 6.7: Knowledge Check

B. False - The guidelines call for the homeowner to be at least 62 years old to be eligible for the reverse mortgage.

Chapter 6 Quiz

1. **B. A borrower must qualify at the note rate.** – The FHA will only allow a borrower who utilizes a temporary buydown to qualify at the higher note rate and payment, not the temporary rate and payment.

2. **B. index** - The index is the component of an ARM that is designed to adjust at pre-determined intervals to allow the lender to keep pace with the cost of money and the economy.

3. **C. margin/interest rate charged** - The formula for determining the adjustable rate for an ARM is: Index + Margin = Interest Rate Charged (Note Rate).

4. **D. the payment made does not cover the interest due for that period.** - Negative amortization occurs when the monthly principal and interest payment is not a large enough amount to pay the interest due for the previous month. Payments that do not cover the interest charge lead to negative amortization.

5. **B. allow for more risk.** - Subprime, or below prime, mortgages allow for more risk factors than are allowed for conforming loans sold on the secondary market.

6. **A. A buyer makes payments to the seller in exchange for the right to occupy, use, and enjoy the property, but no deed or title transfers until a specified portion of payments have been made.** - A contract between a vendor (seller) and vendee (buyer) where payments are made by the buyer to the seller in exchange for the right to occupy and enjoy a property is known as a land contract.

7. **D. reverse mortgage.** - A reverse mortgage provides a borrower with either a monthly check, a line of credit, or a lump sum payment with no monthly payments required of the borrower.

8. **C. higher FICO® scores required.** - Subprime loans possess one or more of the following risky features: high interest rates, high debt-to-income ratios, low down payment requirements, little or no verification of ability to repay the mortgage debt, excessive loan fees, lower FICO® scores allowed, hybrid loan features.

Chapter 7

Exercise 7.1: Knowledge Check

1. **C. obtain the lowest interest rate.** - RESPA's purpose is to help borrowers be better informed, compare options, and shop for settlement services. Obtaining the lowest interest rate is not a specific goal of the Act.

2. **D. landscaping companies.** - Any entity that provides a service after the loan closes is not a settlement service provider, according to RESPA guidelines.

Exercise 7.2: Apply Your Knowledge

1. **When referrals are made in return for a kickback or fee, the borrower's right to shop for the best service and lowest transaction fees is taken from them.** Marketing arrangements and agreements affect the consumer by concealing or omitting information that could cause the consumer to make an erroneous decision or that might cause unreasonable harm to the consumer. When an unearned fee or referral is paid to a settlement service provider, the costs of the transaction are likely to increase.

2. Response:
   - Required all consumers to apply for and obtain a preapproval from Prospect.
   - Required agents to participate in an "exclusivity contract" with Prospect.
   - Required brokers to refer to Prospect as an exclusive or preferred lender.
   - Required brokers to only submit real estate offers that had a preapproval from Prospect.
   - Urged brokers to use seller credits for only a buyer who would obtain a loan from Prospect.

3. The methods that Prospect used included:
   - Fees paid through "lead agreements."
   - Fees paid to brokers were distributed to referring agents by reduced or no rent for their office, $20 bills paid to them at sales meetings, and a fee paid per referral.
   - Fees paid through Marketing Service Agreements (MSAs).
   - Fees paid through higher than market rent for office space.
   - Fees paid on behalf of the agents for marketing efforts, such as third-party websites.

4. The MLO should learn the concepts of a kickback and the penalties for paying "anything of value" in exchange for referrals of settlement service business. An MLO should learn what a kickback looks like and the many forms that a payment for a referral can take.

Exercise 7.3: Knowledge Check

B. the process for resolution of a servicing complaint. - 12 CFR § 1024.33(a) states the Mortgage Servicing Disclosure Statement must indicate whether the servicing of the loan may be assigned, sold, or transferred to any other person at any time while the loan is outstanding.

Exercise 7.4: Knowledge Check

A. help consumers become better and more informed shoppers. - As the Director of the CFPB stated, "To help consumers become better and more informed shoppers, we are improving mortgage disclosures."

Exercise 7.5: Apply Your Knowledge

1. An acceptable changed circumstance for a borrower's request to change the type of loan is permissible. A new Loan Estimate will need to be issued due to the change in loan type and risk-based pricing delivery fees. If a Closing Disclosure has already been delivered to the borrower, a corrected Closing Disclosure with the borrower requested changes will need to be delivered to the borrower and a new three-business-day waiting period will apply.

2. If an originator fails to disclose an increase in fees within three days of receipt of the fee imposition, the originator/creditor will be subject to lender tolerance charges.

3. When an appraisal is received and mortgage insurance is required as a result of a lower appraised value, this is an acceptable changed circumstance and the additional cost and the increase in monthly payment must be re-disclosed to the borrower.

4. An acceptable changed circumstance would be the redisclosure of the increased payment due to a shorter loan term made by the borrower.

Exercise 7.6: Knowledge Check

1. **C. three business days after the email is sent, if not informed of receipt by the borrower sooner.** - A revised Loan Estimate is considered received by the consumer on the day it is provided. If it is mailed or delivered electronically (email, fax, etc.), the consumer is considered to have received it three business days after the disclosures are mailed or transmitted.

2. **B. Closing Disclosure.** - The Closing Disclosure is the document that the actual settlement service provider charges are provided. When the closing costs disclosed to the borrower on the Loan Estimate are lower than the costs provided on the Closing Disclosure, the MLO is considered to have acted in good faith.

3. **D. an MLO neglected to charge an origination fee initially.** - If the MLO initially neglects to charge an origination fee, it may not be added to the Loan Estimate at a later date after it is delivered to the borrower (even in the event that another valid change of circumstance occurs).

4. **D. a lock-in fee.** - A lock-in fee is paid to the lender for locking an interest rate or extending a loan interest rate lock. Since it is retained by the lender and not passed on to a third party, it is not considered a third-party fee.

Exercise 7.7: Knowledge Check

1. **C. deliver a revised Closing Disclosure and apply a new three-day waiting period before consummation.** - If the Closing Disclosure has changed because of the loan's APR, product change, or if a prepayment penalty has been added, the borrower must receive a new Closing

Disclosure and be given a new three-day waiting period prior to loan consummation.

2. **D. make redisclosure.** - If the Closing Disclosure has changed because of a numerical error, creditors must ensure that the consumer receives a corrected Closing Disclosure, but are not required to provide an additional three-day waiting period.

Exercise 7.8: Apply Your Knowledge

1. The combined amounts of the broker fees ($2,600) and the wholesale lender administration fee ($1,000) for a total fee of $3,600.

2. The mortgage broker may not increase the origination charge fee once it has been disclosed to the borrower and accepted. The increase of this fee does not qualify as an acceptable changed circumstance.

3. The closing costs shown in Section B of the Closing Disclosure have zero tolerance for change; therefore, the maximum amount for these charges to the borrower is $4,625.

4. The mortgage broker must pay a tolerance cure of $1,375 at closing or within 60 days of consummation because no increase is allowed on Section B fees at consummation.

Exercise 7.9: Apply Your Knowledge

1. The APR tells a borrower the total cost of financing a loan in percentage terms, as a relationship of the total finance charges to the total amount financed. Therefore, if the term is less, the interest paid and the finance charges will be spread over a shorter period of time, increasing the APR.

2. The total finance charge includes the repayment of interest over the term of the loan. A 30-year mortgage will have increased interest costs due to a longer repayment term.

3. Regardless of the term of the loan or interest repaid, the principal to be repaid is the same amount ($125,000) for each loan. Only the interest charge will vary.

Exercise 7.10: Knowledge Check

1. **C. allow a presumption that the lender followed the Ability-to-Repay guidelines if certain requirements are made.; D. protect the borrower from a loan he may not be able to afford**. - The Ability-to-Repay provision of the Qualified Mortgage Regulation protects the borrower from entering into a loan he cannot afford. It also gives the lender the presumption that it followed the guidelines if certain requirements of the rule are met.

2. **D. maximum loan term.** - The Dodd-Frank Act defines a qualified mortgage by imposing a maximum term of thirty years.

Exercise 7.11: Knowledge Check

D. Regulation Z - Regulation Z, also known as The Truth In Lending Act, regulates advertising terms and disclosures.

Chapter 7 Quiz

1. **D. TILA** - TILA requires the disclosure of the Loan Estimate to borrowers within three business days of a completed application.

2. **A. become better and more informed shoppers for consumer loans.** - The Integrated Disclosures are designed to help consumers become better and more informed shoppers according to Director Cordray of the Consumer Financial Protection Bureau.

3. **B. 3** - Truth in Lending regulations require a three-business-day right of rescission for borrowers after they sign their owner-occupied loan documents.

4. **D. no additional disclosures are required** - When only the APR is advertised, no additional disclosures are required, according to TILA.

5. **D. under no circumstances** - Section 9 of RESPA prohibits the required use of a particular title company under any circumstances.

6. **D. Regulation Z** - Regulation Z - Regulation Z implements the Truth In Lending Act, which requires the use of the Closing Disclosure.

7. **A. 20%.** - The Homeowner's Protection Act permits a borrower to request the cancellation of mortgage insurance when the current loan balance is 80% of the original sale price or appraised value, whichever is less, giving the homeowner 20% equity.

8. **B. credit report fee** - RESPA and TILA regulations both mandate that only the credit report fee (bona fide) can be collected prior to the borrower's receipt of all four mandated disclosures.

9. **B. three business days** - The Truth In Lending Act states that if the final annual percentage rate shown on the Closing Disclosure varies by more than 1/8% for a fixed-rate mortgage or 1/4% for an adjustable rate mortgage from the initial disclosure on the Loan Estimate, then the borrower must be given an additional three-day rescission period to review the new disclosure (Truth in Lending Statement).

10. **C. Lender and mortgage broker fees for the same transaction must be itemized.** - According to TILA, mortgage broker fees and lender fees must be combined on Page 2, Section A of the Loan Estimate.

11. **C. The MLO regretted overlooking certain liabilities in order to qualify the borrower for a better interest rate**. - According to TILA, a changed circumstance does not include a mortgage originator overlooking characteristics or liabilities of the borrower.

12. **A. business day.** - TILA defines a business day as the day the business entity is open for substantially all business operations, for the disclosure of the Loan Estimate, the Special Information Booklet, and the Mortgage Servicing Disclosure Statement.

13. **C. most recent two months of bank statements.** - A "complete application" is defined as the receipt of a borrower's name, social security number (s), gross monthly income, the subject property address, the loan amount, and an estimate of value of the subject. An MLO is prohibited from collecting documents that verify the information related to the application before providing the Loan Estimate.

14. **B. home equity loans.** - A home equity loan, which is a closed-end fixed interest rate loan, usually in a subordinate lien position, is not exempt from the requirements of the Loan Estimate.

15. **A. N/A** - A lender is prohibited from using the term "N/A" on the Loan Estimate. The MLO should leave the space blank rather than insert another phrase.

16. **D. rate lock in information.** - The Closing Disclosure, which is provided at closing, does not contain the rate lock in information, as the loan will already be locked and lock terms are disclosed on the Loan Estimate.

17. **D. total interest percentage.** - Regulation Z defines the total interest percentage as the total amount of interest the consumer will pay expressed as a percentage of the loan amount.

18. **C. the day a business entity is open for business to the public for the purpose of transacting substantially of the entity's business.** - Reg. Z states that for the purposes of disclosing the initial Loan Estimate, a business day is a day the business entity is open for business to the public for the purpose of transacting substantially all of the entity's business.

19. **B. all calendar days except Sundays and legal public holidays.** - Regulation Z states that for the purposes of redisclosing the Loan Estimate, a business day is considered to be all calendar days except Sundays and legal public holidays.

20. **D. 4** - A revised Loan Estimate may not be disclosed within four business days of loan consummation, according to the new guidelines contained in Regulation Z.

21. **A. creditor.** - TILA places the responsibility for the borrower's Closing Disclosure with the creditor.

22. **D. settlement agent.** - TILA places the responsibility for the seller's Closing Disclosure with the settlement agent.

23. **A. all borrowers who have the right to rescind.** - All borrowers who have the right to rescind must have a revised Closing Disclosure delivered to them.

24. **A. expresses an interest in receiving a copy.** - A borrower who expresses an interest in the adjustable rate disclosures may receive a copy of them initially. There is not a requirement that all borrowers receive the initial adjustable rate disclosure forms.

25. **A. borrower becomes contractually obligated on the credit transaction.** - Loan consummation is defined by TILA as the time that a consumer becomes contractually obligated on the credit transaction, but may not necessarily coincide with the settlement or closing of the entire real estate transaction.

26. **B. higher than what is charged on the Closing Disclosure.** - If a loan estimate is made in good faith, the closing costs on the estimate will be higher than what the borrower is actually charged at loan consummation and documented on the Closing Disclosure. If the costs are higher on the Closing Disclosure, then the Loan Estimate was under-quoted.

27. **C. the MLO neglected to inform the borrower of the additional cost and necessity of a review appraisal when requested.** - The neglected disclosure of a new fee will not be allowed as a changed circumstance if not initially disclosed within three business days of discovery.

28. **D. 3** – When a borrower completes a loan application/disclosures but instead of locking the interest rate at the time of application, locks the rate at a later date, a lender has three business days to redisclose the terms of the locked loan.

29. **C. private mortgage insurance.** - Private mortgage insurance is placed in the category of a settlement charge that the borrower is not allowed to choose and therefore, is subject to the 10% tolerance limit.

30. **A. lender processing fee.** - A lender processing fee would be considered a part of Section A, Origination Charges, on Page 2 of Loan Estimate.

31. **B. The fee is deducted from the aggregate amount for the 10% tolerance calculation prior to analyzing the amount for a 10%**

variance. - TILA instructs the creditor to remove fees that are not required or performed for the closing prior to the analysis of the 10% tolerance calculation.

32. **D. within 60 calendar days after consummation.** - 12 CFR § 1026.19(f)(2)(v) allows a creditor a 60-calendar day time period to cure any tolerance violations.

33. **B. 3** - When a creditor discovers a valid changed circumstance, a revised Loan Estimate must be issued to the consumer within three business days of discovery.

34. **C. 3** - Borrowers have three business days to review the Closing Disclosure prior to loan consummation.

35. **D. clerical errors made to the Closing Disclosure.** - Clerical errors do not require a revised Closing Disclosure or additional three-day waiting period to the consumer.

36. **D. the lender will only accept partial payments after foreclosure proceedings have been initiated.** - The options for accepting partial payments are that the lender will or will not accept them or that partial payments will be placed in a special account until a full payment accrues, and then the full payment will be credited to the borrower's account.

37. **A. 5% APR loan available here.** – The Truth in Lending Act requires required disclosures for triggering terms including the amount of the down payment, amount of any payment, number of payments, period of repayment, and the amount of any finance charge. Examples of terms that do not trigger required disclosures include "5% Annual Percentage Rate loan available here," "easy monthly payments," and "terms to fit your budget."

38. **A. a 40-year term loan.** - A qualified mortgage is defined by a maximum loan term of 30 years.

Chapter 8

Exercise 8.1: Knowledge Check

A. True - The FCRA establishes the rights of debtors and responsibilities of creditors involved in consumer lending activities.

Exercise 8.2: Knowledge Check

1. **B. doctor's office.** - A doctor's office or administration is not considered to have a business need for patients' credit reports, according to the FCRA.

2. **A. disputed.** - A consumer reporting agency is required to remove any data reported that is inaccurate, incomplete, or unverifiable. The act of disputing a trade line does not require its removal, only its investigation.

Exercise 8.3: Knowledge Check

1. **B. False** - The primary purpose of the FACT Act is to protect consumers from identity theft.

2. **A. True** -The FACT Act requires that paper loan files be safely disposed of to protect consumer's private information by either shredding or burning the information.

Exercise 8.4: Knowledge Check

1. **B. someone who grants credit.** - The Fair Credit Reporting Act, Regulation V, defines a creditor as one who grants credit.

2. **B. FACTA.** - The Fair and Accurate Credit Transactions Act requires that borrower's information is disposed of in a manner that protects the data.

Exercise 8.5: Apply Your Knowledge

(1) **C. GLB** – Classifies a borrower as either a consumer (who conducts a one-time transaction with a borrower) or a customer (who has an ongoing relationship with the borrower).

(2) **A. FACTA** (Section 114) – Requires a creditor to assess the validity of a borrower's addresses when an alert is reported on the credit report.

(3) **B. FCRA** – Regulates the time period for a credit bureau to report certain derogatory credit items on the report.

(4) **B. FCRA** – Requires a credit reporting bureau to correct information found to be inaccurate or incomplete.

(5) **B. FCRA** – Requires that a creditor issue an adverse action notice.

(6) **B. FCRA** – The required adverse notice must include the contact information for the source of the creditor's decision.

(7) **A. FACTA** – Requires that a paper loan file is burned or shredded after completion of the transaction to protect a consumer's personal information.

Exercise 8.6: Knowledge Check

A. True - The USA PATRIOT Act seeks to prevent the funding of terrorist operations; verifying the identity of customers is a basic part of that effort.

Exercise 8.8: Knowledge Check

B. False - A company's federal DNC list must be updated every three months; internal customer DNC lists must be updated every 30 days.

Chapter 8 Quiz

1. **C. 18 months** - The national DNC regulations allow a mortgage loan originator who has an established business relationship with a consumer whose name is on the national DNC list to solicit further business for a period of 18 months.

2. **A. Fair and Accurate Credit Transactions Act** - The Red Flag Rules are located in Section 114 of the Fair and Accurate Credit Transactions Act.

3. **B. dispute of inaccurate or incomplete information of a report.** - The FCRA allows the consumer to dispute inaccurate or incomplete information found in the credit report.

4. **C. 10 years.** - The Fair Credit Reporting Act provides that derogatory information regarding a discharged bankruptcy be removed after 10 years.

5. **A. an adverse action notice to the borrower who is turned down for a loan.** - FACTA allows borrowers to place fraud alerts or freezes on their credit and requires truncation of credit card numbers on receipts. The FCRA requires a creditor to issue an adverse action for customers who are declined a mortgage loan.

6. **D. Section 114.** - The Red Flag Rules are found in Section 114 of the Fair and Accurate Credit Transactions Act.

7. **B. consumer.** - A consumer is identified by the Gramm-Leach-Bliley Act as a person who only closes a single transaction with a creditor and who does not have an ongoing relationship with the creditor.

8. **D. $16,000.** - The National Do Not Call Registry regulations, administered by the FTC, set the maximum penalty for violations at $16,000 per incident.

Chapter 9

Exercise 9.1: Knowledge Check

B. False - A higher-priced loan is defined as a loan where the APR, as disclosed by the Truth In Lending statement, of a mortgage loan exceeds the average prime offer rate by 1.5% for a first mortgage lien.

Exercise 9.2: Knowledge Check

D. 12.5%. - If the sale price exceeds the seller's acquisition price by more than 10 percent, a creditor shall not extend a next mortgage loan to a consumer to finance the acquisition of the consumer's principal dwelling without obtaining two written appraisals prior to consummation.

Exercise 9.3: Knowledge Check

C. based on the loan amount. - An MLO may only receive compensation based on the loan amount given to the borrower and no other consideration.

Exercise 9.4: Knowledge Check

A. True - This requirement, which protects the borrower's interests, is codified under the Dodd-Frank Act and prohibits compensation based on any other term other than the loan amount.

Exercise 9.5: Apply Your Knowledge

1. The first operation is to determine if the loan is a higher-priced loan. That is done by

performing the following computations:

Current APOR   4.672

                + 1.500

                6.172%   (APOR Threshold)

The APR is greater than the APOR threshold; therefore, it IS a higher-priced loan. As an option, the MLO may use the FFIEC website [see http://www.ffiec.gov/ratespread/newcalc.aspx] to determine if the loan's APR exceeds the threshold and is then a higher-priced loan.

2. If the loan meets the standards of a higher-priced loan, the creditor must verify the borrower's ability to repay the loan and an escrow/impound account must be established for a minimum of five years, according to HOEPA. The loan must meet the other terms of the regulation, such as no balloon payments, etc.

3. A high cost loan is one where the APR exceeds the sum of the APOR + 6.5%. In this scenario, the APR is less than 11.172% (4.672% + 6.5%), so it is not a high cost loan.

4. The loan is a high cost loan in this scenario because the finance charges exceed the 5% guideline:

Closing costs required:	1.5%
Discount points charged:	2.0%
Origination fee charged:	2.0%
Total finance charges	5.50%

Regardless of the loan amount, the finance charges exceed the high cost finance charge guideline of 5%.

5. When a loan is determined to be a high cost loan, the borrower must receive a Section 32 disclosure three business days prior to executing loan documents for the transaction.

During this time, the borrower has a three-day right to rescind the mortgage loan. After the initial rescission period is fulfilled, the borrower may execute documents and disclosures for the mortgage loan and will have the statutory right to rescind the mortgage loan.

Chapter 9 Quiz

1. **D. Regulation Z** - Regulation Z, known as the Truth in Lending Act, was amended by the HOEPA regulations in 1994.

2. **A. defined benefit plan.** - A defined benefit plan is a pension plan with sole contributions and control coming from the employer.

3. **D. uses the average prime offer rate as an index.** - A higher-priced loan is a loan where the annual percentage rate is measured against the current average prime offer rate.

4. **B. current or expected income.** - Current or expected income may be used for determining a borrower's ability to repay the mortgage loan.

5. **C. 20%.** - A seller who acquired a home within three to six months of resale and is selling the home for more than 20% of the original acquisition cost must have a second property appraisal performed on the property.

6. **C. 6.5%.** - The transaction's annual percentage rate exceeds the applicable average prime offer rate by more than 6.5 percentage points for most first lien mortgages.

7. **C. 3** - A creditor shall provide to the consumer a copy of any written appraisal performed in connection with a higher-priced mortgage loan no later than three business days prior to consummation of the loan.

Chapter 10

Exercise 10.1: Knowledge Check

A. True - The SAFE Act defines a loan originator as a natural person who takes a mortgage loan application or negotiates or offers mortgage rates or terms for compensation or in the expectation of compensation.

Exercise 10.2: Apply Your Knowledge

MLO License Term	Description
1. Continuing Education	**H. Two Hours of Ethics Education**
2. Registered MLO	**C. Depository Institution**
3. Loan Originator	**F. Takes a Loan Application**
4. Loan Processor	**B. Clerical/ Administrative Duties**
5. Nontraditional	**A. 3/1 Adjustable Rate Mortgage**
6. Prelicensing	**G. Twenty Hours of Education**
7. SAFE Act	**D. HERA**
8. Unique Identifier Number	**E. NMLS #**
9. UST	**I. Uniform State Test**

Exercise 10.3: Knowledge Check

A. True - An MLO candidate is entitled to try passing the test three times; if he fails all three times, then the candidate must wait at least six (6) months before trying it again.

Chapter 10 Quiz

1. **A. conviction for felony assault**. - A felony conviction from 10 years ago for any crime other than a financial crime would not automatically keep an MLO candidate from obtaining a license.

2. **C. 20** - The prelicensing requirement for education is 20 hours for MLO licensure.

3. **B. evidence of completion of the mandatory eight-hour education requirement.** - For an MLO, eight hours is the continuing education requirement after a license is granted.

4. **D. both A & C** - The SAFE Act defines an MLO as a natural person who takes a residential loan application or offers or negotiates a mortgage loan application.

5. **D. property taxes** - The SAFE Act doesn't designate property taxes as a required topic for MLO continuing education.

6. **B. No, because the state authority has the power to investigate and issue or deny a license and he was a principal of the firm that lost its license** - The state authority can investigate licensees and issue, deny, suspend and revoke mortgage loan originators' licenses. In this scenario, because the applicant was a director/ manager of a company whose license was revoked, the state authority may find culpability on the part of the MLO and not grant a license.

Chapter 11

Exercise 11.1: Knowledge Check

A. True - No advertisement containing an offer to sell a product should be published when the offer is not a bona fide effort to sell the advertised product. Jack baited consumers with his advertisement, which is a violation of 16 CFR §238.1.

Exercise 11.2: Apply Your Knowledge

Scenario 1: Yes, if Jane had never intended to close a so-called "5 for 5" loan and just wanted to get prospective borrowers in the door, her offer was not in good faith.

Scenario 2: Yes, even though Alex is closing some of the loans in the timeframe advertised, he still used deception to bring in more customers, because he never intended to achieve that closing timeframe for most loans. This is an example of bait and switch.

Exercise 11.3: Apply Your Knowledge

1. **NOT**. The advertisement of an APR-only rate considers all other triggering terms in the disclosure of the APR.

2. **DECEPTIVE**. The ad does not give the terms of the loan, such as fixed or adjustable, the APR, the term of the loan, or the down payment required.

3. **DECEPTIVE**. The ad slogan does not state any terms of the loan or whether the payments are based on a low adjustable teaser rate, interest-only terms, or if the interest rate is in fact a low rate 30-year term loan.

4. **NOT**. The Internet follows FTC guidelines by including an obvious and clear link to the Internet page where the disclosures for the advertised loan are displayed.

5. **DECEPTIVE**. The MLO must include the NMLS unique identifier number on all advertising for mortgage services, including on social media on the Internet. Omitting the information deceives the public about the MLO's status with the NMLS.

Exercise 11.4: Knowledge Check

1. **C. property is in a declining market area and no protected class is singled out.** - Lenders may deny loans in neighborhoods where property values are declining, but the denial must be based on objective criteria regarding the condition and value of the property or area, not discriminatory characteristics of the borrower.

2. **A. age.** - The Equal Credit Opportunity Act named age as a protected class. All other choices are protected by the Fair Housing Act.

Exercise 11.5: Apply Your Knowledge

1. ECOA
2. Civil Rights Act of 1866
3. Fair Housing Act
4. None
5. All

Protected Class or Condition	Regulation
Age	1
Color	1,3
Disability	3
Familial status	3
Income from public assistance	1
Marital status	1
National origin/ethnicity	5
Race	5
Religion	1, 3
Separate credit reports	1
Sex	1, 3

Exercise 11.6: Knowledge Check

C. both are violating RESPA. - Section 8 always says that both parties are responsible. The mortgage lender provided "something of value" and the real estate agent accepted "something of value."

Exercise 11.7: Knowledge Check

1. **D. selling the property at market value.** - When a seller places a property on the resale market at a higher than market price, there may be an indication of illegal flipping, especially if the home was purchased at a below market value and only cosmetic repairs were made.

2. **A. the buyer must pay the lender for the second appraisal.** - Under the rules defined in the Federal Register on November 29, 2012 (Vol. 77, No. 230), "The mortgagee may not charge the cost of the second appraisal to the homebuyer. If the mortgagee has ordered a second appraisal to document the increase in value, the mortgagee must not use this appraisal for case processing and must not enter it into FHA Connection."

3. **B. co-signing an auto loan for a relative.** - Co-signing an auto loan for a relative does not include identity theft of another person's identity.

Exercise 11.8: Apply Your Knowledge

Scenario 1: Jack is technically a straw buyer in this situation, since he used his personal information to apply for a loan on a property where he did not intend to live and for which he did not intend to make mortgage payments. Although he may have had pure intentions, since he applied for the loan, Jack was contractually obligated to ensure that the monthly payments were made, whether he lived in the house or not. Additionally, Jack could possibly even be criminally liable for making a fraudulent statement (that he would live in the house, a requirement of an FHA loan) on a matter related to a transaction with a federal agency. At the very least, he's now has a stain on his credit report and no longer has his basement to himself!

Scenario 2: Doug could be on the verge of perpetrating a fraud scheme called a disappearing second. The lender thinks it has an 80% LTV loan, for example, when it may actually be 90% LTV. Stu should be aware that if he goes along with facilitating this deal, he could be guilty of a material omission if he does not inform the lender of seller Doug's plans. Another issue is the fact that the buyer and seller are related. Certainly, there is no law against someone selling his property to a cousin, even at a discounted price. However, mortgage fraud scams often involve family members. So, in these instances, full disclosure is imperative. Purchase contracts between family members should specifically state their relationships so it does not appear intentionally hidden. Stu probably needs to get out of this transaction.

Scenario 3: This is an example of a short sale fraud, and also a flipping scheme. You could even reasonably say that Joe was a straw buyer since he never intended to make payments on the mortgage loan. For the short sale to go through, it's also very likely that Joe and Patrick did not reveal their relationship. Short sales that involve relatives and friends are a significant red flag.

Exercise 11.9: Apply Your Knowledge

Scenario 1: This is an obvious case of predatory lending. The consumer was under duress in this situation, and the lender took advantage of him by changing the loan terms. Furthermore, unless the lender's changes were below the tolerances that require redisclosure of terms, the lender is in violation of the Truth in Lending Act that requires a waiting period of three business days after redisclosure.

Scenario 2: Making loans with a meager tangible benefit that does not resolve the borrower's problem but creates repeat business would be considered predatory lending. More specifically, this is an example of loan flipping, which is a type of equity skimming.

Scenario 3: Borrowers with less than perfect credit may have to pay higher rates to secure a loan. That alone would not necessarily be considered predatory. It does depend on the actual terms of the loan, so more information would be needed to make a definitive call on this situation.

Scenario 4: Legitimate lenders do not require credit insurance, and in fact, many states forbid it since the loan balance would be paid off when the property was sold out of her estate. Therefore, this could be an example of predatory lending. This might also be an example of illegal discrimination if such credit insurance is not required of single men.

Exercise 11.11: Apply Your Knowledge

Scenario, Part 1: You need to be very clear that Velma understands all conditions and terms associated with an adjustable rate mortgage. She needs to understand that the interest rate she will pay when adjusted according to the terms in the note will be set based off a standard index over which neither she nor her lender has any control, and it could be lower, but it could also be higher. You are not required to take her loan application as long as your refusal is not based on Velma's membership in a protected class (race, color, religion, nationality, sex, disability, familial status, source of income). However, you might have a hard time proving that.

Scenario, Part 2: If you submit the loan application, you should take extra special care to confirm that you have made all required disclosures and that she acknowledges the receipt of them.

Chapter 11 Quiz

1. **B. race** - The Civil Rights Act of 1866 prohibited discrimination in the sale or lease of residential or commercial property based on race or ancestry.

2. **C. disability/handicap, familial status, or national origin.** - The Fair Housing Act of 1968 added the protected classes of disability/handicap and familial status to the list of protected classes established by the Civil Rights Act of 1866.

3. **D. Home Mortgage Disclosure Act** - The Home Mortgage Disclosure Act (Regulation C) requires creditors to disclose the race, ethnicity, and gender of the applicant in order to monitor a lender's compliance with the Fair Housing Act and ECOA.

4. **C. Fair Housing Act** - The Fair Housing Act prohibits redlining, blockbusting, and steering in any real estate or mortgage credit transaction.

5. **D. TILA** - The Truth In Lending Act (Regulation Z) is the federal regulation that has the primary responsibility of overseeing advertising.

6. **A. any party to a mortgage loan.** - Mortgage fraud can be committed by any party to a mortgage or real estate transaction, including appraisers, borrowers, lenders, brokers, and other settlement service providers.

7. **D. RESPA** - Chapter 8 of RESPA prohibits the payment or receipt of anything of value (kickbacks) in exchange for referrals.

8. **D. requiring private mortgage insurance.** - Predatory lending involves placing the borrower in a mortgage loan with inferior terms, misrepresenting the loan terms to the borrower by the lender, or collecting high fees such as for origination or processing. Certain loans are legally permitted to require PMI for a loan origination.

9. **A. ABC Mortgage Co. offers a subprime loan to Mark, who is coming out of bankruptcy.** - Offering a higher interest rate or a higher down payment to someone in a mortgage transaction who has completed bankruptcy proceedings would not be predatory lending, as long as the borrower did not qualify for a better loan due to credit or income factors.

10. **A. Ann revises her pay stubs so she can qualify for a loan to buy her dream house.** - A straw buyer involves a third party who allows their name and identity to be used for the purpose of purchasing or refinancing a property. In this case, Ann acts alone, revising her paystubs, and committing fraud for property.

11. **A. No, she can't be held responsible if a client withholds information that does not show on Tom's credit report.** - If Cindy is unaware of the credit entry or the terms of the new loan because Tom did not disclose them to her, she is not guilty of any omission and cannot be held responsible for the omissions of her borrower.

12. **D. requiring mortgage insurance** - Mortgage insurance is required on all first-lien conventional mortgage loans and certain government-insured loans. If this requirement is made of all borrowers in this category, no predatory lending occurs.

13. **D. made available to a reasonable number of qualified applicants.** - An advertised interest rate is not required to be available for a certain time period or to every applicant or payment of a lock-in fee. The interest rate must be made available to qualified applicants who respond to the advertisement in a timely manner.

14. **D. take the application and verify the validity of the Social Security number** - An MLO should complete the application and then verify the validity of the Social Security number provided by the consumer. An MLO should not accuse a consumer of any fraudulent action without a proper investigation.

Chapter 12

Exercise 12.1: Knowledge Check

1. **B. False** - Under the SAFE Act, an MLO is required to be either state-licensed or federally registered.

2. **A. True** - The SAFE Act requires national minimum educational standards for MLOs to enhance consumer protection and reduce fraud.

Exercise 12.2: Knowledge Check

1. **A. True** - The state regulatory authority must effectively supervise and enforce the law under the SAFE Act.

2. **A. federal fund** - A federal fund is not required as a financial protection method under the SAFE Act.

Exercise 12.3: Knowledge Check

A. True - The SAFE Act authorizes states to control the licensing process of the mortgage lending industry.

Exercise 12.4: Apply Your Knowledge

1. **LR**
2. **NLR**
3. **LR**
4. **NLR**
5. **NLR**
6. **LR**
7. **NLR**
8. **NLR**
9. **LR**

Exercise 12.5: Knowledge Check

A. True - Under these conditions, the SAFE Act exempts an individual from holding an MLO license.

Chapter 12 Quiz

1. **C. maintenance of records and enforcement of violations for public access.** - The state regulatory authority must regularly report violations and enforcement actions to the NMLS; maintaining public access to the information is not specified under the SAFE Act.

2. **B. MLO assigns and monitors the individual's clerical tasks** - To prove an individual performs only clerical duties under MLO supervision, an actual nexus must be more than a nominal relationship on an organizational chart. There is an actual nexus when the supervisory licensed or registered MLO assigns, authorizes, and monitors the loan processor or underwriter employee's performance of clerical and support duties.

3. **D. prison sentence** - State (and federal) authorities are not authorized to impose a prison sentence for violations of the law.

4. **D. receives something of value.** - An individual's act is for compensation or gain if the individual receives in connection with their activities any thing of value, including, but not limited to, payment of a salary, bonus, or commission. The concept of "thing of value" is interpreted broadly and is not limited only to payments that are contingent upon the closing of a loan.

5. **D. offering or negotiating loan terms** - Of these options, the only task that requires licensing is offering or negotiating loan terms.

6. **B. communicating directly or indirectly with a borrower in order to reach a mutual understanding about prospective residential mortgage loan terms** - Communicating prospective residential mortgage loan terms to a borrower, whether directly or indirectly, is considered an example of the task of offering or negotiating the terms of a loan.

Chapter 13

Exercise 13.1: Knowledge Check

1. **B. False** - A mortgage servicer must respond to a payoff request within seven (7) business days of receipt of the request.

2. **B. False** - Rules were implemented regarding home foreclosures and requests for modifications as part of the amendment to Regulation X. A mortgage servicer is required to try to establish contact with the borrower no later than 36 days after a missed mortgage payment.

Exercise 13.2: Knowledge Check

A. True - The Mortgage Assistance Relief Service (MARS) Rule requires financial institutions to disclose information that helps consumers make sound decisions when faced with foreclosure or similar conditions.

Exercise 13.3: Knowledge Check

B. False - The BSA requires financial institutions to maintain certain financial records, but report financial transactions greater than $10,000.

Exercise 13.4: Knowledge Check

A. True - Both entities established anti-money laundering regulations to protect financial institutions and U.S. interests from illegal activities.

Chapter 13 Quiz

1. **D. waive a late payment penalty fee when requested by the borrower.** - A mortgage servicer is not required to waive a late payment penalty fee upon borrower request.

2. **D. purchased by a lender when the borrower's insurance lapses.** - Force-placed insurance is purchased by the mortgage servicer when the borrower's insurance lapses.

3. **C. 90** - If a borrower submits an application for assistance, the borrower may seek an independent review of the lender's workout decision. The servicer may not commence any action during this 90-day timeframe.

4. **B. loan modification requests.** - MARS provides regulations for the mortgage modification services of a mortgage originator or lender.

5. **C. has an on-going relationship with a financial institution.** - A customer is a person who has an ongoing relationship with a financial institution.

6. **D. prevent money laundering.** - The Bank Secrecy Act/Anti-Money Laundering legislation regulates money laundering and record retention.

Chapter 14

Exercise 14.1: Knowledge Check

A. annual interest charge. - When the loan amount is multiplied by the note rate, the result is the annual interest charge.

Exercise 14.2: Knowledge Check

D. loan-to-value. - When dividing the loan amount by the lesser of the sale price or the appraised value, the result is the loan-to-value.

Exercise 14.3: Apply Your Knowledge

The qualifying payment is the lesser of the two calculations. In this scenario, the housing ratio provides the lower of the two payments at $846.30 per month.

Calculate the borrower's income:

$15.75 per hour x 40 x 52 = $32,760

$32,760 per year divided by 12 months = $2,730 gross monthly income

$2,730	$2,730.00	
x .31	x .43	
$846.30	$1,173.90	
	– $250.00	Auto loan pmt.
	– $25.00	Credit card pmt.
	$ 898.90	

Exercise 14.4: Knowledge Check

D. housing ratio. - When the PITI payment is divided by the gross monthly income, the result is the housing or front debt-to-income ratio.

Chapter 14 Quiz

1. **A. $4,336** - $216,800 x .02=$4,336

2. **A. $782** - The borrower's monthly debt is $370 and gross monthly income is $3,200. Conventional/conforming qualifying guidelines allow a total housing expense ratio of 28% and a total debt-to-income ratio of 36%, based on gross monthly income. Under the first ratio, the borrower would qualify for $896 ($3,200 x .28). Under the second ratio, the borrower would qualify for $782 ($3,200 x .36 = $1,152; $1,152 – $370 = $782). The borrower must accept whichever is lower.

3. **B. $46.50** - $90,000 x .0062 = $558, which is the PMI annual charge. To obtain the monthly PMI cost, divide $558 by 12, which is $46.50 per month.

4. **C. 75% / 90%** - The LTV is 75% ($90,000 ÷ $120,000 = 75%) where $90,000 is the first mortgage from the primary lender. The CLTV is 90% ($90,000 + $18,000 = $108,000, $180,000 ÷ $120,000 = 90%) where $18,000 is the second mortgage from the seller.

5. **B. $874** - The borrower's monthly debt is $890 (auto loan + VISA + student loan); rent does not count as debt since he will no longer pay it with the house. Conventional qualifying guidelines allow a total housing expense ratio of 28% and a total debt-to-income ratio of 36%, based on gross monthly income. Under the first ratio, the borrower qualifies for $1,372 ($4,900 x .28). Under the second ratio, the borrower qualifies for $874 ($4,900 x .36 = $1,764; $1,764 – $890 = $874). The borrower must accept whichever is lower.

6. **B. $8,872.50** - Using the lesser of the sale price or the appraised value ($253,500) and applying the required FHA down payment of 3.5%, Stu must provide $8,872.50 as a down payment ($253,500 x 3.5% = $8,872.50).

7. **C. $80,000** - The borrower made a $40,000 down payment at the time of purchase, which is his initial equity. The loan balance for the purchase money mortgage is $160,000 ($200,000 sale price - $40,000 down payment). Making interest only payments would maintain the loan balance at $160,000. If the property sells for $240,000, the borrower's equity is $240,000 (current value/sale price) - $160,000 (current loan balance) which is $80,000.

8. **C. $6,916**

   $4,500/week

   X 52/weeks per year

   $234,000 pay per year

   $2,400/bi-weekly

   X 26 pay periods per year

   $62,400 per year

   $234,000

   + 62,400

   $296,400   combined pay per year

   $296,400/12 months per year = $24,700 combined GMI

   $24,700

   x .28

   $6,916

9. **C. $140,272** - To find the answer, multiply the monthly P&I payment by the number of payments the borrower will make (30 x 12 =360)

   $695.20

   x 360

   $250,272   (total P&I payment over the term of the loan)

   $250,272   P&I

   -$110,000 P (original principal amount)

   $140,272   I (Interest paid for 30-year term)

Chapter 15

Exercise 15.1: Apply Your Knowledge

Event	Step
Analyze application information	5
Appraise the property	4
Complete an application	2
Consult with the MLO	1
Disburse funding	7
Process an application	3
Record legal documents	8
Loan settlement	6

Exercise 15.2: Apply Your Knowledge

1. Divide $10,000 by 360 to find the daily interest: $27.7777.

2. He's closing on May 17, so there are 14 affected days: 14 x $27.7777 = $388.89. Bill must bring an additional $388.89 to closing to cover the mortgage interest for the last 14 days in May. Therefore, many buyers prefer to close on the last day of the month

Chapter 15 Quiz

1. **A. cost approach** - The cost approach utilizes the depreciated reproduction cost of a property as replicated on a parcel of land.

2. **A.** A - Flood Zone A is referred to the 100-year flood or an area exceeding a 1% chance of being inundated by a flood. Flood insurance is always required when a borrower has a mortgage lien on his property with a dwelling.

3. **B. change the effective date of the valuation.** – A recertification of value (recert) may be necessary to confirm whether certain conditions in the original appraisal have been met. It does not change the effective date of the valuation.

4. **C. income approach** - The income approach, sometimes called the capitalization approach, is most widely used with commercial or investment properties.

5. **C. mortgage lien** - Of the lien's noted, only a mortgage lien is placed on property voluntarily.

6. **C. continuation** - A continuation, or continuance, is used to bring down the title report from its preliminary issuance to the current date of the settlement to account for any new defects or clouds.

Glossary

A

Abusive Act Action that materially interferes with a consumer's ability to understand the product or service.

Acceleration Clause Clause that gives a lender the right to declare the entire loan balance due immediately because of borrower default or for violation of other contract provisions.

Accrued Expenses Items on a settlement statement for which the cost has been incurred, but the expense has not yet been paid.

Acquisition Cost The total amount needed to purchase property, including down payment, loan amount, and any allowable buyer-paid closing costs.

Adjustable Rate Mortgage (ARM) A mortgage that permits the lender to periodically adjust the interest rate to reflect fluctuations in the cost of money.

Adverse Action The denial of credit or an increased charge for credit based on information obtained from a third party.

Advertisement A commercial message in any medium that promotes, directly or indirectly, a credit transaction.

Alienation Clause In a contract, gives the lender certain stated rights when there is a transfer of ownership in a property. Also called **Due on Sale Clause**.

Alt-A Loan A type of loan in which the risk is greater than prime, but less than subprime. The borrower may have a strong credit history, but the mortgage may have elements that increase risk. Risk issues could include higher loan-to-value and debt-to-income ratios, or lack of documentation about the borrower's income.

Amortization Reduction of the loan balance by paying back, on a regular basis, some of the principal owed.

Application Submission of a borrower's financial information in anticipation of a credit decision.

Appraisal A professional estimate or opinion of the value of a piece of property (parcel of land), as of a certain date, that's supported by objective data.

Appraisal Management Company A business entity that—for a management fee—administers a network of certified and licensed appraisers to fulfill real estate appraisal assignments on behalf of mortgage lending institutions.

Appraiser A person who estimates the value of property, especially a licensed expert qualified to do so by education and experience.

Assets Items of value.

Assumption An action in which one party agrees to take over payments of another party's debt, with terms of the note staying unchanged.

Average Prime Offer Rate (APOR) An annual percentage rate derived from average interest rates, points, and other loan pricing terms that are currently offered to consumers by a representative sample of lenders for mortgage transactions that have low-risk pricing characteristics.

B

Balloon Payment A final lump-sum payment at the end of a loan term to pay off the entire remaining balance of principal and interest not covered by payments during the loan term.

Bankruptcy A court process that cancels debt and provides some relief for creditors; Chapter 7, sometimes called a straight bankruptcy, it is a liquidation proceeding; Chapter 13, sometimes called a reorganization proceeding, is filed by individuals who want to pay off their debts over a period of three to five years.

Bi-Weekly Payment Plan Plan in which payments are made every two weeks instead of once a month.

Bona Fide Offer An offer made in good faith with no element of fraud.

Boot Money and like-kind property exchanged in a transaction; term frequently expressed concerning IRS Section 1031 exchanges.

Buydown, Permanent The payment of points by a borrower to a lender to reduce the interest rate and loan payments for the entire life of the loan.

Buydown, Temporary The payment of points by a borrower to a lender to reduce the interest rate and payments early in a loan, with interest rate and payments rising later. Plans can be level payment, where the interest rate is reduced, but the payment is constant throughout the buydown period, or graduated payment, where payment subsidies in the early years of a loan keep payments low, but payments increase each year until they are sufficient to fully amortize the loan. Payment for the additional points can be made by the borrower or a third party (e.g., seller, builder), subject to the lender's or investor's requirements.

C

Chain of Title A clear and unbroken chronological record of the ownership of a specific piece of property.

Closing The final stage in a real estate transaction where ownership of real property is transferred from seller to buyer according to the terms and conditions set forth in a sales contract or escrow agreement. Also called **Loan Consummation** or **Settlement.**

Closing Costs Expenses incurred in the transfer of real estate in addition to the purchase price (e.g., the appraisal fee, title insurance premiums, broker's commission, transfer tax).

Cloud on the Title A claim, encumbrance, or defect that makes the title to real property unmarketable.

Collateral Property pledged as security for a debt.

Conforming Loan A loan that meets the criteria necessary to be sold in the secondary market.

Consumer Individual who obtains, or has obtained, a financial product or service from a financial institution for personal, family, or household reasons.

Consumer Financial Protection Bureau (CFPB) Independent agency funded by the Federal Reserve with rulemaking and enforcement authority over many consumer financial laws. Established under Title X of the Dodd-Frank Act.

Conventional Loan A loan usually made by a bank or institutional lender that is not insured or guaranteed by a government entity or agency (e.g., FHA, VA).

Conversion Option An ARM option that gives a borrower the right to convert from an adjustable rate loan to a fixed-rate loan.

Correspondent A mortgage banker who originates mortgage loans that are sold to other mortgage bankers or financial institutions.

Cost of Funds Index (COFI) A regional average of interest expenses incurred by financial institutions, which in turn is used as a base for calculating variable rate loans.

Credit Sum of money to be received.

Credit Freeze Places a credit file 'on ice' by preventing the information from being reported to third parties, such as credit grantors and other companies. Lenders are not able to gain access to the credit file unless given permission by the account holder. The credit file can still be disclosed in certain situations, such as for companies (e.g., mortgage, credit card, cell phone) doing business with the account holder and for collection agencies working for one of the companies.

Credit History A person's record of debt repayment, often used as a guide to whether he or she is likely to pay accounts on time in the future.

Credit Scoring A means by which the lender makes certain determinations regarding the creditworthiness of potential borrowers. This involves a lender assigning specified numerical values to different aspects relating to a borrower.

Customer Consumer with a continuing, significant relationship with a financial institution.

D

Debit Sum of money that is owed.

Debt Any recurring monetary obligation that will not be cancelled.

Debt-to-Income Ratio The relationship of a borrower's total monthly debt obligations (including housing and long-term debts with 10 or more payments remaining) to income, expressed as a percentage (Total Debt ÷ Income = Ratio %). Also called **DTI**, **Total Debt Service Ratio**, or **Back-End Ratio**.

Deed of Trust A security instrument placing into the hands of a disinterested third party a specific financial interest in the title to real property as security for the payment of a note. Also called **Trust Deed.**

Defeasance Clause A clause in a legal document that states that in the event a stated condition has been fulfilled, the document becomes null and void.

Demand Clause Any provision that enables a creditor to call due a loan before maturity.

Demand Deposit Money that is immediately accessible by a customer, who may elect to withdraw it from the bank at any time.

Depository Institution Any bank or savings association (the same meaning as in Section 3 of the Federal Deposit Insurance Act) and includes any credit union.

Discount Points A form of pre-paid interest that is charged by a lender to increase the yield on a lower-than-market interest rate loan; one point equals one percent of the loan amount.

Disintermediation The loss of deposits to competing investments that offer higher returns.

Disparate Impact A law that may be neutral on its face, but has a discriminatory effect since it has a greater adverse impact on one group than on others.

Dodd-Frank Wall Street Reform and Consumer Protection Act A federal law with the purpose to promote the financial stability of the United States by improving accountability and transparency in the financial system. It established the Consumer Financial Protection Bureau and new standards concerning a wide range of mortgage lending practices, including compensation of mortgage originators, federal mortgage disclosures, and mortgage servicing.

Dower or Curtesy Rights Interest in the real estate of a deceased spouse given by law to the surviving partner.

Down Payment The amount a buyer pays to obtain a property in addition to the money that the buyer borrows.

Dual Tracking The term used when servicers move forward on a foreclosure at the same time the mortgage servicer is working with a borrower on a workout plan.

Dwelling A residential structure or mobile home, which contains one-to-four family housing units, or individual units of condominiums or cooperatives.

E

Easement The non-ownership right acquired by a person to use the the land of another for a specific purpose. An easement is irrevocable and creates an interest in the property.

Encumbrance Any claim, lien, charge, or liability that affects or limits the fee simple title to real property.

Entitlement A veteran's maximum guaranty amount for a loan guaranteed by the VA.

Equitable Title An interest created in property upon the execution of a valid sales contract, whereby actual title will be transferred by deed at a future date. Also, the vendee's (buyer's) interest in property under a land contract.

Equity Exchange Condition in which value in one property is traded for value in another property. Also called a **tax-deferred exchange**, **tax-free exchange**, **like-kind exchange**, or **Section 1031** (from section number of IRS law).

Exclusionary Zoning Laws Laws that have the effect of denying housing to minorities or other protected classes.

F

Federal Deposit Insurance Corporation (FDIC) A public corporation, established in 1933, that insures up to $250,000 for each depositor for most member commercial banks and S & Ls. The FDIC has its own reserves and can also borrow from the U.S. Treasury.

Federal Home Loan Mortgage Corporation (Freddie Mac) A nonprofit, federally-chartered institution (now privately owned) that functions as buyer and seller of residential mortgages.

Federal Housing Finance Agency (FHFA) Government agency that merged the powers and regulatory authority of the Federal Housing Finance Board (FHFB) and the Office of Federal Housing Enterprise Oversight (OFHEO), as well as the GSE mission office at the Department of Housing and Urban Development (HUD); the conservator of Fannie Mae and Freddie Mac.

Federal National Mortgage Association (Fannie Mae) The nation's largest, privately owned investor in residential mortgages.

Finance Charge The cost of consumer credit as a dollar amount.

First Mortgage A security instrument with a first lien position.

Force-Placed Insurance Type of insurance that covers the lender's interest in the home.

Foreclosure, Judicial A lawsuit filed by a lender or other creditor to foreclose on a mortgage or other lien; a court-ordered sheriff's sale of the property to repay the debt.

Foreclosure, Non-judicial Foreclosure by a trustee under the power of sale clause in a deed of trust, without the involvement of a court. (Not used in some states.)

Fraud Alert Condition attached to a credit report that requires lenders to take extra precautions (e.g., contact by phone) to verify that the identity of the party seeking to establish the credit account is actually the individual who wants the new account.

Fully Indexed Rate In an adjustable rate mortgage, the fully indexed rate is the sum of the current numerical value of the index value used and the margin, as defined in the note.

G

Government National Mortgage Association (Ginnie Mae) Government-owned corporation that guarantees payment of principal and interest to investors who buy its mortgage-backed securities on the secondary market.

Government-Sponsored Enterprise (GSE) A group of financial services corporations created by the United States Congress to enhance the flow of credit to targeted sectors of the economy and to make those segments more efficient and transparent.

H

Hazard Insurance Coverage that compensates for physical damage to a property from fire, wind, vandalism, or other hazards.

High Cost Loans Under the Dodd-Frank Act, HOEPA protections are triggered where a loan's APR exceeds the average prime offer rate by 6.5 percentage points for most first-lien mortgages and 8.5 percentage points for subordinate lien mortgages; where a loan's points and fees exceed 5 percent of the total transaction amount, or a higher threshold for loans below $20,000; or where the creditor may charge a prepayment penalty more than 36 months after loan consummation or account opening, or penalties that exceed more than 2 percent of the amount prepaid.

Higher-Priced Loan A loan where the APR of the mortgage loan exceeds the average prime offer rate by 1.5% for a conventional first lien mortgage, 2.5% for a "jumbo" loan, or 3.5% for a subordinate-lien mortgage.

Home Equity Loan A loan secured by a mortgage on one's principal residence; generally requires a balloon payment.

Home Equity Line of Credit (HELOC) An open-end home equity loan in which borrowers are granted a specific credit limit from which to draw and repay principal only as it is used.

Housing Expense Ratio The relationship of a borrower's total monthly housing expense to income, expressed as a percentage (Total Housing Expense ÷ Income = Ratio %). Also called **Front-End Ratio**.

Hybrid Mortgage (ARM) Mortgage with a combination of fixed and adjustable rates.

Hypothecate Condition in which a debtor pledges personal or real property as security for a debt, typically without giving up possession of it.

I

Identity Theft Condition when someone uses another person's identity on a loan application without the knowledge of the rightful property owner.

Immediate Family Member A spouse, child, sibling, parent, grandparent, or grandchild, including those who are step (stepparents, stepchildren, stepsiblings) and adoptive relationships.

J

Individual A natural person.

Junior Lien Any lien that is a lower priority than another lien.

L

Land Contract A real estate installment agreement in which the buyer makes payments to the seller in exchange for the right to occupy and use the property, but no deed or title is transferred until all, or a specified portion, of the payments have been made.

Lease A contract where one party pays the other rent in exchange for possession of real estate.

Lease/Option Contract in which a seller leases property to someone for a specific term, with an option to buy the property at a predetermined price during the lease term.

Lease/Purchase Contract in which a seller leases property to someone for a specific term, with the tenant agreeing to buy the property at a set price during or following the lease term.

Legal Title Ownership of real property that is enforceable by law.

Liabilities Financial obligations owed by a borrower.

Lien A non-possessory interest in property, giving a lienholder the right to foreclose if the owner does not pay a debt owed the lienholder.

Lien Position The order in which liens are paid off out of the proceeds of a foreclosure sale.

Lis Pendens A notice of a pending legal action.

Loan Inquiry A consumer oral or written discussion about a mortgage loan's rates, terms, or other characteristics.

Loan Processor An individual who performs clerical or support duties as an employee at the direction of and subject to the supervision and instruction of a person licensed, or exempt from licensing under state mortgage licensing laws.

Loan-to-Value (LTV) The relationship between the unpaid principal amount of the mortgage and the appraised value (or sale price, if it is lower) of the property.

Loan Workout Establishment of new payment terms that are mutually agreed upon between the lender and delinquent borrower to get payments back on schedule.

M

Marketable Title A title that is free and clear from undisclosed encumbrances or other defects that would expose a purchaser to litigation or impede a purchaser's ability to enjoy the property or to later sell the property easily.

Money Laundering The process of concealing illicit sources of money to make it appear to be legitimate money.

Mortgage An instrument that creates a voluntary lien on real property to secure repayment of a debt. The parties to a mortgage are the mortgagor (borrower) and mortgagee (lender).

Mortgage-Backed Security (MBS) A Fannie Mae security that represents an undivided interest in a group of mortgages. Principal and interest payments from the individual mortgage loans are grouped and paid out to the MBS holders.

Mortgage Banker Party who originates, sells, and services mortgage loans and usually acts as the originator and servicer of loans on behalf of large investors, such as insurance companies, pension plans, or Fannie Mae.

Mortgage Broker Party who, for a fee, places loans with investors, but typically does not service such loans.

Mortgage Loan Originator (MLO) As defined by the SAFE Act, an individual who either takes a residential mortgage loan application or offers or negotiates terms of a residential mortgage loan for compensation or gain.

Mortgage Servicer When a mortgage escrow account is established, the entity that collects monthly mortgage payments; pays taxes, insurance, and other items as they come due; and notifies the borrower of late payments.

Mortgage Servicing The ongoing relationship between a borrower and the entity that accepts the borrower's payments, pays taxes and insurance (if escrowed), and is the entity that the borrower works with in the event of loan default.

N

Negative Amortization Payments that do not fully pay the interest due on a loan and that cause an increase in the borrower's total principal debt.

Nontraditional Mortgage Product Defined by the SAFE Act as any mortgage product other than a 30-year fixed-rate mortgage; as defined by the Interagency Guidance on Nontraditional Mortgage Product Risk, allows a borrower to defer principal and, sometimes, interest.

O

Option A contract giving one party the right to do something within a designated time period, without obligation to do so.

P

Payment Shock Any significant increase in monthly liability that heightens the risk of loan default.

Periodic/Prepaid Interest The charge a lender makes for the use of the asset (mortgage loan) from the day of funding to the beginning of the next month. Expressed as a dollar charge per day (per diem).

Person Refers to any of the following: Natural person, corporation, company, Limited Liability Company, partnership, or association.

PITI A typical mortgage payment that includes Principal, Interest, Taxes, and Insurance.

Point One percent of the loan amount. A fee charged by a lender for making a loan, calculated based on the loan amount.

Power of Sale Clause A clause that allows the trustee to sell trust deed property, without court supervision, when terms of the trust deed are not kept.

Pre-Approval The process by which a lender determines that potential borrowers can be financed through the lender for a certain amount of money.

Prepaid Expenses The items on a Closing Disclosure the seller has already paid.

Prepayment Clause In a contract, gives the lender the right to charge the borrower a penalty for paying off the loan early, such as when refinancing a loan.

Pre-Qualification The process by which an agent or lender reviews potential borrowers to determine if they are likely to get approved for a loan, and for approximately what amount.

Primary Mortgage Market When lenders make mortgage loans directly to borrowers. Also called **Primary Market**.

Private Mortgage Insurance (PMI) Insurance offered by private companies to insure a lender against default on a loan by a borrower, when there is a loss of value in the repossessed collateral value.

Promissory Note A financing instrument that evidences a promise to pay a specific amount of money to a specific person within a specific time frame. A written, legally binding promise to repay a debt.

Proration The division of expenses between buyer and seller in proportion to the actual usage of the item.

Q

Qualifying Ratios Guidelines applied by lenders to determine how large a loan to grant a homebuyer.

R

Rate Lock Agreement A written or electronically transmitted agreement between a mortgage banker or exempt organization and an applicant for a mortgage loan which, subject to the terms set forth in the agreement, obligates the mortgage banker or exempt organization to make a mortgage loan at a specified rate and a specific number of points, if any. Also called **Lock-In Agreement.**

Reconveyance Clause A clause in a contract that obligates a creditor to release of the property from the lien and convey title to that part back to the debtor once certain provisions of the note or mortgage have been satisfied. Also called **Partial Release** or **Satisfaction.**

Referral Any oral or written action directed to a person, which has the effect of affirmatively influencing the selection of a settlement service or business provider.

Registered Loan Originator A natural person who is employed by a depository institution that is regulated by a federal banking agency and is exempt from state licensing regulation who works with a prospective borrower to gather information, assist with completing applications, and otherwise making or initiating a new loan.

Release A document in which a legal right is given up.

Rescind Take back or withdraw an offer or contract.

Reserves Cash on deposit or other highly liquid assets a borrower must have in order to cover two months of PITI mortgage payments, after theyhe makes the cash down payment and pays all closing costs.

Residential Mortgage A mortgage, loan, or other evidence of a security interest created with respect to a single-family dwelling that is the primary residence of the borrower.

Residential Mortgage Loan Any loan primarily for personal, family, or household use that is secured by a mortgage, deed of trust, or other equivalent consensual security interest on a dwelling (as defined in Section 103(v) of the Truth in Lending Act) or residential real estate upon which is constructed or intended to be constructed a dwelling (as so defined).

Residential Real Estate Any real property located in the state upon which is constructed or intended to be constructed a dwelling (as defined under TILA).

Residual Income The amount of a borrower's income remaining after subtracting taxes, housing expenses, and all recurring debts and obligations.

Reverse Mortgage A vehicle for a borrower who has substantial equity in a property to convert that accumulated equity—at a cost—to cash and additional debt without selling the property and without making payments to the lender. With a typical reverse mortgage, the balance of the loan rises as the borrower receives money from the lender and incurs interest to the outstanding loan balance. Also called a reverse equity mortgage or reverse annuity mortgage. The most popular reverse mortgage program is the HECM.

S

Secondary Financing When a buyer borrows money from another source to pay part of the purchase price or closing costs.

Secondary Mortgage Markets The private investors and government agencies that buy and sell real estate mortgages. Also called **Secondary Markets**.

Securitization Act of pooling mortgages and then selling them as mortgage-backed securities.

Senior Lien Any lien that has a higher position than another lien.

Service Release Premium (SRP) The payment received by a lending institution, such as a bank or retail mortgage lender, on the sale of the right to service a closed mortgage loan.

Servicing The process of collecting payments, keeping records, and handling defaults for loans.

Settlement Agent The person charged with coordinating the activities and documentation necessary for completing a real estate transaction; usually the one who prepares the settlement statement and conducts the closing. Also called **Closing Officer, Closing Agent, Escrow Agent,** or **Title Agent.**

Single-Family Dwelling A residence consisting of a one-family dwelling unit.

Stable Income Income that can reasonably be expected to continue in the future.

State-Licensed Mortgage Loan Originator Any individual who is an MLO; is *not* an employee of a depository institution or a subsidiary that is (a) owned and controlled by a depository institution; and (b) regulated by a federal banking agency.

Steering Influencing, advising, counseling, or directing consumers to accept the terms offered by a particular creditor in order to receive greater compensation than might be available from a different creditor.

Subordinate Financing Debt in which the lender is not the first party due to be repaid by the borrower. In mortgage lending, a second mortgage or home equity loan would be subordinate financing to the first mortgage debt.

Subordination Agreement A written agreement between lienholders on a property that changes the priority of mortgages, judgments, and other liens.

Subprime Loans Loans that have more risks than allowed in the conforming market. Also called **B-C Loans** or **B-C Credit**.

T

Title Insurance An insurance policy that protects lenders and homeowners against losses resulting from undiscovered title defects and encumbrances. Mortgagee policies protect the lender's interest.

Thing of Value Anything (e.g., item, object, payment, service) that is regarded as being worth something by another party.

Title Insurance An insurance policy that protects lenders and homeowners against losses resulting from undiscovered title defects and encumbrances. Mortgagee policies protect the lender's interest.

Traditional Mortgage Product Any 30-year fixed-rate loan, as defined by the SAFE Act.

U

Underwriter An individual who assesses the various risks of each mortgage loan and ensures the loan meets program guidelines before deciding to approve or decline the loan on behalf of the mortgage banker.

Underwriting The process of evaluating documentation, borrower information, and various risk factors associated with a loan in order to make a loan decision.

Unique Identifier A number (or other identifier) assigned by protocols established by the Nationwide Mortgage Licensing System and Registry (NMLS) to a single individual on a nationwide basis.

Y

Yield Spread Premium (YSP) A higher interest rate in return for reducing closing costs. The premium is determined by the difference between the interest rate above the available PAR rate (i.e., reference point in which the interest rate is at zero points; there are no positive or negative adjustments) secured by a mortgage broker for a loan to a borrower. It results in lower closing costs for the borrower. Also called **Lender Credits.**

Index

INDEX

INDEX

INDEX